"This book is a tribute to one of the extraordinary pastors of our generation, who in many ways broke the mold. He has big thoughts about God in a time when God and his glory have been much diminished in the church. His has been a God-centered ministry. In this he has sometimes been unconventional, but the explanation is always that he has insisted on seeking to be true to the truth of God's Word. Though highly imaginative and endowed with a poetic sensibility, he has never let his ideas run away with him but has worked hard to make every thought, and himself, captive to Christ. The result has been a full, rich, and extraordinary ministry that has been owned of God. Pastors like this do not come along very often, and when they do, we need to take note."

David F. Wells, Distinguished Research Professor,
Gordon-Conwell Theological Seminary

"It would be strange if a book that honors a dynamic, intelligent, pious, God-centered, learned, kind, devoted, influential, far-traveled, widely published, and hyper-conscientious pastor like John Piper did not occasionally slip into hagiography. And this book does, but only occasionally. Far more, its authors offer the best sort of tribute by seriously engaging the Scriptures to which Piper is committed, earnestly expounding the classic Calvinistic doctrines into which Piper has breathed such life, and zealously promoting the glory of God to which Piper has devoted his ministry. Here is a volume full of thoughtful reflections on central scriptural themes, Jonathan Edwards, the life of prayer, Christ-honoring preaching, pastoral disciplines, pastoral privileges, Christian hedonism, and more. In the end, it is a tribute that, by stressing the themes John Piper has stressed, draws attention away from him to God."

Mark Noll, Francis A. McAnaney Professor of History,
University of Notre Dame

FOR THE FAME OF GOD'S NAME

FOR THE FAME OF GOD'S NAME

Essays in Honor of John Piper

Edited by

SAM STORMS

and JUSTIN TAYLOR

⁞⁞ CROSSWAY

WHEATON, ILLINOIS

Contents

Contributors

Randy Alcorn, Founder and Director, Eternal Perspectives Ministries (Sandy, OR)

Thabiti Anyabwile, Senior Pastor, First Baptist Church of Grand Cayman (Cayman Islands)

G. K. Beale, Professor of New Testament and Biblical Theology, Westminster Theological Seminary (Philadelphia, PA)

Jon Bloom, Executive Director, Desiring God (Minneapolis, MN)

D. A. Carson, Research Professor of New Testament, Trinity Evangelical Divinity School (Deerfield, IL)

Mark Dever, Senior Pastor, Capitol Hill Baptist Church (Washington, DC)

Sinclair B. Ferguson, Senior Minister, First Presbyterian Church (Columbia, SC)

Wayne Grudem, Research Professor of Theology and Biblical Studies, Phoenix Seminary (Phoenix, AZ)

Scott J. Hafemann, Mary French Rockefeller Distinguished Professor of New Testament, Gordon-Conwell Theological Seminary (South Hamilton, MA)

James M. Hamilton Jr., Associate Professor of Biblical Theology, The Southern Baptist Theological Seminary (Louisville, KY)

David Livingston, South Site Campus Pastor, Bethlehem Baptist Church (Minneapolis, MN)

John MacArthur, Pastor-Teacher, Grace Community Church (Sun Valley, CA)

C. J. Mahaney, President, Sovereign Grace Ministries (Gaithersburg, MD)

11

David Mathis, Executive Pastoral Assistant, Bethlehem Baptist Church (Minneapolis, MN)

David Michael, Pastor for Parenting and Family Discipleship, Bethlehem Baptist Church (Minneapolis, MN)

R. Albert Mohler Jr., President, The Southern Baptist Theological Seminary (Louisville, KY)

William D. Mounce, Vice President of Educational Development, BibleGateway.com

Stephen J. Nichols, Research Professor of Christianity and Culture, Lancaster Bible College and Graduate School (Lancaster, PA)

Ray Ortlund, Pastor, Immanuel Church (Nashville, TN)

David Powlison, Faculty Member and Counselor, Christian Counseling and Education Foundation (Glenside, PA)

Thomas R. Schreiner, James Buchanan Harrison Professor of New Testament Interpretation, The Southern Baptist Theological Seminary (Louisville, KY)

Tom Steller, Pastor for Leadership Development, Bethlehem Baptist Church (Minneapolis, MN)

Sam Storms, Senior Pastor, Bridgeway Church (Oklahoma City, OK)

Mark R. Talbot, Associate Professor of Philosophy, Wheaton College (Wheaton, IL)

Justin Taylor, Vice President of Editorial, Crossway (Wheaton, IL)

Bruce A. Ware, Professor of Theology, The Southern Baptist Theological Seminary (Louisville, KY)

Donald J. Westblade, Assistant Professor of Religion, Hillsdale College (Hillsdale, MI)

A Note to John Piper

John, as you hold this book of essays in your hands for the first time, we suspect your inclination is to turn it back over to us, perhaps with a measure of surprise, even disappointment, that we who know you so well would have ever dreamt that you might approve of what we've done!

But you can't argue with or resist the depths of love that we feel for you. You can't deny or turn aside from the reality of the global impact that your life and ministry have had. Our aim in this book is to follow the example of the apostle Paul, who refused "to speak of anything except what Christ has accomplished" through him (Rom. 15:18). Likewise, we will write only of what Christ has accomplished through you, and that for his glory alone.

We would like for this book of essays to be seen as an expression of gratitude to God for his work in and through you. We deeply appreciate your labor in the grace of God, for the glory of God. We have all been greatly impacted by your life and thought and devotion to Christ, and we believe these essays, which reflect your influence and interact with your theology, are the best way to acknowledge what you have done.

As you yourself hosted conferences to acknowledge and honor the life work of Jonathan Edwards and John Calvin, we present this volume of articles to do the same for you. No one who gave it more than a moment's consideration would ever have concluded from those conferences that your intention was to praise or promote a mere man or to turn our eyes from the splendor of our Savior to the weak and fitful efforts of fallen human beings. It is with that understanding that we undertook this project, hoping and praying that all who read it, and especially you, will know that our goal is the fame of *God's* name, not yours.

As uncomfortable or as unworthy as you might now feel, we lovingly ask you to receive this volume as a simple expression of gratitude on our part.

Some, perhaps even you, might argue that it would have been more appropriate for us to wait for your death before publishing this book. But many who contributed might themselves have entered the presence of Christ before you and thus lost the opportunity to participate. Although it may sound a bit selfish, the fact is that all of us were reluctant to forfeit the joy that we have experienced in being able to reflect and write on themes that are dear to your heart.

As for the contributors, the most difficult task that we as editors faced was their selection. When we first sat down, over three years ago, to draw up a list of those we might consider asking to participate, it was incredibly long. You have countless friends and colleagues and people whose lives have been changed through your faithfulness to the gospel of Christ and the glory of God. Many, no doubt, are disappointed that they did not have the opportunity to express their love by writing for this volume.

We should probably say something about the outline of the book and the essays it comprises. Our aim was to include articles on the variety of themes that have characterized your work these many decades, but even then we were compelled to limit ourselves to a choice few.

Among the numerous issues that deserve our attention, we simply couldn't envision a book of this sort without a focus on Christian hedonism, the glory of God, the suffering to which God has called us, prayer, the sovereignty of God, justification, Jonathan Edwards, the life and focus of the local church pastor, and—well, you get the picture. We pray that you are pleased with the efforts of those involved, even if you don't agree with everything each has said.

Finally, we believe that the apostle Paul has given us a strong and biblical precedent for what this book is designed to accomplish. He wrote to the Philippian church concerning Epaphroditus, having drawn attention to his tireless efforts for the sake of the gospel and the fact that "he nearly died for the work of Christ" (Phil. 2:30). "Honor such men" (Phil. 2:29), Paul instructed the church. Yes, it is possible to "honor" men such as you without detracting from the centrality and supremacy of our Lord. We hope that we have done this successfully. Please know that this project was conceived and birthed in love.

For the supremacy of God in all things,

Sam Storms
Justin Taylor

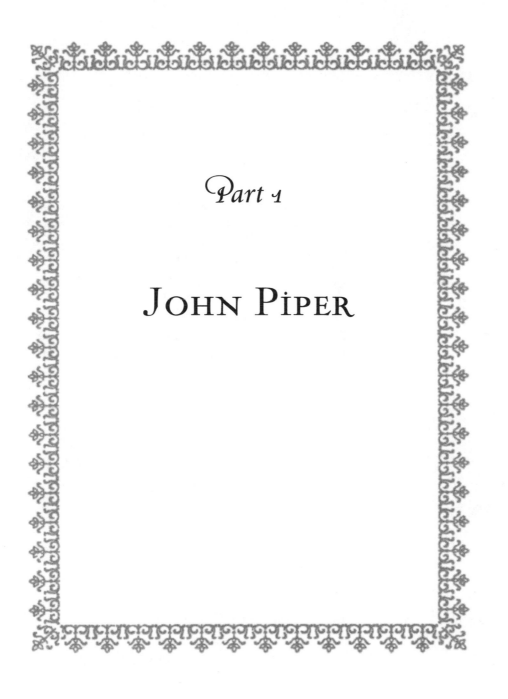

Part 1

JOHN PIPER

1

A PERSONAL TRIBUTE TO THE PRAISE OF GOD'S INFINITE GLORY AND ABOUNDING GRACE

David Michael

It was March 23, 1980. Our pastor was out of town for what was otherwise an ordinary Sunday morning. We appreciated the opportunities our church offered for meaningful engagement in urban ministry, but after two years our souls were parched. Certainly we were not aware that in the next hour a course would be set that would shape our marriage, our ministry, our relationships, our experiences, and our biblical and theological worldview for the next thirty years. Before the guest preacher took the pulpit, our congregation was informed that he would be resigning his position at Bethel College and in July become the senior pastor at one of our urban neighbor churches, Bethlehem Baptist. The introduction ended, a wiry thirty-four-year-old stepped to the pulpit, and Sally and I settled in for what we expected to be another spiritually arid sermon from a PhD Bible professor whom we had never heard of. But within minutes the Word of God was gushing forth like streams in the desert and watering our thirsty souls.

From the outside, Bethlehem seemed like so many of the other twenty-two churches in our community—limited resources, aging congregation, and little or no gospel influence on the neighbors they no longer knew or understood. Though their building remained, their pastors and people had long since moved to safer and more pleasant places. If there was doubt that we would visit Bethlehem to get another drink of what we tasted in March, it vanished when we learned this new pastor bought a home a few blocks from the church. A senior pastor who could faithfully preach the Word of God with such power *and* who was living in the neighborhood offered us hope that Bethlehem could be spiritually alive and fruitfully invested for the cause of Christ in the city. As soon as we heard this, Sally and I made plans to visit Bethlehem the following Sunday.

The course was set, and to the praise of God's infinite glory and abounding grace we would never be the same again. We became members of Bethlehem that fall. Six years later I came onto the staff as pastor for urban and social ministry. A decade later, in 1996, Sally joined the staff, and together we assumed responsibility for parenting and children's discipleship, which was later expanded to include our present responsibilities.

It would be difficult to overstate the influence John Piper's radically God-centered preaching and teaching ministry has had on us and on the people of Bethlehem. It would likewise be difficult to exaggerate the joy it has been to serve as a pastor among people who are experiencing the influence of such radically God-centered preaching and teaching. Being engaged in ministry alongside John and other faithful comrades whose hearts are knit together for serving a great church, in a great cause, to the fame and glory of our great King, has been an indubitable privilege.

It is my joy to give tribute to a man who has devoted his life to helping me (and the rest of the world) see God as the center and source of all things and therefore as the only One to whom all honor and glory and thanks belong. Therein, however, lies the challenge. For me to spend these limited words praising such a man would not only offend the man but, even worse, offend his God. It seems more fitting to honor a faithful pastor and fellow servant in Christ and in the gospel ministry by devoting the rest of my allotted words to praising the One whom I and countless others have come to see more clearly and admire more deeply through the faithful ministry of John Piper. Therefore I would like to lead us in the following prayer of praise and thanksgiving.

Almighty God and Everlasting Father,

I want to bow before you to worship you as the Giver of every good gift, including thirty years of ministry through a man who has taught us to exalt you in everything that we do, from drinking orange juice to giving tribute to a man who has influenced untold numbers of people to the praise of your infinite glory and abounding grace. I join with all who read this book not to honor John Piper, but to honor John Piper's God, who created him and sustained his life for these sixty-five years.

You are the God who works wonders! You have made known your strength among the peoples. You cause the sun to rule by day and the moon and stars at night. You brought water out of solid rock and multiplied food to feed thousands. You split waters and calmed seas. You made the blind to see, the lame to walk, the dead to live again. And, among the myriad wonders you have performed according to your glorious plans formed long ago, you created John Piper.

Thank you for Ruth and Bill Piper, who introduced John to Jesus, faithfully taught him the fear of the Lord from his youth, and gave him Galatians 2:20 on his fifteenth birthday to inspire him to live by faith in the Son of God, who loved him and delivered himself up for him.

Thank you for the awkward and difficult years of adolescence that you used to humble him and keep him from the pitfalls of vanity, worldliness, and self-reliance.

Thank you for the courage you gave John forty-four years ago to pray in Wheaton's chapel service. Thank you for using that prayer to deliver him from the paralyzing fear of man and to loosen his tongue to declare your glory with a passion that you have sustained in him to this day.

Thank you for laying him aside with mono in 1966 and for using the biblical exposition of Harold John Ockenga to grip his heart with a desire to teach and preach the Word.

Thank you for the insight that was given, the faith that was deepened, the theology that was refined, and the doctrine that was established during his years at Fuller Seminary and the University of Munich.

Thank you for six years of fruitful Bible teaching at Bethel and for all his wrestling with Romans 9, which ignited a passion to herald the Word of God and witness its power to create authentic people.

Thank you for opening Bethlehem's pulpit at just the right time and for directing the will of the search committee to recommend that John be called to the position of preaching pastor.

Thank you for thirty years of faithful prayers and for multiplied hours of preparation that gave us glimpses of your glory in over thirteen hundred

Sundays of sermons, dozens of advent poems, untold numbers of articles, classes, seminars, Bible studies, wedding homilies, funeral meditations, and devotions off the "front burner." Through these means, you opened our eyes to see you as an "all-satisfying God" who is "most glorified in us when we are most satisfied in him" and who "works for those who wait for him." Our hearts found joy in the confidence that you "always have a way" and work all things for good "even when things don't go the way they should." You nourished our minds and strengthened our hearts through these means. You gave us a hope in you and a delight in your ways. You awakened a hunger and desire for you. You stirred in us a joy in your Son, a reliance on your Spirit, and a love for your Truth. You gave us knowledge and understanding of your Word. You granted grace for every circumstance and a "white-hot passion" for your supremacy in all things.

I praise you, Lord Jesus, for giving me and my colleagues the unspeakable privilege of serving this church and leading ministries that were sustained week after week, year after year, and decade after decade by faithful, passionate preaching, fueled by your Word and ignited by your Spirit. I will forever bless you for the joy you have given me in serving alongside a people who have been so consistently inspired to be "coronary Christians" going "hard after God," living a "wartime lifestyle," "risking all for the cause of Christ," willing to go "outside the camp, bearing the reproach that Christ endured," forsaking gold because "copper will do," moving "toward need, not comfort," "living by faith in future grace," employing prayer as "a wartime walkie-talkie not a domestic intercom," declaring your glory among the nations with "undistracting excellence," "gutsy guilt," and "brokenhearted boldness."

I praise you for giving us a pastor who is passionate about raising a generation of young people who will "live courageously in the world even under pressure to conform" and who will "thoughtfully and effectively engage the culture for the sake of the gospel." I praise you for a pastor who prays and labors for a generation of "Christ-exalting, God-glorifying, Bible-saturated, truth-driven, doctrinally grounded, faith-filled, God-centered, mission-minded, soul-winning, justice-pursuing, God-fearing, Christ-treasuring, joyfully self-forgetting, passion-spreading, spiritually fruitful servants who are devoted to spreading a passion for the supremacy of God in all things for the joy of all peoples through Jesus Christ."

Thank you for John's example of faithful pastoral ministry that has encouraged the timid, helped the weak, warned the idle, disciplined the wayward, comforted the sick, strengthened the dying, given hope for the grieving, and brought the light of the Word to bear on innumerable decisions and problems and circumstances of life that have troubled your people over these years.

Thank you for three decades of faithful leadership that have consistently challenged the church and the culture with truth. Thank you for his courageous stand against the rising spirit of indifference, alienation, and hostility, a stand that has inspired thoughtful and biblical engagement for racial harmony and protection for the unborn.

I praise you for the most earnest, least visible, most impactful, least noticed, most fruitful, least recognized, most appreciated daily prayers for his family, for his church, and for the advancement of your kingdom to the ends of the earth. Thank you for countless daily intercessions on behalf of fellow pastors, ministry assistants, custodians, elders, missionaries, neighbors, friends, and family members in the hope that all might be kept from "sin, Satan, and sabotage."

Thank you for thirty years of leadership development and a contagious vision for the supremacy of God in preaching and pastoral ministry and Christian education, and for dozens of conferences and thousands of published pages and endless hours invested in strengthening the church and spreading your praise across the nation and around the world to this generation and to the generations to come.

Thank you for thirty years of prayer-soaked, vision-driven staff meetings, board meetings, committee meetings, elder meetings, and prayer meetings that were influenced by a quality of leadership alert to trajectories and kept us on course through Project 84, Span 1, Span 2, Span 3, Freeing the Future, Education for Exultation, Treasuring Christ Together, and countless other ideas and initiatives that have shaped our church.

Thank you for mingling these thirty years with severe mercies and bitter providences that broke us, softened us, delivered us from pride, weaned us from the temporary things of the world, and fixed our minds more on the eternal matters of salvation, holiness, and the lostness of the peoples.

Thank you for thirty years of grace that has kept our pastor firm in faith and sustained what seemed like an indomitable hope that inspired us to lift up our eyes and secure our confidence in the One who made heaven and earth.

Thank you for giving him the grace to practice what he preached and for keeping him from giving in to the temptations of the flesh that could have consumed his soul, ruined his ministry, and brought shame upon your Bride and on your holy name.

Thank you for giving John a wife who has faithfully stood with her husband for more than forty-two years. A wife who has labored with him, ministered with him, shed tears with him, shared joys with him, and prayed with him night after night. A wife who managed the household, faithfully cared for their sons and daughter, welcomed guests, edited manuscripts, and freed her husband to study and pray. Thank you for the blessing of Noël's sacrifice and love that served us, spread a table for us, encouraged us with grace, and blessed us with wisdom and writings.

Lord Jesus, without yet exhausting the praise and thanksgiving remaining in my heart, I ask that your hand of blessing remain on John and on his family and on his ministry. Be pleased to keep the fruit of his unwasted life abounding until the end of the age.

Keep piercing souls with your Word and stirring up hunger for you. Let the river of life continue to overflow into more dead hearts. Make them finally alive with a desire for you and a delight in you as the gospel. Give them eyes to see and souls to savor Jesus Christ. May praise forever be on our lips to the One who shed his blood so that we might die to our spectacular sins, be justified by faith, be counted righteous by grace, and benefit from the forty-seven other reasons Jesus came to die.

Aim more lives in a Godward direction and take pleasure in bringing forth generations of Christian hedonists with a God-entranced vision for their lives. Engage them in the dangerous duty of delight, and inflame them with a passion for your glory so that the unreached may be reached and the nations may be glad.

Grant that biblical manhood and womanhood would be fully recovered, and raise up increasing numbers of men and women who embrace the difference in their momentary marriages. Expand the legacy of sovereign joy through those who battle unbelief under the hidden smile of God. Let them taste your mercy in the midst of misery, and give them glimpses of your glory even when the darkness will not lift. Sink the roots of their endurance deep into your love so that they can stand in the days of testing.

I praise you, Lord Jesus, for sparing our church from a professionalism these past thirty years. Instead, you were pleased to give us a pastor who exalted your supremacy in his preaching and your sovereignty in his suffering. O God, may your church never be without men who stay within your bounds, seeking you like silver and making plain what Jesus demands from this postmodern world, faithfully contending for our all.

Father, we acknowledge that John's life, like ours, is a vapor and the number of his days is in your hands. As I close this prayer, I ask that you would please sustain in John the pace and the grace to finish the race. Keep guarding him from ungodliness and worldly passions. Keep lifting him from the power of every sin. Keep him practicing what he preaches. Keep him alert in prayer with all perseverance. Keep him happy, not because he is spared affliction but because his joy is rooted in you and his feet are walking in your light. Keep his heart exulting in your glory and his mouth filled with your praise. Keep his tongue telling of your righteousness and his lips declaring the wondrous deeds of your salvation to all who come behind him. Come upon John in this final stretch with great power, and let your Word have its free course to run and be glorified for the eternal praise of Jesus Christ and for the sake of his name—in which I pray, Amen.

> *Now to him who is able to keep ⸢John⸥ from stumbling*
> *and to present ⸢John⸥ blameless before the*
> *presence of his glory with great joy,*
> *to the only God, our Savior,*
> *through Jesus Christ our Lord,*
> *be glory, majesty, dominion, and authority,*
> *before all time and now and forever.*
> *Amen.*
> *–Jude 24-25*

2

THREE DOORS DOWN
FROM A POWER PLANT

David Livingston

I have lived three doors down from John Piper for over twenty years. I recall a mutual friend once laughingly remarking to me, "It must be like living next to a nuclear reactor." And given my neighbor's intense, restless, competitive, probing, and usually forceful impact on others, and his high-powered, virtual nonstop generation of compelling spoken and written words, I do see the energetic aptness of "Piper, the power plant."

What follows is an effort to plot the progress of John Piper's implanted power, like successive upward "conversions," from *cold* to *candle* to *coal* to *plutonium*—or, in other words, from *lost* to *found* to *Calvinism* to *Christian hedonism*.

Crucified with Christ
January 11, 1946—just eleven days after the commencement of that seismic demographic tidal wave called the Baby Boom—John Stephen Piper was born in Chattanooga, Tennessee, the second child of Bill and Ruth Piper. The family moved later that year to Greenville, South Carolina. Five years

later they built a house just across the highway from Bob Jones University, where Bill had been elected a trustee. There Bill and Ruth raised John and his older sister Beverly, three years his senior.

Resembling his itinerant evangelist daddy, William Solomon Hottle Piper (1919–2007), Johnny grew up on the short[1] and scrappy side of Southern life. He learned two things from his daddy: to be happy and to be blood-earnest. Despite his dad's being gone two-thirds of the time,[2] John says that his parents "were the happiest people I have ever known."[3]

The lasting influence of his "omni-competent"[4] mother, Ruth Eulalia Mohn Piper (1918–1974), was to instill in him a strong work ethic along with high expectations of character. This woman who gave him first birth was alone with him for his second—in their motel room on a family vacation in Fort Lauderdale, Florida, during the summer of 1952. There her strong-willed, six-year-old boy uttered a "sinner's prayer," Johnny's first embrace of eternal life.

On his fifteenth birthday his parents gave him a beautiful leather-bound KJV Bible with his name printed on the front. In the front leaf his mother wrote,

Happy Birthday, Son,
January 11, 1961.

This book will keep you from sin,
or sin will keep you from this book.

Mother and Daddy.

On the second leaf of the Bible, John wrote Galatians 2:20.

White Oak Baptist, John's home church, and Wade Hampton High School were both within a mile of his home. It was at school that John experienced the beginnings of an intellectual and emotional awakening. His tenth-grade geometry class—with its "process of reasoning from axioms and postulates and corollaries in order to turn theorems into proofs"—was "explosively exciting" to John, awakening in him a love

---

[1] In boyhood, young Bill Piper epitomized himself and his ball-playing teammates with the nickname "Small Potatoes, but Hard to Peel."

[2] "Life," John recounts, "was a rhythm of Daddy's leaving for one week or two weeks or as long as four weeks, almost always on Saturday, and then coming home on Monday." See John's biographical address on his father, "Evangelist Bill Piper: Fundamentalist Full of Grace and Joy," available at www.desiringGod.org.

[3] Ibid.

[4] John Piper, *What's the Difference?* (Wheaton, IL: Crossway, 1990), 11.

for *precise thinking.*[5] His advanced biology class with Mrs. Hinton taught him to slow down and to see what is before his eyes with *painstaking observation.* His father, a romantic poet, had planted the seeds of poetry, but that lay largely dormant until the spring of 1963, when Mrs. Crandall's English class stirred within him "a passion for conceptually clear and emotionally moving expression in writing," which he expressed through a desire to read serious books and to write serious poems and essays.[6]

In the fall of 1964, John started at Wheaton College, by then a serious, studious, self-conscious eighteen-year-old introvert. His freshman year he was introduced to *Mere Christianity* by C. S. Lewis, the famed apologist who had died one year earlier. "For the next five or six years," he writes, "I was almost never without a Lewis book near at hand. I think that without his influence I would not have lived my life with as much joy and usefulness as I have. . . . I will never cease to thank God for this remarkable man who came onto my path at the perfect moment."[7] From Lewis he learned that "rigorous, precise, penetrating logic is not opposed to deep, soul-stirring feeling and vivid, lively—even playful imagination."[8]

At the end of his sophomore year (1966), John was sure he'd learned God's vocational direction for his life:

> In May I had felt a joyful confidence that my life would be most useful as a medical doctor. I loved biology; I loved the idea of healing people. I loved knowing, at last, what I was doing in college. So I quickly took general chemistry in summer school so I could catch up and take organic chemistry that fall.[9]

It was that summer that he met eighteen-year-old Noël Francis Henry, the "adventuresome, fearless, unflappable"[10] oldest daughter of ten children from Barnesville, Georgia. It was June 6,[11] and John was in Fisher Hall, reading Paul Tournier's *Guilt and Grace*, when he heard his future wife's lilting (and probably, pleading) accent coming from the adjacent hall, explaining to the attendant at the desk that "they've locked up Williston [Hall] and I can't get my things." John, who had never once dated,

---

[5] John Piper, "The Pastor as Scholar: A Personal Journey," April 23, 2009, available at www.desiringGod.org.

[6] Most of John's poetic writings are family birthday and special event poetry for Noël and the children, but Bethlehem has heard personally recited "Advent Poems" in four-week cycles since his first twenty-one-verse effort, "Advent Beauty" (November 28, 1982).

[7] John Piper, *Don't Waste Your Life* (Wheaton, IL: Crossway, 2003), 19–20.

[8] Ibid., 19.

[9] Ibid., 21.

[10] John Piper, n.d., "Mark Driscoll Interview with John Piper," available at The Resurgence Web site, http://theresurgence.com/interview_with_john_piper_video (accessed March 13, 2009).

[11] 6-6-66, as John likes to note!

fearing rejection, eventually mustered up the courage to approach her after church one night and asked her to go to The Little Popcorn Store in downtown Wheaton. She said yes, and John was soon in love.

That summer of '66 was notable not just as the dawning of love but as the death of a phobia. Strange, even fanciful, as it may seem to those who hear him today, John had a debilitating physiological, psychological inability to speak for any length of time in front of a group. Throughout junior high and high school John battled this "horrible and humiliating disability"[12]—his throat would close up, his voice would break up, his hands would shake, he could see his shirt moving over his rapidly beating heart. Once as his turn to speak in class approached, he scampered out of class to the bathroom and cried. At home he would cry and pray with his mother. But these prayers began to be answered at Wheaton. First came the ability to deliver a short speech in his Spanish class during his freshman year. Then the decisive breakthrough came when John was approached by Evan Welsh, the sixty-one-year-old beloved chaplain of Wheaton with a gray-haired flattop. He asked John to pray in the summer school chapel before five hundred students and faculty. John surprised himself by answering Welsh's request with, "How long does the prayer have to be?" Welsh responded that it could be as short as thirty seconds, provided it was from his heart. John found himself somehow saying yes. In preparation for praying, he paced the campus praying for God's help. He vowed that if God would get him through this prayer, he would never again turn down an opportunity to speak because of fear. He memorized the prayer word for word, took a tight hold of the pulpit in Edman Chapel, and made it through. "This prayer," John later wrote, "proved to be a decisive turning point in my life."[13] Who can calculate the implications of God's work in those brief classroom moments, or in pacing across Wheaton's front campus, as such subsequent good for Christ was made possible when, like the beggar "walking and leaping and praising God" (Acts 3:8), John Piper's paralysis (of speech) passed away?

The next turning point in John's life came in September 1966, at the start of his junior year. Instead of being in class he ended up spending three weeks in the health center, flat on his back with mononucleosis. "The life plan that I was so sure of four months earlier," he writes, "unraveled in my fevered hands."[14]

---

[12]John Piper, *Future Grace* (Sisters, OR: Multnomah, 1995), 51.
[13]Ibid.
[14]Piper, *Don't Waste Your Life*, 21.

While recovering in the infirmary, he received a visit from Chaplain Welsh, who talked and prayed with him. As Welsh got up to leave he stopped at the door and turned around. "John," he asked, "do you have a favorite Bible verse?"

John hadn't been asked that question for years, but without hesitation he responded by citing the verse he had written in the front of his Bible as a teenager: "Galatians 2:20—I have been crucified with Christ; it is no longer I who live, but Christ who lives in me; and the life I now live in the flesh I live by faith in the Son of God, who loved me and gave himself for me" (RSV).

While in the infirmary, John turned on the bedside radio to the campus station, WETN. Harold John Ockenga (1905–1985), the pastor of Park Street Church in Boston, was preaching each morning for the traditional Spiritual Emphasis Week (September 26–30). John recounts the result of listening to this preaching for five days in a row: "Never had I heard exposition of the Scriptures like this. Suddenly all the glorious objectivity of Reality centered for me on the Word of God. I lay there feeling as if I had awakened from a dream, and knew, now that I was awake, what I was to do."[15] At the end of the week John told Noël that he was sensing a new calling—to study the Bible and be able to teach from it as Ockenga had—a calling that would take him to seminary, as he dropped organic chemistry and all of his premed plans. "From that moment on," he writes, "I have never doubted that my calling in life is to be a minister of the Word of God."[16]

On May 18, 1968—three weeks before he would graduate from Wheaton—John took Noël to a lagoon for a date. Underneath a great oak tree on that drizzly Saturday he read her a poem and proposed to her with a diamond ring. She said yes, and they were engaged.

But they would be apart during the fall semester as John moved to Pasadena, California, to begin his studies at Fuller Seminary while Noël stayed in Wheaton to complete her final semester of college. On December 20 of that year they were married in Midway Baptist Church outside Barnesville, Georgia, taking joy in the God of Habakkuk 3:17–19 (read at the wedding).

Mercy on Whom I Have Mercy
Even though John had been freed from the paralysis of public speaking, this one freedom didn't yet mean all freedom; he remained a plodding

---

[15]Ibid., 21–22.
[16]Ibid., 22.

reader.[17] His compensating habits, since 1966, have been to keep a journal and to methodically annotate books as he reads them, disciplines that enable him to record, reflect on, and recall immense amounts of previously developed thoughts for use in later speaking and writing.

Thus equipped, John and Noël commenced their graduate study years (1968–1973) wherein the slog-paced reader mastered an even slower reading technique of the Bible, especially Romans 9. Starting at Fuller Seminary in Pasadena, California, John brought along his incipient Arminian belief in the self-determining nature of his own will, so that God was free to do only what John gave him permission for. Then came Daniel Fuller's class on Philippians and Jaymes Morgan's course on the doctrine of salvation:

> In Philippians I was confronted with the intractable ground clause of chapter 2 verse 13 . . . which made God the will beneath my will and the worker beneath my work. . . . In the class on salvation . . . Romans 9 was the watershed text and the one that changed my life forever. . . .
>
> Emotions run high when you feel your man-centered world crumbling around you. I met Dr. Morgan in the hall one day. After a few minutes of heated argument about the freedom of my will, I held a pen in front of his face and dropped it to the floor. Then I said, with not as much respect as a student ought to have, "I [!] dropped it." Somehow that was supposed to prove that my choice to drop the pen was not governed by anything but my sovereign self.
>
> But thanks be to God's mercy and patience, at the end of the semester I wrote in my blue book for the final exam, "*Romans 9 is like a tiger going about devouring free-willers like me.*" That was the end of my love affair with human autonomy and the ultimate self-determination of my will. My worldview simply could not stand against the scriptures, especially Romans 9. And it was the beginning of a lifelong passion to see and savor the supremacy of God in absolutely everything.[18]

Observe that Piper's Calvinism neither began with nor primarily fed or flourished on theological formulae alone. His was a biblical and exegetical pathway to a Reformed outlook, learned inductively via Daniel Fuller's hermeneutical method:

---

[17]"To this day I cannot read faster than I can talk. Something short-circuits in my ability to perceive accurately what's on the page when I try to push beyond to go faster" ("The Pastor as Scholar").

[18]John Piper, "The Absolute Sovereignty of God: What Is Romans Nine About?" a sermon at Bethlehem Baptist Church, November 3, 2002, available at www.desiringGod.org.

Not only did he introduce me to E. D. Hirsch [i.e., his 1967 book, *Validity in Interpretation*] and force me to read him with rigor, but he also taught me how to read the Bible with what Matthew Arnold called "severe discipline." He showed me the obvious: that the verses of the Bible are not strung pearls but links in a chain. The writers developed unified patterns of thought. . . . This meant that, in each paragraph of Scripture, one should ask how each part related to the other parts in order to say one coherent thing. And then the chapters, then the books, and so on until the unity of the Bible is found on its own terms. . . . I felt like my little brown path of life had entered an orchard, a vineyard, a garden with mind-blowing, heart-thrilling, life-changing fruit to be picked everywhere. Never had I seen so much truth and so much beauty condensed in so small a sphere. The Bible seemed to me then, and it seems today, inexhaustible. . . . In course after course the pieces were put into place. What a gift those three years of seminary were![19]

Two Congregational church pastors played life-changing roles in those seminary years as well, one far away in Northampton, Massachusetts, the other only walking distance from the campus in Pasadena, California—the Pasadena pastor very much alive, the Massachusetts man over 250 years in his grave. Regarding the latter, John said, "Jonathan Edwards came into my life at this point. . . . For me he has become the most important dead teacher outside the Bible. No one outside Scripture has shaped my vision of God and the Christian life more than Jonathan Edwards."[20]

The other Congregational pastor was a contemporary: Ray Ortlund Sr. (1923–2007), senior pastor of Lake Avenue Congregational Church, which John and Noël began attending in the spring semester of 1969. "What stunned me," John wrote later of Ortlund, "was his manifest love for the church and his overflowing joy in the privilege of being an undershepherd of Jesus Christ for the sake of his body. He simply loved doing what he did. I had never seen any pastor so manifestly thrilled to be called into the service of the church."[21] It was there that John discovered the priority of the local church (reject the church and you reject Christ) and the meaning of true worship (God is to be worshiped as an end in himself). And it was also there that John discovered his gift of teaching. In addition to teaching some Greek at Fuller in his role as William LaSor's teaching assistant, at Lake Avenue he taught various Sunday school classes (seventh-grade boys, then ninth-grade boys, and then the Galilean class).

[19]Piper, *Don't Waste Your Life*, 26.
[20]Ibid., 29.
[21]John Piper, "Thanks to God for Ray Ortlund," blog posted July 26, 2007, www.desiringGod.org.

In July of 1975, between his first and second years of teaching at Bethel, he returned to Lake Avenue to be ordained in the Conservative Congregational Christian Conference under Dr. Ortlund's leadership. John's ordination certificate hangs prominently in his office while the DTheol degree remains in its original cylindrical mailer in a closet. One represents to him a celebration of the church's confirmation of his divine call; the other was simply John's admission ticket to the academic guild.

Fullness of Joy and Pleasures Forevermore

The second and third Piper conversions almost overlapped. When John realized God's supremacy in all things, it was a short step to also recognizing God as the source of his own supreme joy.

In the fall of 1968 he was standing in the famous Vroman's Bookstore on Colorado Avenue in Pasadena. There he picked up a thin blue copy of C. S. Lewis's book *The Weight of Glory* and began to read the address that Lewis had delivered at a church in Oxford twenty-seven years before. The words on the first page changed his life:

> If there lurks in most modern minds the notion that to desire our own good and earnestly to hope for the enjoyment of it is a bad thing, I submit that this notion has crept in from Kant and the Stoics and is no part of the Christian faith. Indeed, if we consider the unblushing promises of reward and the staggering nature of the rewards promised in the Gospels, it would seem that our Lord finds our desires not too strong, but too weak. We are halfhearted creatures, fooling about with drink and sex and ambition when infinite joy is offered us, like an ignorant child who wants to go on making mud pies in a slum because he cannot imagine what is meant by the offer of a holiday at the sea. We are far too easily pleased.[22]

A catalytic mix of insights came in seminary, beginning the first quarter of his first year with Blaise Pascal (1623–1662) and culminating when, as a senior, John took the class "The Unity of the Bible," taught by Daniel Fuller (1925–). Sentences in a single paragraph of Fuller's later-published book by the same name

> were the seeds of my future. The driving passion of my life was rooted here. One of the seeds was in the word "glory"—God's aim in history was to "fully display his glory." Another seed was in the word "delight"—God's aim was that his people "delight in him with all their heart." The passion of my life has been to understand and live and teach and preach how these

---

[22]C. S. Lewis, *The Weight of Glory* (London: Society for Promoting Christian Knowledge, 1942).

two aims of God related to each other—indeed, how they are not two but one. . . . If my life was to have a single, all-satisfying, unifying passion, it would have to be God's passion. And, if Daniel Fuller was right, God's passion was the display of his own glory and the delight of my heart.

All of my life since that discovery has been spent experiencing and examining and explaining that truth. It has become clearer and more certain and more demanding with every year. It has become clearer that God being glorified and God being enjoyed are not separate categories. They relate to each other not like fruit and animals, but like fruit and apples. Apples are one kind of fruit. Enjoying God supremely is one way to glorify him. Enjoying God makes him look supremely valuable.[23]

With his life permanently magnetized to this brightest of doctrinal pole stars, John and Noël then flew off to Germany in 1971.[24] Leonhard Goppelt (1911–1973) was his "Herr Doctor Professor" at the University of Munich. By 1973 John completed his program, having written his dissertation entitled *Love Your Enemies: Jesus' Love Command in the Synoptic Gospels and Early Christian Paraenesis.*[25] Noël was also busy in Germany, giving birth to and caring for their first son, Karsten Luke (born in 1972).

John sent inquiries to about thirty churches, denominations, missions, colleges, and seminaries, and one door opened: a year-long sabbatical replacement, teaching New Testament at Bethel College in Saint Paul, Minnesota. He took the job and has been in the Twin Cities ever since. It was there that the twenty-seven-year-old new daddy and doctor began his six-year teaching career in the Bible department at Bethel. A notoriously demanding teacher and hard grader, John was nevertheless a student favorite,[26] well known for defending clearly defined theological and ethical positions compared to the doctrinal vagueness characterizing some of the other faculty members and administration.[27] Additionally, he was

---

[23]Piper, *Don't Waste Your Life*, 26–28.
[24]On July 27, 1971, John waited nervously for their trans-Atlantic flight at Radio City Music Hall in New York City. Sitting with his wife, his mother, and his grandmother, John called his father, who was on an evangelistic crusade, and his father gave him three passages to read: Isaiah 41:10; Isaiah 50:7; and 2 Timothy 4:1–5. Over the years, Isaiah 41:10 proved especially significant for steadying his heart's trust in God in moments of anxiety.
[25]Published in 1979 by Cambridge University Press.
[26]See the reflections in this volume by two of his former Bethel students, Scott Hafemann and Tom Steller (chaps. 12 and 27).
[27]Over the years John has defended numerous theological positions, some with controversy. For example, Reformed soteriology, male headship in the family and in church eldership, no biblical grounds for remarriage after divorce, God's exhaustive foreknowledge, and the imputation of Christ's righteousness by faith alone.

appreciated for the insights and passion of his class-starting devotional thoughts.[28]

In his sabbatical year, at age thirty-three, John was busy writing a book on Romans 9. Second-born son Benjamin John had come (1975) and Abraham Christian (1979) was on the way when the unexpected happened again.[29]

> As I studied Romans 9 day after day, I began to see a God so majestic and so free and so absolutely sovereign that my analysis merged into worship and the Lord said, in effect: "I will not simply be analyzed, I will be adored. I will not simply be pondered, I will be proclaimed. My sovereignty is not simply to be scrutinized, it is to be heralded. It is not grist for the mill of controversy, it is gospel for sinners who know that their only hope is the sovereign triumph of God's grace over their rebellious will." This is when Bethlehem [Baptist Church] contacted me at the end of 1979. And I do not hesitate to say that because of Romans 9 I left teaching and became a pastor. The God of Romans 9 has been the Rock-solid foundation of all I have said and done in the last 22 years.[30]

On January 27, 1980, in his candidating sermon on Philippians 1:20–21, John raised the question, "Is death better than life? Is departing to be with Christ better than staying here?" He answered:

> If I didn't believe that, how could I dare to aspire to the role of pastor—anywhere—not to mention at Bethlehem Baptist Church where 108 members are over 80 and another 171 over 65? But I do believe it, and say to every gray-haired believer in this church, with all the authority of Christ's apostle, the best is yet to come! And I don't mean a fat pension and a luxury condominium. I mean Christ.[31]

Now three decades of pastoral ministry ago, John's first move was from the Saint Paul suburbs to inner-city Minneapolis, into a house that's a short walk from the church. On the parking lot side of a building Bethlehem had moved into almost a century earlier, John eventually put "Hope in God" (Ps. 42:5) in big, bold letters. He was braced by those words as the insecure, inexperienced "rookie" pastor he knew himself to be. Yet, within three years the average age of the congregation dropped into the

---

[28]John has never lost his affection for and influence with students, as evidenced by his reception at such massive student rallies as Passion '97, '98, '99, '05, '07, Passion Twenty Ten, and OneDay 2000 and 2003.
[29]The youngest of the boys, Barnabas William, was born in 1983.
[30]Piper, "The Absolute Sovereignty of God."
[31]Piper, *Don't Waste Your Life*, 67–68.

twenties as hundreds of former students and their young families began to rejuvenate this old "flagship church" of the Minnesota Baptist Conference. A loyal, long-term team of associate pastors began climbing aboard in the years that followed, and today Bethlehem continues to grow as a multisite church of several thousand.

Six and a half years into his pulpit ministry, John's *Desiring God: Meditations of a Christian Hedonist* was published. It was an initial launching point for his now worldwide reputation as a writer and conference speaker.[32] Two years later, John started targeting pastors and church leaders. A mere seventy of them gathered April 14–16, 1988, in Bethlehem's modest auxiliary chapel to hear J. I. Packer, Ralph Winter, John Armstrong, and Piper himself give lectures on the theme "By Grace through Faith." Now the Desiring God Conference for Pastors annually draws thousands to Minneapolis's Convention Center, usually on the coldest week of a Minnesota winter.

Another significant year in this brief history is 1994. It was Bethlehem's "year of tears," when a moral failure on the staff wrenched John, his colleagues, and the whole congregation more painfully than anything before or since. But in that same year, the retirement of Arnie and Olive Nelson from a dozen years of copying and mailing out audio cassettes of Pastor John's Sunday sermons led to the birth of Desiring God Ministries. John had asked his ministry assistant, Jon Bloom, to pick up the Nelsons' task. Jon requested and received permission to proliferate John's vision of God and Christian living far beyond that little, local work. The result is now a superbly attractive, aggressive, generous, tech-savvy, international enterprise whose history you can read elsewhere in this volume.[33]

Two years later, in 1996, when John was fifty, the Pipers adopted a baby girl.[34] Now their nuclear family was complete—and here we are, back to "nuclear," where I think John hopes always to be.

Conclusion

Has there been a "cooling" to John Piper's flaming and focused exertions over the years? Perhaps. The joys of marriage with Noël have come mingled with struggles alongside such a driven man. With most parents, they've ached together with (and for) their children. He has survived a

---

[32]Bethlehem annually grants him a month-long writing leave from which he usually returns with at least one or two manuscripts that have so far turned into over thirty published books. He has authored books on theology, Christian biography, missions, devotional life, and Christian living.

[33]See chap. 26.

[34]Talitha Ruth is middle-named for the grandmother she never knew, who was tragically killed in a truck-bus accident in Israel on December 16, 1974, the saddest day of John's life until then.

recent brush with prostate cancer. And he still awakens to a daily warfare against the worst of his enemies, himself. So yes, today's battles are waged with the goal of less anger and more ardor—a calmer head along with a warmer heart.

Nevertheless, this martyr-admiring, passion-spreading, culture-confronting, hyphenated-expression-creating pastor three doors down still cannot help but know and go nuclear with Christ at his core as the glad and glorious "blazing center."

3

WHO IS JOHN PIPER?

David Mathis

A ware of the distastefulness of both hagiography and exposé, I write as John's assistant in answer to the question Who is John Piper? John is both boss and friend, pastor and mentor. So, the task is fraught with difficulty—like everyday life.

Admittedly I don't approach the topic impartially. No feigned neutrality here. I work for the man because I love the vision of God and mission that flows from his heart and life. Such are the strengths and weaknesses of learning about a man from those who know him best.

I'm close enough to see more warts than most, but this is hardly the place for cataloging those. However, being close enough to see the faults others don't see also means being close enough to see evidences of God's grace that others may miss. With that grace in mind, I offer here my thanks to God for some of John's gifts and strengths.

From Three Distances

I'll answer the question Who is John Piper? from the three distances at which I have known him in the last decade. Unlike many who have known John only in a personal context or mainly in the large-church atmosphere of Bethlehem, I first knew (of) him from far away, when I was a student at Furman University in Greenville, South Carolina. And unlike most who have known him only from a distance, I've also known John as one of his students and as a member at Bethlehem. And unlike most at Bethlehem and beyond, I've had the privilege of getting to know John much better over the last four years while working with him day in and day out, at home and on the road.

I begin from the greatest distance, likely the distance shared by most readers of this chapter: "Piper" the far-away prophet. Then I'll move in closer, to "Pastor John," the nearby shepherd. And finally, I'll occupy most of my space with "John"—boss, mentor, and friend.

Piper the Prophetic Voice Far Away

Piper the distant prophet is the "Reformed rock star" (coined by Mark Dever, I believe) who speaks at major conferences and publishes book after book. This is the most out-of-focus perspective on Piper, no doubt, but inevitably the main version most readers of this book can know. You've read his books, listened to possibly hundreds of his sermons, and maybe seen him speak live at conferences. His son Abraham once introduced him by saying that some see his dad as "a kind of disembodied idea machine." One classic sermon after another, at Bethlehem and on the road, made available at the Desiring God Web site. Several books a year. Blog post after blog post. And most recently, tweet after tweet. He exudes seemingly endless angles on the glory of God, the centrality of the gospel, and how our joy in the crucified Christ both satisfies our soul and glorifies our Father in heaven.

My first exposure to this distant "Piper" came when I was a freshman at Furman reading *Desiring God* and having my little world turned upside down. The Piper I got to know was the Christian hedonist wielding words like *joy*, *delight*, *treasure*, *glory*, *praise*, and *magnify* in a way I'd never seen—and complete with a barrage of hyphenated adjectives. Piper was the one giving my duty-laden version of Christianity a whole new take on God, the world, sin, faith, and everyday life. I became a Christian hedonist first, and only later a Calvinist.

By the time I graduated from Furman in May 2003, a relationship between Bethlehem and Campus Outreach (the college ministry I was involved with) had developed, and a team of ten of us left South Carolina for Minnesota in August of 2003 to start Campus Outreach Minneapolis. Now the distant "Piper" would become "Pastor John."

Piper the Pastor

One of the first things I learned after arriving at Bethlehem in the fall of 2003 was that "Pastor John" was not nearly as celebrated in Minneapolis as "Piper" was in parts of the Bible Belt. He seemed relatively unknown in the Twin Cities, and his South Minneapolis neighborhood was largely unaware it had an author in its midst so well known in other parts of the country—a prophet without honor in his hometown, I supposed.

Having soaked up pages upon pages of Piper from afar, I was amazed how nonchalant the Bethlehemites were about reading Pastor John's most recent books. Of course, they loved him—but as pastor, not as far-off prophet. And it was so good for me to see this Pastor John in this element—this more realistic context—participating as one of the twenty-plus pastors at staff meetings, sitting among the elders as a peer and equal (even though clearly first among them), graciously evaluating rookie preachers in his preaching class.

At Bethlehem I found the more everyday Pastor John, not merely the Big Name who rocked the Big Event with sixty minutes of preaching and book after book. I quickly learned that John is first and foremost pastor, not conference speaker or best-selling author. His speaking and writing flow from his everyday practice of steeping his soul in the Bible and shepherding the needs of his flock at Bethlehem.

In addition to doing part-time college ministry at the University of Minnesota with Campus Outreach, I started that fall as a student at The Bethlehem Institute (TBI), now Bethlehem Seminary.[1] Thursday lunch hour was (and still is) "Table Talk," where the seminary students brought a bag lunch, sat around a big circle of tables with Pastor John, heard what was on his "front burner" of life and ministry, and asked questions to our hearts' content—or until the end of the hour, which always seemed to come first. It was during these more intimate Q&A times, and in seeing Pastor John deliver a sermon to our hungry congregation weekend after weekend, in the ups and downs of church life, that I got to see his profound pastor's heart.

The biggest takeaway was Pastor John's contagious love for the Bible. Again and again, I went away from Table Talk wanting to be a man of the Scriptures. When asked a question, his mind defaulted to biblical texts, not to confessional formulations, quoting Ephesians and the Gospel of John, not Westminster, to solve a theological problem. This taught

---

[1]For more on TBI and Bethlehem College and Seminary, see chap. 27, "The Vision and History of the Bethlehem Institute," by Tom Steller.

me an invaluable lesson about the baptistic Reformed theology Pastor John loved and proclaimed: however good the Reformed system is, our ultimate authority is always Scripture and Scripture alone. It was clear to us seminarians that Pastor John not only believed in *Sola Scriptura* but practiced it.

John

From January to August 2006, I transitioned from college ministry to working as John's assistant. It was that February that he underwent surgery for prostate cancer. The following month, he left for Cambridge, England, for a five-month sabbatical (where he wrote *What Jesus Demands from the World* and the first draft of his response to N. T. Wright, which grew into *The Future of Justification*), and we kept in close correspondence while he was away. It was this season when "Pastor John" began to become just "John."

This is the John who gave me the Dairy Queen coupons I used to treat Megan, now my wife, to one of our first dates. He was one of the first we called when we got engaged. He officiated at our wedding. Most recently, we traveled together with our wives (and the Pipers' daughter Talitha) for two weeks in Germany and Russia.

This is the everyday life context for the main things I've learned from tagging along with John. Everyday life is complex. It was John's writing and preaching that first taught me explicitly that heart (feeling) is not at odds with head (thinking), that my joy is not at odds with God's glory, and that duty is not at odds with delight. These are the kinds of discoveries I have continued to make in getting to know John better. The rest of this chapter gives seven of those findings in telling who John Piper is.

Seven Lessons Learned from John Piper

From a distance we are inclined to reduce the complexity of personhood to make someone understandable to us on the basis of the little information we have. As I brainstormed the main things I've learned about John, and from him, in the last four years, they brought together realities that we often think of as being in tension or in contradiction rather than in complementary union.[2]

---

[2] John himself put this well in the introduction to a biographical address about his father: "It seems to me that any serious analysis or exploration of a human being's life will always deal in paradoxes. It will see tensions. Again and again, the serious effort to understand another person will meet with ironic realities. . . . Every serious effort to understand another person—especially a Christian—forces us to deal in irony or paradox." John Piper, "Evangelist Bill Piper: Fundamentalist Full of Grace and Joy," available in manuscript, audio, and video form at www.desiringGod.org.

Rigorous Study and Reliance on the Spirit

First, serious study is not at odds with prayerful dependence on the Holy Spirit. Spend much time around John, and soon you'll hear 2 Timothy 2:7, "Think over what [the Bible says], for the Lord will give you understanding in everything." Not our thinking only, and not God's giving only, but both. *God gives* us insight in *our thinking*. Rigorous study and reliance on the Spirit aren't contradictory, but complementary and vital.[3]

The first time I entered John's study in his home, I saw in the middle of his decades-old, dark-brown wooden desk a gray-rimmed monitor with a yellow sticky note that said, "Help!" It is John's reminder that with every e-mail and every line of every sermon, he needs God's help. And this kind of continual plea for God's help in no way disinclines us from hard work, but rather energizes us for it as we study in hope that God will be pleased to lead us in truth and grant us understanding.

Fridays are John's sermon prep days. We block off the day for him to craft his message for the weekend and type it out in manuscript form. John won't go to sleep Friday night until the first draft is done. Sometimes it's late night Friday, but often he's finished around dinnertime.

Only on occasion will John take a Friday lunch appointment away from the sacred day of preparation. Several times as I've driven him to one of these Friday lunch parentheses in his preparation, he's recounted a discovery made over the years. I've heard it several times now, but I enjoy every time he shares it. He says he often senses that God gives him breakthroughs in his sermon preparation because he is working to feed the flock that weekend—not merely to publish and provide some new academic research, but being in desperate need of God's immediate help. When he left the academy for pastoral ministry, he thought he was giving up the extra time he would need for exegetical and theological breakthroughs, but he sees now that God is often pleased to give preachers in a moment an insight that might have taken them hours or days to come to otherwise. God loves to give gifts of insight to his flock's undershepherds when the weekend is fast approaching.

Connected to this Spirit reliance in study is prayer. In many ways John is a man of prayer. Perhaps he will feel that statement is overly generous, but he seems to surpass many of us at Bethlehem in his public and private devotion to prayer. Weekly he attends, on average, five half-hour prayer meetings at Bethlehem—two early mornings and three preservice

---

[3]John writes most extensively about this relationship between God's gift of illumination and our role in thinking in the book *Think: The Life of the Mind and the Love of God* (Wheaton, IL: Crossway, 2010).

gatherings—and our brief but frequent prayer times on the road are one of the most memorable parts of traveling with John. Before we leave the room for any appointment or speaking event, we pray for God's help, that the unbelieving would believe, that the saints would be sanctified, that Jesus would be honored, and that the gospel would run and triumph.

I've found that maybe the most amazing thing about John in relation to his studies is not his raw intellectual power but his profound "spirituality" (for lack of a better word). John has a kind of *spiritual* brilliance—a deep reliance on the Spirit combined with years of wrestling with biblical texts—mingled with discipline and a desire for learning that has made him an unusually effective pastor, writer, and speaker.

John may be the paragon of lifelong learning. He's constantly curious, always wanting to grow, always eager to learn more, ever ready to give undivided attention to some fresh article, book, or speaker. In some ways, the odds are stacked against him intellectually. Growing up, he was a sharp student, but not a standout; he is a very slow reader; and he may have a below-average memory. But the Holy Spirit can make up for our weaknesses when he chooses, and even turn them to strengths. Slow readers, be encouraged. Weak memories, take heart. Less than world-class intellects, don't give up.

Introversion and Relational Investment

Second, being an introvert is not at odds with being increasingly relational and bringing great good into others' lives in people-intensive contexts. It's no secret that John is an introvert. He'd prefer to stay along the periphery of the crowd than work the room. He'd rather pray through prespeaking butterflies than jabber them away. And what I've seen in John is that one doesn't have to be an extrovert to make serious impact in others' lives in relationally demanding situations. Introversion is not at odds with personal investment in people.

It was April 2009 at Park Church in Chicago. Don Carson and John were speaking to a packed house (even multiple overflow rooms were filled) on the topic of the pastor as theologian and the theologian as pastor. At the conclusion of the night, the front was crawling with eager faces wanting a piece of John and Don. I don't know whether that's Don's favorite setting (I suspect not), but it's clearly not John's. Two younger friends of John's were in attendance, and so we opted to sneak away and spend several hours with them. We stayed up so late, in fact, that John got sick the next day and coughed his way through the next week or so. It wasn't that John the introvert evaded the crowd to get alone, but he bowed out of the celebrity hoopla to make the most of a chance to invest a few hours in some younger men.

Working with John, I've seen his intentionality in caring for younger men, both seminarians and young pastors. His investment in the young—whether seminary students at Table Talk and in his preaching class, or the younger generation of guys who work at Desiring God, or Acts 29 church planters—evidences the heart of a man who not only has invested himself in the masses through his writing and preaching, but also desires to invest himself in the few within more relational contexts.[4]

Publishing and Pastoring

Third, in relation to the previous points, I've seen that writing and pastoring are not at odds. For many years now, the Bethlehem elders have granted John a month away each year to write (four consecutive weekends out of the pulpit). The church has not suffered because of these leaves, but benefited immensely. John uses these times to go deep with God in the Book, and to work hard at saying in fresh ways the same old glorious central truths about God, the world, our sin, and Christ that have sustained Christians for centuries.

John's pastoral ministry flows from his writing—from his day-in, day-out crafting of fresh formulations of gospel truth in articles and blog posts and tweets, to his weekly written preparation for sermons, to his annual month-long writing leave.

Theology and Everyday Life

Fourth, theology is not mainly for the ivory tower, but for everyday life. John is indeed not the disembodied-idea machine, but a husband, father, and aging Baby Boomer with all the pains and stresses of marital tension, parental difficulties, and frequent doctor visits and prescriptions.

When I stop by his house on Monday mornings to pick up the sermon manuscript from the weekend to get it ready for posting on the Web, John often has on a damp shirt and drops of sweat running off his long nose from his morning jog. He's the John who loves pizza, a greasy burger with fries, and his Diet Coke with lime. And he's the John who—despite his weaknesses and sins, which he seems to stay aware of daily—tries again and again, day after day, to live 1 Corinthians 10:31: "Whether you eat or drink, or whatever you do, do all to the glory of God." The John who produces the seeming theological masterpieces in sermon and book is

---

[4]On the relational front, one more important thing to note is John's weekly face-to-face investment in the people of Bethlehem in his postservice availability. Week after week, service after service, John stands at the front after the benediction to shake hands, pray with the hurting, meet new people, and greet old friends. He stays as long as people linger to talk, usually forty-five minutes or more, often over an hour.

the same John who does the theology of everyday life every day, running errands, finding flowers for Noël, working through (almost constant) computer snafus, and visiting the dying at the hospital.

Productivity and Family

A fifth lesson is that occupational productivity is not necessarily at odds with care for family. True, there can be tension—tension enough to take drastic measures in pursuit of resolution. But seeing John wrestle forward on both fronts gives me hope for the complementarity of the two. From far away, John appears to many to be a blazing ball of productivity. Another sermon. Another article. Three more blog posts. A dozen more tweets. And another book, seemingly all in a week's work. Well, it's not quite that simple.

Maybe only Noël sees the extent to which apparently normal days can get drowned by new requests and pastoral demands and emotional strains and distraction after distraction that make productivity seem to evaporate. From an insider, you should know that John may not be as productive as you think. He often feels like he's squandered time and not made the most of the day. And he knows well how to copy and paste, using some old material from his thirty-plus-year pastoral reservoir with some fresh life when needed.[5]

And you may be surprised how drastic a step such a seemingly productive man is willing to take in pursuit of extended time away with wife and family. On March 28, 2010, John announced to the church that he had requested of the elders, and they had granted him, an eight-month leave of absence "because of a growing sense that my soul, my marriage, my family, and my ministry-pattern need a reality check from the Holy Spirit." John said that one of the goals of such a leave was that "I want to say to Noël that she is precious to me in a way that, at this point in our 41-year pilgrimage, can be said best by stepping back for a season from virtually all public commitments." As this book goes to press, John is on that leave, tending "the precious garden" of his home. When the strain between home life and ministry rose to an acute season of difficulty, it was public ministry that took the backseat, not wife and family. We are praying that God is richly blessing John's time away.[6]

At various points I've heard him say that he wishes he'd done more with his family over the years, but that hasn't taken away from how

---

[5]Younger pastors aspiring to emulate John's mass of material should note that such a reservoir isn't developed overnight. John's deep well of theological and pastoral content stems from forty-plus years of frequent journaling, the practice of reading the Bible through every year, thirty years of weekly expository preaching through biblical texts, and the discipline of regular writing.

[6]John Piper, "John Piper's Upcoming Leave," blog posted March 28, 2010, at www.desiringGod.org.

encouraging it has been for me as a young husband to see the priority
he places on family, and how he is willing to stand firm, even with his
pastoral heart, against the many assaults on his calendar to preserve it,
even to the point of taking the significant step he recently has.[7]

Passion for Truth and Capacities for Kindness

Sixth, passion for truth is not at odds with great capacities for kindness.
It is God-like—reflecting a holy God who loves sinners. John is known
for his passion for truth, but those who know him well know he can
be a surprisingly warmhearted man. In the last four years, we've spent
hours and hours together on the road and around town, and John has
been amazingly gracious with this inadequate, weak, naïve, flawed, sinful assistant.

John is the kind of leader who is able to maintain high expectations of
those under his charge while showing them astounding grace. His style
shows that good leadership doesn't manipulate behavior but captivates
the heart. He seeks to effect change from the inside out, rather than just
jerry-rigging the externals of moral conformity.

Perhaps somewhat analogous is John's "brokenhearted boldness"—a
phrase he uses frequently to describe the inner dynamics of the Christian
life in a world where God is sovereign, sin remains, pain is prominent,
and the work of Christ has been accomplished. As John's life authentically demonstrates, the Christian has great reason for boldness, as well
as for brokenness. John is a crier and knows what it's like to have your
heart broken by friends, family, and congregants. But he also is a man
of great boldness, at least in the pulpit, as those who have heard his
preaching will testify. Biblically the two belong together this side of the
King's return.

---

[7]I'm frequently asked what John's calendar looks like. His weekly (nontravel) routine has changed a lot
over the years, I'm told, but our rhythm up until early 2010 looks roughly like this: Sundays, preaching
twice in the mornings, lunch and afternoon with the family, occasional evening commitment like monthly
pastors' small group; Mondays, day off, lunch with Noël, errands, time with family; Tuesdays, morning
pastoral staff meeting (and staff lunch), afternoon meeting with pastoral leadership team and appointment
slots with Bethlehem members, evening elders' meeting (every third week); Wednesdays, writing the weekly
Taste & See article, possible lunch meeting or video shoot at Desiring God, afternoons for e-mail catch-up
or preparing a special message for an upcoming speaking event, Wednesday night church; Thursdays,
chapel and preaching class with the seminarians, Table Talk at lunch, afternoon for appointments and
catch-up, evening at home; Fridays, sermon prep and time at home; Saturdays, reviewing sermon in the
morning, lunch with his daughter Talitha, sermon rehearsal in the afternoon, preaching Saturday night,
bowl of cereal at home afterward.
    When we travel, we try our best not to leave until at least Tuesday morning (to preserve his day off
and time with family) and to return home by Thursday evening (to preserve Friday for sermon preparation). Because of this, John normally does not accept weekend engagements and does his best to keep
from being away on Monday. In recent years the elders have granted John five weekends each year (in
addition to vacation and writing leave) to be away at special Desiring God events, one local, two domestic,
and two international.

Life for Christ and Death as Gain

Seventh, living for Christ and seeing death as gain flow from the same heart—the heart that counts Jesus as our greatest treasure and in doing so supremely honors the Savior. John gave his candidating sermon at Bethlehem in January of 1980 from Philippians 1. He shared then that his greatest desire in life is to say with the apostle Paul that "it is my eager expectation and hope that . . . Christ will be honored in my body, whether by life or by death. For to me to live is Christ, and to die is gain" (Phil. 1:20–21). The common thread that makes our living to be honoring to Jesus and our dying to be gain is our being satisfied in, delighting in, enjoying Jesus more than anything else this life has to offer.

When he received word on December 21, 2005, that he had prostate cancer and needed surgery, his mind went to 1 Thessalonians 5:9–10: "God has not destined us for wrath, but to obtain salvation through our Lord Jesus Christ, who died for us so that whether we are awake or asleep we might live with him." Whether awake or asleep—with Jesus. John truly has a contagious love for Jesus.

The greatest single benefit from working with John the last four years is that I love Jesus more. I could never tally all the benefits, but at the top of that unfinished list is John's infectious love for, admiration for, praise of, and delight in Jesus, who loved us and gave himself for us. In this is Jesus supremely magnified. And in this, and only in this, are our hearts most deeply satisfied. Thank you, John, for turning my eyes again and again to Jesus.

Part 2

CHRISTIAN HEDONISM

4

CHRISTIAN·HEDONISM

Piper and Edwards on the Pursuit of Joy in God

Sam Storms

John Piper is known for many things. The mention of his name will prompt some to think of his rigorously biblical defense of the sovereignty of God. Others will point to his passionate and always expository preaching, or perhaps his commitment to the pro-life movement, or even his influence among the youth today as seen by his presence at the many Passion Conferences through the years. More recently he's become widely known for his articulation of the doctrine of justification and his response to those who seek to redefine it.

Some would likely mention the fact that he's never owned a television! I vividly remember my first visit to John's home in 1992. He had invited me to speak at his annual pastor's conference which, as it turns out, is regularly scheduled during the week following the Super Bowl. Upon arriving at his home after the Sunday service, I told John that I had been looking forward for quite some time to watching the game with him. "Not at my house," he said. "We don't have a TV." After I recovered from the initial shock, John graciously agreed to take me to the home of a church member where I could indulge myself in this annual affair. And yes, John stayed and actually watched the game![1]

But if there is any single subject or theme most readily associated with the name of John Piper, it is assuredly that of *Christian hedonism*. John's deliberately provocative[2] choice of terms in labeling his view has not been applauded by everyone, while others reject outright the concept itself, regardless of what it is called. Yet there are those, such as myself, whose lives have been forever changed by John's defense of Christian hedonism. Aside from my conversion to Christ in 1960, nothing has so greatly affected my Christian life as my reading, in 1986, of *Desiring God: Meditations of a Christian Hedonist*.[3]

What Is Christian Hedonism?

There was a time when I thought the verb *enjoy* and the noun *God* should never be used in the same sentence. I could understand *fearing* God and *obeying* God, even *loving* God. But enjoying God struck me as inconsistent with the biblical mandates both to glorify God, on the one hand, and to deny myself, on the other. How could I be committed above all else to seeking God's glory if I were concerned about my own joy? My gladness and God's glory seemed to cancel each other out. I had to choose between one and the other, but embracing them both struck me as out of the question. Worse still, enjoying God sounded a bit too lighthearted, almost casual, perhaps even flippant, and I knew that Christianity was serious business.

Then I read Jonathan Edwards (1703–1758). Something he said hit me like a bolt of lightning. I'm not a Christian hedonist because of Jonathan Edwards or John Piper. I'm a Christian hedonist because I believe Psalm 16:11 (among countless other texts):

> You make known to me the path of life;
>> in your presence there is fullness of joy;
>> at your right hand are pleasures forevermore.

---

[1] As strange as it may sound to those unacquainted with Piper, his decision to rid his home of the influence of television was not from a disdain for pleasure, but an expression of his radical pursuit of it. What John regards as the banal and mind-numbing distractions of TV serve only to diminish his capacity to enjoy the one preeminent delight that never fails to satisfy, namely, the mind-expanding and ever-fascinating knowledge of God as revealed in the face of Jesus Christ. The rationale for this will, I pray, become clearer in the course of reading this chapter. See also John's article, "Why I Don't Have a Television and Rarely Go to Movies," June 25, 2009, available at www.desiringGod.org.

[2] See appendix 5, "Why Call It Christian Hedonism?" in *Desiring God: Meditations of a Christian Hedonist*, 3d ed. (Sisters, OR: Multnomah, 2003), 365–69.

[3] There are several instances throughout this chapter where I use language, particularly short phrases or vivid imagery (often either alliterative or hyphenated), that many will recognize has come from John Piper and for which he is justifiably famous. I mention it here rather than cite each instance and source.

This text is more than a declaration of truth: it is an incentive to pursue God. More on this later.

My point is simply that Scripture always has been and will remain the final authority in my life. But Edwards helped me to see that God's glory and my gladness are not antithetical. He helped me see that at the core of Scripture is the truth that my heart's passion for pleasure (which is God-given and *not* the result of sin) and God's passion for praise converge in a way that alone makes sense of human existence. I should let you read it for yourself:

> Now what is glorifying God, but a rejoicing at that glory he has displayed? An understanding of the perfections of God, merely, cannot be the end of the creation; for he had as good [i.e., might as well] not understand it, as see it and not be at all moved with joy at the sight. Neither can the highest end of creation be the declaring God's glory to others; for the declaring God's glory is good for nothing otherwise than to raise joy in ourselves and others at what is declared.[4]

Here it is again, phrased in a slightly different way:

> God is glorified not only by his glory's being seen, but by its being rejoiced in. When those that see it delight in it, God is more glorified than if they only see it. God made the world that he might communicate, and the creature receive, his glory . . . both [with] the mind and the heart. He that testifies his having an idea of God's glory [doesn't] glorify God so much as he that testifies also his approbation [i.e., his heartfelt commendation or praise] of it and his delight in it.[5]

Edwards's point is that *passionate and joyful admiration of God, and not merely intellectual apprehension, is the aim of our existence.* If God is to be supremely glorified in us, it is critically essential that we be supremely glad in him and in what he has done for us in Jesus. This is Christian hedonism. Enjoying God is not a secondary, tangential endeavor. It is central to everything we do. We do not do other things hoping that joy in God will emerge as a by-product. Our reason for the pursuit of God and obedience to him is precisely the joy that is found in him alone. To come to God or to worship him or to yield to his moral will for any reason other than the joy that is found in who he is, is sinful.

---

[4] Jonathan Edwards, *The Works of Jonathan Edwards*, vol. 13, *The "Miscellanies": Entry Nos. a–z, aa–zz, 1–500*, ed. Thomas A. Schafer (New Haven: Yale University Press, 1994), no. 3, p. 200.
[5] Ibid., no. 448, p. 495.

My aim in this chapter is to account for what John Piper means when he speaks and writes about Christian hedonism. I'm not here to defend his choice of terms or to take up his cause against the critics who have challenged his thesis. I simply want to articulate what Piper means. I hope in doing so that the misunderstandings of this concept and the negative response to it may be put to rest. My approach will be to summarize Christian hedonism in seven propositions or theses. I'll follow this, with the considerable help of Jonathan Edwards, by demonstrating the immense practical and sanctifying power of Piper's idea.

Seven Theses on Christian Hedonism[6]
All People Desire Happiness

This is as much a law of human nature, shaped and fashioned in the image of God, as gravity is a law of physics. Many have rejected Christian hedonism due to their misguided belief that to the degree they seek their own well-being they diminish the virtue or moral value of a choice or deed. Doing something because we enjoy it threatens to empty the deed of its moral worth, or so they think. Christian hedonism contends that nothing could be further from the truth. Piper is often heard citing the words of Blaise Pascal in this respect, and we should listen carefully:

> All men seek happiness. This is without exception. Whatever different means they employ, they all tend to this end. The cause of some going to war, and of others avoiding it, is the same desire in both, attended with different views. The will never takes the least step but to this object. This is the motive of every action of every man, even of those who hang themselves.[7]

The immediate response of many is to say, "But don't people commit suicide because they are *un*happy?" Yes, but they choose suicide precisely because they are persuaded that death will bring them more happiness than life ever could. Or perhaps it would be better to say that they believe death will deliver them from the miseries of life. In either case, they hang themselves because they can no longer endure the misery and depression that life has created, and they believe that nothing can be done to bring them the happiness and sense of value and meaning they so desperately desire.

---

[6]Some of what follows has been adapted from what I've written on this subject in my books *Pleasures Evermore: The Life-Changing Power of Enjoying God* (Colorado Springs: NavPress, 2000), and *One Thing: Developing a Passion for the Beauty of God* (Fearn, Ross-shire: Christian Focus, 2004).
[7]Blaise Pascal, *Pascal's Pensées*, trans. W. F. Trotter (New York: E. P. Dutton, 1958), 113 (thought no. 425).

Although what I'm describing may sound unfamiliar to some, even unspiritual, Christian hedonism has a rich heritage in the church. Perhaps no one understood it as clearly or expressed it as vividly as did Edwards. In a sermon entitled "Nothing upon Earth Can Represent the Glories of Heaven," he makes a breathtaking assertion. "God," says Edwards, "created man for nothing else but happiness. He created him only that he might communicate happiness to him."[8] The soul of every man, says Edwards, "necessarily craves happiness. This is a universal appetite of human nature, that is alike in the good and the bad."[9] Observe his use of the words "necessarily" and "universal." When it comes to happiness, *everybody must* seek it. In fact, he goes on to say:

> It is not only natural to all mankind, but to the angels; it is universal among all reasonable, intelligent beings, in heaven, earth, or hell, because it flows necessarily from an intelligent nature. There is no rational being . . . without a love and desire for happiness. It is impossible that there should be any creature made that should love misery, or not love happiness, since it implies a manifest contradiction; for the very notion of misery is to be in a state that nature abhors, and the notion of happiness is to be in such a state as is most agreeable to nature.[10]

This desire for happiness is "insuperable . . . never can be changed, . . . never can be overcome, or in any way abated. Young and old love happiness alike, and good and bad, wise and unwise."[11] Certainly people have different notions of what constitutes happiness and will pursue it according to their particular appetites, but this in no way alters the fact that its presence is universal among mankind.[12]

---

[8]Jonathan Edwards, *The Works of Jonathan Edwards*, vol. 14, *Sermons and Discourses 1723–1729*, ed. Kenneth P. Minkema (New Haven: Yale University Press, 1997), 145–46.
[9]Jonathan Edwards, "Safety, Fulness, and Sweet Refreshment, to Be Found in Christ," in *Jonathan Edwards on Knowing Christ* (Edinburgh: Banner of Truth, 1990), 166.
[10]Ibid., 166–67.
[11]Ibid., 167.
[12]Edwards was only eighteen years old when he preached a sermon entitled "Christian Happiness," in which he affirmed the inescapable yearning for happiness among both the righteous and the wicked: "They certainly are the wisest men that do those things that make most for their happiness, and this in effect is acknowledged by all men in the world, for there is no man upon the earth who isn't earnestly seeking after happiness, and it appears abundantly by the variety of ways they so vigorously seek it; they will twist and turn every way, ply all instruments, to make themselves happy men. Some will wander all over the face of the earth to find it: they will seek it in the waters and dry land, under the waters and in the bowels of the earth, and although the true way to happiness lies right before them and they might easily step into it and walk in it and be brought into as great a happiness as they desire, and greater than they can conceive of, yet they will not enter into it. They try all the false paths; they will spend and be spent, labor all their lives' time, endanger their lives, will pass over mountains and valleys, go through fire and water, seeking for happiness amongst vanities, and are always disappointed, never find what they seek for; but yet like fools and madmen they violently rush forward, still in the same ways. But the righteous are not so; these only, have the wisdom to find the right paths to happiness." *The Works of Jonathan Edwards*, vol. 10, *Sermons and Discourses 1720–1723*, ed. Wilson H. Kimnach (New Haven: Yale University Press, 1992), 303.

It is this ruthless determination among the wicked to find happiness in whatever sinful or perverse experience imaginable that hardens the believing heart against its own impulse for pleasure. Not wanting to be classed among those who reject Jesus, many Christians have wrongly assumed the problem is in their passion and have taken whatever steps they believe will effectively suppress and stifle its expression. But the righteous, says Edwards, ought to differ from the lost in choosing "the right paths to happiness," not in seeking to rid themselves of the desire itself. The problem isn't in the passion; it's in the paths.

People struggle with this because it strikes them as experientially misguided. "How can you say I want happiness and joy and satisfaction when I'm always making decisions that I know are painful and sacrificial?" The answer is that we always choose what we think will *ultimately* maximize personal happiness and minimize personal misery. If you make a decision that is immediately painful and uncomfortable or unsettling, I assure you it is because you believe that such a choice in the long term will generate more pleasure than not. In other words, you gladly forgo present pleasures if you believe the long-term benefits outweigh whatever short-term discomfort you might experience or sacrifice you might make. Likewise, you will ignore long-term consequences if you believe the immediate pleasures of a decision are worth the risk.

Neither Satan nor sin is responsible for this. God is. God made you this way so that you would choose him and his soul-satisfying pleasures in lieu of those fleeting pleasures that ultimately leave you empty and miserable. *The alternative to resisting the passing pleasures of sin isn't religious misery but relishing the permanent pleasures of God.*

God Places No Restraints on the Depths of Delight in Himself That He Commands Us to Pursue

When it comes to satisfying our spiritual appetites, *there is no such thing as excess*. There are no limitations placed on us by God. There are no rules of temperance or laws requiring moderation or boundaries beyond which we cannot go in seeking to enjoy him. We need never pause to inquire whether we've crossed a line or become overindulgent. You need never fear feeling too good about God.

That's not to say our *sensual* appetites should be left unchecked. The Bible is full of prohibitions and restrictions on how and to what extent we indulge our fleshly and bodily desires. But no such rules exist for our *spiritual* appetites. *Christianity forbids us no pleasures, save those that lead to temporal misery and eternal woe.* You cannot desire pleasure too much. You *can* desire the *wrong kind* of pleasure. You can rely on the wrong things to satisfy your soul, things that God has forbidden. But the intensity of the soul's search for joy cannot be too great or too deep or too sharp or too powerful. The divine invitation is that we would satisfy our voracious appetite for spiritual delight by indulging our souls in every delicacy that God has to offer. He bids us to imbibe the waters of spiritual refreshment from a well that never runs dry. He points us to the river of his delights (Ps. 36:8) and says, "Drink!" We are urged to immerse and soak and saturate ourselves in the spiritual pleasures and blessings that he lavishly and abundantly and happily pours forth through Jesus and the power of the Holy Spirit.

Contrary to popular opinion, this is not sin. Sin is the misguided and selfish determination to seek happiness in places where ultimately only emptiness and disillusionment are found. Spiritual hunger is not sin. Sin is declining God's offer of a filet mignon to fill our spiritual bellies with rancid ground beef.

Some respond by pointing to Paul's warning in 2 Timothy 3:4 that in the last days there will appear people who are "lovers of pleasure rather than lovers of God." The key words in this verse are "rather than," for they highlight options that are mutually exclusive. The "pleasure" that people love, and Paul condemns, is sensual, self-indulgent satisfaction that shuts God out. The "pleasure" that I have in mind, and Paul approves, is precisely pleasure in God as God. *He* is our exceeding great reward. *He* is the treasure (and pleasure) we seek. Christian hedonism deplores any pursuit of pleasure that does not have God as the foundation and focus of its enjoyment.

Paul rightly denounces lovers of pleasure *without* God. Christian hedonism rightly applauds lovers of pleasure *in* God. To be a "lover of God" rather than "pleasure" is to find in him, not it, the satisfaction our souls so desperately crave. God is loved when he is the rock on which we stand, the shelter in whom we seek refuge, the oasis where we find refreshment. Second Timothy 3:4, therefore, is not a problem for Christian hedonism but a proof text!

Even Self-Denial Is a Hedonistic Choice

I say this in response to those who argue that the words of Jesus in Mark 8:34–37 contradict Christian hedonism:

> And calling the crowd to him with his disciples, he said to them, "If anyone would come after me, let him deny himself and take up his cross and follow me. For whoever would save his life will lose it, but whoever loses his

life for my sake and the gospel's will save it. For what does it profit a man to gain the whole world and forfeit his soul? For what can a man give in return for his soul?"

Our Lord's appeal that we deny ourselves and take up our cross is actually grounded upon the concern that each person inescapably has for his or her own soul. The only way you can respond appropriately to his call for "self"-denial is to be wholeheartedly committed to the happiness and eternal welfare of your "self." If you lack concern for the eternal welfare of your soul, you will lose all incentive for obeying Christ's command. His exhortation is persuasive because of the intensely passionate concern you have for what might happen if you don't obey. Jesus calls on us to deny ourselves because otherwise we'll die! We must "lose" our lives if we hope to "save" them. And it is the legitimacy of that personal hope on which Jesus bases his appeal. Clearly, Jesus grounds his exhortation in the inescapable reality of human desire for one's own welfare and happiness and well-being. (Let us never forget that self-interest is not the same as selfishness.) C. S. Lewis, another formative influence on Piper's conception of Christian hedonism, explains it this way: "The New Testament has lots to say about self-denial, but not about self-denial as an end in itself. We are told to deny ourselves and to take up our crosses in order that we may follow Christ; and nearly every description of what we shall ultimately find if we do so contains an appeal to desire."[13]

Jesus is aware that we desire what is best for ourselves. He neither rebukes us for it nor calls for repentance as if it were sinful. In fact, he intentionally targets that universal desire and entreats us on the basis of its undeniable presence in our souls. His somewhat paradoxical advice is that the best thing you can do for your "self" is to deny "self"! Eternal life is the best and most advantageous thing you can obtain for your "self," but it may cost you temporal life and the passing pleasures of sinful self-indulgence.

What possible profit is there from enhancing your physical life now if it costs you eternal life in the age to come? Self-denial, Piper reminds us, "has value precisely in proportion to the superiority of the reality embraced above the one desired. Self-denial that is not based on a desire for some superior goal will become the ground of boasting."[14]

---

[13]C. S. Lewis, "The Weight of Glory," in *The Weight of Glory and Other Addresses*, ed. Walter Hooper (New York: Simon & Schuster, 1996), 25.
[14]Piper, *Desiring God*, 296.

Jesus is simply asking that you sacrifice the lesser blessings of temporal and earthly comforts in order to gain the greater blessings of eternal and unending pleasure. Do what is best for your "self," says Jesus, and deny your "self"! To refuse to follow Jesus is to deny your "self" the greatest imaginable joy. His call is for us to renounce our vain attempt to satisfy our souls through illicit sex and ambition and earthly fortune. Instead, do yourself a favor. Follow Jesus and gain true life, true joy, true pleasure. Jesus, if I may say this reverently, is not a Buddhist! He is not telling us to ignore our needs or to repress our longings but to fulfill them . . . in him! Again, Lewis says:

> If there lurks in most modern minds the notion that to desire our own good and earnestly to hope for the enjoyment of it is a bad thing, I submit that this notion has crept in from Kant and the Stoics and is no part of the Christian faith. Indeed, if we consider the unblushing promises of reward and the staggering nature of the rewards promised in the Gospels, it would seem that Our Lord finds our desires not too strong, but too weak. We are half-hearted creatures, fooling about with drink and sex and ambition when infinite joy is offered [to] us, like an ignorant child who wants to go on making mud pies in a slum because he cannot imagine what is meant by the offer of a holiday at the sea. *We are far too easily pleased.*[15]

God Is Most Glorified in Us When We Are Most Satisfied in Him

Or again, as Piper has said: "Pleasure is the measure of our treasure."[16] The best gauge or standard by which to judge the value of any treasure is the intensity and depth of the pleasure it evokes. Thus the greatness and glory and majesty of God are most clearly seen in the extent to which our souls find satisfaction in him and all that he is for us in Jesus. Or, to put it in other terms, *God's preeminent glory is in our passionate gladness in him.*

Piper himself provides a helpful illustration in making this point. Consider the difference between a microscope and a telescope and how it relates to our knowledge and enjoyment of God, and what it means to glorify him.[17] Both a microscope and a telescope are designed to magnify objects. So, too, are we. The Bible repeatedly calls on us, especially in the Psalms, to magnify the Lord:

> Oh, magnify the LORD with me,
>   and let us exalt his name together! (Ps. 34:3; cf. 35:27)

---

[15]Lewis, "The Weight of Glory," 25–26, my emphasis.
[16]From Piper's sermon, "There Is No Greater Satisfaction," October 1, 1990, available at www.desiring-God.org.
[17]Piper, *The Dangerous Duty of Delight* (Sisters, OR: Multnomah, 2001), 17.

I will praise the name of God with a song;
  I will magnify him with thanksgiving. (Ps. 69:30)

My soul magnifies the Lord,
  and my spirit rejoices in God my Savior. (Luke 1:46–47)

But there are two entirely different ways of magnifying God, one of which exalts him and the other demeans him. First, you can magnify God the way a microscope does by focusing on something quite small, most often invisible to the naked eye, and causing it to look much, much bigger than it really is. This is magnification by distortion! This is *not* how we are to magnify God! Tragically, though, that's how many Christians think of God and how they are to worship him. They think that in their lives and in their prayers and in their praise they are causing God to look bigger and greater and more glorious than he really is, in and of himself. Worship is not like blowing up a balloon. God is not honored by human inflation, as if the breath of our praise enhances and expands his visibility and worth. To think that apart from our praise God remains shrunken and shriveled is to dishonor him who "gives to all mankind life and breath and everything" (Acts 17:25).

But you can also magnify God the way a telescope would. A telescope helps people who are small and distant to see something indescribably huge and massive by making it to appear as it really and truly is. A telescope peers into the distant realms of our universe and displays before our eyes the massive, unfathomable, indescribable dimensions of what is there. Only in this latter sense are we called to magnify the Lord. Of course, the analogy breaks down, as all analogies eventually do, because God is infinitely greater than anything you can see through a telescope. Indeed, he created and fashioned everything you can see through a telescope. But I trust you get my point.

Let's change words for a moment and put in place of *magnify* and *glorify* the word *exalt*. What is the most biblical and effective way to exalt God? How might we engage in the exaltation of the Creator? Piper's answer is found in another word, the spelling of which differs in only one letter from our first word: *exult*. This is not semantic nitpicking. The Christian life hangs suspended on it.

To exult is to rejoice and to celebrate. We exult when we find deep satisfaction in an individual or experience. Whether we say it, shout it, or merely sigh with a profound sense of delight, there are fascination and joy and gladness of heart. There is an emotionally explosive dimension to exultation. To exult in something or someone is to find in that thing or person happiness, gladness, joy, complete and utter satisfaction; it is to savor the object of exultation.

Christian hedonism contends that *exulting* in God is the most biblical and effective means for *exalting* him! Or to put it in other terms: *God is praised when he is prized!*[18] Understanding God is but a means to enjoying God. We tell others of this glory so that we might elevate and intensify joy in both their hearts and our own.

How do you measure the value of something you hold dear? How do you assess the worth of a prize? Is it not by the depth of delight it induces in your heart? Is it not by the intensity and quality of your joy in what it is? Is it not by how excited and enthralled and thrilled you are in the manifold display of its attributes, characteristics, and properties? Is it not by the extent of the sacrifice you are willing to make to gain it, to guard it, and to keep it? In other words, your satisfaction in what the treasure is and does for you is the standard or gauge by which its glory (worth and value) is revealed. The treasure, which is God, is most glorified in and by you when your pleasure in him is maximal and optimal.

That is why if you want to elevate God, celebrate God! Treasure him. Prize him. Delight in him. Enjoy him. In doing so you magnify him, you show him to be the most wonderful and sweet and all-sufficient being in the universe. Enjoying God is not a momentary diversion from more important responsibilities you have as a Christian. Enjoying God is not a means to a higher end. This *is* the end. Enjoying is not a pathway to the pinnacle. It is the pinnacle, the purpose for which you and I live. As such, it is the solution to our struggle with sin. The antidote to apathy is the enjoyment of God. It is the divine catalyst for human change.

Christian Hedonism Insists That We Be Deadly Serious about Joy

Why is joy so central to Christian hedonism? What is it about joy or delight in God that makes it so important? Or again, what is it about joy in God rather than simple obedience or fear or service that uniquely honors and exalts him? Several things are worthy of note.

Joy, unlike any other human experience, requires the engagement and expression of the whole soul. There are things that I understand but in which I find no joy. There are things that I choose, such as eating squash, which bring me no immediate delight whatsoever. But when I genuinely enjoy something, there is both intellectual and volitional, as well as emotional, satisfaction. Simply put, joy is more holistic than any

---

[18]John Piper, "The Inner Essence of Worship," November 16, 1997, available at www.desiringGod.org.

other human experience. We must also remember that there is no such thing as hypocritical or insincere joy. You can pretend to have joy when you really don't (as when I'll pretend to enjoy the squash you serve me at your home). You can fake having joy, but you can't have fake joy. There's something pure and sincere and authentic and genuine about joy that isn't the case with any other human affection.

Most importantly, joy—more clearly and thoroughly than any other response—reveals the worth and value and splendor of whatever has captivated your heart. When you experience and express joy in God, perhaps in the midst of suffering or loss, others may take note and ask, What must this God be like that he is deemed worthy not simply of acknowledgment but delight, not simply of recognition but rejoicing? Or, as Piper has put it: "Joy is the clearest witness to the worth of what we enjoy. It is the deepest reverberation in the heart of man of the value of God's glory."[19]

We must also be clear about the meaning of this joy that is so central to Christian hedonism. We are talking here about a *deep* (not superficial or merely surface), *durable* (it sustains you in the worst of times, no less than in the best of times) *delight* (not merely duty or following God out of a sense of moral obligation) *in the splendor of God* (not in the stuff or goodies or achievements that occupy so many today) *that utterly ruins you for anything else.* It is a whole-souled savoring of the spiritual sweetness of Jesus that drives out all competing pleasures and leads the soul to rest content with the knowledge of God and the blessings of intimacy with him. This is the kind of joy that, rather than being dependent on material and physical comfort, actually frees you from bondage to it and liberates you from sinful reliance on worldly conveniences and gadgets and gold.

As noted earlier, according to Christian hedonism, there is in every soul an insatiable hunger for happiness, a chronic and unending ache for joy and delight. God has hardwired into us a yearning and longing and unrelenting passion for pleasure. It's part of what it means to be created in his image. Thus the problem is not that we have deep, passionate, and powerful desires for joy and pleasure. The problem is that we are far, far, far too easily satisfied. We have settled for pathetic little pleasures like illicit sex and drunkenness and earthly wealth when God offers us fullness of joy and pleasures that never lose their capacity to satisfy and enthrall. The counsel of Christian hedonism is that we pursue God's presence where "fullness of joy" may be found (Ps. 16:11) and that we

---

[19]John Piper, "Joy and the Supremacy of Christ in a Postmodern World," in *The Supremacy of Christ in a Postmodern World*, ed. John Piper and Justin Taylor (Wheaton, IL: Crossway, 2007), 78.

"taste and see that the LORD is good" (Ps. 34:8) and that we "delight [ourselves] in the LORD" (Ps. 37:4) and that we "drink from the river of [God's] delights" (Ps. 36:8).

The Foundation of Our Delight in God Is God's Delight in Himself

To come straight to the point, our glad-hearted passion for God is exceeded only by *God's* glad-hearted passion for God. If the chief end of man is to glorify God by enjoying him forever, the chief end of God is to glorify God and to enjoy himself forever! What is the preeminent passion in God's heart? What is God's greatest pleasure? In what does God take supreme delight? Piper and Christian hedonism suggest that the preeminent passion in God's heart is his own glory. God is at the center of his own affections. The supreme love of God's life is God. God is preeminently committed to the fame of his name. God is himself the end for which God created the world. Better still, God's immediate goal in all he does is his own glory. God relentlessly and unceasingly creates, rules, orders, directs, speaks, judges, saves, destroys, and delivers in order to make known who he is and to secure from the whole of the universe the praise, honor, and glory of which he and he alone is ultimately and infinitely worthy.

The proof for this bold proposition is the multitude of biblical texts that explicitly affirm it, which I will not cite here for the sake of space.[20] What is of immediate concern, however, is the objection this assertion provokes, to wit, that if God is so utterly consumed with his own glory, he cannot possibly be committed to our good. Or again, if God is so completely in love with himself, how can he be in love with us? This important question leads directly into our seventh and concluding thesis concerning Christian hedonism.

God's Passion for His Glory Is the Consummate Expression of Love for His People

Piper has often said that God is the one being in the universe for whom self-exaltation is the supremely loving act. No one has explained this with greater clarity than C. S. Lewis. Early in his Christian life Lewis was extremely puzzled, even agitated, by the recurring demand by Christians that we all "praise God." That was bad enough. What made it even worse is that God himself called for praise of God himself. This was almost more than Lewis could stomach. What kind of God is it who incessantly demands that his people tell him how great he is?

---

[20]For a survey of those many biblical texts, see my book, *Pleasures Evermore*, 81–101. See also Tom Schreiner's essay in this present volume.

Lewis describes his struggle and how he worked through it in an extraordinary passage from the essay "The Problem of Praise in the Psalms."[21]

> We all despise the man who demands continued assurance of his own virtue, intelligence or delightfulness; we despise still more the crowd of people round every dictator, every millionaire, every celebrity, who gratify that demand. Thus a picture, at once ludicrous and horrible, both of God and His worshippers, threatened to appear in my mind. The Psalms were especially troublesome in this way—"Praise the Lord," "O praise the Lord with me," "Praise Him." . . . Worse still was the statement put into God's own mouth, "whoso offereth me thanks and praise, he honoureth me" (50:23). It was hideously like saying, "What I most want is to be told that I am good and great." . . . It was extremely distressing. It made one think what one least wanted to think. Gratitude to God, reverence to Him, obedience to Him, I thought I could understand; not this perpetual eulogy. . . .

I suspect this strikes us as problematic, as it did Lewis, because we want to think that God is preeminently concerned with us, not himself. We want a God who is man-centered, not God-centered. Worse still, we can't fathom how God could possibly love us the way we think he should if he is so unapologetically obsessed with the praise and glory of his own name. How can God love *me* if all his infinite energy is expended in the love of *himself*? Part of Lewis's problem, as he himself confesses, was that he did not see that

> it is in the process of being worshipped that God communicates His presence to men. It is not of course the only way. But for many people at many times the "fair beauty of the Lord" is revealed chiefly or only while they worship Him together. Even in Judaism the essence of the sacrifice was not really that men gave bulls and goats to God, but that by their so doing God gave Himself to men; in the central act of our own worship of course this is far clearer—there it is manifestly, even physically, God who gives and we who receive. The miserable idea that God should in any sense need, or crave for, our worship like a vain woman wanting compliments, or a vain author presenting his new books to people who never met or heard him, is implicitly answered by the words, "If I be hungry I will not tell *thee*" (50:12). Even if such an absurd Deity could be conceived, He would hardly come to *us*, the lowest of rational creatures, to gratify His appetite. I don't want my dog to bark approval of my books.

[21]Found in *Reflections on the Psalms* (New York: Harcourt, Brace and World, 1958), 90–98.

Lewis is addressing, somewhat indirectly, the question, How, or better yet, *why*, do you worship a God who needs nothing? If God is altogether self-sufficient and cannot be served by human hands as if he needed anything (Acts 17:24–25; Rom. 11:33–36), least of all glory, why does he command our worship and praise of him? Lewis continues:

> But the most obvious fact about praise—whether of God or anything—strangely escaped me. I thought of it in terms of compliment, approval, or the giving of honour. I had never noticed that *all enjoyment spontaneously overflows into praise unless* . . . shyness or the fear of boring others is deliberately brought in to check it. The world rings with praise—lovers praising their mistresses [Romeo praising Juliet and vice versa], readers their favourite poet, walkers praising the countryside, players praising their favourite game—praise of weather, wines, dishes, actors, motors, horses, colleges, countries, historical personages, children, flowers, mountains, rare stamps, rare beetles, even sometimes politicians or scholars. . . . Except where intolerably adverse circumstances interfere, praise almost seems to be inner health made audible. . . . I had not noticed either that just as men spontaneously praise whatever they value, so they spontaneously urge us to join them in praising it: "Isn't she lovely? Wasn't it glorious? Don't you think that magnificent?" The Psalmists in telling everyone to praise God are doing what all men do when they speak of what they care about. My whole, more general, difficulty about the praise of God depended on my absurdly denying to us, as regards the supremely Valuable, what we delight to do, what indeed we can't help doing, about everything else we value.

What Lewis is touching on here is how the love of God for sinners like you and me is ultimately made manifest. God desires our greatest good. But what greater good is there in the universe than God himself? So, if God is truly to love us, he must give us himself. But merely giving us of himself is only the first step in the expression of his affection for sinners. He must work to elicit from our hearts rapturous praise and superlative delight because, as Lewis said, *"all enjoyment spontaneously overflows into praise."* That's the way God made us. We can't help but praise and rejoice in what we most enjoy. The enjoyment itself is stunted and hindered if it is never expressed in joyful celebration. Here's how Lewis explained it:

> I think we delight to praise what we enjoy because *the praise not merely expresses but completes the enjoyment; it is its appointed consummation.* It is not out of compliment that lovers keep on telling one another how beautiful they are; the delight is incomplete till it is expressed. It is frustrat-

ing to have discovered a new author and not to be able to tell anyone how good he is; to come suddenly, at the turn of the road, upon some mountain valley of unexpected grandeur and then to have to keep silent because the people with you care for it no more than for a tin can in the ditch; to hear a good joke and find no one to share it with. . . .

If it were possible for a created soul fully . . . to "appreciate," that is to love and delight in, the worthiest object of all, and simultaneously at every moment to give this delight perfect expression, then that soul would be in supreme beatitude. . . . To see what the doctrine really means, we must suppose ourselves to be in perfect love with God—drunk with, drowned in, dissolved by, that delight which, far from remaining pent up within ourselves as incommunicable, hence hardly tolerable, bliss, flows out from us incessantly again in effortless and perfect expression; our joy is no more separable from the praise in which it liberates and utters itself than the brightness a mirror receives is separable from the brightness it sheds. The Scotch catechism says that man's chief end is "to glorify God and enjoy Him forever." But we shall then know that these are the same thing. Fully to enjoy is to glorify. In commanding us to glorify Him, God is inviting us to enjoy Him.

God's pursuit of my praise of him is not weak self-seeking but the epitome of self-giving love! If my satisfaction in him is incomplete until expressed in praise of him for satisfying me with himself (note well: with *himself*, not his gifts or blessings, but the intrinsic beauty and splendor of God as God), then God's effort to elicit my worship (what Lewis before thought was inexcusable selfishness) is both the most loving thing he could possibly do for me and the most glorifying thing he could possibly do for himself. For in my gladness in him (not his gifts) is his glory in me.

If God is to love you optimally, he must bestow or impart the best gift he has, the greatest prize, the most precious treasure, the most exalted and worthy thing within his power to give. That gift, of course, is himself. Nothing in the universe is as beautiful and captivating and satisfying as God! So, if God loves you he will give himself to you and then work in your soul to awaken you to his beauty and all-sufficiency. In other words, he will strive by all manner and means to intensify and expand and enlarge your joy in him. All of which is to say (as I've heard Piper do so many times) that God's love for you is seen not in his making much of you, but in his graciously enabling you to enjoy making much of him forever.

How could it be otherwise? If God is as excellent and gloriously ineffable and unfathomably majestic as Scripture contends, he wouldn't love us unless he did whatever was necessary to bring us into the knowledge and experience and enjoyment of himself. All other, lesser gifts, such as being made much of, would not be the ultimate expression of divine love. God is the gospel![22] Having God is the good news! All other, necessarily lesser, gifts are good only to the extent that they facilitate the higher, indeed highest, goal of getting God! Making himself known to us in Jesus and working through his Spirit to bring us into white-hot admiration and enjoyment of who he is (that's worship, by the way) is the ultimate and unparalleled act of love.

Therefore, God comes to us and says: "Here I am in all my glory: incomparable, infinite, immeasurable, and unsurpassed. See me! Be satisfied with me! Enjoy me! Celebrate who I am! Experience the height and depth and width and breadth of savoring and relishing me!" Does that sound like God pursuing his own glory? Yes. But it also sounds like God loving you perfectly and passionately. The only way it is not real love is if there is something for you better than God: something more beautiful than God that he can show you, something more pleasing and satisfying than God with which he can fill your heart, something more glorious and majestic than God with which you can occupy yourself for eternity. But there is no such thing! Anywhere! Ever! Thus, as Piper himself has said on countless occasions, the reason God seeks our praise is not that he won't be complete until he *gets* it. Rather, he is seeking our praise because we won't be happy until we *give* it. This is not arrogance on God's part. It is love.

In summary, your greatest good is in the enjoyment of God. God's greatest glory is in being enjoyed. So, for God to seek his glory in your worship of him is the most loving thing he can do for you. Only by seeking his glory preeminently can God seek your good passionately. For God to work for your enjoyment of him (that's his love for you) and for God to work for his glory in being enjoyed (that's his love for himself) are not properly distinct.

The Practical, Sin-Killing Power of Christian Hedonism: With Help from Jonathan Edwards

Christians have typically employed one of two tactics in their attempt to motivate one another to walk in the path of righteousness. On the one hand, many have labored to portray immorality in the ugliest and most unappealing terms possible, hoping this would frighten us away from the decadent and destructive ways of our society. Others have taken a slightly

---

[22]On this point, see especially Piper's *God Is the Gospel: Meditations on God's Love as the Gift of Himself* (Wheaton, IL: Crossway, 2005).

different approach. Rather than constructing elaborate and graphic images of the horrors of sin, they argue that the problem is the presence of desire in the human soul, in particular the desire for pleasure. The target of their loud and often angry harangues is the longing, the yearning, the passion in the human heart for joy and happiness and fascination and excitement. Typically they deal with this "problem" by insisting that all such impulses are themselves sinful and must either be ruthlessly suppressed or exorcised (as if they were the product of a demonic presence).

In response to these largely ineffective proposals, Piper has been greatly influenced by Jonathan Edwards. Permit me to explain this Edwardsean/Piperean alternative approach by appealing to a sermon of the former entitled "Youth and the Pleasures of Piety" (preached first in May 1734, but later on multiple occasions throughout colonial New England). As all know, Edwards could portray the horrific consequences of sin in the most vivid and graphic imagery imaginable (and some of it unimaginable; witness his famous sermon "Sinners in the Hands of an Angry God"). But far more dominant in his ministry was his appeal to the superior pleasure and joy to be found in true "religion" (a word Edwards uses positively).

Edwards believed that the greatest objection voiced by young people to the pursuit of religion was their fear that it would undermine their pursuit of pleasure:

> This is what they aim at, to spend their youth pleasantly; and they think, if they should forsake sin and youthful vanity, and betake themselves to a religious course of life, this will hinder them in this pursuit. They look upon religion as a very dull, melancholy thing, and think, if they embrace it, that they must have done in a great measure with their pleasures.[23]

His principal argument in this little-known sermon is that religion, far from being a hindrance to the experience of pleasure, is the most direct and effective way to attain it. The sermon is based on Proverbs 24:13–14:

> My son, eat honey, for it is good,
>   and the drippings of the honeycomb are sweet to your taste.
> Know that wisdom is such to your soul;
>   if you find it, there will be a future,
>   and your hope will not be cut off.

---

[23]Jonathan Edwards, *The Works of Jonathan Edwards*, vol. 19, *Sermons and Discourses, 1734–1738*, ed. M. X. Lesser (New Haven: Yale University Press, 2001), 89. In the rest of this essay, parenthetical numbers after the quotations indicate references from this source, and italics indicate my emphasis. If a paragraph has multiple quotations but only one page number, all the quotations are from that page.

We eat honey because it is sweet and pleasant to the taste. No one has to pay us to eat it, nor do we eat it to attain some greater pleasure than the one that comes from tasting its sweetness. So, too, says the proverb, "it is with respect to piety or wisdom: 'tis as much worth the while to practice this for the sake of the pleasure of it" (82).

Edwards acknowledges that many young people will find his argument strange and paradoxical. To suggest that "spending youth in the practice of religion and virtue . . . is the way to obtain pleasures vastly more excellent than by spending youth in sin and vanity" (82) sounds more than a little odd to most people, regardless of their age.

The approach Edwards took was as unusual in his day as it is in ours. He proceeds to argue at length that the problem isn't the pursuit of pleasure but the willingness of uninformed minds to settle for comparatively inferior joys when God offers unsurpassed and far more durable delights. The pursuit of God brings "delights of a *more* sublime nature" (82), "pleasures that are *more* solid and substantial . . . vastly sweeter, and *more* exquisitely delighting, and are of a *more* satisfying nature . . . that *exceed* the pleasures of the vain, sensual youth, as much as gold and pearls do dirt and dung" (83). Don't abandon your desire for pleasure. (By the way, you couldn't, even if you wanted to.) Rather, seek those pleasures that are greater and more satisfying and capable of bringing fulfillment and joy that exceed the best this world has to offer.

Edwards points to the way in which young people in particular are obsessed with outward adornment, "in making a fine appearance." But by embracing true religion "they would have the graces of God's Spirit, the beauty and ornaments of angels, and the lovely image of God." Don't abandon your desire for beauty, he counsels, but seek the beauty "that would render [you] far *more* lovely than the greatest outward beauty possible," namely, "that beauty that would render [you] lovely in the eyes of Jesus Christ, and the angels, and all wise men." What this world offers is "vile in comparison [with] the beauty of the graces of God's Spirit" (83).

True religion will also bring "the sweetest delights of love and friendship" (83). Loving God "is an affection that is of a *more* sublime and excellent nature" than the love of any earthly object. Such love is always mutual, and thus the love one receives from Christ "vastly exceeds the love of any earthly lover" (84).

Furthermore, by pursuing the true religion of knowing Jesus Christ, young people obtain the sweetest gratification of appetite; not of carnal, sensual appetites, but of those that are *more* excellent, of spiritual and divine appetites, holy desires and inclinations; those that, as they are *more* excellent in themselves, [are] *more* suitable to the nature of man, and are far *more* extensive, so are capable of gratification and enjoyments *more* exquisite sweet, and delighting. They that truly embrace religion and virtue, there are infused into them new appetites after heavenly enjoyments. (84)

Have you noticed how often Edwards employs the word "more"? He does not say, seek God "instead" of pleasure, as if they were two mutually exclusive options, but rather seek your pleasure *in God*, for the latter is always "more" exquisite and "more" extensive and "more" excellent and "more" sublime and "more" solid and substantial and "more" satisfying.

Another ground of appeal is the company and friendship one gains in the pursuit of true religion, specifically, intimacy with God himself. The Father and the Son, according to John 14:21–23, come to "make their abode" with young people and to "manifest themselves to them." Those who embrace true religion "with a spiritual eye do see Christ and have access to him to converse; and Christ by his spirit communicates himself to them." And would this not be "the pleasantest and the happiest company" possible? "Is not the God that made us, able to give us *more* pleasure in intercourse [=conversation] with himself than we have in conversation with a worm of the dust?" (85).

Some fear that the pursuit of God will deprive them of the enjoyment of things in this world. But Edwards is quick to point out that "religion doesn't forbid the use of outward enjoyments but only the abuse of them." Indeed, "the senses and animal appetites may be gratified in a manner religion allows of" (85). "Outward enjoyments," notes Edwards, "are much sweeter, and really afford more pleasure, when regularly used than when abused." In other words, temporal delights are better and more satisfying when they are experienced virtuously. "Vice," says Edwards, "destroys the sweetness of outward enjoyments" (86).

Biblical piety, contends Edwards, even "sweetens" solitude! Many who indulge their sensual appetites in unbiblical ways "are afraid of solitude . . . for they have nothing to entertain them [when] alone." But those who pursue God enjoy times of solitude "for then they have the better opportunity to fix their minds on divine objects, to withdraw their thoughts from worldly things, and the more uninterruptedly to delight themselves in divine contemplations, and holy exercise and converse with God" (87).

The peace that comes from knowing that one's sins are forgiven "is enough to give quietness and cheerfulness" wherever you are or whatever you are doing. Even what Edwards calls our "diversions"—by which he has in view hobbies and leisure activities, etc.—"are abundantly sweetest when virtue moderates and guides them," for it regulates them "according to the rules of wisdom and virtue, and would direct them to suitable and worthy ends, and make them subservient to excellent purposes" (87).

Edwards doesn't hesitate to exhort the young to "forsake all ways of vice and youthful vanity, [and] to renounce all licentious practices in sinful indulgences of carnal appetites." He encourages young people not to employ their minds "when alone, in vain imaginations and sinful thoughts" and to "avoid lewd ways of using [their] tongue" (88). But here is why forsaking such sinful ways is wise and appealing and the only sensible thing to do: because then you will have "the gracious presence of God and his smiles, a good conscience, and a sense of God's favor, accompanying the pleasure you have in outward things, which will unspeakably sweeten them. Seek that divine grace in your heart, whereby your soul may be beautified, and adorned, and rendered lovely in the eyes of God; and whereby you may live a life of divine love, a life of love to Christ, and communion with him" (89). Sin can exert a powerful vise-grip on the human heart, one that mere shouts of denunciation and threats of divine wrath fail to dislodge. The promise and allure of sensual gratification must be countered by the promise and allure of a gratification in God that is sweeter, more sublime, more beautiful, more exquisite, more excellent, more solid, more substantive, and more satisfying.

One can only wonder at the impact of the church on this younger generation (and the older one as well) if such were our strategy for dealing with sin. Christian hedonism, whether Edwardsean or found in Piper, insists that we not demonize their desire for joy and pleasure, but point them to him in whose presence there is "fullness of joy" and at whose right hand are "pleasures forevermore" (Ps. 16:11).

5

WHEN ALL HOPE HAS DIED

Meditations on Profound Christian Suffering

Mark R. Talbot

If we are faithless, he remains faithful—
for he cannot deny himself.
—2 TIMOTHY 2:13

John Piper's breakthrough book, *Desiring God: Meditations of a Christian Hedonist*, was first published in 1986. I am unsure when I first read it, but as I read the third edition (published in 2003) in preparation for writing this chapter, I was astounded by how much essential ground the book covers, as well as by how much John knows and how well he communicates it. Like the proverbial adult child who confessed that as he grew older his father seemed to him to grow wiser and wiser, I find that now, when I know much more Scripture and theology than I did twenty years ago, I appreciate John's book even more. A lot of the truths that I have come to treasure over the past twenty years are truths that John has delighted in for a very long time.

Yet I am still troubled by the phrase "Christian hedonism." Part of my trouble involves still feeling that the secular connotations of the term *hedonism* are so deeply entrenched that it is practically impossible for us to convert it to Christian usage—and this in spite of John's argument to the contrary and all of his careful qualifications about what he does and does not mean by the term. Yet even if I lay that concern aside and take the term to mean exactly what John writes that he intends it to mean, it still troubles me. This chapter will develop what I take to be Christian hedonism's most troubling implication—an implication that arises when we consider a specific kind of Christian suffering, a kind that I call "profound Christian suffering." In the process of explaining that term and drawing out its implications for Christian hedonism, I will say some things about all Christian suffering that, so far as I know, no one else has said.[1] And so this chapter has two goals: first, I want to help all of us to think through Christian suffering in fresh ways that, I hope, are spiritually enlightening and encouraging; and, second, I want to take John's thinking about Christian hedonism as seriously as I take, for example, Augustine's thinking about providence or Calvin's thinking about our twofold knowledge of God or Warfield's thinking about the inspiration of Scripture. And that requires me to determine where I think John's thinking goes wrong as well as where I think it goes right. This is my tribute, John, to your fine mind and your deep, godly heart.

Christian Hedonism: Definition and Appreciation

In the fifth appendix to the third edition of *Desiring God*, Piper characterizes hedonism in terms of "living for pleasure." He then says:

> I would be happy with the following definition as a starting point for my own usage of the word: *Hedonism* is "a theory according to which a person is motivated to produce one state of affairs in preference to another if, and only if, he thinks it will be more pleasant, or less unpleasant for himself." I

---

[1]Much of what I say about suffering in this chapter is taken from a book that I am currently writing, tentatively entitled *Unsought Gifts: Christian Suffering*, which will be published by Crossway.

A word about my footnotes: I would like to see Christian academics take Piper's work more seriously. As a very thoughtful working pastor who is attempting in all things to be faithful to the Scriptures and who is obviously connecting with many Christians, what he has to say represents an important theological perspective. But in order for it to be clear that his work deserves serious academic attention, some of us must show how it can prompt sustained and careful academic work. Many of my footnotes are meant to supply some of the "scholarly boilerplate" that shows Piper's thinking to be worthy of academic attention. Readers who find the notes confusing or distracting rather than helpful should simply skip them. I have tried to write the text in such a way that it can be understood by itself.

would only want to add "forever." For there are deeds God calls us to do that in the short run are painful.[2]

Let us take this as correctly capturing the ordinary meaning of hedonism as well as introducing one qualification needed in order for it to represent Christian hedonism. My primary concern is with Piper's endorsement of the *Encyclopedia of Philosophy*'s "only if." This "only if" means that Piper's Christian hedonism maintains that the pursuit of personal pleasure plays a necessary role in all human motivation. In other words, no one ever does anything unless he thinks that it will bring him pleasure. In addition, in the first chapter of *Desiring God* Piper seems to take the prospect of personal pleasure to be the only consideration that is sufficient to motivate us. Someone will be motivated to do something, in other words, only if she thinks that it will give her pleasure.[3] By adding "forever," Piper makes Christian hedonism prescriptive as well as descriptive. Christian hedonism goes from merely *describing* what it thinks actually motivates human beings to *prescribing* what should motivate them. So from what Piper says in his fifth appendix and his first chapter, his position seems to be that the pursuit of personal pleasure is both essential to and decisive for human motivation (this is the descriptive portion of the theory) and, furthermore, human beings should be motivated by nothing other than the pursuit of everlasting pleasure (this is the prescriptive part). More particularly, self-conscious Christian hedonists won't do anything unless they think that doing it will maximize their pleasure everlastingly.[4]

---

[2]John Piper, *Desiring God: Meditations of a Christian Hedonist*, 3d ed. (Sisters, OR: Multnomah, 2003), 365f. This appendix, entitled "Why Call It Christian Hedonism?" was part of the first edition of Piper's book and remains substantially unchanged. The internal quotation is from the article on hedonism in the *Encyclopedia of Philosophy*, 8 vols., ed. Paul Edwards (New York: Macmillan, 1967), 3:433. Henceforth, I shall give the page references to the third edition of *Desiring God* parenthetically in my text.

[3]I infer this from two passages in Piper's first chapter. In the first he says: "When I was in college, I had a vague, pervasive notion that if I did something good because it would make me happy, I would ruin its goodness.

"I figured that the goodness of my moral action was lessened to the degree that I was motivated by a desire for my own pleasure. . . .

"This was a problem for me because *I couldn't formulate an alternative motive that worked*" (19, my emphasis).

In other words, Piper found that only a desire for his own pleasure could move him to act.

The second passage quotes Pascal approvingly when he wrote, "All men seek happiness. This is without exception. . . . *The will never takes the least step but to this object*" (20, my emphasis). The second sentence of this quotation emphasizes the role that pursuing pleasure necessarily plays in all human motivation, and the third sentence emphasizes that only the prospect of personal pleasure is sufficient to motivate us. In the language that I am about to use in the text, the second and third sentences of the Pascal quotation are both *describing* (according to Pascal and Piper's Christian hedonism) aspects of what actually motivates human beings.

[4]Usually, Piper does not write that hedonism attempts to *maximize* pleasure, although he does use this phrase in the chapter on suffering he added to the second and third editions of *Desiring God*, saying, for instance, that "Christianity as Paul understands it is not the best way to maximize pleasure if this life is all there is" (260).

Ultimately, I shall be arguing, the credibility of Christian hedonism as a *prescriptive* account of what should always motivate human beings will stand or fall with the more basic issue of whether hedonism's *descriptive* claims are true. Is the pursuit of personal pleasure both essential to and decisive for human motivation?[5] If it is, then if the pursuit of some pleasure is not motivating us, then nothing is. And, of course, if nothing is motivating us, then we will stop seeking anything, including even remaining faithfully Christian. The claim that the pursuit of pleasure is (and should be) the only sufficient human motivator is the one I shall finally challenge.[6]

---

[5]In Piper's response to what he calls Objection Three to Christian hedonism on 296–99, he attempts to deal with the biblical texts where Moses and Paul seem to have been willing to give up all prospect of their own future pleasure under certain conditions (see Ex. 32:32 and Rom. 9:3). He needs to deal with these texts given his declaration that "every claim to truth that flies under the banner of Christian hedonism must be solidly rooted in the Christian Scripture, the Bible" (369). But, to my mind at least, Piper's attempt to meet the challenge that these two biblical texts present to Christian hedonism is far from conclusive both because he has not adequately confronted and answered the most common interpretations of these passages and because even those whom we might expect to agree with him on his interpretations of these passages tend to interpret them differently.

For instance, Jonathan Edwards would apparently disagree with Piper on whether someone, seemingly following the apostle's example in Romans 9:3, ought to be willing to be damned for God's glory, for Edwards listed such a willingness under "high attainments in religion," all the rest of which he clearly took to be truly such, as long as they were accompanied by confirming signs of godliness (see *Religious Affections* [New Haven: Yale University Press, 1959], 370). Once Edwards seems to agree with Piper's interpretation of Exodus 32:32 (see *Ethical Writings* [New Haven: Yale University Press, 1989], 261). But at other times, he takes that passage as meaning that Moses was willing to be accursed for the Israelites. In fact, Edwards observes that Moses' willingness to be so accursed and blotted out of God's book involves a willingness to "make atonement for . . . sin, which is to do the part of a mediator" (see *Notes on Scriptures* [New Haven: Yale University Press, 1998], 523)—in other words, it involves a willingness to be damned in their place. This counters Piper's interpretation of this passage as involving nothing more than Moses' expressing (in the words of the nineteenth-century Bible commentator George Bush, whom Piper is quoting here) "the wish rather to die than witness the destruction of the people" (297).

Moreover, when Piper writes that one of his problems before he was converted to Christian hedonism was that, while he thought that "to be motivated by a desire for happiness or pleasure . . . seemed selfish, utilitarian, [and] mercenary," he "couldn't formulate an alternative motive that worked" (18), he may not be recognizing the degree to which this may have been due to his spiritual immaturity. And thus, for instance, while the great Puritan Thomas Goodwin agrees with Piper that a desire for our own pleasure and happiness is the supreme law of human nature, he then claims that the apostle Paul's wish to be "accursed and cut off from Christ for the sake of my brothers, my kinsmen according to the flesh" (Rom. 9:3) represents "one of the supremest laws *in the new creature*. For," he says, "both love to God and love to others, do, in the fullest stream and channel, meet in this. It was the salvation of such a bulk of mankind, in whom God's name was interested, as were the Jews, and the continuance of the gospel to them in future ages, for their salvation, that [Paul] here prefers to his own salvation. He wisheth himself accursed from Christ; and because, *to have the new creature wound up to so high a note, without cracking and breaking nature itself, that the prerogative law thereof should so prevail and overrule the supreme law of nature itself, would (as he knew) be a wonder*, and [even] incredible to the most of Christians, he therefore makes the solemnest protestation, that this was real in his heart, that ever was made by man." Thomas Goodwin, *The Works of Thomas Goodwin*, vol. 6, *The Work of the Holy Ghost in Our Salvation* (Eureka, CA: Tanski, 1996), 513, my emphases.

In other words, Goodwin thought that it was possible only for a regenerate person to be motivated by something other than the prospect of his own pleasure and happiness—namely, by his love for God and others—even if to be so motivated was, even for a Christian, very rare. For more on what is at stake with these two passages and their interpretation, see John E. Hare, *God and Morality: A Philosophical History* (Oxford: Blackwell, 2007), 91–93.

[6]Unfortunately, Piper's claims in his fifth appendix seem to exhibit some conceptual confusion. For instance, in addition to the claims that I have just highlighted in my text, he also says, "The article on hedonism in *The Encyclopedia of Philosophy* shows that the term does not refer to a single precise philosophy. It is a general term to cover a wide variety of teachings that *have elevated pleasure very high*" (365, my emphasis). This is a bit of a misinterpretation of what the encyclopedia's article is showing. But even if

I agree with most of Piper's other claims about the proper place of pleasure in the Christian life. For instance, I heartily affirm his claim that "*God is most glorified in[7] me when I am most satisfied in Him*" (10). The way that *I* most glorify God is by its being manifest that I take him for my "chosen portion" (Ps. 16:5; cf. 119:57), that though my flesh and heart may fail, I find God to be "the strength of my heart and my portion forever" (Ps. 73:26; cf. Lam. 3:22–24), and, consequently, that not only do I find that a day in God's courts is better than a thousand elsewhere, but also that

> I would rather be a gatekeeper in the house of my God
> than live the good life in the homes of the wicked.
>   (Ps. 84:10 NLT)

If our lives manifest this sort of complete and total satisfaction in God, then it is apparent that we love the Lord our God above everything else—and, since God alone is worthy of this sort of unqualified love from us, our loving him in this way glorifies him as he alone should be glorified. So we should, as Piper urges again and again, strive to find all of our satisfaction, all of our pleasure, all of our happiness, and all of our delight, in God.[8]

---

we let it stand, the idea of *elevating pleasure very high* is not equivalent to claiming that pleasure is (and ought to be) the only human motivator. It is quite possible to elevate pleasure very high and yet not take pleasure to be the only possible human motivator.

Piper then quotes C. S. Lewis and Vernard Eller as endorsing the idea of Christian hedonism without addressing the crucial question, Do Lewis and Eller take the prospect of maximizing pleasure to be the only human motivator? For instance, when Eller declares that "the sole motive of Christian simplicity is the enjoyment of God himself (and if that be *hedonism*, let's make the most of it!)" (quoted by Piper on 367), this is not obviously to make enjoyment or pleasure the sole motivator of the entire Christian life. Consequently, unless they explicitly subscribe to the *Encyclopedia of Philosophy*'s "if, and only if" formula, we cannot assume that Lewis and Eller are endorsing hedonism as a theory of all possible human motivation. They may mean to do no more than elevate the pursuit of pleasure very high.

In fact, this seems to me to be the most natural interpretation of the Lewis quotation and the one that is most probable, given Lewis's own statement that he didn't become a Christian—or remain one—because he thought that it would make him happy (see, e.g., *God in the Dock: Essays on Theology and Ethics* [Grand Rapids: Eerdmans, 1970], 58, 90f.).

[7] Piper quotes Charles Williams's *Place of the Lion* about using prepositions accurately as the epigraph for *Desiring God*'s introductory chapter. Williams's point will become crucial near the end of my piece, since I will there distinguish between how God is most glorified *in* us and how he may be most glorified *with regard to* us.

[8] As Paul Helm has pointed out to me, the claim made in this sentence seems to suggest that no one subscribing to it could, for instance, pursue friendship with another human person as an end in itself. This seems to flout the very idea of friendship. Yet Helm himself supplies the appropriate response: if God has intended human friendship as a kind of good in itself, then delighting in the gift of a friend can at the same time involve delighting even more in God as the Giver of this, as well as of every other, good thing (see James 1:17 with Ps. 104:14–15, 24–30; Matt. 7:11; and 1 Tim. 4:4). For a superb analysis of the different ways in which something can be an end in itself, see Jonathan Edwards's dissertation on *The End for Which God Created the World* in John Piper, *God's Passion for His Glory* (Wheaton, IL: Crossway, 1998), 125–36.

I agree, moreover, that the acid test of whether we have really been converted is whether we have received Jesus as our treasure and thus have come to delight in God (55). Piper is profoundly right to stress that "we are surrounded by unconverted people who think they *do* believe in Jesus"[9] and that it "does no good to tell these people to believe in the Lord Jesus" because that phrase does nothing to confront them with the reality of their unregenerate hearts (54f.). The remainder of Piper's chapter on conversion as the creation of a Christian hedonist is a model of how to drive home each human's desperate need, God's provision in Christ for that need, and then to sort out what God does and what we must do if we are to be right with God. Piper correctly stresses that far too many people "try to define true Christianity in terms of decisions" (299), even though someone can make a decision for Christ without being inwardly transformed. As he says, conversion, "understood as the coming into being of a new nature . . . that will obey Christ, is no mere human decision. It is a human decision—but, oh, so much more! Repentant faith . . . is based on an awesome miracle performed by the sovereign God. It is the breath of a new creature in Christ" (68). And he is right that "the newness of the new creature is that it has a new taste" (72)—a taste for God himself and thus for "the hidden treasure of holy joy" that alone can satisfy our deepest desires (73).[10] True Christians delight in God and not only or primarily in God's gifts. So saving faith, as Piper emphasizes, "is the heartfelt conviction not only that Christ is reliable, but also that He is desirable" (73). As his final section heading in chapter 2 puts it, true Christians have "a new passion for the pleasure of God's presence" (73).[11] And we will inevitably experience that pleasure if we have been born again.[12]

---

[9]Piper's examples are arresting: "Drunks on the street say they believe. Unmarried couples sleeping together say they believe. Elderly people who haven't sought worship or fellowship for forty years say they believe. All kinds of lukewarm, world-loving church attenders say they believe" (54). Of course, the fact that someone is a drunkard or sexually immoral or outside Christian fellowship is not itself proof that the person is unconverted.

[10]In a theologically profound footnote, Piper says: "It is worth musing over the implications that the Holy Spirit is the divine Workman who gives us a new heart of faith and is Himself the personification of the joy that the Father and the Son have in each other. We might say that the change that must occur in the human heart to make saving faith possible is permeation by the Holy Spirit, *which is nothing less than a permeation by the very joy that God the Father and God the Son have in each other's beauty. In other words, the taste for God that begets saving faith is God's very taste for Himself, imparted to us in measure by the Holy Spirit*" (73n18, my emphasis).

[11]As Piper (following his great spiritual mentor, Jonathan Edwards) later puts it, "Affections are essential to the Christian life, not optional" (299). Consequently, "Minimizing the importance of transformed feelings makes Christian conversion less supernatural and less radical" than it actually is (89). For a book-length treatment of what it means to be born again, see Piper's *Finally Alive: What Happens When We Are Born Again* (Fearn, Ross-shire: Christian Focus, 2009).

[12]I think it is the offensiveness of this claim, rather than the offensiveness of the term "Christian hedonism" (which may or may not accurately capture the essence of this claim), that is so threatening to nominal Christians (see 367f.). Hesitation about the appropriateness of the concept of Christian hedonism is not equivalent to hesitation about the biblical truth that has prompted Piper to coin the concept.

To cite just two more agreements. I agree that the pleasures of worship are the true Christian's feast. If God has regenerated our hearts to delight in him, then (as C. S. Lewis stressed) our delight will spontaneously over-flow into praise (21). Led by the indwelling Holy Spirit, we will begin to find what will become literally endless pleasure in celebrating—both individually and corporately—the infinite glories of God and what he has done for us in the earthly work of his Son, Jesus Christ. And I agree that God's Word, both spoken and written, is (in Piper's fine phrase) the kindling for our godly pleasure. God's Word is the Christian's life and an inexhaustible source of joy. It is to be sweeter to us than honey (Ps. 19:10). Furthermore, as Piper says, "the Word . . . breaks the power of counterfeit pleasures" (150). Piper's fifth chapter, which emphasizes all of this and much more, is to my mind one of the finest incentives I know for getting Christians to seek life, comfort, hope, peace, wisdom, freedom, victory, restoration, and renewal by seeking the happiness that can be ours through daily feeding on God's Word.

So I shall be urging no more than that Piper should revise one small but (I think) absolutely crucial element in his claims about Christian hedonism. And even though I think that this should lead him to consider abandoning the term, I emphasize that this would leave intact most of the theology of *Desiring God*. We do "find in the Bible a divine command to be [pleasure seekers]," and that does mean that we must be willing "to sell everything 'with joy' (Matt. 13:44) in order to have the kingdom of heaven and thus 'enter into the joy of [our] master' (Matt. 25:21, 23)" (25).[13] I simply think that the term "Christian hedonism," understood as Piper wants us to understand it, carries us beyond Scripture's own depic-tion of the place that pleasure properly plays in Christian life.

Suffering: What It Is and How It Affects Us

In the preface to the third edition of *Desiring God*, Piper observes, "Bib-lically, it is plain that God has appointed suffering for all His children" (10) and, consequently, "if Christian Hedonism is to have any credibility, it must give an account of itself in this [post–9/11] world of fear and suf-fering" (10). Already in the preface to the second edition he had declared, "Biblically, I have not been able to escape, in these passing years, that

---

[13]Here, from quite a different theological perspective, is a similar emphasis: "Whatever else Christianity may be, it is a set of emotions. It is love of God and neighbor, grief about one's own waywardness, joy in the merciful salvation of our God, gratitude, hope, and peace. So if I don't love God and my neighbor, abhor my sins, and rejoice in my redemption, if I am not grateful, hopeful, and at peace with God and myself, then it follows that I am alienated from Christianity, though I was born and bred in the bosom of the Presbyterian Church, am baptized and confirmed and willing in good conscience to affirm the articles of the Creed." Robert C. Roberts, *Spirituality and Human Emotion* (Grand Rapids: Eerdmans, 1982), 1f.

we are appointed to suffer for the advancement of the kingdom in the world." He had also noted that it was clearer to him then, as the third millennium was about to dawn, than it had ever been before "that the final saving purposes of God in the world will triumph only through the loving sacrifice of suffering."[14] Consequently, he wrote a new chapter for that edition entitled "Suffering: The Sacrifice of Christian Hedonism." But even with the addition of that chapter, I don't think that Piper has recognized how some instances of profound suffering impact the concept of Christian hedonism.

In every edition, Piper has observed, "The quickest way to the heart is through a wound."[15] In the second and third editions he adds, "The deep things of life in God are discovered in suffering."[16] Insofar as these claims are true, *why* are they true?

Think for a moment about what suffering is. Of course, there are different kinds and degrees of suffering. For instance, there is physical suffering and there is mental suffering, and either can be mild or intense, brief or enduring. There is also what I shall call "profound suffering," which we shall consider later. But what is common to all of the kinds and degrees of suffering—physical or mental, mild or intense, brief or enduring, or profound?

All suffering, I suggest, involves something disrupting our life's pleasantness to the point where we find that disruption disagreeable and thus—in some sense and to some degree—want it to cease.[17]

Suffering is thus obviously relevant to Christian hedonism. For if hedonists aim to maximize pleasure, then no hedonist is going to seek in and

---

[14]The second edition appeared in 1996. These two quotations are both found on page 10.

[15]Pages 80 in the third edition, 63 in the first edition, 75 in the second. Piper makes this observation while recounting Jesus' encounter with the Samaritan woman in John 4. Whether Christ's words caused the Samaritan woman pain or just struck at the heart of her predicament is a question I shall not try to answer.

[16]Pages 223, second edition; 267, third edition.

[17]Someone may object that this characterization of suffering is tautological because it characterizes suffering by means of another term ("disrupting our life's pleasantness") that in this context is little other than a synonym for the word *suffering*. But, to put it philosophically, I am not trying to give a reductive analysis of the concept of suffering. Instead, I am trying to characterize suffering in a way that illuminates what suffering feels like.

Jamie Mayerfeld characterizes suffering similarly in the first chapter of his *Suffering and Moral Responsibility* (New York: Oxford University Press, 1999). Mayerfeld says that he is going to "use the terms 'happiness' and 'suffering' to refer to overall states of feeling at a particular moment" (14). He then writes that, as a first approximation, "let us say that happiness refers to a state of feeling good overall, or agreeable overall feeling, while suffering refers to a state of feeling bad overall, or disagreeable overall feeling" (14). I think we can assume that, in some sense and to some degree, we want states of feeling bad overall to end. Both Mayerfeld's and my characterizations of suffering approach C. S. Lewis's characterization as "any experience, whether physical or mental, which the patient dislikes." C. S. Lewis, *The Problem of Pain* (New York: HarperCollins, 2001), 87.

Suffering usually functions as a threshold concept, which means that very low degrees of unpleasantness or overall bad feeling are not usually considered suffering. But for our purposes such subtleties are unimportant.

for itself the unpleasantness that suffering brings.[18] Of course, a Christian hedonist will not try to avoid all suffering, for as Piper says, "there are deeds God calls us to do that in the short run are painful." Yet insofar as anything is disagreeable to us, we do *in some sense and to some degree* want it to end. Neither Christian hedonists nor any other normal persons embrace unpleasantness as such. Indeed, since some suffering is very disagreeable to us, we may very much want it to end; and, as Christians, we may beg God to remove it, even as we remind ourselves that it may be good for us in some more inclusive way.[19] Christians are not masochists. But we are also not to be cowards. We often need to acknowledge that good comes at the price of pain.

So suffering is unpleasant and disagreeable to us. Yet how does it wound us in a way that gets at our hearts—in other words, that gets at the deepest part of us?

Suppose that you are prone to mild headaches. Normally, if you are having a headache and you are considering just it,[20] then you want it to end. For to the degree that it is unpleasant, its mere presence casts a disagreeable shadow over your present and your future as you live with and anticipate continuing to live with the pain.

But now, in addition, suppose that occasionally when you get one of these mild headaches, it turns into a full-blown migraine that lands you moaning on your stomach in bed. Under those circumstances, what does getting a mild headache do to you?

It probably disconcerts you in a way that exceeds the disagreeableness arising directly from the pain. Why? Because now the mild unpleasantness you are experiencing may be pointing beyond itself. It is no longer just a matter of your hurting a little in a particular way; it is now a matter of that pain possibly heralding something worse to come—more pain and, indeed, disabling pain. This prospect can make your getting a mild

---

[18]The crucial words here are "in and for itself." Piper's agreement with my claim can be gleaned from his chapter on suffering, where he says, among other things, that it was not normal—indeed, it was "utterly unnatural" (283)—for the apostle Paul to choose a path that led to trouble and pain virtually every day of his life, since human beings normally flee suffering (see 262).

[19]Thus, Paul pleaded with God to remove his thorn in the flesh even though he also was able eventually to write that we rejoice in our sufferings because we know what they produce (see 2 Cor. 12:7–10 with Rom. 5:3–5).

[20]As C. S. Lewis pointed out, we can welcome and even find pleasurable very low levels of the sorts of sensations that we know would become painful at higher levels (see *Problem of Pain*, 23, 87). So perhaps someone might welcome a very mild headache, considered in itself.

Even with much more painful headaches, you may welcome them, if you aren't considering them just in themselves. For instance, one of my students once told me that if he hadn't had a migraine in quite a while, then he actually welcomed getting one because he knew that, when it was over, he was not going to have another one for a very long time. But then he wasn't considering just the migraine itself. He was considering what having the migraine meant for his prospect of being headache-free for some period of time thereafter.

headache more than mildly unpleasant. It serves as a reminder that you don't completely control your life's course and quality.

But now vary the picture again. Suppose that you had a brain tumor several years ago that first started to manifest itself in mild headaches that eventually became severe migraines. Surgery removed the tumor, with radiation therapy following, but of course there was no guarantee that the tumor wouldn't regrow. If you were to get a headache now, especially if it seemed to be threatening to develop into a migraine, then how would that tend to affect you?

Unless you were certain that this headache was not being caused by the regrowth of your tumor, it would tend to unsettle your hopes and plans and dreams. Your whole future would seem foreshortened. Future events as close as car shopping next week or as far off as anticipating attending a toddler's college graduation would lose some of their attraction or certainty. And if you were to find out that this headache was in fact being caused by the regrowth of your tumor, you would probably find yourself reconsidering and then revising or abandoning many of your hopes and plans.

So, as at least a first approximation, we can conclude that pain and suffering—and particularly whatever seems to be potentially ominous pain or whatever threatens to turn into significant longer-term suffering—gets at our hearts by disturbing our equanimity, our "evenness of mind." It does this partly by its mere unpleasantness, but it does it even more because we are creatures on the hunt for goods—that is, needy, "wanty" creatures, full of desires and longings,[21] who live—and *must* live—by projecting ourselves into futures where we hope that our desires and longings will be met. Suffering challenges our shallowly confident projections. It gets at our hearts by disturbing life's pleasantness and, if it is serious enough, unsettling our hopes and plans. As the suffering Job declared:

---

[21]The second-most-frequent Hebrew word applied to human beings in the Old Testament is *nefesh*, which is traditionally translated "soul" but which, Hans Walter Wolff argues, really refers to us as creatures with endless desires (see Eccles. 6:7) and ardent longings (see, e.g., Gen. 34:8; Job 7:2; Pss. 12:5; 84:2). Wolff argues that Scripture characterizes us in terms of such desire and longing so consistently that ultimately we are not so much seen to have *nefesh* as to be *nefesh* (see his *Anthropology of the Old Testament* [Philadelphia: Fortress, 1974], 21f.). He summarizes his survey of the use of *nefesh* in the Old Testament like this: "If we survey the wide context in which the [*nefesh*] of man and man as [*nefesh*] can be observed, we see above all man marked out as the individual living being who has neither acquired, nor can preserve, life by himself, but who is eager for life, spurred on by vital desire. . . . In this way [*nefesh*] shows man primarily in his need and desire, [including] his emotional excitability and vulnerability" (24f.).

These desires and longings, properly directed, are not bad for they kick us off dead center and drive us to hope and plan and act (see, e.g., Prov. 16:26—"It is good for workers to have an appetite [lit., a *nefesh*]; an empty stomach drives them on" [NLT] and Ps. 42:1–2—"As a deer pants for flowing streams, so pants my soul [lit., my *nefesh*] for you, O God. My soul [*nefesh*] thirsts for God, for the living God. When shall I come and appear before God?"). I encourage my readers to think through how this corroborates Piper's claims that "it is not a bad thing to desire our own good" (20) nor is our "persistent and undeniable yearning for happiness . . . to be suppressed, but [rather it should be] glutted—on God!" (21).

[God] has made me a byword of the peoples,
   and I am one before whom men spit.
My eye has grown dim from vexation,
   and all my members are like a shadow. . . .
My days are past; *my plans are broken off,*
   the desires of my heart. . . .
Where then is my hope?
   Who will see my hope?
Will it go down to the bars of Sheol?
   Shall we descend together into the dust?
         (Job 17:6–7, 11, 15–16; cf. 19:10)

As we shall see, suffering can be especially corrosive to our distinctively human need to project hopeful futures. Everything living is needy: plants need food and water, and animals experience their needs and wants as appetite and desire (Pss. 104:10–11; 145:15–16). Yet even the higher animals live primarily by instinct; they are more or less "hardwired" to live as they do. They don't need to take thought for the morrow. We, by contrast, possess relatively little "hardwiring"; and so we alone of all of the creatures in the visible creation live—and, indeed, *should* live[22]—by thinking and hoping and planning.[23] And so hopes—large and small, true and false, wise and foolish—run like a variegated thread throughout the Scriptures. In the end, we are all (to borrow a phrase from Zechariah) "prisoners of hope" who must return to hope's proper stronghold—that is, to trust in God the Father of Christ Jesus—if our souls are to have "a sure and steadfast anchor" (Zech. 9:12 with Heb. 6:19). And so insofar as suffering strikes at our hopes, it does indeed strike at our very hearts, prompting us to discover life's deeper truths.

Chosen versus Unchosen Suffering

Piper opens his chapter on suffering by recounting a meeting he and a group of pastors had with Richard Wurmbrand. Wurmbrand was a Romanian evangelical Lutheran pastor of Jewish descent whom the Communists imprisoned for fourteen years for his faith. Piper writes that during their

---

[22]See, for instance, 1 Corinthians 9:10: "The plowman should plow in hope and the thresher thresh in hope of sharing in the crop." Biblical passages like Matthew 6:34—"Take therefore no thought for the morrow: for the morrow shall take thought for the things of itself" (KJV)—and James 4:13–15 (quoted below) may seem to discourage or prohibit our doing any planning, yet properly interpreted in full biblical context (see, e.g., Prov. 6:6–8; 10:1–5; 30:25; 1 Tim. 5:8) they do not. In fact, at Luke 14:28–32 our Lord presupposed that human beings are obliged to make plans based on their careful assessments of the situations they are in.

[23]Insofar as we are biological creatures like the higher animals, we share some instincts with them—such as the urge to mate—even if our creation in God's image affects how we ought to experience and govern such instincts very radically (see Jude 10).

meeting Wurmbrand stressed repeatedly that Jesus chose suffering, and then asked the group sitting before him if they would choose suffering for Christ's sake.

In Scripture and especially in the New Testament, God's people are often encouraged to endure or embrace or even choose suffering.[24] As Piper argues, we, like the apostle Paul, can and should freely choose to suffer in ways that go beyond anything that human beings ordinarily have to experience in this life—in other words, for our Lord's sake (Phil. 1:29) we can and should freely choose to undergo any of the sorts of unpleasantness that may result from our identifying with him (Mark 10:28–30; John 15:20; Rom. 8:17; 2 Cor. 1:7; 2 Tim. 1:8–12; 2:3; 3:12; Heb. 11:24–27; 13:12–13). And we may do this with the assurance that if we endure such suffering, then we will reign with Christ and be glorified with him (2 Tim. 2:12; Rom. 8:17; 2 Cor. 4:16–18).[25]

Such suffering, Piper says, is the sort that "Christians accept as part of a choice to be openly Christian in risky situations" (256). But what about the sorts of suffering that we do not deliberately choose, such as getting a headache or—to use Piper's own examples (256)—contracting cancer or losing a child in a car accident or suffering severe depression?

Piper claims that these sorts of suffering are not essentially different from those where our deliberate choice to be openly Christian involves knowingly choosing "a way of life that accepts suffering" (256). He argues that a Christian's ordinary choice "to follow Christ in the way He directs" involves choosing to live under God's sovereign providence—and thus "all suffering that comes in the path of obedience . . . is 'chosen' [in the sense that] we willingly take the path of obedience where the suffering befalls us, and we do not murmur against God" (257). Of course, we "may pray—as Paul did—that the suffering be removed . . . ; but if God wills, we embrace it in the end as part of the cost of discipleship in the path of obedience on the way to heaven" (257). Thus, "all suffering, of every kind, that we may endure in the path of our Christian calling . . . tests and proves our allegiance to His goodness and power," and our allegiance thereby reveals that we take God's goodness and Christ's preciousness—and God's goodness and Christ's preciousness alone—to be "an all-sufficient compensation and prize" (257) for whatever he may ordain for us. In other words, our response to any sort

---

[24]On enduring suffering, see 2 Corinthians 1:6; 2 Thessalonians 1:3–7; 2 Timothy 4:5; James 5:10–11; 1 Peter 2:19–20; and Revelation 1:9; on embracing it, see Matthew 5:10–12; Acts 5:41; Romans 5:3–5; and 1 Peter 4:13–14, 16; and on freely choosing it, see Romans 15:1–3 and Philippians 2:5–8.

[25]Of course, Piper needs to maintain that all of our choices to suffer should be motivated by our belief that it will maximize our pleasure, so he concludes that "we do not choose suffering simply because we are told to, but because the One who tells us to describes it as the path to everlasting joy" (287).

of suffering should show God being most glorified in us because, in spite of our suffering, we are resting most satisfied in him.

This is, indeed, how we should respond to any sort of suffering, for it shows that we have placed our ultimate hope in God, both in the sense of our trusting him to work out everything for our good (Rom. 8:28) and in the sense of our taking him and his purposes to be the final object of all of our hopes or, in other words, in the sense of our taking him to be our treasure (Matt. 13:44).[26] But sometimes—and especially, as we shall see, in situations of profound suffering—we fail suffering's test and it thereby becomes apparent that either we are not trusting God to work out everything for our good or we are not taking him right now for our final hope or treasure. So what is left for us then?

In order to answer this question, we need to think more about how suffering affects us.

Why Suffering Is Usually Good for Us

"All experiences of suffering in the path of Christian obedience," Piper claims, "have this in common: They all threaten our faith in the goodness of God and tempt us to leave the path of obedience" (257). I have been partially paraplegic for over forty years, and this is not my experience.

As I have recounted in greater detail elsewhere, from the first moment of the accident that has left me this way, I have always sensed God's love for me both in my accident's occurrence and in the disabilities that have followed on it.[27] Before I was hurt, I was doubting God's existence, but the suffering arising from my accident has conveyed to me a steady sense of God's gracious presence. Even now whenever my physical condition spawns new worries, I find that those worries, rather than threatening my faith in God's goodness and tempting me to leave the path of obedience, inevitably reassure me that God is good and that I must obey him. And so I find myself confessing with the psalmist:

> You have dealt well with your servant,
> O LORD. . . .
> Before I was afflicted I went astray,
> but now I keep your word.
> You are good and do good. . . .

---

[26]As 1 Peter 1:3 makes clear, our having this sort of hope is caused by—and therefore a proof of—our spiritual rebirth (see above). Part of what I shall argue a couple of sections hence is that our lacking such hope is not proof that we are not reborn.

[27]See my "True Freedom: The Liberty That Scripture Portrays as Worth Having," in *Beyond the Bounds: Open Theism and the Undermining of Biblical Christianity*, ed. John Piper, Justin Taylor, and Paul Kjoss Helseth (Wheaton, IL: Crossway, 2003), 78–79, 83–84.

It is good for me that I was afflicted,
  that I might learn your statutes.
The law of your mouth is better to me
  than thousands of gold and silver pieces. . . .
I know, O Lord, . . .
  . . . that in faithfulness you have afflicted me.
      (Ps. 119:65, 67–68a, 71–72, 75)

Of course, my experience with my paralysis is not every sufferer's experience, just as it has not always been my experience with other kinds of suffering. Yet I think that it is eventually the experience of most Christian sufferers (as corroborated by many Christian testimonies) that, although they (quite correctly) would never have deliberately chosen to suffer in the ways that they have, they also would not choose now not to have so suffered. Suffering—especially in the forms of potentially ominous pain or significant longer-term suffering—tends to produce clear benefits.[28] So how does it do this?

It does it in part by challenging our shallow confidences. As long as things seem to be going well for us, we tend to harbor a number of false beliefs. One of them is that our lives are largely in our own control. As the apostle James understands, we all too readily tend to say, "Today or tomorrow we will go into such and such a town and spend a year there and trade and make a profit." Yet, James reminds us, we "do not know what tomorrow will bring." Human life, James tells his readers, is only a mist that appears for a little while and then vanishes. Consequently, he writes, we ought to say, "*If the Lord wills*"—and only then—"will we live and do this or that." Yet we tend to boast in our arrogance, even though all such boasting is sinful (James 4:13–16). In such situations, a good stab of potentially ominous pain tends to remind us of life's fragility and thus can begin to quench our arrogance.

Again, when things are going well for us, we tend to believe that life's ordinary goods can satisfy us. Ease and prosperity all too quickly seduce us into falling for the illusion that we have secured our own happiness

---

[28]This is often even the experience of non-Christians, as when someone says, "My cancer was the best thing that ever happened to me!" C. S. Lewis does a particularly good job in explaining why pain and suffering are usually good for people. See especially chapter 6 of his *Problem of Pain*, along with the appendix written by his medical friend, R. Havard. Havard observes that for people in general, and not just for Christians, "if the cause [of mental pain] is accepted and faced, the conflict will strengthen and purify the character," and chronic mental pain can lead some to "produce brilliant work and strengthen, harden, and sharpen their characters till they become like tempered steel" (161). He concludes his observations with the words that "pain provides an opportunity for heroism; the opportunity is seized with surprising frequency" (162).

and all we need is more of the same.[29] And so, borrowing a phrase from wise old Matthew Henry, we need our mouths "put . . . out of taste" for worldly delights.[30] We must come to see through the illusion that life's ordinary pleasures are enough for us. And this is another part of what significant and especially chronic suffering can do: when our lives begin to be significantly and perhaps rather consistently unpleasant, our quest for life's ordinary pleasures tends to lose its appeal and our Lord's declaration that "one's life does not consist in the abundance of his possessions" may begin to strike home (Luke 12:15; see, e.g., Ps. 107:17–20). Moreover, the new taste of the new creature in Christ—the taste, that is, for God himself and thus for "the hidden treasure of holy joy" that alone can satisfy our deepest desires—tends to grow as we lose taste for merely mundane satisfactions. Pain often affords us our first real taste for the things of God.[31]

Thus suffering often causes us to reconsider the course and quality of our lives. For us as needy, "wanty" creatures, full of desires and longings, who live—and *must* live—by projecting ourselves into futures where we hope that our desires and longings will be met, suffering can be, as C. S. Lewis so memorably put it, "God's megaphone" through which he commands our attention and urges us to reconsider the trajectory of our lives. In this way, suffering is generally good for human beings, and especially for Christians, for it disturbs our equanimity and thus prompts us to reset our frame of mind. "My own experience," Lewis confessed, "is something like this":

> I am progressing along the path of life in my ordinary contentedly fallen and godless condition, absorbed in a merry meeting with my friends for the morrow or a bit of work that tickles my vanity today, a holiday or a new book, when suddenly a stab of abdominal pain that threatens serious disease, or a headline in the newspapers that threatens us all with

---

[29]For Old Testament recognitions of this, see, e.g., Moses' warning that Israel must not allow her future ease and prosperity to lead her to credit her wealth to herself (see Deut. 8:11–17; cf. Jer. 22:21) as well as the Deuteronomic prohibition against any future king of Israel acquiring too many horses or wives or too much silver and gold lest these acquisitions turn his heart away from God and back to Egypt (Deut. 17:16–17; cf. Ps. 30:6).

[30]Quoted by Piper in *Desiring God*, 12. The phrase is found twice in Henry's *Commentary on the Whole Bible*, once with reference to Song of Solomon 2:3–7 and once with reference to Mark 14:25 on the institution of the Lord's Supper.

[31]Although his application of his words to Job may be questioned, Elihu articulated a very similar perspective in Job 33:19–20, 29–30. In Psalm 102, David's physical and mental distress made him forget even to seek minor pleasures such as eating (see v. 4) and yet, at the same time, threw God's eternity into high relief (see vv. 12, 24–27). This eclipse of ordinary pleasure can happen through old age as well as sickness (see, e.g., Eccles. 12:1 and 2 Sam. 19:35). However it comes about, the potential graciousness of having our mouths put out of taste for such pleasures should be clear from what our Lord observed about the way that life's cares and riches and pleasures can choke our spiritual fruitfulness (Luke 8:14).

destruction, sends this whole pack of cards tumbling down. At first I am overwhelmed, and all my little happinesses look like broken toys. Then, slowly and reluctantly, bit by bit, I try to bring myself into the frame of mind that I should be in at all times. I remind myself that all these toys were never intended to possess my heart, that my true good is in another world and my only real treasure is Christ.[32]

Yet, as Lewis observed, the moment the pain or anxiety ceases, we leap back to our toys, and thus "the terrible necessity of tribulation"—of repeated or chronic suffering—"is only too clear." Without the ballast of suffering, we are all too prone to emulate the rich fool in Christ's parable who can't get it through his thick head that tonight his soul, shorn of all the earthly goods that have been giving him pleasure, may be required of him (Luke 12:13–21).

   Thus suffering can be God's gift to us because by its means he may burn the sinful, idolatrous fat off our hearts. Life's more significant hurts and worries have the capacity to burn away our false confidences and illusions. So even though many atheists would claim that suffering is a main motive for disbelief, the paradox is that by God's grace suffering can be crucial for stable and earnest belief.[33] In Psalm 119 it is the insolent who, in the undisturbed tranquility of their minds, have hearts unfeeling like fat, while it is the suffering psalmist who has thereby learned to delight in God's law. His affliction led him to learn God's statutes, and that made God's law more precious to him than any amount of money (Ps. 119:69–72; cf. James 5:1–5). By his suffering he came in effect to know, deep down in his heart, that "here we have no lasting city" (Heb. 13:14) and that we are likely to enter God's kingdom only through many tribulations (Acts 14:22). In short, it became clear for him, as it can become clear to us, both that "life is hard and God is good" (10).

Profound Suffering: What It Is and How It Can Affect Us

In Scripture, our hearts are the core of our personal beings. They are thus central to every crucial aspect of our humanity: our inner life and character (1 Sam. 16:7; Matt. 15:19; 1 Pet. 3:4), our feelings and emo-

---

[32]Lewis, *The Problem of Pain*, 106–7. The idea of pain being "God's megaphone" occurs earlier. "Pain," Lewis observed, "is not only immediately recognisable evil, but evil impossible to ignore. We can rest contentedly in our sins and in our stupidities; and anyone who has watched gluttons shoveling down the most exquisite foods as if they did not know what they were eating, will admit that we can ignore even pleasure. But pain insists upon being attended to. God whispers to us in our pleasures, speaks in our conscience, but shouts in our pain: it is His megaphone to rouse a deaf world" (90–91).

[33]Near the end of the *Problem of Pain*'s sixth chapter, after he had made most of his case for the usually beneficial effects of pain, Lewis concluded that "the real problem is not why some humble, pious, believing people suffer, but why some do *not*" (104).

tions (Pss. 4:7; 13:2; 25:17; 2 Cor. 6:11), our intellectual faculties and activities (Pss. 49:3; 53:1; Prov. 2:2; Mark 2:6; Luke 1:51; 2:51), and our desires and will and purposes (Pss. 27:8; 37:4; 57:7; John 13:2; Acts 5:3f.). "It was essentially the whole man, with all his attributes, physical, intellectual, and psychological, of which the Hebrew thought and spoke, and the heart was conceived of as the governing centre for all of these. It is the heart which makes a man . . . what he is, and governs all his actions (Pr. 4:23)."[34]

Whatever affects our hearts, then, affects everything about us, including our hopes and plans and dreams.[35] In fact, it has only been through the frustration that came with disability and chronic suffering that some of us have learned this truth:

> Many are the plans in a man's heart,
>   but it is the LORD's purpose that prevails.
>   (Prov. 19:21 NIV; cf. 16:9)

So to put the lessons from the previous section in other words: by prompting us to rethink our shallow confidences and see through the illusions that usually fool us, suffering should lead us to revise both the ground and content of our hopes. We should progress from grounding them in ourselves or in any principality or power, real or imagined, to grounding them in the perfectly good although humanly unfathomable will of the one and only living God (Eccles. 3:11; 8:16–17; Rom. 11:33); and we should abandon the sinful dream that anything other than the everlasting enjoyment of the triune God and his people can ultimately satisfy us (see, e.g., Ps. 145:3–6; 1 Tim. 6:17).

In general, the fact that we are needy and "wanty" creatures gets us off our duffs and on the hunt for goods; and it is the prospect of enjoying particular goods, whether temporal or eternal, that arouses our hopes and thus lures us to act in specific ways. Scripture recognizes the centrality of hope to human life and covers its full range, noting—in addition to all of the commendable ones—some hopes that are false or vain (see, e.g., Pss. 33:17; 62:10; Isa. 20:5–6; Jer. 23:16), some that are paltry or uncertain (Acts 24:26; 1 Tim. 6:17), and some that we may lose or abandon (Acts 16:19; 27:20). It also records cases of what I shall call "profound suffering" where all hope may die.

---

[34]B. O. Banwell, "Heart," in *New Bible Dictionary*, 3d ed., ed. J. D. Douglas et al. (Downers Grove, IL: InterVarsity, 1996), 456. The New Testament follows the Old concerning the centrality of our hearts.
[35]For believers, it is when the eyes of our hearts have been enlightened that we come to know what is the hope to which God has called us (see Eph. 1:18).

Not all profound suffering causes all hope to die, yet it always involves experiencing a hurt so deep and disruptive that its presence at least for a time dominates and threatens to overwhelm the sufferer's life. Biblical cases include:

- Naomi, whose calamity weighed on her so heavily that she may have been unrecognizable to her old friends;[36]
- Job, who in his suffering and grief longed for death (3:20–22) and cursed the day of his conception, as well as the fact that he had ever been born (3:1–26; 10:18–22);
- the writer of Psalm 88, whose life was so troubled from his youth up that he became a horror to his companions and found darkness his closest friend;[37]
- Jeremiah, who emerged from torture so traumatized that he cursed the man who brought his father news of his birth for not having killed him and his mother before he was born;[38] and
- our Lord with his sweat like blood in the garden and his cry of dereliction from the cross (Luke 22:39–44; Mark 15:33–37).[39]

---

[36]See Ruth 1, especially verses 19–21: "So [Naomi and her daughter-in-law Ruth] went on until they came to Bethlehem. And when they came to Bethlehem, the whole town was stirred because of them. And the women said, 'Is this Naomi?' She said to them, 'Do not call me Naomi [which means "pleasant"]; call me Mara [which means "bitter"], for the Almighty has dealt very bitterly with me. I went away full, and the LORD has brought me back empty. Why call me Naomi, when the LORD has testified against me and the Almighty has brought calamity upon me?'"

I am not claiming that Naomi's suffering was so profound that all of her hope had at least temporarily died, but since one of my readers thought that I was and said, "She obviously has not lost all hope, for she continues to bear witness that God is 'Almighty,' that he is the 'Lord,'" I would say this: It follows from passages such as James 2:19; Mark 5:7; and Acts 16:17 that even those who have lost all hope of salvation can still have some correct beliefs about God, such as that he is one, almighty, and the absolute sovereign. The fact that Naomi also calls God by his covenant name "LORD" suggests that she also still possessed some saving faith in the God of Israel, who is indeed "strong to save" (see Ps. 31:1–2). If this is so, then she should have, like David (see the whole of Psalm 31), continued to hope in God's salvation. Yet it seems probable that she, again like David (see Ps. 31:21–22), temporarily lost her hope, only to regain it when she experienced through the events related in the subsequent chapters of Ruth (and especially in chap. 4) the fact that God had been with her all along. Naomi, then, would be an Old Testament instance of a case somewhat like what is given in the verse that serves as this chapter's epigraph: "If we are faithless, he remains faithful—for he cannot deny himself" (2 Tim. 2:13).

[37]See the final clause in the NIV: "the darkness is my closest friend."

[38]See Jeremiah 20, especially verses 14–18. This chapter is very difficult to understand and so it has spawned a large number of conflicting interpretations. For one thoughtful interpretation, see Philip Graham Ryken, *Jeremiah and Lamentations: From Sorrow to Hope* (Wheaton, IL: Crossway, 2001), chap. 29, "Dark Night of the Soul." Ryken explains that when Jeremiah was put in stocks (see 20:2) it involved more "than just locking him up. The Hebrew word refers to twisting. They put Jeremiah on the rack, clamping his wrists and twisting his body into painful contortions" (314). It was torture, in other words. And it was this, it seems, that led Jeremiah—shockingly, since as a godly man he was aware of the respect that God has commanded us to show to each other (see, e.g., Gen. 9:4–6)—to curse another human being made in God's image for not killing his mother before he was born in order to prevent his birth and eventual torture.

[39]Lest I be misunderstood: I am not claiming that our Lord lost all hope. In fact, it is a clear implication of Hebrews 12:1–2 that he did not. But, of course, there are many things that were true of our incarnate Lord that may not be true of us, even if they should be.

Nonbiblical cases include C. S. Lewis's profound grief after the death of his wife as he chronicled it in *A Grief Observed*, and Elie Wiesel's expressions of utter desolation in *Night*, his searing first book recounting his experiences in the Holocaust.

A careful reading of the biblical cases makes clear that even profound suffering does not inevitably undermine the sufferers' belief in God's goodness or cause them to leave the path of obedience:[40]

- in spite of the fact that she understood her own suffering in terms of the Lord's hand having gone out against her[41] and her apparent despair about her own life improving, Naomi continued to believe that God was good and kind (Ruth 1:8–9, 12–13), and the book of Ruth gives no indication that she was tempted toward disobedience;
- the writer of Psalm 88 opened his psalm with the words, "O LORD, God of my salvation" and then appealed to God's steadfast love,

---

[40]One of my readers thought that the examples that follow contradict my piece's title. But they do not, as long as profound suffering does not inevitably cause all hope to die.

[41]In all of the biblical cases we are considering, the person who was suffering profoundly had no doubt that his or her suffering was ultimately ordained by God and, indeed, this is the consistent witness of the Scriptures (see, e.g., Job 42:11). For a survey of some of the Scriptures that corroborate this claim, see my "True Freedom," cited in footnote 27.

The distinction between someone's continuing to believe that God is good and someone's believing that God will be good to him is crucial for a proper assessment of Christian hedonism, as should become clear to readers of footnote 56. Naomi seems to be a clear case of someone's believing the former without believing the latter.

In response to my claiming that Naomi seems to be a clear case of someone continuing to believe that God is good without continuing to believe that God would be good to her, one of my readers has written: "I'm not sure that this distinction ultimately holds up. I assume [that to] believe 'that God is good' is not merely an intellectual, notional form of faith. But if it's not, then there is an element of trusting God, taking him at his word. Does it really make sense to say that someone can believe 'that God is good' (in general? to others? as an abstract affirmation of an attribute?) but to refuse to believe 'that God is good to me'? I don't know that we really know enough about Naomi's mind to conclude that she doubted God's goodness to her—though it is quite clear that she believed God was bringing hard things on her." Four considerations seem important here. First, the fact that Naomi seems to have wanted her name permanently changed from "Pleasant" to "Bitter" suggests strongly that she was at least for a time doubting God's goodness to her. Second, Naomi is not the only Old Testament saint who seems to have continued believing in God and his goodness without having continued to believe that God would be good to her. Job clearly never lost his faith in God and his goodness, and yet if we take the biblical text at face value (rather than read it in the grip of a theory), he as clearly at times lost his belief that God would still be good to him; note, for instance, his claim, "My eye will never again see good" (7:7; cf. Lam. 3:18). Third, saints in the midst of profound suffering who no longer can confess that God is being good to them are not necessarily deliberately refusing to believe; they may just find themselves not to be able to believe for some period of time. Last, let me concede, just for argument's sake, that it does not "really make sense" to say that a saint can believe that *God is good* and yet disbelieve that *God is good to me*. "Does not really make sense" here can mean at least two different things: (a) it is impossible for a saint to believe *God is good* and not also to believe *God is good to me*; (b) it would be senseless—that is, irrational, illogical, unreasonable—for a saint to believe *God is good* and not also to believe *God is good to me*. Regarding (a), Naomi and Job seem to be clear biblical cases that saints can affirm the former belief and deny the latter. Regarding (b), even saints can be senseless in this way. E.g., note the psalmist's confession after he found himself envying the wicked: "When my heart was grieved and my spirit embittered, I was senseless and ignorant; I was a brute beast before you" (73:21–22 NIV).

faithfulness, and righteousness (vv. 1–2, 9–13), in spite of his confusion over why God continued to afflict him so relentlessly (vv. 6–9, 14–18); and

- our Lord's cry of dereliction from the cross, "My God, my God, why have you forsaken me?" no doubt was uttered by him with the whole context of Psalm 22 in mind, including its confidence that God will surely rescue those who keep trusting him.[42]

Yet, as the words of Job and Jeremiah make especially clear, profound suffering can challenge our lives at very deep levels.

Both Job and Jeremiah cursed the days of their births (Job 3:1; Jer. 20:14), questioning why they were ever born, given the suffering they were currently undergoing (Job 3:13, 16–19; Jer. 20:18). Each experienced a hurt so deep and disruptive that its presence at least for a time dominated his life. For Job, it seems that it was the length of his suffering and grief that especially wore away at him; and so we find him making statements like these:

I am allotted months of emptiness,
    and nights of misery are apportioned to me. (7:3)

He has set darkness upon my paths. (19:8)

And now my soul is poured out within me;
    days of affliction have taken hold of me.
The night racks my bones,
    and the pain that gnaws me takes no rest. . . .
God has cast me into the mire,
    and I have become like dust and ashes. (30:16–17, 19)

These verses show that Job never doubted that his suffering came from God (see also 1:20–21; 2:10). Yet he also never wholeheartedly questioned God's goodness and justice (23:1–12; James 5:11), even though his suffer-

---

[42]The full significance of our Lord's having uttered the opening words of Psalm 22 becomes clear only as we read the rest of the psalm and thus find the psalmist repeatedly affirming that God rescues and vindicates those who trust in him. For instance, after affirming that his Israelite ancestors trusted in God and God then delivered them, the psalmist declares, "You made me trust you at my mother's breasts" (v. 9), which invites us to draw the conclusion that God will deliver him, too. In fact, the more carefully we read this psalm, the more apparent it becomes that while the suffering that prompted the psalmist's opening cry was indeed dominating his consciousness, yet he understood his current distress to involve his being forsaken *only at one point in time*, with every expectation that God would ultimately save and vindicate him (cf. Heb. 12:2). This is another indication that while our Lord suffered profoundly, his hope did not die. No doubt it should be the same for us, even if we have to confess that it is not.

ing made him feel afraid and helpless (9:27–31; 23:13–16), and its sheer unremitting ceaselessness led him to lose all hope:[43]

> My days are swifter than a weaver's shuttle
>   and come to their end without hope. . . .
>   *my eye will never again see good.* (7:6, 7b)

> The mountain falls and crumbles away,
>   and the rock is removed from its place;
> the waters wear away the stones;
>   the torrents wash away the soil of the earth;
>   so *you destroy the hope of man.*
> *You prevail forever against him,* and he passes;
>   you change his countenance, and send him away.
> His sons come to honor, and he does not know it;
>   they are brought low, and he perceives it not.
> He feels only the pain of his own body,
>   and he mourns only for himself. (14:18–22)

> He breaks me down on every side, and I am gone,
>   and *my hope has he pulled up like a tree.* (19:10)

These verses, combined with Job's third chapter, show that Job's suffering was making the course of his life completely opaque to him (3:23; 7:20b–21a), throwing into question its whole worth and meaning (9:13–24; 10:2–18a). This led him not only to loathe it (7:16; 9:21), but also to declare that he would choose strangling and death over more suffering (7:15).

Given Jeremiah's circumstances as reported in chapter 20, his cursing seems to have been prompted more by the intensity than the length of his suffering. Yet the dynamics of his despair were similar to Job's. Jeremiah's torture at Pashhur's hand (20:2) seems to have been the final straw in crushing his hope that his prophetic ministry would be properly received (20:8–10). For a while, it seems, he rallied in his hope that God would vindicate him (20:11–13). But then he succumbed to life-cursing

---

[43]One of my readers commented here: "I would be inclined to say that Job *felt as if* he lost all hope. Aren't there indications that he felt at least a faint flicker of God's redeeming justice even in the midst of the pain?" I think that the following passages are far too strongly worded to allow us to say that Job merely *felt as if* he had lost all hope when he uttered them. I agree that there are indications that at times he felt at least a faint flicker of God's redeeming justice even in the midst of his pain. But that is not to say that he felt that flicker at the same time as he made these declarations. They certainly seem to require us to say that at the time he made them, his hope had died.

despair (20:14–18), apparently because he abandoned all hope that his life would end well:

> Why did I ever come out of the womb
>> to see trouble and sorrow
>> and *to end my days in shame*? (20:18 NIV)

A few chapters later, Jeremiah attested to the centrality of hope to human life in recording God's declaration to the exiles, "I know the plans I have for you, . . . plans for welfare and not for evil, to give you a future and a hope" (29:11; cf. 31:17; Prov. 23:18). And so, whether or not Jeremiah penned these words that accompany his prophecy, he clearly would have understood them:

> I have become the laughingstock of all peoples,
>> the object of their taunts all day long.
> [God] has filled me with bitterness;
>> he has sated me with wormwood.
> He has made my teeth grind on gravel,
>> and made me cower in ashes;
> my soul is bereft of peace;
>> *I have forgotten what happiness is;*
> *so I say, "My endurance has perished;*
>> *so has my hope from the Lord."* (Lam. 3:14–18)

For this unidentified writer, as well as for Jeremiah and Job, profound suffering at least momentarily eclipsed the horizon of his hope. As Job plaintively summarized it:

> Yet does not one in a heap of ruins stretch out his hand,
>> and in his disaster cry for help? . . .
> But when I hoped for good, evil came,
>> and when I waited for light, darkness came. (30:24, 26)

Profound suffering thus presents the limit case of Solomon's proverb that while "a desire fulfilled is a tree of life," "hope deferred makes the heart sick" (Prov. 13:12).

When All Hope Dies

As this proverb implies, hope deferred makes the heart sick by cutting our most common source of motivation, which is our hope of fulfilling some desire by securing some good. As needy, "wanty" creatures who must be constantly on the hunt for goods, we generally orient ourselves in life by identifying our desires and then judging which of them we think we can and should fulfill. These judgments fuel our hopes, large and small, true and false, wise and foolish. Given the centrality of hope in human life and our sinful tendency to place our hope in the wrong things, suffering (as I argued two sections ago) is often good for us because it challenges our shallow confidences and puts our mouths out of taste for earthly and sinful pleasures that cannot fully satisfy. So, as C. S. Lewis observed, most suffering prompts us to reorient ourselves in clearly beneficial ways. But what happens if we suffer so profoundly that we are at risk of losing all hope? What happens if we experience hurts so deep that their presence not only dominates our lives but also tempts us to conclude, Job-like, that our eyes will not see good—that is, that we will not feel any real peace or pleasure or happiness or joy or satisfaction—ever again?

Such suffering can be profoundly disorienting because it strikes at the nerve of our thinking and hoping and planning by tempting us no longer to believe that any of it will produce any good.[44] So to the degree that our hope dies because we despair that any of our more significant desires or longings will be met, then to that degree we lose our usual motivation.

This happens in severe depression,[45] and it seems to have been what happened (or at least very nearly happened) to Job and Jeremiah and the writer of Lamentations 3. Such despair may also be accompanied by doubts about God's goodness and temptations to leave the path of obedience.[46] For instance, C. S. Lewis's grief over his wife's death not only made all the rest of his life seem worthless; it also tempted him to doubt God's goodness, as he noted when he wrote that he was not "in much danger of ceasing to believe in God" (in spite of the fact that in his intense grief God seemed to him to be utterly absent), but "the real danger is coming to believe such dreadful things about Him"—such as that God is, perhaps, a kind of "Cosmic Sadist." "The conclusion I dread," Lewis wrote, "is not 'So there's no God after all,' but 'So this is what God's really like.

---

[44]This seems to be part of what happened to Job. See 9:25–29, and especially its concluding question: "Why then do I labor in vain?"

[45]For more on the relationship between hope and depression, see my "Starting from Scripture," in *Limning the Psyche: Explorations in Christian Psychology*, ed. Robert C. Roberts and Mark R. Talbot (Grand Rapids: Eerdmans, 1997), 102–22.

[46]Profound suffering can be but is not necessarily accompanied by either one of these or both. On some interpretations of Jeremiah 20:7, Jeremiah was doubting God's goodness (see, e.g., Ryken, *Jeremiah and Lamentations*, 316), and it seems that he was tempted to be disobedient to his call as a prophet in verses 8–9.

Deceive yourself no longer.'"[47] Later, he sounded a note similar to Job's and Jeremiah's: "Reality, looked at steadily, is unbearable. And how or why did such a reality blossom (or fester) here and there into the terrible phenomenon called consciousness? Why did it produce things like us who can see it and, seeing it, recoil in loathing?" A page later, he wrote, "Sooner or later I must face the question in plain language. What reason have we, except our own desperate wishes, to believe that God is, by any standard we can conceive, 'good'?"

By the end of the record of thoughts that make up *A Grief Observed*, Lewis was beginning to recover from his grief. What initially disoriented him ultimately did not. For Elie Wiesel, the evils he suffered in the Holocaust at least at first seemed more like what the Christian philosopher Marilyn McCord Adams calls "horrendous evil"—suffering that is so profound that it gives the sufferer a seemingly permanent reason to doubt that his or her life can be good overall.[48] Wiesel tells us that when he, as a fifteen-year-old, emerged from the cattle car that had carried him to

---

[47] *A Grief Observed*, published under the pseudonym N. W. Clerk (Greenwich, CT: Seabury, 1963), 9–10. The possibility that God is a Cosmic Sadist arises on page 32, the quotation about reality being unbearable is found on page 25, and my final quotation is from page 26.

Lewis captured very well the way that profound suffering disturbs and disorients us. His book opens like this: "No one ever told me that grief felt so like fear. I am not afraid, but the sensation is like being afraid. The same fluttering in the stomach, the same restlessness, the yawning. I keep on swallowing.

"At other times it feels like being mildly drunk, or concussed. There is a sort of invisible blanket between the world and me. I find it hard to take in what anyone says. Or perhaps, hard to want to take it in. *It is so uninteresting*" (7, my emphasis).

Again: "And no one ever told me about the laziness of grief. Except at my job—where the machine seems to run on much as usual—*I loathe the slightest effort*. . . . [Grief] gives life a permanently provisional feeling. *It doesn't seem worth starting anything*. I can't settle down. I yawn, I fidget. . . . Up till this I always had too little time. Now there is nothing but time. Almost pure time, empty successiveness" (8, 29, my emphases). The descriptions I have emphasized show that Lewis's motivation was cut by his grief. He felt that the only good he really wanted had been snatched away from him, and so his hope for any significant future good died.

Lewis's statements gain impact when we remember that he recorded the thoughts that make up *A Grief Observed* over twenty years after writing his *Problem of Pain*. This shows that our having some idea of what our intellectual response to suffering should be does not protect us from suffering—and suffering profoundly. As Lewis himself observed, "You never know how much you really believe anything until its truth or falsehood becomes a matter of life and death to you" (*Grief Observed*, 21).

[48] See Marilyn McCord Adams, "Horrendous Evils and the Goodness of God," in *The Problem of Evil*, ed. Marilyn McCord Adams and Robert Merrihew Adams (Oxford: Oxford University Press, 1990), 209–21. I am taking a little liberty with Adams's characterization in order to have it illuminate the issues I am discussing. Her own characterization goes like this: "For present purposes, I define 'horrendous evils' as 'evils the participation in (the doing or suffering of) which gives one reason prima facie to doubt whether one's life could (given their inclusion in it) be a great good to one on the whole'" (211). She goes on: "Such reasonable doubt arises because it is so difficult humanly to conceive how such evils could be overcome . . . [for such evils] seem prima facie . . . to engulf the positive value of a participant's life. Nevertheless, that very horrendous proportion, by which they threaten to rob a person's life of positive meaning, cries out . . . to be made meaningful" (211).

Adams lists some "paradigmatic horrors": "the rape of a woman and axing off of her arms, psychophysical torture whose ultimate goal is the disintegration of personality, . . . cannibalizing one's own offspring, child abuse of the sort described by Ivan Karamazov, . . . parental incest, slow death by starvation, participation in the Nazi death camps, . . . having to choose which of one's children shall live and which be executed by terrorists, being the accidental and/or unwitting agent of the disfigurement or death of those one loves best" (211–12). Her ultimate solution to these evils is, to my mind, an unacceptable amalgam of Christian and secular thinking.

the Nazi death camp of Birkenau, he could smell burning human flesh and see ditches with huge flames where babies were being dumped alive. He writes:

> Never shall I forget that night, the first night in camp, that turned my life into one long night seven times sealed. . . .
>
> Never shall I forget those flames that consumed my faith forever. Never shall I forget the nocturnal silence that deprived me for all eternity of the desire to live.
>
> Never shall I forget those moments that murdered my God and my soul and turned my dreams to ashes.

When morning finally broke, the intensity of the horrors he had witnessed had turned him into "a different person. The student of the Talmud, the child I was, had been consumed by the flames. All that was left was a shape that resembled me. My soul had been invaded—and devoured— by a huge black flame."[49] Later, when he realized that his father had died while huddled beside him, he writes that suddenly "the evidence overwhelmed me: there was no longer any reason to live, any reason to fight." As Wiesel portrays it in *Night*, his experience in Birkenau hurt him and his faith so deeply that he lost all of his faith and hope as well as all of his motivation to live.

The Lesson for Christian Hedonists
In spite of how it appears in *Night*, Wiesel's faith and hope and motivation did not die forever: he was later motivated by his desire to have the world improve itself through its memory of the Holocaust, and he said that he believed and hoped in God, even if he described his faith as a "wounded faith."[50] So how things seem to us in the very midst of profound suffering

---

[49] Elie Wiesel, *Night* (New York: Hill and Wang, 2006), 34, 37. The next quotation is found on page 99. I reflect more on Wiesel's experience in my "All the Good That Is Ours in Christ," in *Suffering and the Sovereignty of God*, ed. John Piper and Justin Taylor (Wheaton, IL: Crossway, 2006).

[50] See, e.g., the interview that Wiesel had with Jeff Diamant on July 29, 2006 as found at http://www. thestar.com/life/religion/article/126609. To Diamant's question, "In what ways has the world not responded properly to the Holocaust?" Wiesel answers: "I was convinced that if the world was to receive the testimony of the Holocaust, it would improve itself, it would become a better world. And it hasn't." Then in answer to the question, "What is it like having strangers ask you if or why you believe in God?" Wiesel responds: "You know who asks me the most? It's children. Children ask, 'How can you still believe in God?' In *All the Rivers Run to the Sea*, I speak about it. There are all the reasons in the world for me to give up on God. I have the same reasons to give up on man, and on culture and on education. And yet . . . I don't give up on humanity, I don't give up on culture, I don't give up on journalism . . . I don't give up on it. I have the reasons. I don't use them." Later, in response to another question, Wiesel says that only religious people with some anxiety or doubt ask him how he can still believe in God. Such people want "to know how I deal with that anxiety or doubt. And I say, 'Look, I have faith. It's a wounded faith.'"

In mentioning Wiesel and his experiences, I am making no judgment about his standing before God. What happened to him in the Holocaust seems, however, to be paradigmatic of the kinds of experiences that are so horrible that they tempt human beings to lose all hope in God.

and how they seem to us if (and, usually, when) we emerge from it can be quite different. Likewise, when Naomi took Ruth's infant Obed into her arms near the end of the story that opened with her profound grief, her life began to be restored and nourished by the same God who had made it so bitter. It again became no irony to call her "Pleasant."

Indeed, as Paul stresses, a saint's suffering will show itself over time to be an unsought gift[51]—a gift that, by God's grace, produces in Christians endurance, character, and hope (Rom. 5:3–5). This was Paul's own experience, as becomes clear near the beginning of 2 Corinthians:

> We do not want you to be ignorant, brothers and sisters, of the affliction we experienced in Asia. For we were so utterly burdened beyond our strength that we despaired of life itself. Indeed, we felt that we had received the sentence of death. But that was to make us rely not on ourselves but on God who raises the dead. He delivered us from such a deadly peril, and he will deliver us. On him we have set our hope that he will deliver us again. (1:8–10)

In God's saints, suffering ultimately tends to produce hope that is steadfastly "set on the living God," which enables us to labor and strive in godly ways both in this life and for the life to come (1 Tim. 4:10; see the context from 4:7b–10). The hope that God himself causes by regeneration to live within us becomes (in no small part by the suffering he gives us) what orients us by anchoring our souls (Heb. 6:18–19).[52]

Yet we now have seen from both Scripture and two autobiographical reports of personal experience that cases of profound suffering may eclipse all hope at least temporarily. Even Christians may find themselves unable to hope[53] that they will ever know any real peace or pleasure or happiness or joy or satisfaction again. If this happens, we may still retain our faith in God's goodness, as Naomi did, or we, like C. S. Lewis, may find our faith threatened. At its outermost limit, such suffering, like Wiesel's

---

[51]Philippians 1:29 considers suffering a gift, as Piper emphasizes: "When writing to the Philippians, Paul, incredibly, calls suffering a gift, just like faith is a *gift*: 'To you it has been *granted* (*echaristhē* = freely given) for Christ's sake, not only to believe in Him but also to *suffer* for His sake' (Philippians 1:29, NASB)" (263).

[52]Virtually all of the claims of this paragraph are pulled together in 1 Peter 1:3–9, which I would urge my readers to consider very carefully.

[53]This phrase "unable to hope" should be understood like "unable not to sin." Every human being is commanded and required not to sin, but of course no human beings—not even the regenerate—are able in this lifetime to avoid all sin. We are commanded (see Pss. 130:7; 131:3; Heb. 10:23; 1 Peter 1:13) and required (see Col. 1:23; 1 Thess. 4:13; Heb. 3:6) to hope in God, just as we are commanded and required to have faith in him. No doubt, for a saint temporarily to lose all faith and hope involves sin. But that isn't to say that it can't and doesn't happen to God's saints anymore than we can say that God's people can't and won't sin in other ways.

during the Holocaust, may appear so horrendous that it will seem to have deprived us for all eternity of our faith, hope, and desire to live.

In cases like these, appeals to Christian hedonism will not motivate profoundly suffering Christians because they have at least temporarily lost all motivation to produce one state of affairs in preference to any other in the hope that producing that state of affairs will maximize their pleasure, everlastingly or not. For such sufferers have abandoned pursuing any pleasure because they have lost all hope of feeling any pleasure again.

Acknowledgment of Truth as a Distinct Source of Motivation

If the pursuit of pleasure is, then, in fact the only sufficient human motivator and indeed no one ever does anything unless he thinks that it will bring him pleasure, then such sufferers will not be motivated to seek anything, not even remaining faithfully Christian. But then Old Testament saints like Naomi, Job, and Jeremiah would in the midst of their profound suffering have had no motive to remain faithful to God. And so, I conclude, we should hope that Christian hedonism is false insofar as it maintains that the prospect of personal pleasure plays an essential and decisive role in all human motivation.

Yet these Old Testament believers remained faithful: nothing in the book of Ruth suggests that Naomi's faith in the God of Israel wavered; Job is indeed commended for his endurance at James 5:11; and Jeremiah persisted in declaring God's word to the exiles in spite of his resolutions and feelings.

Moreover, the author of Lamentations 3 recovered even his hope right after he said, "My endurance has perished; so has my hope from the LORD." For he continued by saying:

> Remember my affliction and my wanderings,
>   the wormwood and the gall!
> My soul continually remembers it
>   and is bowed down within me.
> But *this I call to mind,*
>   *and therefore I have hope:*
> *The steadfast love of the Lord never ceases;*
>   *his mercies never come to an end;*
> *they are new every morning;*
>   *great is your faithfulness.* (Lam. 3:19–23)

What, then, held these saints' faith in place?

Truth. God had graciously regenerated their hearts so that they persistently acknowledged specific great and crucial specially revealed truths, and so their confession of and allegiance to the God of Israel remained in place, in spite of suffering so profoundly that their suffering at least temporarily eclipsed their capacity to feel any hope.

Consider, for instance, what happened to the writer of Lamentations 3: He called to mind his convictions about the God of Israel's love, mercy, and faithfulness—and these convictions reignited his hope: "This"—the God of Israel's love, mercy, and faithfulness—"I call to mind," he says, *"and therefore* I have hope."[54] Here the *acknowledgment of truth* (see also v. 33) precedes and grounds the writer's hope for future pleasure (see especially vv. 25–26, 29, 31–32), which in turn motivates his patience (vv. 27–30), rather than the *pursuit of pleasure* leading and motivating all else.

A similar insistence on affirming and defending truth is what seems to have constituted Job's commendable endurance. On a quick reading, James may seem to be commending Job for the steadfastness of his hope (James 5:7–11), yet this would run up against Job's not infrequent expressions of having lost all hope. This difficulty disappears, however, if James is commending Job's steadfast insistence on maintaining and defending some absolutely crucial truths about God and himself in spite of the persistent attacks of his friends and his recurrent bouts of utter despair. Although he not merely doubted but actually denied that he himself would ever see good again, Job never seriously questioned God's justice and his own innocence (in spite of the false assertions of his friends), and this stubborn unwillingness to compromise the truth is what grounds the lessons that the book of Job teaches. The book emphasizes not how steadfastly Job hoped but how doggedly he believed.[55]

Likewise, Jeremiah found God's truth to be so powerful that he was compelled to proclaim it, in spite of the temporary loss of all of his hope:

If I say, "I will not mention him,
    or speak any more in his name,"

---

[54] I anticipate that Christian hedonists will maintain that this writer's next declaration that the Lord was his portion means that he continued to hope for pleasure in God. This does not necessarily follow for reasons I don't have space to give here, but even if it did, the writer's affirmations about God's love, mercy, and faithfulness contain no essential reference to himself. The logic of the declaration that I am focusing on moves from the writer's affirmation of God's goodness to a sense of assurance about God's goodness to him.

[55] See, e.g., 42:7: "After the LORD had spoken these words to Job, the LORD said to Eliphaz the Temanite: 'My anger burns against you and against your two friends, *for you have not spoken of me what is right*, as my servant Job has.'" The emphasis here is on asserting what is right rather than hoping unfailingly.

there is in my heart as it were a burning fire
    shut up in my bones,
and I am weary with holding it in,
    and I cannot. (20:9)

Something similar must have gripped and governed Naomi, since her faith in Israel's God never wavered in spite of her false belief that pleasure would never be hers again. And so, in each of these cases, acknowledgment of the truth motivated or (perhaps better) constituted godly faithfulness, even when the hope of all future personal pleasure was gone.[56]

No doubt, God is most glorified *in* us when we are most satisfied in him. Indeed, how could we glorify God more than to show that he remains our "chosen portion" in spite of the fact that we, like Naomi, recognize that his hand has gone out against us to take from us the hope of any more worldly pleasure? Yet God is also glorified in us when, like Job and Jeremiah, we continue faithfully to acknowledge and proclaim his truth in spite of the fact that we are unable to conceive how any alteration to our future circumstances could make our lives seem good and pleasurable again.[57]

---

[56]In a careful effort to defend Christian hedonism, Donald Westblade has written to me in personal correspondence that to hope on God's Word—in other words, to hope on the basis of not just believing God's Word but also trusting that it is true—is ultimately motivationally identical with hoping that some course of action will produce a specific good because "the object of trust or faith must logically always be a promise. . . . And it is in the essential nature of a promise to hold up a future benefit (as its counterpart, the threat, holds up a future danger or loss). To 'hope on the basis of trusting God's word, taken as true,' in other words, can be nothing other than hoping in a promise that the truth counted trustworthy will yield a specific good or benefit." He thus claims that my distinguishing between being motivated by an acknowledgment of the truth and being motivated by the pursuit of pleasure involves setting up a false dichotomy.

But the fact that the writer of Lamentations 3 was motivated to have hope on the basis of the truths that he called to mind establishes that he was not conflating faith in the sense of acknowledging and trusting God's Word as true with hope in the sense of anticipating a specific personal good or benefit. And, indeed, although faith, hope, and love are in Scripture somewhat mutually interpenetrative, they remain three distinct concepts.

One of Westblade's motives for conflating faith and hope involves his wanting to distinguish faith from the sort of "mere mental assent . . . that even demons can exercise" (see James 2:19). I agree that saving faith involves an element additional to mere mental assent, but I disagree that that element should be reduced to an expectation of a future personal benefit, for we have every reason to take Naomi to have been exercising saving faith throughout the book of Ruth although she was for some fair stretch of it convinced (albeit falsely) that her future would include no such benefits. Specifying precisely what the additional element in saving faith is would require an additional paper. (For a good start on such a specification, see the articles on faith and hope in *The International Standard Bible Encyclopedia*, rev. ed., vol. 2 [Grand Rapids: Eerdmans, 1982], although some of the statements found there—such as that "hope . . . is [faith's] forward-looking aspect"—need careful qualification if my claims are true.) Yet, contrary to Westblade's own analysis, even the demons do not merely mentally assent to various truths about God, since they believe "and shudder," no doubt on the basis of the fact that they cannot shake their belief that those of God's threats that concern themselves are true.

[57]The phrase "unable to conceive" in this sentence needs the same sorts of qualifications as "unable to hope" received in footnote 53. As shall become clear in the next section, the phrase "unable to conceive how any alteration to our future circumstances could make our lives seem good and pleasurable again" is meant to include even those alterations that might take place in the eschaton. In other words, even God's saints can, in profound suffering, find some evils so horrendous that they can be (at least temporarily) unable to conceive of how God could ever put them right.

How God Is Glorified When (and Perhaps Especially When) Even Our Faith Fails

Yet sometimes our suffering can be so profound that we fail even the test of faith. Some suffering can seem so horrendous that it leaves even previously faithful, long-term Christians unable to acknowledge core biblical truths, even truths as fundamental as the truth that God is good. I know a couple who lost their son to suicide a few years ago. He had been plagued for years with a besetting temptation. In the end, after a valiant and poignant struggle, he despaired, it seems, and then took his life by stepping in front of a train.

How, these parents cry, can our deeply committed son's struggle be reconciled with these words of our Lord?

> Ask, and it will be given to you; seek, and you will find; knock, and it will be opened to you. For everyone who asks receives, and the one who seeks finds, and to the one who knocks it will be opened. Or which one of you, if his son asks him for bread, will give him a stone? Or if he asks for a fish, will give him a serpent? If you then, who are evil, know how to give good gifts to your children, how much more will your Father who is in heaven give good things to those who ask him! (Matt. 7:7–11)

Here, they point out, our Lord seems to promise that God will be a loving Father to his children—a loving Father who will not give serpents to those who ask for fish or stones for bread. They know that God could have intervened to deliver their son from his temptation and thus to save his life. They know how hard he prayed and they prayed for his deliverance. And yet God seems to have given them serpents for fish and stones for bread. And so, they ask: What can we believe? What can we trust as God's promises? And who is God if he allowed or ordained this to happen to our son? How can God be good, and how can he be someone whom we can love, if he didn't intervene to stop all of this from happening to our son?

For these parents who are still in the midst of profoundly disorienting grief, it is not merely a question of whether God will ever again be good to them; it is right now a question of whether God is good, period.[58] Although they do not doubt that their son is with God, they are unable to conceive right now how anything—even the prospect of everlasting life with God and their son—could after this tragedy possibly bring them true

---

[58]This was also C. S. Lewis's question after the death of his wife, as noted above. In these sorts of states, the sufferer cannot be comforted by the prospect of everlasting personal pleasure in God because he or she is unable to conceive of finding any pleasure in God.

happiness again. And so while they have not denied their Lord, a living, vibrant faith that acknowledges and proclaims God's righteousness and goodness seems for now closed to them.

In the midst of their profound grief, no answer that I give satisfies them.[59] I know, from some profound suffering of my own, that only God can restore their faith. Yet because of my own experience I also know that their faith and their ultimate happiness do not depend on whether God is right now being glorified *in* them. Their future with God does not depend on their manifesting right now their complete and total satisfaction in him, nor does it depend on their obedience, nor even on their being able to acknowledge God's goodness. It depends only on God's continued faithfulness to them.

During Jeremiah's dark night of the soul, Philip Ryken writes, he "questioned his creation, his salvation, and his vocation." Yet, Ryken continues, *"Although suffering can place a question mark over existence, it never has the last word.* Chapter 20 ends with a question that Jeremiah himself was in no shape to answer," namely,

> Why did I come out from the womb
>   to see toil and sorrow,
>   and spend my days in shame? (Jer. 20:18)

Yet, Ryken reminds us, Scripture does have an answer—and it is one that God had given to Jeremiah when he first called him:

> Before I formed you in the womb I knew you,
>   and before you were born I consecrated you;
>   I appointed you a prophet to the nations. (Jer. 1:5)

"Jeremiah," Ryken notes, "traced his troubles back to the womb. But he did not go back far enough! God could trace his promises [to Jeremiah] back *before* the womb. He'd had a purpose for Jeremiah's life since before the beginning of time. . . . The prophet needed to be reminded that from all eternity, the Lord had set him apart for salvation and ministry."[60] From before the beginning of time, God had had plans for Jeremiah, "plans for welfare and not for evil, to give [him as well as the exiled Israelites] a future and a hope."

---

[59]This is not to say that there is no satisfactory answer, for I believe there is one, which I will give in my forthcoming book. But an answer can *be* satisfactory without necessarily *seeming* satisfactory to those who need it, as all of us who are parents know when we have given satisfactory answers to our children's questions without their finding them satisfactory.

[60]Ryken, *Jeremiah and Lamentations*, 321–22.

In the clamor of his suffering, Jeremiah may not have been able to hear that reminder, no matter how clearly it was spoken. Yet, if the Christian faith is true, Jeremiah hears it now. And he has heard it ever since he heard our God bid him to come into his presence, where there are fullness of joy and pleasures forevermore.

As I think every day of my profoundly grieving Christian friends, I pray—and I believe—that in spite of the darkness that has descended on them, quenching their faith as well as for now completely eclipsing their horizons of hope, God will continue to be faithful to them. And as I stand beside them, trying to bear their burden with them, I find myself encouraged by Paul's profound declaration,

> Remember Jesus Christ, risen from the dead, . . . as preached in my gospel . . . . [And this] saying is trustworthy . . . :
>
> If we have died with him, we will also live with him;
> if we endure, we will also reign with him;
> if we deny him, he also will deny us;
> *if we are faithless, he remains faithful—*
>
> for he cannot deny himself. (2 Tim. 2:8, 11–13)

And so, in the spirit of your own proposal to amend the first question of the Westminster Shorter Catechism, John, I offer to you my own proposal to amend your declaration that God is most glorified in us when we are most satisfied in him. Yes, I affirm, God is indeed most glorified *in* us when we are most satisfied in him. But, I venture to propose, perhaps God is even more glorified *with regard to* us when our hope and perhaps even our faith have failed—and yet he remains faithful because of who he alone is. Let us seek everlasting pleasure as much as we can, but may our lives be monuments to his glory even when we can't.[61]

---

[61] I thank Noah Toly, Paul Helm, Ron Jones, Don Westblade, and especially Justin Taylor and Sam Storms for their careful comments on this chapter. Thanks also to my current and former students Andrew Formica, Aaron Griffiths, Rose Acquavella, and Nick Martin for their comments.

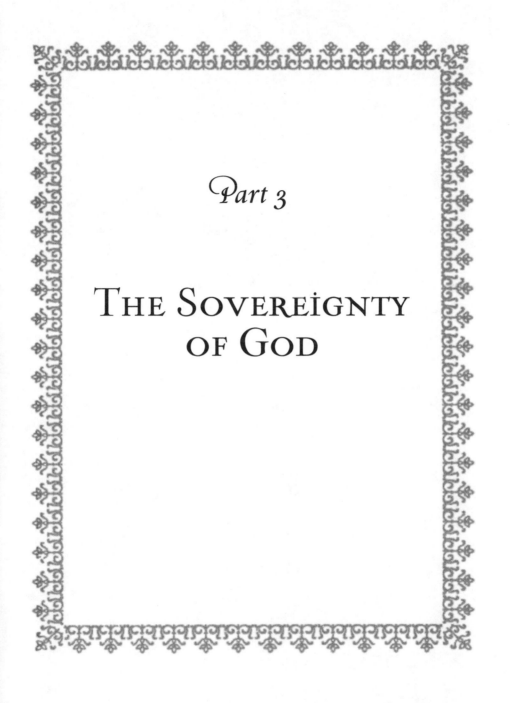

Part 3

THE SOVEREIGNTY
OF GOD

6

THE SOVEREIGNTY OF GOD IN THE THEOLOGY OF JONATHAN EDWARDS

Donald J. Westblade

The LORD has established his throne in the heavens,
and his kingdom rules over all.
−PSALM 103:19

A bsolute sovereignty is what I love to ascribe to God."[1] By this well-known declaration the Puritan pastor of Northampton, Jonathan Edwards, describes the conviction to which he awakened as these words of Scripture opened the window of his soul to the bright rays of the glory of God: "Now unto the King eternal, immortal, invisible, the only wise God, be honour and glory for ever and ever. Amen" (1 Tim. 1:17 KJV).

I offer this essay with gratitude beyond expression for John Piper's camaraderie in the gospel, shared for nearly four decades with two dozen others gathered around Dan Fuller in the "Fellowship of the Arc," some of whom are already enjoying the direct fellowship of the Father, but all of whom learned together with John to draw deeply from the biblical wisdom and devotion of Jonathan Edwards.
[1]Jonathan Edwards, "Personal Narrative," in *The Works of Jonathan Edwards*, vol. 16, *Letters and Personal Writings*, ed. George S. Claghorn (New Haven: Yale University Press, 1998), 792.

By Edwards's own testimony in his "Personal Narrative," this love that came to consume his life and ministry had to find him. His own early affections were seeking their object elsewhere, in religious duties: in prayer, in spiritual conversation, in disciplines of denial, and in self-examination. These, too, were loves and types of delight. He found it easy, he says, to mistake them for grace. But the vision of ultimate majesty that broke in upon the eyes of his soul—as "God's excellency, wisdom, purity, and love" displaced every excellency of his own religious efforts—outshone Edwards's youthful delights in a manner he could compare only with the sight of beautiful color breaking in upon a blind man.

Says Edwards, "Those former delights never reached the heart; and did not arise from any sight of the divine excellency of the things of God; or any taste of the soul-satisfying and life-giving good there is in them."[2] In sharp contrast, he calls his new sense of the absolute sovereignty of God exceedingly pleasant, bright, sweet, and delightful. So powerful was his contemplation that all things rest in God's loving control that its promise sustained him in the highest joy and comfort through a lifetime of ministry challenges, personal injustices, attacks of physical illness, the sorrows of unfaithful and dying parishioners, and in the end the anticipation of his own death while still at the prime of his life.

Along the path of his earlier pursuits, however, this soul-satisfying vision of the sovereignty of God had brought Edwards revulsion instead of satisfaction. "It used to appear like a horrible doctrine to me," he avows. "From my childhood up, my mind had been full of objections against the doctrine of God's sovereignty, in choosing whom he would to eternal life; and rejecting whom he pleased; leaving them eternally to perish, and be everlastingly tormented in hell."[3] Before him loomed a vision not majestic but arbitrary, enslaving, unloving, even absurd.

Nevertheless, over time—in a manner that recalls the apostle Paul's experience on the Damascus road—a transformed perspective on the sovereignty of God dawned upon Edwards not merely because a divine and supernatural light from heaven flashed around him (Acts 9:3; 22:6; 26:13), but because the Word of God and the Ananiases on his library shelves provided the means of compellingly preached arguments through which the light of God was pleased to find its way to the reasoning of his mind and from there to the affections of his heart. Indeed, despite the deep certainty that this new sense "came into" him and "would often of a sudden kindle up" wholly apart from his own prompting or ability

---

[2]Edwards, "Personal Narrative," 795.
[3]Ibid., 791–92.

"to give an account how, or by what means, [he] was thus convinced," Edwards professes that he became "fully satisfied as to this sovereignty of God and his justice in thus eternally disposing of men, according to his sovereign pleasure," and that his "reason apprehended the justice and reasonableness of it." One could accurately describe his new conviction as a submission of his will to the authority of an almighty God, but not if by that one meant a blind acquiescence. Edwards insists out of his experience that his "mind rested in it; and it put an end to all those cavils and objections."[4]

By Edwards's own report this new, joyful light on an old, seemingly horrible doctrine did not fully dawn upon a sudden morning. Rather he speaks of this conviction of divine things as a sense that "gradually increased" and that imperceptibly "became more and more lively, and had more of that inward sweetness." Edwards attributes his first new apprehensions and freshly envisioned thoughts about Christ and his redemptive work to the glory that poured forth to him out of the doxology of Paul in his first letter to Timothy (1:17). But this was only the beginning. He further recounts frequent, ongoing occasions throughout the course of his pastoral ministry when his sense of delight in the sovereign and universal providence of God grew and deepened through his continuing study and prayer.

The fruits of Edwards's labors over this and other questions have become increasingly familiar to modern readers, thanks both to the active publication of his treatises and sermons[5] and to a flourishing production of introductions, abridgments, and other secondary studies of Edwards's writings.[6] Beneath the fruit of these formally published treatises and publicly preached sermons of Edwards and nourishing them lay a seedbed of his more private theological journaling in notebooks. These records of his running theological deliberations have become transcribed and included in the volumes of Yale's edition only within the last generation, under

---

[4]Ibid., 792.

[5]A scholarly edition of *The Works of Jonathan Edwards* in twenty-six volumes was completed by Yale University Press in time for the three hundredth anniversary of Edwards's birth, in 2003. The eight to ten volumes of *The Works of President Edwards* published at Worcester have been available since the early nineteenth century. An especially accessible reprinting of a substantial segment of *The Works of Jonathan Edwards* (1834) in two volumes was published by the Banner of Truth Trust in 1974 (and republished by Hendrickson Press in 1998). Most recently the Jonathan Edwards Project at Yale University has made its entire transcribed corpus of the writings of Jonathan Edwards accessible (without cost, to date) through a searchable Internet Web site: http://edwards.yale.edu/research. To all of these the present article owes an incalculable debt of gratitude.

[6]Exemplary among such introductory editions that have proved especially successful in broadening readership and understanding of Edwards's works are: John Piper, *God's Passion for His Glory: Living the Vision of Jonathan Edwards (with the complete text of* The End for Which God Created the World) (Wheaton, IL: Crossway, 1998); and Gerald R. McDermott, *Seeing God* (with a paraphrased text of the *Treatise concerning Religious Affections*) (Downers Grove, IL: InterVarsity, 1995).

Edwards's own title, the *Miscellanies* (hereafter identified parenthetically by the numbers Edwards assigned them as he wrote).[7]

In the hundreds of entries in these notebooks one may witness Edwards's mind at work on the arguments that eventually emerge in his published writings. Here, in particular, one can observe the growing collection of reasons and the increasing sense of joyful delight through which the Holy Spirit gradually, indiscernibly, but inexorably put an end to all his earlier cavils and objections against the sweetness of the sovereignty of God and set his mind and heart at rest in this doctrine that became paramount in all his thought and practice.

The full flower of Edwards's defense of the reasonableness and goodness of the absolute sovereignty of God may be found in his more well-known treatises and above all in the 1754 work entitled *The Freedom of the Will*.[8] With an interest in the development of his arguments in the seedbed from which that flower blossomed, however, we turn our attention primarily to the *Miscellanies*, on our knees with Edwards in prayer that his arguments there might serve for us, as for him, as the means by which God can shine in the full glory and sweetness of his absolute sovereignty over all that he surveys.

What Does Jonathan Edwards Mean by Sovereignty?

Edwards has nothing eccentric in view in his use of the word *sovereignty*, and as always he is nothing less than precise in defining his terms. By the sovereignty of God, Edwards understands God's absolute right and power to dispose over all things as he wills. Sovereignty presupposes God's all-sufficiency, his utter independence from all influences, motives, standards, and resources outside of himself, an inexhaustible power to create as he wills, to assign purposes to all he creates, and to serve as cause to every effect in his creation, and an unlimited title to dispose over creation according to the designs he intends for each part. In entry no. 1263 Edwards expresses the sum of God's sovereignty like this: In God "there is no other law than only the law of the infinite wisdom of the omniscient first cause and supreme disposer of all things who in one,

---

[7]Quotations from Edwards's entries have been altered here to modernize spelling and to clarify punctuation. *The Works of Jonathan Edwards*, vol. 13, *The "Miscellanies": Entry Nos. a–z, aa–zz, 1–500*, ed. Thomas A. Schafer (New Haven: Yale University Press, 1994); vol. 18, *The "Miscellanies": Entry Nos. 501–832*, ed. Ava Chamberlain (New Haven, CT: Yale University Press, 2000); vol. 20, *The "Miscellanies": Entry Nos. 833–1152*, ed. Amy Plantinga Pauw (New Haven: Yale University Press, 2002); vol. 23, *The "Miscellanies": Entry Nos. 1153–1360*, ed. Douglas A. Sweeney (New Haven: Yale University Press, 2004).

[8]Jonathan Edwards, *The Works of Jonathan Edwards*, vol. 1, *A Careful and Strict Inquiry into the Prevailing Notions of the Freedom of the Will*, ed. Paul Ramsey (New Haven: Yale University Press, 1957).

simple, unchangeable, perpetual view comprehends all existence in its utmost compass and extent and infinite series."

In Edwards's mind this comprehensive sweep of God's sovereignty implies a crucial theological corollary. In that God designed creation to commit all things to Christ so that Christ "might dispose of it to the purposes and designs of his work of redemption and procuring the salvation and glory of his church," and in that "the creation of the world in strictness cannot be distinguished from his government and disposal of all things" (no. 1039), Edwards perceives the providence of God in entrusting the creation of the world itself to Christ (John 1:1–3). As a result, Christ, as Head of his body, the church, "has the absolute possession of all and rules over all and disposes all things according to his will" (no. 1072). Christ the Son, in other words, shares altogether in the absolute sovereignty of the Godhead.

Unlike his disciples, Jesus Christ works his signs and wonders by his own power and in his own name (no. 518). Even those distinguishing works that demonstrate the sovereignty of God in the Old Testament Edwards finds spoken of as "the work and glory of the Messiah" (Psalm 72; Isaiah 11; Psalm 45; no. 1194). Jesus' high-priestly prayers confirm for Edwards that Jesus "knew that he was the sovereign Lord of heaven and earth and was to reign as such as God-man" (no. 791). In his incarnation and identification with humanity, Christ sets many exercises of his sovereignty aside, but "as respects his divine nature" all that Edwards affirms of the sovereignty of God he affirms of all three persons of the Trinity.

God exercises his sovereignty over nature by creating the very laws that govern it. Because he is their author he commands them and not they him. When it pleases his purposes to set the laws of nature aside, nothing prevents his performing the miraculous in their place. More radically yet, the influence of Nicolas Malebranche[9] engenders in Edwards a functional "occasionalism" by which all causation is reserved to God. By this he means that the laws of physics do not identify cause-effect relationships in matter. Rather,

> in natural things means of effects in metaphysical strictness are not proper causes of the effects, but only occasions. God produces all effects, but yet he ties natural events to the operation of such means, or causes them to be consequent on such means, according to fixed, determinate, and unchangeable rules which are called the laws of nature. (no. 629)

---

[9]Nicolas Malebranche, *Entretiens sur la Metaphysique: Dialogues on Metaphysics* (New York: Abaris, 1980).

God reigns in utter control over the physical world he has created. Yet freedom from obligation to its laws of nature or to any other external necessity speaks only of a negative and derivative expression of the sovereignty of God. The root and positive expression of sovereignty in Edwards's understanding reside in the unfettered exercise of "God's mere good pleasure" (no. 1127) and the utter dependence of all things upon the counsel of his will. "For he is not seen to be the sovereign ruler of the universe or God over all any otherwise than he is seen to be arbitrary" (no. 1263).

The growing evidence in which Edwards found positive arguments to convince him of the truth of God's absolute sovereignty fills his notebooks. The disposition of the world toward final causes or future goods presupposes a cause in an intelligent and voluntary or designing agent antecedent to the world: a God who sovereignly disposes the world to ends (no. 749). Even non-Christian peoples acknowledge, through ancient tradition and the light of nature, God's moral government over the world as its supreme Head and fountain of laws and judgments (no. 954). It is evident to reason that there is but one eternal, self-existent, independent, infinite being upon whom all else is dependent (no. 1156). Scripture clearly teaches that God rules in absolute sovereignty (nos. 683, 710). The record of his miracles (no. 1190), the fulfillment of biblical predictions (no. 1194), the beauty and proportion of natural laws (no. 1196), the extraordinariness of Moses' laws and Jewish doctrine that unlike any other ancient religion wholly savor, magnify, and exalt God rather than great people or people in power (no. 1300), all together serve as distinguishing marks of a God who reigns in reality with the serenity of sovereignty. Even the traditions of the Chinese, in particular of Confucius, about which Edwards read in his *Monthly Review*, confirm reason's conviction of a supreme, holy, intelligent, invisible sustainer of all things, including an expectation that "in the West the holy one will appear" (no. 1200). And, as to the sovereignty of this deity, "as it is absurd to suppose that an infinitely wise being should make creatures for no end at all so it is equally absurd to imagine that he does not conduct them to the end designed by his providence" (no. 1184).

Does Absolute Sovereignty Attribute the Origin of Evil to God?
Still, Edwards appreciates that the doctrine invites objections. He had had them himself. One potential reason for Edwards's objections and cavils against the doctrine of God's sovereignty might have presented itself to him from his metaphysical notion that all causation belongs to God. The

denial of causation to any source but God threatens an implication that even evil must then have its origin with God. If this were among his earlier objections, it does not appear much to preoccupy his thinking. Augustine's customary response lays the issue to rest for Edwards wherever the threat seems to loom. Recognizing that in numerous places Scripture does speak of God's "creating evil" and other contraries of good (Num. 16:30; Isa. 41:20; 45:8; 48:7; 54:16; 57:19; Jer. 31:22), Edwards is content to counter that "God makes wicked men in no other sense than he creates darkness, which is not by any positive effecting, but only ordering by withholding light, for darkness is only a negative."[10] What after all can a theist of any stripe offer as an alternative to a single ultimate origin of good and evil beside the Manichaean heresy of an independent, competing principle that co-occupies eternity with God? At all events, Edwards denies any need to reason that God's allowing of evil makes him the author of it for its own sake or need saddle him with any culpability for it. Commenting on the most explicit text in Isaiah 45:7, he concludes, "It doesn't appear that this scripture will justify such an expression as that, that God made some men to damn them."[11]

Four other objections, focused less upon God's sovereignty over nature and more upon his sovereignty over the human will, attract the greater energy and passion of Edwards's intellect: (1) If God is sovereign over the will and "turns [the heart] wherever he will" (Prov. 21:1), do humans not then act under coercion and thereby lose their responsibility? (2) If the distinguishing principle of God's sovereignty consists in the arbitrary freedom of his will (no. 1263), does that not subject humanity to an untrustworthy God of whim and caprice? (3) If God is sovereign and thus "infinitely greater than all other beings and . . . as it were the sum of all being," does it not "follow that a proper regard to himself is the sum of his regard" (no. 1077) and that therefore God's purposes are ulti-mately selfish rather than aimed at love for his creatures? And (4) does the doctrine of the sovereignty of God not entail so much mystery and complexity that it ought simply to be rejected as absurd and beyond our understanding?

Do We Act under Coercion If God Is Sovereign?

Jonathan Edwards encountered a "prevailing notion" of the freedom of the will in his time that still prevails in popular reasoning today: *Respon-*

---

[10]Jonathan Edwards, *The Works of Jonathan Edwards*, vol. 24, *The Blank Bible*, ed. Stephen J. Stein (New Haven: Yale University Press, 2006), 561; cf. 679; *Miscellanies* no. 761.
[11]Ibid.

sibility presupposes ability. If the abilities of our will are subject to the sovereignty of God and are not determined by our own agency, then we would lack ability and ought not to count ourselves responsible. Since we do consider ourselves responsible, the problem must lie with the premise: our human wills must be free from the sovereign direction of God and fall instead under our own determination. Augustine's assessment that fallen humanity sins because we are "not able not to sin" must surely misdiagnose our condition.

Edwards exposes the flaws in the logic of this objection from two directions. First, he argues that the inability of the will we fallen humans suffer from apart from the enablement of the Holy Spirit does not conform to the expectations we have when we experience physical or natural inabilities. And, second, he argues that the freedom that popular reasoning wants to locate in a capacity for self-determination apart from outside influences turns out to be a freedom that, defended in one way, fails of self-contradiction and, defended in another, no one would ever desire.

Edwards develops the distinction between natural and physical ability on the one hand and moral ability on the other in greater detail in his treatise on *The Freedom of the Will* than he did in the *Miscellanies*, but the nature of moral inability and its compatibility with responsibility receives a long treatment in *Miscellanies* no. 1153. Edwards acknowledges that natural and physical inabilities do properly diminish responsibility. An inability to yield apples on command will produce guilt in no one. Humans do not share the nature of apple trees. Neither will an inability to lift more than one's own weight or to swim the Atlantic Ocean on command produce guilt since—despite natural abilities to lift and to swim—the feats in question ordinarily defy our human physical strength. Our first instinct that follows from this is therefore conditioned to assume that a moral inability should follow a similar logic. Nevertheless, actual experience confirms that it does not.

Moral ability refers to the ability of the will. The prophet Isaiah asks,

> Can a woman forget her nursing child,
>> that she should have no compassion on the son of her womb?
>>> (Isa. 49:15)

She has scarcely any moral ability at all to do so, he clearly implies. But if she is morally unable to abandon remembrance and compassion, then is our first instinct right, that she lacks responsibility or is not praiseworthy for those acts of care? No. This sort of inability, Edwards points out to our common sense, puts no constraints whatsoever on our responsibility. If anything, it elevates it.

If I find myself morally unable to complete my homework because I cannot tear myself away from my favorite television program, I do not arrive in class expecting my teachers to absolve me for that inability. A physical ailment or a natural incapacity might encourage that expectation. The awareness of a "lazy will" only aggravates my feelings of responsibility and guilt. If I find myself morally unable to betray my best friend, I do not count myself involuntarily coerced into faithfulness to our friendship, nor a mere puppet manipulated by strings of loyalty. The constraints of a loyal nature that cannot betray a friend characterize deliberate and voluntary choices of my will.

Edwards hears Augustine's *not able*s in just this sense. Our fallen condition does not hinder us by nature or by strength from obeying God in trust (much as the term *sin nature* might invite that assumption). Christ's incarnation in fully human nature stands against the conclusion that our human nature by itself precludes a life free from sin. We are not able *not* to sin only in the sense that our will lacks a motive to do other than sin. The weakness of our will can of course also put us into circumstances where physical hindrances to faithful obedience grow and contribute even further to sin. For this reason Scripture admonishes us to "seek the LORD while he may be found" (Isa. 55:6). Still, when we face the question honestly, we ourselves lay ultimate responsibility upon our own moral inability whence those physical habits and hindrances originally sprang. When we rightly understand inability in this sense, the objection against Augustine that our inability not to sin would rob us of responsibility loses all its force.

Referring in the same sense to moral inability, one can say that neither God the Father nor God the Son is able to sin. This concerns no deficiency in God's power to do as he wills. It affirms only that sin could never be what he wills. God's infinite wisdom and unbridled passion for his own glory would never let loose of such a prize as the enjoyment of himself to settle for a lesser object of joy.

Likewise, Augustine describes Adam prior to the fall as "able to sin and able not to sin." By this description Augustine would not in Edwards's understanding make Adam the world's only Pelagian, indifferent at all moments to all influences upon his will and making his choices wholly free from any causes that might disturb his equilibrium in favor of any preference. Edwards must see Adam rather as a man subject to the influences of circumstances beyond him and to the finite short-sightedness of his vision and commitment to his own benefit. Unlike his progeny, he might have continued in his inclination toward God indefinitely. He could have. He had only to fix his vision upon God to find God's soul-satisfying beauty irresistible. Yet at the moment the external influences of immediate, momentary allurements attracted his preferences away from the deeper but sometimes hidden joys of eternity, a new motive overtook him, and with it he could not do otherwise than sample the fleeting sweetness of moral independence that grew upon the Tree of the Knowledge of Good and Evil. He fell and henceforth was cursed, and we in him, to be morally able to do no other. The argument by no means resolves the mystery why Adam chose the lesser joy over the mightily greater one. It only expresses the mystery in a way that we can recognize its inexplicable but undeniable reality as we repeat it so often and so foolishly in our own experience.[12]

Edwards's demonstration that an inability of the will does not, as the prevailing notion would have it, imply any reduction of responsibility points the way to a second flaw in the popular logic: it operates with a notion of freedom that cannot reasonably be attributed to the will. The will does not need to be free from prior influences in order to act responsibly; in fact, it *cannot* be free from external determination as the popular view imagines it.

Only two alternatives to the will's being determined by causes external to it present themselves, Edwards reasons. The will can be determined by a cause internal to it, namely itself, or it is simply not determined at all by anything.

Edwards wrestles often and at great length against the supposition that the will must be self-determining to be free. One can discern from the attention he pays the idea how widely he found it to prevail in popular thinking. The modern reader may not realize it from the usual abbreviated name we employ, but the title of his treatise on *The Freedom of the Will* promises not his own positive definition of the phrase but "a careful and strict enquiry into the modern prevailing notions of that freedom of will which is supposed to be essential to moral agency, virtue and vice, reward and punishment, praise and blame" (but that is altogether mistaken in that presupposition). He devotes all of parts 2, 3, and 4 of this 5-part treatise to a defense of his negative answer to the question "whether there is or can be any such sort of freedom of the will" consist-

---

[12]It thus also provides evidence that the mystery represents no final paradox or antinomy. See John Piper, "A Response to J. I. Packer on the So-Called Antinomy between the Sovereignty of God and Human Responsibility," March 1, 1976, available at www.desiringGod.org.

ing in self-determination, "and whether any such thing ever was, or can be conceived of." A dozen lengthy entries concern the question in the *Miscellanies*, and a blank space was left at no. 1155 to go back and add even more. Perhaps he had entertained the idea himself in the days when the prospect that the sovereignty of God might determine the will had appeared to him so horrible and unfree. But as his mind considered this alternative, its logic slid again and again into circularity.

If the freedom of the will consists in the will's power to determine itself, then, for example, "that determination of itself is an act of the will, and the freedom must attach to that act; but then what determines that act must also be a self-determining act of the will and what determines that determining act is a further act and so on in an infinite circle of logic" (no. 1075b). Either there must be a first act that determines the rest, which cannot be free if it is not the first act but one determined by some preceding act of choice; or the first act must be determined in a manner that is not free in the sense presupposed because it was not determined by the will.[13]

The alternative—that the will is neither externally determined nor self-determined but simply not determined at all by anything—might mean that the will up and chooses for no particular reason. Yet few would content themselves with—let alone want—a will whose actions arose at random, with no determining connection to one's circumstances, purposes, or expected outcomes.

A more appealing formulation of this alternative therefore maintains that the will's freedom consists in a "state of indifference antecedent to the act of choice." Edwards discovered that this formulation, too, devolves in a circular way, albeit not to a contradiction but to another undesirable conclusion. He forged the reasoning that undercut this construction of freedom in *Miscellanies* no. 830, an entry that proved one of the earliest and most important preparatory steps toward his published treatise.

Here he argued that, by this formulation of the will's freedom, any natural disposition that might be found in a person—whether the maliciousness of an ill nature or the good cheer and virtue of an excellent spirit—would count as evidence that the person could not be accorded any responsibility—whether blame or praise—for these acts because they arose not from indifference but from a determining nature. In particular, Christ himself would be unworthy of praise on the grounds that his actions do not arise from a freedom of indifference but are determined

---

[13]Cf. his similar argument in *The Freedom of the Will*, 172.

by his holy state. Similarly, if circumstances swayed the will from its state of sovereign indifference, its choices would no longer be exercises of its own sovereignty, but be determined by the influences of external inducements that diminished the indifference in which the will's freedom was presumed to consist.

The logical difficulties that beset any view of freedom that disconnects the will's choices from prior, determining causes convinced Edwards that the formulation of freedom itself needed rethinking. Despite stereotypes that a doctrine of absolute sovereignty must commit Edwards to determinism or fatalism, Edwards was certainly not convinced that he needed to deny freedom. He took for granted that humans universally experience themselves as distinct from inert matter that conforms only to physical laws of nature.[14] Against the accusations of his Arminian objectors, he insisted that "man is entirely, perfectly and unspeakably different from a mere machine, in that he has reason and understanding, and has a faculty of will, and so is capable of volition and choice." Moreover, in that his actions are subject to his will, every human has, Edwards affirms, "liberty to act according to his choice, and to do what he pleases."[15] The liberty humans enjoy must simply be rethought and understood in a manner that is compatible with the will's choices being determined by motives and with those motives' being subject to the absolute sovereignty of God.

Choice, Edwards has persuasively demonstrated, is in no way at odds with having a nature or a preference that is out of equilibrium. Indeed choice logically presupposes a preference for the option that one chooses. For the same reason choice is in no way at odds with being determined by a preponderance of attractive circumstances. We think of people as hindered or unfree when we see them faced with an attractive and beneficial option yet making a choice that seems contrary to it. We say it doesn't make sense to us. We think if they were free they would let the evidence in favor of the beneficial option influence them. And just there we have arrived at Edwards's more relevant, important, and practical formulation of freedom as it applies to the will. Add to the common-sense requirement (that one be free from physical and natural hindrance) this moral requirement (that one is free to the degree that one's choices succeed in assisting one toward objective benefit), and Edwards's reformulation of

---

[14]See, for example, the premises on which he builds his argument for "The Importance of Christian Knowledge" in his sermon (by that simpler title in earlier editions) "The Importance and Advantage of a Thorough Knowledge of Divine Truth," in *The Works of Jonathan Edwards*, vol. 22, *Sermons and Discourses, 1739–1742*, ed. Harry S. Stout (New Haven: Yale University Press, 2003), 90.
[15]Edwards, *The Freedom of the Will*, 370.

freedom compellingly expresses what we ordinarily mean when we speak of our wills as free.

This means that responsible, voluntary choice is in no way at odds with the will's being determined by the ordering of divine providence, if the work of providence consists in the ordering of circumstances and the bestowing of nature and of motives—all of which thoughtful observers have always recognized are given to us.[16] We do not *cause* ourselves to have such things. We *find* ourselves to have them. From whence are they given? From whence do we find ourselves to have them? Edwards's penetrating inquiries brought him to the inescapable answer: from God alone who, through the natural means of circumstances, motives, preferences, and other influences prior to and presupposed in our choosing, rules in absolute sovereignty over human wills.

Does the Sovereignty of God Subject Us to Mere Arbitrary Whims of Divine Caprice?

We have heard Edwards locate the heart of God's sovereignty in the "arbitrary" quality of his rule over the universe. God's absolute sovereignty in those terms means that his will prevails freely over all things without exception. "Arbitrary operation being every way the highest," he reasons, "it is that wherein God is most glorified. 'Tis the glory of God that he is an arbitrary being, that originally he in all things acts as being limited and directed in nothing" (no. 1263). In this freedom of God to be what he will be (cf. Ex. 3:14–15; 33:19) Edwards sees the pinnacle of the glorious nature of God.[17]

Edwards often expresses the same thought in different terms by stressing (as in no. 537) that, paramount above all his other acts, "God will make his sovereign-right here more eminently to appear, in the bestowment of [grace]." Here in the freedom of grace Edwards sees the "best communication of God's nature." For "there is no gift or benefit that is so much in God, that is so much of himself [and] of his nature, that is so much a communication of the Deity, as grace is: 'tis as much a communication of the Deity, as light [is] a communication of the sun."

Just as Edwards epitomizes the freedom of God's will by emphasizing its arbitrary character, so too does he stress that the "means of grace are not

---

[16]See, for example, Aristotle's analysis of motivation for the purposes of persuasive rhetoric: "some end must be given"—θέμενοι τέλος τι (*Nicomachean Ethics* 3.3.11).

[17]See further the incisive treatment of these Exodus texts in the same light of the sovereignty of God in chap. 4 of John Piper's *The Justification of God*, 2d ed. (Grand Rapids: Baker, 1993), 75–89. "It is the glory of God and his essential nature mainly to dispense mercy . . . on whomever he pleases apart from any constraint originating outside his own will. This is the essence of what it means to be God" (88–89).

means of the exercises of grace [in the same way that natural means are the causes of the exercises of natural principles,] for the actings of the Spirit of God in the heart are more arbitrary and are not tied to such and such means by such laws or rules" (no. 629). Again, "The exercises and operations of this Spirit are after the manner of a natural principle in many respects, but yet there is that in it that shows it [to] be something supernatural, not only in such a sense as to be a principle besides all the principles of human nature as such, but also so as to be above all nature, above all laws of any nature and all natural principles whatsoever" (no. 818).

The more, however, one elevates the freedom of God's will and accentuates its arbitrary quality, the more one invites the objection that God then operates by mere caprice and whim. The doctrine of God's absolute sovereignty may well have stung Edwards early on with apprehensions that such a God whose will is free to act in any manner whatsoever might prove himself unpredictable and therefore untrustworthy.

Edwards's path to overcoming this objection about God's will lay along the same route as his reasoning concerning the human will. If, that is, the freedom of the human will consists in some degree of absence of natural and physical *constraint* in the act of choosing and some degree of success in attaining objective *benefit* from the choice, one may then ask, in what does the freedom of God's arbitrary will consist?

The threat of capriciousness in God might stand if reason were to permit Edwards to ascribe an Arminian view of freedom to God, as though God begins his choices from a position of utter indifference. A God unconstrained not only by the laws of nature he authored but also by his own nature and loves and sense of order, whose will made its choices spontaneously apart from any motives, would indeed be utterly free—even of the consistency of keeping promises and covenants. To such a God his subjects may be obliged to bow. They surely, however, would find in him few grounds for trust.

Nevertheless, even God cannot conform to this Arminian notion of freedom. Edwards's rejection of any alleged freedom of *self-determination* or of *absent determination and indifferent equilibrium* in the human will had no recourse to a deficiency in the human. The deficiency he exposed lay in the logic. As little sense as he found in the self-determination or indifference of the human will in its choices, so little does he also find in either account of the divine will.

But if the freedom of God resembles, because it is the source and inspiration of, the human freedom Edwards found fully compatible with a prior nature and all its preferences and commitments, then Edwards has grounds for his important clarification in *Miscellanies* no. 1263: "When I speak of arbitrary operation, I don't mean arbitrary in opposition to an operation directed by wisdom but in opposition to an operation confined to and limited by those fixed establishments and laws commonly called the laws of nature." To Edwards's understanding of the sovereignty of God the distinction is key, and he labels it with the terms "arbitrary operation" and "natural operation."

In the material world, natural operations dominate our observation. The laws that govern natural operations have a limiting quality that, on the one hand, confers immense benefit: science becomes possible because the limit of regularity makes natural outcomes predictable and replicable; on the other hand, humans abhor an imposition of the same limit upon ourselves: we disavow every suggestion that we can be reduced to the mere effect of our natural causes and refuse to be treated as machines or science experiments. Our operations, we prefer to think, can be arbitrary after the pattern of God's. We have a will.

Edwards has made clear that our will has a necessary and desirable connection to, not an unwelcome coercion from, our nature and preferences when it acts freely to choose that which it perceives to be to its benefit. He therefore finds it altogether reasonable to discover the same principle in the free action of God's sovereign will. "'Tis the glory of God that he is an arbitrary being, that originally he in all things acts as being limited and directed in nothing *but his own wisdom*, tied to no other rules and laws *but the directions of his own infinite understanding*" (no. 1263, emphasis added).

Caprice furthermore vanishes when one observes how scrupulously God attends to—and in a sense is pleased to limit himself by—the proper fitness of his choice of means to the ends that are given to his will by his holy nature. "If free grace, exercised in a way of mere sovereignty without regard to propriety, was all that was requisite, there would have been no need of the means and methods provided for man's salvation in the admirable scheme which infinite wisdom hath contrived" (no. 1346). In the same entry Edwards illustrates the point:

> God saw it necessary . . . that the Mediator should die for sinners. And, if the sinner was saved on his account, it was not possible that that cup should pass from him, because propriety required it. So God will not bestow the benefits of the Mediator on them that are not united to him, because there is no propriety in it. It is not proper that they should have communion with Christ who have no union with him. And furthermore God will not look on those as in a state of union with the Mediator and treat them as persons

united to him who don't cordially receive him and cleave to him but reject him, because it is not proper that he should so do. There can be no propriety in looking on intelligent beings capable of act and choice as united to Christ that don't consent to it and while their hearts are disunited. Therefore active voluntary union is insisted on. But neither does this in the least infringe on any possible freedom of grace in the method of salvation.

The conclusion Edwards reaches here has crucial significance for his understanding of God's justification of the elect through faith alone. God's limiting himself to observe particular means in his choice to give grace in a most noncapricious way to certain people under the condition of certain qualifications does to no degree, Edwards is arguing, diminish the freedom of God's arbitrary exercise of his sovereignty. That is because, unlike natural means that necessarily conform to the laws of nature, the means of grace are arbitrary: "Not only the principle of grace but every exercise of it is the immediate effect of the sovereign acting of the Spirit of God" (no. 629). Still, they are not arbitrary in the sense that God, for instance, simply appointed that faith shall have some peculiar influence, as if any of God's graces might have served just as suitably as a means of uniting a person to Christ. Faith stands in a relationship to being united with Christ that Edwards calls a "natural fitness." God looks on believers rather than others as united to Christ because he recognizes a "natural suitableness in faith to unite to Christ" (no. 1092).

This does not mean that a fitness between faith and union with Christ had its ground in a nature to which God had to conform and thus did not originate in God's good pleasure, as if God could not have decreed otherwise. The fitness of faith's receptivity to the accepting of Christ's offer of grace depended upon a prior deliberation of God's will whether to give humanity his Son in the first place as a Savior and Head in whom the body of believers might be counted righteous (no. 831).

Neither does it mean that God exercises any obligation to faith in itself. Faith is indeed a virtuous thing, but, Edwards insists, in respecting it as the means by which a person is set rightly into union with Christ, God has no respect to faith's own virtue, much less any virtue of the person who exercises it. Such a respect for the excellence of a thing itself or for the goodness of the person who exercises it Edwards calls instead a "moral fitness" (no. 877).

For all of faith's inherent virtue and potential for moral inducement, in looking at a believer as united with Christ, God has respect not at all to faith's own moral suitableness to be respected but only to the natural fitness anyone would acknowledge of the receptive posture of a beneficiary to the gracious generosity of a benefactor.[18] In honoring the propriety of the relationship between the means he wisely fits to his ends and those ends he by nature pursues, God obligates himself to the beauty of that propriety he himself established and not to the nature or the goodness of the human who employs those means.

The freedom of grace in God's exercise of his sovereign will, Edwards concludes, is undiminished by the necessity that certain conditions should influence it, provided those conditions are necessary by a natural rather than a moral fitness. If by a charge of capriciousness one alleges that God's sovereignty implies a will that acts in utter independence of an omniscient wisdom and disposition to pursue the end of his own glorification or of the propriety of the means he might ordain to his ends, Edwards concludes that "'tis unreasonable to suppose that [God in] Christ is in this sense arbitrary" (no. 1092). God's will acts purposefully, and it is wholly reasonable to rely upon him as unshakably trustworthy.

Can a Sovereign God Who Puts Himself First Still Love Us?

In *Miscellanies* no. 1208, Edwards poses a question of central importance: "What would it have been fit and proper for God to have a chief respect to and make his highest end in creating a world (if he did create one) and in establishing a system of intelligent creatures?" He poses the question to a hypothetical third party who would come to the inquiry with perfect wisdom, holy motives, and completely disinterested objectivity. The answer he believes such an arbiter must reach is this: "As he is every way the first and supreme Being and his excellence is in all respects the original excellence, the fountain of all good, and the supreme beauty and glory, so he must in all respects have the supreme regard, as he is God over all" (no. 1208; cf. no. 1077). The absolute sovereignty of God demands that God place himself and his own glory at the center of his attention and esteem. To give honor anywhere else would fail to give all credit where

---

[18]Remarkably, Edwards follows the logic of the distinction even to argue that our works might be required in order to attain our salvation. In Edwards's terms, works may be counted "as necessary in order to a natural fitness or proper capacity for the benefit, without any consideration of a moral value, fitness or amiableness recommending; and they may be connected as having a natural tendency so to fit us for the benefit as to enhance it and increase the sweetness of it and our relish of it and delight in it." Convictions of sin along with all their suffering don't detract from free grace because "converting grace isn't consequent on them as the reward of something profitable to God or as something recommending the sinner to God by their value [i.e., their moral fitness] but by the propriety of their humility to receive a benefit of grace [i.e., their natural fitness]" (no. 1070). The defense of this entry helps lessen the reservations many have about Edwards's arguments in the third section of his 1734 treatise on "Justification by Faith Alone," in *The Works of Jonathan Edwards*, vol. 19, *Sermons and Discourses, 1734–1738*, ed. M. X. Lesser (New Haven: Yale University Press, 2001).

it is due and render God unjust. To seek the satisfaction of his happiness from any other source would require him to settle for less.

Edwards brings his exposition of this key insight to its full fruit in the treatise entitled *The End for Which God Created the World*.[19] Along the way to its publication, we find Edwards working in his *Miscellanies*, particularly in the entry just cited, to come to terms first with another challenge he would have to meet from the sovereignty of God. He sets a first objection before himself with force:

> An indifferent third being might fitly determine that 'tis proper that God should be the supreme object of respect . . . [and] that this would [be] no other than equal and just in it self, but yet that it might show a noble generosity in God, when he himself orders and regulates all things, to deny himself, forego his own right, and make the good of his creatures his last end. Seeing it is so that God himself is the supreme determiner in his own cause, it would look like selfishness in him in his actions to prefer himself to all other beings. (no. 1208)

To the student of morals tutored in altruism, the objection seems to carry substantial weight. Does not Paul's ethic of imitating Christ call his churches to elevate love over rights and to sacrifice their own advantage for the benefit of others? But Edwards quite quickly discerns the error in this objection's mistaken understanding of selfishness. Selfishness, he notes, is vicious only where the importance of the self eclipses a greater public good. In the case of God's infinite worth, however, that is to an infinite degree never the case. Furthermore, to forgo one's own interest for the sake of others has no more title to be called generosity than does treating things according to reason and according to them what they are worth. True generosity means valuing and protecting the infinite worth of God, inasmuch as it is the very gift that his most generous expression of love has to offer and without which his generosity instead suffers.

A second objection conveys comparable force. Since God has no needs and cannot be improved by making him one's end,

> it would be improper and foolish . . . to seek that which can't possibly be obtained and which doesn't need to be obtained. The highest good that can be brought to pass by any thing that can be done by either God or created beings is the happiness of the creature. Therefore this is properly made the highest end by both. (no. 1208)

---

[19]See Jonathan Edwards, *The Works of Jonathan Edwards*, vol. 8, *Ethical Writings*, ed. Paul Ramsey (New Haven: Yale University Press, 1989), 403–536.

In response, Edwards protests the inaccuracy of assuming that God can rejoice only in his own goodness directly and delight only directly in himself. Scripture portrays him also rejoicing in the good of his creatures and delighting in our happiness as well. What is more, since our greatest good and highest joy lie in God, God's delight in our creaturely happiness resolves into a delight in himself.

Edwards's insight into this God-centered revolution in understanding the purpose of creation and human history arrives at a liberating conclusion: the end of the happiness of the creature is one with the end of the glorifying of God.

> This one supreme end consists in two things, namely, in God's infinite perfection being exerted and manifested, that is, in God's glorifying himself; and, second, his infinite happiness being communicated and so making the creature happy. Both are sometimes in scripture included in one word, namely, God's being glorified. (no. 1066; cf. no. 1218)

Edwards relates the unity to the character of the Trinity itself: "That which proceeds from God *ad extra* is agreeable to the twofold subsistences which proceed from him *ad intra*, which is the Son and the Holy Spirit, the Son being the idea of God or the knowledge of God, and the Holy Ghost which is the love of God and joy in God" (no. 1218). *Miscellanies* no. 1275 suggests that the insight into this happy confluence of God's ends came to him from the writings of Thomas Goodwin.[20] To the twenty-first century the insight has become especially well known through the watchword of John Piper at Bethlehem Baptist Church: "God is most glorified in us when we are most satisfied in him."[21]

Must I Finally Sacrifice My Intellect to Believe in the Mysterious Sovereignty of God?

Even such an extraordinary intellect as Jonathan Edwards's appreciated the depths of the riches and wisdom and knowledge of God, unsearchable in his judgments and inscrutable in his ways (Rom. 11:33). "It may reasonably be expected" that a doctrine so bound up with the supremacy and infinity of the ruler of the universe should "contain many mysteries" (no. 1340). The wisdom of Providence towers above our meager human imaginations and orders its designs more than we could ask or think. In the main we see its benefit and wisdom. Who could have arranged it such

---

[20]Thomas Goodwin, *The Works of Thomas Goodwin*, 12 vols. (1681; repr., Eureka, CA: Tanski, 1996).

[21]This is the message of John Piper's book, *Desiring God*, 3d ed. (Sisters, OR: Multnomah, 2003), 10.

that Pilate would place over Jesus' cross a sign that read not "he says he is . . ." but simply, and more truly than he knew, "King of the Jews" (no. 629)? But we also meet with heights and depths that confound us by their mystery and complexity. Why should Adam have turned from the most delicious of all joys for a momentary bite that would turn so bitter? Why would Esau exchange a birthright for a dish of stew? Why do I turn away from the gold of God's promises to the tin of the world's? How do we reconcile the givenness of our motives with the responsibility we nonetheless take for them?

As the questions multiply, two sorts of temptations can arise with them. On the one hand, one may be tempted to despair of believing in the sovereignty of God because belief in a doctrine so incomprehensible would seem absurd. On the other hand, one may be tempted to redefine belief to mean a simple acquiescence in the incomprehensible and so believe because of the apparent absurdity. Edwards refused the resort to either path. To the contrary, he pronounced "the doctrines of regeneration and the sovereign grace of God in it exceedingly rational" (no. 1156; cf. no. 1346).

By that he did not mean that answers are always apparent. He recounts his experience of attempting to convince a thirteen-year-old boy that a cube of 2-inch sides had eight times the volume of a cube with 1-inch sides. Nothing he said or demonstrated could prevail on the boy to accept this as a truth and not an absurdity. "And why should we not suppose that there may be some things that are true that may be as much above our understandings and as difficult to them as this truth was to this boy?" he asks (no. 652). Many adults have the same experience with works of literature and art (no. 1340).

His evidence for the rationality of these mysterious doctrines lies not with the answers he has discovered but rather in the correspondence of the mysteries to his own curious experience in being human. "The doctrine of Original Sin and the exceeding depravity and corruption of human nature is so agreeable to experience and also man's obstinacy in sin and folly under all manner of means" (no. 1156). Perhaps we do not know *how* human responsibility squares with moral inability, but we do know *that* we make choices whose deliberate foolishness can only be the acts of an unfree slave to sin, and nonetheless we own our responsibility for them. Scripture speaks exactly of such sin and lawlessness as "the mystery" (2 Thess. 2:7). At least we have this biblical reassurance of having sorted the mystery into the right drawer.

Perhaps, Edwards muses, our failure to find answers on earth, or to achieve the great happiness for which we sense we were made, simply proves that "God reserves happiness to be bestowed hereafter; that is the appointed time for it, and that is the reason he doesn't give it now" (no. 585).

Conclusion

In the end, none of Edwards's youthful objections to the absolute sovereignty of God survived the intellectual rigors of his daily writing, studying, thinking, and journaling, always in the context of the Scriptures and prayer. The sovereignty of God, he learned, does not attribute evil to God; it does not cause us to act under coercion; it does not give us a God of arbitrary caprice; in it there is no absence of love; nor is it guilty of absurdity. To the contrary, it came to provide Edwards with the only sufficiently firm foundation for his faith, the only hope by which to withstand earth's trials, and a soul-satisfying vision to capture the eyes of his mind and heart with the majestic beauty of holiness. Absolute sovereignty is what Edwards loved to ascribe to God. Few statements more than this so unite the passions of the man who is the subject of this article and the man whose ministry its writing celebrates.[22] I venture that the beauty of this natural fitness would have delighted Jonathan Edwards, "whose ghost" in the words of J. I. Packer, "walks through most of Piper's pages."[23]

---

[22]At the time this essay was written, an Internet search on the key terms *absolute sovereignty*, *God*, and *love* in any given search engine typically yielded two names at the head of the resulting list: Jonathan Edwards and John Piper.

[23]Bookjacket of the 1986 edition of *Desiring God*.

7

PRAYER AND THE SOVEREIGNTY OF GOD

Bruce A. Ware

*Words fail to explain how necessary prayer is, and in how many
ways the exercise of prayer is profitable. Surely, with good reason the
Heavenly Father affirms that the only stronghold of safety
is in calling upon his name {Joel 2:32}. By so doing we invoke the
presence of both his* providence, *through which he watches over and
guards our affairs, and of his* power, *through which he sustains
us, weak as we are and well-nigh overcome, and of his* goodness,
*through which he receives us, miserably burdened with sins,
unto grace; and, in short, it is by prayer that we call him to reveal
himself as wholly present to us. Hence comes an extraordinary
peace and repose to our consciences. For having disclosed to the Lord
the necessity that was pressing upon us, we even rest fully
in the thought that none of our ills is hid from him who, we are
convinced, has both the* will *and the* power *to take the best care of us.*[1]

–JOHN CALVIN

---

[1]John Calvin, *Institutes of the Christian Religion*, ed. John T. McNeill, trans. Ford Lewis Battles (Philadelphia: Westminster, 1960), 3.20.2, my emphasis.

*It is indeed a very wonderful thing, that so great a God
should be so ready to hear our prayers, though we are so despicable
and unworthy. That he should give free access at all times to
everyone; should allow us to be importunate without esteeming it an
indecent boldness; should be so rich in mercy to them
that call upon him; that worms of the dust should have such power
with God by prayer, that he should do such great things in answer to
their prayers, and should show himself, as it were, overcome
by them. This is very wonderful, when we consider the distance
between God and us, and how we have provoked him by our sins, and
how unworthy we are of the least gracious notice. It cannot
be from any need that God stands in of us, for our goodness extends
not to him. Neither can it be from anything in us to incline the heart
of God to us. It cannot be from any worthiness in our prayers,
which are in themselves polluted things. But it is because God
delights in mercy and condescension. He is herein infinitely
distinguished from all other Gods. He is the great fountain
of all good, from whom goodness flows as light from the sun.*[2]

–Jonathan Edwards

*Christians who spend time in prayer do it because they see that
God is a great Giver and that Christ is wise and merciful
and powerful beyond measure. And therefore their prayer glorifies
Christ and honors His Father. The chief end of man is to glorify God.
Therefore, when we become what God created us to be we become
people of prayer. . . . Prayer is the very heart of Christian Hedonism.
God gets the glory; we get the delight. He gets the glory
precisely because He shows Himself full and strong to deliver us
into joy. And we attain fullness of joy precisely because He is the all-
glorious source and goal of life. Here is a great discovery. We do
not glorify God by providing His needs, but by praying that
He would provide ours–and trusting Him to answer.*[3]

–John Piper

---

[2] Jonathan Edwards, "The Most High a Prayer-Hearing God," in *The Works of Jonathan Edwards*, 2 vols. (repr., Peabody, MA: Hendrickson, 2006), 2:116.
[3] John Piper, *Desiring God: Meditations of a Christian Hedonist*, 2d ed. (Sisters, OR: Multnomah, 1996), 162–63.

If God is sovereign so that he controls all that takes place, what is the purpose or point of prayer? Why pray if God has already ordained all that will happen? How can prayer make a difference in a world ruled by a sovereign God? What meaning is there to prayer if God has already decided everything that will occur in our lives and in all of human history?

These represent one category of commonly raised questions within discussions of the sovereignty of God. Far from being spurious or wrongheaded, these questions are fully legitimate and deserve thoughtful and biblical responses. Indeed, it is absolutely true: if God has ordained from before the foundation of the world all that will take place, and if God rules the world he has created in such a way that he fulfills all, but only and exactly, what he has ordained, then it does rightly raise the question of how prayer can possibly be meaningful and purposeful. Why pray, or better, why is there prayer at all in a world over which an exhaustively sovereign God reigns supreme? In order to be as clear as we can be on the main question this chapter seeks to address, we should have before us definitions both of the "sovereignty of God" and of "prayer" so that readers may know more precisely just how these concepts are understood here.

Divine sovereignty may be defined as follows:

> God exhaustively plans and meticulously carries out his perfect will as he alone knows is best, regarding all that is in heaven and on earth, and he does so without failure or defeat, accomplishing his purposes in all of creation from the smallest details to the grand purposes of his plan for the whole of the created order.

One might think of this understanding of divine sovereignty as a full or strong view of sovereignty, one in which God's design and control of the world are both exhaustive ("over all that is in heaven and on earth") and meticulous ("from the smallest details to the grand purposes of his plan for the whole of the created order"). Ruled out, then, would be any conception of divine sovereignty in which God relinquishes exhaustive planning of what will happen and/or meticulous control over what will occur, either because God does not know exhaustively all that will take place in the future (e.g., as in open theism) or because God has granted a kind of freedom to moral creatures by which he is rendered incapable of controlling what they freely choose and do (e.g., as in both open theism and classic Arminianism with their common commitment to libertarian freedom). Rather, God plans exhaustively everything that will take place throughout the whole of the universe and in all of time, doing so by the infinite knowledge and wisdom that is his exclusively, and he carries out meticulously and exactly every detail of what he has planned, by his invincible power and sovereign control, throughout the entire universe and for all of time. The conception of divine sovereignty understood here, then, might be summarized by the phrase "exhaustive, meticulous divine sovereignty."

Implicit in this conception of exhaustive and meticulous divine sovereignty is also the idea of God as fully self-sufficient: God possesses within himself, intrinsically (i.e., by nature, or by virtue of his being God) and eternally, all qualities or perfections; and his possession of these qualities is without measure, restriction, or limitation. That is, for God to be fully sovereign he must also be fully self-sufficient. If God lacked some qualities or if others possessed something that God needed and would have to "get" from them, then God would be dependent upon others. And if God were to be lacking or dependent, he thereby could not guarantee either that he could plan exactly what he thought best or bring to pass precisely what he had planned. But since God is fully self-sufficient, he indeed possesses absolutely everything needed for the exhaustive planning and meticulous execution of all that he intends to do as God. Exhaustive and meticulous divine sovereignty can be achieved only by a totally self-sufficient God, and the God of the Bible is that.

Prayer, as it is being discussed here, focuses most directly on petitionary prayer, since the main question is whether what we ask of God, or petition God to do, makes sense if God is sovereign as we have so understood him to be. So, *petitionary prayer* may be defined as follows:

> Requesting or petitioning God, on behalf of oneself or others, to act in some specific manner in order to bring about some specific result, where the action and result are seen as brought about by God's own will and action while they are also, in certain instances, causally tied to the petition that was brought before God and requested of him.

Care is needed in this discussion not to imply that prayer is necessary for everything that God does in the world. Clearly God does much of what he does in the world totally apart from prayer, simply as the outworking of his perfect will.[4] But this is to say that some portion of what God has willed to accomplish he has also willed to be brought about only through and not apart from prayer. Petitionary prayer, as understood here, envisions occasions in which the prayer itself is one of the necessary conditions for God to act and bring about what the prayer seeks. That is, if God has willed certain things to happen, and if he has willed that they happen only *because* his people pray and not apart from their prayers, then there are occasions when prayer becomes necessary—contingently necessary (i.e., contingent upon God's will that certain actions happen only with and not apart from prayer) to God's actions in the world in fulfilling what God has willed. And furthermore, while prayer in certain instances is a necessary condition (albeit contingently necessary) for the fulfillment of God's will, by no means is prayer by itself ever sufficient to bring about the desired result. The so-called power of prayer then is really the "power of God" that is requested and granted when prayers are answered by God.

How Prayer Does Not and Cannot Function

Given these understandings of divine sovereignty and of petitionary prayer, let's be clear on some ways in which prayer does not and cannot function.

First, prayer simply cannot be necessary in an absolute sense to the fulfillment of anything God intends to bring to pass or accomplish. While prayer may be seen as a *contingent* necessity in the fulfillment of God's plans, prayer simply cannot be an *absolute* necessity in bringing to pass what God intends to do. Since prayer does not and cannot provide God with anything he lacks, prayer simply cannot rightly be understood as some element that is absolutely essential in the fulfillment of anything God intends to do. In other words, God could accomplish all of the actions in human history that he plans to do totally apart from prayer. Yes, God desires our prayers; yes, God commands us to pray; but no, God does not need our prayers to "help" him in the execution of his perfect plans. We must look, then, for some other reason or reasons for prayer than to think that God needs prayer (in an absolute sense) or is dependent on his people's praying in order to fulfill what he wants to bring to pass

---

[4]Surely the vast majority of the events that occur in the universe as a whole, and much of what happens in the natural realm and even in human affairs on earth, are governed by God totally apart from any human prayers that may have been involved in the carrying out of God's will in these matters.

in human history. No, God can just do anything he wishes, and prayer simply cannot contribute to God something that he lacks.

Second, even where prayer is rightly seen as contingently necessary to the fulfillment of God's will, care is needed not to imply that God's hands are tied (so to speak), such that whether we pray or not ultimately determines whether God's perfect plan can be done. Rather, just as God determines not only his own will, and not only whether certain aspects of that will are accomplished through prayer or apart from prayer, he also ultimately controls whether people pray for those very aspects of his will that he has ordained can be brought about only by prayer. The God who can turn the king's heart "wherever he will" as he does a stream of water (Prov. 21:1) can turn one person or another to prayer. If God has willed that some particular divine action will occur only through and not apart from prayer, God will work in the hearts of his people to ensure that the prayers needed for the accomplishment of his plans will be offered.

Third, given God's omniscience—which includes God's exhaustive definite foreknowledge of all future actions and events, including all future free choices and actions to be performed by his moral creatures (e.g., Isa. 41:21–29; 46:5–11)—prayer simply cannot function to inform God of something of which he was previously ignorant, providing him with needed information he lacked in order to help him decide what is best to do. In short, God doesn't need our input to inform him of something he really should know in order to make his plans or decide what he should do! He knows it all. His knowledge is comprehensive and perfect. We cannot provide God information he lacks, for indeed he lacks none. As the psalmist declares,

> Great is our Lord, and abundant in power;
>   his understanding is beyond measure. (Ps. 147:5)

Fourth, and related, God's infinite and perfect wisdom is such that he knows how best to use the comprehensive knowledge he has at his disposal to plan and execute what truly is best in any and every situation. He doesn't need us to provide him knowledge he supposedly lacks, nor can he benefit from any insight or discernment or perspective we have, as if these could add to the fullness of his infinite wisdom. As God declares through the prophet Isaiah:

> Who has measured the Spirit of the LORD,
>   or what man shows him his counsel?

Whom did he consult,
  and who made him understand?
Who taught him the path of justice,
  and taught him knowledge,
  and showed him the way of understanding?
        (Isa. 40:13–14)

God's knowledge is infinite, and his wisdom is impeccable. We simply cannot rightly understand prayer to provide God any item of information or insight that would assist him in determining what is best to do. As I've noted elsewhere, when Jesus instructs his disciples how to pray, he does not encourage them to pray, "Your will be *formed*," but rather "Your will be *done*"![5] Prayer cannot rightly be seen as a source of added knowledge or wisdom for God. God alone knows *all*, and he alone knows *best*. Period.

Compatibility of Petitionary Prayer with God's Perfect Knowledge, Wisdom, and Control

Having seen how prayer cannot function in the Christian life, we now ask the question of whether petitionary prayer is compatible with divine sovereignty. That is, do we have reason to think that prayer "fits" within a theological understanding that would uphold God as knowing and declaring all that will take place? In Matthew 6:7–8 Jesus instructs his disciples, "And when you pray, do not heap up empty phrases as the Gentiles do, for they think that they will be heard for their many words. Do not be like them, for *your Father knows what you need before you ask him*." How fascinating this is. One might think that since Jesus has just told the disciples that the Father knows what they need before they pray, he might follow this by saying:

> So, since the Father already knows your needs, and since you simply cannot tell him anything he doesn't already perfectly and fully know, therefore, there really is no point in bringing your requests to him in prayer. After all, since you cannot inform the Father of anything or assist him in knowing what is best to do, petitionary prayer, then, is superfluous, unnecessary, and pointless. So quit pestering the Father! Quit asking him to meet the needs in your life. He knows what you need already, so there's no point in praying for them.

---

[5]Bruce A. Ware, *God's Lesser Glory: The Diminished God of Open Theism* (Wheaton, IL: Crossway, 2000), 170.

But as we know, Jesus doesn't say this! Instead, after instructing his disciples how to pray, as a part of which they are to petition the Father, he immediately follows with:

Give us this day our daily bread,
and forgive us our debts,
    as we also have forgiven our debtors.
And lead us not into temptation,
    but deliver us from evil. (Matt. 6:11–13)

Far from seeing the Father's prior knowledge of the disciples' needs as indications of the futility of prayer, Jesus rather sees God's knowledge of what they need as grounding the disciples' confidence in God as they pray. When they pray, "Give us this day our daily bread," they know that the Father already knows their need for what they ask, so their request can come with confidence and assurance that the Father knows exactly what they need and what is best to provide. And when they pray, "Lead us not into temptation," they know that the Father already knows the temptations they will face and his plan to assist them in facing these, so they can be sure of the divine help that will come. Therefore, prayer is not rendered futile or superfluous because God knows in advance the needs of which prayer speaks and the provisions that prayer seeks. Rather, petitionary prayer is fully compatible with God's infinite knowledge, impeccable wisdom, and full control over all that takes place.

The Purposes of Petitionary Prayer in Light of God's Sovereignty

But our earlier questions remain: If God controls all that takes place, and if prayer cannot add anything to his knowledge or wisdom, then why did God institute petitionary prayer and make this an essential part of his people's life of faith before him? If the purpose of prayer cannot be assisting God either in forming or in fulfilling his will, what reasons did God have in mind when he came up with the idea of his people petitioning him with prayer? Allow me here to suggest at least two fundamental purposes God has for petitionary prayer.[6]

1. *God has devised prayer as a means to draw us into close and intimate relationship with him, the self-sufficient God who possesses all.* Scripture teaches clearly that God is fully self-sufficient. God exists eternally indepen-

---

[6]These two points are adapted from Bruce A. Ware, *God's Greater Glory: The Exalted God of Scripture and the Christian Faith* (Wheaton, IL: Crossway, 2004), 186–94.

dent of creation, possessing within himself, intrinsically and eternally, every quality and perfection in infinite measure. All goodness is God's goodness, and he possesses it intrinsically, eternally, and in infinite measure. All beauty is God's beauty, and he possesses it intrinsically, eternally, and in infinite measure. All power and wisdom and every perfection or quality that exists, exists in God intrinsically, who possesses each and every one infinitely and eternally. Therefore, God needs none of what he has made, and nothing external to God can contribute anything to him, for in principle nothing can be added to this One who already possesses every quality without measure. Instead, everything that exists external to God does so only because God has granted it existence and has filled it with any and every quality it possesses. As the apostle Paul puts it, God is not "served by human hands, as though he needed anything, since he himself gives to all mankind life and breath and everything" (Acts 17:25).

Concerning the self-sufficiency of God and our corresponding dependence on God, John Piper writes:

> God has no needs that I could ever be required to satisfy. God has no deficiencies that I might be required to supply. He is complete in himself. He is overflowing with happiness in the fellowship of the Trinity. The upshot of this is that God is a mountain spring, not a watering trough. A mountain spring is self-replenishing. It constantly overflows and supplies others. But a watering trough needs to be filled with a pump or bucket brigade. . . . And since that is the way God is, we are not surprised to learn from Scripture—and our faith is strengthened to hold fast—that the way to please God is to come to him to get and not to give, to drink and not to water. He is most glorified in us when we are most satisfied in him.[7]

Given these truths about God, we should marvel at the fact that this self-sufficient God has created us, has redeemed us in his Son, and loves us dearly. Though he doesn't need us, and though we can add nothing to the infinite fullness that is his, he loves us and wants us to experience the fullest life possible for his finite image bearers to know. And here is exactly where petitionary prayer comes in. Although God already knows our needs, and already knows every request we could ever make, nonetheless he commands us to bring these very needs and requests before him. Why? Certainly not so that he can learn from us what our needs are. Rather, the God who does not need us is nevertheless passionate about relationship with us. Although he cannot gain or benefit from what we bring to

---

[7]John Piper, *The Pleasures of God: Meditations on God's Delight in Being God*, rev. ed. (Sisters, OR: Multnomah, 2000), 208–9.

him, he deeply desires us to come before him with all of our concerns. Admonitions like "cast . . . your anxieties on him, because he cares for you" (1 Pet. 5:7) and "do not be anxious about anything, but in everything by prayer and supplication with thanksgiving let your requests be made known to God" (Phil. 4:6) instruct us on how serious God is that we come before him with each and every need of our hearts. He longs for us to demonstrate our dependence upon him and our absolute trust in his character by coming to him in petitionary prayer.

Clearly, God does not need us to bring our concerns to him in order for him to know what we need or to know how best to act. He is God! He knows perfectly our backgrounds, our families, our friends, our circumstances, our jobs, our relationships, our struggles, our difficulties, our needs, our desires, our fears, our dreams, our longings, our strengths, our weaknesses, our successes, our failures, our sins, and everything else, both internal and external, related to our lives. He doesn't need us to pray. He doesn't learn anything when we do. He isn't helped in knowing better what course of action to take. The fact is, nothing that we are or have or give can benefit God in any respect whatsoever, and our prayers are no exception. Therefore, God's purpose in instituting prayer, and in longing for us to pray, simply cannot have anything to do with helping him.

Rather, one of the most startling and wondrous realizations that any Christian can have is that much of the purpose of prayer has to do with one simple thing: *relationship*—that is, relationship *coram Deo* (before the face of God). One great and glorious reason God devised prayer was to use it as a mechanism to draw us to himself, to help us see how much we need him, to set before us constantly the realization that he is everything we are not, and he possesses everything that we lack. We are weak, but he is strong; we are foolish, but he is wise; we are untrustworthy, but he is faithful; we are ignorant, but he is infinitely knowledgeable; we are poor and empty, but he is rich and full. Imagine this: although God does not need any of what we bring to him in prayer, he longs for us to bring everything that we do bring to him and so much more! He wants us to pray without ceasing (1 Thess. 5:17), in part because our need for him never ceases. Prayer is not instituted, then, as a means of helping God out. Just the opposite: it is for our sake, and for ours alone. In fact, God commands us to pray! And he does so, not out of some supposed benefit he derives from our praying, but because he longs for us to learn the discipline and joy of dependence upon him for everything we lack, all of which he possesses in infinite measure! We are compelled, then, by the force of divine authority to come and drink of the living water that

our souls thirst after, to receive bread from heaven that sustains us day
by day, and to realize afresh moment by moment by moment that all we
are longing for, and everything that is good, is found in one and only
one place: in God.

This is like no human relationship on earth, to be sure. In no human
relationship is one of the parties self-sufficient! No husband or wife or
friend is "needless." But God is. Romans 11:36 declares that "from him
and through him and to him are *all things*." Acts 17:25 says that God
is not "served by human hands, as though he needed anything, since he
himself gives to all mankind life and breath and everything." And James
1:17 affirms that "every good gift and every perfect gift is from above,
coming down from the Father of lights with whom there is no variation
or shadow due to change." Indeed, in this relationship one of the parties
has it all (literally) and the other is desperately needy. God knows this
better than we do, given our propensity to pretension (otherwise known
as sinful pride), and so he calls us, summons us, commands us, woos us,
entices us, admonishes us, and in every way longs for us to pray.

What he wants for us so much in our praying is simply to see him
for who he is, and in light of that glorious vision, to see ourselves for
who we are. The prophet Isaiah, who was granted a vision of the Lord
sitting on his throne lofty and exalted, with the train of his robe filling
the temple, and seraphim hovering with eyes and feet covered, exclaim-
ing, "Holy, holy, holy is the LORD of hosts; the whole earth is full of his
glory!" having beheld God in his splendor and majesty, then fell before
this glorious and holy God and confessed, "Woe is me! For I am lost;
for I am a man of unclean lips, and I dwell in the midst of a people of
unclean lips; for my eyes have seen the King, the LORD of hosts!" (Isa.
6:1–5). God longs for us, similarly, to know the incomparable wisdom
and wealth, the glory and goodness, the majesty and mercy, the sufficiency and supremacy, the compassion and kindness that are exclusively
and infinitely his. And with this, he longs for us to know and embrace,
within the very depths of our own souls, the immensity of our total
dependency upon him.

But that's not all. Amazingly, God longs for us to know yet one more
thing, and it is this: God loves to share the bounty. He loves being the
Giver. He loves granting to his humble and dependent children what is
best for them. He takes great pleasure in being the source of "every good
gift and every perfect gift" (James 1:17), and he is lavish and generous
and gracious and compassionate so that

no good thing does he withhold
  from those who walk uprightly. (Ps. 84:11)

Therefore, he summons his people to pray.

Listen afresh to the heart of God from the teaching of our Savior:

> Ask, and it will be given to you; seek, and you will find; knock, and it will
> be opened to you. For everyone who asks receives, and the one who seeks
> finds, and to the one who knocks it will be opened. Or which one of you,
> if his son asks him for bread, will give him a stone? Or if he asks for a fish,
> will give him a serpent? If you then, who are evil, know how to give good
> gifts to your children, how much more will your Father who is in heaven
> give good things to those who ask him! (Matt. 7:7–11)

This is much of what prayer is about. To know the riches of God and the
poverty of our human lives is one of the key foundation pillars for prayer,
and through prayer, for the glorifying of God and the blessing of God's
people. As we pray in humble dependence, God bestows his gifts from the
storehouse of his treasury. And as we are enriched by God, in all the ways
that we are, we then give to him our heartfelt thanksgiving and honor
and worship. Yes, God is most glorified in us as we are most satisfied in
him, and the mechanism God has put in place by which our satisfaction
in God is met is petitionary prayer. Though God cannot benefit from our
praying, through it he can accomplish one of his primary goals—that his
people come to him to receive what he alone has to offer, so they might
be filled with him, to the glory of his name.

Commenting on prayer as a sweet aroma to God, John Piper says:

> When God hungers for some special satisfaction, he seeks out a prayer to
> answer. Our prayer is the sweet aroma from the kitchen ascending up into
> the King's chambers making him hungry for the meal. But the actual enjoy-
> ment of the meal is his own glorious work in answering our prayer. The
> food of God is to answer our prayers. The most wonderful thing about the
> Bible is that it reveals a God who satisfies his appetite for joy by answer-
> ing prayers. He has no deficiency in himself that he needs to fill up, so he
> gets his satisfaction by magnifying the glory of his riches by filling up the
> deficiencies of people who pray.[8]

Relationship *coram Deo*—knowing God truly for who he is as the
infinitely rich provider to those who look to him alone for their hope and

---

[8]Ibid., 216.

joy—is what God longs to further through prayer. Prayer is not an end in itself but a God-ordained, God-designed means of grace. Through prayer, God gives himself to us and we are drawn into his presence and his fullness. We do ourselves no favor, then, when we hold on to pretenses of self-ability and self-attainment, for in any and every way that we refuse to humble ourselves before God, we lose. But God, in his grace, wants us to gain! And therefore, God in his grace wants us to want him! "Come to me!" is heard not only on Jesus' lips to Jerusalem (Matt. 11:28), but it echoes throughout the Scriptures. Listen again to the heart of God, and may our response be to hear, and to heed, and to come, and, yes, to pray:

> Come, everyone who thirsts,
>   come to the waters;
> and he who has no money,
>   come, buy and eat!
> Come, buy wine and milk
>   without money and without price.
> Why do you spend your money for that which is not bread,
>   and your labor for that which does not satisfy?
> Listen diligently to me, and eat what is good,
>   and delight yourselves in rich food.
> Incline your ear, and come to me;
>   hear, that your soul may live. (Isa. 55:1–3a)

2. *God has devised prayer as a means of enlisting us as participants in the work he has ordained, as part of the outworking of his sovereign rulership over all.* Marvel at the fact that although God possesses absolute authority, wisdom, and power—by which he devises exactly the plan of his choosing for all of his creation for all of its history, and by which he carries out that plan in meticulous detail, without failure or defeat—nonetheless, he commands his people to pray because whether they pray or not makes a difference! But, some will say, surely prayer cannot really make a difference, and surely prayer must actually be an exercise in futility if prayer is offered in a universe over which God exercises absolute sovereign control. If God "does according to his will among the host of heaven and among the inhabitants of the earth; and none can stay his hand or say to him, 'What have you done?'" (Dan. 4:35), then why pray?

The relationship between divine sovereignty and petitionary prayer can be stated by this word: *participation.* Being the sovereign God that he is, God simply is in no need of our participation with him in accomplishing his work. Sometimes we think so because we mistakenly confuse the *call* of God to work for him with a *need* in God for us so to work. Take the call of God to missions as an example. Does God call some of his children to serve him by crossing cultural boundaries in order to bring the gospel of Jesus Christ to those who have never heard? Absolutely yes! From Matthew 28:18–20, to Acts 1:8, to Paul's own conversion and calling in Acts 9:1–19 to the spread of the gospel through much of the known world by the end of the history recorded in the book of Acts—yes, God calls some of his children to serve in the missionary enterprise. But must God call some to serve as missionaries in order for others to hear the gospel and be saved?

We must be very careful in how we think about this question. It is not a simple one. The answer, it seems, must be yes and no simultaneously, but in different senses. In light of God's design and purpose that the lost hear the gospel as missionaries are called and sent out to preach, then yes, God must call some as missionaries for this work to be done. That is, given the fact that God has designed this means of the lost hearing the gospel, then yes, missionaries must go. But no, in the sense that God could have chosen a different mechanism to get the gospel to lost people. After all, he is sovereign, and he could accomplish this task in a multitude of ways. He could, for example, write the gospel in the sky, or proclaim it from a heavenly loudspeaker, or send the message by way of angels, or speak the gospel directly and in perfect dialect into the ears and minds of every individual person throughout the world simultaneously! But God has designed not to do it in these ways. Rather, he has designed for the gospel to be spread through his call on the hearts of some to go and preach, so that others might hear and believe and call upon the name of the Lord and be saved (Rom. 10:13–15).

So, because God is sovereign, he can rule the world unilaterally with no participation from anyone at all. His infinite wisdom and power, along with his uncontested authority, give him all he needs to accomplish everything he wants to do without your help or mine. His sovereignty, then, renders prayer unnecessary—in principle. But here is where the wonder and amazement at prayer increases further. Although God is fully capable of "doing it on his own," nonetheless, he enlists his people to join him in the work that alone is his. And one of the chief means that he employs for our participation with him in this work is prayer.

How God Uses Prayer to Enlist Our Participation in His Work
How does prayer function, then, as a tool designed by God to enlist our participation in his work? Consider the following answers:

1. *God has designed not only that his people pray, but that, as we indicated earlier, prayer sometimes be a necessary means for accomplishing the ends that God has ordained.* In other words, God purposely designed the manner by which his ordained works would be accomplished, so that some of what he accomplishes can be brought to pass only as people pray. All of the commands and admonitions in Scripture to pray certainly indicate that this is the case. Consider, for example, James 5:14–15: "Is anyone among you sick? Let him call for the elders of the church, and let them pray over him, anointing him with oil in the name of the Lord. And the prayer of faith will save the one who is sick, and the Lord will raise him up." Surely this implies that prayer (of the elders, in this case) is part of the God-ordained means by which God's healing of the sick would occur. If prayer were not linked with the outcome (i.e., healing), then why admonish the sick to call for the elders to pray? But notice another important point: since God is sovereign, he could just heal this sick person as he wills, fully apart from whether anyone prays or not. God's power to heal is not subject to or hindered by lack of prayer, in the absolute sense. Yet it is clear here that God has so chosen that the fulfillment of his work is tied—by his good pleasure and will—to the prayer that is offered on behalf of the sick. Some of God's work, then, is designed by God to be fulfilled only as people pray to God.

One area of biblical teaching on divine sovereignty that John Piper has particularly linked to the necessity of prayer is the doctrine of election:

> When we believe in the sovereignty of God—in the right and power of God to elect and then bring hardened sinners to faith and salvation—then we will be able to pray with no inconsistency, and with great biblical promises for the conversion of the lost. Thus God has pleasure in this kind of praying because it ascribes to him the right and honor to be the free and sovereign God that he is in election and salvation.[9]

Indeed, God does have the right and honor to save those whom he chooses. And he could do so without prayer. Yet God has deemed it good and wise that Christian people pray for the salvation of the lost. For example, Paul asks others to pray that words may be given him in boldly proclaiming the mystery of the gospel (Eph. 6:19), and for a door to be open to speak forth the gospel in words that are clear (Col. 4:3–4). Clearly Paul knows that God works all things after the counsel of his will (Eph. 1:11), yet Paul requests prayer for God's leading and empowerment in gospel proclama-

---

[9]Ibid., 220.

tion. God's election of sinners to salvation does not preclude the necessity of prayer; rather, divine election provides the surety and confidence that prayers for faithfulness in gospel proclamation for the salvation of the lost will be heard and answered.

2. *In prayer we are led, by the Spirit, to have our minds and wills reshaped to the mind and will of God.* Recall that in our Lord's prayer he told us to pray,

> Your kingdom come,
> *your will be done,*
>   on earth as it is in heaven. (Matt. 6:10)

This indicates that the perfect will of God precedes my praying and yours. As indicated earlier, Jesus does not say to pray, "your will be *formed*," but "your will be done." As should be abundantly clear from our preceding discussion on God's self-sufficiency and prayer, God doesn't need us to inform him about the state of affairs of some situation, nor does he need (or want!) advice regarding what is best to do.

If anyone thinks that somehow, in a literal sort of sense, our prayers can change God's mind, I would like to ask that person: Who do you think you are?! What could you (or I) possibly know that has escaped God's attention? What perspective do you (or I) have that he lacks? When we consider the extremely limited knowledge we have, our lack of foresight compared to God's perfect foreknowledge, our record of poor decisions and bad judgment in far more cases than we'd like to admit, not to mention our morally twisted natures and as-yet unreformed affections and values, do we really want God to listen to our advice regarding what might be best to do? Honestly, I believe that I could not act more foolishly than to come to God in prayer suggesting to him that he see things my way and insisting that he do as I want. No, "your will be done" means that Another's will precedes mine, and thankfully, this will has been formed out of an omniscient (all-knowing) and omnisapient (all-wise) mind and heart so that we can be assured it cannot be improved. In prayer, we seek to pray "according to God's will" and "in Jesus' name," indicating our longing to have our minds, desires, affections, and wills reshaped to be more like God's.

3. *In prayer for other people and their needs, we minister the grace of God to them.* Ministers of grace—what a privilege and precious calling

this is. And one way God has enabled his people to join him in his work and ministry is through prayer by which God's work goes forth. Bear in mind the first point above. It is only because prayer functions necessarily as a God-ordained means for the fulfillment of some of God's work that this ministry of prayer on behalf of others can take place. But by God's grace, he has so chosen to minister some of his grace to others through the prayers that you or I offer before his throne of grace to the honor of his name. When you hear someone say something like, "Well, all I could do is pray," remember that while this statement makes it sound as though nothing really useful is being done when a person prays, from heaven's vantage point, one of God's most important and strategic means of accomplishing his work in fact is being employed. Why is prayer this important? The answer, as we have seen, is captured in one word: participation. God has willed to enlist our participation with him in the work he is doing, and prayer has been designed by God to get us onto the front lines, deeply involved in his work.

4. *Prayer makes us more fully aware of what God is doing, and so, as a result, we can offer praise to God when it is accomplished.* Just think if God did his work unilaterally without using prayer. So much of what he accomplished would take place with little if any notice by his people, and little if any praise to God for the great work he had done. But by designing prayer, he allows us the privileged position of being insiders to kingdom strategy and kingdom operations. We are drawn into the unfolding of the plans, we sense the great stakes that are faced, and we realize how important it is for God to act and work and reign. And when prayers are answered and God's work is done, we will be able to praise and worship him for the things we have seen accomplished, having anticipated the need for the answer, and having been attuned to the marvelous work that God has now done. Great joy is ours both in being enlisted to pray and in seeing the results of prayer.

5. *Prayer is a means of sanctifying grace as we persist in prayer, sometimes for long periods and through agonizing trials.* Through these times of persevering prayer, God ministers his grace, comfort, peace, and hope to us, even when his answer to our deep longings, ultimately, is no. Paul prayed earnestly three times for his thorn in the flesh to be removed, and when God said no, Paul had grown much as a result (2 Cor. 12:7–10). Prayer, then, is as much a tool of our sanctification by God's grace as it is a tool of ministering God's grace to others.

Conclusion

By prayer, then, we are drawn into relationship with the One from whom all blessings flow; and by prayer we are called into participation in the work of the One by whom all sovereign rulership is exercised. Because God is self-sufficient, we come in prayer with joyous anticipation, knowing that in God's grace he offers his fullness for our emptiness, his strength for our weakness, and his wisdom for our folly. We believe the word announced, that God "rewards those who seek him" (Heb. 11:6), and so we come and seek God in prayer, and we find in him our comfort, our strength, our direction, our forgiveness, our joy, indeed our life. And because God is sovereign, we come in prayer believing that God has ordained this instrument as a gracious tool by which he enlists us into participation in his glorious work. We are not fundamentally bystanders, though many of God's works unfold before us merely as we are granted eyes to see and to rejoice. But mostly we are involved participants through prayer in the very work of God himself, as prayer is made a necessary means for accomplishing much of God's ordained work.

Why pray if God is sovereign? In the end, the answer to this question is as deeply devastating to our sense of self-attainment as it is strengthening to our sense of dependence upon God. Though God doesn't need our prayers—he is sovereign and could accomplish all he does without ever instituting prayer or enlisting us to pray—he longs for his people to pray. He loves us deeply and wants us to share in the work, his very work, which is the most meaningful and important work in all of the world to do. What a privilege we have been given in this marvelous gift of prayer by which we enter into closer relationship with and heartfelt dependence upon God, and by which we are allowed—indeed, called—to participate in the outworking of the very eternal plans and purposes of God. As the self-sufficient God, he cannot benefit from our prayers, and as the sovereign God, he doesn't need our prayers. But as the fully self-sufficient and sovereign God who also loves his people so very deeply, he calls us into greater relationship and participation with him through the acts of petitionary prayer that God establishes as necessary to the fulfillment of some portion of his work.

May God grant us greater vision for prayer. May we see more of the greatness of God through his grace manifest in calling us to pray. And may we give greater glory to God as we understand the privilege of prayer and the necessity of prayer. And in the end, may prayer cause us to be satisfied and strengthened more fully in God that he may be glorified more fully in our lives.

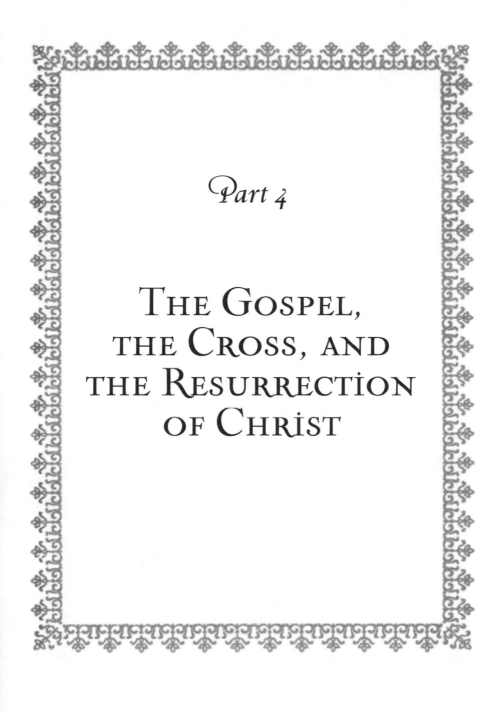

Part 4

THE GOSPEL,
THE CROSS, AND
THE RESURRECTION
OF CHRIST

8

WHAT IS THE GOSPEL?–REVISITED

D. A. Carson

The word "revisited" in the title is my way of reminding myself that I have addressed this question before. Not long ago I wrote an editorial for *Themelios* that briefly focuses on how the gospel is the announcement of what God has done, and must not be confused with our responses.[1] A little over two years ago I prepared a sermon on 1 Corinthians 15:1–19, under the title "What Is the Gospel?"[2] More than a dozen years ago I wrote an essay titled "The Biblical Gospel."[3] So what will be different or fresh about the approach I adopt here?

This essay is more than an excuse to honor my friend and colleague John Piper, who has been preaching the gospel for decades and thinking about it penetratingly.[4] It is also the beginning of a fresh probe into the

---

[1] "Editorial," *Themelios* 34, no. 1 (2009): 1–2, available online at http://www.thegospelcoalition.org/publications/themelios.

[2] "The Gospel of Jesus Christ (1 Cor. 15:1–19)," a lightly edited manuscript of a sermon preached at The Gospel Coalition conference in Deerfield, Illinois, on May 23, 2007; text, audio, and video are available online at http://www.thegospelcoalition.org/resources/a/what_is_the_gospel_1#.

[3] "The Biblical Gospel," in *For Such a Time as This: Perspectives on Evangelicalism, Past, Present, and Future*, ed. Steve Brady and Harold Rowdon (London: Scripture Union, 1996), 75–85; available online at http://s3.amazonaws.com/tgc-documents/carson/1996_biblical_gospel.pdf.

[4] One thinks, for instance, not only of his recent material on justification, but of *God Is the Gospel: Meditations on God's Love as the Gift of Himself* (Wheaton, IL: Crossway, 2005); *Finally Alive: What Happens When We Are Born Again* (Fearn, Ross-shire: Christian Focus, 2009); and much more.

subject by looking at "gospel" words—at εὐαγγέλιον and cognates. In my mind this is part of two larger projects aimed at showing (a) how the New Testament relates these gospel words to a wide swath of theological and pastoral themes and (b) how we would be wiser to stop talking so much about what "evangelicalism" is without deeper reflection on what the "evangel" is, what "the gospel" is. Those larger projects are merely hinted at in this chapter, of course.

Gospel Words

For reasons of brevity I shall restrict myself to the Septuagint (LXX) and the New Testament. The "gospel words" I shall survey are εὐαγγέλιον, εὐαγγελίζω, and εὐαγγελιστής. The meaning and distribution of these words in the LXX and New Testament can be presented as shown in figure 1:[5]

Fig. 1.

Word	Form	Meaning	LXX	NT
εὐαγγέλιον	noun	"gospel," "good news," "evangel"	1x	76x
εὐαγγελίζω	verb	"to preach/proclaim the gospel"	23x	54x
εὐαγγελιστής	noun	"one who preaches/proclaims the gospel," "evangelist"	—	3x

Gospel Words in the LXX

Εὐαγγέλιον in the LXX

The single occurrence of εὐαγγέλιον in the LXX is found in 2 Samuel 4:10. In the context, Rekab and Baanah have killed Ish-Bosheth and run to David with the news, thinking he would be pleased. David responds by drawing an analogy with the way he had acted when someone had told him the news that Saul was dead, thinking he was bringing good news to the king (ὡς εὐαγγελιζόμενος ἐνώπιόν μου): he put the man to death. "That was the reward I gave him for his news [εὐαγγέλια]!"

Εὐαγγελίζω in the LXX

The verb εὐαγγελίζω does not occur in the LXX of the Pentateuch. In the historical books, it refers to the announcing of good news, or news that is perceived by some, at least, to be good news—news that is usually political or military, for example, related to the deaths of enemies. Not surprisingly, such news is often announced to the king (e.g., 2 Sam. 4:10, the passage cited above; also 2 Sam. 18:19, 20, 26, 31). When pagans

---

[5] I am grateful to Andy Naselli for compiling the raw data for me.

receive the news of the destruction of their enemies (e.g., King Saul), they rush to tell it to the house of their idols and their people (1 Sam. 31:9; 1 Chron. 10:9). Whether the news is perceived to be good or bad can depend on the perspective of the viewer: in 2 Samuel 1:20, David takes up a lament at the death of Saul:

> Tell it not in Gath,
>   proclaim it not in the streets of Ashkelon,
> lest the daughters of the Philistines be glad,
>   lest the daughters of the uncircumcised rejoice.[6]

The LXX reads "and tell it not as glad tidings [μὴ εὐαγγελίσησθε] in the streets of Ascalon." Clearly, what might be good news in Ashkelon is not good news to David. A similar tension, we have already seen, is found in 2 Samuel 4:10.

When we turn to occurrences of the verb εὐαγγελίζω in the Psalms, the usage becomes more overtly theological. Translating the Hebrew of Psalm 40:9a, the TNIV reads, "I proclaim your saving acts in the great assembly," and the ESV,

> I have told the glad news of deliverance
>   in the great congregation.

The corresponding LXX passage, Psalm 39:10 LXX, reads, "I have preached righteousness in the great congregation [εὐηγγελισάμην δικαιοσύνην ἐν ἐκκλησίᾳ μεγάλῃ]." Those to whom the Lord gives the word to preach it are designated τοῖς εὐαγγελιζομένοις in Psalm 67:12 LXX (they appear to be women in Hebrew, Ps. 68:11). If the Hebrew of Psalm 96:2 commands us to proclaim the Lord's salvation day after day, the corresponding Septuagintal text renders "proclaim salvation" by the one word εὐαγγελίζεσθε (Ps. 95:2 LXX). Something similar can be said for the "proclaiming" of the "good news" that God is merciful to Israel in Psalm of Solomon 11:1 LXX.

Turning to the prophets, occasionally the LXX offers a "proclaim good news" clause not found in the Hebrew (e.g., Joel 3:5 LXX; compare Joel 2:32 in most English versions). Many of the occurrences of the Greek verb in the prophets have to do with bringing good news to Judah and/ or Jerusalem/Zion to the effect that the years of her punishment are ended or will end in due course (e.g., Nah. 1:15 [LXX 2:1]; Isa. 40:9).

---

[6]Unless otherwise noted, Scripture quotations in this chapter are from the TNIV translation.

Some of these passages, initially attached to the return from exile, are so bound up with eschatological salvation that it is not surprising they are tied by the New Testament to broader themes (e.g., "as the feet of one preaching glad tidings of peace, as one preaching good news: for I will publish your salvation, saying, O Sion, your God shall reign" [ὡς πόδες εὐαγγελιζομένου ἀκοὴν εἰρήνης ὡς εὐαγγελιζόμενος ἀγαθά ὅτι ἀκουστὴν ποιήσω τὴν σωτηρίαν σου λέγων Σιων βασιλεύσει σου ὁ θεός]) (Isa. 52:7 LXX; cf. similarly Isa. 60:6; 61:1). One prophetic passage in which the "good news" is read differently by different people is the hyperbolic lament in Jeremiah 20:15.

Gospel Words in the New Testament
Εὐαγγέλιον outside Paul's Letters
Turning to the New Testament, we discover that the noun εὐαγγέλιον is found only twelve times in the Gospels—four times in Matthew and seven or eight times in Mark, never in Luke or John—and only two times in Acts and once each in 1 Peter and Revelation. The rest of the occurrences are found in Paul—at least once in each of the canonical Pauline Epistles save Titus. In other words, it is a distinctively (though not an exclusively) Pauline word. Before we survey the usage in Paul, however, we should take note of its occurrence in the rest of the New Testament.

In Matthew, three of the four occurrences find the noun embedded in the larger expression "the gospel of the kingdom" (τὸ εὐαγγέλιον τῆς βασιλείας, 4:23; 9:35; 24:14). Once the expression is "this gospel" (τὸ εὐαγγέλιον τοῦτο, 26:13), but transparently the referent must be similar. The first two occurrences are in summary statements of Jesus' ministry: Jesus went through Galilee, or through all their cities and villages, teaching in their synagogues, proclaiming (κηρύσσων) *the gospel of the kingdom*, and healing every sickness and disease. In 24:14, "this gospel of the kingdom" will be preached (κηρυχθήσεται) in the whole world (ἐν ὅλῃ τῇ οἰκουμένῃ); in 26:13, Jesus describes what will take place wherever "this gospel" is preached (κηρυχθῇ) in the whole world (ἐν ὅλῳ τῷ κόσμῳ).

Interestingly enough, none of the eight occurrences of εὐαγγέλιον in Mark link the word so directly with the kingdom (though one is close: see Mark 1:15, below). The opening line of Mark introduces readers to the word: "The beginning of the gospel about Jesus the Messiah" (1:1). By 1:14 we are told that Jesus came into Galilee "proclaiming the gospel of God [κηρύσσων τὸ εὐαγγέλιον τοῦ θεοῦ]." In the next verse, 1:15, the content of Jesus' preaching is given: "The time has come, and the kingdom of God has come near. Repent and believe the gospel [πιστεύετε ἐν τῷ εὐαγγελίῳ]." In 8:35 and 10:29, the gospel is something so valuable that someone might suffer deprivation or lose life itself for the gospel's sake. In 13:10 and 14:9, the gospel will be preached in the whole world (with minor verbal variations from Matthew). The only other occurrence in Mark is in the so-called long ending: Mark 16:15 finds Jesus commanding his disciples to "preach the gospel [κηρύξατε τὸ εὐαγγέλιον] to all creation."

In the first of the two occurrences in Acts, Peter declares, at the Jerusalem Council, that God ordained that by his mouth "the Gentiles might hear the word of the gospel [τὸν λόγον τοῦ εὐαγγελίου] and believe" (Acts 15:7). In the other, Paul declares to the Ephesian elders how he wished to complete the task the Lord Jesus had given him, "to testify to the gospel of the grace of God [διαμαρτύρασθαι τὸ εὐαγγέλιον τῆς χάριτος τοῦ θεοῦ]" (Acts 20:24). In 1 Peter 4:17, judgment is threatened to those who do not obey "the gospel of God [τῷ τοῦ θεοῦ εὐαγγελίῳ]."

The final New Testament occurrence, in Revelation 14:6, has generated some controversy. We are introduced to an angel "with the eternal gospel [εὐαγγέλιον αἰώνιον] to proclaim to those who live on the earth—to every nation, tribe, language and people." The next verse (14:7) tells us what the angel said in a loud voice: "Fear God and give him glory, because the hour of his judgment has come. Worship him who made the heavens, the earth, the sea and the springs of water." Some have argued that verse 7 gives us the content of "the eternal gospel" mentioned in verse 6. The substance of this "eternal gospel," then, is simply the command to fear God and give him glory. In the light of the rest of New Testament usage, this interpretation is singularly unlikely. It is much more plausible to hold that the substance of "the eternal gospel" is roughly in line with the news of God's redeeming act in Christ and all that flows from it, and verse 7 gives us not the content of that gospel but the motive for responding: the hour of final judgment is near.

Εὐαγγελίζω outside Paul's Letters

Before turning to Paul, it is worth briefly scanning the uses of the verb εὐαγγελίζω that are found outside the Pauline corpus. Εὐαγγελίζω occurs once in Matthew, 11:5, which picks up the language of Isaiah 61:1: the good news is preached to the poor (πτωχοὶ εὐαγγελίζονται).

The verb is found in neither Mark nor John, but occurs twenty-five times in Luke–Acts. Good news is announced to Zechariah regarding the birth of his son John (Luke 1:19) and to the angels regarding the birth of Jesus (2:10). John the Baptist preached the good news of the impending

arrival of one whose sandals he was unworthy to untie, one who would
baptize in the Holy Spirit and burn up the chaff on his threshing floor
(3:18). Luke 4:18 finds Jesus applying Isaiah 61:1 (regarding the good
news preached to the poor) to himself; the same Old Testament passage
is picked up again in 7:22 (parallel to Matt. 11:5, cited above). In Luke
4:43 Jesus announces that he must preach the good news of the kingdom
to other towns; the construction is rather different from that found in
Matthew: Καὶ ταῖς ἑτέραις πόλεσιν εὐαγγελίσασθαί με δεῖ τὴν βασιλείαν τοῦ
θεοῦ, "for I was sent for this purpose" (ESV; similarly Luke 8:1; 16:16).
"Preaching the gospel" (bound up in the verb) is often used absolutely
(e.g., 20:1), and sometimes in a list of Jesus' activities (e.g., preaching
and healing, 9:6).

Acts 5:42 says that the believers never stopped "teaching and preaching that the Messiah is Jesus" (as the Greek really must be rendered:
οὐκ ἐπαύοντο διδάσκοντες καὶ εὐαγγελιζόμενοι τὸν Χριστόν, Ἰησοῦν).
Christians are found preaching the word (εὐαγγελιζόμενοι τὸν λόγον,
8:4), Philip is preaching the good news about the kingdom of God
(εὐαγγελιζομένῳ περὶ τῆς βασιλείας τοῦ θεοῦ, 8:12), and, once again,
the verb is found without modifiers, meaning simply "to preach the
gospel" or the like (8:25, 40; 14:7, 21; 16:10). The range of the content
of the preaching connected with this verb is of some interest: preach
Jesus (8:35), preach good news of peace through Jesus Christ (10:36),
preach the Lord Jesus (11:20), preach that what God promised to the
fathers he has now fulfilled to this generation (13:32), teaching and
preaching the word of the Lord (15:35), preaching Jesus and the resurrection (17:18).

The verb appears twice in Hebrews (4:2 and 4:6), where it is used to
draw a comparison between the "good news" that was preached to the
Israelites in the desert and the good news preached about Jesus to the
author's readers. It shows up three times in 1 Peter (1:12, 25; 4:6), always
absolutely, identified as the word of the Lord. Finally, it shows up twice in
Revelation, once in connection with the "eternal gospel" already discussed
(εὐαγγέλιον αἰώνιον εὐαγγελίσαι, 14:6) and once as the announcement of
"the mystery of God" to God's servants, the prophets (10:7).

Εὐαγγέλιον and Εὐαγγελίζω in Paul's Letters
That brings us to Paul, where the noun εὐαγγέλιον occurs twenty-three
times and the verb εὐαγγελίζω occurs fifty-four times. Limitation of space
prohibits an equally exhaustive catalog of the usages in this corpus.

Εὐαγγέλιον in Paul's Letters. In the first verse of the first Pauline letter to appear in the canon, Paul declares that he is a servant of Jesus Christ, called to be an apostle and "set apart for the gospel of God [ἀφωρισμένος εἰς εὐαγγέλιον θεοῦ]" (Rom. 1:1). Paul serves God with his spirit "in the gospel of his Son" (1:9 ESV), the gospel of which he is not ashamed (1:16). According to Paul, his gospel declares that God judges everyone's secrets (2:16); indeed, in line with Isaiah 53:1, Paul recognizes that not all have obeyed the gospel (Rom. 10:16), and some Jews in Paul's day remain enemies of the gospel (11:28). The apostle's evangelistic efforts can be understood to be his priestly service of the gospel of God (ἱερουργοῦντα τὸ εὐαγγέλιον τοῦ θεοῦ, 15:16). By preaching as he has, Paul has fulfilled the ministry of the gospel of Christ (15:19). In the final doxology of his letter to the Romans, Paul addresses himself to God who is able to establish his readers "in accordance with my gospel, the message I proclaim about Jesus Christ," which is itself simultaneously in line with the revelation of the mystery long hidden and entirely in line with the Scriptures already given (16:25–27).

The Corinthian letters have an abundance of references to the gospel (1 Cor. 4:15; 9:12, 14, 18, 23; 15:1; 2 Cor. 2:12; 4:3, 4; 8:18; 9:13; 10:14; 11:4, 7). First Corinthians 15 is especially powerful in laying out the matters "of first importance" in connection with this gospel: it is Christ-centered, bound up with Jesus' death and resurrection, apostolic, biblical, transforming, and so forth. First Corinthians 9 depicts Paul's own example, precisely because he is a gospel-shaped apostle, not to use his rights but to put them aside, mirroring how Jesus set aside his own rights—a reality at the heart of the cross and thus at the heart of the gospel.

Small wonder the letter to the Galatians finds Paul saying that any other "gospel" is really no gospel at all (1:6–7). This gospel that Paul preaches (κηρύσσω) among the Gentiles (2:2) must preserve the exclusive sufficiency of Christ (2:5) and is preached to Jews and Gentiles alike (2:7). Christian life must be lived according to the truth of the gospel (πρὸς τὴν ἀλήθειαν τοῦ εὐαγγελίου), or one is acting hypocritically (2:14; cf. Col. 1:5).

The "word of truth" is "the gospel of your salvation" in Ephesians 1:13; unity between Jews and Gentiles is accomplished because both are "partakers of the promise in Christ Jesus through the gospel" (3:6), this "gospel of peace" (6:15). Paul's purpose is to make known the mystery of the gospel (γνωρίσαι τὸ μυστήριον τοῦ εὐαγγελίου, 6:19).

When believers share their assets and gifts to promote the gospel, as the Philippians supported Paul, they enter into a partnership in the gospel (Phil. 1:5; 4:15). Paul is determined to remain in defense and confirmation of this gospel (1:7, 16); even his imprisonment seems light if it serves to advance the gospel (1:12). The apostle knows full well that believers ought to live a life worthy of the gospel of Christ (1:27) as they learn to strive side by side "for the faith of the gospel" (1:27; cf. 2:22; 4:3; 1 Thess. 3:2).

Believers must not move away from the hope held out in the gospel (Col. 1:23). Ideally, when that gospel is proclaimed, it is also experienced in power (1 Thess. 1:5) and proclaimed with courage (2:2), for we have been entrusted with it (2:4). Those who understand it best want to share not only the gospel but themselves as well (2:8–9). God calls us to be saved through the sanctifying work of the Spirit and belief in the truth, calling us to this through the apostolic gospel to the end that we might share in the glory of our Lord Jesus Christ (2 Thess. 2:14).

Small wonder Paul wants believers to live in line with sound doctrine that conforms to the gospel concerning the glory of the blessed God (1 Tim. 1:11). This gospel is well worth suffering for (2 Tim. 1:8; Philem. 13); Christ Jesus has abolished death and brought life and immortality to light through the gospel (2 Tim. 1:10). The gospel can be summarized in a number of ways, but is always deeply Christocentric: for example, "Remember Jesus Christ, raised from the dead, descended from David, according to my gospel" (2 Tim. 2:8, my translation).

Εὐαγγελίζω in Paul's Letters. The verbal form εὐαγγελίζω is less frequent in the Pauline letters than in Luke–Acts. Paul wants to preach the gospel to those in Rome (Rom. 1:15; cf. 10:15); indeed, it is his ambition to preach the gospel where Christ is not known (15:20; cf. 2 Cor. 10:16). In his preaching, the apostle is determined to do so without manipulative eloquence lest the cross of Christ be emptied of its power (1 Cor. 1:17—which again shows a tremendously tight tie between the gospel and the cross of Christ; cf. also 1 Cor. 9:16, 18; 15:1–2). The other Pauline occurrences of the verb are in line with the noun uses.

Εὐαγγελιστής in the New Testament

Finally, for the sake of completeness, I should list the three instances of the noun εὐαγγελιστής, referring to the preacher of the good news. Our English versions traditionally render the Greek word as "evangelist." Philip is labeled "the evangelist" (Acts 21:8); God has given to the church apostles, prophets, evangelists, shepherds, and teachers (Eph. 4:11); Timothy is to do the work of an evangelist (2 Tim. 4:5).

Preliminary Observations on These Gospel Words

This bare-bones list of word usages could easily be considered shallow, even slightly boring. Yet I fear that some of the nonsense about what the gospel is today turns on *not* having worked through the way the word-group is actually used. What we must now do is offer some preliminary observations on these raw data, and then probe the evidence a little more deeply.

Word Study Fallacies

This side of James Barr, we are all aware of the common mistakes in word studies. We must not, for instance, merely assume that each instance of the gospel word-group means exactly the same thing as every other instance: even a cursory glance over the list discloses substantial diversity. Nor do we have the right merely to add up the various contextually determined meanings in order to establish a synthetic whole. Nowadays, however, converse dangers are perhaps more common. Some scholars display a penchant for assuming nothing in common between one usage and another unless it is specifically spelled out. For example, in 1 Corinthians 2 Paul declares that he is determined to know nothing except Jesus and him crucified. By contrast, in 2 Timothy 2:8 Paul declares that what is in line with his gospel, what is according to his gospel, is "Jesus Christ, raised from the dead, descended from David"—with no mention of the cross. This confirms some scholars in their belief that the apostle could not have written the Pastoral Epistles: the "gospel" found in each of the two passages is different from the other "gospel." A more sober assessment recognizes that Jesus can hardly be resurrected unless he dies first; that Paul—whether in the Pastorals or in his undisputed writings—is interested in Jesus' incarnation not only as a model in humility but as the supreme act of divine self-disclosure that makes the redemptive act of the cross possible (and hence "descended from David" is entirely in line with Pauline thought). If the gospel word-group in the New Testament is taken to mean the (good) news of what God has done, supremely in Jesus, including his coming, death, and resurrection and all that he does that flows from this sacrifice, we have a category broad enough to embrace almost all the uses while allowing subtle refinements in individual passages.

Nevertheless there is frustration in the survey I have just provided, for I have not had the space to tease out the significance of fascinating expressions that are regularly tied to the gospel—what it means, for instance, to say that the gospel is the mystery of God,[7] or for Paul to say that his function is that of a διάκονος ("servant") of the new covenant and thus of the gospel, or what it means to speak of the οἰκονομία ("stewardship") of the gospel, and much more. We could usefully explore how the "gospel" relates to the "promise," how "preaching the gospel" relates to preaching/ proclaiming (κηρύσσω). We have noted a substantial number of passages where the gospel focuses on the cross, and that in turn ought to draw us into discussion of what the cross achieves, how it is tied to, say, justification. And of course one could usefully undertake a full-scale exegesis of each passage where the gospel words occur. Thus our understanding of what "the gospel" is must, in a full-scale treatment, run down each of these lanes, for otherwise our treatment is in danger of being little more than cliché. But one must start somewhere.

Literary Genre

One small matter should be raised if only to set it aside. Today one common use of "gospel" is to refer to the ostensible literary genre of the first four books of the New Testament: we speak of the four canonical Gospels. It is now widely recognized that there is no evidence that anyone in the first century used the word "gospel" that way. Each of what we call the four Gospels was called "The Gospel according to Matthew," "The Gospel according to Mark," and so on: there was *one* gospel, the gospel of Jesus Christ, according to Matthew, Mark, Luke, and John. There is little harm in preserving usage that sprang up in the second century and continues to this day, but we should not succumb to the anachronism that thinks such usage has any bearing whatsoever on how the word was understood in the first century.

The Gospel and the Imperial Cult

Some have pointed out that the word εὐαγγέλιον, "gospel," is never used with theological significance in the LXX, and they therefore conclude that New Testament usage likely springs from its occurrence in the imperial cult.[8] The argument has little validity. For a start, the noun εὐαγγέλιον occurs only once in the LXX, so to speak of it "never" being used with theological significance, while formally correct, is more than a little misleading. Moreover, our survey of the use of the entire word-group in

---

[7]See D. A. Carson, "Mystery and Fulfillment: Toward a More Comprehensive Paradigm of Paul's Understanding of the Old and the New," in *Justification and Variegated Nomism*, vol. 2, *The Paradoxes of Paul*, Wissenschaftliche Untersuchungen zum Neuen Testament 181, ed. D. A. Carson, Peter T. O'Brien, and Mark A. Seifrid (Tübingen: Mohr Siebeck/Grand Rapids: Baker, 2004), 393–436.

[8]So U. Becker, "Gospel, Evangelize, Evangelist," in *The New Testament Dictionary of New Testament Theology*, 3 vols., ed. Colin Brown (Grand Rapids: Eerdmans, 1976), 2:109.

the LXX shows that the psalmists and prophets happily use the cognate verb with theological significance, while the historical books tend not to. Many of the relevant LXX uses reflect Hebrew בָּשַׂר ("bring good news"), often deployed to refer to Yahweh's eschatological activity, the announcement of the dawning of eschatological joy (e.g., Joel 2:32; Nah. 1:15; Isa. 40:9; 52:7; 60:6; 61:1).[9] Conceivably, Paul and his readers could have picked up allusive overtones to the imperial cult and delighted by contrast in proclaiming the *real* good news, but there is no valid reason to look beyond the Old Testament/LXX for the dominant influence on Paul's usage of the word-group.

Gospel Content and Gospel Proclamation

Douglas Moo rightly points out,

> The noun [εὐαγγέλιον, "gospel"] in the NT denotes the "good news" of the saving intervention of God in Christ, referring usually to the message about Christ (1 Cor. 15:1; Gal. 1:11; 2:2) and, by extension, to the act of preaching that message (1 Cor. 9:14 [second occurrence]; 2 Cor. 2:12; 8:18; Phil. 1:5[?]; 4:3[?]).[10]

In some Pauline contexts it is notoriously difficult to decide which emphasis takes preeminence: the good news itself or the proclamation of that good news. In Romans 1:1, for instance, when the apostle tells us that he was "set apart for [εἰς] the gospel," does he mean that he was set apart (by God) to preach the gospel, or that he was set apart (by God) for the gospel itself—that is, for the advantage of the gospel, for the advance of the gospel? Perhaps it is not necessary to choose. The word "gospel" can become so comprehensive that it becomes more or less equivalent to "Christ" or to "God's redeeming and transforming work in Christ" (see Rom 1:9; Phil. 1:27). The "gospel," which is *the good news about* God's redeeming work in Christ, becomes shorthand for God's redeeming work in Christ itself. When that happens, to say that Paul was set apart (by God) *for* this gospel inevitably carries overtones of both the content of what God has done and the promotion and declaration of it.

---

[9]See Peter Stuhlmacher, *Das paulinische Evangelium. I: Vorgeschichte*, Forschungen zur Religion und Literatur des Alten und Neuen Testaments 95 (Göttingen: Vandenhoeck & Ruprecht, 1968), 152–53, 177–79, 204–6; R. P. Martin, "Gospel," in *International Standard Bible Encyclopedia*, 2:530.
[10]Douglas J. Moo, *The Epistle to the Romans*, New International Commentary on the New Testament (Grand Rapids: Eerdmans, 1996), 43n16.

More Probing Observations on These Gospel Words
The Gospel Is Heraldic Proclamation

Because the gospel is news, good news (even if some will hear it as bad news), it is to be announced: that's what one does with news. The essentially heraldic element in preaching is bound up with the fact that the core message is not a code of ethics to be debated, still less a list of aphorisms to be admired and pondered, and certainly not a systematic theology to be outlined and schematized. Though it properly grounds ethics, aphorisms, and systematics, it is none of these three: it is *news*, good news, and therefore must be publicly announced. That is why εὐαγγέλιον κηρύσσειν, "to preach the gospel," is the functional equivalent of εὐαγγελίζω. Paul reminds us that it is by the foolishness of what is *preached* that people are saved (1 Cor. 1:21). True, the focus of the participial construction (in Greek) is not on the foolishness of *preaching*, that is, the activity, but on the foolishness of "what was preached," that is, the gospel. Nevertheless, it is not surprising that Paul speaks of the foolishness of what was preached rather than the foolishness of what was taught, or discussed, or reasoned over. I hasten to add that the Bible includes a handful of verbs that pick up such activity. When all is said and done, however, the gospel is primarily displayed in heraldic proclamation: the gospel is announced, proclaimed, preached, precisely because it is God's spectacular news.

So when one hears the frequently repeated slogan, "Preach the gospel—use words if necessary,"[11] one has to say, as gently but as firmly as one can, that this is smug nonsense.[12] The element of truth in it, of course, is that words alone, divorced from the credibility that is gained by believers acting Christianly (i.e., in line with the gospel), may engender a great deal of cynicism. Even this element of truth is belied by advising readers to use words "if necessary": the very nature of announcing or proclaiming (good) news—whether εὐαγγελίζω or κηρύσσω—is that words are the primary medium. What we might call the logocentrism of Scripture is massively reinforced by the nature of the gospel itself: it is news, good news, to be proclaimed.[13]

---

[11]The expression is often attributed to St. Francis of Assisi. Mark Galli, the author of a biographical guide to Francis, has nicely debunked this notion (available online at http://www.christianitytoday.com/ct/2009/mayweb-only/120–42.0.html). Galli suggests that the saying has been attached to Francis because many of us entertain a highly sentimentalized mental picture of the man.

[12]First Peter 3:1 is not an exception. That passage says that husbands who do not believe the word may be won over by the Christian conduct of their wives. That presupposes that the words have been uttered (probably again and again!). Peter is not saying that the first priority is the conduct, with words added only if necessary.

[13]One recalls the recent blog post by Justin Taylor: "'Gospel' means 'good *news*.' If so, the saying 'Preach the gospel at all times; use words if necessary' makes about as much sense as telling a reporter he should broadcast the news but that words are optional" (available online at http://thegospelcoalition.org/blogs/justintaylor/).

The Gospel in Its Wide and Narrow Senses

For some time there has been interesting and sometimes complex discussion about how "big" or "robust" or "focused" the gospel really is. Some of this discussion, it must be said, pays too little attention to the gospel words and their contexts. Not long ago I had occasion to ask a Christian leader what he thought the gospel was. He replied that it is first of all about Christ dying on the cross for our sins, about people being justified before God because of that death, of people being born again. "But," he added, "there is also the gospel of social justice." That the Bible says quite a lot of important things about justice is not in dispute. The question, rather, is whether it ever labels the demand for justice "gospel." Frankly, it does not.

One or two well-known leaders in the emerging church movement have been known to draw attention to Jesus' teaching regarding the greatest two commandments—to love God with heart and mind and soul and strength, and to love our neighbors as ourselves (Mark 12:28–34). These commandments, they say, are the gospel. Far be it from any of us to depreciate what the Lord Jesus himself identifies as the greatest two commandments. Nevertheless they are not the gospel. The gospel is the news of what God has done; it is not the stipulation that God requires.

During the last couple of years *Christianity Today* has run a series of interesting essays under the rubric "The Christian Vision Project." Although the series has cast up numerous helpful insights, on the whole it has been remarkably devoid of robust biblical or theological reflection. Fleming Rutledge, for instance, projects the common polarization: "Some Christians emphasize the gospel as purely a matter of individual salvation; others see it essentially in terms of community and social justice."[14] She then goes on to point out how the leaders of the civil rights struggles believed, for the most part, that "God was on the move," and that conservative Christians need to give more attention to this dimension of the gospel. Sadly, she devotes no space to demonstrating that the Bible itself emphasizes the gospel "as purely a matter of individual salvation" or sees it "essentially in terms of community and social justice." That the Bible addresses both of these topics is beyond dispute. What is more doubtful is that the Bible treats *either* as the gospel. The better question asks the extent to which the Bible insists that there are both individual and communal *outcomes* to the preaching of the gospel, *neither of which is the gospel itself*. Another contribution, by David Fitch,[15] turns the table

---

[14]"When God Disturbs the Peace," *Christianity Today* 52, no. 6 (June 2008): 30–33, esp. 33.
[15]"Missional Misstep," *Christianity Today* 52, no. 8 (September 2008): 36–39.

on the series question, "Is our gospel too small?" by suggesting that the mainline emphasis on the breadth of the gospel has made it almost impossible to press individuals into receiving it at all. Doubtless there is some pastoral insight here, but once again there is no reflection on what the Bible explicitly says about the gospel.

Many writers begin with the expression "the gospel of the kingdom"— which, as we have seen, occurs only three times (and is hinted at in a fourth), all in Matthew's Gospel, though there are rough parallels in three other passages—and then expound the gospel entirely in terms of what they judge to be central to the kingdom. Commonly this is carried out by focusing on the social and communal values of the kingdom, and the word "kingdom" becomes an adjective: kingdom ethics, kingdom justice, kingdom community, kingdom gospel. It is certainly right to ask what is bound up with the kingdom. Immediately one learns from the canonical Gospels, however, that one of the dominant notes in passages about the kingdom is that, contrary to belief then popular, the kingdom of God was not yet coming as a climactic apocalyptic event, but was dawning more slowly, subtly, like wheat amid the weeds, like a treasure to be pursued, like yeast in a lump of dough—all brought about by King Jesus who goes to the cross, and reigns from the cross in a massive reversal of what "reign" commonly means among us human rebels, with Jesus not being served but serving and giving his life as a ransom for many. In other words, all that the canonical Gospels say must be read in the light of the plotline of these books: they move inevitably toward Jesus' cross and resurrection, which provides forgiveness and the remission of sins. That is why it is so hermeneutically backward to try to understand the teaching of Jesus in a manner cut off from what he accomplished; it is hermeneutically backward to divorce the sayings of Jesus in the Gospels from the plotline of the Gospels.[16]

A more helpful analysis of the problem of defining how broad or how focused the gospel is comes from a series of posts by Greg Gilbert on the 9Marks blog.[17] He argues that some passages where "gospel" is used focus on the message a person must believe to be saved, while others focus on the message that is "the whole good news of Christianity." (I would

---

[16]One thinks, for instance, of Brian D. McLaren, *The Secret Message of Jesus: Uncovering the Truth That Could Change Everything* (Nashville: W. Group, 2006). Similarly, Edmund K. Neufeld, "The Gospel in the Gospels: Answering the Question 'What Must I Do to Be Saved?' from the Synoptics," *Journal of the Evangelical Theological Society* 41 (2008): 267–96, concludes, "The Synoptics normally teach that one receives eternal life, or eschatological salvation, or that one enters the kingdom of God, by some kind of active obedience" (291).

[17]Greg Gilbert, "Appendix: The Gospel in Its Broader and Narrower Senses," in Mark Dever, J. Ligon Duncan III, R. Albert Mohler Jr., and C. J. Mahaney, *Proclaiming a Cross-Centered Theology* (Wheaton, IL: Crossway, 2009), 121–30; available online at http://blog.9marks.org/2009/03/what-is-the-gospel.html. See now Gilbert's popular-level book-length treatment, *What Is the Gospel?* (Wheaton, IL: Crossway, 2010).

prefer to say something like "the whole good news of what God has done in Christ Jesus and in consequence will do.") The first list includes, for example, texts like Acts 10:36–43; Romans 1:16–17; 1 Corinthians 1:17–18; 15:1–5—all passages having to do with the forgiveness of sins, how to be saved, how a person is justified, and so forth. In Gilbert's analysis, one group of believers, whom he designates Group A, rightly argues that "the gospel is the good news that God is reconciling sinners to himself through the substitutionary death of Jesus." A second group of believers, whom Gilbert designates Group B, rightly argues that "the gospel is the good news that God is going to renew and remake the whole world through Christ." The two groups tend to talk past each other. When a Group A believer asks the question What is the gospel? and hears the answer provided by a Group B person, inevitably he or she feels the cross has been lost; when a Group B believer asks the question What is the gospel? and hears the answer provided by a Group A person, inevitably he or she feels the response is too individualistic, too constrained, not driven by the sweep of eschatological expectation and ultimate hope.

The problem is subtler yet. Sometimes Group B Christians, rightly discerning the communal and eschatological sweep of the promises of a new creation, then work backward in time to the ordering of life *now*. There are surely right and wrong ways of doing this. The gospel of grace that Paul expounds in Ephesians, for instance, a gospel that reconciles to God those who are by nature children of wrath, also reconciles Jews and Gentiles into one new humanity, a new humanity being built up into a holy temple in which God dwells by his Spirit. The entailments of Christ's cross work must be developed in transformed, reconciled churches. But it is no help to blur the distinction between the church and the world, then blur the distinction between the gospel and its entailments, and conclude that the gospel *is* the message of racial reconciliation. The fact is that neither Paul nor anyone else in the New Testament says, "This is my gospel: that human beings are racially reconciled." I hesitate to write so boldly (though what I have said is, quite simply, the truth), because some might take what I have just written out of its context to justify indifference about racial reconciliation.

Gilbert's point is that although one can discern two foci in "gospel" texts—both having to do with the message of what *God* has done or is doing, but one more focused on Christ and his cross and how people are saved, the other taking in the broadest sweep of restoration in the new heaven and the new earth—these are not two separate and competing gospels, two distinguishable and complementary gospels. There is but one gospel of Jesus Christ. The narrower focus draws you to Jesus—his incarnation, his death and resurrection, his session and reign—as that from which all the elements of what God is doing are drawn. The broader focus sketches in the mighty dimensions of what Christ has secured. But this means that if one preaches the gospel in the broader sense without also emphasizing the gospel in the more focused sense of what God has done to bring about such sweeping transformation, one actually sacrifices the gospel. To preach the gospel as if this were equivalent to preaching, say, the demands of the kingdom or the characteristics and promises of the kingdom, both now in its inauguration and finally in its consummation, without making clear what secures the whole, is not to preach the gospel but only a tired and tiring moralism. Perhaps that is why Paul, talking of what the gospel is, feels free to identify the matters of first importance: Christ crucified and risen again.

The heart of the gospel is what God has done in Jesus, supremely in his death and resurrection. Period. It is not personal testimony about our repentance; it is not a few words about our faith response; it is not obedience; it is not the cultural mandate or any other mandate. Repentance, faith, and obedience are of course essential, and must be rightly related in the light of Scripture, but they are not the good news. The gospel is the good news about what *God* has done. Because of what God has done in Christ Jesus, the gospel necessarily includes the good that has been secured by Christ and his cross work. Thus it has a present and an eschatological dimension. We announce the gospel.

Yet we must be careful not to make the lines too crisp. Does preaching the gospel include, say, *the demand* for repentance, faith, and obedience? Some will respond negatively: the gospel focuses exclusively on what God has done. But what God has done in Christ Jesus has an intrinsic demand built into it. If in God's mercy Christ has come to bear the sins of his people and risen in vindicated glory to call together a new covenant people and usher in the consummated kingdom, intrinsic to God's work in Christ is an appeal for the ends of earth to turn to him and be saved. Their actual turning is not the gospel; their transformed living is not the gospel, however much it is the fruit of the gospel. But the "good news" is not just like the news, say, that there has been an accident on the Dan Ryan Expressway. That sort of news does not intrinsically demand anything of us (unless we happen to know the victims). By contrast, the gospel, the good news, has an *intrinsic* demand to it, such that our rearticulation of the demand for repentance, faith, and obedience cannot be divorced from the gospel itself. Of course, the demand for repentance, faith, and obedience *divorced from Christ and his cross work* is no more the gospel than hope for a consummation divorced from Christ and his cross work is the gospel. But I do not see how one can be said to be truly preaching the gospel without spelling out the demands that the gospel makes.

The Gospel Is Not Simply Important News, but Good News

There is another dimension to the discussion about the breadth of the gospel. Some have objected to rendering εὐαγγέλιον by "good news." It should be rendered, they say, simply by "news," for in some contexts the news is not good at all, but threatens judgment.[18] Mark 1:1 announces the beginning of the gospel of Jesus Christ, the Son of God, and promptly reports the preaching of John the Baptist, who preached Jesus. In preaching Jesus, the Baptist not only insisted that people believe in him, but warned that Jesus himself would separate out the chaff and burn it with unquenchable fire. This was huge news, big news—but it was *good* news only to those who believed. John the Baptist announced the dawning of the kingdom. But the dawning of the kingdom meant, for both John and Jesus, that everyone was called to repent: "Repent, for the kingdom of heaven is at hand." The announcement that Jesus is King cannot be isolated from the announcement that Jesus is the final Judge. On the last day, Jesus himself is the one who will tell some people to depart because he never knew them (Matt. 7:21–23). When Felix invites Paul to address the court "about faith in Christ Jesus" (Acts 24:24), the apostle discourses "about righteousness, self-control and the judgment to come," and in consequence Felix becomes afraid (24:25). If Paul were doing nothing but preaching good news, there would be no reason for Felix to fear. We have already seen that Paul speaks of "the day when God will judge the secrets of men and women by Jesus Christ"—according to Paul's *gospel* (Rom. 2:16). Much more evidence could be adduced.

What shall we make of this suggestion that εὐαγγέλιον is better thought of as "news" or "important news" than as "good news"? Five observations will help.

First, there is a valid dimension to the argument. Our ready talk of "good news" sometimes entices us to overlook the plentiful biblical threats, the promise of final judgment, and the raw alternative to receiving the salvation that Jesus alone brings. If John 3:16 tells us that God so loved the world that he gave his Son, John 3:36 reminds us that the wrath of God remains on all who reject the Son. The question, however, is whether

---

[18]Above all see D. Broughton Knox, "The Gospel of the New Testament," in *D. B. Knox: Selected Works* (Kingsford: Matthias Media, 2006), 3:9–60. In condensed form the material occurs as "What Is the Gospel?" *The Briefing* 343 (April 2007): 10–14.

being faithful to the biblical emphasis on the imminence of judgment warrants the conclusion that we should not think of the εὐαγγέλιον itself as good news, but take it, more neutrally, as highly important news.

Second, several passages speak clearly of how Jesus rescues us from the coming wrath (e.g., 1 Thess. 1:10; cf. 2 Thess. 1:8). Surely that is spectacularly good news.

Third, if one objects that it is not good news to those who perish, we must remember how even in the Old Testament there were instances where the news was perceived to be good by some and bad by others. That did not stop it from being good news; it merely stopped it from being good news to everyone.

Fourth, although etymology is rarely determinative for the meaning of a word, if our authors had simply wanted to say "news," one wonders why they did not use the simpler form ἀγγελία or the like, or, perhaps, for "great news," coin μεγαγγέλιον or something of that order.

Above all, fifth, one wonders if this neutral rendering of εὐαγγέλιον as "important news" focuses too much attention either on the *coming* of Jesus (whether in blessing or judgment) or on the *results* of the coming of Jesus (some are saved and some are lost), and too little attention on the *cross and resurrection* of Jesus. Paul says that God "uses us to spread the aroma of the knowledge of him everywhere. For we are to God the pleasing aroma of Christ among those who are being saved and those who are perishing. To the one we are an aroma that brings death; to the other, an aroma that bring life. And who is equal to such a task?" (2 Cor. 2:14–16). But Paul is certainly not suggesting that the aroma is neutral, a strong smell that might be either good or bad. It *is* good. If it is a stench to those who are perishing, that says something about them, not about the nature of the smell itself.

The Gospel Is Not Just for Unbelievers, but Also for Believers

The gospel is not a minor theme that deals with the point of entry into the Christian way, to be followed by a lot of material that actually brings about the life transformation. Very large swaths of evangelicalism simply presuppose that this is the case. Preaching the gospel, it is argued, is announcing how to be saved from God's condemnation; believing the gospel guarantees you won't go to hell. But for actual transformation to take place, you need to take a lot of discipleship courses, spiritual enrichment courses, "Go deep" spiritual disciplines courses, and the like. You need to learn journaling, or asceticism, or the simple lifestyle, or Scripture memorization; you need to join a small group, an accountability group, or a women's Bible study. Not for a moment would I speak against the potential for good of all of these steps; rather, I am speaking against the tendency to treat these as postgospel disciplines, disciplines divorced from what God has done in Christ Jesus in the gospel of the crucified and resurrected Lord. We have already caught a glimpse of the way our living ought to be tied to the gospel in the several texts that speak of living a life in line with the gospel, worthy of the gospel (e.g., Gal. 2:14; Phil. 1:27). Moreover, the gospel is regularly presented not only as truth to be received and believed, but the very power of God to transform (see 1 Corinthians 2; 1 Thess. 2:4).[19]

Failure to see this point has huge and deleterious consequences. I shall mention only two. First, if the gospel becomes that by which we slip into the kingdom, but all the business of transformation turns on postgospel disciplines and strategies, then we shall constantly be directing the attention of people *away* from the gospel, *away* from the cross and resurrection. Soon the gospel will be something that we quietly assume is necessary for salvation, but not what we are excited about, not what we are preaching, not the power of God. What is really important are the spiritual disciplines. Of course, when we point this out to someone for whom techniques and disciplines are of paramount importance, there is likely to be instant indignation. *Of course* I believe in the cross and resurrection of Jesus, they say. And doubtless they do. Yet the question remains: What are they excited about? Where do they rest their confidence? On what does their hope of transformation depend? When I read, say, Julian of Norwich, I find an example of just how far an alleged spirituality may be pursued, in medieval form, directly attempting to connect with God *apart* from self-conscious dependence on the substitutionary death and resurrection of Jesus—the very matters the apostle labels "of first importance." Wherever contemporary pursuit of spirituality becomes similarly distanced from the gospel, it is taking a dangerous turn.

One of the most urgently needed things today is a careful treatment of how the gospel, biblically and richly understood, ought to shape everything we do in the local church, all of our ethics, all of our priorities.

Second, a rich grasp of what it means to "preach the gospel" (εὐαγγε-λίζω) ought to be definitive for establishing our strategy.[20] We are con-

---

[19]See, e.g., Jerry Bridges, *The Gospel for Real Life: Turn to the Liberating Power of the Cross . . . Every Day* (Colorado Springs: NavPress, 2003); C. J. Mahaney, *Living the Cross-Centered Life: Keeping the Gospel the Main Thing* (Sisters, OR: Multnomah, 2006); Milton Vincent, *A Gospel Primer for Christians: Learning to See the Glories of God's Love* (Bemidji, MN: Focus, 2008).
[20]It is well worth reading Phillip D. Jensen, "The Strategy of God," *The Briefing* 358 (July–August 2008): 13–18.

stantly urged to develop mission strategies, vision documents, strategic plans, and the like. At a certain level, I am all for such encouragement, *so long as the primary strategy of God, disclosed in Scripture, is preserved*, such that what we are really doing is nothing more than carefully working out tactics in submission to the grand strategy that God himself has laid down. That gospel strategy, laid out again and again, is the heraldic announcement of the gospel. It is gospeling; it is εὐαγγελίζω in the most comprehensive sense.

"Evangelists" in the New Testament Are Simply Proclaimers of the Gospel

We should at this juncture cast another glance at εὐαγγελιστής, regularly rendered "evangelist." The advantage of this rendering is that it is almost an easy transliteration of the Greek. The problem is that in contemporary English "evangelist" calls to mind someone who preaches the "gospel" to unbelievers with the aim of seeing them converted. On this view, if Paul tells Timothy to do the work of an evangelist (2 Tim. 4:5), he is telling him that, among his other pastoral responsibilities, he is not to neglect trying to win outsiders to place their faith in Jesus. He must be not only a "pastor" but an "evangelist." Similarly, Philip "the evangelist" (Acts 21:8) may not be a systematic teacher of the Bible or a good pastor, but his calling is to win outsiders to faith in Jesus.

I have come to suspect, however, that we are in danger of reading back into the Greek word εὐαγγελιστής what the English transliteration "evangelist" means. If instead we understand εὐαγγελιστής in terms of its cognates εὐαγγέλιον and εὐαγγελίζω, then a εὐαγγελιστής is simply someone who proclaims the εὐαγγέλιον, the gospel. If we are not thinking of "the gospel" in some simplistic or reduced sense, then an "evangelist" (in the Greek sense), precisely because he or she focuses on proclaiming the gospel, will inevitably provide at least some such proclamation to outsiders, and thus be doing evangelistic work, the work of an "evangelist" in the contemporary sense. Nevertheless, such an "evangelist" will still be proclaiming the gospel even when such proclamation is not directed toward outsiders with the aim of their conversion. In short, an "evangelist" in the New Testament sense is simply a gospel-preacher, an announcer of the gospel. That is what Philip does: he begins with the text presented him by the Ethiopian eunuch (viz., Isaiah 53) and preaches Jesus: he has thought through how the Scriptures (for him, what we call the Old Testament) point forward to Jesus, his person and work, and the good news Jesus is and brings, and he announces this good news.

The Gospel Is Not Only Revelation, but Also History

In the contemporary climate it would be irresponsible of me not to mention an intrinsic, nonnegotiable element in this heraldic proclamation of the gospel. While we proclaim what God has done in Christ, there are elements of what God has done in Christ *that have taken place in history*; what we proclaim, in other words, are not only truths that can be known exclusively by revelation (e.g., God accepted Christ's death as a sacrifice on behalf of his people), but truths that we come to know, in large part, because they took place in history and were witnessed (e.g., Jesus died on a cross; he rose again the third day). Gospel proclamation cannot ignore either pole because both elements are intrinsic to the good news of what God has done in Christ.

This has been a challenge for a long time. For example, for more than a century many scholars have used the expression "salvation history" to mean something like "salvation as purported to be history in the Bible even though it is not real history that takes place in the space-time continuum."[21] There are many offshoots of this heritage. Most recently Luke Timothy Johnson, whose voluminous writings are invariably lucid and insightful, and frequently helpful, published an essay that, regrettably, falls along this axis. Johnson's title is "How Is the Bible True? Let Me Count the Ways."[22] He sketches out a rather stereotypical contrast between American fundamentalists, who are interested in defending the truth about details and establishing the veracity of predictive prophecy, and American modernists/liberals, who never get beyond the truth of "broad principles they derive from Scripture."[23] Johnson proposes "another approach to the truth of the Bible, one which works in and through literary imagination. Such an approach would focus neither on the world that created the Bible nor on the world that the Bible might predict, but rather on the world that the Bible *itself* creates."[24] This Johnson ties to postmodern epistemology, for "all great history and all great science depend on fantasy and imagination . . . just as every human life is driven by fantasy and imagination more than by sets of facts."[25] In this sort of world, what might we mean by suggesting that the Bible is true? We might ask if the Bible imagines a true world. This could not mean that the Bible imagines a true three-decker universe: we would have to let the language fire our

---

[21]See especially the important analysis of the problem by Robert W. Yarbrough, *The Salvation Historical Fallacy? Reassessing the History of New Testament Theology*, History of Interpretation 2 (Leidendorp: Deo, 2004).
[22]*Commonweal* 136, no. 10 (May 22, 2009): 12–16.
[23]Ibid., 13.
[24]Ibid., 14.
[25]Ibid., 15.

imagination to enable us to grasp the mythic dimensions of reality, the inner and outer dimensions of the universe. Again, do we read the Bible truly? This will demand that we undertake a reading that is responsible to the text, a reading that demands we recognize the Bible's otherness, a reading that is responsible to the community of other readers past and present. Yet again: Do we act truly as readers of the Bible? Are we morally competent to read? Among other things, this means we must "be in the process of being transformed by the world that Scripture imagines."[26]

Oh, dear. Among the questions that Johnson's piece calls to mind:

1. Does the Bible (assuming it has been given by God) *intend* primarily to incite the human imagination? Even at the human level, without appealing to God as the Bible's ultimate author: Do the biblical writers *intend* primarily to spark human beings to exercise their imagination? Or do they have a variety of goals, including provoking imagination, but also including, say, moral exhortation, disclosing the nature of God, making historical claims, and so forth? What precisely sanctions such a high valuation of imagination? One might argue that heavily symbol-laden literature, such as apocalyptic, is more vested in sparking the imagination than, say, genealogical lists. But even apocalyptic demonstrably has other intentions built into the genre. In other words, Johnson is short-circuiting serious discussion of literary genre. Granted that, say, Proverbs is not interested *primarily* in making historical claims, what forms of Scripture *are* interested in making historical claims? How does one decide? Johnson's essay begins to appear like a horrible piece of reductionism.

2. Can one afford to stand quite this loose to at least some biblical historical claims? Consider, for a prime example, the resurrection of Jesus from the dead. Paul goes so far as to say that if one believes this to have happened (i.e., in history), when in fact it has not happened (i.e., in history), then we remain in our sins, the apostles are liars, our faith is futile, and we are of all people most to be pitied (1 Cor. 15:14–19). In other words, in this context one of the validating factors in faith is the historical truthfulness of faith's object. In this domain, if you believe something that isn't true, then even if it fires your imagination, you remain an object of the apostle's pity. Must we not say something similar about the *historical* nature of the incarnation? Further, there are many theological, imagination-engendering arguments in the Bible that depend absolutely on the validity of a certain historical sequence (e.g., Galatians 3; Heb. 4:1–13; 7:1–25). For instance, if the Pentateuch is not telling the truth about entering into the "rest" of

---

[26]Ibid., 16.

the Promised Land, and if the report of it was not written until *after* Psalm 95, then the argument of Hebrews 4 makes no sense.

3. Johnson's argument is a profoundly intellectualist argument. We are not saved by stirring ideas about the death and resurrection of the incarnate Son of God, but by the death and resurrection of the incarnate Son of God. In other words, the heart of what saves us, the heart of the gospel, is not a set of ideas that fire the imagination, but the extratextual realities to which the text points. The Bible expounds the ideas, not because ideas themselves reconcile us to God, but because the ideas are about Christ, and he reconciles us to God. Once we get such matters clear in our minds, then of course we can say all sorts of useful things about the power of imagination, the use of words to stir and shape us, and so forth; that is, in part, what good preaching does. But if one says such things *at the expense of* the extratextual referentiality, it's a bit like trying to build a skyscraper after destroying the foundation. Only intellectuals can believe such nonsense *about Christianity*. If you are a Buddhist, of course, and someone proved that Gautama the Buddha never lived, it would not devastate your Buddhism: Buddhism depends for its believability not a whit on historical claims. But that cannot be said of Christianity. Either prove that Christ never lived, never died, and never rose from the dead, or declare that such details are unimportant, and you have destroyed Christianity utterly.

4. Should we not also reflect on how old-fashioned Johnson's treatment of epistemology appears to be? He seems to accept the absolute polarizations between modernism and postmodernism that were far more common in the 1970s and early 1980s, without acknowledging that modernism has become chastened modernism and is better analyzed in terms of critical realism, while postmodernism remains absurdist (If one can never speak of the truth, how does one speak of the truth of postmodernism?) unless it becomes "soft" postmodernism. While American undergraduates are still fed a régime of Lyotard, Derrida, and Foucault, university students in France have long since given them up. Johnson is capable of first-class biblical scholarship, but this piece is no more than kitsch.

What the Gospel Rescues Us From, and What It Saves Us For

Finally, if the gospel is the good news about what God is doing in Christ to rescue and redeem his rebellious image bearers, we must constantly bear in mind what it is we are being rescued from. The reason is that we will gain a clearer grasp of the gospel if we hold a clear grasp of the desperate situation the gospel addresses. If we see that we are guilty, we will understand that for the gospel to be effective it must clear us of our guilt; if we are alienated from God, we must be reconciled to him; if we stand under his judicial wrath, that wrath must be propitiated; if we are estranged from one another, we must be reconciled to one another; if the entire created order lies under the curse, the curse must be lifted and the created order transformed; if we are, morally speaking, weak and helpless (as well as guilty), we must be empowered and strengthened; if we are dead, we must be made alive; if the heart of our idolatry is abysmal self-focus and the de-godding of God, God must be restored in our vision and life to his rightful glory. In other words, we gain clarity regarding the gospel when we discern what the gospel addresses, what it fixes. If we focus on just one element of the desperate need—say, our broken horizontal relationships—then by ignoring all the other dimensions of our sin, including the most fundamental dimension, namely, our rebellion against God and the consequent wrath we have rightly incurred, we may marginalize or even abandon crucial elements of the gospel that address our sin. After all, the Bible speaks of the wrath of God more than six hundred times. If we cannot grasp how the gospel of Jesus Christ addresses all these dimensions of our desperate need, we will invariably promulgate an anemic and truncated gospel.

By the same token, many of the themes with which the gospel words are associated in the Scriptures bear out the same connection—the connection between plight and solution—from the other end. Thus the gospel not only forgives us, but holds out the hope of resurrection existence (Col. 1:22–23; 2 Thess. 2:14; cf. Romans 8; 1 Corinthians 15); the gospel of the cross not only justifies us, it is the power of God that transforms us (1 Thess. 1:5; 1 Cor. 1:18ff.). It not only draws faith from us, but commands our obedience (Rom. 10:16; 1 Pet. 4:17) in line with its truth (Gal. 2:14; Phil. 1:27; 1 Tim. 1:11). It calls us not only to preach the unique suffering of Christ, but also to participate in his suffering (1 Cor. 9:23; Phil. 3:9–10; 1 Thess. 2:8–9; 2 Tim. 1:8; Philemon 13). In it God himself is vindicated and his own righteousness revealed (Rom. 1:17; 3:21–26).

Small wonder the apostle boldly declares that he is not ashamed of the gospel "because it is the power of God that brings salvation to everyone who believes" (Rom. 1:16).

9

Christus Victor et Propitiator

The Death of Christ, Substitute and Conqueror

Sinclair B. Ferguson

What was the reason the Son of God appeared? In what sense did the cross put authorities to open shame? Why did the Son of God share in our humanity?

Hidden within these questions are, of course, phrases from texts of the New Testament that provide us with the answers: "The reason the Son of God appeared was to destroy the works of the devil" (1 John 3:8); "He disarmed the rulers and authorities and put them to open shame, by triumphing over them in him" (Col. 2:15); "Since therefore the children share in flesh and blood, he himself likewise partook of the same things, that through death he might destroy the one who has the power of death, that is, the devil, and deliver all those who through fear of death were subject to lifelong slavery" (Heb. 2:14–15).

The Reformed Tradition

Theologians of an antisupernatural bent will immediately dismiss such statements as mythological—modern man could hardly be expected to believe that the work of Christ terminated on the Devil.

For a variety of reasons, however, even systematic theologians in the Reformed tradition, who resolutely believe in the supernatural, have given relatively little attention to this aspect of Christ's work. The standard textbooks from Francis Turretin through Charles Hodge to Louis Berkhof[1] do not explore it in any detail, despite the insistence of the apostle John that the destruction of the Devil's works is a key reason for the incarnation.

There are at least three identifiable causes of this lack of interest:

1. The first is that the agenda for discussing the work of Christ was already settled in the twelfth century following the benchmark interpretations of the atonement by Anselm of Canterbury in his *Cur Deus Homo* (around 1090) and shortly afterward by Peter Abelard in his controversial response in his exposition of Romans 3:19–26.[2]

Anselm stressed that the atonement was a satisfaction of God's honor. Abelard, on the other hand, argued that the cross is the supreme manifestation of God's love. The dialectic thus set up has dominated theological discussion ever since, and interpretations of the meaning of Christ's death have therefore tended to argue that its effect terminates either on God or on man, the so-called objective and subjective views of the atonement. Post-Reformation controversies over the atonement have also been waged within these parameters, and the theme of Christ's defeat of Satan has been largely neglected.

2. In the Reformed thinking of the seventeenth century, some development of interest is apparent. Often this is expressed within the context of a shift of focus from *historia salutis* (history of salvation) to *ordo salutis* (order of salvation). That, in my judgment, is too simple an analysis.[3] But it is certainly true that there developed in the seventeenth century a sophisticated pastoral theology that gave greater attention to

---

[1]Turretin, in his exposition of the work of Christ in *Institutio Theologiae Elencticae*, topic 14, does not concern himself with the issue. Charles Hodge divides the theories of the atonement into five groups (*Systematic Theology*, 3 vols. [New York, 1872–73], 2:563–91), but deals with the effect of the atonement on Satan only under the heading "The Doctrine of Some of the Fathers." In this he is followed by B. B. Warfield (*The Person and Work of Christ* [Philadelphia: Presbyterian and Reformed, 1952], 356ff.), as well as by Berkhof, who lists seven views of the atonement, including the "Ransom-to-Satan" view; but his own exposition makes no reference to the effect of the cross on Satan (*Systematic Theology* [Grand Rapids: Eerdmans, 1939], 384–99). The Westminster Confession of Faith (1647), albeit briefly, does note in its chapter "Of Christ the Mediator" that the *protevangelium* is a reference to Christ's victory over the Devil, "wherein he was revealed and signified to be the seed of the woman, which should bruise the serpent's head" (8.6).

[2]Abelard's understanding is expressed in powerful eloquence. But even when it is recognized that the criticisms of Abelard's teaching, which begin with Bernard of Clairvaux, wrongly accuse him of holding an exemplary view of the atonement *simpliciter*, his exposition of Romans 3:19–26 makes redemption take place through the effect of divine love itself rather than by the payment made in love for the penalty for sin. See *A Scholastic Miscellany: Anselm to Ockham*, ed. and trans. E. R. Fairweather (Philadelphia: Westminster, 1956), 276–87, for an accessible translation. For a modern treatment of Abelard, see R. E. Weingart, *The Logic of Divine Love: A Critical Analysis of the Soteriology of Peter Abailard* (Oxford: Clarendon, 1970).

[3]It ignores, for example, the solid expositions of the person and work of Christ that are found in the writings of the seventeenth-century Reformed divines, particularly, but by no means exclusively, Thomas Goodwin and John Owen.

expounding the Christian's conflict with and victory over Satan than it did to Christ's triumph over him, albeit rooted in the latter. Titles such as John Bunyan's *The Holy War*, Thomas Brooks's *Precious Remedies against Satan's Devices*, and William Gurnall's *The Christian in Complete Armour* provide a commentary on this transition, as do the words of many later evangelical hymns (perhaps even more potent shapers of evangelical piety).

3. The third and probably most important reason is the discrediting of the early Fathers' view of how it is that Christ's work was a conquest of the Devil.

The Early Fathers

The teaching that the work of Christ was a conflict with and conquest of Satan is found in some of the greatest of the early Christian Fathers like Justin Martyr[4] and Irenaeus.[5] The latter particularly saw the work of Christ as a recapitulation of Eden, a rerun of the conflict between the Serpent and Adam and Eve. His ingenious development of Romans 5:12–21 and 1 Corinthians 15:20–49, in which he traced parallels not only between Adam and Christ but also between Eve and Mary, was to provide the basis for many later developments, not always with happy consequences.

It fell to Origen—Origen of the allegorical hermeneutic and the universal restoration—to develop the theme of Christ's death as a ransom paid to Satan. He rightly saw the death of Christ in Johannine terms as "the first blow in the conflict which is to overthrow the power of that evil spirit the devil, who had obtained dominion over the whole world."[6] But, as in other areas, Origen went astray because he gave the wrong answer to profoundly important and difficult questions. Lesser theologians would give more accurate answers than did Origen. In fairness to him, however, it should be said that he did seek to distinguish between the catholic faith (i.e., the orthodox teaching confessed by the whole church) and his own speculation.

---

[4]Justin writes of the righteous reversal of the fall in a style that would become beloved of the Fathers: "He became man by the Virgin in order that the disobedience which proceeded from the serpent might receive its destruction in the same manner in which it derived its origin." See *Dialogue with Trypho* 100, in *Ante-Nicene Fathers*, ed. A. Roberts and J. Donaldson, rev. A. C. Coxe, 1:249 (cf. also 45:4; 49:8; 85:1; 103:6; 125:4).
[5]See *Adversus Haereses* 3.22.3–4, in *Ante-Nicene Fathers*, 1:455, and for his working out of the Eve-Mary parallel, 5.19.1, 1:547.
[6]Origen, *Contra Celsum* 7.16, in *Ante-Nicene Fathers*, 4:617. Origen affirms that the Devil was deceived by the cross. At the same time, however, Christ also was a spotless sacrifice that served as a propitiation before God. Origen thus seems to have grasped the necessity of both propitiation to deal with guilt and a redemption price to set us free from bondage, but failed to see the actual nature and logic of the inner connection between propitiation and liberation.

The classic exposition of the "ransom to Satan" view, and the one most easily caricatured, is to be found in Gregory of Nyssa (335–395), the youngest of the three Cappadocian Fathers.[7] In his *Great Catechism* he describes how Satan accepted the incarnate Christ as a ransom for the souls of men, but did so without taking account of the fact that Christ's humanity concealed his deity. Like a ravenous fish, Satan gulped down the flesh of Christ, only to discover that with that flesh he had swallowed the hook of indestructible deity by which he himself would be destroyed! Thus he was both deceived and defeated.[8]

Although the problem of the righteousness of such deception troubled even his friend Gregory Nazianzus,[9] Gregory of Nyssa rejoiced in its fittingness. After all, this was the *lex talionis* par excellence: an eye for an eye! How fitting that in overcoming the one who himself had used deceit to entrap Eve in the garden of Eden, God himself proved to have more guile than even the Serpent! By way of an *apologia pro Deo*, as it were, Gregory argues that just as two persons may mix poison with food for different motives—one to murder, the other as an antidote to bring healing—so, since this deception is the antidote to the fall, it is altogether righteous.

In any event, Gregory of Nyssa's case was in his own eyes somewhat ameliorated by his sharing with Origen (and Clement of Alexandria before him)[10] the expectation of a universal salvation, Satan included. The deceived deceiver would also in the end be undeceived and redeemed.

This ransom tradition recurs in Ambrose of Milan and Rufinus.[11] In it Augustine also stood,[12] albeit giving it a more sophisticated and acceptable interpretation. It endured until the time of Anselm and Abelard, but thereafter largely, although by no means entirely, disappeared.[13]

---

[7]Basil of Caesarea and his younger brother, Gregory of Nyssa, along with their friend Gregory Nazianzus.

[8]See his *Great Catechism*, chaps. 22–26 (*Ante-Nicene and Post-Nicene Fathers*, 2d series, 5:492–509). The idea of deception was by no means original to Gregory. Traces of it can be found as early as Ignatius of Antioch, *To the Ephesians*, 19.

[9]Gregory was cautious about overextending the ransom idea to the point of identifying a recipient. The idea that it was paid to the Devil he believed was "outrageous." "But if the price is offered to the Father, I ask first of all, how? For it was not the Father who held us captive. . . . What remains to be said shall be covered with a reverent silence." *Second Oration on Easter* 22, in *Ante-Nicene and Post-Nicene Fathers*, 2d series, 7:431.

[10]See his *Stromateis* (Miscellanies) 1.17, in *Ante-Nicene Fathers*, 2:319–20.

[11]Ambrose saw the hungering of Christ in the desert as a deliberate snare set to catch the Devil. For the views of Rufinus, see his *Commentary on the Apostles' Creed* 16, *in Nicene and Post-Nicene Fathers*, 3:550.

[12]See, for example, *On the Trinity* 13.13–15.

[13]Interesting examples of its reluctance to die can be found in such figures as Lancelot Andrewes (1555–1626) as well as in the Puritan evangelical tradition.

Aulén's *Christus Victor*

Sixty years ago, in a famous series of lectures, later to be published as *Christus Victor*,[14] the Swedish Lutheran theologian Gustav Aulén (1879–1977) sought to rehabilitate the Patristic view, purged of its excesses. He argued that historical theology was in error to see either the Anselmic or the Abelardian views, the so-called objective and subjective views, as the classical interpretations of the work of Christ. On the contrary, he argued that the "dramatic view"—Christ's work viewed as the conquest of the powers of darkness—was the truly classical teaching. This, he maintained, was in fact the view of Martin Luther.

Aulén stated that his only interest in this question was historical and not apologetic. But it seems clear enough from the theological construction in his later systematic study *The Faith of the Christian Church*[15] that he operated within his own theological agenda. In arguing that Luther held to the dramatic view he was denying that Luther's view was merely a continuation of the Anselmic view. The implication was that later orthodoxy, with its emphasis on the idea of satisfaction, was neither the view of historic Christianity nor that of the founder of Lutheranism. The net effect of Aulén's exposition, then, was to deny that penal substitution is the classical atonement doctrine of the Christian church as a whole.

In arguing thus, Aulén was surely mistaken on several counts. In particular he missed the key point in the Patristic teaching. Curiously, Charles Hodge grasped this point well, although he dismissed the teaching as such. (Indeed, Hodge confuses Gregory of Nyssa with Gregory Nazianzus in the process, a further indication of his lack of real interest in the theme.) But Hodge nevertheless recognized a key point: the Patristic view "was intended only as a solution to the question *how Christ delivers us from the power of Satan.*"[16]

The Fathers, therefore, had asked a correct and important question, to which they gave an imperfect answer. Hodge, as I think we shall see, actually knew the right answer, but did not show sufficient interest in the question. Aulén, by contrast, for all the benefits of his drawing attention to this theme, did not well state the right question and failed to elicit the biblical answer to it.

Against this background I want to explore this important dimension of Christ's work by examining (1) the Gospel record of Christ's conflict with

---

[14]Gustav Aulén, *Christus Victor*, trans. A. G. Hebert (London: S.P.C.K., 1931).

[15]Gustav Aulén, *The Faith of the Christian Church*, trans. E. H. Wahlstrom (Philadelphia: Muhlenberg, 1948).

[16]Hodge, *Systematic Theology*, 2:565, my emphasis.

Satan and (2) the apostolic understanding of his victory, before drawing (3) some brief but important conclusions.

The Gospel Record of Christ's Conflict with Satan

In the Gospels, the whole of Christ's ministry is seen as a conflict with Satan. This is obviously true of the Synoptic Gospels, where the multidimensional conflict motif is a dominant theme.

The Synoptic Gospels

All three Synoptics open their accounts of our Lord's public ministry by reference to his baptism and temptations. In his baptism he is anointed with the Spirit for messianic ministry. Immediately he is driven out into the wilderness to be tempted by the Devil.

Geerhardus Vos has rightly commented here that in interpreting Christ's temptations the mistake has frequently been made of viewing them primarily as analogous to our own.[17] But whatever exemplary lessons may be appropriately learned (and there are many), it must be emphasized that this event is sui generis—of a unique kind. It is deliberately set before us as a recapitulation and a rerun of the Eden temptation.

This is evident from various signals in the narrative. In Luke the baptism of Jesus as Messiah, climaxing with the words from heaven, "You are my beloved Son" (Luke 3:22), leads to the temptation narrative by way of his genealogy. This significantly traces Jesus back to Adam, who is also seen as "the son of God" (Luke 3:38). The setting of this last Adam's temptations—in the wilderness, surrounded by wild beasts and starving from forty days without nourishment—not only echoes the testing of Moses and Elijah in the wilderness, but points up the stark contrast between the conditions in which this Man faces Satan and those in which the first Adam was confronted by him. The hissing of the tempter "Take, eat" is set in a context a diameter removed from Eden.

But what is even more striking is the Synoptic writers' stress on the fact that Jesus, as the Man full of the Spirit (Luke 4:1), was driven into the desert *by the Holy Spirit*. Temptation does not merely "come" to him; he goes to it. He attacks it. "He entered the lists in the name of His whole Church," writes Calvin.[18] He appears as the divine champion, as it were, entering into enemy-occupied territory under the guidance of the Spirit as the director of spiritual intelligence. Miss this, and we miss the point of the narrative: it is a declaration of war, an attack on the one who claims

---

[17]Geerhardus Vos, *Biblical Theology* (Grand Rapids: Eerdmans, 1948), 358.
[18]John Calvin, *Harmony of the Gospels Matthew, Mark and Luke*, ed. D. W. Torrance and T. F. Torrance, trans. A. W. Morrison (Edinburgh: Saint Andrews Press), 1:135.

to be the ruler of this world (Luke 4:6). Rather than overcome Jesus, Satan is comprehensively defeated, and in sovereign manner dismissed by his conqueror with the words, "Away from me, Satan!" (Matt. 4:10 NIV).

This is Jesus' first step in binding the strong man. He is armed in order that he may systematically despoil him of his goods (Matt. 12:29) and "undeceive" the nations (Rev. 20:3) although the final victory will not be won without continued opposition (Luke 4:13). The heel of the Seed must be crushed before the head of the Serpent is.

These three Gospels also give us hints of the reverberations Christ's victory caused in the kingdom of darkness. The fact that the wilderness conflict is soon followed in each of the Synoptics by the widespread manifestation of the presence of demons and the exorcism of them is surely significant here. This is the sign that the kingdom of God has come (Matt. 12:28; Luke 11:20). The demons know who Jesus is (Luke 4:41) and react in terror in the consciousness that he has already won a signal victory and plans to finalize it. They know, fear, and confess that he has come to destroy them (Mark 1:24; 5:7; Luke 4:34; 8:28).

This preview of Christ's final victory is probably the most coherent explanation for the extraordinary measure of demonic activity that seems to have taken place during our Lord's ministry. It is not essential for a legion of demons to indwell a man in order to destroy him. One is sufficient. But Legion experiences multiple indwelling because it is Christ and his kingdom, not simply Legion as an individual, who is the object of satanic assault (Mark 5:1–20). Yet even here we are given only fleeting glimpses of the nature of this conflict. In Luke 10:18, for example, Jesus tells his disciples who are rejoicing in the power they have exercised over the demons, that he had seen "Satan fall like lightning from heaven."

What is sometimes overlooked in this connection is that the Gospel narratives give us two signals which at first sight—but only at first sight—seem to be in tension with each other. The first signal is that Satan's efforts, through various means, appear to be geared to preventing Jesus from going to the cross. Is it reading too much into the text to see the hand of Satan behind the infant pogrom instituted by Herod? John's words in Revelation 12:4, "And the dragon stood before the woman who was about to give birth, so that when she bore her child he might devour it," suggest such a view. Another such effort is the wilderness temptation in which Satan seeks to divert Christ from the way of the cross as an act of obedience to his Father. Later Satan speaks again, this time through the lips of Simon Peter, seeking to divert Jesus from the path of the Suffering Servant Messiah (Mark 8:33).

The second signal paradoxically reveals Satan's activity in actually seeking to bring the cross to pass, but now as an act of his satanic will rather than an act of Jesus' obedience. This he does through human instrumentality, doubtless including the religious leaders, but specifically through Judas Iscariot, into whose heart, Luke tells us, Satan comes to complete his malevolent work (Luke 22:3).

In both of these aspects Satan is intent on opposing the solemn resolve of Christ to give his life as "a ransom for many." This in itself should have prevented the Fathers from the excesses of their "ransom to Satan" theory. The truth is, the Gospels view Satan as *opposing the payment of a ransom.*

It is clear, then, in the Synoptic Gospels, that the whole of Jesus' ministry is one of conflict. Here two quotations from my own New Testament teachers are apposite: "In acting as the bringer of the kingdom of God," writes I. Howard Marshall, "Jesus placed himself in total opposition to the kingdom of Satan. . . . The task of Jesus was to dethrone 'the prince of this world.' . . . From this point of view the whole of the ministry of Jesus was a campaign against Satanic power."[19] In a similar vein are the words of A. M. Hunter:

> The emergent picture of the Chief Figure in the campaign, so far from being that of a high-souled teacher patiently indoctrinating the multitudes with truths of timeless wisdom, is rather that of the Strong Son of God, armed with his Father's power, spear-heading the attack against the devil and all his works, and calling men to decide on whose side of the battle they will be.[20]

What is not so clear in the Synoptics, however, is an explanation of the *means* by which Christ overcomes Satan. To this question we will return. But we ought not to lose sight of it as we consider the conflict theme as it is traced in John's Gospel.

John's Gospel

The Gospel of John is sometimes divided into two sections or volumes: chapters 1–12, the Book of Signs; chapters 13–21, the Book of Glory.[21] Significantly the first volume ends with a focus on the conflict motif, which will be developed in volume 2: the time for "the judgment on this world" had come. Here is a development of the Synoptics' driving back

---

[19] I. H. Marshall, *The Work of Christ* (Exeter: Paternoster, 1969), 31.
[20] A. M. Hunter, *Introducing New Testament Theology* (London: SCM , 1945), 17–18.
[21] E.g., by Raymond Brown, *The Gospel according to John*, Anchor Bible, 2 vols. (New York: Doubleday, 1966, 1970).

of Satan in the wilderness. Jesus now advances further, saying, "Now will the ruler of this world be cast out" (John 12:31).

Here too, consistent with the testimony of the Synoptics, the final denouement of the conflict focuses on the activity of Judas Iscariot. In John 13:2 we are told that Satan had already put it into his heart to betray Jesus. By 13:27, Satan has entered him—a satanic indwelling, set significantly in the very context in which Jesus will speak to his disciples about his indwelling of his disciples by the Spirit (John 14:20). But just as in the Synoptics our Lord regally dismissed Satan and his demons from his presence, so in the same way in John he gives the sop to Judas and sovereignly dismisses him to his task: "What you are going to do, do quickly" (John 13:27). He is in as complete control of the situation here as he had been in the temptations. He chooses the moment when the conflict will reach its ultimate climax.

In this context C. H. Dodd's interpretation of John 14:30–31 is theologically attractive, although it does not seem to have found favor among other New Testament commentators as a solution to the puzzling setting of the words: "The ruler of this world is coming. He has no claim on me, but I do as the Father has commanded me, so that the world may know that I love the Father. Rise, let us go from here." As the narrative stands, the disciples do not appear to go anywhere until 18:1. "When Jesus had spoken these words, he went out" has, as its most natural antecedent of place, the same location as the entire previous conversation (from 13:1). Dodd makes the suggestion that the words ἐγείρεσθε ἄγωμεν ("Rise, let us go from here") be understood in a quasi-military sense. According to Dodd, the verb ἄγω is used in extrabiblical sources of marching, of advancing.[22] Interestingly, the same words occur in a conflict context in Mark 14:41–42: "The Son of Man is betrayed into the hands of sinners. Rise, let us be going [ἐγείρεσθε ἄγωμεν]; see, my betrayer is at hand." The picture is of Jesus advancing to meet his oncoming human enemy, not as a hapless victim but as one who has "found new resources of arms. . . . He advances of His own accord to meet death," as Calvin finely says.[23] C. F. D. Moule agrees, if with less vivid expression: "Jesus sees the situation as a great campaign—the battle of the kingdom of God. His friends are summoned to 'advance' like soldiers entering battle. But it is a battle in which Jesus will not use physical force but only the weapon of loyalty to God's will."[24]

---

[22] C. H. Dodd, *The Interpretation of the Fourth Gospel* (Cambridge: Cambridge University Press, 1953), 407–9.
[23] Calvin, *Harmony of the Gospels*, 3:155–56.
[24] C. F. D. Moule, *The Gospel according to Mark*, 2d ed., Cambridge Bible Commentary (Cambridge: Cambridge University Press, 1969), 118.

In John, however, it is not simply Judas whom Jesus goes to meet. He goes to do battle with Satan: "The ruler of this world is coming. . . . Rise! Let us advance to meet the enemy!"

We have now seen that in the Synoptics Satan suffers defeat in the wilderness, is repelled on later occasions, and finally enters into Judas (Luke 22:3). But his purposes are resisted and overcome by Jesus. No further exposition is offered to us to explain the mechanism of his defeat.

On the other hand, while omitting the wilderness temptations, John does provide such added exposition. The judgment and driving out of Satan will take place not simply by Jesus' refusal of Satan's temptations and his storming of the positions that the demons have occupied. Rather it will be specifically when the Son of Man is lifted up on the cross (John 12:31–32). It is in the event of his going to the Father *by way of a death thus interpreted* that Jesus arises and advances to meet and defeat his enemy (John 14:31).

In John that triumphant military advance begins when Judas appears with a detachment of soldiers carrying weapons (John 18:3). In response to Jesus' lordly ἐγώ εἰμι, I am! (His words echo—indeed more than echo— Exodus 3:14: Jesus is Yahweh!), the advancing forces draw back and fall to the ground (John 18:5–6). As in the last day, so now, Christ's human enemies are "destroyed"—blown away as it were by the breath of his divine mouth (cf. 2 Thess. 2:8!). But the supernatural enemy himself must be faced in the agony of death.

This lends special significance to the words "It is finished" (John 19:30; cf. 17:4). Following them, in regal dignity, Christ "bowed his head and gave up his spirit" (John 19:30). Thus, in John, Satan is driven out as the King is exalted.

John therefore advances the insight given to us in the Synoptics. By means of the complex of actions involved in his crucifixion Christ judges, condemns, and casts out Satan. But again we are forced to probe more deeply into the question: How? By what means does the death of Christ thus affect Satan?

It should now be a little clearer why it was possible for the early Fathers of the church to give a misleading answer to this question. Christ is set forward in the Gospels as one who conquers Satan. But there is little reflection on precisely how he does so. In the proclamation of the gospel the *fact* of Satan's downfall is of greater immediate moment than the precise *mechanism* by which it takes place. But when we turn to the rest of the New Testament, we do receive more specific light on this aspect of the work of Christ.

The Apostolic Understanding of Christ's Victory

In the Epistles the nature of Christ's conquest of Satan is more fully explored. Here we may focus on the three key biblical statements with which we began.

1 John 3:8

John says that "the reason the Son of God appeared was to destroy the works of the devil." This statement is paralleled by 1 John 3:5: "He appeared to take away sins, and in him there is no sin." What lies behind these words is explained in 1 John 4:10: God "sent his Son to be the propitiation for our sins." Interestingly, 1 John 3:5 is also reminiscent of Jesus' statement in John 14:30 that "the ruler of this world is coming. He has no claim on me."

For John, then, the work of Christ has these two aspects: it is a propitiatory sacrifice made by the sinless one; in addition, in that same act, the Devil's work is destroyed by the one in whom he could find no foothold. The altar of propitiation of God is at one and the same time the arena of conflict against and victory over Satan. In essence then, for John, since it is by the cross that Satan is defeated, it is through the propitiatory character of Christ's sacrifice that this is accomplished.

Hebrews 2:14–15

This hypothesis is strengthened by the teaching of Hebrews 2:14–15. Here the author underlines that it is not only by Christ's incarnation, viewed narrowly as his assuming of our flesh, but particularly and specifically by his death that the Devil, the one who has the power of death, is destroyed or disarmed.

There is an echo in these words of the principle enunciated first in Genesis 3:15—whether one sees that promise as a specific prophecy of Christ, as the Fathers did, or as Calvin seems to have done, as a more general prophecy that is in fact consummated in Christ. The Serpent[25] crushes the heel of the Seed of the woman; but the Seed of the woman crushes the head of the Serpent. Victory is gained only through injury; it is in being crushed that Christ crushes Satan. The Prince of Death is defeated by means of Christ's "defeat." As Johann Bengel somewhere notes, "Jesus, who suffered death, conquers; the Devil, who wields death, succumbs to it."

But how is it that Christ's death is thus the means for Satan's overthrow? The answer lies in the book of Hebrews' understanding of the nature of

---

[25]It is surely significant here that it is the Serpent himself, not the seed of the Serpent, who crushes the heel of the Seed of the woman. The antithesis at this point is not the seed of the Serpent against the Seed of the woman, but the Serpent ("you") against the Seed of the woman.

that death. The constant appeal of Hebrews to the sacrificial system of the Old Testament underlines that Christ's death is a sacrifice for the guilt of sin. Man is destined to die and face judgment because death implies guilt, and guilt evokes condemnation and condign punishment. This is why Christ was "offered once to bear the sins of many" (Heb. 9:28; cf. Isa. 53:12). He has made purification for our sins (Heb. 1:3) as the sacrifice that has turned aside God's wrath, making "propitiation for the sins of the people" (Heb. 2:17).

The death that overthrows Satan is specifically the Godward sacrificial and propitiatory death of Jesus for the guilt of his people. The result is that his blood cleanses their guilty consciences (Heb. 9:14). Believers now have confidence to enter into the presence of God, by his blood (Heb. 10:19). This boldness, or confidence, in approaching God is the antithesis of the fear of death that the guilt of sin and the knowledge of judgment had engendered (Heb. 2:14–15).

For the author of Hebrews, this death not only cleanses guilty consciences but also liberates from fear because it destroys ("renders ineffectual") the one who held the power of death (Heb. 2:14–15). It must therefore be Christ's death as a propitiatory sacrifice that renders powerless the one who has brought humanity into captivity to fear.

It is the older exegetes who tend to provide serious reflection on this dual aspect of Christ's work. Here is a sample from the Puritan genius John Owen:

> When the sinner ceaseth to be obnoxious unto death, the power of Satan ceaseth also. And this every one doth that hath an interest in the death of Christ: for "there is no condemnation unto them that are in Christ Jesus," Rom. viii.1; and this because he died. He died for their sins, took that death upon himself which was due unto them; which being conquered thereby, and their obligation thereunto ceasing, the power of Satan is therewith dissolved.
>
> (1) The first branch of his power consisted in the bringing of sin into the world. This is dissolved by Christ's "taking away the sin of the world," John i.29; which he did as "the Lamb of God," by the sacrifice of himself in his death, typified by the paschal lamb and all other sacrifices of old.
>
> (2) Again, his power consisted in his rule in the world, as cast under sin and death. From this he was cast out, John xii.31, in the death of Christ. When contending with him for the continuance of his sovereignty, he was conquered, the ground whereon he stood, even the guilt of sin, being taken away from under him, and his title defeated. . . .

(3) Nor can he longer make use of death as penal, as threatened in the curse of the law, to terrify and affright the consciences of men: for "being justified by faith" in the death of Christ, "they have peace with God," Rom. v.1. Christ making peace between God and us by the blood of his cross, Eph. ii.14, 15, 2 Cor. v.19–21, the weapons of this part of his power are wrested out of his hand, seeing death hath no power to terrify the conscience, but as it expresseth the curse of God.

(4) And, lastly, his final execution of the sentence of death upon sinners is utterly taken out of his hand by the death of Christ, inasmuch as they for whom he died shall never undergo death penally. And thus was Satan, as to his power over death, fully destroyed by the death of Christ.[26]

Colossians 2:14–15

This is confirmed in the third passage, Colossians 2:14–15. Here, forgiveness through the cross coalesces in Paul's thought with the disarming of Satan. Through the cross sins are forgiven (Col. 2:13); in the cross Christ disarms Satan and triumphs over him. A similar combination of ideas is found in Colossians 1:13–14. In Christ the saints are rescued from the dominion of darkness and brought into Christ's kingdom; in Christ we have redemption through the forgiveness of sins. Thus the work of Christ which brings forgiveness effects redemptive deliverance and does so precisely because it brings forgiveness.

But how does the propitiation which effects forgiveness simultaneously effect release from Satan?

It was here that many of the Fathers took their wrong turn, assuming that if the work of Christ terminated on Satan and the ransom effected deliverance from Satan, then the ransom itself must have been paid to Satan. They did not give careful enough attention at this point to the reasons why Satan is able to exercise his tyrannical dominion over the human race, or to the biblical witness that Christ triumphed over Satan by removing the guilt and dominion of sin that made his reign possible.

Few commentators explore this aspect of the theological (in addition to the grammatical) significance of Colossians 2:14–15. One who did in a previous generation was George Smeaton (1814–1889), professor of exegetical theology in New College, Edinburgh. He comments on this passage in a way that reminds one of Owen before him and, as we shall see, John Murray after him:

---

[26]John Owen, "The Epistle to the Hebrews," in *The Works of John Owen*, ed. William H. Goold, 24 vols. (Edinburgh: Johnstone & Hunter, 1850–1855; reprint by Banner of Truth, 1965, 1991), 20:450ff.; numeration added for clarification.

How did the cross effect the results recounted in the three several clauses [that Christ disarmed the powers and authorities, made a public spectacle of them, and triumphed over them in the cross]? I answer: Sin was the ground of Satan's dominion, the sphere of his power, and the secret of his strength; and no sooner was the guilt lying on us extinguished, than his throne was undermined, as Jesus Himself said (John xii.31). When the guilt of sin was abolished, Satan's dominion over God's people was ended; for the ground of his authority was the law which had been violated, and the guilt which had been incurred. This points the way to the right interpretation; for all the mistakes have arisen from not perceiving with sufficient clearness how the triumph could be celebrated on His cross. . . . It was on God's part at once a victory and a display of all God's attributes, to the irretrievable ruin, dismay, and confusion of satanic powers.[27]

"Paul with good reason, therefore," writes Calvin, "magnificently proclaims the triumph that Christ obtained for himself on the cross, as if the cross, which was full of shame, had been changed into a triumphal chariot."[28]

That it is by Christ' propitiation and expiation that Satan is conquered and people are set free is both confirmed and uniquely portrayed in the vision of John in Revelation 12. Here the Evil One is named and described in the sinister multifaceted nature of his work: as the ancient Serpent who has now grown into the dragon (12:3–4, 7–9) who sought to destroy the Christ, but failed; as Satan, the prosecuting counsel who accuses believers (v. 4); as the Devil, who hurls his fiery darts of temptation against them (v. 4); and as the accuser of the brethren who fills his diary with a record of their sins in order to blackmail them (v. 10).

Yet the brethren overcame him. How? "By the blood of the Lamb," said the loud voice in heaven, "and by the word of their testimony, for they loved not their lives even unto death" (Rev. 12:10–12). This is the sacrificial blood of the Lamb slain (Rev. 5:6), by which they were freed from their sins (Rev. 1:5).

Thus, through his death as it dealt with our guilt and its implications in relationship to God, Christ disarms him who had the power of death, and releases his people from their lifelong bondage to the fear of death (cf. Heb. 2:15).

---

[27]George Smeaton, *The Apostles' Doctrine of the Atonement* (Edinburgh: T. & T. Clark, 1870), 307–8.
[28] John Calvin, *Institutes of the Christian Religion*, ed. John T. McNeill, trans. Ford Lewis Battles (Philadelphia: Westminster, 1960), 2.16.6.

This explains how those who, by Christ's blood, overcame Satan, did not love their lives so much as to shrink even from death (cf. Rev. 12:11). From fear of it they had been most gloriously delivered!

Here, then, the theology and the experience of the early Christians were one.

Implications of Christ's Victory
In the light of this, we may briefly draw attention to four implications of the victory of Christ.

Theology
Any adequate understanding of the atonement must include within it this aspect of Christ's disarming of the powers of darkness. It is personally gratifying in this context to be able to quote some apt words from the late Professor John Murray:

> Redemption from sin cannot be adequately conceived or formulated except as it comprehends the victory which Christ secured once for all over him who is the god of this world, the prince of the power of the air. . . . It is impossible to speak in terms of redemption from the power of sin except as there comes within the range of this redemptive accomplishment the destruction of the power of darkness.[29]

A comprehensively biblical exposition of the work of Christ recognizes that the atonement, which terminates on God (in propitiation) and on man (in forgiveness), also terminates on Satan (in the destruction of his sway over believers). And it does this last precisely because it does the first two.

In this respect, Aulén's view was seriously inadequate. He displaced the motif of penal satisfaction with that of victory. But, as we have seen, in Scripture the satisfaction of divine justice, the forgiveness of our sins, and Christ's defeat of Satan are not mutually exclusive but complementary. Each is an essential dimension of Christ's work. Each is vital for our salvation, and each provides an aspect of the atonement from which the other aspects may be seen with greater clarity and richness. Moreover, these aspects are interrelated at the profoundest level. For the New Testament the dramatic aspect of the atonement involves a triumph that is secured through propitiation. Aulén therefore failed to recognize that in setting the dramatic view over against the penal view of the atonement he inevitably enervated the dramatic view of its true dynamic.

---

[29]John Murray, *Redemption—Accomplished and Applied* (Grand Rapids: Eerdmans, 1955), 50.

Doxology

Worship is theology set to music. The praises of Christ are christology in song since we praise him for who he is and for what he has done. Praise is therefore energized and expanded by an increased vision of his accomplishments, and correspondingly limited whenever it fails to show forth the totality of his work.

The fact that Christ's death terminated on Satan and delivers us from him needs to be recovered in our spirituality and our worship. Here, *ordo salutis* concerns appear to have dominated our hymnology, to the neglect of *historia salutis*. To a degree that is true even of Luther's great hymn "A Mighty Fortress Is Our God." Although it does speak of "the Right Man on our side" fighting for us, the emphasis is on the present aspect of his kingly ministry rather than on his already accomplished triumph. True, Christ exercises his kingly office on behalf of his people. But even more fundamentally, he has already fought for us in his life, death, and resurrection and gained the victory.

The motif of Christ's conflict and victory is more often expressed in the ancient Catholic tradition, and in more modern guise in John Henry Newman's hymn "Praise to the Holiest in the Height," theologically deficient though it may be in other respects:

> O loving wisdom of our God!
> When all was sin and shame,
> A second Adam to the fight
> And to the rescue came.
>
> O wisest love! that flesh and blood,
> Which did in Adam fail,
> Should strive afresh against the foe,
> Should strive and should prevail.
>
> O generous love! that He who smote
> In man, for man, the foe,
> The double agony in Man
> For man should undergo.[30]

We surely need to rekindle this classical theme in our praises today.

---

[30]From his poem "The Dream of Gerontius," written in 1865 and later set to music by Edward Elgar for his oratorio of the same name.

Ministry

The significance of Hebrews 2:14–15 for pastoral counseling can hardly be overestimated. The thesis of the author is that through the fear of death men and women are subject to lifelong bondage. Our deepest fear, the fear of death, is a mother phobia which gives birth to all the phobias of life. "An overdose of fear," writes Calvin again, with insight, "comes from ignorance of the grace of Christ."[31] The angst of man, and many of the spiritual neuroses of our day, must therefore be analyzed in these terms as aspects and symptoms of bondage to Satan, or as aspects of his malevolent efforts to hinder Christian believers and to rob them of their joy in Christ. The ministry of the Word, and the work done confidentially in pastoral counseling, must accordingly be sensitive to this whole dimension of Christian life and warfare, and provide "precious remedies against Satan's devices."[32]

Christ is not offered to us in the gospel as a panacea for our fears. But he is a deliverer from that bondage to Satan which engenders the fear of death and gives rise to all manner of other fears. Pastoral counseling must always therefore have the one great fear in view, and Jesus Christ the deliverer as the divinely appointed remedy. We need to appreciate at the deepest level the fact that the words "fear not" were so frequently on his lips.

Missiology

There is a final implication of Christ's victory over Satan. Through the judgment of Satan and his being cast out, all men are now to be drawn to the Savior—that is, men and women from every tribe and tongue and people and nation. In some definitive sense we can say that since Christ has finished his work, and in the light of his death, resurrection, ascension, and the gift of the Spirit, Satan is already bound and the undeceiving of the nations has begun (Rev. 20:2–3). This is implied in the wording of the Great Commission. All authority in heaven and earth is now Christ's; we are to penetrate "all nations" with the gospel (Matt. 28:18–20). Satan has been overcome. Jesus has asked the Father for the nations as his inheritance in accordance with the promise of Psalm 2:8. He has poured out the Spirit on all flesh to bring it to pass, and now waits for his enemies to be made his footstool.

---

[31]John Calvin, *The Epistle of Paul the Apostle to the Hebrews and The First and Second Epistles of St. Peter*, trans. W. B. Johnston, Calvin's Commentaries, ed. D. W. Torrance and T. F. Torrance (Grand Rapids: Eerdmans, 1963), 31 (*ad* Heb. 2:15).

[32]The allusion is to the book of this name by the Puritan author Thomas Brooks.

No doubt what Richard B. Gaffin Jr. has, in another connection, called "the staging principle that marks the coming of the kingdom of God"[33] is operative here also, and we must continue to pray, "Your kingdom come. . . . Deliver us from [the] evil [One]." But in a profound sense, surely, the kingdom has already been established. Christ has already bound the strong man armed and is even now, through the sword that issues from his mouth (that is, the Word in the hands of the Spirit whom Christ has breathed out on us), spoiling his goods.

In the light of their sense of Christ's victory over Satan and the powers of darkness, the early disciples went into the world proclaiming Christ the Redeemer and Conqueror. If we share their appreciation for Christ's triumph, we will also share their passion to proclaim it. For we live in the light of this fact: Jesus has triumphed over Satan.

We too may therefore ask the questions Paul does in Romans 8:31–35. Here, significantly, in the light of the cross seen as a triumph over Satan, Paul uses the personal interrogative pronoun. Does he have Satan specifically in mind? *Who* can be against us? *Who* will bring any charge against those whom God has chosen? *Who is he* that condemns? *Who* shall separate us from the love of Christ?

Satan certainly cannot; for by his death Christ disarmed him of the weapons that would otherwise enable him to do so. Christ has conquered! And in him we are more than conquerors!

> No, in all these things we are more than conquerors through him who loved us. For I am sure that neither death nor life, nor angels nor rulers, nor things present nor things to come, nor powers, nor height nor depth, nor anything else in all creation, will be able to separate us from the love of God in Christ Jesus our Lord. (Rom. 8:37–39)

Christus Victor indeed!

Dear John,
These reflections on the work of Christ are gladly dedicated to you, in gratitude for your ministry, example, and friendship over the years.

---

[33]Richard B. Gaffin Jr., *Perspectives on Pentecost* (Phillipsburg, NJ: Presbyterian and Reformed, 1978), 40.

To a remarkable degree the implications that flow from a biblical under-standing of Christ's propitiation and victory have suffused your life and ministry. Theology, doxology, missiology, ministry have formed central threads in your exposition of the seamless garment of the gospel of Jesus Christ.

It is a privilege to be included in the company of friends who honor you.

With them and with countless others I thank God for you and for all he has done for you, in you, and through you. *Soli Deo gloria*!

Warmly and gratefully, in Christ,
Sinclair

10

THE ROLE OF RESURRECTION IN THE ALREADY-AND-NOT-YET PHASES OF JUSTIFICATION

G. K. Beale

I am happy to contribute to this Festschrift for John Piper.[1] I am grateful to John because his writings have influenced me to understand more deeply the glory of God as it is revealed in Scripture. I am also indebted to his writings on justification.

This chapter is not an exhaustive essay on the nature of justification, but rather a discussion of how the resurrection of Christ—and the resurrection of believers represented by Christ—helps us to better understand both the inaugurated eschatological phase and the consummated eschatological phase of justification.

The Inaugurated Eschatological Nature of Justification in Relation to Resurrection
Christ the Righteous, Representative Last Adam Commences the New Creation

I have argued elsewhere that Christ as the righteous last Adam who represents the saints is a good example of the eschaton breaking into

---

[1]This essay is adapted from a larger chapter in my forthcoming book tentatively titled *Eschatology and the New Creation: A Biblical Theology for the New Testament* (Grand Rapids: Baker Academic, a division of Baker Publishing Group). It is reprinted in this revised form by permission.

history.[2] Christ's role as the last Adam indicates that another new creation has begun, breaking into the old age of the fallen creation. Complete righteousness was something humans could achieve only in the eternal new creation, which has begun in Christ and vicariously through Christ for his people.

The Cross of Christ Begins the Eschatological Judgment

Before focusing on resurrection in connection to justification, there is another aspect of inaugurated eschatology that also deserves mention: the final judgment that was to occur at the very end of history has been pushed back into history at the cross of Christ. This is expressed in Romans 3:21–26:

> [21] But now apart from the Law the righteousness of God has been manifested, being witnessed by the Law and the Prophets, [22] even the righteousness of God through faith in Jesus Christ for all those who believe; for there is no distinction; [23] for all have sinned and fall short of the glory of God, [24] being justified as a gift by His grace through the redemption which is in Christ Jesus; [25] whom God displayed publicly as a propitiation in His blood through faith. This was to demonstrate His righteousness, because in the forbearance of God He passed over the sins previously committed; [26] for the demonstration, I say, of His righteousness at the present time, so that He would be just and the justifier of the one who has faith in Jesus.[3]

God in his "forbearance" has "passed over the sins previously committed," which, according to Old Testament and Jewish expectation, would be punished in the last great judgment. This great judgment, however, has begun to be executed upon the Messiah on behalf of his people (v. 25) before the watching world, which shows that, despite delaying judgment for a time during the Old Testament epoch, God does punish sin after all and is vindicated as righteous. This is the case despite the fact that the judgment that Jesus suffers is on behalf of those who believe (vv. 22, 26). Thus the eschatological judgment has begun in Jesus but will be consummated in the judgment of unbelievers at the end of the age, directly preceding the establishment of the new creation. Hence the final judgment is staggered for "all the world," which is "accountable" to God for its sin: the sin of believers is judged first in Christ's death in the first century, and unbelievers suffer this judgment in their own persons at the climax of history.

---

[2]See my forthcoming *Eschatology and the New Creation*.
[3]Unless otherwise indicated, Scripture quotations in this chapter are from the NASB.

Further confirmation that Romans 3 is speaking of the eschatological judgment that commences with Jesus on behalf of the faithful comes from observing the *inclusio* consisting of end-time temporal language framing verses 21–26. Verse 21 starts with "now" (Νυνì), and verse 26 contains virtually the same word but in expanded form, "the present [now] time" (τῷ νῦν καιρῷ). The first "now" of verse 21 highlights that the recently "manifested . . . righteousness of God" was prophetically "witnessed" to by the Old Testament, which indicates that this "righteousness" is part of prophetic eschatological fulfillment (which is pointed to further by the similar statement in Rom. 16:25–26). The "now," therefore, indicates the commencement of latter-day expectations. Likewise, "the present [now] time" of verse 26 is also linked to a climax of the demonstration of the righteousness of God in contrast to the past period of redemptive history when "God passed over the sins previously committed."

While there are varying uses of "now" in the New Testament (a logical use, a reference to mere present time, etc.), the eschatological use of "now" to demarcate the beginning of an age in contrast to a former old age occurs elsewhere in Paul and the New Testament. The combination of "now" with "time" appears in Paul six other times, most of them clearly in connection to latter-day contexts.[4] The use of "now" by itself can often have the same temporal association.[5] Thus, Paul's use of an eschatological "now" in Romans 3:21 and 26 fits naturally into his other such uses.

The Resurrection of Christ Inaugurates the Eschatological Vindication

In addition to the two inaugurated latter-day facets of justification discussed above, I want to focus on a third aspect. Resurrection is one of the most highly charged inaugurated eschatological concepts in the New Testament, since, for example, the resurrection that was to occur at the

---

[4]The use in Romans 8:18 is part of the time period when resurrection existence for God's people is beginning (8:10–11), as is their experience of the end-time Spirit (8:5–17, 22–23). Romans 13:11–12a is fairly straightforward in this respect: "Do this, knowing the time, that it is already the hour for you to awaken from sleep; for now salvation is nearer to us than when we believed. The night is almost gone, and the day is near." Second Corinthians 6:2 refers to the present time, when the latter-day Isaiah prophecy about God helping his servant was beginning realization (Isa. 49:8), which continues the earlier reference to the "now" of the inaugurated resurrection life and new creation, when proper evaluative judgments about Christ will be made (5:14–18). The "now" of 2 Thessalonians 2:6 is the same time when "the mystery of lawlessness is already at work," which is a beginning fulfillment of the end-time opponent prophecy of Daniel 11:36 (for further discussion of resurrection and the Spirit in Romans 8, as well as of 2 Corinthians 5:14–6:2 and 2 Thessalonians 2, see my forthcoming *Eschatology and the New Creation*). The uses in Romans 11:5 and 2 Corinthians 8:14 are not explicitly eschatological but are susceptible of such a meaning.

[5]The more obvious examples of this use of "now" (νῦν) are Romans 16:25–26; Ephesians 3:5, 10; Colossians 1:26; and outside of Paul, see John 4:23; 5:25; 12:31; 1 John 2:18; 4:3; with respect to the alternate form of "now" (Νυνì), see Romans 7:6; 1 Corinthians 15:20; Ephesians 2:13; Colossians 1:22; outside of Paul see Hebrews 9:26: "Otherwise, He would have needed to suffer often since the foundation of the world; but now once at the consummation of the ages He has been manifested to put away sin by the sacrifice of Himself."

very end of the world has begun in Jesus' bodily resurrection. Jesus' own resurrection was an end-time event that "vindicated" or "justified" him from the wrong verdict pronounced by the world's courts. The vindication of God's people against the unjust verdicts of their accusers was to happen at the eschaton,[6] but this has been pushed back to Christ's resurrection and applied to him.

1 Timothy 3:16

Particularly pertinent in this regard is 1 Timothy 3:16:

> By common confession, great is the mystery of godliness:
>
> > He who was revealed in the flesh,
> > *Was vindicated [declared righteous = ἐδικαιώθη]*[7] *by the Spirit,*
> > Seen by angels,
> > Proclaimed among the nations,
> > Believed on in the world,
> > Taken up in glory.

The phrase "was vindicated by the Spirit" refers to the Spirit's raising Christ from the dead (as in Rom. 1:4), which was a vindication from the wrongful verdict[8] that had been issued against him by the sinful human court and a declaration of his righteousness.[9] Geerhardus Vos has said in this connection:

> Christ's resurrection was the *de facto* declaration of God in regard to his being just. His quickening bears in itself the testimony of his justification. God, through suspending the forces of death operating on Him, declared that the ultimate, the supreme consequence of sin had reached its termination. In other words, resurrection had annulled the sentence of condemnation.[10]

Acts 17:31

Acts 17:31 expresses a similar notion: "because He has fixed a day in which He will judge the world in righteousness through a Man whom He has appointed, having furnished proof to all men by raising Him from the dead." The proof that God "will judge the world" on the last "day"

---

[6]As prophesied by Isaiah 40–53, discussed later in this chapter.
[7]Here and in the following discussion some Greek words cited singly will be put not in their lexical form but in the exact form in which they occur in the Greek text.
[8]For the unjust verdict against Christ, see Matthew 27:24; Mark 15:4, 14; Luke 23:24; John 18:29–31; 19:4; Acts 13:27–29; 1 Timothy 6:13.
[9]For persuasive elaboration on this point, see Richard B. Gaffin Jr., *The Centrality of the Resurrection: A Study in Paul's Soteriology* (Grand Rapids: Baker, 1978), 119–22. Acts 13:27–30 likely refers to the same vindication but without the technical language of "justification."
[10]Geerhardus Vos, *The Pauline Eschatology* (Grand Rapids: Eerdmans, 1953), 151.

by his "appointed" human agent is that this agent of judgment has been "raised from the dead." That is, the logic appears to presuppose that Christ's resurrection has demonstrated him to be just and, therefore, one who will exercise justice at the last judgment.

Isaiah 50

This thought of vindication by God from an unjust verdict that comes from giving life after death has precedence in Isaiah. For example, the Servant Song in Isaiah 50 portrays the Servant as having been "obedient" to God's call to suffer unjust persecution (50:4–6) and unjust accusation (vv. 8–9) from which he will be "vindicated" by God (vv. 7–11) and be seen as truly righteous. In this respect, verses 8–9 affirm,

> He who *vindicates* [δικαιώσας] Me is near;
> Who will contend with Me? . . .
> Who is he who condemns Me?

The Lord "helps" the Servant (vv. 7, 9) to overturn the false condemnation, thus vindicating his Servant.

Isaiah 53

Likewise, the famous Suffering Servant passage of Isaiah 53 makes the same point conceptually, and the Greek Old Testament (LXX) specifies that God will "justify [δικαιῶσαι] the just one [the Servant]"[11] from the wrongful legal persecution under which he will suffer (cf. 53:11 with vv. 7–9, 12), showing him to be absolutely righteous after all. This vindication consists in causing the Servant to enjoy victory even after and despite his own death (vv. 10–12; e.g., v. 12a, "I will allot Him a portion with the great, and He will divide the booty with the strong"). Though he would die (vv. 5, 8–9), he would be given this victory, which includes seeing life after his painful death:

> He will see His seed [LXX has "long-lived seed"],
> He will prolong His days . . .
> He will see [light].[12] (vv. 10–11)

---

[11]The Hebrew at this point has "the righteous one, my servant, will justify the many"; in place of the Hebrew "the righteous one . . . will justify," the LXX has δικαιῶσαι δίκαιον, which is best rendered "to vindicate [justify] the just one" (so L. C. L. Brenton, *The Septuagint with Apocrypha: Greek and English*; likewise almost identically the New English Translation of the Septuagint; though it is possible to render the Greek by "the just one to justify," it would be awkward, as well as not being in line with the parallelism of the preceding two infinitives). The LXX here is probably interpreting the Hebrew by saying that the one who will justify will himself be justified, which may be inspired by the preceding Servant passage in Isaiah 50:8 ("He who vindicates Me is near").

[12]1QIsa[a], 1QIsa[b], and 4QIsa[d] all add "light" after "he will see" : "he will see light." The LXX has almost identically "to show him light."

The New Testament doubtless understands this victory to be resurrection. Since Isaiah says elsewhere that the Spirit was to be the empowering agent of the Servant's ministry (Isa. 11:2; 42:1; 48:16; 61:1), it is not unreasonable to think that this Spirit would play a role in vindicating this ministry.

This all comes very close to what 1 Timothy 3:16 has said above. Even though Paul likely does not allude here to Isaiah, Isaiah stands as precedence even before the time of Paul for thinking that the Messiah's "justification/vindication" would consist, at least partly, in his resumption of a prosperous life after his death.[13]

The Meanings of δικαιόω. It is fitting at this point that a word be said about the possible meanings of δικαιόω, which is often translated in Paul as "justify." The standard lexicon of the Greek New Testament gives the following ranges of meaning: (1) "to take up a legal cause, show justice, do justice, take up a cause"; (2) "to render a favorable verdict, vindicate"; (3) "to cause someone to be released from personal or institutional claims that are no longer to be considered pertinent or valid, make free, pure"; (4) "to demonstrate to be morally right, prove to be right."[14] All of the uses in Paul can be reduced to "vindicate" or "declare righteous," both referring to rendering a favorable verdict. This translation is as applicable to Christ as it is to believers. The obvious difference is that the resurrection vindicates Christ's innocence, thus overturning the unjust verdict against him. On the other hand, the saints were justly accused of sin and guilt and sentenced to death. Nevertheless, they have been vindicated by Christ's work, declared not guilty but innocent because he suffered the penalty of death due to them and represents them in his resurrected being with his own innocence (i.e., righteousness), which has been vindicated by his own resurrection. In this respect, Michael F. Bird has likewise rightly focused on Christ's vindication from a wrong verdict by resurrection with which believers are identified: "Thus, believers are justified only for the reason that they share a corporate solidarity with the justified Messiah and what is true of him is true of God's people,"[15] "because they are 'in-Christ'"[16]—though, as noted above, unlike Christ, they themselves deserved the guilty verdict.

---

[13]I have also found that Michael F. Bird, "Justification as Forensic Declaration and Covenant Membership," *Tyndale Bulletin* 57 (2006): 115, has made the same observation from Isaiah 53:11. Bird's essay is available online: http://www.tyndalehouse.com/TynBul/Library/TynBull_2006_57_1_06_Bird_JustificationCovenantPaul.pdf.

[14]*A Greek-English Lexicon of the New Testament and Other Early Christian Literature*, ed. F. W. Danker, 3d ed. (Chicago: University of Chicago Press, 2000), 249.

[15]Bird, "Justification as Forensic Declaration," 114.

[16]Ibid., 120.

Romans 4:25

The relation between the believer and Christ's resurrection as a "justi-fying" event is reflected in Romans 4:25: "He who was delivered over because of [διὰ] our transgressions, and was raised because of [διὰ] our justification." Some commentators understand the dual use of διὰ to be identical ("because of"), while others understand the first διὰ to be causal ("because of") and the second as final or purposive ("for the sake of," "with a view to"). Some commentators suggest that Christ's resurrec-tion is mentioned after his vicarious death because the former confirms that the latter is effective, since he was no longer bound by the penalty of death himself.

Though the last clause of this verse has been debated because of its vagueness, Richard Gaffin gives probably the most persuasive assessment of it, arguing that we must do justice to both sides of the parallelism within the context of Paul's broader theology. Jesus' dying "on account of our transgressions" identified him with believers in the *punishment* due for those transgressions. Correspondingly, Christ's resurrection "on account of our justification" identifies him with saints in the *verdict* of justification, which was given to him for his establishing of righ-teousness. The unexpressed assumption in verse 25b, Gaffin argues, is that "Jesus' resurrection is his justification."[17] Since Christ's resurrection justified him, believers are justified in Christ when they identify with his resurrection.[18]

The Future Consummated Eschatological Nature of Justification in Relation to Resurrection

To understand better the believers' vindication we must also look at how it is related to the very end of the age and the believers' own resurrection. The following represents the "not yet" aspect of the justification of the Christian, which remains to be consummated in the future. There are three aspects of future "justification," each of which has three parts (fig. 2). I will be able to develop only the first and part of the third of these three aspects in this article.[19]

---

[17]Gaffin, *Centrality of the Resurrection*, 123.
[18]Gaffin acknowledges that his point was anticipated, among others, by H. Heppe, *Reformed Dogmatics* (London: Allen and Unwin, 1950), 499, who says, "Just as by giving the Son to death the Father actually condemned all our sins in him, the Father also by raising Christ up from the dead, acquitted Christ of our sin-guilt and us in Christ. . . . So Christ's resurrection is our righteousness, because God further regards us in the perfection in which Christ rose" (citing Rom. 4:25 in support).
[19]A fuller development of all three aspects can be found in my forthcoming *Eschatology and the New Creation*. Though part 2 will not be developed here, brief comment is warranted. Whereas the announce-ment of the believer's justification/vindication in the present age is directed only to the community of the

Fig. 2.

Action	Means	Location
justification/vindication	bodily *resurrection* of believers	publicly displayed
justification/vindication	God's *announcement*	publicly announced before all the world
justification/vindication	*good works* by believers	publicly demonstrated before the entire cosmos

The Final Resurrection as Justification/Vindication of the Saints

God's people are "vindicated" from the sentence of condemnation due their sin when they believe at any point during the age leading up to Christ's final return.

Our Vindication Is Definitive. On the one hand, this vindication is once for all and definitive. It is definitive in the sense that believers are declared *not guilty* from God's perspective because Christ suffered the penalty of their sin. And, just as definitively, they are also *declared righteous*, and accordingly righteousness is imputed to them because Christ achieved representative righteousness for them in his resurrected person and was vindicated from injustice (showing he had been righteous all along), a vindication with which the saints are also identified.

Our Vindication Is Incomplete. But on the other hand, there is a sense in which this vindication is not completed, especially in the sense that the world does not recognize God's vindication of his people. Just as happened to Jesus, the ungodly world has judged the saints' faith and obedience to God to be in the wrong, which has been expressed through persecution of God's people. As was the case with Christ, so with his followers, their final resurrection will vindicate the truth of their faith and confirm that their obedience was a necessary outgrowth of this faith. That is, though they had been declared righteous in God's sight when they believed, the world continued to declare them guilty. Their physical resurrection will be undeniable proof of the validity of their faith, which had already declared them righteous in their past life.

This follows the pattern of Christ's own vindication from the unjust verdict pronounced against him. He had already been perfectly innocent during his life leading up to death and before his vindicating resurrection.

church, this announcement of the church's final vindication is made publicly to the cosmos at the very end (see Rom. 2:13). Thus, God's verbal declaration of righteousness has an already-and-not-yet dimension.

Likewise, saints will have been already declared as completely righteous by God before their deaths and their resurrection, the latter of which will vindicate that their prior justified status was in fact true despite the world's verdict about their faith. Of course, the vindication of *their* righteous status is different in one important respect from the vindication of *Christ's* righteous standing: they were originally guilty of sin. Therefore their vindication is not a defense of their own innate righteousness but rather an *identification* with Christ's righteousness (especially as represented by his resurrected person), with which they have been clothed, and a *vindication* that the works they performed through the Spirit, while not being perfect, were faithful deeds and not evil, as the world had judged them.

Romans 5:18b

The link between the saints' justification and their final resurrection is also expressed in Romans 5:18b: "Through one act of righteousness there resulted justification leading to life[20] for all men" (my translation). This refers to the notion that those who are truly justified will receive resurrection life, which begins spiritually in the present (Rom. 8:6, 10–11) and will be completed with physical regenerated life in the future (Rom. 8:11, 13, 23). This "life" is not merely a necessary consequence of justification but, I would suggest, functions to demonstrate that the one resurrected has already been justified in the past age. It is especially the final form of bodily resurrection that is the final vindication of true justifying faith, the reality of which the world and the powers of evil have denied. The final resurrection shows that the world was wrong and that the saints were right after all in placing their justifying faith in Christ.

Romans 8:29–30

Romans 8:29–30 also suggests the very close link between justification and resurrection:

> [29] For those whom He foreknew, He also predestined to become conformed to the image of His Son, so that He would be the firstborn among many brethren; [30] and these whom He predestined, He also called; and these whom He called, He also justified; and these whom He justified, He also glorified.

The inextricable linking here of sonship (v. 29), justification, and glorification (v. 30) supports the notion that justification leads to glorification.

---

[20]It is not unusual to take the phrase "justification of life" in Romans 5:18 as genitive of result (e.g., see D. Moo, *Romans 1–8* [Chicago: Moody, 1991], 355, who also cites others in support. This is borne out by Romans 5:21b: "even so grace might reign through *righteousness to eternal life* through Jesus Christ our Lord."

The glorification of Romans 8:30 should be understood probably in the light of Romans 8:17–18, 21, since this is the last time Paul has mentioned "glory" (three times). There "glory" clearly refers to the glory of their final resurrection bodies (as clarified by vv. 21–23). Thus, though "glorification" is placed directly after "justification" without any statement about their precise relation, it is likely that verse 30 includes the notion that justification will result in the final glorification of saints in their resurrection bodies. Another way to say this is that the glorious final resurrection of true saints is an eschatological declaration that necessarily results from and vindicates their prior justified status.[21]

Romans 8:32–34
There remains one more relevant passage to discuss, which follows right on the heels of Romans 8:17–30. The text is Romans 8:32–34:

> [32] He who did not spare His own Son, but delivered Him over for us all, how will He not also with Him freely give us all things? [33] Who will bring a charge against God's elect? God is the one who justifies; [34] who is the one who condemns? Christ Jesus is He who died, yes, rather who was raised, who is at the right hand of God, who also intercedes for us.

The crucial wording for our purposes comes in verses 33–34, which are an allusion to the Greek version of Isaiah 50:8 (fig. 3).

Fig. 3.

Isaiah 50:8 (LXX)	Romans 8:33–34
"for *He who has justified* [ὁ δικαιώσας] Me draws near . . .	"God is *the one who justifies* [ὁ δικαιῶν];
who is the one condemning[22] [τίς ὁ κρινόμενός] Me? . . .	*who is the one condemning* [τίς ὁ κατακρινῶν]?

22

It is probable, as a number of commentators think,[23] that the Romans passage is a clear reference to the Isaiah passage, which is validated by

---

[21]It would appear too in the directly following verses (8:31–34) that mention of Christ's death *and resurrection* as the basis for believers not being able to be condemned is significant, on which see the directly following discussion.

[22]For rendering κρίνω as "condemn, judge, pass judgment, punish, contend," see J. Lust, E. Eynike, and K. Hauspie, *A Greek-English Lexicon of the Septuagint*, pt. 2 (Stuttgart: Deutsche Bibelgesellschaft, 1996), 267–68.

[23]So F. F. Bruce, *Romans*, Tyndale New Testament Commentaries (Leicester: Inter-Varsity, 1989), 169; C. E. B. Cranfield, *The Epistle to the Romans*, International Critical Commentary, 2 vols. (Edinburgh: T. & T. Clark, 1975), 1:437–38; J. D. G. Dunn, *Romans 1–8*, Word Biblical Commentary (Dallas: Word Books, 1988), 503; B. Byrne, *Romans*, Sacra Pagina (Collegeville, MN: Liturgical Press, 1996), 276; see also R. Jewett, *Romans*, Hermeneia (Minneapolis: Fortress, 2007), 541; and E. Käsemann, *Commentary*

observing that nowhere in all of the Greek Old Testament does the verb *justify* (indeed, in the participial form) occur in syntactical relation to the phrase "who is the one condemning?" The verb δικαιόω, rendered above as "justified," can just as easily be translated "vindicated."[24]

This part of the Servant Song from Isaiah 50 was discussed above with respect to the vindication of the messianic Servant prophesied by Isaiah. We saw that the Servant was obedient to the divine call to suffer unjust persecution (vv. 4–6) and unjust accusation (vv. 8–9), though he would be "vindicated" by God (vv. 7–11) and viewed as in the right after all. We concluded that Jesus' resurrection was the means that God used to vindicate him in overturning false and unjust condemnation.

Now, however, in Romans 8:33–34 Paul applies this prophecy about the Servant's vindication to believers. What was prophesied of the Servant's vindication now becomes true of the believers' vindication. The likely reason for this application is that Christ, as the Servant, represented his people by his obedience through wrongfully imposed suffering in the face of false accusation and condemnation followed by vindication. Whereas Christ's vindication occurred through his resurrection, the believers' vindication occurs through their identification with both his death and his vindicating resurrection from the dead. Both Christ's death and resurrection form the basis of the believer's justification/vindication, as is apparent from noticing that the mention of their justification and lack of condemnation in verses 33b–34a is sandwiched between references to Christ's death and resurrection. Verse 32 refers to God who "delivered Him up for us all" and asks "how will He not also with Him freely give us all things?" This "giving of all things" because they are "with Him" certainly includes reference to their identification with the resurrected Christ through whom come all future blessings of the new creation, which has been inaugurated by Christ's resurrection.[25] Verse 34b repeats this

---

on Romans (Grand Rapids: Eerdmans, 1980), 248, who both cite others seeing a clear reference to Isaiah 50:8, though they themselves are tentative about seeing an echo.

[24] See Lust, Eynike, and Hauspie, *Lexicon of the Septuagint*, pt. 2, 115.

[25] The phrase "will He not also with Him freely give us all things?" likely includes the final resurrection hoped for in 8:18–25, and this probably relates directly to not being condemned in the future, as well as the present, the latter of which is the emphasis of verses 30–34. Strikingly, see Byrne, *Romans*, 276, who says that when verse 32 is seen in light of the following lists (vv. 35–39) and particularly in view of 1 Corinthians 3:21–23, where the apostle says "all things are yours" with a focus on inheritance of the coming world, then "all things" in Romans 8:32 likely refers to the physical inheritance of the earth (already anticipated in Rom. 4:13), which belongs to Christians as "fellow-heirs with Christ" (Rom. 8:17; cf. "with Him [Christ]" in v. 32), and Romans 8:17b–23 sees such heirship focused on the obtaining of resurrection bodies in a new creation (so likewise see the τὰ πάντα in 2 Cor. 5:17–18, though underscoring inaugurated eschatology with specific reference to the "new creation," which has been launched through Christ's resurrection). So also Dunn, *Romans 1–8*, 502, who sees all of the coming new creation to be in mind. So similarly, Cranfield, *Romans*, 436–37, though he finally sees Romans 5:10 as the closest parallel, where "saved by His [Christ's] life" is the focal point, which is a reference to being saved by his resurrection life.

double reference to Christ's death and resurrection: "Christ . . . died . . . [and] was raised" and "is at the right hand of God," which is a further explanation of how they are identified "with Him" from verse 32. This shows further that the "giving of all things" in verse 32 includes identification with the benefits of Christ's resurrected and ascended position of rule at God's right hand.

> [God] delivered Him up for us all . . .
> > how will [God] not also with [the resurrected Christ] freely give us all things?

> > It is God who justifies.
> > Who is to condemn?

> Christ . . . died . . .
> > [and] was raised [and] is at the right hand of God.

The significance of this dual mention of Christ's death and resurrection both before (v. 32) and after (v. 34b) mention of God's justification/vindication of saints and their noncondemnation (vv. 33–34b) is that the guilty verdict of the world against them and the world's unjust persecution of them have begun to be overturned in Christ's suffering and condemnation on their behalf; furthermore, their already-and-not-yet identification with Jesus' resurrected status as the obedient Servant, which has overturned the world's guilty verdict on him, has begun to overturn the world's verdict against them, a guilty verdict especially expressed through the persecution described in Romans 8:35–39. In contrast to the world's "persecution" and Christians' being "put to death all day long" (Rom. 8:35–36), the final bodily resurrection of the saints represents the climactic stage of their vindication against the world's unrighteous evaluation of them. That the saints' physical resurrection at the eschaton is in mind here is evident from the expression "will He [God] not also with Him [the resurrected Christ] freely give us all things" (8:32), which, as noted above, continues the theme of the "redemption of the body" from 8:17–25. At this time when they receive "immortality" and "eternal [resurrection] life," they will also be "glorified" (Rom. 8:30; cf. 2:7, 10) and given "honor" before those who had unrighteously mistreated and shamed them.[26]

That neither "angels nor principalities . . . shall be able to separate" believers "from the love of God" in Christ (Rom. 8:38–39) indicates that

---

[26]See Bird, "Justification as Forensic Declaration," 122, with whom I have found significant agreement here on the significance of Romans 8.

Satan and his angelic hosts are among those who had maliciously treated and wrongly accused Christians and whose slander will be nullified at the vindication of the final resurrection. No one, including Satan, can "bring a charge against God's elect" now (Rom. 8:33, on which see also Rev. 12:7–10) or on the last day. The consummation of this inaugurated inability to accuse God's faithful ones is likely included in Romans 16:20: "And the God of peace will soon crush Satan under your feet." At this time, the Devil will be "thrown into the lake of fire and brimstone" (Rev. 20:10), which means he will have no prosecuting or condemnatory function in the final judgment. It is not coincidental that in Revelation 20:11–15, which is a picture of the judgment at the final resurrection, not only is Satan conspicuously absent, but those raised who are "written in the book of life" are exempted from the judgment.

The final bodily resurrection of the saints vindicates them before the on-looking world in that it is an "enfleshing" or "incarnation"[27] of their prior spiritual identification with Christ's vindicating resurrection, which was not seen or recognized by the ungodly powers. That is, spiritual resurrection that was invisible but to the eyes of faith (2 Cor. 4:6–11, 16–18) will become visible to all eyes in the consummated form of physical resurrection (2 Cor. 4:14; 5:1–5), which is foundational to a person's being judged favorably by Christ at the end.[28]

2 Corinthians 4:16

In particular, 2 Corinthians 4:16 presents a significant paradigm for this understanding: "For we do not lose heart, but even though our outer man is decaying, nevertheless our inner man is being renewed day by day." In the light of this, the believer has a two-sided existence: the inner man, which is the unseen immaterial aspect, and the outer man, the visible bodily aspect. Accordingly, though this verse refers to the unseen progressive resurrection renewal, we may speak more broadly and say that the identification of believers with Christ's resurrection in this age (discussed earlier in this section) pertains to the believer's inner man and, therefore, that initial resurrection identification and existence is the beginning invisible evidence of justification. The granting of spiritual life is an overturning of the verdict of spiritual death in that the believer has been delivered from the execution of that death verdict.

---

[27]Bird (ibid.) has used this word in referring to the resurrection being "the incarnation of the justification of the saints."

[28]On this subject, see further discussion of 2 Corinthians 4:6–5:10 toward the conclusion of this chapter.

But though Christians have been *declared* not guilty of sin (both spiritual and physical), they have not yet been *delivered* from the physical death penalty of sin that has been carried out upon them, the decaying effects of which they live under. What this means is that their physical resurrection is the final overturning of the death penalty—the actual verdict from which they had already been declared as having been justified. This removing of the execution of the physical death penalty is a final part of the two-stage already-and-not-yet effects of justification: (1) resurrection of the inner man followed by (2) resurrection of the outer man.[29] Gaffin refers to this double justification as "justified by faith" and "yet to be justified by sight."[30] In that the complete overturning of the death penalty lies still in the future, there is a sense in which the full justification/vindication from that penalty is also yet to be carried out, though this carrying out is ultimately an effect of the earlier declaration of justification from the complete penalty of sin that comes by faith. Figure 4 displays this double justification.

Fig. 4.

Justification by faith	resurrection of the inner man	declared innocent of the penalty of sin
Justification by sight	resurrection of the outer man	delivered from the penalty of sin, vindicated from the world's wrong verdict

An illustration here may be helpful. A man has been wrongfully convicted of a crime and has begun to serve a jail sentence. When new evidence is adduced to demonstrate his innocence, the court nullifies the former verdict and declares him not guilty. However, because of the necessary administrative paperwork, the actual release of the prisoner does not take place for another three weeks. Thus, the prisoner's justification occurs in two stages: (1) the court's announced verdict of not guilty and (2) the subsequent release from the prison (the imprisonment was a punishment of the former guilty verdict that was decisively overturned three weeks earlier, the full effects of which are now carried out).[31]

---

[29] Romans 8:10–11, 23 refers to the same kind of two-stage process (following R. B. Gaffin, *By Faith, Not by Sight* [Milton Keynes, UK: Paternoster, 2006], 86).
[30] Ibid., 88.
[31] I am indebted to Gaffin (ibid., 86–92) for the ideas in the last two paragraphs.

The Final Resurrection and Good Works in Connection
  to the Justification/Vindication of the Saints
We have thus seen that the believers' bodily resurrection is a consummative
end-time manifestation of their "already" justified status. "Good works"
are part of this final "manifestive justification." There are a few texts that
speak of a future end-time justification of Christians. For example, Romans
2:13 says, "for it is not the hearers of the Law who are just before God,
but the doers of the Law will be justified."[32] Paul also repeatedly speaks
of the believers' appearing "before the judgment seat" of God or Christ
(Rom. 14:10, 12; 2 Cor. 5:10). James 2:14–26 also speaks of the close
link between justification and good works (e.g., v. 14, "a man is justified
by works and not by faith alone"). This text is also likely focusing on a
final justification at the end of time.[33]

How can believers be said to be "judged by works" and yet be justified
by faith? There is much more to be said than can be elaborated on here
about the believer's righteous works in connection to this consummate,
manifestive stage of justification, and the following is just the beginning
of an answer to that question. An illustration must suffice for now to
summarize my own view of this connection. In the United States there are
large discount food stores that require people to pay an annual fee to have
the privilege of buying food there. Once this fee is paid, the member must
present a card as evidence of having paid the fee; only then is entrance
to the store allowed. The card is necessary to get into the store, but it is
not the ultimate reason that the person is granted access. The paid fee
is the ultimate reason for entrance, and the card is the evidence that the
fee has been paid. We may refer to the fee paid as the necessary causal
condition of entrance into the store and the evidence-testifying card as
the necessary condition (but not the necessary causal condition).[34] The
card is the external manifestation or proof that the prior price was paid,
so that both the money paid and the card are necessary for admittance,
but they do not have the same conditional force for allowing entrance.
One could refer to the fee paid as a "first-order condition" and the card
as a "second-order condition."[35]

---

[32]This refers to a future "justification" (to which the context of Rom. 2:3–10, 15–16 strongly points)
and likely not, as some hold, to a principle that if people are to be justified by keeping the law, it is by a
perfect doing of the law.
[33]Though there is not space to demonstrate this, see D. J. Moo, *The Letter of James*, Pillar New Testament Commentary (Grand Rapids: Eerdmans, 2000), 134–36, 144; see also Moo, *The Letter of James*,
Tyndale New Testament Commentaries (Grand Rapids: Eerdmans, 1985), 99–101.
[34]In this respect, Jonathan Edwards proposes "a distinction between causal conditionality and non-causal
conditionality." Samuel T. Logan, "The Doctrine of Justification in the Theology of Jonathan Edwards,"
Westminster Theological Journal 46 (1984): 32.
[35]For the latter category, see ibid., 38.

Likewise, Christ's justifying penal death (together with his imputed obedient life through identification with his vindicating resurrection) is the price paid "once for all" (Heb. 9:12; cf. vv. 26–28), and the good works done within the context of Christian faith become the inevitable evidence of such faith at the final judicial evaluation. Christ's work is the necessary causal condition for justification and the believer's works are a necessary condition for it. Jonathan Edwards helpfully referred to Christ's work as "causal justification" and the believer's obedience at the end of the age as "manifestive justification."[36] This manifestive evidence is not only part of a judicial process, but it also becomes evidence that overturns the wrong verdict of the world on the believers' faith and works done in obedience to Christ.

A full-orbed discussion of good works in relation to justification cannot be set forth here. Accordingly, the following discussion is limited to the link of such works to the saints' resurrection. In particular, the following passages reveal an inextricable connection between the believers' bodily resurrection and their final judgment according to works. I believe that this connection sheds further light on the question about how believers can be said to be "judged by works" and yet be "justified by faith."

2 Corinthians 4:6–5:10

Paul in 2 Corinthians 4:6–5:10 closely links the saints' final resurrection and their judgment according to works. As noted earlier, the spiritual resurrection in the present age, not recognized in the eyes of the world (2 Cor. 4:6–11, 16–18), will become manifest in the final form of bodily resurrection (2 Cor. 4:14; 5:1–5). Particularly important here is 2 Corinthians 5:1–10.

> [1] For we know that if the earthly tent which is our house is torn down, we have a building from God, a house not made with hands, eternal in the heavens. [2] For indeed in this house we groan, longing to be clothed with our dwelling from heaven, [3] inasmuch as we, having put it on, will not be found naked. [4] For indeed while we are in this tent, we groan, being burdened, because we do not want to be unclothed but to be clothed, so that what is mortal will be swallowed up by life. [5] Now He who prepared us for this very purpose is God, who gave to us the Spirit as a pledge. [6] Therefore, being always of good courage, and knowing that while we are at home in the body we are absent from the Lord— [7] for we walk by faith, not by sight— [8] we are of good courage, I say, and prefer rather to be absent from

---

[36] Ibid., 39. Or, one could refer to this as "internal justification," which is seen or recognized only by God and the believing community, and "external justification," which manifests the internal verdict through the believer's works to all the world at the eschaton.

the body and to be at home with the Lord. [9] Therefore we also have as
our ambition, whether at home or absent, to be pleasing to Him. [10] For we
must all appear before the judgment seat of Christ, so that each one may
be recompensed for his deeds in the body, according to what he has done,
whether good or bad.

On the basis of (note the significance of the οὖν in v. 6) the consummate resurrection elaborated upon in verses 1–5, believers are to be of
"good courage" (v. 6), "for," verse 7 asserts, in the present age "we walk
by faith, not by sight" (in recognizing our present spiritual resurrection
and especially its inevitable final expression in bodily resurrection). Thus,
both verses 1–5 and verse 7 are the basis for being of "good courage"
in verse 6, which is confidence in the fact of resurrection, particularly as
this is realized bodily in the future. Then verse 8 repeats being "of good
courage," which again is based on verses 1–5 concerning the coming
resurrection. Such "courage" is necessary in the face of affliction (2 Cor.
4:7–12, 16–17). Verse 9 continues the argument by affirming that, on
the basis of (note the διὸ) being of good courage (vv. 6 and 8) because of
confidence in the coming bodily resurrection (vv. 1–5), believers should
strive "to be pleasing to Him [God]." Courage inspired by confidence in
the coming resurrection motivates one to be pleasing to God: since God
will act favorably on behalf of believers by raising them from the dead, they
should now want to show their gratitude by doing those things "pleasing"
to him (the same rationale is straightforwardly given in 2 Cor. 4:14–15,
though there the language of "giving thanks" is expressed instead of being
"pleasing"). Verse 10 gives a further reason that Christians should want
to please God: "because" (γὰρ) they must all appear before the bar of
the divine law court "so that each one may be recompensed" for good or
bad deeds. They should be motivated to "please" God by doing "good"
deeds because they will be called to account for how they live.

A point not often observed in this passage is that "pleasing" God, and
thus doing "good" works, is based not only on the confidence in future
resurrection but also on the fact that resurrection existence has already
begun. Accordingly, it is out of the renewing power of such inaugurated
resurrection existence (so 4:16!)—which shows identification and solidarity with Christ's resurrection existence now (2 Cor. 4:10–11; 5:14–15)
and proleptically on the last day (4:14)—that the desire to "please" God
and do good works arises.

Paul believed that true believers who are truly identified in an unseen
manner with Christ's resurrection now and will be identified with his

bodily resurrection at the last great assize, will thus appear before the "judgment seat" *in such resurrection bodies*. Considering the broader context of Paul, such people will be judged not on whether their deeds have been perfect, but on whether they have borne the fruit of good works in keeping with and as a result of their resurrection existence. Thus, what is being evaluated is the character (i.e., the "in Christ" resurrection character) from which the works arose.[37] The believer's future "building from God . . . not made with hands" (2 Cor. 5:1), with which they "long to be clothed" (5:2; so also 5:3–4), is none other than their resurrection body: they want "to be clothed, in order that what is mortal may be swallowed up *by life*" (5:4) and "not be found naked" (5:3). Thus, in the light of 5:1–4, 5:10 includes the notion that what "clothes" persons is their good deeds pleasing to God, inextricably linked to and arising from their resurrection character, which is "manifested" bodily[38] on the last day. And, since they are "manifested before the judgment seat of Christ," the resurrected Christ himself acknowledges their resurrection identification with him (see also 1 Cor. 15:22–23) and evaluates them and their works positively.

This means that believers are first resurrected immediately before the "recompensing for their deeds" takes place. As we have discussed, Paul elsewhere sees the believers' resurrection to be part of their justification, vindicating them from the wrong verdict declared over them by the world and vindicating them from the penalty of bodily death as a result of their own sin against God. Thus, believers appear as already openly justified in their resurrection bodies immediately preceding their examination before "the judgment seat of Christ." In this respect, the last judgment for believers, which is according to works, is "reflective of and further attesting their justification that has been openly manifested in their bodily resurrection."[39]

In addition, we observed earlier that believers begin to be in Christ's restored image during the present age and consummately and perfectly so at the final resurrection.[40] This means that as they appear before the

---

[37]In this respect, the change from the plural deeds (ἃ, literally "what things") to the singular "good or bad" (ἀγαθὸν εἴτε φαῦλον) would appear to suggest that "conduct will be judged as a whole," so that it is not distinct acts but character that will be punished or rewarded (following M. J. Harris, *The Second Epistle to the Corinthians*, New Greek Testament Commentary [Grand Rapids: Eerdmans, 2005], 407–8).

[38]Just as Christ's resurrection life had begun to be "manifested" (see the aorist passive of φανερόω) spiritually or in an unseen manner through the saints while in their earthly bodies (2 Cor. 4:10–11), so it will be fully "manifested" (again, the aorist passive of φανερόω) in their resurrection bodies at the end of the age (2 Cor. 5:10).

[39]Gaffin, *By Faith, Not by Sight*, 99–100.

[40]For the former, see 2 Corinthians 3:18; for the latter, see 1 Corinthians 15:45–54; for both, see Romans 8:29.

judgment seat in their resurrected body, they are also now in the perfect image of the last Adam, which further includes a testimony to their righteous, obedient character. Such righteous obedience begins during the interadvent age, as a result of beginning to be in Christ's image during the same age.[41]

In contrast, others who profess to have been identified with Christ's resurrection but who do not bear such fruit will "be found naked," that is, not found resurrected "in Christ" and lacking new life-bearing works. As a consequence, they will "fail the test" of this judicial evaluation (2 Cor. 13:5; cf. 1 Cor. 11:19) because they have "received the grace of God in vain" (2 Cor. 6:1) and, consequently, are still "yoked together with unbelievers," are in "fellowship with darkness," are characterized by "lawlessness" (2 Cor. 6:14), and identified with the Devil (2 Cor. 6:15; 11:13–15).[42] Such people will suffer judgment with the world of unbelievers, since they have "disguised themselves as servants of righteousness, whose end shall be according to their deeds," since such deeds reveal their true unbelieving character (2 Cor. 11:15; see also Matt. 7:15–23).[43]

This means that 2 Corinthians 5:10 is not a passage about Christ distributing differing awards to Christians, all of whom are "saved" according to their differing works. Rather, some will be found to be true believers, while others will not. With respect to true believers it is suitable to refer to this passage as expressing the notion of a future "manifestive justification or vindication" through judgment. First Corinthians 3:13 expresses a very similar idea: "Each man's work will become manifest [φανερὸν]; for the day will show it because it is to be revealed with fire, and the fire itself will test the quality of each man's work." This refers to some who are saved and others judged at the eschaton.[44]

Revelation 20:11–15

This is another important passage concerning the judgment by works in relation to the Christian's standing at the final judgment. The saints' identification with Christ's death and resurrection at the time of final judgment is sometimes stressed so much that they are viewed as being

---

[41]This paragraph is indebted to the thought of Gaffin, *By Faith, Not by Sight*, 99–101.

[42]Second Corinthians 11:13–15 refers specifically to the false Jewish-Christian teachers but may be applicable to those in the Corinthian church who follow them and thus identify with them (on which cf. 2 Cor. 11:3–4).

[43]For the connection of the "clothing" in 2 Corinthians 5:1–4, I have generally followed S. J. Hafemann, *2 Corinthians*, New International Version Application Commentary (Grand Rapids: Zondervan, 2000), 217.

[44]Unfortunately, there is not space to elaborate further on my view of 1 Corinthians 3:10–17, though see in part Charles Hodge, *A Commentary on the First Epistle to the Corinthians* (London: Banner of Truth, 1958), 56–57.

excluded from being judged "according to their works" in the way that unbelievers are so judged. The Revelation text is a classic expression of such a passage:

> [11] Then I saw a great white throne and Him who sat upon it, from whose presence earth and heaven fled away, and no place was found for them. [12] And I saw the dead, the great and the small, standing before the throne, and books were opened; and another book was opened, which is the book of life; and the dead were judged from the things which were written in the books, according to their deeds. [13] And the sea gave up the dead which were in it, and death and Hades gave up the dead which were in them; and they were judged, every one of them according to their deeds. [14] Then death and Hades were thrown into the lake of fire. This is the second death, the lake of fire. [15] And if anyone's name was not found written in the book of life, he was thrown into the lake of fire.

That John sees "the dead, the great and the small, standing before the throne" in verse 12 presupposes that the last, great resurrection of the unrighteous and the righteous is finally about to take place (in light of Rev. 20:5; Dan. 12:2; John 5:28–29; and Acts 24:15). The idea is reinforced by the Lamb's "standing" before a "throne," expressing resurrection existence (Rev. 5:6). Revelation 20:13 makes clearer that resurrected people are standing before God's throne.

The clauses "the books were opened; and another book was opened, which is the book of life" in Revelation 20:12 combine allusion to Daniel 7:10 ("the books were opened") and Daniel 12:1–2 ("everyone who is found written in the book . . . will be rescued . . . to everlasting life"). The point of "the books" in Daniel 7 is to focus on the evil deeds of the end-time persecutor(s) of God's people for which he (they) would be judged. It is only the deeds of unbelievers that are recorded in these plural "books," and it is these sinful deeds that will be the basis for their judgment. The book of Daniel 12:1 also concerns the end time, but is an image of redemption. Those "written in the book" will be given life but those excluded from the book will suffer final judgment (Dan. 12:1–2), especially because they will be judged on the basis of their evil works, which are recorded in the "books" of Daniel 7:10. Those whose names are written in the singular "book" of those destined to be resurrected will not be subject to such an examination based on the recorded ungodly works in the "books" of Daniel 7. The same is true for those "judged from the things which were written in the books, according to their [sinful] deeds" here in Revelation 20:12. And, likewise, those identified with the "book of life" will not be subject to the same kind of judgment of works as are unbelievers, though we must continue to elaborate on the nature of this distinction.

Therefore, this vision in Revelation 20:11–15 gives assurance that Daniel's prophecy of final judgment and redemption will occur. The "opening of the book" in Revelation 5:1–9 referred partly to the inauguration of judgment, but the image there connoted more broadly the decree involving all facets of judgment and redemption during the era preceding Christ's final return and culminating at the end of history (see 5:1–8). The judgment at the end is what is highlighted here in 20:12, though final salvation is secondarily included.[45] As in 13:8 and 17:8 the "book of life" is introduced to bring attention to those excluded from it, though, of course, it includes reference secondarily to those who have been included in the book.

The phrase "the dead were judged" reveals the focus on judgment and shows Revelation 20:11–15 to be an amplification of the earlier shorter account of final judgment in 11:18 (which contains the almost identical phrase "the time [came] for the dead to be judged"). Even though both 11:18 and 20:11–15 focus on the judgment of the wicked, the former adds that "the reward" will be given to God's "servants the prophets and to the saints and to the ones fearing" God. Strikingly, the same phrase "the small and the great" refers to all classes of believers in 11:18 and to all classes of unbelievers in 19:18, so that the same wording in 20:12 may be an all-inclusive reference to both believers and unbelievers. The basis (κατὰ) for judgment of the impious is the record of their evil deeds "having been written in the books." The record books are metaphorical for God's memory which never fails and at the end provides the account of the misdeeds of the wicked which is presented before them.

In verse 15, as in verses 12–14, the note of final judgment is rung once more for emphasis. All who are "not found written in the book of life" were cast "into the lake of fire."[46] This implies that all who are found written in the book of life are spared from the judgment, which 3:5 and 21:27 make explicit (see 3:5, "I will not erase his [the overcomer's] name from the book of life," and 21:27, "those [who overcome, 21:7] whose names are written in the Lamb's book of life"). The implication that those written in the book of life do not go through the same judgment

---

[45]For full Old Testament and Jewish background on the two "books" in Revelation see G. K. Beale, *The Book of Revelation*, New International Greek Testament Commentary (Grand Rapids: Eerdmans, 1999), on 3:5; 13:8; 17:8; and 20:12, 15.

[46]Similarly Targum Ezekiel 13:9 says, "In the inscription for eternal life which is inscribed for the righteous . . . they [false prophets] shall not be inscribed."

process as the ungodly is warranted by the positive form of the statement in Daniel 12:1 (LXX): "all the people will be saved, *whoever should be found having been written in the book.*"

What is it about the book of life that spares true saints? The fuller title for the book is "the book of life of the Lamb having been slain" (13:8, and 21:27 has "book of life of the Lamb"). The added description is a genitive of possession or source. The life granted them in association with the book comes from their identification with the Lamb's righteous deeds (note the Lamb's "worthiness" qualifying him "to open the book" in Rev. 5:4–9; cf. 5:12), and especially identification with his death on their behalf, which means likewise that they are identified with his resurrection life that "overcame" death (cf. 5:5–13). They do not suffer judgment for their evil deeds because the Lamb has already suffered it for them: he was slain on their behalf (so esp. 1:5 and 5:9; see further on 13:8). The Lamb acknowledges before God all who are written in the book (3:5) and who are identified with his righteousness (i.e., "worthiness"), his death, and his resurrection life.

That the believers' identification with the Lamb's resurrection life is clearly also intended by their inclusion in the book is obvious from three observations: (1) the very name of the book: the "book of life" (on which see the same name in Rev. 3:5; 13:8; 17:8; 21:27); (2) the Daniel 12:1–2 allusion: "Everyone who is found written in the book will be rescued . . . and . . . will awake to everlasting life"; (3) the Lamb who first "opens the book" (also an allusion to Dan. 7:10 and 12:1–2) has been "slain" but is able to possess "the book" because of his "standing" in resurrection existence (Rev. 5:5–9).[47] The inevitable conclusion is that the saints written in the book are identified with the Lamb's resurrection life.

At the end God recognizes those who have taken refuge in the Lamb and have been recorded in the book for an inheritance of eternal life. While we have seen that Paul and James can conceive of true believers going through a judgment according to works, Revelation gives another perspective on this by saying that saints' works are not evaluated in the way unbelievers' works are, but they are evaluated according to their placement in the book of life, which identifies them with the Lamb's perfect worthiness, his penal death, and his resurrection on their behalf. Thus, those who have "their faith in Jesus" and "who die in the Lord . . . may rest from their labors, for their works [ἔργα] follow with them" (Rev. 14:12–13). Consequently, any evaluation of their works on the last

---

[47]However, for the difference between the book in Revelation 5:2–9 and the books in Revelation 20:12, 15, see Beale, *Revelation*.

day views the saints as identified with the risen Lamb and their works as done "in the [risen] Lord." This is also a conclusion that we reached with respect to the Pauline "judgment according to works" passages. The Pauline texts focus more on the evaluation of the believers' works and the Revelation text on identification with Christ's worthiness, death, and resurrection.

What Douglas Moo has said about James 2 is also a good summary of what we have said so far in this section:

> The believer, in himself, will always deserve God's judgment: our conformity to the "royal law" is never perfect, as it must be (vv. 10–11). But our merciful attitude and actions [= good works] will count as evidence of the presence of Christ within us. And it is on the [ultimate] basis of this union with the [resurrected] One who perfectly fulfilled the law for us that we can have confidence for vindication at the judgment.[48]

Conclusion

Initial justification and final justification (or twofold justification) are grounded in the believer's union with the resurrected Christ, the former coming by faith and the latter through the threefold demonstration of the believers' bodily resurrection, public announcement to the cosmos, and evaluation of works. In this essay, I have been able to develop only the aspect of resurrection and to some degree how good works relate to resurrection and, hence, justification. This, in part, is an example of already-and-not-yet eschatology.

---

[48]Moo, *James* (2000), 118 (the second bracketed wording is my addition).

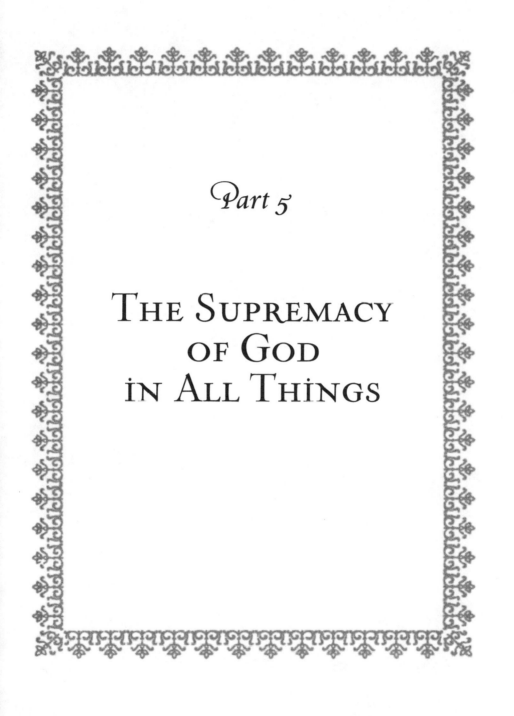

Part 5

THE SUPREMACY
OF GOD
IN ALL THINGS

11

A BIBLICAL THEOLOGY OF
THE GLORY OF GOD

Thomas R. Schreiner

I would like to begin with a personal word of appreciation for John Piper. I had the privilege of being a member of Bethlehem Baptist Church for eleven years (1986–1997) and of serving together with John as an elder. John's deeply impassioned preaching of the Word had an immense impact on me. During each week I looked forward with great anticipation to Sundays. What a joy and a challenge to be confronted week after week with the Word of the Lord. I am forever grateful to John, for God used him to renew and deepen my love for the Lord. And now that my children are older, I am doubly grateful, for John's preaching and writing are bearing fruit in their lives. Furthermore, a remarkable number of students at Southern Seminary, where I serve as a professor, have told me that the greatest influence in their life is John Piper. Nor can John's impact be confined to his words. He lives what he preaches: his godliness and radical commitment to the glory of God adorn the gospel. I have often thought that what makes John's preaching most effective is the ethos of his preaching. In other words, the Word of God comes with power because it is evident that John himself has been powerfully transformed by it (1 Thess. 1:5).

My essay on "A Biblical Theology of the Glory of God" really functions as a footnote to and repetition of what John has written on the glory of God. I am not writing anything new here! All of us who have heard and read John know that his message is God-centered, for he calls upon us to live for the glory and honor of the Lord's name. My intention in this essay, then, is simply to call attention to the message that John has proclaimed throughout his ministry. I could footnote virtually everything said here from John's writings,[1] but I trust that my words at the beginning signal my debt to and gratefulness for John Piper's ministry.

My purpose in this chapter is to trace out theologically the God-centeredness of the Scriptures by looking at the Old and New Testaments in terms of biblical theology. In other words, as we consider the storyline of the Scriptures, the aim of this essay is to trace out the ultimate reason for the Lord's work in salvation and judgment. We shall see that God does everything for his praise, his glory, his honor—for the sake of his great name. If we were to confine ourselves only to a study of the term *glory*, the fullness of the biblical witness on the centrality of God would be overlooked.[2] Therefore this essay does not restrict itself to "the glory of God" linguistically but considers the theme theologically. This is not to say that we are straying from exegesis! Since the glory of God is foundational in Scripture, the thoughts here are sketched in, for a short essay cannot do justice to the fullness and richness of the theme before us. I would define the glory of God as the beauty, majesty, and greatness of who he is; therefore, in all he does, whether in salvation or in judgment, the greatness of his being is demonstrated.

God's Glory in Creation

The Scriptures commence with the account of the creation of the world in six days in Genesis 1:1–2:3. As we gaze upon and ponder the created world, we are struck again and again with the intense beauty, marvelous intricacy, and grandeur of creation. The natural response to such beauty is praise for the Creator. Genesis itself does not say that creation is for the sake of the glory of God, but drawing such a conclusion cannot be criticized as eisegesis (reading into the text), for such a conclusion is often drawn elsewhere in the Scriptures. For instance, Psalm 104 considers the handiwork

---

[1]In particular see John Piper, *Desiring God: Meditations of a Christian Hedonist*, 3d ed. (Sisters, OR: Multnomah, 2003), 308–21.

[2]For a study of the term *glory* in both the Old Testament and the New, see Gerhard Kittel and Gerhard von Rad, "*doxa-doxazo*," in *Theological Dictionary of the New Testament*, 2:233–55.

of God in creation, reflecting on the origin of majestic mountains, verdant valleys, gushing springs, and the manifold creatures the Lord has made. And the work of God lifts up the psalmist's soul to the Lord in praise, for the psalm begins with the call to "Bless the LORD, O my soul," confessing that the Lord is "very great" (v. 1). And the psalm concludes,

> Bless the LORD, O my soul!
> Praise the LORD! (v. 35)

When the psalmist considers God's handiwork, he sees in it the glory of God, for he exclaims,

> May the glory of the LORD endure forever;
>   may the LORD rejoice in his works. (v. 31)

As Piper has reminded us constantly, God's greatest joy is in seeing his glory maximized, and hence the Lord rejoices in his creative work because it redounds to the glory of his name. And the Lord's glory cannot be restricted to intellectual contemplation; in considering the Lord's creative work the psalmist bursts forth with praise,

> I will sing to the LORD as long as I live;
>   I will sing praise to my God while I have being. (v. 33)

The glory of God in creation permeates the biblical witness. Perhaps one other text will suffice to make the point. Revelation 4 brings readers into the very throne room of God, and it is dazzling indeed. The radiance of the Lord cannot be captured in human language; he is compared to magnificent stones and to the rainbow (v. 3). Mysterious beings serve him, like the twenty-four elders and the four living beings (v. 4), and approaching God's throne is frightening, for lightning and thunder and flashes of fire proceed from it (v. 5). And what is happening in the great throne room where the ruler of all is seated? The four living creatures are engrossed with God and cry out,

> Holy, holy, holy, is the Lord God Almighty,
>   who was and is and is to come! (v. 8)

Ascribing holiness to God is further defined in verse 9 as giving "glory and honor and thanks to him who is seated on the throne" (v. 9). And the four living creatures are joined in their worship by the twenty-four elders, who

> fall down before him who is seated on the throne and worship him who lives forever and ever. They cast their crowns before the throne, saying,
>
> "Worthy are you, our Lord and God,
>   to receive glory and honor and power,
> for you created all things,
>   and by your will they existed and were created."
>   (vv. 10–11)

When the twenty-four elders see God in all his majesty and might, they praise him as the Creator of all, as the sovereign One who willed all things into existence. They are constrained to prostrate themselves before him and to give him all the glory and honor and praise as the Creator.

The Lord created human beings in the image of God (Gen. 1:26–27). It is not my intention here to delve into the controversial discussion on the meaning of the image of God. We can say, however, that Genesis itself emphasizes that human beings image God as they rule the world for him.[3] Human beings are God's vice-regents, and they are to extend his sovereignty over the world. If Adam and Eve were called to rule the world for God, then it follows that in exercising dominion they reflect the glory and likeness of their Creator. Such a conclusion fits with God's purpose in making man, for he declares that he created his people "for my glory" (Isa. 43:7).

The Fall as a Refusal to Glorify God

When we reflect on the storyline of the Bible, the themes of creation, fall, redemption, and new creation stand out. We have already seen above that God created the world for his glory. The next major event in redemptive history is the fall, in which Adam and Eve sinned against God by disobeying the command not to eat of the tree of knowledge of good and evil.

What is the nature of the sin committed in the garden? The Serpent promises Eve that if she eats of the forbidden fruit, she "will be like God, knowing good and evil" (Gen. 3:5). Eve succumbed and ate of the fruit since it would "make [her] wise" (Gen. 3:6). As Daniel Fuller observes, knowledge of good and evil is possessed by God (Gen. 3:22) and angels

---

[3]See the discussion in Kenneth A. Mathews, *Genesis 1–11:26*, New American Commentary (Nashville: Broadman and Holman, 1996), 163–72. See also Scott Hafemann's essay in this present volume: "The Kingdom of God as the Mission of God" (chap. 12).

(2 Sam. 14:17), and is given to Solomon in answer to prayer (1 Kings 3:9). But young children and the old do not have it (Deut. 1:39; Isa. 7:15; 2 Sam. 19:35).[4] Adam and Eve's lack of such knowledge demonstrates that they needed to depend upon God for everything, just as little children rely upon their parents (Matt. 18:3). In other words, Adam and Eve sinned against God because they did not trust in him. They desired to be independent of him, to be "gods" on their own. In not relying upon the Lord, they dishonored him.

This accords with Paul's reflection on the fundamental nature of sin. Unbelievers do not "honor him as God or give thanks to him" (Rom. 1:21; cf. Ps. 106:20). At its root, sin does not acknowledge the Godness of God, refusing to give him the glory and honor and praise he deserves. Sin exalts self over God, which explains why C. S. Lewis was profoundly right in identifying pride as "The Great Sin."[5] In a summarizing statement on the nature of sin Paul affirms that sin consists of the failure to glorify God: "for all have sinned and fall short of the glory of God" (Rom. 3:23). The sin of Adam and Eve (and indeed all sin) robs God of his glory and puts man on the throne instead, for sin exalts self rather than God as the center of the universe.[6]

God's Glory in Judgment

If creation and fall are the first two major movements in redemptive history, then redemption is clearly the third. The Lord promises Adam and Eve that the offspring of the woman will triumph over the offspring of the Serpent (Gen. 3:15).[7] The promise of redemption is worked out in the covenants the Lord made with his people, particularly the covenant with Abraham (Gen. 12:1–3), the Sinai covenant (Exodus 19–24), the covenant ratified with David (2 Samuel 7; Psalms 89, 132), and the new covenant (Jer. 31:31–34).[8] If we pick up the story from Adam and Eve, we see that the offspring of the Serpent seems to be winning the victory. Cain slays his brother Abel, and then the offspring of the Serpent multiply so rapidly that Noah and his family are the only ones left on earth that are righteous (Genesis 6–9). The Lord reigns over all, bringing judgment by

---

[4]Daniel P. Fuller, *Unity of the Bible: Unfolding God's Plan for Humanity* (Grand Rapids: Zondervan, 1992), 182–83.

[5]C. S. Lewis, *Mere Christianity* (New York: Macmillan, 1952), 108–14.

[6]We are not surprised to learn, then, that the fundamental sin in building the Tower of Babel was the desire to "make a name for ourselves" (Gen. 11:4). The fundamental sin consists in the desire to advance our reputation and to "de-god" God.

[7]For the working out of this theme in the Scriptures, see James M. Hamilton Jr., "The Skull-Crushing Seed of the Woman: Inner-Biblical Interpretation of Genesis 3:15," *Southern Baptist Journal of Theology* 10, no. 2 (2006): 30–54.

[8]Other texts could be listed for the various covenants. Those cited are merely representative.

a cataclysmic flood that destroys those who have sinned and refused to glorify him. Here we see the theme that runs through the Scriptures that the Lord displays his glory in judging sinners. No one can disregard his name and escape the wrath of the Lord. As Psalm 76:10 says, "Surely the wrath of man shall praise you." No one defies God and ends up triumphing over him. For instance, Herod Agrippa is put to death for failing to glorify God and arrogating the glory to himself (Acts 12:23).

Satan and his hosts win only apparent victories; the wisdom of God shines in both salvation and judgment. Pharaoh, as the offspring of the Serpent, seems to triumph over Israel, but ultimately God gets "glory over Pharaoh" (Ex. 14:18) by inundating his chariots and horsemen in the sea. Paul, citing Exodus 9:16, indicates that the resistance of Pharaoh did not ultimately undo God's purposes but carried them out: "For the Scripture says to Pharaoh, 'For this very purpose I have raised you up, that I might show my power in you, and that my name might be proclaimed in all the earth'" (Rom. 9:17). The wonder of God's salvation shines against the black backdrop of Pharaoh's resistance. In judging Pharaoh, the Lord's name and awesome power were declared among the nations. No one resists the Lord and escapes unscathed.

Nor is God's glory in judgment restricted to temporal judgments in history. In Romans 9:14–23 the judgment of Pharaoh is explicated in a context where Paul reflects on final judgment (vv. 21–22). And the judgment of the flood functions as a type of the final judgment (2 Pet. 2:5, 9). Indeed, in Revelation the saints and angels exclaim "Hallelujah" and praise the Lord for the final and eternal judgment of Babylon (which represents the city of man that persecutes and hates the city of God; see Rev. 18:20; 19:1–4). They praise God with great joy because his judgment of Babylon is just and right. We have gotten ahead of ourselves in the story of redemption, but the point just made is a crucial one. *God is glorified in the judgment of the wicked.* The defiant resistance against the Lord by some does not rob him of glory but actually manifests it, for his justice is displayed in the punishment of the ungodly (Rom. 1:18). Here we see a problem with any biblical theology that posits salvation as the foundational theme of Scripture. How is judgment integrated into such a reading of Scripture? If the glory of God is foundational, however, then his glory is featured in both judgment and salvation.

As we return to the storyline of the Scripture and come to the account of the flood, the righteous are restricted to one man (Noah) and his family. Noah becomes a new Adam, representing a new beginning for human beings, and the Lord promises to preserve the human race until his promise of salvation is completed (Genesis 6–9).[9] The fundamental flaw with human beings has not been solved, for Noah, like Adam, sins (Gen. 9:21). By the time of the Tower of Babel (Gen. 11:1–9) the power of sin seems irreversible, and it appears that the seed of the Serpent will defeat the Seed of the woman. But the Lord again shows his glory in judgment by frustrating the designs of those building the tower. Ultimately, evil will not have the final say. Indeed, hope surfaces again with the calling of one man, Abraham (Gen. 12:1–3).

What is the purpose of emphasizing the dominance of evil over good, with the result that once again at the time of Abraham it is one man against the world? First, we learn that human evil cannot be dismissed as a minor peccadillo. The judgment of the flood reveals the true nature of human beings and the destiny deserved by all. Second, the greatness of the redemption promised in Genesis 3:15 and now reaffirmed to Abraham is underlined. Triumphing over evil is no triviality; heaven and earth, so to speak, must be moved to accomplish salvation. Third, the repeated emphasis on one man points us to Jesus Christ, for he is the one Seed of Abraham (Gal. 3:16) who truly accomplishes God's saving purposes.

The storyline, then, highlights God's glory by featuring the wonder and power of his grace. We know that God's glory includes his gracious work of salvation from Exodus 33–34. Moses asks the Lord, "Please show me your glory" (Ex. 33:18). The Lord defines his glory in terms of his goodness and the freedom of his grace and mercy (Ex. 33:19). Hence, God's glory is revealed not only in judgment but particularly in salvation. That God's glory includes both judgment and salvation is reaffirmed in Exodus 34:6–7:

> The LORD, the LORD, a God merciful and gracious, slow to anger, and abounding in steadfast love and faithfulness, keeping steadfast love for thousands, forgiving iniquity and transgression and sin, but who will by no means clear the guilty, visiting the iniquity of the fathers on the children and the children's children, to the third and the fourth generation.

God manifests his glory in judgment, but the emphasis here shows that he demonstrates his glory particularly in pouring his mercy and grace and forgiveness upon his people. Even though Israel sinned against the Lord,

> he saved them for his name's sake,
> that he might make known his mighty power.
>   (Ps. 106:8)

---

[9]For the remarkable parallels between Adam and Noah supporting the idea that we have a new beginning in many respects with Noah, see Gary V. Smith, "Structure and Purpose in Genesis 1–11," *Journal of the Evangelical Theological Society* 20 (1977): 310–11.

God's Glory in the Call of Abraham and in Faith

In calling Abraham the Lord did not summon a man who was righteous. Instead, Abraham was an idolater (Josh. 24:2) and belonged to the category of the ungodly (Rom. 4:5). God's call and promises to Abraham, then, were not on the basis of Abraham's works but his faith (Gen. 15:6; Rom. 4:2–3; Gal. 3:6–9). God did not pay Abraham a wage for believing (Rom. 4:4). On the contrary, Abraham pinned all his hopes on God in trusting him to fulfill his promises. Abraham's faith, as Paul explains in both Romans 4 and Galatians, is paradigmatic for all who will be justified, showing that the only way to be right before God is by faith. What I want to particularly emphasize here is that such faith glorifies God. Paul notes that Abraham "grew strong in his faith as he gave glory to God, fully convinced that God was able to do what he had promised" (Rom. 4:20–21). Paul specifically argues here that faith glorifies God because it honors God as reliable. Disbelief dishonors God because it reckons God's promises to be lies, concluding that he will not carry out what he has pledged. We have already seen that the fundamental sin is the refusal to glorify or thank God (Rom. 1:21). Now in Romans 4:20–21 we learn that faith gives glory to God by trusting him to fulfill his promises. Hence, it makes sense that Paul declares in Romans 14:23 that "whatever does not proceed from faith is sin." We glorify God by trusting in him, and dishonor him by failing to believe in his Word. Hence, whatever we do that is not a result of faith constitutes sin inasmuch as it dishonors God.

Abraham is not only the paradigm of righteousness by faith; Abraham is also the recipient of the promise that all nations (all people groups) would be blessed in him (Gen. 12:3). The promise of universal blessing made to Abraham is fundamental to the story of Genesis, the Pentateuch, and the entire Bible. In particular, God's promise to bless all nations is another way of saying that "all the earth shall be filled with the glory of the LORD" (Num. 14:21). Or as Habakkuk says,

> For the earth will be filled
> with the knowledge of the glory of the LORD
> as the waters cover the sea. (Hab. 2:14)

Malachi 1:11 similarly says, "For from the rising of the sun to its setting my name will be great among the nations." The universal blessing promised to Abraham is fulfilled in the proclamation of the gospel of Jesus Christ (Gal. 3:8). God's name is magnified in the spread of the gospel (fulfilling the promise to Abraham) to the ends of the earth.

God's Glory and the Law

The covenant with Israel (Exodus 19–24), or the Sinai covenant, overlaps with the Abrahamic covenant in content and yet is also distinct from it. Paul, in particular, emphasizes that the Sinai covenant was intended to be in force for only a limited period of time (Gal. 3:15–4:7). The Sinai covenant differs from the Abrahamic covenant in that it focuses especially on the nation of Israel. The Abrahamic covenant has a universal dimension, whereas the Sinai covenant has a nationalistic focus. Furthermore, the commands of the Mosaic covenant call attention to Israel's inability to keep what God commanded (cf. Rom. 2:17–29; 3:9–20; 7:7–25; 2 Cor. 3:6–11; Gal. 3:10–25). Paul's pessimistic perspective on human ability to keep the law matches the Old Testament account. Both Israel (722 B.C.) and Judah (586 B.C.) were sent into exile because of their failure to abide by the stipulations of the Sinai covenant. The Old Testament prophets summoned both Israel and Judah to repentance for their sin, but they failed to return to the Lord and were punished for their hardness of heart. The blessings promised in the Mosaic covenant did not become a reality, for Israel regularly violated what God commanded.

Still, the commands of the law were "holy and righteous and good" (Rom. 7:12). Indeed, the whole of the law is summed up in the first commandment of the Decalogue. "You shall have no other gods before me" (Ex. 20:3). The first commandment insists on the supremacy of God; he brooks no rivals. He must be first. He is a jealous God who demands absolute loyalty (Ex. 34:14). The prohibition against coveting (Ex. 20:17) is just another way of saying that God must have absolute priority in our lives. Whatever we covet is our god, and hence Paul identifies coveting as idolatry (Col. 3:5).

In still another way the law summons its hearers to put God above all else: "You shall love the LORD your God with all your heart and with all your soul and with all your might" (Deut. 6:5). Jesus summarized the message of the entire law with the commands to love God and neighbor (Matt. 22:34–40). God receives glory when we prize him as our treasure, when we find him to be our all in all, when, in short, we love him! But Israel's disobedience revealed that they did not love the Lord, that he was not supreme in their affections, and that they worshiped themselves rather than the true and living God.

God's Glory in the Davidic Covenant and the Promise of a New Exodus

The Davidic covenant advances the storyline of the Bible. Now the universal blessing promised to Abraham will become a reality through a son of David (2 Samuel 7; Psalm 72). If the heir of David who sits on the throne sins, he will be disciplined and reproved, but the covenant will not be revoked or canceled, for the Davidic dynasty will endure forever. Ultimately, every son of David failed to do the will of God. Even David, a man after God's own heart, sinned dramatically in committing adultery with Bathsheba and putting to death her husband, Uriah the Hittite (2 Samuel 11). The promise made to David, as the New Testament emphasizes throughout, is fulfilled in Jesus of Nazareth. He is the true son of David and the inheritor of the promises made to him, and as we shall see, the passion of his life was the glory of God.

If we pursue the storyline of the Old Testament, we see that Israel had its ups and downs, but in the end they failed to please God and hence were sent into exile. The kingdom was divided into the northern and southern kingdoms during the reign of Rehoboam (1 Kings 12). None of the kings in Israel pleased the Lord, and even Judah ultimately failed to do God's will and hence suffered punishment as well. Throughout Israel's history the Lord was patient with his people and did not bring on them the full punishment they deserved. Samuel's words to Israel are representative. The nation has sinned against the Lord by asking for a king. Samuel rebuked them for their sin, but he comforted them as well, "For the LORD will not forsake his people, for his great name's sake, because it has pleased the LORD to make you a people for himself" (1 Sam. 12:22). Ultimately, the Lord will not abandon his people. He will have mercy on them for the sake of his great name—in order to maximize his glory.

The exile of God's people, then, is not the last word. He promises a new covenant (Jer. 31:31–34), a new exodus (e.g., Isa. 11:15–16; 40:3–11; 42:16; 43:2, 5–7, 16–19; 48:20–21; 49:6–11; 51:10), and a new creation (Isa. 65:17; 66:22). The word spoken to Samuel, that the Lord would not abandon his people, was not revoked but reaffirmed. Israel deserved final and irrevocable judgment for its recalcitrance and disobedience. Nevertheless, the grace of God, not the judgment of God, is the final word. In two crucial passages we learn why this is the case. Isaiah declares:

> For my name's sake I defer my anger,
>   for the sake of my praise I restrain it for you,
>   that I may not cut you off.
> Behold, I have refined you, but not as silver;
>   I have tried you in the furnace of affliction.

> For my own sake, for my own sake, I do it,
>   for how should my name be profaned?
> My glory I will not give to another. (Isa. 48:9–11)

The Lord promises a new exodus—a return from Babylonian captivity, for his own name's sake. In other words, the Lord acts as he does "for the sake of [his] praise" so that his name will not be "profaned." He preserves Israel because he will not give his glory to anyone else. So, when we come to the fundamental ground for the preservation of Israel, we see that he saves his people for the glory of his name. Hence, the salvation of human beings is not God's ultimate concern but the majesty of his glorious name.

The same theme is evident in Ezekiel. Again the Lord pledges that he will rescue his people from exile. He will establish with them "a covenant of peace" (Ezek. 34:25; 37:26). This is likely just another way of describing the new covenant found in Jeremiah (31:31–34). In this covenant the Lord will put the law within his people so that they do his will and keep his laws. Ezekiel teaches the same truth but expands upon it by emphasizing that the Lord will give his Spirit to his people, and thereby they will be enabled to observe God's commands (Ezek. 11:19–20; 36:26–27). But what explains God's graciousness to his people? Ezekiel provides an explanation.

> Therefore say to the house of Israel, Thus says the Lord GOD: It is not for your sake, O house of Israel, that I am about to act, but for the sake of my holy name, which you have profaned among the nations to which you came. And I will vindicate the holiness of my great name, which has been profaned among the nations, and which you have profaned among them. And the nations will know that I am the LORD, declares the Lord GOD, when through you I vindicate my holiness before their eyes. (Ezek. 36:22–23)

This text reaffirms what we saw in Isaiah. God's ultimate concern is the greatness of his holy name. The Lord's desire is to vindicate his name since it has been trampled in the dust by Israel. The good news is that the glory of God's name, because of his gracious will, is tied to the fortunes of his people, just as we saw in 1 Samuel 12:22. Hence, we can rejoice that God's ultimate commitment is the glory of his name, for he vindicates his holiness, according to Ezekiel, in showing mercy to his people.[10]

---

[10]Ezekiel emphasizes repeatedly (seventy-two times!) that God does what he does so that people will "know that I am the LORD." The God-centeredness of his vision is evident in the repetition of this expression. The expression goes back to the exodus, where the Lord delivers Israel from Egypt so that both the Israelites and the Egyptians will "know that I am the LORD" (Ex. 6:7; 7:5, 17; 8:22; 10:2; 14:4, 18). Again, this phrase emphasizes the lordship and sovereignty of God. John Frame argues that God's lordship is the central theme in Scripture. Such a claim accords with what is being said here. See John M. Frame, *The Doctrine of God* (Phillipsburg, NJ: P&R, 2002).

God's Glory in the Psalms and Wisdom Literature

We have been concentrating on the storyline of Scripture, but does the theme of this chapter fit with the Psalms and the Wisdom Literature? It has often been pointed out that the Wisdom Literature fits awkwardly with many of the centers postulated for the Old Testament. For instance, Walther Eichrodt suggested that covenant is the central theme of the Old Testament,[11] but the covenantal theme is scarcely central in Proverbs, Ecclesiastes, and Job. Similarly, Walter Kaiser has focused on God's promise, which again does not clearly accord with the Wisdom Literature.[12] Does the focus on God's glory and the centrality of God meet the same fate? I would argue that it does not. The centrality of God is prominent in both the Psalms and the Wisdom Literature. A detailed argument is hardly necessary for the Psalms because the Psalms call upon people to praise the Lord! In other words, the Lord is to be central to their affections. They are to sing and honor and glorify him with their praises. The God-centeredness of the Psalms is quite obvious, since the call to praise God resounds throughout them, showing that the purpose of life is to magnify the Lord. The Psalms verify what Piper has argued relentlessly. God is glorified in our praise, in our thanksgiving, and in our joy. When we praise something or someone, we honor the object of our praise. Hence, Psalms fits beautifully with the theme that God's glory is paramount in his affections.[13]

But what about Proverbs, Job, and Ecclesiastes? Do they share the same God-centered worldview? They do not share such a worldview if these books constitute secular wisdom—if they convey wisdom that is separated from Yahweh as Lord. Virtually all acknowledge, of course, that wisdom writers drew on the learning of other cultures, and many of the lessons drawn are gleaned from observing everyday life. We must beware, however, of segregating everyday life from God's realm, since he is the Creator of all. "Secular" life is not a category recognized in the Old Testament Scriptures. All of life belongs to the Lord. Indeed, a number of scholars have recognized that the wisdom writers draw on the theme of creation.[14] Yahweh is the Lord of all. Everyday wisdom is not separated from his sovereignty. Most important, the wisdom writers do not merely

---

[11]Walther Eichrodt, *Theology of the Old Testament*, 2 vols., trans. J. A. Baker (Philadelphia: Westminster, 1961, 1967).
[12]Walter C. Kaiser Jr., *Toward an Old Testament Theology* (Grand Rapids: Eerdmans, 1978); *The Promise-Plan of God: A Biblical Theology of the Old and New Testaments* (Grand Rapids: Zondervan, 2008). Kaiser attempts to fold wisdom into the theology of promise, but how it fits on his model remains unclear.
[13]Piper credits Lewis's work (see *Reflections on the Psalms*) as confirming his understanding of Christian hedonism.
[14]For instance, see Gerhard von Rad, *Wisdom in Israel* (Nashville: Abingdon, 1972), 144–76.

provide observations regarding everyday life. Such a view of their writings badly misrepresents their aims and purposes.

Proverbs begins with the claim that "the fear of the LORD is the beginning of knowledge" (Prov. 1:7). And Proverbs 9:10 adds,

> The fear of the LORD is the beginning of wisdom,
>   and the knowledge of the Holy One is insight.

Proverbs cannot be reduced to a secular perspective on wisdom. True wisdom fears and honors and obeys the Lord.

The book of Job corrects a possible misreading of Proverbs, reminding us that we cannot necessarily discern why human beings suffer. We read in Job 28:28,

> Behold, the fear of the Lord, that is wisdom,
>   and to turn away from evil is understanding.

Many things in life elude the intellect of human beings, but we are to center our lives on the fear of the Lord.

The wisdom of Ecclesiastes is quite similar. The author emphasizes how nothing in this life ultimately satisfies, and he laments the tragic and absurd in human existence. The human intellect cannot plumb the depths of truth. Human life since the fall is full of meaninglessness, where there is "sound and fury signifying nothing." Still, the conclusion of the book should not be sheared off from the rest of it. The final reflections of the author are fundamental. The meaning of life is frustrating and elusive. Still, the author communicates the most important truth in life, a truth that can be known, in the conclusion of the book: "The end of the matter; all has been heard. Fear God and keep his commandments, for this is the whole duty of man" (Eccles. 12:13). Remarkably, Ecclesiastes, Job, and Proverbs all concur on what is most important in life: fearing the Lord. It seems, then, that the Wisdom Literature does fit with the theme advanced here. God is central in life. He is the Lord of all. He is the judge on the final day. Hence, human beings must fear him and give him all the honor and glory.

God's Glory in the Kingdom and His Son

We return from the interlude granted by the Psalms and Wisdom Literature to the storyline of the Bible. The Lord fulfilled his promise and Israel did return from Babylon. Yet the fullness of what was promised in the new exodus, the new covenant, and the new creation did not become a reality. Life in the days of Zerubbabel, Ezra, and Nehemiah was good in many ways, and yet the great promises (such as we find in Isaiah 40–66) were clearly not fulfilled in their entirety. Hence, when the New Testament opens, the Jewish people are still longing for the fulfillment of all that God had promised.

The term used in the Synoptic Gospels to express what was promised in the new exodus, the new covenant, and the new creation is the "kingdom of God."[15] When Jesus taught that the kingdom was at hand, he promised that the day of salvation and judgment was near. In particular, Jesus emphasized the fulfillment of God's saving promises when he proclaimed the kingdom of God, for the in-breaking of the kingdom is manifested in the forgiveness of sins, the healing of the sick, the exorcism of demons, and the proclamation of the gospel (Mark 1:15).[16] The coming of the kingdom brings glory to God. Believers are to pray that God's name is "hallowed" (Matt. 6:9), and his name is hallowed when his kingdom comes (Matt. 6:10). If we put together what the Gospels teach about the kingdom with the Old Testament, it is clear that the kingdom's inauguration redounds to the glory of God's name. As we saw in Isaiah (48:9–11) and Ezekiel (36:22–23), when God restores his people in the new exodus, he vindicates the holiness of his name. Since the coming kingdom fulfills what is said about the new exodus, God's great name is hallowed with the arrival of the kingdom.[17]

What must not be missed at this juncture, however, is that God is glorified especially in the Son. In other words, what we see in the Synoptic Gospels is God being magnified in Christ. Jesus is the central figure in the Gospels: he is the new Moses, the wisdom of God, the prophet of Deuteronomy 18:15, the Messiah—the Son of David, the Son of Man, the Son of God, Lord, and Immanuel, God with us. It would be a grave mistake to speak of God's ultimate concern as his own glory if the glory of Jesus is left out of the equation. We scarcely need a detailed argument to say that Christ is central in the Synoptic Gospels, for the decisive issue before Israel is whether they will confess Jesus as Lord, Messiah, Son of God, Son of Man, and Son of David. When Jesus heals the paralytic and

---

[15]Matthew, of course, uses the term "kingdom of heaven." For a study of "kingdom of heaven" in Matthew, see Jonathan Pennington, *Heaven and Earth in the Gospel of Matthew*, Novum Testamentum Supplement 126 (Leiden: Brill, 2007; Grand Rapids: Baker, 2009).

[16]Indeed, the link between gospel and kingdom indicates that the kingdom fulfills the promises made to Israel, for in Isaiah the gospel proclaimed is return from exile (Isa. 40:9; 52:7). Note how the rule of God follows the proclamation of the good news in Isaiah 40:10, showing that God's saving rule of his people and judgment of his enemies are in view.

[17]As many scholars have argued, the kingdom is inaugurated but not consummated, but that theme is not our concern here.

forgives his sin, the people glorify God (Mark 2:12). Similarly, the manifold healings of Jesus provoke people to glorify God (Matt. 15:29–31; cf. Luke 7:16; 13:13; 18:43). The angels exult in the birth of Jesus and exclaim, "Glory to God in the highest" (Luke 2:14; cf. Luke 2:20). Obviously the argument here does not depend lexically on the presence of the word "glory," since the supremacy of Christ dominates the Synoptics. Nevertheless, the texts cited here show that the centrality of Christ does not diminish God's glory but enhances it. This is precisely what we expect since the Father is "well pleased" with his Son (Mark 1:11).

God's Glory in Christ in the Gospel of John

In the Gospel of John the kingdom theme recedes, and John often refers to eternal life. Eternal life is obtained only by believing in the Son (John 3:15–16; 5:24; 6:47, etc.). The high christology of John is acknowledged by all. Jesus is Lord, Son of Man, the Son of God, the Messiah, and the eternal Logos. And life is obtained only by believing in him. John emphasizes that Jesus' aim in life was to do the Father's will. He did not act on his own initiative but always did the Father's will and only did what was pleasing to the Father (John 5:19–43; 8:29, 50). One of the characteristic themes of John is that the Father sent the Son, so that Jesus came from God (John 5:23–24, 30; 6:39, etc.; cf. also 1 John 4:9–10, 14). Indeed, Jesus' aim in life was to glorify God, and he did so by accomplishing the work God intended for him to do (John 17:4).

On the one hand, Jesus glorified the Father and depended on him, showing that the glory of God was the passion of his life. And yet the Father is also glorified when the Son is glorified, particularly in his death on the cross (John 13:31–32; 17:5). The Son glorifies the Father, but the Father's glory is also enhanced when the Son is honored (John 8:54). Those who refuse to honor the Son do not honor the Father (John 5:23), which is truly one of the most astonishing statements in Scripture. And it is the Father's will that Jesus' disciples see the radiance of his glory (John 17:24). The Son prays that the Father would glorify him (John 17:5), for the Father's glory is maximized in the glory of the Son (John 17:1; cf. 14:13). The Father is glorified when disciples bear fruit, showing that they are *Jesus'* disciples (John 15:8), and he is honored when people receive life by believing in Jesus as the Christ and the Son of God (John 20:30–31).

It is abundantly clear, then, that God is glorified in Christ. Jesus glorifies God in the cross, and his being lifted up on the tree is also his exaltation (John 8:28; 12:32). God is particularly glorified in the cross, for the cross underlines Jesus' radical dependence on and obedience to the Father. The cross also glorifies God by revealing his love (John 3:16). Eternal life consists not merely in knowing God but also in knowing his Son, Jesus Christ (John 17:3). John could scarcely be clearer: God's glory must not be abstracted from Christ. Indeed, the Spirit's role is not to bring glory to himself but to glorify Christ (John 16:14), so that the focus is not on the Spirit but on the Son.[18]

God's Glory in the Epistles

What can we say about the glory of God in the Epistles, particularly in Paul's writings? We have already seen that sin consists in the failure to glorify and praise God (Rom. 1:23)—in the exaltation of the creature over the Creator (Rom. 1:25). Faith, on the other hand, glorifies God because it depends on him and trusts him to fulfill his promises (Rom. 4:20–21). Such faith for Paul has a particular texture. It is faith in the crucified and risen Jesus that brings honor to God (Rom. 4:25). The glory of God in the New Testament is christological and cross-centered. God is glorified when believers put their trust in Christ Jesus for the forgiveness of their sins. We cannot harbor any doubts about the importance of God's glory, for Paul specifically says that we are "to do all to the glory of God" (1 Cor. 10:31), including such matters here as eating and drinking! And doing all to the glory of God does not leave out Jesus Christ.

Paul expresses a parallel thought in Colossians 3:17: "And whatever you do, in word or deed, do everything in the name of the Lord Jesus, giving thanks to God the Father through him." We are to do everything to the glory of God (1 Cor. 10:31) and everything in Jesus' name (Col. 3:17). It follows, then, that when we act in the name of Jesus, God is glorified. Therefore, it is clear that God is glorified in Christ. Peter expresses the same truth when he says that all our serving and speaking is to be such "that in everything God may be glorified through Jesus Christ" (1 Pet. 4:11). Again, note that God is glorified in Christ, and that such glory to God is rendered in proclamation and service. Indeed, all our good works are carried out for the glory of God (Matt. 5:16). Every arena of life is designed to bring God glory, and so believers are enjoined to accept and welcome one another to bring glory to God (Rom. 15:7), and to honor God with their bodies by abstaining from sexual sin and using their bodies for God's sake (1 Cor. 6:20).

The significance of God's glory is occasionally indicated by the crucial places where it is found in the letters. Peter sums up his second letter by

---

[18]The New Testament does not emphasize that the Spirit is to be glorified, but it clearly teaches that the Spirit is divine and shares in the nature of God (Matt. 28:19; 2 Cor. 13:14). Hence, the Spirit, too, is to be worshiped as God.

exhorting the readers to "grow in the grace and knowledge of our Lord and Savior Jesus Christ." And then he concludes the whole letter by praying that all the glory will go to Christ. "To him be the glory both now and to the day of eternity. Amen" (2 Pet. 3:18).

Paul, after disclosing God's purposes regarding the election of both Jews and Gentiles in Romans 9:1–11:32, concentrating particularly on his faithfulness to the Jews, stands amazed at God's incomprehensible wisdom in his plan for all of history (Rom. 11:33–35). And naturally, in reflecting on God's purposes in all history he breaks forth in praise, "For from him and through him and to him are all things. To him be glory forever. Amen" (Rom. 11:36). Since everything is from God and comes into reality by means of him and is done for his sake, then it follows that he deserves the glory forever. In the same way it is not surprising that Romans concludes with a doxology. After setting forth God's great plan of salvation for both Jews and Gentiles, the deliverance from sin through Jesus Christ, and the new life believers should live, Paul ends, "to the only wise God be glory forevermore through Jesus Christ! Amen" (Rom. 16:27).

The centrality of Christ and the cross blazes throughout Paul's writings. He longs to preach only Christ and him crucified, for that is the heart of his message[19] (1 Cor. 1:17–18, 23; 2:2), but in the same context Paul emphasizes that we should boast not in ourselves but only in the Lord (1 Cor. 1:29–31). Clearly, we boast and exult in God when Jesus Christ is "[our] wisdom from God, [our] righteousness and sanctification and redemption" (1 Cor. 1:30). Perhaps the most important paragraph in the Bible is Romans 3:25–26, where Paul emphasizes that Christ satisfied the wrath of God in his death to demonstrate the righteousness of God. In other words, Jesus' death vindicated the holiness of God and the beauty of his justice. At the same time his death accomplished salvation or justification for those who belong to God. God's splendor redounds in the death of Christ, for both his justice and mercy meet in the cross. God's justice is satisfied in Christ taking the penalty upon himself that human beings deserve because of their sin (Gal. 3:10, 13; 2 Cor. 5:21). His mercy is also dispensed because the cross displays the love of God and the glory of his grace.

The Christ-centered passion of Paul permeates Philippians. Paul finds his joy in knowing that others are preaching Christ (Phil. 1:18), even though their motives are stained with envy and selfish ambition. Paul's exceeding

---

[19]J. I. Packer calls it "the best part of the best news," in J. I. Packer and Mark Dever, *In My Place Condemned He Stood* (Wheaton, IL: Crossway, 2008), 21.

joy in Christ bursts forth when he exclaims, "For me to live is Christ" (Phil. 1:21).[20] He considers all things as garbage in comparison to Christ (Phil. 3:7–9), gladly leaving all his past accomplishments behind to gain Christ. Believers gain Christ by trusting in his work on the cross and depending on his righteousness, for Paul exults in the fact that his righteousness is not his own but comes from Jesus Christ. Christ is the supreme exemplar for believers in terms of his humiliation and exaltation (Phil. 2:5–11). What is significant here is that God has exalted Christ as Lord of all. Does the Christ-centered passion of Philippians push the Father to the margins? By no means. The great Philippian hymn or poem concludes by informing us that all that happened to Christ was "to the glory of God the Father" (Phil. 2:11).

The glory of God in Christ is found virtually everywhere we turn. All of God's promises receive their "Yes" and "Amen" through Christ (2 Cor. 1:20). The glory of Christ outshines the glory of Moses (2 Cor. 3:10–11; cf. 3:18; 4:4–6). In Galatians the replacement of circumcision is not baptism but the cross-work of Jesus Christ (Gal. 1:4; 2:21; 3:1, 13; 4:4–5; 5:11; 6:14). Paul's only boast is in the cross (Gal. 6:14), for God receives glory when believers depend upon Jesus for salvation (Gal. 1:4–5).

Paul reaffirms what we noticed in the Old Testament regarding the relationship between salvation and God's glory. God elects, redeems, and grants the Spirit for the praise of his glorious grace (Eph. 1:6, 12, 14). What is ultimate, therefore, is God's glory, not the saving of his people (though, of course, his glory is featured in the salvation of his people). Paul marvels at the free grace of God, which has inducted believers into God's presence and gives joy even in trials (Rom. 5:1–5). God's love finds its anchor in the cross of Christ whereby the weak, sinners, ungodly, and his enemies are justified and reconciled (Rom. 5:6–10). The saving work of God provokes believers to "rejoice in God through our Lord Jesus Christ" (Rom. 5:11). This joy and exultation in God is the final aim and goal for believers. God is glorified when we rejoice in him, and it is clear once again that salvation is not God's ultimate purpose, for God saves and justifies so that we will exult and glory in him. Further, the joy is not merely in the Father but believers rejoice in the Father through Jesus Christ and his redeeming work.

God's Glory in Missions and Worship

As Piper has argued in his book *Let the Nations Be Glad*, "Missions is not the ultimate goal of the church. Worship is. Missions exists because

---

[20]We find a similar sentiment in Colossians where Christ is identified as "your life" (Col. 3:4). If space permitted, the preeminence of Christ in Colossians could be unfolded. Consider the Christ-hymn in Colossians 1:15–20 and the claim that our fullness is in Christ in Colossians 2:9–10.

worship doesn't."[21] Missions is done for the name of Christ (Rom. 1:5). The psalms regularly exhort readers to declare God's deeds among the nations, so that he will be praised (Pss. 9:11; 66:8). His "glory" and "marvelous works" must be proclaimed to "all the peoples" (Ps. 96:3). All people must "ascribe to the LORD the glory due his name" (Ps. 96:8). All nations and peoples are summoned to praise the Lord (Ps. 117:1). We find the same message in Isaiah 12:4:

> Give thanks to the LORD,
>   call upon his name,
> make known his deeds among the peoples,
>   proclaim that his name is exalted.

The call to missions is a call to testify to the beauty and splendor of the Lord and his Christ. And we pray that the Spirit will convict unbelievers so that they see the glory of God in the face of Christ (2 Cor. 4:4–6; cf. 1 Pet. 2:12).

The final book in the canonical Scriptures, Revelation, highlights the centrality of worship, for in worship we are exulting in and praising our God. We have already touched on some of the texts in Revelation. Revelation 4 is redolent of Isaiah 6 as angels worship God as Creator. But worship and praise are not confined to the Father, for in Revelation 5 Christ is worshiped as Redeemer, showing again that God is glorified in Christ. Such worship of Christ shows that he shares the same status and nature as God, for angels are not to be worshiped (Rev. 19:10; 22:9). All angels and all of creation worship the slain Lamb and give him praise (Rev. 5:12–14). The Lord is praised and honored for wrapping up all of history, for rewarding his saints, and for judging the wicked (Rev. 11:16–18). God's glory, then, cannot be restricted only to salvation, but must also include judgment.

Conclusion

We have seen in this chapter that the glory of God is the heartbeat of all of biblical revelation. Whether we speak of creation, the fall, redemption, or the final restoration, God's purpose is to bring glory to his name. God's name is honored in both salvation and in judgment. And yet the Scriptures focus on the glory of God in saving his people, and hence it is not surprising to discover that God is particularly glorified in Jesus

---

[21] John Piper, *Let the Nations Be Glad! The Supremacy of God in Missions*, 3d ed. (Grand Rapids: Baker, 2010), 15, 35.

Christ, and particularly in the salvation he accomplished in his cross and resurrection. As believers put their trust in what God has done in Christ through the power of the Holy Spirit, they are filled with joy. As John Piper has often preached and written, our final destiny is delight, awe, and joy. "*God is most glorified in us when we are most satisfied in him.*"[22] And we find satisfaction in what we worship, in what we treasure, and what we delight in. We glorify God most by enjoying him, and that is why Piper is on target in saying that "*the chief end of man is to glorify God* by *enjoying him forever.*"[23]

---

[22]John Piper, *When I Don't Desire God: How to Fight for Joy* (Wheaton, IL: Crossway, 2004), 13, his emphasis.
[23]Piper, *Desiring God*, 18, his emphasis.

12

The Kingdom of God
as the Mission of God

Scott J. Hafemann

The LORD reigns, let the earth rejoice;
let the many coastlands be glad!
—Psalm 97:1

It was John Piper who introduced me to God's unswerving commitment to uphold the glory of his own character as the foundation, driving focus, and climactic finish of creation, redemption, and new creation. To that end, as one of his students at Bethel College from 1973 to 1976, I was introduced also to the fact that inaugurated eschatology (the kingdom of God is here, albeit not yet in all its fullness!) is the key to understanding the history of salvation, through which God glorifies himself now and forever. To this end, we read the Gospel of Luke, Ephesians, Romans 9–11, Daniel Fuller, Jonathan Edwards, John Bright, Oscar Cullmann, George Ladd, and many mimeographed pages of his own material, the ideas of which would one day end up in *Desiring God*.

I will be forever grateful for this life-changing perspective of a God-centered universe grounded in the hermeneutic of a historically based, biblical theology. I have never learned anything more practical for pursuing the life of faith to the "praise of his glorious grace" (Eph. 1:6). In tribute, this modest essay attempts to apply this hermeneutic to the biblical concept of the kingdom of God as the outworking of the realization that "missions is the overflow of God's delight in being God."[1] We begin at the beginning, with the establishment of the kingdom of God at creation. There we see that "missions" is *God's* mission in the world and that God's *mission* is to glorify himself by creating a people who obey the commands of God their King and thereby exercise a dominion characterized by dependence on God himself.

The Kingdom of God at Creation

In Genesis 1:26–27, God creates male and female equally in his "likeness" and then, as a result, grants them "dominion" over the rest of creation. This link between God's likeness and humanity's dominion makes it clear that to see mankind ruling over the world was to see a mirror image of God's own sovereign rule over all things. Moreover, the following verses emphasize that Adam and Eve are not called to rule the world in order to provide for themselves out of their own authority and ingenuity. Rather, their call to "be fruitful and multiply and fill the earth" is based on God's promise that his sovereign provision had already granted them everything they needed to accomplish God's command (Gen. 1:28–31).

As the consequence of God's creative acts on days one through six, Adam and Eve rule, under God, over a home already prepared for them. Like the kings of the ancient world who mimicked him, God demonstrated his supreme power and beneficent love by providing for his subjects, who ruled over his realm in his name. In turn, the glory of God as King is manifest through mankind's "dominion of dependence," in which their rule over the rest of creation is an expression of the sufficiency of the Lord's sovereign provision. Mankind's mandate is God's mission in the world. As an interpretation of Genesis 1:26–28, Psalm 8 therefore frames the glory and honor of *mankind*, who has been crowned to rule over the earth, with declarations of *God's* majesty, since the former reveals the latter.

The mission mandate to exercise dominion over God's creation by obeying God's commands, as made possible by God's provisions, is the consequence of establishment of the kingdom of God. The God-centered nature of the universe cannot be more evident. Briefly put, the kingdom of God is the rule of God (the exercise of his sovereignty), which creates

---

[1] John Piper, *Let the Nations Be Glad: The Supremacy of God in Missions*, 3d ed. (Grand Rapids: Baker, 2010), 39.

the reign of God (the sphere of his sovereignty) in God's realm (the space of his sovereignty), all of which is reflected in the obedience of his people. By establishing his kingdom, God reveals his glory in the world through creating a people who will obey his commands as the expression of their confidence in his sovereignty. "Ethics" (obedience to God's commands) is the embodiment of the kingdom of God as the mission of God in the world: the glory of the invisible God is made visible in the trusting obedience of his people. To be created in God's image is to be given the role of ruling over the rest of creation under God's authority by relying on God's provisions. Against this backdrop kingdom therefore becomes the primary biblical metaphor by which God will make known his glory to and through his people. *The historical revelation of God's glory as King through the obedience of his people* thus becomes the central theme of the Scriptures, from which the themes of creation, judgment, redemption, covenant, and new creation all derive and are held together, like the spokes of a wheel radiating from the hub.

The establishment of the kingdom of God at creation reaches its climax when God rests on the seventh day, thereby declaring the glory of his sovereign rule as demonstrated in the sufficiency of his provisions—there is nothing more to provide. For God to sit serenely on his throne in his own sanctuary, rather than having to go out to do battle against the enemies that threaten his people, is the posture of the king at rest (cf. God's corresponding promise to David in 2 Sam. 7:1–16 and God's taking up his resting place in the temple in Ps. 132:7–8, 13–14).[2] The King's rest on the Sabbath day of creation declares the good news that under his sovereign reign everything in his realm is as it should be.[3] In Eden, God keeps the Sabbath as a result of providing for his people; in response, Adam and Eve are to keep the Sabbath not by inactivity, but by exercising dominion under God's reign through obedience to his commandments (Gen. 2:16; 3:2). In this way, Adam and Eve's obedience to the King's commands, as the expression of their trust in the sufficiency of his provisions, will glorify God as the sovereign Giver of all good and sufficient gifts (cf. the creation imagery in James 1:16–18).

Nonetheless, in spite of God's provisions as their sovereign King, and in a tragedy beyond description, Eve and Adam fell prey to Satan's lie

---

[2]For this latter reference I am indebted to G. K. Beale, *The Temple and the Church's Mission: A Biblical Theology of the Dwelling Place of God* (Downers Grove, IL: InterVarsity, 2004), 61–62. Beale points as well to 1 Chronicles 28:2; 2 Chronicles 6:41; Isaiah 66:1; Judith 9:8.

[3]So too Beale, *Temple*, 62: "God's rest both at the conclusion of creation in Genesis 1–2 and later in Israel's temple indicates not mere inactivity but that he had demonstrated his sovereignty over the forces of chaos (e.g., the enemies of Israel) and now has assumed a position of *kingly* rest further revealing his *sovereign* power" (my emphasis).

that God's commands were driven not by his sovereign love for his creation (see Deut. 10:12–14) but by a fearful, self-protective regard for his own status. Satan maintained that God had therefore lied about the death-producing consequences of rebelling against God's commands (Gen. 3:1–5). In response to Satan's cunning, and driven by their own desires for independence, Adam and Eve broke their Sabbath relationship with God by disobeying his commandments because of their lack of trust in his word (Gen. 3:6–7). As a result of their fall into disobedience as the expression of their disbelief, God's mission, though launched at creation, remained unfulfilled.

Nevertheless, in spite of humanity's sin, and in an act of mercy equally beyond description, God did not abandon his mission of revealing his glory by establishing his rule in the world through the obedience of his people. And so, to accomplish his mission, God's rule in overcoming chaos at creation would now extend to overcoming the effects of the fall. Under his sovereign and gracious reign, God creates an unfolding history of redemption in the midst of the ongoing history of mankind's rebellion. Beginning with the redemption of Adam and Eve themselves, therefore, a battle will now take place between the kingdom of this world, made up of the people now under the rule of the Evil One, and the kingdom of God, made up of the seed of Eve who, by God's mercy (Gen. 3:20–21), are brought back under his rule (Gen. 3:15a). Though God's ultimate victory through his Seed is clear (Gen. 3:15b), the people of God, as a minority within God's own world, will have to fight the fight of faith in the midst of the many nations who continue their self-rule.

The Kingdom of God in the Life of Abraham

As Bruce Waltke points out in his introductory sentence to the Abrahamic narratives, "The Bible is all about the irrupting kingdom of God, and Genesis is all about the elect 'seed,' a metaphor for the people of God who constitute that kingdom."[4] The election and call of Abraham and the ensuing patriarchal narratives continue God's mission of revealing his glory through reestablishing his rule by creating a people who will obey his commands as they learn to trust his provisions and promises. If Genesis 1–11 presents the problem, Genesis 12–50 presents God's solution.[5]

---

[4]Bruce K. Waltke, *An Old Testament Theology* (Grand Rapids: Zondervan, 2007), 305.
[5]Similarly, ibid., 307. Cf. H. W. Wolff's observation that the fivefold repetition of the language of blessing in Genesis 12:1–3 responds to the five curses in Genesis 1–11 (Gen. 3:14, 17; 4:11; 5:29; 9:25), as cited by Roy E. Ciampa, "The History of Redemption," in *Central Themes in Biblical Theology: Mapping Unity in Diversity*, ed. Scott J. Hafemann and Paul R. House (Grand Rapids: Baker, 2007), 254–308, 264.

God's sovereign call of Abraham back from the *east* (i.e., from Ur in southern Babylon) to a land of God's own provision is God's response to his own judgment on the tower of the city of Babel (= Babylon; *babel* means "to confuse" or "to mix"), by which humanity had sought on its own to overcome God's earlier dispersal of Adam and Eve *east* of Eden (cf. Gen. 3:24 with 11:1 and 11:31–12:1). Humanity had found its own land and sought to build its own city of brick, with its own man-made mountain into the heavens, in order to make a name for itself (Gen. 11:1–4); God calls Abraham to live as a nomad on other people's land he will provide and then promises that he will make Abraham's name great (Gen. 12:2). In this way, the kingdom of God, first established at creation, once again continues with a single family. As an allusion back to creation itself, God's command to go to the land he will provide is followed by seven promises, the central one of which is the missional statement that Abraham will not remain alone but become an instrument of blessing to others, who will encounter the reality of God's rule through Abraham's life of faith.

Having left the security of his earthly "father's house" (Gen. 12:1), Abraham will become the "father" of a great nation; indeed, Abraham will be "the father of a multitude of nations" (Gen. 12:2–3; 17:4–5). Moreover, as Roy Ciampa observes:

> God's promises to Abram in Genesis 12:2–3 suggest blessings that one great suzerain might confer upon another. [Gordon] Wenham points out that "what Abram is here promised was the hope of many an oriental monarch." He will become a great nation, blessed by his divine Suzerain, including the blessing of the common royal aspiration of a great name, so that he might become "the mediator of blessing for mankind." In fact, others will be blessed or cursed depending on their relationship to Abram, as though they were all bound to him by a suzerainty treaty with blessings or curses depending on the attitude taken with respect to Abram as *their* suzerain. This clearly anticipates the later biblical material about the ideal Davidic king . . . , as does God's promise to Abraham in 17:6 that "kings shall come from you."[6]

God's promises to Abraham make clear that God is continuing his mission "to govern a world through a human vice-regent who would come to have dominion over and bring blessing to his creation."[7]

---

[6]Ciampa, "History," 265.
[7]Ibid. In support, Ciampa, 266 and 266n29, points to the fact that the motif of "being fruitful" and "multiplying" from Genesis 1:28 is frequently used in connection with Abraham and his seed, so that

To that end, Abraham must learn to trust God's promises as his divine King, in the midst of the increasing adversities that call them into question (Genesis 13), and to hold out for a miracle baby to be his heir as time creeps on (Gen. 15:1–21:7). Having experienced God's deliverance in the past (Gen. 15:7: "I am the LORD who brought you out from Ur of the Chaldeans to give you this land to possess"), Abraham learns to trust God in the present (Gen. 15:1, 6: "Fear not, Abram, I am your shield. . . . And he believed the LORD, and he counted it to him as righteousness"), as he hopes in God's promises for the future (Gen. 15:1, 5: "Your reward shall be very great. . . . number the stars . . . . So shall your offspring be"). Indeed Abraham's faith is seen in his obedience to God's command not to give his inheritance to Eliezer or Ishmael (Gen. 15:2; 16:1–15).

Abraham also fights to rescue Lot from the four kings of the Babylonian (!) region just as they reach the northern border of the Promised Land (Gen. 14:13–16). This leads Melchizedek, the priest-king of Salem (= Jerusalem!), to acknowledge that Abraham is blessed by "God Most High," the "Possessor of heaven and earth," who is to be blessed himself as the one "who has delivered [Abraham's] enemies into [his] hand" (Gen. 14:19–20). Abraham defeats the enemies of God's people by virtue of the provisions of the divine King who, as the ruler over all, grants dominion to Abraham. For this reason, Abraham refuses to take the spoils offered him by the king of Sodom, lest he should say, "I have made Abram rich," when in reality Abraham has lifted up his empty hand to the Lord alone as "the Possessor of heaven and earth" (Gen. 14:22–23). Into Abraham's empty hand, the Lord covenants to grant descendants and a land in fulfillment of his promise, and, in yet another allusion to the kingdom of God at creation, to make Abraham "exceedingly fruitful," which is now interpreted to mean that God will make Abraham "into nations, and kings shall come from you" (Gen. 17:6). As the inauguration of this promise, Abraham's subsequent intercession for Sodom and the ensuing rescue of Lot from its destruction demonstrate how the Lord uses Abraham to be the instrument of blessing and curse in the world, just as Lot himself carries on this calling in relationship to Zoar (Gen. 18:22–19:22).

The narrative makes clear that the Lord has provided for Abraham throughout his life, beginning with his call in Ur and climaxing on the mountain (!) where Abraham offered up Isaac to God, which Abraham appropriately calls "The LORD will provide" (Gen. 22:14). In the context of Abraham's dependence on God's provision, manifest in his obedience

---

"the primaeval blessing has been *reaffirmed* and *reapplied* to Abraham's progeny" (quoting Carol M. Kaminski); cf. Genesis 16:10; 17:2, 20; 22:17; 26:4, 24; 28:3; 35:11; 47:27; 48:4.

to God's command to sacrifice Isaac (Gen. 22:10), Abraham's offspring also receive the promise to "possess the gate of their enemies, and in [their] offspring shall all the nations of the earth be blessed, because [Abraham has] obeyed my voice" (Gen. 22:17–18). The promise to Abraham's offspring in Genesis 22:17–18 forms an *inclusio* with the promise first given to Abraham in Genesis 12:1–3, and in both cases the promise is given in response to Abraham's obedience. In obedience to God's word as his sovereign King (Gen. 12:1), Abraham forsook his father's house and was promised to become the father of many nations, who will be blessed through him (Gen. 12:3; cf. its repetition in Gen. 17:4–5; 18:18). In obedience to God's command (Gen. 22:1–2), Abraham offered up his only son, and his son's descendants are promised to rule over their enemies, so that in them too "the nations of the earth [will] be blessed" (Gen. 22:18; cf. Gen. 26:1–5 for the extension of the covenant promises to Isaac based on Abraham's obedience to God's commandments and Gen. 18:19 for the fulfillment of the promises to Abraham based on the obedience of his descendants).

In calling Abraham, an ungodly moon-worshiper from east of Eden (Josh. 24:2–3), God has chosen a people as an act of unconditional election, and hence unmitigated grace, through whom he promises to establish his rule on the earth. God's people are called to manifest the glory of his sovereignty through their obedience to his commands, since their obedience is made possible by God's ongoing provisions and protection, all of which are expressions of his sovereign mercy. Not surprisingly, then, since Abraham represents the kingly rule of God on earth, the Hittites recognize him to be "a prince of God among us" and seek to honor him by giving him the land needed to bury Sarah (Gen. 23:6). Yet, as God's prince, Abraham will not accept their gift, as if he were dependent on them, but insists on paying full price for the burial cave and its land, thereby securing it for his family's future generations on the basis of what God, his sovereign King, has provided (Abraham, Isaac, Jacob, Rebekah, and Leah will all be buried there).

The Kingdom of God at Sinai

Although Abraham's descendants were granted the Promised Land as the realm of God's reign over them, God himself had declared in his sovereignty that they would end up as slaves under Egypt's rule for four hundred years (Gen. 15:13). But once again God did not forsake his mission, now inextricably tied to his chosen people. To keep his promises to Abraham, God delivers Abraham's descendants from their slavery in

Egypt in order to bring them back into his Promised Land as a nation over which he himself will reign as their King (Ex. 2:23–25). Though there arose a "king over Egypt, who did not know Joseph" (Ex. 1:8), God, Joseph's true King (cf. Gen. 50:20), "saw the people of Israel—and God knew" (Ex. 2:25). As their true ruler, God proves his sovereignty by ten acts of judgment on Egypt's false sources of security and pride, including the destruction of the nation's firstborn sons. Finally, to declare definitively his glory as the King of kings and Lord of lords, God drowns the army of the greatest earthly empire of the day, while Israel stands still to watch the Lord, their divine, royal warrior, fight on their behalf (Ex. 14:4, 13–14, 17–18; cf. Ex. 15:3: "The LORD is a man of war; the LORD is his name"). Hence, "by faith the people crossed the Red Sea as on dry land, but the Egyptians, when they attempted to do the same, were drowned" (Heb. 11:29).

The exodus narrative, which stretches from the crossing of the Red Sea out of Egypt to the crossing of the Jordan River into the Promised Land, is framed by two Songs of Moses (Ex. 15:1–18; Deut 32:1–43). Both harmonize in their emphasis on the exodus as a demonstration of the kingdom of God. In praising the Lord, who has become their salvation (Ex. 15:2), the first describes the Egyptian horse and rider thrown into the sea in terms reminiscent of God's overcoming the original chaos of the world at creation and of God's judgment of rebellious humanity at the flood, where in both cases God drove back the waters to provide dry land for his people (Ex. 15:4–8, 10, 19; cf. Ex. 14:21 with Gen. 1:9 and 8:1–19; Neh. 9:11; Ps. 66:6). Against this backdrop, the redemption of Israel at the exodus once again demonstrates through his provisions for his people that "the LORD will reign forever and ever" (Ex. 15:18). In the same way, the second Song of Moses declares that just as God "created" and "formed" the land at creation, so too, as the "father" of Israel, his own "firstborn son" (Ex. 4:22), God "created," "made," and "established" Israel as his people at the exodus (Deut. 32:6). As the Lord will later declare through Isaiah,

> I am the LORD, your Holy One,
>   the Creator of Israel, your King.
>   (Isa. 43:15; cf. Isa. 43:1)

As the result of God's redemption and rule over his people, rehearsed in the covenant prologue of Exodus 19:4 and 20:2, Israel was to be a "kingdom of priests and a holy nation," mediating God's glory to the world by obeying God's voice and keeping his covenant (Ex. 19:5–6). Her call, specified in the covenant stipulations of the Decalogue and Book of the Covenant (Ex. 20:3–23:33), could be summarized in the great commandments of Deuteronomy 6:4–5 (to love the one true God with all her heart, soul, and might) and Leviticus 19:18 (to love one's neighbor as oneself, since YHWH is Israel's Lord!)—the command that Jacob Milgrom argues is the central verse of the central chapter of the central book of the Torah.[8]

By God's grace, Israel as the descendants of Abraham, her patriarch, is the "new creation" people of God, redeemed to reveal God's glory as King through her obedience to his covenant commands, which are made possible by God's covenant provisions and motivated by his covenant promises. The Sabbath relationship first established in the garden of Eden therefore becomes the sign of the Sinai covenant (Ex. 31:13, 17; Ezek. 20:12, 20; cf. its establishment already in Ex. 16:29 with the provision of manna and quail). So God's "kingdom" mission of creating a people who, like Abraham, will glorify God by keeping his laws and thus inherit his promises continues on through the Sinai covenant (cf. Ex. 19:5; 20:1–17; Lev. 26:1–13; Deut. 4:32–40; 6:1–3; 30:1–20, etc.). Hence, like a patriarch before his death, Moses reminds Israel in his final blessing that the Lord granted Israel his law at Sinai as an expression of his love, so that "the LORD became king in Jeshurun ["the righteous one," a poetic name for Israel],[9] when the heads of the people were gathered, all the tribes of Israel together" (Deut. 33:1–5). God's missional intention, first announced at creation, is reaffirmed at the creation of Israel.

Yet again, however, God's mission, though still moving forward through redemptive history, remained unfulfilled. Despite her declaration that "all that the LORD has spoken we will do" (Ex. 19:8), Israel as a people broke the covenant, the fall of Israel with the golden calf in the wilderness replicating the fall of humanity in the garden of Eden. For as Ezekiel will later lament, Israel's history from the exodus to the exile testifies that, although she had been delivered from slavery in Egypt, Israel as a nation had not been delivered from her slavery to sin (Ezek. 20:1–29; cf. Ps. 106:6–43; Neh. 9:9–37). The exodus had changed her circumstances but not her "stiff neck" (Ex. 32:9; 33:3, 5; 34:9; Deut. 9:6; cf. Acts 7:51). God had judged Adam and Eve for breaking the Sabbath (Gen. 2:1–3) by casting them out of the garden, east of Eden. So too, God judged Judah for breaking

---

[8] Jacob Milgrom, *Leviticus* (Minneapolis: Augsburg Fortress, 2004), 218 (see also 7–8, 175, 180, 219, 235). Milgrom therefore calls Leviticus 19 the writing of "a new 'Decalogue'" (214) and argues that 19:18 "is the ethical summit not only in this chapter but in all of Scripture" (218).
[9] See the *ESV Study Bible* (Wheaton, IL: Crossway, 2008), 378, note on Ex. 32:15–16.

the Sabbath (cf. Ezek. 20:13–16 with 20:30) by sending her into exile in Babylon, east of the Promised Land, not having learned her lesson from the northern tribe's exile in Assyria (2 Kings 17:7–23; 23:26–27).

But again God did not abandon his mission. He preserved a remnant of faithful believers throughout Israel's history, who, "chosen by grace," submitted to God's kingship (Rom. 11:4–5). And he declared that one day he would restore Israel, and the nations with her, fully and finally, through the future reign of a Davidic King, the throne of whose kingdom would last forever (Gen. 49:8–10; Ps. 89:1–4, 29, 36; Isa. 9:6–7; 11:1–5; Jer. 23:3–6; Ezek. 37:24–28, etc.).[10] Through this Messiah, who would represent God as his Son (2 Sam. 7:12–14; Ps. 2:6–7), God would one day rule over all people as Judge, Lawgiver, and King (Isa. 33:13–24; 43:14–21; Ezek. 20:33). To that end, under a new covenant brought about by the messianic King, God will forgive the sins of his people and pour out his Spirit in their lives in order to bring about a renewed obedience to the commandments of his law, by which they will exercise dominion over the land (Jer. 31:31–34; Ezek. 36:25–27).

Jesus and the Kingdom of God

The fulfillment of these promises is clearly marked: Jesus is enthroned as Israel's messianic King at his baptism. As the Spirit descends, God himself declares Jesus to be the royal Son in fulfillment of Psalm 2:7 and 2 Samuel 7:12–14 (Matt. 3:16–17; Mark 1:9–11; Luke 3:21–22; John 1:29–34). In response, Jesus announces that he is fulfilling the call to proclaim "good news to the poor" as promised in Isaiah 61:1–2 (Luke 4:18–21). The parallel passage in Isaiah 52:7, from which we get the word *gospel* (a proclaimed message of good news), stands behind the corresponding summary of Jesus' preaching in Mark 1:14–15. This Isaianic background to Jesus' preaching makes clear that the good news of happiness is the message of salvation from one's enemies that comes about when "your God reigns" (Isa. 52:7), a reference back to the first Song of Moses in Exodus 15:18. For the "herald of good news" is sent to proclaim the One who comes to rule: "'Behold your God!'" (Isa. 40:9–10). For this reason, in the *inclusio* that makes up the first and last verses of the introduction to the Gospel of Mark, the "gospel" about *Jesus* in Mark 1:1 turns out to be Jesus' "gospel" about *God* in Mark 1:14. The good news is that,

---

[10]For the promised Davidic dynasty (genealogy) and the king's dominion (geography) as the key to the structure of the Old Testament canon, which may be summarized under the expression "the kingdom of God," see Stephen G. Dempster, *Dominion and Dynasty: A Biblical Theology of the Hebrew Bible* (Downers Grove, IL: InterVarsity, 2003), 45–51, 62, 193–202.

in and through the Christ, God has come to rule, finally and fully, over his people.

It is no wonder that the people thought that the coming of the messianic King would surely bring a decisive "second exodus" redemption of God's people from her Roman oppressors and the long-awaited establishment of David's kingdom to its rightful place of sovereignty over all nations. The coming of God as King, through his Son, meant the vindication of the righteous through the judgment of the rebellious, disobedient world (Joel 2:18–3:21; Mal. 4:1–6; Isaiah 40). Hence, with God's wrath on the horizon, John the Baptist had prepared for the coming of the Messiah by calling for genuine repentance, manifest in obedience, and offering the forgiveness of sins in response, symbolized by baptism (Matt. 3:1–12; Luke 3:1–18).

In a shocking turn of events, however, Jesus' proclamation of the kingdom does not lead to God's final judgment but to a further call to repentance and trust in the good news of God's reign: "The time is fulfilled, and the kingdom of God is at hand; repent and believe in the gospel" (Mark 1:15). This is the main point of Jesus' ministry. The King has come, but there is still time to come to faith and be forgiven (cf. Mark 2:5)! Although God's eschatological kingdom (i.e., his final and full rule) is dawning, Jesus extends the period of repentance in preparation for God's coming, final judgment by offering God's forgiveness and acceptance to sinners to whom the gospel of God's rule and reign is proclaimed (Mark 2:13–17). Indeed, rather than bringing John's preparation to an end, the main point of Jesus' preaching (Matt. 4:17) was identical to that of John's (Matt. 3:2): "Repent, for the kingdom of heaven is at hand." Inasmuch as the kingdom was not yet coming in all its glory, which was clearly seen in John's own imprisonment and death, even John the Baptist wondered whether Jesus really was the Christ (Matt. 11:2–3).

The Mystery of the Kingdom of God

Jesus' establishment of the kingdom of God is the vantage point from which the entire ministry of Jesus must be understood. The kingdom of God is here because the Messiah—the Son of David as God's Son, whom we come to realize is also the *divine* Son of God (!)—has come. But as demonstrated by Jesus' own continuing call for repentance and faith (rather than his calling forth the wrath of God), the kingdom has not come as expected! Already at Jesus' baptism God himself interprets Jesus' identity as the Son (Ps. 2:7: "You are my [beloved] Son") in terms of the Suffering Servant of the Lord (Isa. 42:1: "in whom my soul delights"), who later in Isaiah is identified with the One who gives his life for the sins of his people (Isa. 52:13–53:12; cf. Mark 1:11 with 10:45). The sign on the cross would unwittingly speak the truth: "This is Jesus, the King of the Jews," since the Son had been sent to die as the Servant (Matt. 27:37). Jesus was in fact bringing the judgment of God, but it would fall on the one person who did not deserve it, so that all who did deserve God's wrath could nevertheless be forgiven and enter into the kingdom of God.

By way of commentary, Jesus' parables of the kingdom reveal that a mystery necessitated by the cross lies at the very heart of Jesus' ministry (Matt. 13:1–33; Mark 2:18–22; 4:1–32; Luke 8:4–18; 13:18–21). Although the final, eschatological kingdom is now here (in Cullmann's analogy, D-Day has taken place), it is not yet here in all its fullness (V-Day is still to come).[11] In other words, the "mystery of the kingdom" is the fact that the new age of the new creation is being realized in the midst of the evil age that still dominates this world. Rather than bringing this age to an end, the new age now overlaps this one, with God's final, eschatological rule first established not by the cataclysmic fire of God's wrath, but by the planting and slow growth of God's word, centered as it is on the kingdom. Jesus has inaugurated the kingdom but its consummation is yet to come.

But it is coming! The mystery of the kingdom also makes clear that God has not given up on his mission: the seed produces a hundredfold, the hidden lamp will be manifest, the grain ripens; the smallest mustard seed becomes the largest plant in the garden (Mark 4:20, 22, 29, 32). Yet just as the seed of the kingdom grows "by itself" (Mark 4:28), so too the consummation of the kingdom comes solely as a result of God's sovereignty, when, in his timing, the harvest is ripe (Mark 4:29; cf. 2 Pet. 3:8–10).

Therefore, only with the return of the divine Son of Man of Daniel 7:13–14 (Jesus' favorite title for himself as the messianic King who is identified with his people!) will the kingdom be established in all its glory (Mark 4:26–29; 8:38; 14:62; Matt. 13:24–30, 47–50; 16:27; Rev. 1:7). Despite its central, cosmic significance, Christ's first coming is still only the ante-climax of the covenant. For in his vision of the coming of the kingdom of God, Daniel saw one "like a son of man," who came, like

---

[11]See Oscar Cullmann, *Christ and Time* (Philadelphia: Westminster, 1975), 3, 10, 141–42, 145. As he rightly observes, "To anyone who does not take clear account of this tension, the entire New Testament is a book with seven seals, for this tension is the silent presupposition that lies behind all that it says" (145–46).

God himself, "with the clouds of heaven" (Dan. 7:13a; cf. Ex. 13:21; 19:16; Lev. 16:2; Pss. 68:4; 104:3–4, etc.).[12]

> To him was given dominion
>   and glory and a kingdom,
> that all peoples, nations, and languages
>   should serve him;
> his dominion is an everlasting dominion,
>   which shall not pass away,
> and his kingdom one
>   that shall not be destroyed. (Dan. 7:14)

Furthermore, the "son of man" in Daniel's vision, like the "servant of the LORD" in Isaiah, represents the people of God, who together with him will rule and reign in God's kingdom forever (Dan. 7:18, 22; cf. 7:9–10). For this reason, the interpretation of the vision concludes with the promise that, just as the kingdom was granted to the divine figure of the "son of man," so too

> the kingdom and the dominion
>   and the greatness of the kingdoms under the whole heaven
>   shall be given to the people of the saints of the Most High;
> their kingdom shall be an everlasting kingdom,
>   and all dominions shall serve and obey them. (Dan. 7:27)

Against this backdrop, the mystery of the kingdom entails that in his first coming, "the Son of Man came not to be served but to serve, and to give his life as a ransom for many" (Mark 10:45). In Mark 10:45 Jesus confirms his baptism by interpreting the Son of Man from Daniel 7:13–14 in terms of the "ransom" of Isaiah 43:3–4 and the Suffering Servant of 53:11–12. The death of the King as a "ransom for many" is what enables God to rule over the lives of sinful people without destroying them. Without the cross the kingdom would be empty and God's mission could not be accomplished. The cross makes it possible for the obedience-producing Spirit to take up his dwelling with the people of the new covenant, who themselves now become "the temple [better: holy of holies!] of the living God" (2 Cor. 6:16). As a result, those who, like Moses, encounter God's

---

[12]For an accessible treatment of the text, making these points, see Tremper Longman III, *Daniel*, New International Version Application Commentary (Grand Rapids: Zondervan, 1999), 186–91, 198. Thus, as in Genesis 1:26–28, God is coming to rule through a man, not through the worldly kingdoms, which are pictured in Daniel as the created beasts over which *adam*, as God's vice-regent, was to exercise dominion. But now that man will be God himself!

glory with an "unveiled face . . . are being transformed into the same image [of God!] from one degree of glory to another. For this comes from the Lord who is the Spirit" (2 Cor. 3:18).

The redeemed fulfill their role as God's image. Because of the atoning consequence of the cross, God is finally fulfilling his mission of revealing his glory through (re-)creating a people who will exercise dominion in his name by keeping his commandments. Whereas humanity failed in the garden and Israel fell in the wilderness, the church, under the sovereignty of Christ, who is "the ruler of kings on earth," will fill the world with the glory of God as "a kingdom, priests to his God and Father" (Rev. 1:5–6; cf. 1:9; 5:10; 12:10). In the words of John's vision from Revelation 11:15, which again recall the "gospel" of Exodus 15:18 and Isaiah 52:7, "The kingdom of the world has become the kingdom of our Lord and of his Christ, and he shall reign forever and ever." The first and second Songs of Moses are finally being fulfilled in a third "song of Moses, the servant of God," which is now expanded to be "the song of the Lamb" (Rev. 15:3a). The first two sang of God's reign over Israel (see above); the third sings of God's reign over the nations. Now, in an echo of Exodus 15:11–16 and Deuteronomy 32:3–4, those who have conquered with Christ sing forth:

> Great and amazing are your deeds,
>   O Lord God the Almighty!
> Just and true are your ways,
>   O *King of the nations!*
> Who will not fear, O Lord,
>   and glorify your name?
> For you alone are holy.
>   All nations will come
>   and *worship* you,
> for your righteous acts have been revealed.
>   (Rev. 15:3b–4)

The Mission of the Kingdom of God

Among John Piper's many insightful theological dictums is his declaration that "missions exists because worship doesn't."[13] In line with the song of Revelation 15, "the goal of missions" can therefore rightly be said to be "worship," since "in missions we simply aim to bring the nations into the white-hot enjoyment of God's glory," which Piper unpacks in terms of the kingdom theme of Psalm 97:1:

---

[13]Piper, *Let the Nations Be Glad*, 15, 35.

> The LORD *reigns*, let the earth rejoice;
> let the many coastlands be glad![14]

Moreover, Psalm 97 makes clear that the worship of God does not yet exist everywhere in the world because the kingdom of God, though a reality within the church, is not yet manifest and recognized everywhere in the world. And the kingdom of God is not yet manifest everywhere because obedience to God's commands, made possible by the King's own presence and provisions, is not yet everywhere being realized, even among those who call themselves Christians.

But God has still not given up on his mission. The main point of Jesus' ministry remains the church's central message: though the kingdom of God is here, there is still time to repent before the day of final judgment dawns as the consummation of God's rule over a rebellious world (2 Pet. 1:19; 3:8–10)! The "Great Commission" is thus the pathway to the global worship of God. The resurrected Jesus commands those disciples who already worship him (Matt. 28:17) to make disciples of all nations by baptizing them in response to their repentance and then by teaching them to "observe" (lit., "to keep" in the sense of "obey") all that the messianic King has "commanded" as the expression of his universal authority (Matt. 28:18–20).[15] It is no accident that Jesus' mission-command is given on a mountain in Galilee after his resurrection (Matt. 28:7, 16). This location signals that the command to make disciples by teaching them to obey Jesus' commandments is simply an extension of the mission-command first given to the disciples themselves on a mountain in Galilee during his earthly ministry: "Let your light shine before others, so that they may see your good works and give glory to your Father who is in heaven" (Matt. 5:16).[16] The "good works" of God's people manifest God's glory in the world as the One who, by reestablishing his reign over their lives in a second-exodus deliverance, has set them free from their slavery to sin. As a result, God gets the glory for his people's obedience. Jesus therefore makes it clear that his call for good works is simply the final realiza-

---

[14]Ibid., referring also to Psalm 67:3–4.

[15]That the Great Commission is a statement concerning the rule of Christ as messianic King, over against the rule of the pagan king Cyrus, the anticlimactic "messiah" of the old covenant (cf. Isa. 44:28–45:1), is confirmed by the fact that 2 Chronicles 36:23, the last verse in the traditional Jewish ordering of the Old Testament canon, provides the backdrop for the Great Commission in Matthew 28:18–20. This has been pointed out by Alan B. Vance in "The Church as the New Temple in Matthew 16:17–19: A Biblical-Theological Consideration of Jesus' Response to Peter's Confession as Recorded by Matthew," ThM thesis, Gordon-Conwell Theological Seminary, 1992.

[16]Having stated this link between Matthew 28:18–20 and 5:16, I was happy to discover that Piper also links these two texts together conceptually in the introduction to his comprehensive survey of the commands of Jesus, which he develops in obedience to Jesus' "last command" in Matthew 28:19–20; see his *What Jesus Demands from the World* (Wheaton, IL: Crossway, 2006), 18.

tion of God's mission in the world, which has already been anticipated throughout the history of redemption:

> Do not think that I have come to abolish the Law or the Prophets; I have not come to abolish them but to fulfill them. . . . Therefore whoever relaxes one of the least of these commandments and teaches others to do the same will be called least in the kingdom of heaven, but whoever does them and teaches them will be called great in the kingdom of heaven. For I tell you, unless your righteousness exceeds that of the scribes and Pharisees, you will never enter the kingdom of heaven. (Matt. 5:17–20)[17]

Jesus' warning in this passage underscores why God's mission is centered on proclaiming the mystery of the kingdom, since the King's cross, validated by the resurrection, is the means by which the good-works-producing power of the Spirit's presence is made possible in the lives of God's people. Only as they are transformed by the cross of Christ and the Spirit of the Lord, may God's people reveal the glory of God's kingdom by doing his will in obedience to his commands. The consummation of the eschatological kingdom in the "new heavens and a new earth in which righteousness dwells" (2 Pet. 3:13), like its establishment in Christ's first coming, is not the work of God's people but the gift of God's grace.

The Dominion of Dependence
Knowing that God alone can establish his kingdom, and at the same time confronting them with the commands of the King, Jesus taught his disciples to pray:

> Our Father in heaven,
> hallowed be your name.
> Your kingdom come,
> your will be done,
>   on earth as it is in heaven.
>   (Matt. 6:9–10)

---

[17]So too, George Eldon Ladd, *The Gospel of the Kingdom* (Grand Rapids: Eerdmans, 1959), 79, commenting on Matthew 5:20: "The qualification for entrance into the future Kingdom is a present righteousness. . . . The righteousness required for entrance into the future realm of God's Kingdom is the righteousness which results from God's reign in our lives. The Kingdom of God gives to us that which it demands; otherwise, we could not attain it." (See, too, 83, 85, 93–94.) For an application of Jesus' warning, see Colossians 1:3–14, where Paul unpacks the gospel—i.e., the good news that God "has delivered us from the domain of darkness and transferred us to the kingdom of his beloved Son, in whom we have redemption, the forgiveness of sins" (vv. 13–14)—in terms of the need to "walk in a manner worthy of the Lord" by bearing "fruit in every good work" (vv. 6, 10; cf. too 1 Thess. 2:12).

The prayer that God would vindicate the holiness of his character is the first and foundational petition of the Lord's Prayer. It is the petition that orientates all the others, since it recognizes that the manifestation of the glory of God's reputation, which is most important to God, is also his people's greatest good. For inasmuch as the King exercises his sovereignty as "our [loving] Father," his people can be confident that his glory is wrapped up in the goodness of his gifts. As Jesus put it, "If you then, who are evil, know how to give good gifts to your children, how much more will the heavenly Father give the Holy Spirit to those who ask him!" (Luke 11:13). This first petition provides the framework for all others. Everything else that we pray, we pray in order that, through the granting of our requests, God's name might be hallowed. For "the most important prayer is that the most important person in the universe do the most important act in the universe."[18]

So after asking that God would glorify his name, we pray for the coming of God's kingdom as the means by which the glory of God's holiness will be realized—since, as we have seen, God's glory is revealed in his rule over his creation. The prayer then acknowledges that the coming of the kingdom, and hence the hallowing of God's name, takes place when God's will is obeyed on earth as it is already being done in the realm of his uncontested rule. All of creation and the history of redemption are summed up in this petition. For God hallows his name by establishing his rule and reign in the realm of the world through obedience to his will.

We pray this not only because we are confident, on the basis of God's mission, that he desires to establish his kingdom on earth without limit but also because he has already begun to do so. God's provisions in the past and present are inextricably tied to his promises for the future, the former being a down payment of the latter. Though the kingdom is not yet consummated, its future realization has already been inaugurated. The plea that God would establish his kingdom is the prayer of those who have already begun to experience God's life-transforming rule over their lives. For this reason, they desperately want God to unleash his reign in *all* its compassionate mercy, strength, holiness, and justice. It is also the prayer of those who grieve over the nominalism that plagues Christ's church in the world.[19] The prayer for the coming of God's kingdom becomes the

---

[18]John Piper, "The Most Important Prayer Request in the World," blog posted March 26, 2009, www.desiringGod.org.

[19]S. Douglas Birdsall, the executive director of the Lausanne Movement, has said in public presentations and private conversation that part of his motivation as he works to bring about the third Lausanne Congress on World Evangelization in Cape Town, 2010, is that "the worst thing that could happen to the future of world evangelization is to bring in 100 million new 'converts' like the last 100 million, since their superficiality obscures rather than reveals the glory of God" (quoted by permission).

prayer of those who are tired of the sin in their own lives and of the pain, greed, hunger, injustice, killing, lust, corruption, poverty, false religions, and godlessness that result from the idolatrous independence infesting our world.

The "disciples' prayer" is therefore also the prayer of hope, as we join those who, from the first days of the church, have cried out, "Maranatha," which translated means "Our Lord, come!" (1 Cor. 16:22). Indeed, dependent on "the grace of the Lord Jesus," "Maranatha" is the cry of the kingdom of God, as we look forward to the day when God's mission climaxes in universal worship (Rev. 22:20–21).

13

The Mystery of Marriage

James M. Hamilton Jr.

Marriage holds a unique place in all the Bible: what else joins two image bearers together as one, serves as a key concept for understanding the relationship between Yahweh and Israel, and then between Christ and the church, and consequently affords to every married couple the opportunity to live out the gospel? God sets himself on display in marriage, which means that God shows his glory in marriage. Thus, the thesis of this essay is that *marriage exists as a unique display of God's glory.*[1] In order to establish and exposit this thesis we will look first at the way that marriage joins two persons in the likeness of God as one. From there the second section explores the way that Yahweh's relationship to Israel is treated as a marriage, and the third section of this

---

[1] I am humbled to have this opportunity to honor John Piper. The Lord has used him mightily in my life, mainly as I have listened to recorded sermons and addresses across the years. In this preaching, the Lord has used John Piper to herald again and again the infinite glory of God in Christ. I cannot adequately thank him for showing me such glory, but I can join him in praising this glorious God, this worthy Savior, and this powerful Spirit, three persons, ever one God, worthy of all praise. And praise be to God for John Piper! I am also grateful to write on the topic of marriage in honor of Piper, since his chapter on marriage in *Desiring God* provided a key insight I have pursued in my own marriage and announced at every wedding at which it has been my privilege to speak: love seeks its joy in the joy of the beloved. "The reason there is so much misery in marriage is not that husbands and wives seek their own pleasure, but that they do not seek it in the pleasure of their spouses." John Piper, *Desiring God*, 2d ed. (Sisters, OR: Multnomah, 1996), 175–76. See also John Piper, *This Momentary Marriage: A Parable of Permanence* (Wheaton, IL: Crossway, 2009).

essay will examine the way that marriage exists to portray the relationship between Christ and the church. The final section will look at marriages as minidramas of the gospel.[2]

The current that flows through the four sections of this essay is constant: the energy all comes from God's intention to display his glory. God's character is displayed by his image bearers, and this display is augmented when two become one. God's character is displayed in his relations with Israel, where he shows himself to be just and merciful, a faithful husband to a wayward wife. And God's character is displayed as Christ weds himself to the church, laying down his life to present her to himself as a spotless bride. That bride will one day descend from heaven, and the Lamb will be the lamp, radiating glory, giving light to his beloved.

Adam and Eve: Two Become One

God built the universe as a realm in which he would commune with his image-bearing likeness. The world was designed as a cosmic temple[3] in the sense that the universe was intended as a place for God to be known, worshiped, and served. There are many indications that the tabernacle and temple were symbolic microcosms of the universe, and several statements in the Bible imply as much. For instance, the ark of the covenant within the Holy of Holies is referred to as God's "footstool" (1 Chron. 28:2; Pss. 99:5; 132:7). This imagery suggests that the Holy of Holies is part of God's throne room.[4] This means that when Yahweh declares through Isaiah,

> Heaven is my throne,
>   and the earth is my footstool, (Isa. 66:1)

the earth is seen to be pictured as Yahweh's cosmic temple.

It seems, then, that when he made the world, Yahweh built a cosmic temple into which he placed his image and likeness. This next point is so basic that it is easy to move past without reflection, but it needs to be asserted: Yahweh's image and likeness manifest Yahweh's glory. What other god has created the cosmos as a theater for the display of his majesty?

---

[2]For a wider discussion of marriage in the Old Testament, see Paul R. House, *Old Testament Theology* (Downers Grove, IL: InterVarsity, 1998), 466–69. For a broader discussion of marriage that takes up the issues of divorce, qualifications for elders, and children, see Thomas R. Schreiner, *New Testament Theology: Magnifying God in Christ* (Grand Rapids: Baker, 2008), 776–86.

[3]See esp. G. K. Beale, *The Temple and the Church's Mission: A Biblical Theology of the Dwelling Place of God* (Downers Grove, IL: InterVarsity, 2004).

[4]See further J. M. Hamilton, "Divine Presence," *Dictionary of the Old Testament: Wisdom, Poetry and Writings*, ed. Tremper Longman III and Peter Enns (Downers Grove, IL: InterVarsity, 2008), 117–18.

What other god has created human beings as those who represent him, embodying aspects of who he is? Not only has no other god created anything like the world we inhabit, or anything like us as human beings, but no other god has created anything at all. The creation of human beings in the image and likeness of God is an astonishing display of skill, wisdom, power, engineering ability, and material mastery. To take one example of God's creative prowess, what other substance is both as resilient and as light as bone, which even grows back together when broken? And bones are not even unique to human beings.

What is so glorious about human beings? What does it mean that they are in the image and likeness of God? Peter Gentry has argued that image and likeness have to do with worship and relationship—worship to God and relationship to other humans and the rest of creation.[5] Humanity is unique in its ability to worship God: what other species devises musical instruments, melodic tunes, and rhythmic poetry to sing the praise of its Creator? And humans are unique in their ability to relate to other human beings: what other species has anything like marriage? Humans display the glory of God in all the ways they exercise intelligence, spirituality, sensitivity, and morality, especially as they worship God and relate to other human beings. Marriage, however, is a unique display of God's glory.

God put the man in the garden to work and keep it (Gen. 2:15); then he made the woman to help the man (2:18). It was the Lord himself who brought the woman to the man (2:22), like a father walking his daughter down the aisle. The man then poetically sang his solidarity with and authority over the woman:

> This at last is bone of my bones
> and flesh of my flesh;
> she shall be called Woman,
> because she was taken out of Man. (2:23)

The statement of solidarity is in the first clause, stressing that the man and woman are made of the same substance and thus equal before God. The statement of authority comes in the second, when the man announces what the woman will be called, just as God had earlier announced that the light would be called day (Gen. 1:5). In the garden, then—before sin, before the curse, before the expulsion from God's presence in Eden—there was a harmonious union that worked itself out in different roles:

---

[5]Peter J. Gentry, "Kingdom through Covenant: Humanity as the Divine Image," *Southern Baptist Journal of Theology* 12, no. 1 (2008): 28–30.

the man working and keeping, and the woman helping.[6] These roles, moreover, were undertaken within a hierarchical structure of authority. The man acted in God's place to name God's creation, even to the point of naming the woman, created in the image of God and made to be his helper.

The narrator of Genesis then draws a conclusion from the primordial scene he has depicted: "Therefore a man shall leave his father and his mother and hold fast to his wife, and they shall become one flesh. And the man and his wife were both naked and were not ashamed" (Gen. 2:24–25).[7] This conclusion shows the narrator's understanding of what took place between Adam and Eve, and what we see is that the narrator holds that this event has implications for others. Because of the way the Lord made the man, made the woman, then brought the woman to the man, a man is to separate himself from his parents, cleave to his wife, and the two become one. Genesis 2:24 asserts that the primordial pattern exemplifies what should take place between man and woman.

In marriage two human beings are united to become one flesh. At the level of whole Bible theology, this can be seen as another way in which humanity is in the image of God. The married two in one become a living picture of the way the three persons of the Godhead are one in essence, equal in power, glory, and every perfection. God spoke the world into being by his word, and by the same creative power of his word, God declares that when a man and a woman enter into the holy covenant of marriage, the two shall become one flesh.[8]

At a linguistic level, the same Hebrew term for "one" (אֶחָד) in the declaration that the two become "one flesh" appears again in the *shema*, "Hear, O Israel: Yahweh our God, Yahweh is one" (Deut. 6:4).[9] From this we can observe that the use of the word "one" does not exclude a plurality within unity. The transcendent reality that God exists as a Trinity, as one God who is three persons, is embodied in a profound way when two of God's image bearers—a man and a woman—are united to

---

[6]Similarly Andreas J. Köstenberger with David W. Jones, *God, Marriage, and Family: Rebuilding the Biblical Foundation* (Wheaton, IL: Crossway, 2004), 34–37.

[7]For searching reflections on the original shamelessness and the meaning of clothing, see Piper, *This Momentary Marriage*, 32–38.

[8]Commenting on Genesis 2:24, C. John Collins, *Genesis 1–4: A Linguistic, Literary, and Theological Commentary* (Phillipsburg, NJ: P&R, 2006), 108n36) writes, "I take this to be the narrator's comment, speaking on behalf of God (typical of the narrator in the Hebrew Bible), and this explains why Jesus in Matt. 19:4–5 attributes this saying to the Creator himself (he had a high view of Scripture)." For a helpful discussion of Genesis 2:24 and Proverbs; Malachi 2:14–16; Matthew 19:3–9; 1 Corinthians 6:16–17; and Ephesians 5:31, see ibid., 142–45.

[9]In this and similar passages I am substituting the divine name Yahweh for LORD in the ESV text.

become one flesh in the holy covenant of marriage.[10] Marriage displays the glory of God.

God charged the man and the woman with the task of filling the earth and subduing it (Gen. 1:28). They were to expand the borders of Eden so that the glory of Yahweh would cover the dry lands as the waters cover the sea (cf. Num. 14:21). Eve's fall into temptation and Adam's headlong plunge into sin radically disrupted God's good creation. God had promised that disobedience would be punished by death (Gen. 2:17), but in the curse on the Serpent, God announced that the Seed of the woman would crush the Serpent's head (Gen. 3:15).[11] Adam heard in this judgment on the snake the news that the woman would have off-spring, which meant they would live to have offspring. Thus, when he named his wife "Eve, because she was the mother of all living" (Gen. 3:20), he acted on faith.[12] Adam trusted the word of God, the promise of a delivering descendant.

God cursed the Serpent, but rather than cursing the man and the woman, God made their roles more difficult. The woman's role of help-ing the man and joining with him to fill the earth was made difficult in that she would have pain in childbearing and would desire to control the man the way sin desired to control Cain, while the man would rule over her the way that Cain was called to rule over sin (cf. Gen. 3:16 and 4:7).

Expelled from the garden of Eden, Adam and Eve no longer had the opportunity to extend its borders. Yahweh's promises to Abraham in Genesis 12:1–3 announced that he would overcome the curses of Genesis 3:14–19 through Abraham and his Seed.[13] The Seed of Abraham would not only roll back the curse, he would renew harmony in marriage, a theme sung in the most sublime Song (cf. Gen. 3:16 and Song 7:10).[14] Yahweh thus initiated a relationship with the family of Abraham through which he pursued the task of covering the dry lands with his glory. Then, in a remarkable development at Sinai, as the Mosaic covenant was inaugu-rated, Yahweh married Israel.

---

[10]For discussion of the nature of marriage as a sacrament, contract, or covenant, concluding that the biblical concept of marriage is best described as a covenant, see Köstenberger with Jones, *God, Marriage, and Family*, 81–91. So also Robin Routledge, *Old Testament Theology: A Thematic Approach* (Downers Grove, IL: InterVarsity, 2008), 163–64.

[11]See James M. Hamilton Jr., "The Skull-Crushing Seed of the Woman: Inner-Biblical Interpretation of Genesis 3:15," *Southern Baptist Journal of Theology* 10, no. 2 (2006): 30–54.

[12]Stephen G. Dempster, *Dominion and Dynasty: A Biblical Theology of the Hebrew Bible* (Downers Grove, IL: InterVarsity, 2003), 68.

[13]See James M. Hamilton Jr., "The Seed of the Woman and the Blessing of Abraham," *Tyndale Bulletin* 58, no. 2 (2007): 253–73.

[14]James M. Hamilton Jr., "The Messianic Music of the Song of Songs: A Non-Allegorical Interpretation," *Westminster Theological Journal* 68, no. 2 (2006): 331–45.

Yahweh and Israel: Covenant Broken and Kept

Perhaps the most prominent treatment of the covenant between Yahweh and Israel as a marriage in the Old Testament is found in the book of Hosea.[15] The likening of the covenant between Israel and Yahweh to the closest of human relationships captures the inexpressible intimacy Israel was to enjoy with her covenant Lord. It also gives emotional traction to the shock of their betrayal and idolatry.

The prophet Hosea became a living picture of the way that Yahweh loved his people, and this was at Yahweh's instigation. The book of Hosea teaches that marriage is a picture of the relationship between God and his people, and it teaches the significance of both male and female contributions to this picture. In Hosea's case, his personal history with Gomer presents Yahweh's history with Israel in miniature. As these themes are intertwined in Hosea 1–3, Hosea's understanding of Israel's history and Israel's future is extrapolated from his own experiences with Gomer. As we go forward, we will see Hosea's personal experience with Gomer in Hosea 1 applied to Israel's history and future in Hosea 2; then in Hosea 3 his experience is resumed and applied to Israel's future.

Hosea 1: Hosea and Gomer

Yahweh instructed Hosea to take a "wife of whoredom and have children of whoredom, for the land commits great whoredom by forsaking Yahweh" (Hos. 1:2).[16] So Hosea married Gomer, and Yahweh told him to name her children Jezreel (1:3–4), No Mercy (1:6–7), and Not My People (1:8–9). With the naming of Not My People Yahweh explained, "for you are not my people, and I am not your God."

These judgments were announced because the nation had forsaken Yahweh by relying on the Baals to provide rain, grain, and new wine. Yahweh regarded this as spiritual adultery, and Hosea lived out the heart-rending realities of the emotional devastation brought on by infidelity.

Hosea's reputation with friends and neighbors would have been affected by his marriage to Gomer, and the same applies to what happens to Yahweh's reputation when he takes for himself the unimpressive nation of Israel. This is compounded when the nation proves unfaithful. Not only would Hosea's judgment be called into serious question when he engaged in such a marriage, but the offense would be aggravated by the strange names given to the children. The firstborn child had a rather strange name, Jezreel. The

---

[15]For a study of this theme that focuses on Malachi, see Gordon P. Hugenberger, *Marriage as a Covenant: Biblical Law and Ethics as Developed from Malachi* (Grand Rapids: Baker, 1998).

[16]See the compelling argument that "Gomer was already a promiscuous woman when Hosea married her," in Duane A. Garrett, *Hosea, Joel*, New American Commentary (Nashville: Broadman and Holman, 1997), 44–49.

second child's name was shocking, No Mercy. And the third child's name essentially declared that Gomer had not been faithful, Not My People.

The identifications in this enacted parable are not difficult: Hosea represents Yahweh. Gomer represents the nation of Israel, and the children born to Gomer point to the people of Israel and the judgment that Yahweh will bring on them.

Whatever else we might say about the name Jezreel (Hos. 1:4; cf. 1 Kings 21 and 2 Kings 9–10), we can affirm that what took place there in Israel's history hardly matches what we would expect from the nation charged to spread the glory of Yahweh over the dry lands as the waters cover the sea.[17] The naming of No Mercy shouts the termination of Yahweh's patience, and then Not My People means just that. Yahweh has disowned the children of Israel. All of this is informed by the history of Israel related in Exodus through Kings.

Historically speaking, Hosea prophesied before the fall of the northern kingdom of Israel to Assyria in 721 B.C. (1:1, 6–7). Though he promised mercy to Judah (1:7), the southern kingdom did not learn from Yahweh's treatment of their northern kinsmen. Judah's adultery eventually bore the same fruit as Israel's.

Though Yahweh's mercy came to an end and the children of Israel were disowned, still Yahweh announced a hope for Israel beyond judgment. Through the judgment of the coming exile, Israel would be restored to the land, shown mercy, acknowledged as "Children of the living God," and encouraged that "great shall be the day of Jezreel" (1:10–2:1).

Hosea 2: Israel's History and Future

The covenant infidelity of the nation takes center stage in Hosea 2 as Israel's idolatry brought an end to the marriage of Yahweh and Israel. Yahweh denounced Israel in Hosea 2:2:

> Plead with your mother, plead—
> > for she is not my wife,
> > and I am not her husband—
> that she put away her whoring from her face,
> > and her adultery from between her breasts.

This statement treats the nation's reliance upon other gods as "whoring" and "adultery." This is a figurative description of the way the nation has spiritually broken their covenant with Yahweh.

---

[17]See the discussion in Raymond C. Ortlund Jr., *God's Unfaithful Wife: A Biblical Theology of Spiritual Adultery* (Downers Grove, IL: InterVarsity, 1996), 51–52.

All through Hosea 2 we find two kinds of overlapping imagery. On the one hand there is the imagery of Israel's *adultery*, with her lovers, her lewdness, and her bastard children. On the other hand is the *exile* imagery that arises from the consequences of the broken covenant. Both kinds of imagery are on display in Hosea 2:3 when Yahweh warns that in response to Israel's adultery he will "strip her naked." With Israel depicted as a scandalous wife who will be publicly humiliated, the exile comes into view when the shaming of the adulterous wife is exposited with the words:

> and make her like a wilderness,
>   and make her like a parched land.

The whore will be stripped naked and exposed to shame, which means that the nation is going to be depopulated by an invading army, with the result that the cultivated cities will be thrown down and revert to wilderness because the inhabitants have been killed or carried away captive.

Yahweh himself will thwart Israel's efforts to play the whore (Hos. 2:4–6), with the result that she will return to him (2:7). Israel thinks that her "lovers"—foreign gods—have caused the rain to fall so that the grain, vines, and olive trees grow, but in reality it was Yahweh who gave her the gifts she used for the worship of Baal (2:8). Yahweh promised to exile Israel for these adulterous deeds (2:9–13), but in wrath he remembered mercy.

Yahweh swore to "allure" Israel into the wilderness and to "speak tenderly to her" (2:14). Hosea 2:15 describes Israel's point of entry into the land that was marked by Achan's sin, the Valley of Achor (cf. Josh 7:25–26), as "a door of hope," suggesting a new conquest. This suggestion is strengthened as the verse goes on to state, "And there she shall answer as in the days of her youth, as at the time when she came out of the land of Egypt" (2:15). The two statements in Hosea 2:15—first the Valley of Achor being a door of hope, and second the reminder of the way Israel answered when she came out of Egypt—both assume that Israel will be exiled and return to the land. They will enter the land as they did before, and they will respond to Yahweh as they did before.

This response to Yahweh recalls the way that Israel gladly agreed to Yahweh's terms at Sinai, and the answer Israel gave there seems to have functioned as consent to Israel's marriage to Yahweh.[18] This view is strengthened as Hosea 2:16 states, "And in that day, declares Yahweh, you

---

[18]Similarly Routledge, *Old Testament Theology*, 270.

will call me 'My Husband,' and no longer will you call me 'My Baal.'"
When they answer as they did when they came out of Egypt (2:15), Yahweh will be their husband.

Yahweh promises to cleanse his bride of idolatry (Hos. 2:17), protect her from the beasts, birds, and creeping things, and abolish the implements of war as he establishes a safe place for his beloved (2:18). Yahweh then declares his intention to betroth his people to himself in Hosea 2:19–20: "And I will betroth you to me forever. I will betroth you to me in righteousness and in justice, in steadfast love and in mercy. I will betroth you to me in faithfulness. And you shall know Yahweh." Yahweh's promise to Israel to enter into this new covenant with Israel begins with the assertion that this betrothal will be forever, and it ends with the assertion that he will be faithful. Between the bookends of this promise of everlasting faithfulness are assertions that the betrothal will display Yahweh's severity and his kindness, with two terms for holiness ("in righteousness and in justice") and two terms for kindness ("in steadfast love and in mercy"). The final statement that Israel will "know" Yahweh resonates with the intimacy of two becoming one flesh, but it also states that Israel will know Yahweh in his steadfast love and mercy, his refusal to clear the guilty, and his forever faithfulness (cf. Ex. 34:6–7).

These are the very attributes of Yahweh that have been displayed all through his marriage to Israel. He has upheld justice and truth and righteousness, resulting in his willingness to state that Israel has ceased to be his wife. Thus comes his judgment in the form of the exile, when the whoring wife is stripped naked by the lovers she sought. And Yahweh also displays his mercy and love for Israel by promising to bring them back after exile, to accomplish a new exodus from bondage, a new conquest of the land, replete with a new marriage covenant between Yahweh and Israel.

Perhaps no other metaphor for Yahweh's relationship to Israel could capture the pain of betrayal and the wonder of forgiveness the way that marriage does. Where are betrayal and forgiveness more poignantly displayed than when adultery happens, justice is done, and mercy and forgiveness flow in restoration?

Hosea 3: Hosea and Israel's Future
Marriage exists for the glory of God, and when Hosea married Gomer this truth was put on display. The consequences of Gomer's whoredom made it necessary for Hosea to buy her back, which he did (Hos. 3:1–3), and this action is likened to the way that Yahweh will deal with Israel (3:4).

Indeed, this will bring Israel to repentance. Israel will be saved through judgment for Yahweh's glory:[19] "Afterward the children of Israel shall return and seek Yahweh their God, and David their king, and they shall come in fear to Yahweh and to his goodness in the latter days" (3:5). Israel's latter-day salvation will include a *new redemption*, like Hosea buying Gomer back (3:2); a *new exodus*, as the children of Israel again "go up from the land" (1:11; cf. Ex. 1:10); a *new conquest*, as the Valley of Achor becomes a door of hope (Hos. 2:15); a *new covenant*, as Yahweh betroths himself to his people in forever faithfulness with justice and mercy (2:19–20) and Israel repents and seeks her *new David* (3:5). Yahweh sends his whoring wife into exile to discipline her, but he will bring her back for a fuller and deeper experience of marital intimacy.[20]

When Jesus comes, these promises are fulfilled in unexpected ways. We turn to the New Testament for further exploration of the way that Yahweh's glory is uniquely displayed in marriage.

Jesus and the Church: Marriage and the Gospel

In order to understand marriage in the broader context of biblical theology, we must briefly consider the way that the New Testament presents Jesus as the fulfillment of Old Testament expectation. This broader context will regulate the atmospheric pressure of our thoughts so that when we consider Paul's comments on the meaning of marriage, we will not experience vertigo from the sudden plunge into the great deep.[21]

The Fulfillment of Old Testament Expectation

It is interesting that Jesus came calling himself the bridegroom (Matt. 9:15). It would seem that Jesus and the authors of the New Testament understood his death in terms of the fulfillment of the exile—the moment when the temple would be destroyed (John 2:19). Simultaneously, as Jesus died he accomplished an "exodus" (Luke 9:31), and Paul can assert that "Christ, our Passover lamb, has been sacrificed" (1 Cor. 5:7). In Jesus the exile is fulfilled, the new exodus dawns, and the return from exile begins. Like Moses, Jesus ascended the mountain and gave teaching from God (Matthew 5–7). Like Joshua, Jesus began the process of cleansing the

---

[19]See further James M. Hamilton Jr., "The Glory of God in Salvation through Judgment: The Centre of Biblical Theology?" *Tyndale Bulletin* 57, no. 1 (2006): 57–84, and *God's Glory in Salvation through Judgment: A Biblical Theology* (Wheaton, IL: Crossway, 2010).

[20]For discussion of Israel's spiritual adultery in other Old Testament prophets, see Ortlund, *God's Unfaithful Wife*, 77–136.

[21]For discussion of other New Testament texts on marriage (e.g., Matt. 19; 1 Pet. 3:1–7; 1 Cor. 7; 1 Tim. 2, 4), see Köstenberger with Jones, *God, Marriage, and Family*, 61–66, and see the extensive discussion of marriage in the Pauline texts in Thomas R. Schreiner, *Paul, Apostle of God's Glory in Christ: A Pauline Theology* (Downers Grove, IL: InterVarsity, 2001), 413–31.

land (e.g., Matthew 8–10), and one day he will return to finish the work (Revelation 19). At that point his people will receive the Promised Land, the new heavens and the new earth (Revelation 21–22).

In fulfillment of the hopes of the Old Testament prophets, the New Testament authors present what has taken place in Jesus as the completion of the exile, the beginning of the return from exile, and the new exodus, replete with the new covenant and the new David—Jesus himself—leading his people to a new conquest of the new heavens and the new earth. All this will culminate in the marriage supper of the Lamb (Rev. 19:9), when Jesus will consummate his relationship with his blood-bought bride.

The Deep Waters of the Meaning of Marriage

As he reflects on Spirit-filled relations in the church (Eph. 5:18), Paul begins his discussion of households with the relationship between husbands and wives in marriage (Eph. 5:21–33). From there he will go on to discuss parents and children (6:1–4) and slaves and masters (6:5–9).

Having discussed the way that husbands and wives should model their behavior on the relationship between Christ and the church (Eph. 5:22–30), Paul quotes Genesis 2:24 (in Eph. 5:31) and then states the meaning of marriage in Ephesians 5:32–33. In order to understand Paul's conclusion in Ephesians 5:31–33, we must follow the argument he makes in 5:21–30.

Paul begins with the instruction that being filled with the Spirit results in "submitting to one another in the fear of Christ" (v. 21).[22] He then explains that wives are to submit to their husbands (vv. 22–24), while husbands are to die for their wives (vv. 25–30).

In Ephesians 5:22–24 Paul explains the way that wives are to submit to their husbands (v. 22), the reason they should do so (v. 23), and then restates the way that wives are to submit (v. 24). The first statement of the way that wives are to submit is a simple assertion that fills out the verbal idea in Ephesians 5:21, "submitting to one another in the fear of Christ," with the words "wives to their own husbands as to the Lord" (v. 22). This statement presents us with the first of several comparisons using the little word "as." The comparison dictates that a wife is to submit to her husband in the same way that she would submit to the Lord.

The reason for this sacred submission is stated in Ephesians 5:23: "because a husband is the head of the wife, as also Christ is the head

---

[22]Throughout this discussion of Ephesians 5:21–33 I present my own intentionally wooden rendering of the Greek text.

of the church, himself the Savior of the body." This reason fills out the comparison that will be developed throughout the passage: a husband is to his wife as Christ is to the church and vice versa. The husband being head of the wife is here compared to Christ being the Head of the church, and this Christlike headship grounds the submission articulated in 5:22. What this means for the way that husbands are to relate to their wives is anticipated in the final clause of 5:23 when Paul states that Christ is "the Savior of the body." Christ saved his body by laying down his life, and Paul will elaborate on that in Ephesians 5:25–30. Having introduced the idea in Ephesians 5:22 and given the reason for it in 5:23, Paul restates the concept in 5:24: "but as the church is subject to Christ, so also the wives to their husbands in everything." This call for a wife to submit to her husband as the church submits to Christ is nothing less than comprehensive. That scope is astonishing.[23] The reason that Paul calls for this all-encompassing churchlike posture from wives will become clear as he continues. At this point we can observe that whatever the reason is, it must merit what it demands. That is, if Paul is going to call wives to submit to their own husbands as the church submits to Christ, something massively significant must be at stake. What would necessitate a wife submitting to her husband as she submits to Christ?

This question begins to be answered as Paul turns to address husbands, filling in the details of the comparison he is making and tracing out the true meaning of marriage. He writes in Ephesians 5:25, "Husbands, love your wives, as also Christ loved the church and gave himself for her." If the wife's duty to submit is all-encompassing, the husband's duty to love is all-consuming. A wife's submission to her husband demands the sacrifice of her freedom. A husband's love for his wife demands his life. Here Paul's reasons for calling wives to such submission and husbands to such sacrifice begin to come into view. The beauty of living out the gospel in marriage—and that is what happens when husbands lay down their lives and their wives submit to them—is that the benefits of the gospel are unleashed in the lives of husbands and wives who live it. By submitting to Christ, the church finds freedom in obedience, freedom from the tyranny of sin. The commands of Christ the King, the loving husband, become a wide, safe place, in which those who embrace his reign run free

---

[23]See the discussion of six things that submission is not (from 1 Pet. 3:1–6) in Piper, *This Momentary Marriage*, 99–101: (1) it does not mean agreeing with everything the husband says; (2) it does not mean total surrender of brain and will; (3) it does not mean the wife does not try to see her husband change for the better; (4) it does not mean putting the husband's will before Christ's; (5) it does not mean the wife gets her spiritual strength primarily from her husband; and (6) it does not mean the wife is to act from fear.

and fearless. G. K. Chesterton describes Christianity's beliefs and ethical requirements as

> the walls of a playground. . . . We might fancy some children playing on the flat grassy top of some tall island in the sea. So long as there was a wall round the cliff's edge they could fling themselves into every frantic game and make the place the noisiest of nurseries. But the walls were knocked down, leaving the naked peril of the precipice. They did not fall over; but when their friends returned to them they were all huddled in terror in the centre of the island; and their song had ceased.[24]

Paul is teaching that the freedom that women should seek is the freedom that comes from what the flesh wrongly perceives as the surrender of freedom. Obviously women are not to submit to their husbands if their husbands order them to do something that would dishonor God, something sinful or inappropriate. Nor is God honored by women who cease to think, who cease to have desires, leaving the exercise of will and intelligence to their husbands. And obviously husbands do not carry the authority of Christ himself. Still, the path to freedom starts at the biblical point of submission, and submission sustains the guardrails on that straight and narrow path through the mountains. The same is true of what Paul calls husbands to do. What looks like death gives way to life. Just as the death of Jesus opened the gates of life, so also the husband's death-to-self love for his wife puts gospel life in his heart. There is an awe-inspiring symbiosis in this, too, for the wife who knows her husband is ready to lay down his life for her will gladly submit to such a man.

Christ's self-sacrificial love for the church did not exploit the church but met her deepest need. Christ did not love the church by doing what he wanted but by doing what the church needed. Nothing Christ could have done for the church could have benefited her more—indeed, anything else would have been meaningless. Had Christ not gone to the cross for his bride, no adornments, no privileges, no worldly status would have kept her from going to hell. Jesus laid down his life for the church, paying the penalty for her sin and reconciling her to the Father, and this self-sacrificial church-benefiting love provides the pattern husbands are to follow as they love their wives.

In Ephesians 5:26–27, Paul states two purposes Christ pursued as he laid down his life for the church. First, Christ gave his life for the church "that he might *sanctify her*, having washed her with water by the

---

[24]G. K. Chesterton, *Orthodoxy* (1908; repr., Colorado Springs: Waterbrook, 2001), 220 (chap. 9).

word." This purpose statement focuses on what the church gains from Christ's laying down his life, and it states the way that Christ prepared the church for the status she gained. Christ died for the church to "sanctify her," which means that his death sets the church apart for God. It is as though the church was in an unclean state, separated from God by sin and death, banished from his holy presence, and not qualified to enter the clean realm, proceed through the Holy Place, and worship in the Holy of Holies. Christ prepared the church for her new status of holiness by washing her with water by the word.

The church is here personified, depicted in terms drawn from the Levitical system of sacrifice. Like one who had become unclean, the church needed a ritual washing to enter the clean realm. The cleansing that Christ provided was a cleansing accomplished by the word of promise, for no external lustration could accomplish what was necessary. The church will be saved by faith, and the word with which Christ washed the church accomplishes the necessary cleansing. Christ calls the faith of the church into existence by his word, and by his word he has provided the content of the church's faith. Christ washed the church by the word, removing her uncleanness by giving her faith. That done, he offered the only sacrifice that could sanctify her: himself. Thus the church is no longer banished to the realm of the dead outside the camp. She has been cleansed by the word of Christ, which gives her the right to enter the camp. She has been sanctified by his death, which gives her access to the Holy of Holies. By Christ's work she is holy.

The second purpose statement in Ephesians 5:27 focuses on how Christ benefits from his love for the church. He laid down his life for his bride, "that he might present to himself *the church in glory*, not having stain or wrinkle or any such thing, but that she might be *holy and blameless*" (Eph. 5:27). Christ's service to the church does benefit him. It benefits him in that having cleansed the church by his word and sanctified her by his death, he then presents her to himself.

Here is a paradox: by sacrificing himself Christ wins for himself a glorious church. Jesus gains what is desirable from an undesirable death. The very things that selfish people desire for themselves—good things that are desired inordinately and sinfully—are the things that Jesus gains by being unselfish. The very things that keep men from behaving in an unselfish way, from being concerned for the welfare of their wives first, are gained by Christ because he was unselfish. A selfish husband desires to be served and satisfied by a glorious wife. By unselfishly giving himself for his wife, Christ creates for himself just such a wife.

But it is not as though Christ alone benefits from this—the church gets a husband like no other. The church is made clean and holy, and then she is presented to a husband who has demonstrated himself to be supremely concerned for her welfare, supremely devoted to her good, supremely worthy of her trust. By laying down his life for his bride, Jesus makes the church glorious, stainless, spotless. He cleanses her of the stain of sin. He wins for her a resurrection body, magnificent like his own. Sanctified by the death of Jesus, the church is presented to him, holy to the Lord and blameless—there will be no grounds for satanic accusation against those for whom Christ died.

Just as Paul *called* wives to submit to their husbands as the church does to Christ (Eph. 5:22), gave the *reason* for that submission (v. 23), then *restated* the call to submit (v. 24), so now having *called* for husbands to love their wives as Christ loved the church (v. 25), and explained *why* Christ did that (vv. 26–27), Paul *restates* the call for husbands to love their wives as Christ loved the church: "In this way husbands are to love their own wives like their own bodies. The one who loves his wife loves himself" (v. 28). This statement assumes and anticipates the reference to the one-flesh union between man and wife that Paul will articulate in verse 31. So on the one hand, the one-flesh union between man and wife makes it so that the one who loves his wife loves himself. On the other hand, the blessings that follow loving one's wife as Christ loved the church validate the truth that "the one who loves his wife loves himself."

This dynamic is pressed home in Paul's next statement, where assuming the one-flesh union and the joy of having a wife who knows she is loved, who trusts her husband, Paul writes in Ephesians 5:29, "For no one ever hated his own flesh but nourishes and cares for it, just as Christ also the church." No one ever hated his own flesh, but those who treat their wives hatefully do so without realizing it. The fool exalts himself over his wife, mocks her, demands service, and speaks in derogatory ways of her. Without realizing it, such fools are hating themselves. They demean their wives and suffer the consequences: highlighting the flaws of their wives only causes their wives to become less attractive as they grow more bitter, more discouraged, more frightened, and more suspicious. A one-flesh union with a bitter, discouraged, frightened, suspicious woman is hardly pleasant. Fools hate themselves. And wives of fools will have a difficult time respecting and submitting to husbands who treat them hatefully. When fools present their wives to themselves, they get what they have created for themselves: misery. Only by the abundance of God's common grace do fools get any blessing from the wives they have abused. They have hated themselves. They suffer for it.

Paul calls the Ephesian husbands to recognize these truths and love their wives the way Christ loves the church. He calls on them to recognize the one-flesh union between themselves and their wives and to treat their wives as they treat their own bodies—not hating them but nourishing and caring for them. At the end of Ephesians 5:29 Paul again compares the way that husbands are to love their wives with the way that Christ loves the church, and then he gives the reason for Christ's beneficent treatment of the church in verse 30: "because we are members of his body." Paul here calls husbands to recognize that those who are united to Christ by faith have not been treated by him as they deserve. If anyone deserves to be treated hatefully, sinful rebels against almighty God do. But rather than give them what they deserve, much less treat them hatefully, Christ has cleansed them with his word and sanctified them by his death, uniting them to himself, making them members of his own body. He then treats them as he would treat his own body, nourishing, caring, sacrificing, loving. This calls any man who deems his wife unworthy of tender care, unworthy of special attention, unworthy of extraordinary sacrifice to look at the way that Christ has loved wretches, rebels, and revolutionaries.

Christ cleansed. Christ died. Christ made his bride spotless and then presented her to himself. In this way husbands are to love their wives. So goes Paul's argument in Ephesians 5:22–30. After this argument, which comprises so many comparisons between man and wife, Christ and the church, the depths are sounded in Paul's conclusion. This comes in Ephesians 5:31–32: "On account of this a man shall leave his father and mother and be joined to his wife, and the two shall be one flesh. This mystery is great, but I speak concerning Christ and the church." The connection between Ephesians 5:29b–30 and 5:31–32 is the point where the plunge is taken. This connection is such that having described the way that Christ has loved the church, Paul says that it is because of Christ's love for the church that the words of Genesis 2:24 exist. This amounts to a declaration that God created humans as gendered persons who would unite in a one-flesh union as one man, one woman, in covenant marriage, the two becoming one, *so that the world would have a category for understanding the relationship between Christ and the church.*[25]

Marriage was made the way that a novelist describes political buildup to war, battlements, strategies, troop deployments, and the personalities

---

[25]Similarly Schreiner, *Paul*, 425.

and backgrounds of different soldiers, all to provide a backdrop against which shines the courage in the daring charge of the hero. The heroism and courage will not be understood without context. And marriage is part of the context that God writes into creation to highlight the heroism of Christ. Marriage exists so that people will understand Christ's love for his unworthy bride and his ability to cleanse, sanctify, and transform the lost and broken so that he presents her to himself as a thing of beauty and glory. And he does this not in selfishness but in unselfishness, not in pride but in humility, at no cost to the bride but at the cost of his own life.

These realities provide the answer to the question posed above as to what could possibly warrant absolute submission from a wife and to-the-death sacrificial love from a husband. What warrants churchlike submission and Christlike taking up the cross is the fact that marriage exists as a picture of the gospel. This is the mystery: that speaking about necessary behavior in marital relations is speaking about Christ and the church (Eph. 5:32). Paul presses home the implications this has for the way that wives and husbands relate in Ephesians 5:33: "Still, each one of you, each his own wife in this way he must love as himself; and the wife, that she might fear her husband." Paul is speaking of Christ and the church, but that does not nullify the need for husbands to love their wives and wives to submit to their husbands. That Paul is speaking of Christ and the church is precisely what creates the need for such behavior.[26]

Paul's words in Ephesians 5:31–32 also reflect a profound interpretation of the way that Old Testament passages such as Hosea 3 are fulfilled in Christ. Jesus will one day have his messianic banquet, the marriage supper of the Lamb (Rev. 19:7; 21:2, 9–10; cf. Luke 22:16). All the promises of God find their yes and amen in him (2 Cor. 1:20).

The Gospel and Marriage

Every marriage, then, should be a minidrama of the gospel. Christlikeness is displayed to the world as selfish men are transformed into the image of Christ and unselfishly set aside their own needs and desires in order to pursue the good of their wives. The transformation of the church is on display as Christlike men love their wives, who are not necessarily worthy of Christlike treatment, but who are transformed by such love into confident women who know their husbands seek first their good. These ladies are well thought of by all around because their husbands speak well of them; they shine with the glory of Christ's own church, lovely as

---

[26]Similarly Ortlund, *God's Unfaithful Wife*, 152–59.

Jerusalem, awesome as an army with banners (Song 6:4), because they have been loved with an extravagant transforming love.

There are also implications from this in a negative direction: foolish husbands misrepresent the One who is the bridegroom. Unsubmissive wives give a false impression about how the church is to relate to Christ. Like liberal churches in which Christ's Word does not mediate his lordship, wives who do not submit to their husbands set themselves against the very purpose of marriage. And unbiblical divorce tells the lie that a regenerate person could somehow be made unregenerate.

Conclusion

The mystery of marriage, then, is that in it the gospel is proclaimed as a wife submits to her husband as the church submits to Christ and as a husband loves his wife as Christ loves the church, giving himself up for her. Herein is displayed not only the love of Christ for the church, but also the love of Yahweh for Israel, and the latter is fulfilled in the former.

We await the marriage supper of the Lamb, the great wedding day for which the world was made. Marriage is about the glory of God in Christ. As men love their wives as Christ loved the church, and as women submit to their husbands as the church submits to Christ, the age-old curse on gender relations in Genesis 3:16 is overcome. Through faith in Christ, by the power of the Spirit, for the glory of the Father, married couples who live this way find their lives blooming like the garden of Eden.

Marriage is a unique display of God's glory. It is a living picture of the way Christ has died for and transformed his people. The Spirit and the bride say, "Come, Lord Jesus" (Rev. 22:12, 17, 20).

An Attempt at a Poetic Postscript

In a volume honoring John Piper, hopefully imitation will be a high compliment. In his recent book of poems to his wife, *Velvet Steel: The Joy of Being Married to You* (Wheaton, IL: Crossway, 2009), we are given an intimate look at the marriage between John and Noël Piper.

My own attempt below seeks to capture the glory of God and the gospel in marriage.

Marriage

Like land and sea and stars above
And all else he has made,
This too is for the glory of
The one who has displayed

A love not based on beauty's shades
Nor driven by some debt,
A love before there were yet days
Like none else ever met.

The archetype for man and wife
Is Christ's love for his bride.
To Christ her Lord the church submits,
And for her life he died.

And for this reason, man should leave
His parents and his kin,
And to his wife then he shall cleave
Never to leave again.

14

PLEASING GOD
BY OUR OBEDIENCE

A Neglected New Testament Teaching

Wayne Grudem

I t is a privilege to write this essay in honor of my friend John Piper. He has been an encouragement and an example of godly living to me since the days when we were both young faculty members at Bethel College in St. Paul (John was teaching New Testament and I taught systematic theology).

I arrived in January of 1977 at Bethel College, where John was already teaching, and though we had met prior to that time, our friendship and partnership in the work of the kingdom really began at Bethel and has grown deeper and stronger over the last thirty-three years. We worked together in the founding of the Council on Biblical Manhood and Womanhood (CBMW), in the drafting of the Danvers Statement for CBMW, in co-editing the book *Recovering Biblical Manhood and Womanhood*, in cautiously exploring what God was doing through the Vineyard Movement (John with more caution than I!), in meeting together at various sessions of the Evangelical Theological Society, in supporting one another regarding our opposition to the gender language changes in the TNIV Bible, in helping to lay the initial groundwork for the translation of the English Standard Version, in speaking together at the funeral after the tragic accidental death of my daughter-in-law, Rachael Grudem (a time when John was such a great comfort to my son Alexander), and in countless instances of mutual prayer and counsel and encouragement over many years. I am so very thankful to God for John's faithful, strong, winsome, wise, thoughtful, persuasive, articulate proclamation of "the whole counsel of God" (Acts 20:27).

In John's influential book *The Pleasures of God* he has a chapter on "The Pleasure of God in Personal Obedience and Public Justice."[1] In that chapter he points out that God takes pleasure in the obedience of his children. I was thankful for the emphasis in that chapter because in the evangelical world generally today I see and hear very little emphasis on God's taking pleasure in our obedience as Christian believers.

Therefore I thought it might be appropriate in this chapter to add to what John wrote in *The Pleasures of God* by carrying out a more extensive examination of the New Testament teaching on God's pleasure in our obedience. John's study was largely based on 1 Samuel 15:22:

> Has the LORD as great delight in burnt offerings and sacrifices,
>   as in obeying the voice of the Lord?

It was an excellent study of Samuel's words in that context, and it included a helpful explanation of the fact that obedience must come by faith and not "by works,"[2] but it did not provide an extensive survey of the New Testament data on this teaching. That is what I propose to do in this chapter.

This topic seems important to me because I think that evangelicals today are generally afraid of teaching about "pleasing God by obedience," for fear of sounding as if they disagree with justification by faith alone. But when the need to please God by obedience is neglected, we have millions of Christians in our churches who fail to see the importance of obedience to God in their daily lives.

Another reason why I am writing on this topic in this book is that John Piper's own life has been for many of his friends (including me) a significant example of a life that is pleasing to God.

---

[1]John Piper, *The Pleasures of God*, 2d ed. (Sisters, OR: Multnomah, 2000), 241–67.
[2]Ibid., 251–57.

Pleasing God Is a Frequent Motivation for Obedience
in the New Testament
A Wide Range of Verses on Pleasing God

The New Testament authors often encourage Christian believers to try to please God by what they do. It may surprise us to find how frequent this emphasis is in the New Testament:

> The unmarried man is anxious about the things of the Lord, *how to please the Lord . . .* how to be holy in body and spirit. (1 Cor. 7:32, 34)

> Try to discern *what is pleasing to the Lord*. (Eph. 5:10)

> It is God who works in you, both to will and to work for *his good pleasure*. (Phil. 2:13)

> I am well supplied, having received from Epaphroditus the gifts you sent, a fragrant offering, a sacrifice acceptable and *pleasing to God*. (Phil. 4:18)

> Walk in a manner worthy of the Lord, *fully pleasing to him*, bearing fruit in every good work and increasing in the knowledge of God. (Col. 1:10)

> Children, obey your parents in everything, *for this pleases the Lord*. (Col. 3:20)

> We ask and urge you in the Lord Jesus, that as you received from us how you ought to walk and *to please God*, just as you are doing, that you do so more and more. (1 Thess. 4:1)

> [Grateful prayer] is good, and it is *pleasing in the sight of God our Savior.* (1 Tim. 2:3)

> But if a widow has children or grandchildren, let them first learn to show godliness to their own household and to make some return to their parents, for *this is pleasing in the sight of God*. (1 Tim. 5:4)

> Now before [Enoch] was taken he was commended as having *pleased God*. (Heb. 11:5)

> And without faith it is impossible *to please him.* . . . (Heb. 11:6; cf. Rom. 8:8–9, which implies that believers who are not "in the flesh" can please God)

> Do not neglect to do good and to share what you have, for such sacrifices are *pleasing to God*. (Heb. 13:16)

... equip you with everything good that you may do his will, working in us *that which is pleasing in his sight*, through Jesus Christ, to whom be glory forever and ever. Amen. (Heb. 13:21)

And whatever we ask we receive from him, because we keep his commandments and do *what pleases him*. (1 John 3:22)

Other New Testament passages speak of what is "acceptable" to God, and these verses also use the same Greek term *euarestos* ("pleasing, acceptable") that was used in several of the passages above (namely, Eph. 5:10; Phil. 4:18; Col. 3:20; Heb. 13:21; the related verb *euaresteō* was used in Heb. 11:5, 6; 13:16):

I appeal to you therefore, brothers, by the mercies of God, to present your bodies as a living sacrifice, holy and *acceptable* [Gk. *euarestos*] *to God*, which is your spiritual worship. Do not be conformed to this world, but be transformed by the renewal of your mind, that by testing you may discern what is the will of God, what is good and *acceptable* [Gk. *euarestos*] and perfect. (Rom. 12:1–2)

Whoever thus serves Christ is *acceptable* [Gk. *euarestos*] to God and approved by men. (Rom. 14:18)[3]

Let us offer to God acceptable [Gk. *euarestōs*, the related adverb] worship, with reverence and awe. (Heb. 12:28)

Still other verses talk about the actions of Christians that are "acceptable" to God, using another term, *euprosdektos*, "capable of eliciting favorable acceptance, acceptable." For example, Peter says that we are "to offer spiritual sacrifices *acceptable to God* through Jesus Christ" (1 Pet. 2:5).

In addition, Paul seems to characterize his entire life and ministry as one of seeking to please God by what he does.

But on some points I have written to you very boldly by way of reminder, because of the grace given me by God to be a minister of Christ Jesus to the Gentiles in the priestly service of the gospel of God, so that the offering of the Gentiles may be *acceptable* [*euprosdektos*], sanctified by the Holy Spirit. (Rom. 15:15–16)

---

[3]This is referring to someone who refrains from putting a stumbling block or hindrance in the way of a brother because of what he eats.

So whether we are at home or away, we make it our aim *to please him.*
(2 Cor. 5:9; cf. Gal. 1:10)

But just as we have been approved by God to be entrusted with the gospel,
so we speak, not to please man, but *to please God* who tests our hearts.
(1 Thess. 2:4)

The supreme pattern of a life pleasing to God is found, of course, only
in Jesus Christ himself. He alone could say, "He has not left me alone,
for *I always do the things that are pleasing to him*" (John 8:29). And at
Jesus' baptism the voice of God the Father came from heaven, saying,
"This is my beloved Son, with whom I am *well pleased*" (Matt. 3:17; cf.
Matt. 12:18; 17:5; Mark 1:11; Luke 3:22; 2 Pet. 1:17).

The Desire to Please God Is Used to Motivate Christian Obedience
Such a desire to please God is explicitly used as a motivation for Christians to obey God in several places. For example:

Children, obey your parents in everything, *for* this pleases the Lord. (Col.
3:20)

Do not neglect to do good and to share what you have, *for* such sacrifices
are pleasing to God. (Heb. 13:16)

. . . and whatever we ask we receive from him, *because* we keep his commandments and do what pleases him. (1 John 3:22)

But if a widow has children or grandchildren, let them first learn to show
godliness to their own household and to make some return to their parents,
for this is pleasing in the sight of God. (1 Tim. 5:4)

The idea of pleasing God as a motivation for obedience is also implicit
in all those other verses above that encourage Christian believers to seek
to please God. The New Testament authors simply assume that believers
would want God to be pleased with them, and therefore they would do
those things that will result in his good pleasure.

What Kinds of Things Please God?
What kinds of things are said to please God? We find a variety of specific
kinds of obedience that touch all areas of life. In addition, some general
statements include all forms of obedience to God's will for our lives.
Consider how many diverse items are on the following list:

1. Presenting our bodies as a "living sacrifice" to God (Rom. 12:1).
2. Not being conformed to this world but being transformed by the renewal of our minds, and thereby learning by practice what the will of God is (Rom. 12:2).
3. Not putting a stumbling block in the way of a brother's Christian life (Rom. 14:18).
4. Being holy in body and spirit (the implication of 1 Cor. 7:34 with v. 32).
5. Preaching the true gospel and not adding to it the requirement of circumcision (Gal. 1:10).
6. Sending a financial gift to support Paul's ministry (Phil. 4:18).
7. Walking in a manner worthy of the Lord, and leading a life that bears fruit in every good work and increases in the knowledge of God (Col. 1:10).
8. Obeying one's parents (Col. 3:20).
9. Speaking and teaching all of God's truth faithfully (1 Thess. 2:4).
10. Having a pure heart before God in one's ministry (1 Thess. 2:4).
11. Praying for civil government authorities (1 Tim. 2:3).
12. Supporting one's own parents or grandparents who are in need (1 Tim. 5:4).
13. Believing that God exists and rewards those who seek him (Heb. 11:6).
14. Offering pleasing worship to God "with reverence and awe" (Heb. 12:28).
15. Doing good (Heb. 13:16).
16. Sharing what you have with others (Heb. 13:16).
17. Doing God's will (Heb. 13:21).
18. Keeping his commandments (1 John 3:22).

This list is so broad that it implies that all kinds of obedience to God's will as revealed in Scripture, as well as daily trust in God, are all pleasing to him.

Pleasing God by Obedience Is Complementary, not Contradictory, to Justification by Faith Alone

I suspect that the main reason for the neglect of this doctrine in evangelical circles today is that pastors and teachers and writers are afraid of compromising the great doctrine of justification by faith alone. If we can please God by works, doesn't that sound like justification by works?

No, it does not, or else the New Testament authors would not put so much emphasis on telling Christians to please God by their obedience! The key to understanding this is to distinguish clearly between justification (on the one hand) and sanctification and our daily relationship to God as Christians (on the other hand).

Justification Is by Faith Alone

The New Testament is clear that our justification comes through faith alone: Paul says, "So we also have believed in Christ Jesus, in order to be *justified by faith in Christ* and not by works of the law, because *by works of the law no one will be justified*" (Gal. 2:16). Paul says also, "Since we have been *justified by faith*, we have peace with God through our Lord Jesus Christ" (Rom. 5:1).

But justification by faith alone does not mean that we are *sanctified* by faith alone, because in sanctification, active obedience on our part is required.

And justification by faith alone does not mean that we *please God in our daily lives* by faith alone, for obedience to God is also required.

And justification by faith alone does not mean that our *daily relationship with God* depends on faith alone, for our obedience is also important.

The Importance of Good Works

Although the New Testament is emphatic that we cannot be justified before God on the basis of works (Gk. *ex ergōn*, Rom. 3:20; 9:32; 11:6; Gal. 2:16; 3:10; Eph. 2:9), on the other hand, the New Testament authors frequently insist that "good works" (*erga kala* or *erga agatha*) are very important for the Christian life:

> In the same way, let your light shine before others, so that they may see your good works and give glory to your Father who is in heaven. (Matt. 5:16)

> [Tabitha] was full of *good works* and acts of charity. (Acts 9:36)

> For we are his workmanship, created in Christ Jesus *for good works*, which God prepared beforehand, that we should walk in them. (Eph. 2:10)

> They are to do good, to be rich in *good works*, to be generous and ready to share. (1 Tim. 6:18)

> Show yourself in all respects to be a model of *good works*. . . . (Titus 2:7)

[Christ] gave himself for us to redeem us from all lawlessness and to purify for himself a people for his own possession who are zealous for *good works.* (Titus 2:14)

The saying is trustworthy, and I want you to insist on these things, so that those who have believed in God may be careful to devote themselves to *good works.* These things are excellent and profitable for people. (Titus 3:8)

And let our people learn to devote themselves to *good works,* so as to help cases of urgent need, and not be unfruitful. (Titus 3:14)

And let us consider how to stir up one another to love and *good works.* (Heb. 10:24)

With such a frequent emphasis on the importance of "good works," it should not surprise us to think that good works *done by Christians who are already eternally justified* are pleasing to God.

Our Good Works Can Actually Be Pleasing to God
Sometimes Christians assume that they can do absolutely nothing in this life that will please God. They think that God counts even their faithful obedience as totally worthless, totally unworthy of his approval. But that assumption is surely wrong, both because the New Testament so frequently speaks about "pleasing" God and because such an assumption tends to deny the genuine goodness of the work that Christ has done in redeeming us and making us acceptable before him. Such a view would maximize our sinfulness to the extent that it is even greater than Christ's redemptive work, "who gave himself for us to redeem us from all lawlessness and to purify for himself a people for his own possession who are zealous for *good works*" (Titus 2:14).

I suspect that just as Satan accuses Christians and wants them to feel false guilt and false accusation, so he also seeks to keep them from the great joy of knowing the favor of God on their daily activities, of knowing that God is pleased with their obedience. In this way he seeks to hinder our personal relationship with God, for the ability to take pleasure in another person is an essential component of any genuine personal relationship.

Is Christ not capable of producing in us works that are genuinely "*good works*"? All the verses cited above with reference to the "good works" of believers would indicate that he is, for such works are not called "bad works" but "good works"! Though they are imperfect, they are certainly not 100 percent evil and sinful, especially when they proceed from faith and are motivated by a love for God and for other people.

The Westminster Confession of Faith also speaks of God's acceptance of our good works, imperfect though they are:

> Notwithstanding, the persons of believers being accepted through Christ, *their good works also are accepted in Him*; not as though they were in this life wholly unblameable and unreproveable in God's sight; but that He, looking upon them in His Son, is pleased to accept and reward that which is sincere, although accompanied with many weaknesses and imperfections.[4]

Paul can even use the language of "worthiness" in speaking of the conduct of obedient believers before God, implying that our conduct can actually be "worthy" of God's approval:

> I therefore, a prisoner for the Lord, urge you to walk in a manner *worthy* [Gk. *axiōs*, "worthily, in a manner worthy of"] of the calling to which you have been called. (Eph. 4:1)

> . . . walk in a manner *worthy* of the Lord, fully pleasing to him, bearing fruit in every good work and increasing in the knowledge of God. (Col. 1:10; cf. Phil. 1:27; 1 Thess. 2:12; 2 Thess. 1:11)

We may conclude that God delights in our good works, that he is pleased with them, that he accepts them in Christ, and that, according to the evaluation of his own Word, we should think of them not as "evil works" but as what he himself calls them, "*good* works."

If we boldly teach that justified Christians can and should seek to please God by their obedience, we will not obscure justification by faith alone! Zeal to protect one great biblical teaching should never cause us to neglect another great biblical teaching. In fact, if we fear to teach something that is clearly taught in the New Testament, we probably need exactly that teaching to keep us from an unbalanced and misleading emphasis on the doctrine we are so zealous to protect. In this case, such an unbalanced emphasis can lead us to a wrongful neglect of the importance of obedience to God in the Christian life, and a neglect of the great truth that we actually can live lives that are pleasing to God each day. It can rob us of a great motive for obedience and also rob us of the great joy of knowing that we at this very moment actually are pleasing God!

---

[4]Westminster Confession of Faith, 16.6, my emphasis.

Pleasing God by Obedience Is a Skill That Can Be Learned

The apostle Paul assumes that pleasing God by obedience is a skill that needs to be taught to Christians, a skill that they can develop over time: "Finally, then, brothers, we ask and urge you in the Lord Jesus, that *as you received from us how you ought to walk and to please God*, just as you are doing, *that you do so more and more*" (1 Thess. 4:1). In other words, their entire lives should be devoted to increasing in the skill of pleasing God.

This is similar to Paul's very first statement of life application to the Christians in Rome immediately after he finished his magnificent summary of the truths of salvation in Romans 1–11. In Romans 12:1–2 he appeals to them, on the basis of all God has done, to seek to please God more and more in their daily lives:

> I appeal to you therefore, brothers, by the mercies of God, to present your bodies as a living sacrifice, holy and acceptable [Gk. *euarestos*, "pleasing, acceptable"] to God, which is your spiritual worship. Do not be conformed to this world, but be transformed by the renewal of your mind, that *by testing you may discern* what is the will of God, what is good and acceptable [Gk. *euarestos*, "pleasing, acceptable"] and perfect. (Rom. 12:1–2)

The expression "by testing you may discern" is the ESV's helpful attempt to capture the force of Greek *dokimazō*, which has the idea of trying something out in the actual events of life and, by that test, discovering a good result (other translations attempt to express this by "prove" or "test and approve"). The idea is that as we seek daily to obey "the will of God" (v. 2), we will gain greater skill in *knowing by experience* when we are walking in conformity to God's will, and thereby we will discover again and again that the sacrifice of our bodies to follow God's will is not only "pleasing" or "acceptable" to God (v. 1), but also "good and acceptable and perfect" (or pleasing) both in God's sight and in ours.

In another place Paul writes to the Christians in Ephesus, "*Try to discern* what is pleasing to the Lord" (Eph. 5:10). Here again we find the same verb (Gk. *dokimazō*), which shows that while we seek daily to "walk as children of light" (Eph. 5:8), we will learn over time, by the practice of obedience, to experience and give approval to "what is pleasing to the Lord."

In other passages Paul implied that it was his constant goal to please God: "So whether we are at home or away, we make it our aim [Gk. *philotimeomai*, "have as one's ambition, consider it an honor, aspire"] to please him" (2 Cor. 5:9; cf. Gal. 1:10).

In practical terms in our ministries today, it seems to me that this New Testament pattern means that we ought to be teaching our people that they should daily be seeking to please God by their obedience. As we teach the moral standards of Scripture, we should be saying, "Do this, for this pleases God." Or, to put it even more bluntly, "Walk in obedience to God every day, because God will be happy with you if you do!" And should we not desire to live each day under the light of God's good pleasure, experiencing his favor and his delight in our lives?

Pleasing God by Obedience Must Flow from Faith in God and Must Rely on the Power That Comes from God

However, the New Testament teaching about pleasing God by obedience must never be taught as if it were something we could do in our own strength. In fact, Paul is emphatic in saying that we of ourselves, apart from the Spirit of God within us, have no ability to please God: "Those who are in the flesh *cannot please God*" (Rom. 8:8). And the author of Hebrews says bluntly, ". . . and without faith it is *impossible to please him*, for whoever would draw near to God must believe that he exists and that he rewards those who seek him" (Heb. 11:6). Similarly, Paul says, "Whatever does not proceed from faith is sin" (Rom. 14:23).

And Jesus clearly reminded his disciples, "I am the vine; you are the branches. Whoever abides in me and I in him, he it is that bears much fruit, for *apart from me you can do nothing*" (John 15:5).

When speaking of his own obedience to Christ, Paul reminded his readers that it was not by his own strength that he was able to do this but by the power of God working in him: "But by the grace of God I am what I am, and his grace toward me was not in vain. On the contrary, I worked harder than any of them, *though it was not I, but the grace of God that is with me*" (1 Cor. 15:10).

Similarly, he spoke of living by the power of Christ within him: "I have been crucified with Christ. It is no longer I who live, *but Christ who lives in me*. And the life I now live in the flesh *I live by faith in the Son of God*, who loved me and gave himself for me" (Gal. 2:19–20).

So the New Testament teaches a combination of (a) active effort on our part to walk in obedience to God and also (b) a firm trust in God for his power to enable us to do what we could not do on our own. That is why Paul could encourage the Philippians to make continual progress along the path of sanctification, "*for* it is God who works in you, both to will and to work for his good pleasure" (Phil. 2:13). Apart from God's power, and apart from trust in him to work within us, we could not please him.

But because of God's power within us, we can work to please him, and we can, again and again each day, please him by our actual obedience.

The other side of this teaching is also important: there is some "obedience" that is not pleasing to God because it is not fully consistent with the teaching of his Word. Mere outward conformity to some rules of Scripture, but with a cold heart, is not pleasing to God:

> This people honors me with their lips,
>   but their heart is far from me. (Matt. 15:8)

And legalistic obedience that adds to the commands of Scripture does not please God: Jesus told the Pharisees who had added multiple commands to Scripture, "For the sake of your tradition you have made void the word of God" (Matt. 15:6).

We Can Also Displease God by Our Disobedience

If the New Testament teaches that our obedience pleases God, then it should not be surprising to find that our disobedience is displeasing to him. Paul writes, "And *do not grieve the Holy Spirit of God*, by whom you were sealed for the day of redemption" (Eph. 4:30). The implication is that sin in our lives will cause the Holy Spirit to be grieved with us—something far different from his being pleased with us.

Similarly, the risen Lord Jesus, in his words to the church in Laodicea that was "neither cold nor hot" (Rev. 3:15), and that was "wretched, pitiable, poor, blind, and naked" (Rev. 3:17), issued this warning: "*Those whom I love, I reprove and discipline*, so be zealous and repent" (Rev. 3:19). Though they still were experiencing the love of Christ (Rom. 8:35–39), in this case it was a disciplinary love, a love that flowed from Christ's displeasure at their continued sin. (As any parent can attest, or as any husband or wife can attest, it is possible to love someone deeply and yet be displeased with that person at the same time! So it is here with Christ and a disobedient church.)

In the same way, God in his love sometimes puts us through painful discipline "for our good, that we may share his holiness" (Heb. 12:10). When we disobey God, we can experience his love as a disapproving, disciplinary love that flows from his fatherly care for us. (Compare also the painful discipline of God on the Corinthian church for its abuse of the Lord's Supper in 1 Cor. 11:30–32.)

The authors of the Westminster Confession of Faith understood this in 1646 when they included the following in the article on "justification":

God doth continue to forgive the sins of those that are justified; and, although they can never fall from the state of justification, yet they may, by their sins, fall under *God's fatherly displeasure*, and not have the light of His countenance restored unto them, until they humble themselves, confess their sins, beg pardon, and renew their faith and repentance.[5]

To have "the light of His countenance restored" unto us is another way of expressing the idea of moving from what the confession wisely calls "fatherly displeasure" back into a situation in which he is once again pleased with us because our previous sins have been confessed and forgiven, and because we have forsaken those sins and have begun to walk in obedience once again.

This of course is why Jesus tells us that we should daily ask God to forgive us our sins (Matt. 6:12), and it is why the promise of forgiveness in 1 John is so precious to believers and so necessary if we are ever to experience God's pleasure in our lives: "If we confess our sins, he is faithful and just to forgive us our sins and to cleanse us from all unrighteousness" (1 John 1:9). We should seek to please God by our obedience, and we should also pray each day that he would forgive us for those ways in which we have not pleased him, so that our relationship with him might be restored and we might enjoy his favor once again. Another way of saying this is that when God is displeased with our sin, although our spiritual *union* with God by virtue of being "in Christ" is not lost, our *communion* with God can be disrupted.

Pleasing God by Obedience Will Result in Experiencing More of His Favor (or "Grace") on Our Lives

Someone might object that what I have said to this point seems inconsistent with the New Testament emphasis on grace (Gk. *charis*) in the Christian life. Haven't we been told that grace is God's unmerited favor? How then can we say that God gives more grace or more favor to those who are obedient?

Grace Also Includes the Idea of Favor from God

The New Testament term *charis* is often translated "grace," but we must realize that there is always a nuance of "favor" in it as well, and in fact, in earlier Greek literature, the sense of "favor" is more central to the meaning of the term than the nuance of something that is undeserved. The Liddell-Scott *Greek-English Lexicon* does not even mention the idea of favor being unde-

---

[5]Westminster Confession of Faith, 11.5.

served or unmerited in its definition of *charis*, but gives the meaning "*grace, kindness, goodwill . . . for* or *towards* [someone]."[6] And the current edition of the Bauer *Greek-English Lexicon of the New Testament* defines *charis* as "a beneficent disposition towards someone, *favor, grace, gracious care/ help, good will.*"[7] While it adds that in the New Testament *charis* generally includes the idea of doing something that is "not otherwise obligatory,"[8] it clearly also retains the sense of "favor" or "a favorable disposition toward someone," which can be seen in most or all of its uses in the New Testament. While it often has the sense of going *beyond* what is deserved, the word itself does not mean something that is *totally* undeserved.

The sense of "favor" in *charis* is evident in passages like the following:

> And the child grew and became strong, filled with wisdom. And the *favor* [Gk. *charis*] of God was upon him. (Luke 2:40)

> And Jesus increased in wisdom and in stature and in *favor* [Gk. charis] with God and man. (Luke 2:52)

But we would hardly want to say that God's favor on Jesus was unmerited or undeserved favor!

In the Old Testament, *charis* is the regular Septuagint translation of Hebrew *khēn*, which means "favor, acceptance" either with God or with other people, as in the following verses:

> But Noah found *favor* in the eyes of the Lord. (Gen. 6:8)

> And the LORD said to Moses, "This very thing that you have spoken I will do, for you have found *favor* in my sight, and I know you by name." (Ex. 33:17; see also v. 12)

> Toward the scorners he is scornful,
>   but to the humble he gives *favor*. (Prov. 3:34)

> A good man obtains favor from the LORD,
>   but a man of evil devices he condemns. (Prov. 12:2)

All of these verses in the Septuagint have the term *charis*, "grace, favor," and the sense of the word in these verses would have been in the

---

[6]Liddell-Scott-Jones, *Greek-English Lexicon*, p. 1978, meaning 2.1.
[7]Bauer, Arndt, Gingrich, and Danker, *Greek-English Lexicon of the New Testament*, 3d ed. (Chicago: University of Chicago Press, 2000), 1079.
[8]Ibid.

background for the New Testament authors and readers when they used the term *charis*, which is so frequently rendered "grace" in our English Bibles. They would have clearly heard the nuance of "favor" also connected to this term, and would not have thought of it as something that had to be totally undeserved.

Grace in Justification Is Totally Unmerited Favor from God

It is certainly true, however, that God's grace in justification is entirely unmerited, for "all have sinned and fall short of the glory of God" (Rom. 3:23), and so we must be justified as a free gift: we "are justified *by his grace as a gift*, through the redemption that is in Christ Jesus" (Rom. 3:24). Because we deserve nothing but the condemnation of hell, our salvation must be a totally free gift: "For the wages of sin is death, but the *free gift* of God is eternal life in Christ Jesus our Lord" (Rom. 6:23). So justification cannot be based in any part on our works: "But if it is by grace, *it is no longer on the basis of works*; otherwise grace would no longer be grace" (Rom. 11:6).

And in a larger sense, the totality of all that we receive in salvation is an undeserved gift from God. Paul says, "For by grace you have been saved through faith. And this is not your own doing; it is the gift of God, not a result of works, so that no one may boast" (Eph. 2:8–9). Paul reminds the Corinthians that all that they have is a result of God's gift: "What do you have that you did not receive? If then you received it, why do you boast as if you did not receive it?" (1 Cor. 4:7).

Grace (God's Favor) after Justification Is Given in Greater Measure to Those Who Please God by Obedience

However, after we are justified, God can choose to give more favor and more blessing to whomever he wishes. After all, he is the Lord! Therefore, if "grace" has both the sense of "going beyond what is deserved" and the sense of "favor" from God, it is not surprising that many verses in the New Testament can speak of receiving more grace from God or of having grace increase or abound in our lives.

How does God decide to whom he will give more favor in this lifetime? Is it entirely random and arbitrary? No, there seems to be a connection between God's being pleased with his children (when they trust him and obey him) and his bestowal of more favor on them. Just as the Old Testament narratives demonstrate over and over again that God rewards covenant faithfulness on the part of his people, several New Testament passages also reinforce that teaching. *God's favor is often directly related to our obedience*—obedience that has been made possible by Christ's great salvation and his power at work within us. During our lives here on earth, there seems to be a pattern whereby God chooses to give more favor (or we could say more grace) to those who trust him and walk in obedience to him.

This is seen in a number of passages. For example: "But he gives *more grace*. Therefore it says, 'God opposes the proud, but *gives grace* to the humble'" (James 4:6; see also 1 Pet. 5:5, both quoting Prov. 3:34). Humility brings us more favor from God.

Prayer is also a factor in receiving more grace from God, because the author of Hebrews encourages us to "draw near to the throne of grace" in order that "we may receive mercy *and find grace* to help in time of need" (Heb. 4:16), implying that through prayer we can receive more grace or favor from God.

Peter also says that God gives additional "favor" (or "grace"; Gk. *charis*) to those who patiently endure suffering for doing good:

> For this finds favor [Gk. *charis*], if for the sake of conscience toward God a person bears up under sorrows when suffering unjustly. For what credit is there if, when you sin and are harshly treated, you endure it with patience? But if when you do what is right and suffer for it you patiently endure it, this finds favor [Gk. *charis*] with God. (1 Pet. 2:19–20 NASB)

Peter can also say, "May *grace* and peace be *multiplied to you*" (2 Pet. 1:2), and can encourage his readers that they should "*grow in the grace* and knowledge of our Lord and Savior Jesus Christ" (2 Pet. 3:18). In other words, Peter assumes that Christians can grow in the experience of God's favor on their lives each day.

Spiritual gifts can be understood as the result of varying degrees and varying types of favor that come from God: "As each has received a gift, use it to serve one another, as good stewards of God's varied grace [*charis*]" (1 Pet. 4:10). All of the spiritual gifts are gifts of God's favor/grace upon us, for Paul says, "having gifts [plural of *charisma*, "that which is freely and graciously given, favor bestowed, gift"] that differ according to the grace [or "favor," Gk. *charis*] given to us, let us use them . . ." (Rom. 12:6). Different kinds and measures of grace result in different spiritual gifts.

In the early church, extraordinary measures of grace were seen in some believers:

> And with great power the apostles were giving their testimony to the resurrection of the Lord Jesus, and *great grace was upon them all*. (Acts 4:33)

> And Stephen, *full of grace* and power, was doing great wonders and signs among the people. (Acts 6:8)

On the other hand, we can also pray for God's grace to be given to others, for every epistle that Paul wrote opens with a greeting in which he expresses the desire that God would give blessing to his readers: "*Grace to you* and peace from God our Father and the Lord Jesus Christ" (Rom. 1:7). And he closes every epistle with a similar prayer or expression of desire for more grace from God to come to them, "The *grace* of our Lord Jesus Christ be with you" (Rom. 16:20). Such verses show that we can pray for God's grace to be given to others, and also that grace can come to us in increasing measure throughout our Christian lives. We *stand* in the grace of justification (Rom. 5:1) and *grow* in the grace of sanctification and in the increasing favor of God on our lives (see 2 Pet. 3:18).

Pleasing God by Obedience Will Bring Various Blessings of Other Kinds
Other passages speak of other kinds of blessings that God gives to believers who faithfully obey him. For example, Peter affirms another section of Old Testament Wisdom Literature in which God rewards faithful obedience with blessings in this life, and then he applies this passage to New Testament believers, saying that if they are obedient (if they have things like "brotherly love" and a "humble mind" and do not return evil for evil), God will watch over them with his providential protection ("the eyes of the Lord are on the righteous") and will be more ready to hear and answer their prayers ("and his ears are open to their prayer"). Here is the entire passage, emphasizing the importance of living in love and humility and not repaying evil for evil:

> Finally, all of you, have unity of mind, sympathy, brotherly love, a tender heart, and a humble mind. Do not repay evil for evil or reviling for reviling, but on the contrary, bless, for to this you were called, *that you may obtain a blessing. For*
>
> > "Whoever desires *to love life*
> >   and see good days,
> > let him keep his tongue from evil
> >   and his lips from speaking deceit;
> > let him turn away from evil and do good;
> >   let him seek peace and pursue it.
> > For the eyes of the Lord are on the righteous,
> >   and his ears are open to their prayer.
> > But the face of the Lord is against those who do evil."
> >   (1 Pet. 3:8–12, quoting Ps. 34:12–16)

Peter explicitly encourages his readers to live in obedience to God "that you may obtain a blessing" (1 Pet. 3:9), and he then illustrates that with examples of blessing that will occur in this lifetime (God's protection and answers to prayer), not just at the final judgment.

Paul seems to connect pleasing the Lord by obedience with a different kind of blessing, that is, fruitfulness in one's own life and ministry. He prays that the Colossians would be "filled with the knowledge of his will in all spiritual wisdom and understanding" (Col. 1:9) so that they would "walk in a manner worthy of the Lord, *fully pleasing* to him, *bearing fruit in every good work* and increasing in the knowledge of God" (Col. 1:10).

In writing to the Corinthian church about their financial contributions to the offering that Paul was collecting for the poor in Jerusalem, he encourages them to give generously and cheerfully and implies that then God will also meet their needs, for he says that God is able "to make all grace abound to you" so that they would have enough to supply their own needs and to supply the needs of other good works as well:

> The point is this: whoever sows sparingly will also reap sparingly, and *whoever sows bountifully will also reap bountifully.* Each one must give as he has decided in his heart, not reluctantly or under compulsion, for God loves a cheerful giver. And *God is able to make all grace abound to you, so that having all sufficiency in all things at all times, you may abound in every good work. . . .* He who supplies seed to the sower and bread for food will supply and multiply your seed for sowing and increase the harvest of your righteousness. *You will be enriched in every way* to be generous in every way, which through us will produce thanksgiving to God. (2 Cor. 9:6–8, 10–11)

Here, "enriched in every way" is not limited to material provision (for it surely includes spiritual blessings as well), but it must include material provisions for their needs.

In one passage the author of Hebrews seems to appeal to God's own justice in expecting blessings to come *in this life* for the faithful believers among his readers: "For God is *not unjust* so as to overlook your work and the love that you have shown for his name in serving the saints, as you still do" (Heb. 6:10). The implication seems to be that if God were to give no blessing for their work and love, this would not be truly just. Apparently he is able to say this because he understands the whole-Bible pattern of God in blessing and rewarding those who obey him in daily life.

The author of Hebrews also indicates that part of pleasing God is believing that he will reward those who "draw near" to him and who "seek" him: "And without faith it is impossible to please him, for whoever would *draw near* to God must believe that he exists and that *he rewards those who seek him*" (Heb. 11:6). In the context of the book of Hebrews, to "draw near" to God is connected to genuine worship and prayer in this lifetime, for the same Greek verb (*proserchomai*) is connected with drawing near to God in prayer and worship in Hebrews 4:16; 7:25; 10:22; and 12:22.

John also sees the blessing of answered prayers as a result of obeying God's commandments and doing "what pleases him" in the following passage: "Beloved, if our heart does not condemn us, we have confidence before God; and whatever we ask we receive from him, *because we keep his commandments and do what pleases him*" (1 John 3:21–22).

Therefore the pattern of Scripture seems to be that God is pleased to give more of his favor and more of his other blessings to those who please him by living lives of obedience to his commandments.

Why should this surprise us? By giving additional blessing to obedience, God encourages us to obey him, which brings glory to him and is good for us as well. Although all of our obedience is still imperfect, and our hearts are never completely pure, and we can never demand that God grant us any measure of blessing, nevertheless, after we have been justified as an entirely free gift of God's grace, these verses indicate a pattern in which God does bestow additional blessings in this life on those who obey him, and withholds blessing and brings discipline upon those who disobey him. Why do we not hear this taught more often in evangelical churches?

Pleasing God by Obedience May Lead Us on the Path of Suffering

Lest we misunderstand the fullness of New Testament teaching on this matter, it is important to remember that the New Testament authors also frequently warned that believers should be ready to experience hardship and suffering as part of the Christian life. This is not an indication that God's favor on them has diminished, for our Savior Jesus Christ was himself "full of grace and truth" (John 1:14), yet he followed the path of obedience to God even to the point of death.

Peter can say, "If when you do what is right and suffer for it you patiently endure it, this finds *favor* with God" (1 Pet. 2:20 NASB). The reason for this is that we have been called to follow in Christ's steps: "Christ also suffered for you, leaving you an example, so that you might follow in his steps" (1 Pet. 2:21). And the Holy Spirit will rest in unusual measure on those who suffer for Christ's sake: "If you are insulted for the name of Christ, you are blessed, because the Spirit of glory and of God rests upon you" (1 Pet. 4:14).

Paul told the Philippian Christians, "It has been granted to you that for the sake of Christ you should not only believe in him but also suffer for his sake" (Phil 1:29; the term "granted" translates Gk. *charizomai*, "graciously given"!). And Paul himself, who knew the abundant favor of God on his ministry, experienced extensive suffering throughout his life (see 2 Cor. 11:23–29; 2 Tim. 1:12; 3:10–13).

Therefore when we teach believers that their obedience to God will please him and will bring more of his favor and blessing in their lives, we must also make it clear that the life of Christ, the example of Paul and the other apostles, the teaching of the New Testament, and the entire history of the church show that God's blessing in this life is not a guarantee that we will live a life of ease or prosperity or perfect health, or be able to avoid suffering and hardship! But it is a guarantee that God will be with us and strengthen us and make his presence known to us even in times of great difficulty. In fact, it will often be at such times that our awareness of God's favor and his wonderful presence will be the strongest.

Pleasing God by Obedience Gives Us the Joy of Thinking That God Is Pleased with Us Most of the Time

The New Testament teaching on pleasing God by obedience should have a profound effect on how Christians think of their relationship to God throughout each day. Of course, whenever we sin we need to confess that sin and ask God's forgiveness at once (Matt. 6:12; 1 John 1:9). But often we will be walking in conscious obedience to God and God's commands insofar as we understand them and how they apply to our lives.

During those times when we are obeying God to the best of our knowledge, how should we think of God's relationship toward us? What should we think of his attitude toward us at this very moment?

It seems to me that these verses on pleasing God should encourage us to think that our heavenly Father is actually pleased with us at this very moment. He takes pleasure in the good work that he has done in us through Jesus Christ and by the power of the Holy Spirit. He takes pleasure in our sincere desire to obey him. He takes pleasure in the increasing manifestation of his own character in our lives. He takes pleasure in the acts of obedience that we daily offer him as "spiritual sacrifices acceptable to God through Jesus Christ" (1 Pet. 2:5). He takes pleasure in the fact that he is daily equipping us with "everything good" that we "may do his will, working in us that which is pleasing in his sight, through Jesus Christ, to whom be glory forever and ever" (Heb. 13:21). He takes pleasure in the fact that we have learned how we "ought to walk and to please God, just as you are doing" (1 Thess. 4:1). He takes pleasure that, like John's readers, we can say, "We keep his commandments and do what pleases him" (1 John 3:22).

And just as we may expect that at the last day he will look over our life and say, "Well done, good and faithful servant" (Matt. 25:21), so it does not seem wrong for us to be able to think, at the end of a day when we have sincerely sought to obey him, that he is pleased with our work done by trusting in Christ's power within us, and is saying to us at the end of that day, "Well done."

15

THE GLORY AND SUPREMACY OF JESUS CHRIST IN ETHNIC DISTINCTIONS AND OVER ETHNIC IDENTITIES

Thabiti Anyabwile

Paltry is the number of white evangelical pastors, preachers, and leaders who deal effectively and directly with race, racism, and racial reconciliation. To my knowledge, very few have addressed this issue with anything resembling the legitimate fervor, consistency, and intentionality used to address other issues like homosexuality or abortion. Still fewer have made racial reconciliation or racial harmony a centerpiece of their preaching ministry, church objectives, or writing projects.

Pastor John Piper belongs to a class of brilliant exceptions in all of this. Each year Bethlehem Baptist Church in Minneapolis, Minnesota, celebrates Racial Harmony Weekend during the annual Martin Luther King Jr. observance. This special weekend works as a bookend with Sanctity of Life Weekend, dedicated to the elimination of abortion in practice and thinking.[1] Under Piper's leadership, the church makes these two great issues of our time equally important and central to the church's prophetic witness in the community.

John Piper repeatedly addresses race and racism from the large platform God has given him in the white evangelical world. He deserves commendation for his courage, emulation of his zeal, and admiration for his love. This chapter celebrates the supremacy of Jesus Christ over the ethnic distinctions that have so often divided us, and the ministry of one who has worked to point us to Jesus' supremacy in all things.

Where Are We Now?

The spring 2006 issue of *The American Scholar* contains two rather interesting articles under the feature section entitled "Beyond Race." In the first article, Amitai Etzioni, university professor at George Washington University, argues that "treating people differently according to their race is as un-American as a hereditary aristocracy, and as American as slavery."[2] In his view, America is a meritocracy, a place where the national ideal is that people are defined by what they achieve rather than by where they have been. He says, "Achievement matters, not origin." Etzioni proposes that one first step in the way forward out of the racial quagmire engulfing us is to remove racial categories from American public life, especially in things like the U.S. Census. These categories, he suggests, divide people unhelpfully and artificially. And with the rise of significant numbers of "brown people," Hispanics, there comes an opportunity to rethink racial categories and forge a new vision of America that lives up to its ideals.

In the second article, Nancy Honicker, an English professor at the University of Paris, takes a look at the November 2005 riots in suburban Paris.[3] Honicker points out that African immigrants from Senegal and the Ivory Coast populate these suburbs in large percentages. France, however, maintains precisely the policy that Professor Etzioni advocates in his article. The French government keeps no official statistics on race, religion, or the ethnic origins of its citizens. And in most cases public law forbids the collection of such data by private institutions. This policy, Professor Honicker argues, contributes to rather than diminishes the racial discrimination that many immigrants face in France. Honicker maintains that the invisibility of immigrant populations, caused in part by the absence of statistical information, allows for unfettered mistreat-

---

[1]See chap. 17, Justin Taylor's essay on Piper and abortion.
[2]Amitai Etzioni, "Leaving Race Behind," *The American Scholar* (Spring 2006): 20–30. Available online at http://www.theamericanscholar.org/leaving-race-behind/.
[3]Nancy Honicker, "On the Outside Looking In," *The American Scholar* (Spring 2006): 31–40.

ment of immigrants. The policy allows the country to adopt "an abstract model of citizenship" where citizens pretend not to see ethnic immigrants, while all the time they do see black- and brown-skinned peoples they systematically reject.

It seems that the famous African American sociologist W. E. B. DuBois was a bit of a prophet when he remarked in 1903 that "the problem of the twentieth century is the problem of the color-line."[4] I'm not sure DuBois intended to suggest that the problem of race would be solved in the twentieth century, but we're well into the twenty-first and the problem is very much with us.

And it is not just the problem of the color line—as if the issue only embroiled blacks and whites. That was certainly DuBois's context. And that was something of the context for a young John Piper growing up in South Carolina.

> I grew up in Greenville, South Carolina. You need to know something of the psyche of this state where I spent the first eighteen years of my life. The population of South Carolina in 1860 was about 700,000. Sixty percent of these were African Americans (420,000) and all but 9,000 of these were slaves. That's a mere 140 years ago. On December 20, 1860, South Carolina was the first state to secede from the Union, largely in protest over Abraham Lincoln's election as an anti-slavery president. And it was in Charleston, South Carolina, that the Civil War began. Ninety-five years later, when I was nine years old in Greenville, the segregation was absolute: drinking fountains, public rest rooms, public schools, bus seating, housing, restaurants, waiting rooms and—worst of all—churches, including mine.
>
> And I can tell you from the inside that, for all the rationalized glosses, it was not "separate but equal," it was not respectful, and it was not Christian. It was ugly and demeaning. I have much to be sorry about, and I feel a burden to work against the mindset and the condition of heart that I was so much a part of in those years.[5]

One admires God's grace in John Piper's life, prompting him to deal honestly and consistently with his history and his present. The alienation he felt then is very much a present reality.

However, ours is the problem of the color lines (plural) and the even more nebulous cultural lines (plural). Thinking merely in terms of black and white, and occasionally brown, is far too simplistic today.

---

[4] W. E. B. DuBois, *The Souls of Black Folk* (New York: New American Library, 1903), 19.
[5] John Piper, "Race and Cross," sermon delivered January 16, 2000, during Racial Harmony Weekend; this and other sermons cited are available at www.desiringGod.org.

Shifting and Shading

Issues involving ethnicity, and what is commonly called race, have a way of shifting and shading and even blurring in today's rapidly changing international society. DuBois's "color line" is sometimes drawn right down the middle of individual people. What about those who are multiracial? How do we class those individuals? And should we?

Many members of various minority groups are trying to shuffle their way through the personal identity maze created by all of this. Several recent books define and explore the personal identity problem. For example, Mark Smith's work *How Race Is Made: Slavery, Segregation, and the Senses*[6] argues that whites of all classes, from the colonial period to the mid-twentieth century, used not just sight but all of their senses to construct an artificial binary of "black" and "white" to justify slavery and establish social, political, and economic hierarchies.

Deborah Dickerson, in her iconoclastic reflection on W. E. B. DuBois entitled *The End of Blackness*,[7] calls for the return of the souls of black folks to their rightful owners by redefining blackness and rejecting white ideas about what it means to be black. A spouse in an interracial marriage, Dickerson writes candidly about the confusing and sometimes enraging dynamic of being "post-Black" in a society moving at glacial speed from a very racialized history.

Meanwhile, Eric Goldstein asks, "What does it mean to be Jewish in a nation preoccupied with the categories of black and white?" In his book *The Price of Whiteness*[8] Goldstein takes a look at the history of Jewish racial identification in America by tracing the hard choices and conflicting emotions Jewish immigrants and their children faced as they sought social inclusion. The price of such inclusion, Goldstein argues, was the loss of ethnic distinctiveness.

You see the quagmire, don't you? We live in a complex maze of histories and definitions, counterhistories and redefinitions, all aimed at figuring out who we are without the unintended consequence of further alienation.

Ethnic Strife

The cover story for the May 15, 2006, edition of *The New Republic* was rather striking on this point. Instead of the typical layout for a news magazine—a rather provocative and bold headline with perhaps a clari-

---

[6]Mark M. Smith, *How Race Is Made: Slavery, Segregation, and the Senses* (Chapel Hill: University of North Carolina Press, 2006).
[7]Deborah J. Dickerson, *The End of Blackness: Returning the Souls of Black Folk to Their Rightful Owner* (New York: Anchor, 2004).
[8]Eric L. Goldstein, *The Price of Whiteness: Jews, Race, and American Identity* (Princeton, NJ: Princeton University Press, 2006).

fying subtitle and appropriate cover art—*The New Republic* featured a black cover with large white lettering that read:

> Never again? What nonsense. Again and again is more like it. In Darfur, we are witnessing a genocide again, and again we are witnessing ourselves witnessing it and doing nothing to stop it. Even people who wish to know about the problem do not wish to know about the solution. They prefer the raising of consciousness to the raising of troops. Just as Rwanda made a bleak mockery of the lessons of Bosnia, Darfur is making a bleak mockery of the lessons of Rwanda. Some lessons, it seems, are gladly and regularly unlearned. Except, of course, by the perpetrators of evil, who learn the only really enduring lessons about genocide in our time: that the Western response to it is late in coming, or is not coming at all.

So nations or ethnic groups war against other nations or ethnic groups. And some nations stand back as they do. It is as though the earth is not big enough for us all and someone has to be homeless or obliterated. People are alienated, hostile, and angry.

We know on some gut level that our situation is unjust and wrong. We feel its unnatural quality in the pits of our stomachs even if we don't know what to do about it in our heads. And we ask ourselves, "What is the way forward?" "How do we escape this quicksand?" Lots of books are written each year, yet explosive conflicts along the lines of color, ethnicity, culture, and religion continue to plague us.

Is there no way of affirming our unique differences on the one hand and achieving a lasting and permanent peace and unity on the other? Is there no solution for the estrangement and hostility we witness in the world? Is there no solution for the estrangement we witness in ourselves?

The Scripture offers two complementary truths for forging ahead.

The Glory of God in Ethnic Distinctions

One must always remember that the world we now live in is not the world as God created it. The effects of the fall—sin, corruption, death, alienation—mangle and distort God's original creation order. The distortion may be observed in the twisting winds of tornadoes and hurricanes that destroy homes and take lives. The corruption may be witnessed in the perversion of human relationships and intimacies. Sin and death touch all (Rom. 5:12).

And the alienation faced by ethnic groups echoes that great alienation from God that man suffered when Adam and Eve transgressed God's commandment. "Ethnic cleansings," genocides, and wars remind us again and again that things have gone awry; things are not as they should be. The question of ethnic strife troubles us because somewhere deep inside we know there should be a peace where hostility resides and "kindred-ness" where "otherness" dominates. We wonder where the glory of God is seen in all of this ethnic division and tension.

To see God's glory more clearly, we have to view the entire biblical narrative. We must recognize that what we see now is the middle of the story. But there is quite a different beginning and will be quite a different ending to the drama.

The Beginning

In the beginning God created the heavens and the earth. And he created man. Genesis 1:26–27 records the divine intent and design for man:

> Then God said, "Let us make man in our image, after our likeness. And let them have dominion over the fish of the sea and over the birds of the heavens and over the livestock and over all the earth and over every creeping thing that creeps on the earth."
>
> So God created man in his own image,
>   in the image of God he created him;
>   male and female he created them.

Unique among all his creation were the human image bearers of God. There would be only two genders, male and female, both bearing the image of God, both in his likeness. The apex of God's creation would bear God's imprimatur, the divine impress of his image and likeness, exercising dominion over all the earth and all that the earth contains.

And from this original pair, all the peoples of the earth descend. The woman receives the name Eve "because she was the mother of all living" (Gen. 3:20). From her womb comes all mankind. Genesis 5 records the lineage of man from Adam and Eve down to Noah. Genesis 6–9 records the cataclysmic flood of God that destroys all but eight souls (Noah and his family). And Genesis 10 records the Table of Nations, the descendants of Noah's three sons—Shem, Ham, and Japheth—into "their clans, their languages, their lands, and their nations." The first ten chapters of Genesis reveal the biological unity of all mankind, as all the nations of the earth spread over the globe from our original parents, Adam and Eve, through one preserved family, that of Noah.

Whatever we may say about the existence of races or ethnicities, we must assert that the variety we see in peoples is of the sort that magnifies

God's wisdom and power in creation. For God "made from one man every nation of mankind to live on all the face of the earth" (Acts 17:26).

With clear eyes, Piper sees the implications of Genesis 1:27 and Acts 17:26:

> When you put this teaching of Genesis 1 (that God created the first man in his image) together with the teaching of Acts 17:26 (that God made all the ethnic groups from this first ancestor), what emerges is that all members of all ethnic groups are made in the image of God.
>
> No matter what the skin color or facial features or hair texture or other genetic traits, every human being in every ethnic group has an immortal soul in the image of God: a mind with unique, God-like reasoning powers, a heart with capacities for moral judgments and spiritual affections, and a potential for relationship with God that sets every person utterly apart from all the animals which God has made. Every human being, whatever color, shape, age, gender, intelligence, health, or social class, is made in the image of God.[9]

By his manifold wisdom, God himself has worked in our ethnic selves a display of his creative power. The fact that we are one humanity and yet so diverse testifies to the infinite imaginative desires of God. He pleases himself with the diversity of roses—some red, some yellow, some white, some pink. He pleases himself with the variegated species of birds—the ostrich, ravens, sparrows, eagles, parakeets, owls, and so on. And he pleases himself with the various families descended from Adam and Eve.

Why does God do this? Why the creation of so many ethnicities? Why create a world with the possibility of so much confusion and animosity associated with ethnic difference?

Answer: Because God glorifies himself in the differences themselves and is being glorified in the reconciliation of the nations through Jesus Christ, his Son. To see this more clearly, consider the end of the human drama of redemption.

The Ending

The beginning of the end of redemption dawns with the creation of the church. The kingdom of God has come, though its fullness awaits final consummation. This means that the end of ethnic hostility and the hidden plan of God to glorify himself in ethnic difference find penultimate expression in the church of God.

---

[9]John Piper, "Racial Reconciliation: Unfolding Bethlehem's Fresh Initiative #3," January 14, 1996.

Consider Ephesians 3. The apostle Paul writes of his ministry and stewardship of God's grace on behalf of the Gentiles, the non-Jewish *ethnē* or nations. He refers to his stewardship as "the mystery of Christ," hidden to previous generations but now revealed to the apostles and prophets. "This mystery is that the Gentiles are fellow heirs, members of the same body, and partakers of the promise in Christ Jesus through the gospel" (Eph. 3:6). This mystery was previously hidden "in God who created all things." The reason God hid these things in himself is stated in verse 10—"so that through the church the manifold wisdom of God might now be made known to the rulers and authorities in the heavenly places." God concealed his "eternal purpose" (v. 11) in order to one day display his manifold or variegated wisdom to all realms through the church. He kept this purpose hidden until it was "realized in Christ Jesus our Lord" (v. 11). The church, then, becomes a foretaste of that consummated age to come when the nations, assembled around the throne of God, praise the Lamb in eternal song.

However, the ultimate display of God's glory in the nations occurs in the consummated age itself. The arch of God's redemption bends toward the praise of his glorious grace (Eph. 1:6) as every nation, tribe, and language are brought into his awesome presence. Consider the scene in Revelation 5:9–10.

And they sang a new song, saying,

"Worthy are you to take the scroll
    and to open its seals,
for you were slain, and by your blood you ransomed people for God
    from every tribe and language and people and nation,
and you have made them a kingdom and priests to our God,
    and they shall reign on the earth."

This is the end for which the nations are made: to glorify God as one new people through faith and union in his Son. The ethnic and language distinctions remain, but there comes into view an overarching unity in praise and worship of the sovereign redeeming God and Lamb. In some inscrutable way, the very distinctions of language and nation heighten for all eternity the glory of God in redemption.

This is the final chapter of the story. This is where redeemed humanity is headed. The glory of God shines through the hues and tongues of all peoples. Our sin and strife mar the middle of the story. But both the beginning and the end are quite different realities. And in them, God receives glory from all the nations made in his image and likeness.

The Supremacy of Jesus Christ over Ethnic Identities

But what the Scripture teaches about the glory of God *in* ethnic difference must be set alongside another truth. Namely, that Jesus Christ is supreme *over* our ethnic identities. If John Piper has been committed to one thing, it is to helping everyone see the supremacy of Jesus Christ in and over everything. Christ Jesus' supremacy makes no exception of ethnic identity. Christ reigns over our natural heritages just as he reigns over all creation.

The supremacy of Jesus Christ over our ethnic identities may be seen in several ways.

First, *God assigns to all individuals their particular nation with the aim that they might by that very appointment come to find him.* The apostle Paul makes this clear in Acts 17:26–27: "And he made from one man every nation of mankind to live on all the face of the earth, having determined allotted periods and the boundaries of their dwelling place, that they should seek God, in the hope that they might feel their way toward him and find him." God makes us to be who we are and locates us in specific time periods and places *so that* we might seek him and find him. The ultimate thing is not the ethnic identity, but finding God through Christ. Christ is supreme, not ethnicity. This means, then, that there are no accidents of birth. And there are no nations that happen to fall outside the eternal redemptive purposes of God in Christ Jesus. And there are no acceptable justifications for elevating ethnic background over Christian identity. To the contrary, our ethnic identities and locations are gifts of God that maximize our proximity to him through Christ and the gospel. And because we are given such backgrounds as a means to finding Christ, Christ must be a superior gift of God.

Second, *the cross-work of Christ creates a new spiritual ethnicity, a new man, which ends our hostilities and alienation.*

> But now in Christ Jesus you who once were far off have been brought near by the blood of Christ. For he himself is our peace, who has made us both one and has broken down in his flesh the dividing wall of hostility by abolishing the law of commandments expressed in ordinances, that he might *create* in himself one new man in place of the two, so making peace, and might reconcile us both to God in one body through the cross, thereby killing the hostility. (Eph. 2:13–16)

We are no longer Jews and Gentiles in the earthbound, fleshly, divisive, and hostile sense; we are now God's workmanship, a new nation, a new household, and a new creation (2 Cor. 5:17).

This new reality is something already accomplished by Christ. Notice the past tense action of Ephesians 2. Gentile and Jew "have been brought near"; Christ "has made us both one" and "has broken down" the wall of hostility dividing us. These past tense phrases refer back to the cross. The new humanity was created "by the blood of Christ," "in his flesh," "in one body through the cross." In the words of Piper:

> That is what God is aiming at in our salvation: a new people (one new man, verse 15) that is so free from enmity and so united in truth and peace that God himself is there for our joy and for his glory forever. That's the aim of reconciliation: a place for God to live among us and make himself known and enjoyed forever and ever.[10]

Third, *the new spiritual ethnicity created in Christ makes natural ethnic identities secondary.* The apostle Paul makes this point when he writes: "For as many of you as were baptized into Christ have put on Christ. There is neither Jew nor Greek, there is neither slave nor free, there is no male and female, for you are all one in Christ Jesus" (Gal. 3:27–28). "For in one Spirit we were all baptized into one body—Jews or Greeks, slaves or free—and all were made to drink of one Spirit" (1 Cor. 12:13). The apostle does not mean that ethnic, social, and gender distinctions are destroyed, for those realities persist. Rather, Christ subsumes those real differences in a way that makes them secondary to our baptism into Christ and our newfound identity. We are one in him, drinking from the same Spirit. This means we may recognize real ethnic, social, and gender differences without being divided over them. We may celebrate femininity and masculinity, or rejoice in Jewish, Indian, Slavic, Ibo, Kikuyu, Canadian, and other heritages, while simultaneously holding forth a grander vision of unified life flowing from immersion in Christ. Because we have been joined together with Christ, we have been joined together with one another in a way that relativizes other corporate identities.

An illustration from Piper may help on this point:

> Finding your main identity in whiteness or blackness or any other ethnic color or trait is like boasting that you carry a candle to light the cloudless noonday sky. Candles have their place. But not to light the day. So color

---

[10]Piper, "Race and Cross."

and ethnicity have their place, but not as the main glory and wonder of our identity as human beings. The primary glory of who we are is what unites us in our God-like humanity, not what differentiates us in our ethnicity.

This is the most fundamental reason why programs of "diversity training" usually backfire in their attempt to foster mutual respect among ethnic groups. They focus major attention on what is comparatively minor, and virtually no attention on what is infinitely, gloriously major—our common, unique standing among all creation as persons created in the image of God.

If our sons and our daughters have a hundred eggs, let us teach them to put ninety-nine eggs in the basket called personhood in the image of God and one egg in the basket called ethnic distinction.[11]

Fourth, the supremacy of Christ over natural ethnic origin is seen in the fact that *in Christ we are being renewed to the image of God—not made a more pristine ethnic person.* Unity with Christ entails the gradual recovery of the image of God lost in Eden (e.g., 2 Cor. 3:18). Because Jesus Christ is "the radiance of the glory of God and the exact imprint of his nature" (Heb. 1:3), the icon or "image of the invisible God" (Col. 1:15), those united to Christ are also being restored to the image and likeness of God. As Paul explains, this new humanity—these Christians—"have put on the new self, which is being renewed in knowledge after the image of its creator" (Col. 3:10; see also Eph. 4:22, 24). "Here there is not Greek and Jew . . . but Christ is all, and in all" (Col. 3:11). Fundamentally, Christian identity grounds itself not in the old ideas of ethnicity and "race" but in the renewing work of Jesus Christ. "We regard no one according to the flesh," and "all this is from God" (2 Cor. 5:16, 18). The Christian of every hue and nation finds himself being made more like God in Christ and less like man in natural ethnic pose. So, the supremacy of being in and like Christ clearly outshines and outlasts the praiseworthy aspects of God's gift of ethnic identity.

So What?
But does any of this really make any difference? We may willingly admit that God receives glory in making man in all his ethnic variety, and that Christ is supreme over those distinctions. But does that acknowledgment come home in any enduring way? Is it more rhetorical grist for the preaching mill?

---

[11]Piper, "Racial Reconciliation."

The preacher's job is to press Bible truth home in such a way that its implications are unavoidable and undeniable. How often have platitudes been offered Christian people in the place of the cutting, wounding, healing, transforming Word of God? How often do we tend to "play nice" and "affirm" one another without ever peering into the costly and radical implications of God's truth?

Not so with John Piper. He underlines this issue by connecting it with the most marvelous work of God in the soul of man: conversion. The converted "get it" and do something with it. Those who don't "get it" and apply it may not be converted. In his thinking and preaching it is that simple. Consider this extended quote from the pen of John Piper at his pastoral best:

> I think that one of the reasons some Christians have a hard time relating their Christianity to issues like racial harmony and justice is that their view of what happens in conversion to Christ is so superficial. Let me illustrate with the way the apostle Paul handled a misuse that his gospel received. Somewhere along the way, Paul's gospel of justification by grace through faith was distorted like this: "Well, if we are saved by grace alone through faith alone, then let's just sin all the more that grace may abound. The more sin we do, the more grace God shows, and the more glory he gets for his wonderful grace."
>
> Given the way a lot of professing Christians think and feel and act today toward people of other races than themselves, it may be that this distortion is alive and well. Salvation is by grace through faith, so there is no necessity for a change in whether we hate or mistreat people on the basis of race (racism); God forgives and gets more glory for being more gracious.
>
> So how does Paul answer this distortion of his gospel of justification by grace through faith? Listen. I will read it to you from Romans 6:1–2. But get ready, because it is devastating to a superficial view of Christian conversion that reduces it to a "decision for Christ."
>
> Here is what he says, "What shall we say then? Are we to continue in sin so that grace may increase? May it never be! How shall we who died to sin still live in it?" [In other words,] "How shall we who died to racism still live in it?" "How shall we who died to malice, still live in it?" "How shall we who died to unkindness and cruelty and meanness and injustice and ugliness and hard-heartedness and bitterness and hostility and anger still live in it?"
>
> Do you hear what Paul is saying? He is saying: If you justify ongoing sin on the basis of abounding grace, if you minimize the seriousness of sin in the life of a Christian, you don't know what conversion to Christ means. It means death. Death to sin. Let me read it again: "Shall we con-

tinue in sin—in hating or mistreating or slurring other races—because grace abounds? God forbid! How can we who died to sin still live in it?" Conversion means death—not just decision for Jesus, but death with Jesus. One great problem in the church today—not the only one—is that we do not grasp the magnitude and depth and wonder and miracle of what happens in genuine conversion to Christ. And therefore we do not know how to live and work and fight for righteousness as Christians. And we have a hard time connecting issues like racism with our faith, because we got it wrong from the beginning.[12]

"You don't fight for racial harmony and justice because you don't understand conversion." Can you remember the last time you heard that trumpeted from the pulpit? Yet, how could we conclude otherwise given the biblical data?

But to preach this way—and more importantly, to *live* this way—requires that we celebrate God's glory by learning from men like John Piper. Below are four things I personally appreciate about Piper and hope are found in some measure in our lives as we seek to demonstrate the glory of God in human ethnicity and the supremacy of Christ over our ethnic selves.

Personal Reflection and Self-Critique
We take in ethnic bias and racial toxin as regularly as we view mindless sitcoms, participate in office chatter, and observe our closest family and friends. The only escape from this atmosphere of alienation and bias is serious personal reflection and sober self-critique, the kind we see in John Piper's own public statements about how he grew up in South Carolina. And more than reflection, we need repentance and resolve. We must turn from the old life of sin—first seeing it for what it is—and turn toward God in the new life of faith and righteousness in Christ, who includes in himself the redeemed of all nations.

Theological Precision
Ethnicity, like justification and the gospel and christology, requires theological precision. It requires thinking rightly and biblically about the nature of man and God's redemption. Empty platitudes and politically correct niceties will not do. Piper says it best: "Any listener who thinks that the way forward in race relations is to dumb down doctrine, so that you can hang out and not count truth as important, is undermining the very foundation on which we must stand together to make progress

---

[12]John Piper, "Class, Culture and Ethnic Identity in Christ," sermon delivered January 17, 1999, during Racial Harmony Weekend.

against injustice and the forces that destroy families, cities, and kids."[13] Truth matters. Doctrine matters. We will not make meaningful progress until our best theological minds level their gaze at the *theological*—not just social or historical—problem of race and racism. After all, a lot of theological imprecision and malpractice provided for so many years the sustaining fuel for slavery, segregation, and racist attitude.

Church Leadership

If the church is the penultimate display of God's glory in ethnicity and Jesus' supremacy over it, then real leadership will be required for the church to reverse centuries of glory-denying, Christ-belittling, gospel-distorting racist practice. The Lord's church needs men who begin with personal reflection, continue with theological force, and subsequently offer real leadership. The elders of Bethlehem Baptist Church offer one example. Consider what they call "Fresh Initiative 3: *Racial Reconciliation*." The initiative states: "Against the rising spirit of indifference, alienation, and hostility in our land, we will embrace the supremacy of God's love to take new steps personally and corporately toward racial reconciliation, expressed visibly in our community and in our church."[14]

Statements like these must live in the preaching and the witness of the pastors and leaders. Consider John's call to the flock of God at Bethlehem:

> I am aware this Racial Harmony Sunday, as always, that there are more races than white and black, and that the call to racial harmony is very complex and goes deeper than color. But I carry a special burden in my heart for the experience of African Americans and our relationship to each other. And I call us as a church to grow in our understanding of that experience which has a uniquely painful place in the history of our country. I believe the ripple effect of this focus and this understanding will be deeper harmony for all races and cultures represented in our church, and will pull us forward to greater racial diversity and greater racial harmony. At least that's my prayer and my goal.
>
> I can't create this understanding and this relationship by myself. It will be God's work. And you must help me. Join me in prayer, and in reading, and in listening, and in hanging out together across racial lines.[15]

---

[13]John Piper, "What Is Hindering Racial Reconciliation in the Church?" October 26, 2007.
[14]Piper, "Racial Reconciliation."
[15]John Piper, "The Peril of Partiality: Riches and Race in the Christian Church," sermon delivered January 18, 2004, during Racial Harmony Weekend.

How will God's people live out the reconciled redemption we have unless their leaders call them to it?

Courage

No man lacking courage will make this call. It is risky. So many things can go wrong. And yet God requires his stewards to be faithful (1 Cor. 4:1–2). And God has given John Piper courage—"brokenhearted boldness"—to address our racial sins and opportunities amidst all the difficulties and risks and distractions. Visit Desiring God's Web site and you will find sermons on the touchiest issues involving race and ethnicity—sermons on race and abortion; racial harmony and interracial marriage; and articles on affirmative hiring. God has given John Piper the courage to address issues that appear to have no positive, upside potential—unless you view them from the vantage point of God's greater glory and fame, as John does.

Conclusion

I am glad John Piper was born. And I am glad he was born again. God granted him life and new life. And God did this for his own glory. It is exceedingly kind of God to have given the church John Piper so that our generation may see with increasing clarity and awe something of the magnificent greatness and glory of God in the person and work of his Son, Jesus Christ, who reigns supreme over all things—including our ethnic identities.

16

DETHRONING MONEY
TO TREASURE CHRIST ABOVE ALL

Randy Alcorn

When it comes to money and possessions, the Bible is sometimes extreme, and occasionally shocking. It turns people away, interferes with our lives, and makes us feel guilty. To avoid guilt feelings, we invent fancy interpretations that get around plain meanings.

We come to the Bible wanting comfort, not assaults against our worldview. The church should concern itself with what's spiritual and heavenly. Let *God* talk about love and grace and brotherhood, thank you. Let *us* talk about money and possessions—then do with them whatever we please.

Some believers ask each other tough questions: "How are you doing in your marriage? How much time have you been spending in the Word? Sharing your faith? Guarding your sexual purity?" Yet how often do we ask, "Are you winning the battle against materialism?" Or, "Are you cutting your spending and increasing your giving?" Or, "Have you been peeking at those tempting magazines and Internet sites? You know, the ones that entice you to greed?"

Financial stewardship seems to be the last bastion of accountability. People are more open about their sexual struggles than battling materialism. Some churches are talking about getting out of debt. I applaud that. But you can be out of debt and still be stingy and greedy. We don't need to become smarter materialists; we need to repent of materialism.

When it comes to stewardship, money management, and giving, most churches operate under a "don't ask, don't tell" policy. We lack communication, accountability, or modeling. It's as if we have an unspoken agreement—"I won't talk about it if you won't." That way we can go on living guilt-free.

Our Need to See and Become Giving Mentors

Ask people at your church if they can point out prayer warriors. Most can. Now ask them to point out *giving* warriors, people who have chosen a modest lifestyle so they can give away 100 percent above that to God's kingdom. The fact that the term "giving warrior" isn't in our vocabulary says it all, doesn't it?

Where can young Christians go to observe what giving looks like in the life of a believer who treasures Christ above all else? Why are we surprised when, seeing no other example, they take their cues from a materialistic society?

God commands us, "Consider how to stir up one another to love and good works" (Heb. 10:24). Shouldn't we be asking, "How can we stir one another to giving and good stewardship? How can we model scaled-down lifestyles to free investment capital for God's kingdom?"

As high-jump teammates raise the bar for each other, shouldn't we be raising the bar of giving and providing growing Christians something to strive for?

Studies show we have failed to pass the stewardship-and-giving baton to the next generation. The younger church people are, the lower the percentage they give to God. That means we older Christians aren't modeling a giving lifestyle.

Many Christians operate under a serious misinterpretation of Scripture. Certainly we must avoid prideful giving—in the context of giving, prayer, and fasting, Jesus warns us, "Beware of practicing your righteousness before other people in order to be seen by them" (Matt. 6:1). In exactly the same sense that prayer warriors should avoid being proud about prayer, good Bible students about their study, evangelists about their witnessing, and good parents about their parenting, we ought to avoid being proud about giving.

Getting people's applause shouldn't be our reason for doing anything! But this does not mean we should hide joyful obedience and growth in these areas of discipleship. If we do, it's predictable that the church won't learn to pray, study, witness, parent, or give. If we are committed to silence about spiritual disciplines, we'll never be able to hear from those whom God has shown great grace.

Had George Mueller not told of his prayer experiences, Hudson Taylor of his evangelistic encounters, John Paton of his sacrifices for the gospel, or R. G. Letourneau of giving away 90 percent of his income, what a loss it would have been to countless others who have benefited from their examples.

Earlier in the same message, before warning against doing spiritual acts to be seen by men, Jesus said, "Let your light shine before men, that they may see your good deeds and praise your Father in heaven" (Matt. 5:16 NIV). We should let our lights shine and make our good deeds seen never so that we'll be praised, but only so God will be praised!

By spotlighting testimonies involving every spiritual discipline except giving, we fail to mentor people in giving. We violate God's explicit command to emphasize excellence in giving as much as in other areas: "But just as you excel in everything—in faith, in speech, in knowledge, in complete earnestness and in your love for us—see that you also excel in this grace of giving" (2 Cor. 8:7 NIV).

By all means let's be careful to avoid self-praise, but let's not fail to testify to God's gracious empowerment as we follow him in the journey of joyful giving.

The Call to Total Surrender
John Calvin said, "Where riches hold the dominion of the heart, God has lost His authority."[1]

Scripture repeatedly demonstrates the profound relationship between our true spiritual condition and our attitude and actions concerning money and possessions.

Zacchaeus said he would give half his money to the poor and pay back fourfold those whom he had cheated. Jesus didn't say, "Good idea." He said, "Today salvation has come to this house" (Luke 19:9). Jesus judged the reality of Zacchaeus's salvation on the basis of his cheerful eagerness to part with money for the glory of God and the good of others.

In contrast to Zacchaeus stands the rich young ruler (Luke 18:18–30). He earnestly asked Jesus what good thing he could do to get eternal life.

---

[1]John Calvin, *Harmony on the Evangelists*, on Matthew 6:24.

Jesus said, "Go, sell what you possess and give to the poor, and you will have treasure in heaven; and come, follow me" (Matt. 19:21).

Jesus knew that money was the rich young man's god. We can't enthrone the true God in our hearts unless in the process we dethrone our other gods. If Christ is not Lord over our money and possessions, then he is not our Lord. As Jesus used Zacchaeus's willingness to part with his money to gauge his true spiritual condition, he used the rich young ruler's unwillingness to do so to gauge his.

Jesus told his disciples, "Truly, I say to you, only with difficulty will a rich person enter the kingdom of heaven." He said that this was harder than for a camel to go through a needle's eye. This statement left the disciples "greatly astonished" (Matt. 19:23–25). They didn't understand the barrier that wealth presents to genuine spiritual birth and growth. Neither do we.

Jesus sees our hearts and knows us as well as he knew those two men. Our Lord didn't and doesn't call all disciples to give away everything. He does call us to take radical action that breaks our bondage to money and possessions, freeing us to live under his lordship. He calls all of us to a life of dethroning all secondary treasures in order to elevate him as our primary treasure. If we value anything or anyone more than we value Jesus, we are not his disciples.

When people asked John the Baptist what they should do to bear the fruit of repentance, he told them to share their clothes and food with the poor. Then he instructed tax collectors not to collect and pocket extra money. Finally he told the soldiers not to extort money and accuse falsely (probably with the goal of confiscating goods they claimed were stolen), and to be content with their wages (Luke 3:7–14).

No one had asked John about money and possessions. They asked him what they should do to bear the fruit of spiritual transformation. Yet at least five—perhaps all six—answers involve material things. John couldn't talk about spiritual change without addressing how people handle money and possessions.

The Ephesian occultists' willingness to burn their magic books—worth fifty thousand days' wages, equivalent to six million dollars in today's economy—demonstrated the reality of their spiritual conversions (Acts 19:18–20). The early Christians' willingness to surrender money and possessions to help others proved their spiritual transformation (Acts 2:44–45; 4:32–35).

It was no more natural for those Christians to liquidate and disperse assets they'd spent their lives accumulating than it would be for us. That's the point. Conversion and the filling of the Holy Spirit are *super*natural experiences that produce *super*natural responses—whether in the first century or the twenty-first. Joyful giving and voluntary sharing of property became the new norm of supernatural living. Seeing each other's examples of radical giving spurred early Christians onward and upward, toward the Christ they valued over all.

If John the Baptist or a first-century Christian were to visit us today and determine our spiritual condition, what conclusions would he draw about our attitudes and actions regarding money and possessions? Would the evidence convince him we are true followers of Jesus? Or would he see us merely as a baptized version of the world's self-preoccupied materialism?

When you look around our Christian communities today, what do you see in our handling of money and possessions that only the supernatural work of God could explain? When you look at yourself, what do you see?

As thunder follows lightning, giving follows grace. We give because he first gave to us. If your life doesn't resound with the thunder of giving, doesn't that suggest you've not been struck by the lightning of God's grace?

How Would You Advise a Poor Widow and a Rich Businessman?

To test how close your thinking is to Christ's, suppose you have two appointments today, one with an elderly woman, one a middle-aged man. The woman, a widow whose husband left her nothing, says, "The cupboards are bare. I'm down to my last two dollars. Yet I sense God wants me to give them to him."

What would you tell her? Perhaps this: "That's very generous of you, dear. He knows your heart—that you *want* to give. But he desires you use common sense and take care of yourself. God would have you keep those two dollars and buy food. Don't give away the little money he's already provided."

Your next appointment is with a successful, hardworking, middle-aged farmer whose crop production has been stellar. He tells you, "I'm planning to tear down my old barns to build bigger ones so I can save up plenty for the future. Then I can retire early, do some traveling, go to the beach, and play golf. What do you think?"

What's your answer? Perhaps this: "Well, as long as you give 10 percent to the Lord, that sounds good to me! It's your business, crops, and money. If you can save up enough to take care of yourself for the rest of your life, go for it. One day I hope to do the same!"

Doesn't this advice seem reasonable? We don't have to wonder what Christ would say to either of these people. Scripture tells us.

In Mark 12 we meet a poor widow. She put two tiny copper coins, all her money, in the temple offering box. Jesus called his disciples together to teach them a lesson. Did he say she should have been more sensible? No. He gave her an unqualified commendation: "Truly, I say to you, this poor widow has put in more than all those who are contributing to the offering box. For they all contributed out of their abundance, but she out of her poverty has put in everything she had, all she had to live on" (Mark 12:43–44).

Jesus set her up as a model for his disciples to follow. He enshrined her example in God's Word so that future generations might emulate her faith and sacrificial generosity.

In Luke 12 we meet a rich man. We're not told that he gained his wealth dishonestly. Perhaps he went weekly to synagogue and three times yearly to the temple, tithed, and prayed, as most Jews did. Now he wanted to expand his God-blessed business by building bigger barns. His purpose was to accumulate enough wealth to retire early and have a good time. Sounds exactly like the American dream, doesn't it?

What did God say to this man? "Fool! This night your soul is required of you, and the things you have prepared, whose will they be?" Jesus added, "So is the one who lays up treasure for himself and is not rich toward God" (Luke 12:20–21).

By our standards, the widow's actions seem unwise and the rich man's wise. But God regards the poor woman as eternally wise and the rich man as eternally foolish.

If our advice to the poor widow and the rich fool contradicts Christ's, then either he was wrong or we are. (I'm betting it's us.)

Who gets featured more frequently in Christian magazines and talk shows? Who serves on our boards and determines the direction of our ministries? Do we have a scarcity of poor widows and a surplus of rich fools?

In 1986, John Piper (then a mere forty-two years old) wrote his classic book *Desiring God*. I read it immediately. I didn't know John then, but God touched me through his words. He wrote:

The issue is not how much a person makes. Big industry and big salaries are a fact of our times, and they are not necessarily evil. The evil is in being deceived into thinking a $100,000 salary must be accompanied by a $100,000 lifestyle. God has made us to be conduits of his grace. The danger is in thinking the conduit should be lined with gold. It shouldn't. Copper will do.[2]

Christians today face a disturbing question: Can we really put Christ before all, deny ourselves, take up our crosses and follow him, with no apparent effect on what we do with our money and possessions? God's Word answers an emphatic No!

Materialism: The Religion of Greed

Materialists attach the wrong price tags to the things of this world and the things of God. They inflate the value of what's worthless, and depreciate Christ, the universe's greatest treasure.

Materialism is a false god that distracts us from Jesus. The popularity of Christian seminars, books, and messages focused on amassing wealth in this life demonstrates how normal Christianized materialism has become. The Bible sets our hearts not on securities but *security*, not trusts but *trust*, not real estate but *real* estate.

Materialism is manifest not merely in what we say we believe—our doctrinal statement—but in the way we actually live—our worldview. Even true Christians who deny belief in materialism's philosophical underpinnings (they couldn't be Christians if they didn't) may be preoccupied with material things. Materialism is a matter of the heart.

Christ's disciples love people and use things. Materialists love things and use people. Marketing strategists call people consumers, the economic units a company values to the degree they contribute to its profits. Respectable business people market goods without regard to whether consumers (God's image bearers) become addicted, depressed, obese, or diseased as a result.

Our country's materialism may alarm us, but shouldn't surprise us. We cannot reject God's person and truths without rejecting the respect for human dignity that naturally flows from them. We cannot teach and believe that human beings are merely the product of time, chance, and natural forces without treating each other as expendable.

High-sounding courses in ethics or rousing speeches calling on us to restore the moral fiber of our nation will never correct materialism. Changing our view of God, seeing him as far bigger and ourselves as far smaller, is the only cure. We must value Jesus Christ and knowing him

---

[2]John Piper, *Desiring God* (Portland, OR: Multnomah, 1986), 166–67.

above all else: "But whatever gain I had, I counted as loss for the sake of Christ . . . because of the surpassing worth of knowing Christ Jesus my Lord. For his sake I have suffered the loss of all things and count them as rubbish, in order that I may gain Christ . . . that I may know him" (Phil. 3:7–8, 10).

Materialism results from a failure to realize that we were made for one person, Jesus, and one place, heaven. We should never be satisfied with less than Jesus. As C. S. Lewis put it, "We are half-hearted creatures, fooling about with drink and sex and ambition when infinite joy has been offered to us. We are far too easily pleased, like an ignorant child who goes on making mud pies in a slum because he cannot imagine what is meant by an offer of a holiday at the sea."[3]

Satan whispers, "If you had this thing or this person, you'd finally be happy." God says, "Sweet is the sleep of a laborer, whether he eats little or much, but the full stomach of the rich will not let him sleep" (Eccles. 5:12). Jesus plus nothing is everything. Everything minus Jesus is nothing.

Jesus tackled head-on materialism of any form in any age: "Take care, and be on your guard against all covetousness, for one's life does not consist in the abundance of his possessions" (Luke 12:15).

Greed is the passion to possess what God doesn't want for us, and what therefore will harm us. Mall window shoppers and catalog browsers should remind themselves that greed isn't a harmless pastime; it's a serious offense against God. Just as one who lusts is an adulterer (Matt. 5:28), and one who hates is a murderer (1 John 3:15), one who is greedy is an idolater (Col. 3:5). No sin is greater than worshiping false gods and thereby depreciating the only true God. The fact that idol worshipers may surround us doesn't reduce the seriousness of our offense.

Greed violates the first commandment: "I am the LORD your God. . . . You shall have no other gods before me" (Ex. 20:2–3). The eighth commandment prohibits stealing (Ex. 20:15), a product of greed. The tenth commandment forbids covetousness (Ex. 20:17). Remarkably, the ten great laws of God, written in stone, contain no fewer than three prohibitions against materialism.

In that same first edition of *Desiring God*, John Piper pointed out the emptiness of materialism and the immorality it fosters:

> Who do you think has the deepest, most satisfying joy in life, the man who pays $140 for a fortieth-floor suite downtown and spends his evening in the half-lit, smoke-filled lounge impressing strange women with ten-dollar

---

[3]C. S. Lewis, *The Weight of Glory* (New York: Macmillan, 1980), 17–18, 3–4.

cocktails, or the man who chooses the Motel 6 by a vacant lot of sunflowers and spends his evening watching the sunset and writing a love letter to his wife?[4]

Our culture's current financial turbulence is largely the result of our entitlement mentality and its debt addiction. We imagine that if we want to own a new car or a house or a big-screen television, then we have a right to own it. Nothing should get in the way, including the fact that we can't afford it, and that even if we could, God might not want us to have it.

What will happen to the affluent person or society that doesn't rectify its materialism? Physics tells us the answer. The greater the mass, the greater its gravitational pull. The more things we own—the greater their total mass—the more they grip us, hold us, set us in orbit around them. Finally, like a black hole, they mercilessly suck us into themselves, until we become indistinguishable from our things, surrendering ourselves to the gods we've idolized.

In the face of this grim prognosis, Jesus Christ brings us good news. He calls us to look at himself—God incarnate, crucified and risen. Paul reminds us, in the middle of the longest New Testament passage on giving (2 Corinthians 8–9), that God's grace in Christ is the greatest gift, which overshadows and underlies all lesser gifts: "For you know the grace of our Lord Jesus Christ, that though he was rich, yet for your sake he became poor, so that you by his poverty might become rich" (2 Cor. 8:9).

When we gaze upon Christ and see him as he is, and allow ourselves to be transformed into his image, we automatically adopt a giving mindset. Through generous giving, we establish a new orbit around Christ, our primary treasure, who promises us heaven's secondary treasures of eternal reward.[5] Only as we give can we escape the gravitational hold of money and possessions (Matt. 6:19–21).

What keeps us from giving more and living on less? It's not just our love for things; it's our fear of being unwise or looking odd. If simple living were normal, it would be much easier to live simply. A mandate to "live simply" won't do. It's easier to follow footprints than orders. If most people in the church drive new cars and live in beautiful homes and go on expensive vacations, young Christians will think that's standard for the Christian life. We need living examples of Christ-loving people we respect living simpler lifestyles.

---

[4]Piper, *Desiring God*, 157.
[5]Randy Alcorn, *The Law of Rewards* (Carol Stream, IL: Tyndale, 2003), 15–31.

A single man in our church came to Christ in his twenties, read Scripture, and got so excited that he determined to sell his house and give all the money to God (he had a regular income and could easily have rented an apartment). But when he shared this plan with older believers in his Bible study group, something tragic happened: they talked him out of it.

Let's be careful not to quench God's Spirit and rob others of joy and reward that comes from following Christ wholeheartedly. Are we talking them out of something radical because we want to remain comfortable with our own lifestyle choices? Why not watch and learn? Let's lay all of God's assets on the table and ask him which ones he wants us to give away. A disciple doesn't ask, "How much can I keep?" but "How much more can I give?"

We don't like risky faith. We like to have our safety net below us, a backup plan in case God fails. Our instinct for self-preservation leads us to hedge our bets. We will give only as much as we can without really feeling it. We take away the high stakes, and lose the high returns. We miss the adventure of seeing God provide when we've stretched our faith in radical giving.

A. W. Tozer wrote:

> The man of pseudo faith will fight for his verbal creed but refuse flatly to allow himself to get into a predicament where his future must depend upon that creed being true. He always provides himself with secondary ways of escape so he will have a way out if the roof caves in. What we need very badly these days is a company of Christians who are prepared to trust God as completely now as they know they must do at the last day.[6]

Positioning Ourselves for the Turn

> Show me, O Lord, my life's end
>> and the number of my days;
>> let me know how fleeting is my life. . . .
>> Each man's life is but a breath.
> Man is a mere phantom as he goes to and fro: . . .
>> he heaps up wealth, not knowing who will get it.
>> (Ps. 39:4–6 NIV)

Read the obituaries to remind yourself how short our time here is. Visit a junkyard to see where all the material things you chase after will one day end up.

---

[6]A. W. Tozer, *The Root of the Righteous* (Camp Hill, PA: Christian Publications, 1955), 50.

Luke 16:19–31 tells us of a rich man and poor Lazarus. The rich man lives in luxury. Lazarus is a beggar, diseased, dirty, who "desired to be fed with what fell from the rich man's table" (Luke 16:21).

We aren't told that this rich man is worse than average. We don't know that he despises Lazarus; we do know that he ignores him. He lives as if the poor man doesn't exist. He doesn't use his God-provided wealth to care for him.

Both men die. Lazarus goes to paradise, the rich man to hell. When the rich man begs Abraham to send Lazarus across the gulf to relieve his suffering, Abraham replies, "Child, remember that you in your lifetime received your good things, and Lazarus in like manner bad things; but now he is comforted here, and you are in anguish" (Luke 16:25).

This parable presents an overlooked teaching we might call "the reversal doctrine." It reveals that in eternity many of us will find ourselves in conditions opposite to our current ones.

"Blessed are you who are poor," Jesus says, and "Woe to you who are full now," precisely because their status will one day be reversed (Luke 6:20, 25). The poor in spirit, those who mourn, the meek, those who hunger and thirst for righteousness, and the persecuted will find relief and God will reward them in heaven (Matt. 5:3–12). Those praised in this world won't be highly regarded in the next, and vice versa (Matt. 6:1–4, 16–18). Those exalted now will be humbled then; those humbled now will be exalted in heaven (Matt. 23:12).

Who would you rather be, the rich man or Lazarus? If we answer based on their lives before death, we'd answer incorrectly. Their eternal condition should determine our choice.

If we had God's perspective, even for a moment, and looked at how we go through life accumulating and hoarding and displaying things, we'd have the same feelings of horror and pity that any sane person has when he views people in an asylum endlessly beating their heads against the wall.

Seeking fulfillment in money, houses, cars, clothes, and cruises has left us bound and gagged. Like drug addicts, we pathetically imagine that our only hope lies in getting more. Meanwhile, the voice of God—unheard amid the clamor of our possessions—tells us that even if materialism did bring happiness in this life, which it clearly does not, it would leave us woefully unprepared for the next life.

Someday this upside-down world will be turned right-side up. Nothing in all eternity will turn it back again. If we're wise, we will spend our brief lives on earth positioning ourselves for the turn.

Two Masters

Jesus speaks in Matthew 6 of two treasuries (heaven and earth), two perspectives (the good eye and the bad eye), and two masters (God and money). He says that although we might *have* both God and money, we cannot *serve* both God and money.

I may have two jobs, three sisters, or five friends, but only one spouse. Some relationships are, by their nature, exclusive. The most basic of these is our relationship with God. There's room on the throne of each person's life for only one occupant. Christ may be on that throne or money may be on that throne. They cannot share it.

By naming it Mammon, Christ personified money. Mammon is a false god, an antichrist, a Jesus substitute. It's a bogus messiah, rallying its followers, promising them happiness, bringing them ruin.

There's nothing wrong with money. We need it to live on here in this foreign land. God graciously provides it. But like Confederate money near the end of the Civil War, it's only good for a very short period of time, and time's running out. This Confederate currency that runs through our fingers will be utterly worthless once our tour on this battleground is over. We'll live one day on a new earth, but we're here on this present earth with a short-term visa that will soon expire.

Suppose you're an American living in Italy for three months, working and renting a room. You're told that you can't bring anything back to America on your flight home. But you can earn money and mail deposits to your bank in the U.S. Would you fill your rented room in Italy with expensive furniture and wall hangings? Of course not. You'd spend only what you needed on living expenses and your temporary residence, sending your earnings home so they'd be waiting for you.

This is what Jesus says: "Lay up for yourselves treasures in heaven" (Matt. 6:20). He's saying, you can't take it with you, but you can send it on ahead.

Jesus gave us a choice: a life wasted in the pursuit of wealth on earth, or a life invested in the pursuit of wealth in heaven. Every day, the person whose treasure is on earth is headed away from his treasure. Every day, the person whose treasure is in heaven is headed toward his treasure. He who spends his life headed away from his treasure has reason to despair. He who spends his life heading toward his treasure has reason to rejoice.

So . . . every day as the sand falls in your life's hourglass, where are you headed, away from your treasure, or toward it?

Transferring the Title Deed to God

> The earth is the LORD's, and the fullness thereof,
> the world and those who dwell therein. (Ps. 24:1)

> The silver is mine, and the gold is mine, declares the LORD of hosts.
> (Hag. 2:8)

> You shall remember the LORD your God, for it is he who gives you power
> to get wealth. (Deut. 8:18)

When I grasp that I'm a steward, not an owner, when I realize that God graciously grants me even my ability to earn money, I'll no longer ask, "How much of my money shall I, out of the goodness of my heart, give to God?" Rather, I'll ask, "Since all of my money is really yours, Lord, how would you like me to invest your money today?"

When I realize that God has a claim not on a few dollars to throw in an offering plate, not on 10 percent, but 100 percent of my money, it's revolutionary. Suddenly I'm God's money manager. I'm not God. Money isn't God. God is God.

Not only does God own everything, but God controls everything. When catastrophe strikes, I can honestly say, "God has taken only what belonged to him" (cf. Job 1:21).

God's ownership and sovereignty offer a liberating life-changing perspective on the robbed house, the totaled car, the stolen bike . . . or the terminal diagnosis.

The more holdings we have on earth, the more likely we are to forget that we're citizens of another world. If you were traveling through a country on foot, what would your attitude be toward possessions? You wouldn't hate them or think them evil, but you would choose them judiciously. Accumulating unnecessary things would slow your journey or force you to stop.

We live in houses, and build businesses. There's nothing wrong with this. But we must cultivate the traveler's utilitarian view of things. They are tools to use, not treasures to store up. God may or may not call me to move from my home, business, or country. Yet I must be in a position to say yes if he does. I must hold loosely all things, while grasping tightly to Christ my treasure.

Name It and Claim It?

Few things are uglier than Christianized materialism. In health and wealth theology, God is a cosmic slot machine in which you drop a coin, pull the lever, stick out your hands, and catch the winnings while your casino buddies (in this case, fellow Christians) whoop and holler (or say "Amen") and await their turn.

In this worldview, God's reason for existing is to give us what we want. If we had no needs, God would disappear—after all, what purpose would he have? Prosperity theology revises the Westminster Shorter Catechism: "The chief end of God is to give Man whatever he wants, and serve Man forever."

What makes every heresy dangerous is its element of truth. Some passages do link material prosperity with God's blessing. God gave material wealth to some he approved of, including Abraham (Gen. 13:1–7), Isaac (Gen. 26:12–14), Jacob (Gen. 30:43), Joseph (Gen. 39:2–6), Solomon (1 Kings 3:13), and Job (Job 42:10–17).

In Deuteronomy 28:1–13, God tells the Israelites that their reward for obedience would be children, crops, livestock, and victory over their enemies. Then he tacks on fifty-four more verses describing the curses—including diseases, famine, and military defeat—that would come upon the nation if they didn't obey him.

Many believed in a direct cause-and-effect relationship: health and wealth meant that God approved; sickness and poverty meant he didn't. Job's "comforters" thought there must be hidden sin in his life to account for his loss of prosperity. But God called Job blameless (Job 1:8; 42:7). Still, he permitted Satan to bring grief and destruction on him.

Christ's disciples betrayed their assumptions when they asked, "Rabbi, who sinned, this man or his parents, that he was born blind?" (John 9:2). Jesus responded, saying they didn't get it: "It was not that this man sinned, or his parents, but that the works of God might be displayed in him" (John 9:3). God's higher purpose for this man's adversity didn't fit the neat little categories of "Do good and you'll be well off" and "Do bad and you'll suffer."

Are material wealth, fame, and success reliable indicators of God's reward or approval? Material wealth surrounded Hitler, Stalin, Mao, and Pol Pot during their rise to power and at the apex of their regimes. Was God on their side? Is God also on the side of wealthy cultists, dishonest business executives, and immoral rock stars? If wealth is a dependable sign of God's approval and lack of wealth shows his disapproval, then Jesus and Paul were on God's blacklist, and drug dealers and tyrants are the apple of his eye.

How Did the "King's Kid" Live?

There's irony in a saying heard in health-and-wealth gospel circles: "Live like a king's kid." The "King's kid" was Jesus, who lived exactly the opposite of what that phrase means today. The King we serve was stripped down for battle. At the end of the age he will don the royal robes of victory, as will his faithful servants; but now is the time for battle garb, not regalia.

Born in lowly Bethlehem, raised in despised Nazareth, part of a pious, poor family that offered two doves because they couldn't afford a lamb (Lev. 12:6–8; Luke 2:22–24), the King's kid wandered the countryside dependent on others to open their homes, because he didn't have one of his own. "Live like a king's kid"? Whatever king's kid the prosperity proponents are speaking of, it isn't Jesus!

Prosperity theology sees as our model the ascended heavenly Lord rather than the descended earthly servant. Jesus warned his disciples not to follow a lordship model, but his servant model (Mark 10:42–45). In this life, we're to share in his cross—in the next life we'll share in his crown (2 Tim. 2:12).

Verses you won't see embroidered, framed, or posted on refrigerators or dashboards promise persecution, betrayal, flogging, and being dragged before courts and tried for our faith (Matt. 10:16–20). The King warned, "In the world you will have tribulation" (John 16:33). He said, "Any one of you who does not renounce all that he has cannot be my disciple" (Luke 14:33). This is not the stuff of which prosperity sermons are made.

I have no argument with anyone who says that God often chooses to prosper his generous people in material ways. Jesus said so in Luke 6:38, while in the near context he also said, "Blessed are you who are poor" (Luke 6:20). When he does prosper us, the great question is *Why?* When he blesses us financially, what does he expect us to do with the abundance?

Prosperity preachers argue that God expects us to live in luxury, in order to be good witnesses to how God cares for his children. By this standard, Jesus and Paul and most of the apostles were poor witnesses. Many believers suffer precisely because they are Christ's followers. They join ranks with the persecuted and mistreated of whom God says, "The world was not worthy [of them]" (Heb. 11:37–38).

Any gospel that is more true in America and South Korea than in Sudan or Haiti is not the true gospel. And whether a message is proclaimed by an angel, a television evangelist, a pastor, or a fund-raising letter, Scripture makes clear what our response should be to any gospel other than the true one (Gal. 1:6–10).

Why Does God Give Us So Much More Than We Need?

Why does God make many of us rich? We don't have to wonder, since Scripture directly answers: "You will be enriched in every way to be generous in every way, which through us will produce thanksgiving to God" (2 Cor. 9:11). God entrusts to us riches not to raise our standard of living, but to raise our standard of giving.

John Piper wrote in 1986:

> God is not glorified when we keep for ourselves (no matter how thankfully) what we ought to be using to alleviate the misery of unevangelized, uneducated, unmedicated, and unfed millions. The evidence that many professing Christians have been deceived by this doctrine is how little they give and how much they own. . . . They will object: Does not the Old Testament promise that God will prosper his people? Indeed! God increases our yield, so that by giving we can prove our yield is not our god. God does not prosper a man's business so he can move from a Ford to a Cadillac. God prospers a business so that 17,000 unreached peoples can be reached with the gospel. He prospers the business so that 12 percent of the world's population can move a step back from the precipice of starvation.[7]

Suppose you have important items you want to get to people who need them. You wrap them up and hand them over to the FedEx delivery person. What would you think if you found out that instead of delivering those packages, he's been taking them home, opening them, and keeping them for himself?

You confront him and he responds, "Well, if you didn't intend for me to keep those things, you shouldn't have given them to me in the first place."

You'd say, "Those packages don't belong to you. *I* say where they go, *you* get them there. You're not the owner, you're the delivery guy!"

Just because God puts his money into our hands, what makes us think he intends for us to keep it?

Why Giving Is Better Than Receiving

When Jesus said, "It is more blessed to give than to receive," he really meant it (Acts 20:35).

---

[7]Piper, *Desiring God*, 163–64.

What's the biggest misconception Christians have about giving? That when we give money away to a church or ministry, or to help the needy, it's gone. While we hope others will benefit from it, we're quite sure we won't. We think we're divesting ourselves of money. Once it leaves our hands, we imagine, it has no connection to us, no future implications relevant to our lives.

We couldn't be more wrong.

What we think we own will be rudely taken from us—some of it before we die, and the rest when we die. Now is our window of opportunity to invest it in eternity. We don't have to have everything taken from us. We can give it before disaster or death strikes. To paraphrase Jim Elliot, now's our chance to give what we can't keep to gain what we can't lose. Martin Luther said, "I have had many things in my hands, and I have lost them all; but whatever I have been able to place in God's, I still possess."[8]

Paul says, "For this light momentary affliction is preparing for us an eternal weight of glory beyond all comparison" (2 Cor. 4:17). Note the contrasts: "light" versus a "weight beyond comparison"; "momentary" versus "eternal"; "affliction" versus "glory." Soldiers, athletes, and farmers all know that short-term sacrifices are justified in light of their long-term payoffs (2 Tim. 2:3–6). Christ's disciples understand the same.

Where Is Your Heart Headed?

John Wesley once purportedly said, "I judge all things only by the price they shall gain in eternity."

Christ said, "Where your treasure is, there your heart will be also" (Matt. 6:21). What we do with our possessions is a sure indicator of what's in our hearts. Jesus is saying, "Show me your checkbook, and your credit card statement, and I'll show you where your heart is." What we do with our money is a bold statement of what we truly value.

What we do with our money doesn't simply *indicate* where our heart *is*. According to Jesus, it *determines* where our heart *goes*. If our heart is where our treasure is, then when we move our treasure somewhere else, our heart follows our treasure there. This is a remarkable truth. If I want my heart somewhere, I need to put my money there.

I've heard people say, "I want a heart for missions." I respond, "Jesus tells you how; if you put your money in missions, your heart will follow."

Do you wish you had a greater heart for the poor and lost? Then give your money to help the poor and reach the lost. Do you want your heart

---

[8]From a letter written by Luther to Justus Jonas, cited in Jean-Henri Merle d'Aubigné, *History of the Great Reformation of the Sixteenth Century in Germany, Switzerland, Etc.* (R. Carter, 1846), 183.

to be in your church? Put your money there. If most of your money is in mutual funds, retirement, your house, or your hobby, that's where your heart's going to be. You can redirect your heart into God's kingdom by investing your treasures in God's kingdom. If you want to care more about General Mills or Marriott, buy up shares. If you want to care more about God's kingdom, buy up shares through investing your time and money. Gain vested interests in what matters to God.

The Church as a Giving Community

Someone told me, "When I look at the Bible, I get really convicted to change my lifestyle. Then I look all around me at other Christians who live like I do and I think, 'It must be OK—everybody else lives this way too.'"

To turn the tide of materialism in the Christian community, we desperately need bold models of kingdom-centered living. People respond best when they have tangible examples they can follow in their leaders and their peers (Num. 7:3; 1 Chron. 29:9; 2 Chron. 24:10).

I believe the Christian community should be filled with people who set caps on their lifestyles, giving away everything above a reasonable amount to live on. Consider setting a lifestyle finish line. That means if you make a predetermined amount of money or save a certain amount, you won't accumulate or spend beyond that. You'll give away everything else. That isn't sacrificial giving, it's giving according to our ability. Yet this seems so extreme we may not know anyone who lives that way. There are such people. Why not join their ranks?

Bible colleges, Christian liberal arts colleges, and seminaries should develop courses centered not merely on money management, but on a biblical theology of stewardship and giving. We need more than illustrations of budgeting, debt reduction, and retirement planning. We need a Bible-centered, Christ-centered study of money and possessions that gives a vision for kingdom living rather than Christianized materialism.

Jesus says, "One who is faithful in a very little is also faithful in much, and one who is dishonest in a very little is also dishonest in much" (Luke 16:10). God tests us all in little things. If a child can't be trusted to spend his father's money and return the change, neither can he be trusted to stay overnight at a friend's house. If his father can trust him to clean his room and take out garbage, he can trust him with a dog or a bike.

"If only I had a million dollars, I'd give it to my church or missions." The issue is not what I would do with a million dollars, but what I am doing with the hundreds or thousands of dollars I do have. If we are being selfish and unfaithful with what he has entrusted to us, why should he trust us with more?

It's about Jesus, and Eternity

Missionary C. T. Studd said, "Only one life, 'twill soon be past; only what's done for Christ will last."

For some of us, it's time to drop to our knees and ask God's forgiveness for our self-indulgent lifestyles, our indifference to human need, and our short-sightedness about eternity. It's time to commit, or recommit, to a life of obedient and exhilarating discipleship. It's time to trade in our short-term American dream for the long-term kingdom dreams of the risen Christ.

Once more I'm grateful to John Piper for insight in many areas, including this one:

> Three billion people today are outside Jesus Christ. Two-thirds of them have no viable Christian witness in their culture. If they are to hear—and Christ commands that they hear—then cross-cultural missionaries will have to be sent and paid for. All the wealth needed to send this new army of good news ambassadors is already in the church. If we, like Paul, are content with the simple necessities of life, hundreds of millions of dollars in the church would be released to take the gospel to the frontiers. The revolution of joy and freedom it would cause at home would be the best local witness imaginable.[9]

Embrace Christ's invitation: "Give, and it will be given to you" (Luke 6:38). Then, when he gives you more, remind yourself why: "You will be enriched in every way to be generous in every way" (2 Cor. 9:11). When you give, you'll experience his joy. When you give, you'll feel his pleasure.

I spoke with a man who'd read my book on giving, *The Treasure Principle*. He owns a profitable business and believes for the first time that he knows why God has blessed him financially. It's not so he can drive nicer cars and live in a nicer house. It's to give it to build God's kingdom. I told him about a dozen different missions groups and pro-life projects, and ways to help persecuted Christians. I wish you could have heard the excitement in his voice as he walked away determined to liquidate more assets and dramatically expand his eternal investment portfolio.

---

[9]Piper, *Desiring God*, 157.

This man followed through on his commitment and has given more and more over the years. He isn't a reluctant, guilt-ridden giver. He's been liberated from material bondage. He's thrilled to have gotten on board with what matters! He's like the man who finds priceless treasure hidden in the field, "Then in his joy he goes and sells all that he has and buys that field" (Matt. 13:44). Do we pity the man for his sacrifices? On the contrary, we envy him for his treasure and his joy.

Conclusion

If God is speaking to you, listen. We dare not delay obedience. Nothing's more fleeting than the moment of conviction. If we turn our backs on that moment, the next time may not come until we stand before our Lord—when it will be too late to reclaim a lifetime of squandered opportunities.

Five minutes after we die, it will be too late to go back and redo our lives. Gazing into the eyes of the Christ we treasure, we'll know exactly how we should have lived. God has given us his Word so we don't have to wait to die to find out how we should have lived. And he's given us his Spirit to empower us to live that way now.

Ask yourself: Five minutes after I die, what will I wish I would have done with the money and possessions God entrusted to my care? What will I wish I'd given away while I still had the chance?

When you've come up with an answer, why not do it now? Why shouldn't we spend the rest of our lives closing the gap between what we are doing and what we'll wish we would have done for his glory?

17

"ABORTION IS ABOUT GOD"

Piper's Passionate, Prophetic Pro-Life Preaching

Justin Taylor

Evangelicalism—in the Reformed camp or elsewhere—is not exactly overflowing with models of how to preach exegetically faithful, powerfully prophetic, culture-engaging, hope-giving, gospel-centered sermons on the politically charged and personally painful topic of abortion. But for the past twenty years John Piper has been doing just that.[1] In this chapter I want to survey Piper's sermons and writings on abortion as an encouragement and a model for preachers—and all believers—to honor God and defend the defenseless by proclaiming God's Word and engaging the world on the issue of abortion.

In order to let Piper speak as much as possible, I'll quote and para-phrase him extensively in what follows. I begin with a bit of biographi-

---

[1]For a complete list of these sermons, see the list appended to this chapter. Throughout this chapter, I will simply cite the sermons by year in the body of the text. Each sermon can be read or listened to in its entirety for free at the Desiring God Web site.

cal overview, sketching Piper's development as a pro-life pastor. I'll then attempt to summarize the main exegetical arguments in his pro-life sermons, since expositional preaching on abortion is a challenge. Finally, I will suggest some application lessons that pastors can learn from Piper's pro-life preaching.

Piper's Slowly Opening Eyes on the Silent Holocaust of Abortion

Piper was installed as the senior pastor of Bethlehem Baptist Church on July 13, 1980. In 1982 he publicly raised the issue of abortion for the first time in the form of a newsletter article entitled "Abortion, Father's Day, and Infant Doe." It traced the timeline of an infant boy in Minnesota who died when his parents refused an operation for his surgically correctable condition. The reason? He had Down syndrome and his parents didn't want him to live. The couple was not charged with wrongdoing for letting their son die.

Calling abortion "a most grievous sin," Piper wrote, "Abortion is, in my judgment, manslaughter and a breach of the sixth commandment." He connected the increase of abortion to the increase of infanticide and concluded, "The reason abortion has led to the killing of infants is because it already *is* the killing of infants." He then encouraged the people of Bethlehem to respond in the following ways: (1) avoid entertaining even the thought of an abortion; (2) teach your children that abortion is an abomination in God's sight and an assault on his glory; (3) keep informed about pro-life legislation; and (4) support ministries to young women in crisis.

It would be another five years before Piper devoted a sermon to abortion, which he did on January 18, 1987. After explaining what was happening and why, Piper turned to how we should respond. Here his counsel was wider and more proactive than the "modest suggestions" offered in 1982: (1) submit yourself to God, being a visible and audible Christian; (2) pray earnestly and regularly for awakening in the churches; (3) use your imagination to see abortion for what it really is; (4) support alternatives to abortion with money and time and prayers; and (5) use your democratic privileges of free speech and representation and demonstration to press for legal protection for the unborn.

This counsel seems to represent a strategic shift in Piper's thinking whereby Christians are to engage the issues not only in their homes (through sanctification, prayer, teaching, and being informed) and in crisis-pregnancy ministry, but also in the public square through actions that make the case for legally protecting the unborn.

Two years later, after being arrested for peaceful pro-life civil disobedience,[2] Piper referenced an editorial that lamented "the silence of the evangelicals" on abortion. Piper applies this to himself first:

> I want to publicly confess a great blindness and indifference and apathy in my own life and ministry. I am in no position to point my finger at any of you. I bear a greater responsibility as a leader. My silence has been more shameful than yours. I am praying now that I would be forgiven and granted another chance to do my part in ending "the silent holocaust" of abortion.[3]

It is not as if Piper had suddenly become pro-life. The shifting issue in 1989 was over the degree of personal outrage and the resolve to address the issue publicly—both from the pulpit and at the abortion clinics. Signing the article, "With slowly opening eyes, Pastor John," it is clear that Piper had now made a decisive move with regard to his public, pastoral advocacy against abortion. Since 1989, Piper has preached every January on the topic of abortion.

Piper's Exegetical Grounding for Abortion Opposition and Pro-Life Action

Pastors who want to preach against abortion and equip their congregations in the cause for truth and life often struggle with how to do this exegetically. Natural-law arguments are one thing, but how does one address abortion by expositing Scripture when the Bible never explicitly deals with the situation of someone intentionally seeking to kill life in the womb?

Piper's sermons on abortion do not follow a set formula, but most of them contain the following elements: (1) a review of facts and argu-

---

[2]Piper, along with other pastors and members at Bethlehem, was arrested twice (December 19, 1988, and January 20, 1989) for attempting to save the lives of the unborn at Planned Parenthood of Minnesota in St. Paul. In a January 1989 newsletter article he wrote that "[we] simply sat in front of the door to say by our action: without violence we will do what we can to stop child-killing here today. . . . Wouldn't you sit down in front of a door to separate a baby from a killer?" Five days before the second arrest he offered his public justification for such a rescue attempt in his sermon "Rescuing Unborn Children: Required and Right," from Proverbs 24:10–12. Piper argued from the text that rescue is always "right" (i.e., permissible) but is not "required" by direct biblical injunction; rather, it is one way our consciences might dictate that we apply this proverbial command. The following January (1990) Piper preached another sermon prior to a planned rescue, offering justification for showing solidarity with those suffering (namely, the unborn). There he specifically stressed the importance of nonviolence: "This war will not be won by bullets. It will be won by brokenness and humility and sacrifice. It will be won when we identify with the children in our suffering rather than with the abortionist in his killing." The physical rescue movement fizzled after this time, as the method became ineffective due to the swift response of law enforcement in removing protestors and the success of abortion-choice advocates in raising legal charges, including racketeering.
[3]John Piper, "Why Would Three Pastors from Bethlehem Get Arrested?" *Star* [church newsletter], January 9, 1989.

ments about abortion (its definition, prevalence, immorality, etc.); (2) an examination of biblical passages that show why abortion is wrong and why Christians should be involved in exposing this dark work; (3) gospel application for the guilty (for abortion killing, abortion support, or abortion apathy); and (4) practical ways that Christians can take a stand for truth in order to save lives for the glory of God. In the next section I make no attempt to summarize all of Piper's abortion sermons in their entirety, but rather focus on the exegetical work that he does in each. My goal will be to let Piper himself speak as much as possible in these extracts, so that readers can hear his own words and follow his own exegetical arguments.

Understanding Why We Murder the Unborn: James 4:2

In his first sermon on abortion (1987) Piper asks, "Can we say anything from Scripture about what is happening when a life in the womb is aborted?" The first text he turns to is the familiar Psalm 139:13:

> For you formed my inward parts;
>> you knitted me together in my mother's womb.

Piper observes that "the life of the unborn is the knitting of God, and what he is knitting is a human being in his own image, unlike any other creature in the universe." He then turns to a lesser-known text, Job 31:13–15 (summarized in a later section, below). From these two texts Piper concludes that "the destruction of conceived human life—whether embryonic, fetal, or viable—is an assault on the unique person-forming work of God."

For why this is happening, Piper turns to James 4:2: "You desire and do not have, so you murder."

> We kill marriages and we kill unborn babies because they cut across our desires; they stand in the way of our unencumbered self-enhancement. And we live in a culture where self-enhancement and self-advancement is god. And if self-enhancement is god, then the One who is at work in the womb shaping a person in his own image is not God and the assault on his work is not sacrilegious, but obedience to the god of self.

Behind and beneath the rhetoric of abortion is the agenda of Satan, who was a murderer from the beginning (John 8:44). So men and women who cause abortion to abound refuse to submit to their Creator. They worship instead the god of self-enhancement and follow the steps of the ruler of this world (Eph. 2:2–3).

Publicly and Peacefully Identifying with the Unborn: Hebrews 10:32–35
In 1990 Piper focused on rescuing unborn children from slaughter. Hebrews 10:32–35 focuses on two groups within the church: one suffering abuse and affliction through imprisonment, the other publicly and compassionately identifying with their suffering brothers and sisters by visiting them in prison. The latter "joyfully accepted the plundering of [their] property," knowing that they "had a better possession and an abiding one" (v. 34). Piper, expounding and applying the text in light of a planned rescue operation at an abortion clinic, explains their rationale:

> Because when the compassion of Christ for people who are suffering unjustly combines with the confidence of kingdom hope, the power of courage and freedom and meekness is unleashed, and some (not all) are called to let the light of the kingdom shine through peaceful, public solidarity with the unborn, and if necessary, through suffering.

Kingdom compassion requires that Christians intercede and identify in some way.

Listening to God Not Men: Acts 4:13–22
In 1991 Piper's exegetical work explored how to interact with those who reject God's truth. Piper highlighted three things in Acts 4:13–22 that are relevant for life in a secular world, especially with regard to abortion: (1) The kind of people who will stand up to the authorities (v. 13) is not necessarily the educated or skilled but, rather, the bold, forthright, and clear because they have real fellowship and experience with Jesus. (2) The leaders respond to the evidence of truth mounting against them (vv. 16–17) by turning a deaf ear and a blind eye; their minds selectively see what will justify the desires of their heart, and that's what needs to be changed. (3) Our response to the threat of the authorities (v. 19) should be to stand up in public and tell God's truth as we see it without worrying that secular listeners may not agree with even our most basic assumptions. Applying this to abortion as well as other issues, Piper says, "Your job is not to win. Your job is not to control this society. Your job is to say what God wants said. . . . We are not called to win; we are called to witness."

Exposing the Dark and Unfruitful Work of Abortion: Ephesians 5:11
In 1992 Piper built the heart of his sermon around Ephesians 5:11: "Take no part in the unfruitful works of darkness, but instead expose them." Many Christians obey only the first part of this verse, practicing only a "passive avoidance ethic" and ignoring the second part of the duty to actively expose the works of darkness. But walking as children of light

(Eph. 5:8) entails our not doing works of darkness and our exposing the works of darkness that others do. An application is that God is calling all Christians to expose the dark and fruitless work of abortion. In this way Christians serve as the conscience of their culture and the light of the world.

Honoring the President: 1 Peter 2:13–17

Piper's 1993 sermon was delivered just three days before the inauguration of President Bill Clinton, an adamant supporter of abortion on demand. Piper begins his exegetical work in this sermon by recounting the Bible's perspective on human government. Those who rule over us have been given authority by God, and we are to be subject to them (Rom. 13:1, 5; 1 Pet. 2:13–14) as God's servants (Rom. 13:1, 4). We are to pray for them and thank God for them (1 Tim. 2:1–2), and we are to respect and honor them (Rom. 13:7; 1 Pet. 2:17).

But if you believe that aborting a child means killing a child, how then do you honor the president of the United States if he has the power and desire to make abortion more accessible? How do pro-life Christians honor a pro-choice president? Piper offers eight points to his answer, personally addressing them to President Clinton: (1) We will honor the president by humbling ourselves under God's mighty hand, acknowledging that we are ourselves sinners and in need of mercy and forgiveness from God. (2) We will honor the president as an utterly unique human being created in the image and likeness of the living God with untold potential. (3) We will honor the president by acknowledging that government is God's institution and the president is in power by God's appointment. (4) We will honor the president by submitting to the laws of the state and the nation wherever they do not conflict with our higher allegiance to Christ the King of kings and Lord of lords. (5) We will honor the president by not withdrawing into little communes of disengaged isolation from American culture, but (following 1 Pet. 2:15) by trying to do as much good as we possibly can for the unborn, and for unwanted children, and for women in distress, so that we will not be thought insolent or inconsistent in asking from the president what we are not willing to do ourselves. (6) We will honor the president by opposing his position as long as we can with nonviolence instead of violence, with reasoning instead of rocks, with rational passion instead of screaming, with honorable speech instead of obscenities, with forthright clarity of language instead of dodging the tough realities and tough words, with evidence instead of authority, and with scientific portrayals of life instead of authoritarian blackouts (cf.

2 Cor. 4:2). (7) We will honor the president by expecting straightforward answers to straightforward questions. (8) We will honor the president by trusting that the purpose of our sovereign and loving God to defend the fatherless and contend for the defenseless and to exalt the meek will triumph through his presidency.

Beholding the Majesty of God in His Supreme Creation: Psalm 8

In 1994 Piper unpacked Psalm 8, observing that it begins and ends with the same statement:

> O LORD, our Lord,
>   how majestic is your name in all the earth!
>   (vv. 1, 9)

Verses 3–5 teach that God manifested his majesty through his supreme creation, human beings. Piper explains the relevance of Psalm 8 to abortion (and racism):

> The vision is that God is majestic above all the majesties of the universe and this majesty—though dimmed and besmirched and defiled by sin—shines in the glory of God's supreme creation, human beings. And the truth that flows from this vision is that we cannot worship and glorify the majesty of God while treating his supreme creation with contempt.

In verse 4 David asks, "What is man?" and makes three points in response: (1) humans are made by God ("You have made him"); (2) they are radically different from animals ("a little lower than the heavenly beings"); and (3) they are "crowned . . . with glory and honor" (v. 5). This, Piper suggests, is the reason that the infant humans and nursing babies of verse 2 can overcome the enemies of God. Piper says:

> Let all the adversaries of God take note and tremble. If they treat God's supreme creation with contempt, they will lose. They will be silenced. And so I appeal to you, do not join with the adversaries of God in killing unborn children or scorning any race of human beings. Because the truth of this text stands sure: You cannot worship and glorify the majesty of God while treating his supreme creation with contempt.

Fasting for the Safety of Little Ones: Ezra 8:21–23

Piper's 1995 Sanctity of Life sermon was part of a larger 1994–1995 series on fasting (which formed the basis for the book *A Hunger for God*). Piper exegetically connected abortion and fasting by looking at the book of Ezra. In 8:21 Ezra proclaims a fast, "that we might humble ourselves before our God, to seek from him a safe journey for ourselves, our children, and all our goods." It is here that Piper got the idea of fasting for the safety of children, or "little ones" (NASB). The Israelites sought God with life-and-death seriousness and humility, and verse 23 records the result: God listened to their entreaty.

While endorsing pro-life engagement in various ways (education, political action, crisis pregnancy care, sidewalk counseling) Piper insists that "at root the issue we are facing is a spiritual one—the darkness and depravity of the human heart and mind." Piper asks, "Might not the cry of our hearts for such an awakening of conscience and faith be made more full and earnest and fruitful through fasting?"

Boiling in the Spirit for the Cause of Truth and Life: Romans 12:9–11

The text for Piper's 1997 sermon was sparked by his encountering an unfamiliar word in an essay by William Bennett: *acedia* (apathy, boredom). Piper agreed with Bennett that in America today there is a deep cultural acedia—a "cultural yawn." This is contrary to the Christian mind and heart, which calls for zeal, fervency, and strength in the service of Christ and his kingdom. Against this cultural apathy and boredom come the words of Romans 12:11: "Do not be slothful in zeal, be fervent [Gk. ζέοντες, boiling] in spirit, serve the Lord." Those who boil in the Spirit will find ways to pour their lives into the cause of life and truth.

Abortion Is about God: James 4:1–10

In his 1998 sermon Piper expressed gratitude for non-Christian arguments for why abortion is wrong. Nevertheless he is adamant that accounts without God are ultimately trivial. A biblical perspective on abortion recognizes that this issue is ultimately about God, for at least four reasons: (1) the child in the womb is created by God in the image of God; (2) only God can forgive the sin of killing unborn children; (3) the root cause of abortion is a failure to be satisfied in God as our supreme love; (4) the political and cultural events that will make abortion unthinkable and illegal are in God's hands.

In the sermon Piper explains that the ultimate evil of abortion is not that it kills children or that it damages women—which it does. "The ultimate evil," he said, "is that it assaults and demeans God." But that, he says, "is what the gospel of Jesus Christ is about. How God planned and brought about a plan to forgive people who have committed the ultimate outrage of discounting his glory and treating it as less valuable than their own private preferences."

Visiting the Unborn in Their Affliction: James 1:26–27

Piper's 1999 sermon centers on James 1:27: "Religion that is pure and undefiled before God, the Father, is this: to visit orphans and widows in their affliction, and to keep oneself unstained from the world." Piper's application argument proceeds a fortiori (from the greater to the lesser): "If God wants us to care about the orphan whose life is endangered because his parents are dead, he would want all the more that we care about the child whose life is endangered because his parents choose to make him dead."

Piper uses the same form of argument regarding the affliction or distress of the orphan, for there is no greater place of distress than the womb of a woman being given over to abortion. And even the command to care for widows has application for women who choose abortion: "Women who abort are often desperately alone. They are in a worse situation than many widows." If we are to care for orphans and widows, we should also care for babies in the womb and women who are contemplating or have committed abortion.

Engaging Culture for Christ: 1 Peter 2:9–17

In the year 2000 Piper reviewed the arguments for why we know abortion is wrong but then stepped back to provide a wider framework for Christian involvement in society and culture. Using 1 Peter 2:9–17 he showed that (1) we all were once in darkness, along with the whole world; (2) God has called us out of darkness into his marvelous light; then (3) God sends us back to (but not into) that darkness to "proclaim his excellencies." (4) We are to make God's excellencies known to the darkened culture by both avoidance and engagement. (5) Our freedom in Christ does not cancel submission to cultural institutions (state, employers, family, etc.), but puts us on a whole new footing of submission to God. (6) Finally, we are to honor all people, but in ways appropriate to their roles in life.

God's Person-Forming Work in Every Womb: Job 31:15

In 2001 Piper returned to the argument of Job 31:13–15, which he briefly looked at in his first sermon on abortion fourteen years earlier. Job ponders his accountability before God after a servant issues a complaint against him. Job says,

> Did not he who made me in the womb make him?
>   And did not one fashion us in the womb? (v. 15)

Piper makes four observations regarding the argument: (1) The ground of inalienable human rights is traced all the way back to the womb. (2) Job and his servant are both equal in that they are both utterly dependent, derivative creatures made by God. (3) The central, essential, and crucial work in the womb is not natural or biological development but the work of God in creating a person; to attack God's creation is to attack God himself. (4) Job trembles in reverence and fear before God for neglecting or despising the rights of his servant because they are both created in the womb in God's image by God himself.

Piper's exegetical application from all of this is that "this issue of abortion—the taking of the life of the unborn—is a very important issue. It is not just a social issue, or a justice issue, or a woman's issue, or a children's issue, or a health issue; it is, beneath all those and more important than all those, a God issue."

Being Sinfully Ignorant: Luke 23:32–38

In 2002 Piper examined Luke 23:34, where Jesus prays from the cross: "Father, forgive them, for they know not what they do." Piper's preaching frequently involves setting up a problem and then resolving it, and this exposition is no different. He asks, "Why forgive a person for what he does not know he is doing?" If people don't know what they are doing, it seems they are not morally guilty and hence don't need forgiveness. Piper's answer is that they are guilty precisely *because* they don't know what they are doing. They *should* know, and the only explanation for their ignorance in light of so much evidence is that they must not *want* to see it. Piper then applies this principle to abortion:

> Whether we know what we are doing or don't know what we are doing, we are guilty and need forgiveness, because we *should* know what we are doing. Indeed, we do know what we are doing. . . . wrongfully killing unborn human beings whose right to life, liberty, and the pursuit of happiness is a gift of God (Acts 17:25).

Exposing the Darkness of Abortion with the Light of Truth: Ephesians 5:1–16

In his 2003 sermon Piper compares Ephesians 5:8–14 and Matthew 5:13–16 on the roles of light and darkness. Paul says that "you are light in the Lord," and Jesus says that "you are the light of the world." Paul says that "the fruit of light is found in all that is good and right and true," and Jesus says that the fruit of shining our light before others is "that they may see your good works and give glory to your Father who is in heaven." Paul's focus here is on the exposing work of light. Light causes truth to appear and things to be seen as they are, while deceptions and half-truths are exposed and blown away.

Applying this to the issue at hand, Piper argues that the only way for abortion to survive is for the darkness of reasoning and language to survive. As Christians, we must shine our light so that good deeds are done and dark works are revealed and exposed. We need both "the light of good deeds" (crisis pregnancy centers, adoption, sidewalk counseling, education, political engagement) and "the light of loving analysis and critique and exposure" (reading, thinking, conversing, writing).

Piper concludes the exegetical portion of his sermon by briefly commenting on the first three verses of Ephesians 5. Verse 1: "Be imitators of God, as beloved children." We should imitate God by loving children the way he loves his children: "Let us love children: the idea of children, children in the making, and children on the earth." Verse 2: "And walk in love, as Christ loved us and gave himself up for us, a fragrant offering and sacrifice to God." Whereas "Christ died that we might live, . . . abortion kills that someone might live differently." We were weak when we were rescued by Christ's sacrifice (Rom. 5:6), and therefore we should be ready and willing to sacrifice and stand up for the weak. Verse 3: "But sexual immorality and all impurity or covetousness must not even be named among you, as is proper among saints." Sex by itself doesn't make abortion. It's sex plus covetousness. "Illicit sex and unencumbered freedom without children: for these we covet, and abortion is the result."

Eating from the Tree of the Knowledge of Good and Evil: Genesis 3:1–13

Piper's exegetical work in this 2004 sermon is more extensive than in his other sermons, and in my opinion it is perhaps his most profound work on the origin and essence of abortion. Therefore I will summarize it and quote from it at greater length.

He begins with Genesis 2:16–17, where God commanded the man, "You may surely eat of every tree of the garden, but of the tree of the knowledge of good and evil you shall not eat, for in the day that you eat of it you shall surely die." Having "the knowledge of good and evil" means claiming "the independent right to decide for oneself what is good and evil (true and false, ugly and beautiful)." God has this knowledge, but such independent knowledge would be devastating for men. God promised that such knowledge would kill man—and it's still doing so today, both spiritually and physically. "All death is rooted in this insurrection."

God alone is the source of what is objectively true and right and beauti-ful. But Satan suggests that if Adam and Eve eat from this tree, they will be like God (Gen. 3:1–5). Piper responds:

> So true and so false! God is a flower of truth and right and beauty, and he has no roots and needs no water, no sunshine, no soil. He is absolutely self-sufficient. We are planted in God. We get all our water and light and nutrition from him. Yes, we can cut our stem and try to be like him. We can be our own source of life and light and truth and right and beauty. We can. And die.

Piper then turns his attention on the immediate effects of the fall, namely that "the eyes of both were opened, and they knew that they were naked" (v. 7).

> The first result of choosing to be god is the canyon between appearance and pretension. Now that I have chosen to be God, my non-godlike appearance is ridiculous. And humans have spent centuries with fine clothing (cool cloth-ing) and make up and body-building trying to look less like the wreckage we are without God. The root of shame is the pretension to be god—the need to look invulnerable, self-sufficient, god-like (or goddess-like). The essence of the fall of Eve and Adam—and all of us in Adam—is the supreme pleasure we have in being independent, and deciding for ourselves what is true and right and beautiful, rather than finding supreme pleasure in God as the fountain of all that is true and right and beautiful. The essence of the fall is preferring to be god rather than enjoy God.

How does all of this relate to abortion? Piper argues that the link between the modern secular world (rooted in the garden of Eden) and the reality of abortion is found in the word *want*. "I do not *want* this child at this time."

> At this time in American history, that is one of the most powerful sentences a person can speak: "I do not want a child at this time." It's powerful, because in a world without God, and without submission to his will, the will—the "want"—of a mother has become the will of a god. I say it care-fully and calmly and sadly: Our modern, secular, God-dethroning culture has endowed the will (the "want") of a mother not just with sovereignty over her child, but with something vastly greater. We have endowed her will with the right and the power to create human personhood. When God is no longer the Creator of human personhood, endowing it with dignity

and rights in his own image, we must take that role for him, and we have vested it in the will of the mother. She creates personhood.

But then, as is usually the case, Piper closes with the gospel. Staying within the text of Genesis 3, Piper turns to verse 15:

> I will put enmity between you and the woman,
>   and between your offspring and her offspring;
> he shall bruise your head,
>   and you shall bruise his heel.

Instead of saying that the Seed of the woman would someday crush woman for her sin, God makes Eve "a means of salvation, not an object of judgment. The offspring of this woman will crush Satan. Jesus Christ died and rose again to forgive and reverse our love affair with being god instead of enjoying God."

Seeing Abortion as the Outworking of Racism and Sexism: Exodus 1:1–22

In 2005 Piper looked at the connections between abortion, race, and gender by recounting the early events of Exodus 1, observing that the Egyptians (the dominant ethnic group) took four increasingly radical steps to eliminate the threat of the Israelites (the minority ethnic group): (1) they initiated slavery (vv. 1–12), and then (2) they intensified the slavery (vv. 13–14). (3) Pharaoh then instructed the midwives to kill the infant males at birth (vv. 15–16), and (4) he later commanded the entire Egyptian nation to kill the infant male Israelites (v. 22).

Piper sees this Egyptian escalation of infanticide as analogous with our abortion situation, which is often the outworking of racism and sexism. The subtle infanticide against Israel, like abortion today, (1) preceded open infanticide, (2) was selective, and (3) was ethnically specific. Piper also notes that those who disobeyed the authorities by refusing to participate in such infanticide were rewarded by God (Ex. 1:17–21). Piper closes with a contrast between Moses and Jesus in order to show the power and the beauty of the gospel:

> Moses delivered the people who were being oppressed. Jesus delivers oppressed and oppressor.

> Moses delivered the hated race. Jesus delivers the hated and the hater.

Moses couldn't deliver the strangled babies or babies thrown into the Nile, but Jesus delivers the babies, the mothers, the abortion providers, the irresponsible boyfriends. He loves and saves every sinner who trusts in him.

Killing babies is not the path to freedom. Jesus Christ is.

Asking the "Good Samaritan" Question: Luke 10:25–37

Piper's 2006 sermon was on the Good Samaritan. He observes that the parable is framed first by the lawyer seeking self-justification in asking Jesus, "Who is my neighbor?" (v. 29), and ends with Jesus' return question, "Which of these three, do you think, proved to be a neighbor?" (v. 36). The intervening parable changes the question from "What kind of person is my neighbor?" to "What kind of person am I?" "What status of people are worthy of my love?" becomes *"How can I become the kind of person whose compassion disregards status?"* Applying this to abortion, Piper says:

> When all the arguments are said and done about the status of pre-born human life and whether the unborn qualify for our compassion along with mommy and daddy and grandma and granddaddy—when we are done trying to establish, "Is this my neighbor?"—the decisive issue of love remains: What kind of person am I? Does compassion rise in my heart for both mommy and daddy and grandma and granddaddy and this unborn baby? Or do I just get another Coke and change the channel?

Piper also draws attention to the "practical compassion" of the Good Samaritan. The type of people who follow Jesus are willing to practice the concrete, hands-on, get-messy, sacrificial, time-consuming, stressful compassion of verses 34–35. And there is similar work for each of us to do in the practical compassion of caring for the unborn.

Shining the Light of Christ and Truth into the Darkness: Ephesians 5:16–17

In his 2007 sermon Piper sought to put the evil of abortion in light of the gospel of grace, using Paul's letter to the Ephesians. Reflecting on Ephesians 5:2, Piper told his people: "Christ loved us and gave himself up for us"—that is, for sinners, people who need forgiveness, including those who have had abortions, condoned abortions, or even demanded them. But "God in Christ forgave you" (Eph. 4:32). Salvation in Jesus is available for every abortionist and everyone involved in abortion at every level.

When we are forgiven by Christ and called out of darkness, we are called to be light and to walk as children of light (Eph. 5:8–10). In fact, we are to use our light to expose the unfruitful works of darkness (Eph. 5:11–14). Piper observes that "some of the strongest witnesses to the light of life are women who have had abortions and come out of the darkness into the light of forgiveness and light. They have *become* light. They are shining with the truth."

Sacrificing the Innocent Blood of Our Sons and Daughters: Psalm 106
In 2008 Piper used Psalm 106 to show four parallels between child sacrifice and abortion: (1) It is "sacrifice" (v. 37)—the giving up of something valuable to get something better. (2) It is "sons and daughters" who are being sacrificed (v. 37)—sexually different, and members of a family. (3) The sacrifice involves "innocent blood" (v. 38)—these little ones do not deserve to be mistreated by fellow human beings. (4) This innocent blood is sacrificed to demons and idols (vv. 37–38). As Paul teaches in 1 Corinthians 10:19–20, idolatry involves sacrificing to demons. The demons receive tribute when our innocent children are sacrificed for a greater "good."

Piper then turns to the "amazing grace" of verses 44–45:

> Nevertheless [that is, in spite of sacrificing their children to demons], he
>   looked upon their distress,
>   when he heard their cry.
> For their sake he remembered his covenant,
>   and relented according to the abundance of his steadfast love.

This is where we get the strength to stand up and make a difference in the cause of abortion, for this is what Jesus Christ came to achieve for all who will receive it.

Lessons for Pro-Life Pastors
In this final section I want to suggest some lessons that pastors can learn from Piper's pro-life preaching. I'll continue quoting from Piper's sermons to make these points.

Insist That Abortion Is Mainly about God
In my summary of Piper's 1998 sermon, above, I listed his four main points about why abortion is about God. But his explanation is worth quoting at length: "Abortion is mainly about God. Abortion is about God, the Creator of the universe, the Giver and Sustainer of all life, the Judge of the living and the dead, the Father of our Lord, Jesus Christ, and the Redeemer and Forgiver of all who trust him. Abortion is about

God." Piper continues by stating that leaving God out of the picture trivializes abortion.

> All things are trivial without God. God is the ultimate reality over the universe. All other reality is derivative and dependent and has no ultimate meaning at all without reference to God the ultimate reality. In him we live and move and have our being. If we leave him out of account, we know nothing of any lasting significance about ourselves or the world. Therefore the message that I have to give is that abortion is about God. And therefore it is not trivial. . . . The most important things to say about abortion are how it relates to God and how God relates to it.

In all of our labors to protect the unborn, let us remember that this issue—like all others—must be done to his glory, recognizing that all things are from God, through God, and to God (1 Cor. 10:31; Rom. 11:36).

Preach the Word

Many pastors struggle to deal with abortion exegetically because there are no cases in Scripture of someone intentionally trying to kill a baby still in the womb. But Piper's exegetical summaries demonstrate the various ways in which a preacher might unfold the biblical perspective on the value of life and the horror of abortion. In his 1991 sermon Piper provided a concise summary of the evidence regarding God's view of the unborn and their rights:

> Many Christians involved in abortion turn a deaf ear to the Bible when it says that the growing life in the womb is the unique creative work of God knitting together a being in his own image (Psalm 139:13; Job 31:13–15); or when it speaks of babies in the womb with the very same words as babies out of the womb (Genesis 25:22; Luke 1:41; cf. 2:12, 16; 18:15); or when it warns repeatedly against shedding innocent blood (Psalm 106:38); or when it calls again and again for the protection of the weakest and most vulnerable members of the community (Psalm 82:3–4); or when it says that God alone has the right to give and to take human life (Job 1:21).

Faithful preachers will not only expound what the Word says about the value of those within the womb, but also explain to their congregation what it means to be salt and light in a world that wants to destroy the weakest members of the human race.

Do Not Shrink Back Because Some Will Accuse You of Being Political

Some Christians are uncomfortable with churches becoming too engaged on the issue of abortion. Doesn't it bring politics into the pulpit? Doesn't it make the church of Jesus Christ sound like the "Christian Right" in America? Doesn't it confuse the two kingdoms of God (God's rule in the secular realm and his rule in the spiritual realm)?

Piper believes that the "political action of pro-life people is good. God ordains that governments exist for the protection of [their] people from violence (Romans 13:3f.)."[4] Nevertheless, he is a Christian pastor and not a politician, and this affects the way in which he understands his calling with regard to abortion:

> My main job is not to unite believers and unbelievers behind worthwhile causes. Somebody should do this. But that is not my job. Some of you ought to be doing that with a deep sense of Christian calling. My job is to glorify Jesus Christ by calling his people to be distinctively Christian in the way they live their lives.[5]

In his 2003 sermon he said: "I am a Christian pastor who wants to be biblical, and gives not a rip for being Republican or Democrat. Such things mean almost nothing to me. But the glory and will and the rights of Jesus Christ, the King of kings and Judge of all men, mean everything to me." Therefore Piper aims in his sermons and writing to present a distinctively Christian approach to the pro-life cause.

He also argues that obedient Christians cannot help but be political in some sense. In his 1993 sermon he said, "This message does not aim to be political. But I realize that being a Christian today is increasingly putting us at odds with political positions. Just being an obedient Christian is increasingly becoming a social, political, legal issue."

Although Piper supports political action on behalf of the pro-life cause, he does not believe it is the highest calling. As he said in 1998, "For all the great legal work that needs to be done to protect human life, the greatest work that needs to be done is to spread a passion—a satisfaction—for the supremacy of God in all things. That's our calling."

Call Your People to Fast and Pray

Piper calls for fasting and praying about abortion in A Hunger for God:

> I appeal to you to seek the Lord with me concerning the place of fasting and prayer in breaking through the darkened mind that engulfs the modern world, in regard to abortion and a hundred other ills. This is not a call for a collective tantrum that screams at the bad people, "Give me back my

---

[4] 1995.
[5] 1992.

country." It is a call to aliens and exiles in the earth, whose citizenship is in heaven and who await the appearance of their King, to "do business" until he comes (Luke 19:13). And the great business of the Christian is to "do all to the glory of God" (1 Corinthians 10:31), and to pray that God's name be hallowed and his kingdom come and his will be done in the earth (Matthew 6:9–10). And to yearn and work and pray and fast not only for the final revelation of the Son of Man, but in the meantime, for the demonstration of his Spirit and power in the reaching of every people, and the rescuing of the perishing, and the purifying of the church, and the putting right of as many wrongs as God will grant.[6]

We must fast and pray, and call others to do the same, for God to do the humanly impossible.

Work to Destroy the Root of Bad Ideas

Abortion engagement can be a means of preevangelism, preparing the way for the gospel. Piper makes this point in his 1996 sermon:[7]

> If millions of Christians keep sowing seeds of truth . . . there will be a leavening effect that will shape ideas and restrain bad behavior and lead people toward the light.
>
> If the truth is a seamless fabric, then speaking the truth anywhere on any issue will strengthen the cause of truth everywhere on every issue. God only knows how often the gospel of Jesus Christ has been made more hearable because preconditions of truth have been laid down by a thousand prior influences of right speaking. This is part of the salt that preserves the mental life of society so that it can be touched more effectively by the gospel message, which is also salt.

Piper's call here echoes J. Gresham Machen (1881–1937), who wrote about the way in which false ideas are the greatest obstacle to the reception of the gospel in our culture:

> It is true that the decisive thing is the regenerative power of God. That can overcome all lack of preparation, and the absence of that makes even the best preparation useless. But as a matter of fact God usually exerts that power in connection with certain prior conditions of the human mind, and it should be ours to create, so far as we can, with the help of God, those favorable conditions for the reception of the gospel. False ideas are the

---

[6] John Piper, *A Hunger for God: Desiring God through Fasting and Prayer* (Wheaton, IL: Crossway, 1997), 172.

[7] This sermon, "Challenging the Church and Culture with Truth," was the last in a series on six "Fresh Initiatives" that were unveiled in 1995. It was not specifically devoted to abortion, though there is a key section of application, given that it was delivered on Sanctity of Life Sunday.

greatest obstacles to the reception of the gospel. We may preach with all
the fervor of a reformer and yet succeed only in winning a straggler here
and there, if we permit the whole collective thought of the nation or of
the world to be controlled by ideas which, by the resistless force of logic,
prevent Christianity from being regarded as anything more than a harmless delusion. Under such circumstances, what God desires us to do is to
destroy the obstacle at its root.[8]

We must preach the gospel, but we must also work to expose the poison-
ous root of godless ideology.

Expose "Choice" as a Sham Argument That Logically Leads to Anarchy and Tyranny

One recurring theme in Piper's preaching is that the argument and language
of "choice" in this debate is actually a sham. All choices, Piper argued in
1992, are limited by life:

> It is hypocritical to speak as though choice were the untouchable absolute
> in this matter and then turn around and oppose choice in matters of gun-
> control and welfare support and affirmative action and minimum wage and
> dozens of other issues where so-called pro-choice people join the demand
> that people's choices be limited to protect others. It's a sham argument. All
> choices are limited by life.

The following year Piper made essentially the same point: "We submit
to the right of government to limit our right to choose in hundreds of
areas, especially when the good of others is at stake. We understand that
governments exist to limit the right to choose and we submit to that."

But there's more going on here than simply that those who are pro-
choice are hypocritical and inconsistent. Piper argues that pro-choicers
elevate choice to such a degree that anarchy is the logical result. Here's
how he put it in his 1991 sermon: "There will be no law but the law
of individual choice (=anarchy) if the foundation stone of life's value is
destroyed."

Piper likes to illustrate this by referring to a fetal homicide law in Minnesota. The Minneapolis *Star Tribune* once described the effect of the law
in this way: it "makes it murder to kill an embryo or fetus intentionally,
except in cases of abortion." Preaching on this in 1996, Piper examined
the argument and the connection to anarchy:

---

[8]J. Gresham Machen, "Christianity and Culture," in *What Is Christianity and Other Addresses*, ed. Ned
Stonehouse (Grand Rapids: Eerdmans, 1951), 162–63.

Now what makes the difference here? Why is it murder to take the life of an embryo in one case and not murder in the case of abortion? Now watch this carefully, because it reveals the stunning implications of the pro-choice position.

The difference lies in the choice of the mother. If the mother chooses that her fetus live, it is murder to kill it. If she chooses for her fetus not to live, it is not murder to kill it.

In other words in our laws we have now made room for some killing to be justified not on the basis of the crimes of the one killed, but solely on the basis of another person's will or choice. If I choose for the embryo to be dead, it is legal to kill it. If I choose for the embryo to live, it is illegal to kill it. The effective criterion of what is legal or illegal, in this ultimate issue of life and death, is simply this: the will of the strong.

There is a name for this. We call it anarchy. It is the essence of rebellion against objective truth and against God. It takes us back to the Yale law professor who said that modern man is torn between wanting to discover what is right and wanting to create what is right—wanting to be ruled by truth and wanting to rule truth. The pro-choice worldview opts for creating what is right rather than discovering it, and ruling truth rather than being ruled by it.

When the pro-choice philosophy chants, "We will not lose the right to choose," it says in effect that the act of choosing is unfettered and unlimited by objective reality and truth outside the act of choice. The act of choice is absolute in itself. It does not have to conform or submit to law, or human dignity, or God. It is the final statement of rebellion. It says, In my choice I create law. In my choice I create my own human dignity. In my choice I do not bow to God, I become god.

This is ultimately why a church that has a passion for the supremacy of God in all things must speak and act against the standard pro-choice worldview, and for the cause of the unborn.

Piper returned to the "might makes right" theme in his 2004 sermon:

In a world without God, the will of the strong creates (or nullifies) the personhood of the weak. How can there be a fetal homicide law that is not broken by abortion? Why is abortion not fetal homicide? There is one essential answer. In the case of the fetal homicide, the mother wants the baby. In the case of abortion, she does not. The will of the mother is god.

And the awesome thing is that we endow her will not just with sovereignty over her unborn baby, but with the authority to define it: If she wants it, it is a baby, a person. If she does not want it, it is not a baby, not a person.

In other words, in our laws we have now made room for some killing to be justified not on the basis of the rights or crimes of the one killed, but decisively on the basis of the will, the desire, of a stronger person. The decisive criterion of personhood and non-personhood, what is right and wrong, what is legal and what is illegal, is the will of the strong. Might makes right. Might makes personhood. Might makes legal. This is the ultimate statement of anarchy. It is the essence of the original insurrection against God, and against objective truth and right and beauty.

Choice is a good value but a bad god. Pastors must help their congregations to see and explain the difference.

Give Hope to Sinners by Preaching the Gospel

When we talk about abortion, we are talking about not just destructive ideas but a deadly practice, resulting in real people who are being killed every day. We are not just talking about sin, but talking to sinners—those who support the right to abortion, those who promote the practice of abortion, those who have aborted their own children, or those who have sat silently through the holocaust of the unborn. There are no innocent people in the pew. They must be informed, and they must be stirred to action. But faithful preaching also requires setting before sinners (that's all of us) the hope of the gospel of Jesus Christ.

Here are a few examples of how John Piper has extended the gospel with regard to abortion. In 1989 he gave sinners hope that their past need not determine their future: "No one is cut off from Christ because of past sin—any past sin. What cuts a person off from Christ and the fellowship of his people is the endorsement of past sin. For the repentant there is forgiveness and cleansing and hope." In 2002 Piper again reminded the guilty that Jesus stands ready to forgive the repentant: "Jesus offers you forgiveness this morning for aborting your child, or encouraging your girlfriend or your daughter to abort [her] child, or for working in an abortion clinic, or for being apathetic and doing nothing about this great evil and injustice in our society." In 2004 he stressed that God is offering salvation in place of judgment:

> I think God wants every woman, and every man, to take heart this morning that his offer to you is salvation, not judgment. The offspring of the woman, Jesus Christ, came into the world to save women who have dethroned God, taken his place, defined personhood as tissue, and willed the death of their own child. It can't be reversed, but it can be forgiven. That is why Christ died.
>
> Every person listening to me now needs this salvation—men and women and children. Some only feel it more than others. And those who feel it

most are most fortunate. Turn to Christ for forgiveness and embrace him as your Lord and the Treasure of your life.

Gratitude and Prayer

I thank God for John Piper's faithful work in preaching the gospel of Jesus Christ and exploring the whole counsel of God in order to expose the dark work of abortion. May the Lord multiply this work, and may our pulpits across this land be filled with preachers who follow his passionate, prophetic, pro-life preaching. I close with a prayer to God from Piper, expressing our weakness but God's power:

> We are not able in ourselves to win this battle.
>
> We are not able to change hearts or minds.
>
> We are not able to change worldviews and transform culture and save 1.6 million children.
>
> We are not able to reform the judiciary or embolden the legislature or mobilize the slumbering population.
>
> We are not able to heal the endless wounds of godless ideologies and their bloody deeds.
>
> But, O God, you are able!
>
> And we turn from reliance on ourselves to you. And we cry out to you and plead that for the sake of your name, and for the sake of your glory, and for the advancement of your saving purpose in the world, and for the demonstration of your wisdom and your power and your authority over all things, and for the sway of your Truth and the relief of the poor and the helpless, act, O God. This much we hunger for the revelation of your power. With all our thinking and all our writing and all our doing, we pray and we fast. Come. Manifest your glory.[9]

---

[9]Piper, *A Hunger for God*, 171 (paragraph breaks added).

Sermons by John Piper on Abortion (1987–2010)

This chapter was written before Piper's 2009 and 2010 sermons were delivered. They are included here to provide an up-to-date list at the time of publication.

"Abortion: You Desire and Do Not Have, So You Kill," James 4:2 (January 18, 1987)

"Rescuing Unborn Children: Required and Right," Proverbs 24:10–12 (January 15, 1989)

"Kingdom Compassion and the Killing of Children," Hebrews 10:32–35 (January 21, 1990)

"Abortion: Shall We Listen to Men or God?" Acts 4:13–22 (January 27, 1991)

"Exposing the Dark Work of Abortion," Ephesians 5:11 (January 26, 1992)

"Being Pro-Life Christians under a Pro-Choice President," 1 Peter 2:13–17 (January 17, 1993)

"What Is Man? Reflections on Abortion and Racial Reconciliation," Psalm 8 (January 16, 1994)

"Fasting for the Safety of the Little Ones," Ezra 8:21–23 (January 22, 1995)

"Challenging the Church and Culture with Truth" (January 21, 1996)

"Be Strong and Fervent in Spirit in the Case of Truth and Life," Romans 12:9–11 (January 19, 1997)

"Where Does Child Killing Come From?" James 4:1–10 (January 25, 1998)

"Visiting Orphans in a World of AIDS and Abortion," James 1:26–27 (January 24, 1999)

"Christ, Culture, and Abortion," 1 Peter 2:9–17 (January 23, 2000)

"God at Work in Every Womb," Job 31:13–15 (January 21, 2001)

"Father, Forgive, For We Know What We Are Doing," Luke 23:32–38 (January 27, 2002)

"The Darkness of Abortion and the Light of Truth," Ephesians 5:1–16 (January 26, 2003)

"Abortion and the Tree of the Knowledge of Good and Evil," Genesis 3:1–13 (January 25, 2004)

"Abortion, Race, Gender, and Christ," Exodus 1:1–22 (January 23, 2005)

"Love Your Unborn Neighbor," Luke 10:25–37 (January 22, 2006)

"When Is Abortion Racism?" Ephesians 5:16–17 (January 21, 2007)

"Abortion: The Innocent Blood of Our Sons and Daughters," Psalm 106:32–48 (January 27, 2008)

"The Baby in My Womb Leaped for Joy" (January 25, 2009)

"'Born Blind for the Glory of God': Eugenics by Abortion Is an Abomination to God," John 9:1–7 (January 24, 2010)

18

A GOD-CENTERED WORLDVIEW

Recovering the Christian Mind by
Rediscovering the Master Narrative of the Bible

R. Albert Mohler Jr.

To be human is to think, and to think is to operate within a worldview. Every individual operates out of a basic set of convictions about reality, truth, meaning, and how the world works. As thinking creatures we create, perceive, absorb, and base our thinking upon certain intellectual assumptions that allow the world to make sense to us.

There is nothing distinctively Christian about having a worldview. The very process of intellectual activity requires some framework, and no idea is independent of prior assumptions. As human beings, we can hardly begin each moment of intellectual activity without dependence upon assumptions that are, in essence, prephilosophical. This is true for all human beings, regardless of the actual content and shape of their worldviews. The simple fact is that everyone has a worldview, whether he or she is aware of it or not.

The great challenge for the Christian is to craft a worldview that is distinctively Christian in its shape, substance, and structure. This is no easy task, especially in an intellectually complex world that is marked by an incredible diversity of worldviews and ideologies.

As John Piper reminds us, a Christian worldview must, above all else, make much of God. Piper observes that our duty and delight must be "to reflect the value of God's glory—to think and feel and do whatever we must to make much of God."[1] This is one of Piper's most significant contributions to his vision of Christian hedonism—glorifying God by delighting in him. In his preaching, his writing, and his ministry of encouraging us all to desire God, John Piper has simultaneously demanded and demonstrated a pattern of rigorous Christian thinking. In essence, the Christian worldview can be defined as thinking "whatever we must to make much of God."

In this generation, a growing number of Christians understand the responsibility for developing a Christian worldview. Nevertheless, for many of these Christians, the development of a Christian worldview is reduced to certain principles of conviction that are assumed to lead to certain pragmatic conclusions and practical applications. There is no shortage of seminars, books, courses, and curricula directed toward the development of the Christian worldview. There is good reason to be thankful for this recovery of interest in developing a Christian worldview, but there is an even greater need to advance toward a more comprehensive understanding of the Christian worldview that finds its beginning and end in the glory of God and finds its grounding in the master narrative of the Bible.

Christianity and the Life of the Mind

Christianity recognizes and affirms the importance of the intellect. The life of the mind is understood to be a central issue of Christian discipleship. The Christian is not only to live in obedience to Christ, but also to serve Christ through the development of a distinctively Christian mind.

All too many Christians ignore the intellectual component of discipleship. This tragic reality betrays a misunderstanding of the gospel, for the gospel of Jesus Christ itself requires cognitive understanding. In other words, there is a knowledge central and essential to the Christian faith. As the apostle Paul makes clear, faith comes by hearing, and that faith is

---

[1]John Piper, "A God-Entranced Vision of All Things: Why We Need Jonathan Edwards 300 Years Later," in *A God-Entranced Vision of All Things*, ed. John Piper and Justin Taylor (Wheaton, IL: Crossway, 2004), 23.

established upon truth claims that are nonnegotiable and necessary for our salvation (Rom. 10:14–17).

Christian faithfulness requires the development of the believer's intellectual capacities in order that we may understand the Christian faith, develop habits of Christian thought, form intuitions that are based upon biblical truth, and live in faithfulness to all that Christ teaches. This is no easy task, to be sure. Just as Christian discipleship requires growth and development, intellectual faithfulness requires a lifetime of devoted study, consecrated thinking, and analytical reflection.

As Anselm of Canterbury, a leading Christian theologian of the eleventh century, classically affirmed, the Christian task is well defined as "faith seeking understanding."[2] In other words, the Christian faith honors intellectual responsibility and the life of the mind. The faith that justifies sinners is a faith that requires a certain knowledge and then leads to a responsibility to advance in knowledge and understanding in order to move "from milk to meat" in terms of intellectual substance.

All of this is necessary in order that the disciple may grow in grace and in understanding, but it is also necessary in order that Christians grow in intellectual discernment. This intellectual discernment is a necessary component of the Christian's responsibility to know the truth, to love what is true, to discern the difference between truth and error, and to defend the faith "once for all delivered to the saints" (Jude 3).

The Christian affirmation of the life of the mind has produced schools, colleges, universities, seminaries, and a host of other centers of intellectual activity. The rise of the university can be traced directly to the intellectual vigor of medieval Christianity. Christianity honors the life of the mind and has made literacy a central issue of the church's concern. Christianity is a religion of the book—the Bible—and it is a faith that takes the tasks of reading and writing with profound seriousness.

In the end, Christianity honors the life of the mind, not because it celebrates the power of human intellect, but because Christ himself instructed Christians to love God with heart and soul and mind.

The fact that God would command that we love him with our minds indicates in a most profound and unmistakable sense that our Creator has made us to know him in order that we would love him and seek his glory above all else. Understood in this light, our intellectual capacity and the discipleship of the mind are to culminate in the development of a

---

[2]Anselm *Proslogion* 1.

Christian worldview that begins and ends in the glory of the self-revealing God of the Bible.

The Starting Point for All Christian Thinking

One of the most important principles of Christian thinking is the recognition that there is no stance of intellectual neutrality. No human being is capable of achieving a process of thought that requires no presuppositions, assumptions, or inherited intellectual components. All human thinking requires some presupposed framework that defines reality and explains, in the first place, how it is possible that we can know anything at all.

The process of human cogitation and intellectual activity has been, in itself, the focus of intense intellectual concern. In philosophy, the field of study that is directed toward the possibility of human knowledge is epistemology. The ancient philosophers were concerned with the problem of knowledge, but this problem becomes all the more complex and acute in a world of intellectual diversity. In the aftermath of the Enlightenment, the problem of epistemology moved to the very center of philosophical thought.

Are we capable of knowing truth? Is truth, in any objective sense, accessible to us? How is it that different people, different cultures, and different faiths hold to such different understandings and affirm such irreconcilable claims to truth? Does truth even exist at all? If so, can we really know it?

As the modern age gave way to the postmodern, the problem of knowledge became only more complex. Many postmodern thinkers reject the possibility of objective truth and suggest that all truth is nothing more than social construction and the application of political power. Among some, relativism is the reigning understanding of truth. Among others, the recognition of intellectual pluralism leads to an affirmation that all truth claims are trapped within cultural assumptions and can be known only through the lenses of distorted perspective.

In other words, the problem of knowledge is front and center as we think about the responsibility of forming a Christian worldview and loving God with our minds. The good news is this—just as we are saved by grace alone, we find the starting point for all Christian thinking in the grace of God demonstrated to us by means of his self-revelation.

The Self-Revealing God of the Bible

The starting point for all genuinely Christian thinking is the existence of the self-revealing God of the Bible. The foundation of the Christian worldview is the knowledge of the one true and living God. The fact of

God's existence sets the Christian worldview apart from all others—and, from the very beginning, we must affirm that our knowledge of God is entirely dependent upon the gift of divine revelation.

Christian thinking is not reducible to mere theism—belief in the existence of a personal God. To the contrary, authentic Christian thinking begins with the knowledge that the only true God is the God who has revealed himself to us in the Bible.

As the late Carl F. H. Henry reminded us:

> Divine revelation is the source of all truth, the truth of Christianity included; reason is the instrument for recognizing it; Scripture is its verifying principle; logical consistency is a negative test for truth and coherence a subordinate test. The task of Christian theology is to exhibit the content of biblical revelation as an orderly whole.[3]

That same affirmation is true for all Christian thinking. Christianity affirms reason, but divine revelation is the source of all truth. We are given the capacity to know, but we are first known by our Creator before we come to know him by means of his gift of self-revelation.

The Total Truthfulness of the Bible

Once our dependence upon the Bible is made clear, the importance of affirming the total inspiration and truthfulness of the Bible is apparent. Affirming the inerrancy and infallibility of the Bible is not merely a matter of articulating a high view of Scripture. The affirmation of the Bible's total truthfulness is essential for believers to have an adequate confidence that we can know what God would have us to know. Furthermore, our affirmation of the inerrancy of Scripture is based, not only in Scripture's internal claims, but in the very character of God. The God who knew us and loved us long before we came to know him is the God we can trust to give us a completely trustworthy revelation of himself.[4]

Even so, ignorance of basic biblical truth is rampant. Remarkably, this is a problem inside, as well as outside, the church. Many church members seem as ignorant of the true and living God as is the general public. Too many pulpits are silent and compromised. The "ordinary god" of popular belief is the only god known by many.

As Christian Smith and his fellow researchers have documented, the faith of many Americans can be described as "moralistic therapeutic

---

[3]Carl F. H. Henry, *God, Revelation, and Authority*, 6 vols. (1976; repr., Wheaton, IL: Crossway, 1999), 1:215.
[4]See Paul Helm and Carl R. Trueman, eds., *The Trustworthiness of God: Perspectives on the Nature of Scripture* (Grand Rapids: Eerdmans, 2002).

deism"—a system of belief that provides the image of a comfortable, nonthreatening deity who is not terribly concerned with our behavior but does want us to be happy.[5]

The erosion of the Christian worldview in the modern age can be traced directly to a significant shift in the doctrine of God. The God worshiped by millions of modern persons is a deity cut down to postmodern size.

The One True God

The one true God, the God who reveals himself in the Bible, is a God who defines his own existence, sets his own terms, and rules over his own creation. The sheer shallowness of much modern spirituality stands as a monument to the human attempt to rob God of his glory. The Christian worldview cannot be recovered without a profound rediscovery of the knowledge of God.

Inevitably, our concept of God determines our worldview. The question of the existence or nonexistence of God is primary, but so is the question of God's power and character. Theologians speak of the attributes of God, meaning the particulars about God's revealed nature. If we begin with the right concept of God, our worldview will be properly aligned. If our concept of God is subbiblical, our worldview will be subbiblical as well.

God's attributes reveal his power and his character. The God of the Bible is omniscient and omnipotent, and he is also faithful, good, patient, loving, merciful, gracious, majestic, and just.

At the foundation of all the attributes ascribed to God in Scripture are two great truths that form central pillars for all Christian thinking. The first of these is *God's total, final, and undiluted sovereignty.* God's sovereignty is the exercise of his rightful authority. His omnipotence, omniscience, and omnipresence are the instruments of his sovereignty.

The second of these great pillars is *God's holiness.* Just as sovereignty is the great term that includes all of God's attributes of power, holiness includes all of the moral attributes ascribed to God in the Bible. At the first level, holiness defines God as the source of all that is good, true, beautiful, loving, just, righteous, and merciful. In other words, holiness establishes that God is not merely the *possessor* of these moral distinctives—he is the ultimate *source* of them as well. In the end, God is not so much defined by these moral attributes as he defines them by the display of his character in the Bible.

---

[5]Christian Smith with Melinda Lundquist Denton, *Soul Searching: The Religious and Spiritual Lives of American Teenagers* (New York: Oxford University Press, 2005).

In other words, to say that God is righteous is not to say that he passes muster when tested against our own understandings of righteousness. To the contrary, we gain any adequate understanding of righteousness only by coming to know the self-revealing God who is himself righteous. One of the central problems of modern thought is the attempt by human beings to judge God by our own categories of moral perfection. Our proper responsibility is to bring our categories into submission to the reality and revelation of God.

The question of the existence or nonexistence of God is primary, but so is the question of God's power and character. The Christian worldview is structured, first of all, by the revealed knowledge of God. And this means the comprehensive knowledge of the self-revealing God who defines himself and will accept no rivals. There is no other starting point for an authentic Christian worldview—and there is no substitute.

The Unfolding of the Christian Master Narrative

One of the hallmarks of the postmodern age is, as one of its main theorists has explained, "incredulity toward metanarratives."[6] This reflects the postmodern suspicion of any master explanation of world reality and human experience. But, from beginning to end, biblical Christianity is a master narrative. Biblical Christianity is not only a faith that involves essential truths; it is the story of God's purpose to redeem humanity and to bring glory to himself. This narrative is revealed to us as a comprehensive master story that is as vast as the cosmos and so detailed as to include every atom and molecule of creation.

Even as the postmodern age has rejected the metanarrative, most postmodern thinkers accept the fact that human existence is essentially narrative in terms of our consciousness. This is an important insight, for it is impossible to give an account of our individual lives without using the structure of a story. The postmodern resistance to a master narrative is the fear that such a story would be inherently repressive. But the Christian gospel is the most liberating narrative ever heard, and the Bible presents the story, not merely as one account of reality to be put alongside others, but as the one definitive account of God's purposes.

Indeed, the Christian gospel is the story to which all other narratives are accountable. The Scripture narrates the story in the unfolding of God's plan and purposes. The very God who reveals himself as sovereign

---

[6]Jean-François Lyotard, *The Postmodern Condition: A Report on Knowledge*, trans. Geoff Bennington and Brian Massumi (Minneapolis: University of Minnesota Press, 1984).

and holy—the only true God—is the God who has generously shared the knowledge of himself and his purposes with his sinful creatures.

Creation—The Beginning of the Story

Every worldview and metanarrative has a beginning. Without exception, every worldview must give an account of how the cosmos came into being and must answer the question of its meaning. The very existence of the cosmos requires an answer to this question, and this answer determines so much of what follows in the narrative.

The Bible begins with the declaration that "in the beginning, God created the heavens and the earth" (Gen. 1:1). The doctrine of creation forms the starting point for our understanding of the cosmos and our place within it. The Bible's straightforward explanation for the existence of all things is traced to God's own intention to create the cosmos as the theater of his own glory. The Bible rejects all forms of dualism or polytheism, leaving the God of the Bible as the sole explanatory principle of the universe. Nothing that exists does so outside of his sovereignty and intention. The God of the Bible creates ex nihilo (out of nothing) and is not dependent upon any preexistent matter or conditioned by any external force.

As Creator, God takes responsibility for his creation. Furthermore, the Creator remains directly involved with his creation, ruling over all times, places, and authorities. He exercises his rule through a scrupulous providence that includes, as Jesus made clear, even the birds of the air and the lilies of the field (Matt. 6:26, 28).

The Bible also makes clear that the Creator is pleased with his creation. Having created all that exists, he declared his creation to be good. This verdict on creation is a refutation of any worldview that denies the goodness of creation or slanders the material world as unholy. At the same time, the Bible condemns any worship of nature as an end in itself.

The creation of human beings is the climax of the creation narrative. Having created everything else that exists, God crowned his creation when he created human beings as the singular creature made in his own image (Gen. 1:26–27). The Bible clearly and unambiguously reveals that human beings are special creatures—the only creatures made in the image of God. Even as we face contemporary efforts to dethrone humanity from a position of privilege within creation, the Bible makes clear that human beings are made in God's image precisely so that we, alone within all creation, may consciously know and glorify God. Therefore the human creature is given the ability to fabricate and to manipulate the material world. God gave human beings the ability to till the soil, reap a harvest, and bring the earth under dominion. At the same time, God invested human beings with a crucial responsibility to use, enjoy, and care for creation as a matter of essential stewardship.

The Bible also reveals that gender is a part of the goodness of God's creation. God made his human creatures as male and female and invested these creatures with responsibility to enjoy his gifts and to reproduce within the context of marriage (Gen. 1:27–28). Marriage, too, is part of the goodness of God's creation. While other creatures merely mate, humans are called to enter into a covenant of marriage whereby one man and one woman come together to form a union that is pleasing to God.

The biblical portrait of the creating God demonstrates a God of love whose character issues naturally in his creation. The loving character of God is woven into the warp and woof of his creation and the creatures within it. The substance of the biblical teaching focuses on God's creation of the universe and all within it by the power of his word. The product of God's creative activity is a universe of seemingly infinite variety, complexity, and mystery.

Thus, creation is not a brute fact without meaning. It derives its meaning from the divine character and will. As the theater of God's redemptive activity, creation is not static, but is moving toward that goal established by decree before the foundation of the universe. Without the knowledge of divine creation, we would be left to ourselves in terms of discerning or discovering the very purpose for the existence of the material world and the means by which it came to exist.

All worldviews start with this great question and must give some account of beginnings. The naturalistic worldview insists that this account of beginnings must be comprehensively limited to natural and material causes and effects. Such a worldview runs into direct collision with the worldview of the Bible, for the Bible does not flinch from claiming and explaining that all that exists owes its existence ultimately to God himself (e.g., John 1:3).

One interesting aspect of worldview analysis is the recognition that, for the most part, everything that follows is contained within the account of origins. Once we know that God is the solitary explanation at the beginning, we can be confident that he will be the one who brings this story to a close in a way that brings him no less glory.

Sin—Explaining All That Has Gone Wrong

Our experience of the world requires us to perceive that things are not as they should be. We do not experience the world of unblemished perfection that is revealed in the first two chapters of the book of Genesis. To the contrary, we experience a world filled with mosquitoes, viruses, earthquakes, and malevolence in the animal world. We are surrounded by the evidence of death and decay, and we see it in our own bodies.

Furthermore, we see the violence and sin that human beings cause and commit. We are not only those who experience the violence of nature; we know ourselves to be creatures whose own nature is often violent. To observe humanity is to see the undeniable reality that something has gone horribly wrong.

Even as the Bible begins the story with creation, it immediately moves to an explanation of what has gone wrong. Again, such an account is required of every worldview, and every philosophy of life must provide some explanation for why human beings are as we are and why we act as we act.

The Bible directs those who ask this question to the garden of Eden and to the event we know as the fall. When Adam and Eve sinned, they brought corruption and rebellion into the very heart of God's perfect creation. The only creature made in God's own image rebelled against him and sought to rob him of his own glory. The nature of sin is just this—we would deny the Creator his rightful glory and would seek this for ourselves.

The consequences of the fall were immediate and catastrophic. Adam and Eve were expelled from the garden of Eden and cut off from the tree of life (Gen. 3:23–24). The earth, which had freely given of its fruit and crops, would now turn hostile, and human beings would have to work with the sweat of the brow to gain a hard-earned harvest (Gen. 3:17–19). Human reproduction would now be accompanied by pain and labor. Most importantly, the fall explains why human beings are no longer at peace with our Creator. God's verdict on Adam's sin was immediate. As Genesis reveals, when sin came, death came.

Our understanding of the fall and of the sinfulness of humanity is absolutely necessary for any adequate understanding of the human condition. We cannot possibly understand human existence without reference to sin. The Bible steadfastly refuses to allow us to find the cause and substance of the human problem outside of ourselves. Instead, the Bible points directly to our individual culpability, even as it affirms that every single human being inherits Adam's sin and guilt. The complex of human sinfulness is so vast that it encompasses every individual human sin and the totality of human depravity as demonstrated in the rise and fall of nations and the course of human history.

The Bible's account of the human problem goes far beyond a mere explanation of human foibles and failures. In essence, the Bible turns directly to the human creature and offers an indictment of our rebellion against God. Even as Adam and Eve sought to create aprons in order to hide their own nakedness (Gen. 3:7), human beings will attempt any number of creative and desperately asserted explanations for what is wrong with us.

In other words, the Christian account of humanity and human behavior runs into direct collision with all other worldviews. This is particularly evident when we compare the Bible's account of human sin with contemporary attempts to explain the brokenness of humanity by means of economic, sociological, political, or psychotherapeutic explanations. The Bible affirms the inherent goodness of humanity in terms of the pristine goodness of God's creation as it was in the beginning. But the Bible also explains that, after the fall, every single human being is, in his or her own way, a rebel and insurrectionist who is attempting to dethrone God and take his glory as one's own.

Thus, when we look at humanity, read the newspapers, watch the news reports, or tend to our own children, Christians must be constantly aware that what we witness is the working out of sin and a demonstration of the fallenness of humanity. Yet, our most direct evidence for this fallenness is what we see when we look at the reflection in our mirror.

Every worldview must give an account of what is wrong with humanity and why the cosmos demonstrates so much death, decay, and apparent meaninglessness. As Christians, we know that the world as we see it contains vestiges of the glory of God that shine through the corruption of the universe blighted by sin. Nevertheless, we are constantly reminded that the entire universe is groaning under the burden of human sinfulness. We are able to endure this because we are confident that this is not the end of the story.

Redemption—The Hinge of History and the Rescue of Sinners

The third great movement in the Christian metanarrative begins with the affirmation that God's purpose from the beginning was to redeem a people through the blood of his Son in order to show the excellence of his name throughout eternity. The God of the Bible is not a divine strategist ready with a new plan in the event his original plan fails. The God of the Bible is sovereign and completely able to accomplish his purposes. Thus, when we come to the great act of God for our redemption, we come to the heart of God's self-revelation.

Beyond this, an adequate understanding of human sin brings us to the inescapable conclusion that there is absolutely nothing that the human creature can do to rescue himself from his plight. We find ourselves in an insoluble situation and are brought face to face with our own finitude. What is worse, all our efforts to solve the problem on our own lead only into an even deeper complex of sin.

When we come to the rescue of sinners, the Christian narrative points directly to Jesus Christ as the one sent by God to die as a substitutionary sacrifice for sin and to inaugurate the kingdom of God as Israel's Davidic Messiah.

Of course, Jesus Christ does not enter the biblical narrative at this point. As the prologue to the Gospel of John makes clear, Jesus Christ is the eternal Logos through whom the entire cosmos came into being (John 1:1–3). The Word through whom the worlds were made now enters human existence, assuming authentic humanity, in order to identify with us and to save us from our sins.

Redemption is God's act from beginning to end. The gospel explains that God, in order to maintain his own righteousness, was required to exact an adequate punishment for sin. Yet, while we were his enemies, God saved us by providing the very sacrifice that he required.

Just as God revealed himself in the most exclusive terms (monotheism), he also reveals his gospel as exclusive of any other means of salvation. And as at every other point in the story, we are completely dependent upon the Bible for our knowledge of Christ and of the gospel. It is only through the Bible that we come to understand who Jesus is—very God and very man—and to understand the purpose for which he came, suffered, died, and was raised from the dead. We come to understand that the gospel alone explains how the requirements of divine justice can be satisfied and sinful humanity can be rescued from the wrath of God.

Once again, God's sovereignty and holiness are displayed even as the drama of redemption demonstrates God's power and character. The gospel does not reveal God's mere *intention* to save. At every turn, the Bible reveals God's *power* to save and his determination to do so for the glory of his own name.

The plan of redemption is set out in Scripture through a succession of covenants that find their fulfillment only in Christ. As the New Testament makes clear, there is one gospel that is addressed to all people and all peoples. God's determination is to redeem the people from every tongue and tribe and nation in order to show the excellence of his name.

The Christian worldview must also be framed around the fact that God is calling out a people, cleansed by the blood of his Son. Over against the autonomous individualism of contemporary American culture, the Christian narrative establishes our identity in Christ as part of a new humanity. This new humanity is, in this age, established as the church. Those who commit by faith to know the Lord Jesus Christ are incorporated into the life of the church as a foretaste of the fullness of life in Christ that will be known in the kingdom yet to come.

Consummation—The End That Is a Beginning

The reversal of the curse of sin originates in God's sovereign determination to save sinners and is grounded in the cross and resurrection of Christ. The atonement of Jesus Christ accomplishes our salvation from sin. Nevertheless, the New Testament makes clear that we are awaiting the transformation of our bodies and the arrival of the kingdom in fullness.

In understanding the kingdom we benefit by considering the fact that the kingdom is already here, inaugurated by Christ, but is not yet fully come. The "already–not yet" character of the kingdom explains why, though sin is fully defeated, we still experience sin in our lives. Death was defeated at the cross, but we still taste death. The created order continues to cry out for redemption, and the venom of the Serpent still stings.

The Christian doctrine of eschatology provides the Christian worldview with its understanding of history. Every worldview must provide an account of where history is headed and whether human history has any purpose at all. Christianity grounds the meaning of human existence in the fact that we are made in the image of God and points to a final judgment yet to come.

This final judgment is made necessary by the fact of human sin and the infinite reality of God's holiness. The Bible straightforwardly presents the assurance of a final judgment that will demonstrate the perfection of God. This final judgment will demonstrate God's mercy to those who are in Christ and God's wrath righteously poured out upon sin.

This judgment will be so perfect that, in the end, all must know that God alone is righteous and that his decrees are absolutely perfect. God's power will be demonstrated when all authorities are brought under submission to the Lord Jesus Christ, when every earthly kingdom yields and when every knee bows and every tongue confesses that Jesus Christ is Lord to the glory of God the Father (Phil. 2:10–11).

Every single moment of human history cries out for judgment. Every sin and every sinner will be brought before the throne of God and full satisfaction will be made. The demands of the divine justice will be fully met, and the mercy and grace of God will be fully demonstrated. The great dividing line that runs through humanity will be that separating those who are in Christ and those who are not.

The backdrop of eternity puts the span of a human life into perspective. Our time on earth is short, but eternity dignifies time even as it reminds us of our finitude. The concluding movement of the biblical narrative reminds us that we are to yearn for eternity and for the glory that is to come.

On this day of judgment, all human attempts at justice will be shown to fall far short of authentic justice. On this day, God's perfect justice will indeed flood like a mighty river. But God's justice is also restorative, and those who are in Christ will come to know the absolute satisfaction, peace, wholeness, and restoration that are promised to us. Every eye will be dry and every tear will be wiped away (Rev. 7:17; 21:4).

The reversal of the curse and the end of history serve to ground Christians in this age within the secure purposes and the sovereign power of God. In other words, the conclusion of the Christian master narrative reminds believers that we are not to seek ultimate fulfillment in this life. Instead, we are to follow Christ in obedience and give the totality of our lives to the things that will bring glory to God in the midst of this fallen world. We will refrain from optimism grounded in humanity and will rest in the hope that is ours in Christ. We will suffer illness, injury, persecution, and death—but we know ourselves to be completely safe within the purposes of God.

Intellectual Discipleship—Thinking as a Christian

The biblical master narrative serves as a framework for the cognitive principles that allow the formation of an authentically Christian worldview. Many Christians rush to develop what they will call a Christian worldview by arranging isolated Christian truths, doctrines, and convictions in order to create formulas for Christian thinking. No doubt, this is a better approach than is found among so many believers who have very little concern for Christian thinking at all.

A robust and rich model of Christian thinking—the quality of thinking that culminates in a God-centered worldview—requires that we see all truth as interconnected. Ultimately, the systematic wholeness of truth can be traced to the fact that God is himself the author of all truth. Christianity is not a set of doctrines in the sense that a mechanic operates with a set of tools. Instead, Christianity is a comprehensive worldview that grows out of Christian reflection on the Bible and the unfolding plan of God revealed therein.

A God-centered worldview brings every issue, question, and cultural concern into submission to all that the Bible reveals and frames all understanding within the ultimate purpose of bringing greater glory to God. This task of bringing every thought captive to Christ requires more than episodic Christian thinking and is to be understood as the task of the church, and not merely the concern of individual believers. The recovery of the Christian mind and the development of a comprehensive Christian worldview will require the deepest theological reflection, the most consecrated application of scholarship, the most sensitive commitment to compassion, and the courage to face all questions without fear.

Christianity brings the world a distinctive understanding of *time, history, and the meaning of life*. The Christian worldview contributes an understanding of the universe and all it contains that points us far beyond mere materialism and frees us from the intellectual imprisonment of naturalism. Christians understand that the world—including the material world—is dignified by the very fact that God has created it. At the same time, we understand that we are to be stewards of this creation and are not to worship what God has made. We understand that every single human being is made in the image of God and that God is the Lord of life at every stage of human development. We honor the sanctity of human life because we worship the Creator. From the Bible, we draw the essential insight that God takes delight in the ethnic and racial diversity of his human creatures, and so must we.

The Christian worldview contributes a distinctive understanding of *beauty, truth, and goodness*, understanding these to be transcendentals that, in the final analysis, are one and the same. Thus, the Christian worldview disallows the fragmentation that would sever the beautiful from the true or the good. Christians consider the stewardship of cultural gifts, ranging from music and visual art to drama and architecture, as a matter of spiritual responsibility.

The Christian worldview supplies authoritative resources for understanding *our need for law and our proper respect for order*. Informed by the Bible, Christians understand that God has invested government with an urgent and important responsibility. At the same time, Christians come to understand that idolatry and self-aggrandizement are the temptations that come to any regime. Drawing from the Bible's rich teachings concerning money, greed, the dignity of labor, and the importance of work, Christians have much to contribute to a proper understanding of economics. Those who operate from an intentionally biblical worldview cannot reduce human beings to mere economic units, but must understand that our economic lives reflect the fact that we are made in God's image and are thus invested with responsibility to be stewards of all the Creator has given us.

Christian faithfulness requires a deep commitment to serious moral reflection on matters of *war and peace, justice and equity, and the proper operation of a system of laws.* Our intentional effort to develop a Christian worldview requires us to return to first principles again and again in a constant and vigilant effort to ensure that the patterns of our thought are consistent with the Bible and its master narrative.

In the context of cultural conflict, the development of an authentic Christian worldview should enable the church of the Lord Jesus Christ to maintain a responsible and courageous footing in any culture at any period of time. The stewardship of this responsibility is not merely an intellectual challenge; it determines, to a considerable degree, whether or not Christians live and act before the world in a way that brings glory to God and credibility to the gospel of Jesus Christ. Failure at this task represents an abdication of Christian responsibility that dishonors Christ, weakens the church, and compromises Christian witness.

Evangelical failure in this task is just one symptom of a deeper evangelical superficiality. Observers such as David Wells have provided us with a comprehensive diagnosis of evangelical failure in this regard. Yet, even as the failure of evangelical thinking is a symptom of a deeper failure, it is also a cause. Looking at contemporary evangelicalism, John Piper has observed, "What is missing is the mind-shaping knowledge and the all-transforming enjoyment of the weight of the glory of God."[7]

By God's grace, we are allowed to love God with our minds in order that we may serve him with our lives. Christian faithfulness requires the conscious development of a worldview that begins and ends with God at its center.

In other words, Christian faithfulness has a necessary intellectual component. As John Piper reminds us, we must think "whatever we must to make much of God." That is the beginning and the end of the Christian worldview.

---

[7]Piper, "A God-Entranced Vision of All Things," 22.

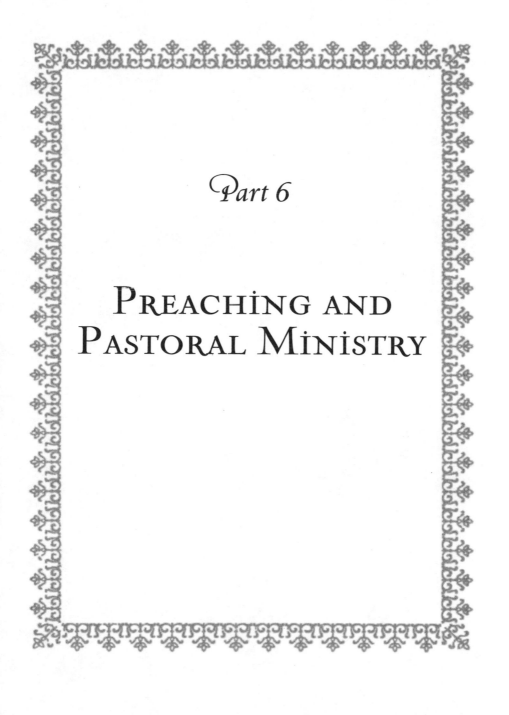

Part 6

PREACHING AND
PASTORAL MINISTRY

19

PROCLAIMING THE GOSPEL AND THE GLORY OF GOD

The Legacy of Jonathan Edwards for Preaching

Stephen J. Nichols

Jonathan Edwards (1703–1758) means many things to many people. To some he is the consummate *Puritan*, in the sense of the worst caricature. Pick out any line from "Sinners in the Hands of an Angry God," and you have made the case for Edwards as a preacher of fire and brimstone, with nostrils flaring and fists clenched. For others, Edwards is the great *philosopher*. To be sure, they recognize that he stepped into the pulpit and spent most of his life there. But to these interpreters, that step was a misstep, and American philosophy lost its best and brightest when Edwards took it. For others still, he's merely a *genius*, a genius who expresses himself in the written word. "Sinners in the Hands of an Angry God" may be full of vitriol, but it also sings with vivid images and startling cadences—Edwards as a man of letters. And then there's

Edwards the *theologian*, plying his great mind to the knotty problems of free will, the origin of sin, and the nature of virtue.[1]

Edwards, however, was first and foremost a *pastor*, and his main genre was the sermon. In fact, some have argued that he nearly perfected his craft of preaching. He certainly had plenty of practice. Harry Stout once said, "Through thousands of closely scribbled pages of text, composed over decades of weekly preaching, Edwards etched words of literary brilliance and spiritual depth that continue to impress the scholar and inspire the believer." Stout also has something to say about the type of preacher that Edwards was. He acknowledges that many see Edwards only as the purveyor of fire and brimstone from "Sinners in the Hands of an Angry God." But then Stout counters by observing, "Edwards was far more concerned that his congregation come to a saving knowledge of God through an awareness of the beauty of God's great and powerful redemptive love for them. Even a cursory scan of the titles of Edwards' sermons will make this point forcefully."[2] Edwards was quick to speak of God's anger, and of sin, wrath, damnation, judgment, and hell. But he was equally quick to speak of God's love, and of joy, delight, pleasure, redemption, and heaven.

I suspect readers of this book tend to see Edwards as a pastor and are well aware that Edwards's vocabulary overflowed with the words *love*, *joy*, *delight*, and *pleasure*. This is primarily due to the fact that many readers of this book, indeed many contemporary evangelicals, were introduced to Jonathan Edwards by John Piper. In other words, I have been preaching to the choir. There may be merit, however, in exploring the legacy of Edwards with regard to the pastor's duty of preaching. The legacy of Jonathan Edwards has much to say to pastors about the types of sermons preached and the goal of preaching. The legacy of Jonathan Edwards also has much to say to contemporary congregations concerning how they are to hear these sermons and, more importantly, what they are to do in response.

Jolting Congregations

George Marsden, Edwards's biographer, draws attention to the goal of Edwards's preaching. He argues that Edwards's preaching intended to

---

[1]See Peter J. Thuesen, "Jonathan Edwards as Great Mirror," *Scottish Journal of Theology* 50, no. 1 (1997): 39–60. For a survey of interpreters and interpretations of Edwards, see also Stephen J. Nichols, *An Absolute Sort of Certainty: The Holy Spirit and the Apologetics of Jonathan Edwards* (Phillipsburg, NJ: P&R, 2003), 5–21.

[2]Harry Stout, "Jonathan Edwards: Preacher," http://edwards.yale.edu/research/about-edwards/preacher.

make an impression that would leave a lasting impact. He puts it this way: "Preaching, . . . [according to Edwards], should be designed primarily to awaken, to shake people out of their blind slumbers in the addictive comforts of their sins. Though only God can give new eyes to see, preaching should be designed to jolt the unconverted or the converted who doze back into their sins (as do all) into recognizing their true estate."[3] And jolt his congregation Edwards did. This jolting, however, consisted more of persuasion than manipulation. The latter may appear to be the easier route, but it runs close to coming under Paul's condemnation when he sadly speaks of so many "peddlers of God's word" in 2 Corinthians 2:17. Edwards was in the group Paul commends, the "men of sincerity," the ones who, "as commissioned by God" and "in the sight of God," "speak in Christ."

Style is one thing; content is another. In addition to those who run afoul by peddling God's Word through manipulative techniques, there are those who fail to preach the gospel, or at least fail to preach the whole gospel for the whole person. Elsewhere Paul speaks of congregations of "itching ears," who will find eager ministers to assure them of their self-righteousness as they pursue their selfish passions, sacrificing the truth and jettisoning sound doctrine along the way (2 Tim. 4:3–4). Nothing could be further from the case in the preaching of Jonathan Edwards. Little wonder that H. Richard Niebuhr was inspired by Edwards when he pronounced his famous dictum over the liberalism of the early twentieth century: "A God without wrath brought men without sin into a kingdom without judgment through the ministrations of a Christ without a cross."[4] No one would accuse Edwards of preaching about a wrathless God, a sinless humanity, a judgment-less eternity, or a cross-less Christ. He could preach damnation with the best of them. But there's more to what Paul is speaking of in 2 Timothy 4 than just keeping sin and hell in sermons.

Paul is pointing Timothy in the direction of preaching that centers on sound doctrine and the gospel and pointing him away from preaching that caters to the natural desire for self-fulfillment and the pursuit of selfish, and hence self-destructive, passions (2 Tim. 4:3). Then Paul tells Timothy something quite intriguing: "Do the work of an evangelist, fulfill your ministry" (2 Tim. 4:5). No doubt the logical relationship between these clauses is complex, and likely better left in the hands of New Testament scholars, so I will only venture a basic interpretation—especially since

---

[3] George Marsden, "Foreword," *The Salvation of Souls: Nine Previously Unpublished Sermons on the Call of Ministry and the Gospel by Jonathan Edwards*, ed. Richard A. Bailey and Gregory A. Wills (Wheaton, IL: Crossway, 2002), 11–12.

[4] H. Richard Niebuhr, *The Kingdom of God in America* (New York: Harper and Row, 1959), 193.

there are some significant New Testament scholars in this book! Being an evangelist, persuasively preaching the gospel, is a significant part of the minister's task. In other words, a minister fulfills his duty by being, among other things, an evangelist. But Paul seems to be pressing something more in this injunction to his protégé, Timothy. Preaching the gospel has something to do with pointing people past themselves, away from the pursuit of fulfilling selfish passions.

Paul, in laying out Timothy's duties as a pastor, is communicating to Timothy the type of preaching he is to engage in: a preaching that is first and foremost the Christ-centered and God-saturated gospel, a preaching that cuts to the quick a self-centered and a self-saturated false gospel. Martin Luther expresses it this way as he closes out the Ninety-Five Theses: "Away, then, with all those who say to the people of Christ, 'Peace, peace,' when there is no peace. Blessed be all those prophets who say to the people of Christ, 'Cross, cross.'"[5] Paul wants ministers who say "cross, cross."

Here enters Edwards on the pastor as preacher. Both in terms of style and in terms of content, this eighteenth-century figure, wearing Geneva bands and donning a powdered wig in the fashion of the colonial Puritan ministers, has something meaningful to say to us living today. His influence has had a profound impact on the ministry and preaching of John Piper. Through Piper and others, Edwards's reach has extended into many lives in the twentieth and twenty-first centuries. In the pages to follow, we'll explore why. This exploration is only partially in the hopes that we will consider Edwards. His voice from the past indeed offers a helpful perspective for us in the present, or perhaps better stated, a helpful perspective for us who tend to be consumed with the present. This exploration of Edwards is ultimately, however, in the hopes that we will consider Christ, the joy of our salvation yesterday, today, and forever.

Preaching the Gospel . . . to Christians, Too

On a wintry Sunday in January of 1758, Jonathan Edwards preached a "Farewell Sermon" to his congregation of mostly Native Americans and a handful of English in the bucolic setting of Stockbridge, Massachusetts. He chose for his text Hebrews 13:7–8, reminding his congregation of the Word of God that Edwards had preached to them over the last seven years and also reminding them, during a time of flux and transition, of the constancy of Jesus Christ, "the same yesterday and today and forever."

---

[5] Martin Luther, "Ninety-Five Theses," nos. 92 and 93, October 31, 1517. Luther is quoting Jeremiah 6:14.

As was his practice, Edwards connected his application to various types of listeners. He made application to "professors of religion," to the ones who have "gone on in drinking," and even "to the young people." Then he addressed a group he referred to as those who "have made it [their] care to live agreeable to the gospel."[6]

The manuscript of this sermon is sketchy, a mere outline, which is profoundly disappointing. So we are left without much to go on in terms of reconstructing the sermon. Even though Edwards wrote down that he wished to address this group, he didn't write down anything that he was going to say to them. While it would have been much better to have the full text, especially from a historian's standpoint, that little phrase "to live agreeable to the gospel" strikes me as offering quite a bit to ponder. It seems that this little phrase may even be enough to serve as a mission statement for Edwards's preaching.

"To live agreeable to the gospel" speaks to a couple of things. The first concerns understanding the gospel, sometimes harder than we might think. The second concerns the "living agreeably to it" part, which may also be harder than we might think. This phrase, it turns out, may well explain John Piper's debt to and enthusiasm for the New England colonial preacher. Piper, too, would undoubtedly concur that having your congregation "live agreeable to the gospel" is both one of any pastor's highest joys and delights and a noble and worthy goal.

Edwards's Ministry Context

Edwards did not come by this phrase "to live agreeable to the gospel" easily. We first need to consider the context of Edwards's ministry. Edwards preached this sermon at Stockbridge, where he spent nearly seven years as minister and missionary to the Indians who lived there. He spent a much longer time forty or so miles to the east at the Congregational church in Northampton, Massachusetts, a prominent town along the Connecticut River Valley. Edwards's tenure at Northampton lasted well over twenty years, spanning from 1726 until 1750. It did not end voluntarily on Edwards's part. His quarrel with his church concerned the Lord's Supper and his putting an end to a practice instituted by his maternal grandfather and predecessor at Northampton, Solomon Stoddard. This so-called communion controversy, concerning which much ink has already been spilt, was only on the surface. What lay beneath tells the real story. Marsden sets

---

[6]Jonathan Edwards, "Farewell Sermon to the Indians" (January 15, 1758), in *The Works of Jonathan Edwards*, vol. 25, *Sermons and Discourses, 1743–1758*, ed. Wilson H. Kimnach (New Haven: Yale University Press, 2006), 714.

up his own telling of the story of Edwards's conflict and eventual ouster with this observation, "As in so much of his thought, [Edwards] seemed determined to demonstrate how the Puritan tradition he had grown up with could work in eighteenth-century settings."[7]

Edwards was intent on being a Puritan minister in a world that was ready to rid itself of the old Puritan ways. The Puritan way may be summed up as endeavoring to establish "pure" churches filled with true saints who take the charge to live holy lives seriously. A. G. Dickens, a historian of English Puritanism, referred to the Puritans as having little interest in establishing a state church like their Anglican counterparts. For them, church was to be a "religious club for athletes"—a serious place for serious people.[8] In New England, these sentiments rang true for many of the early generations of Puritan settlers. By the eighteenth century, other interests began to crowd out these Puritan ideals. Edwards, ministering in the 1730s and 1740s, held to these ideals precisely when much of his congregation, and especially many of those in positions of power in the community, were more than happy to leave them in the past. Whenever a minister and a congregation are locked in a conflict, the reasons tend to be complex, and both sides tend to contribute to the conflict. So it is in the strange case of Jonathan Edwards and the church at Northampton. But it is also true that fundamentally this strife came about because his congregation cared little for the direction Edwards intended to take them. To put this matter directly, Edwards desired his congregation to live agreeably to the gospel, while they desired to live agreeably to their own agenda.[9]

The problem that eventually came to a head in the vote to dismiss him (June 22, 1750) boiled below the surface throughout his ministry. When the church balcony collapsed during a service on March 13, 1737, a new church had to be built. During construction, disputes broke out over the seating arrangement in the new meetinghouse. Puritan churches, or meetinghouses, had assigned pew boxes that were arranged in a hierarchical fashion from the pulpit out. Typical protocol called for age to be the primary criterion for the arrangement. This was in deference both to

---

[7]George Marsden, *Jonathan Edwards: A Life* (New Haven: Yale University Press, 2003), 350.

[8]A. G. Dickens, *The English Reformation*, 2d ed. (University Park: Pennsylvania State University Press, 1989), 376.

[9]For more on the dispute with Edwards and his congregation, see Marsden, *Jonathan Edwards: A Life*, 341–74; Mark Dever, "How Jonathan Edwards Got Fired, and Why It's Important for Us Today," in *A God-Entranced Vision of All Things: The Legacy of Jonathan Edwards*, ed. John Piper and Justin Taylor (Wheaton, IL: Crossway, 2004), 129–44; Stephen J. Nichols, "Heaven Is a World of Love, Congregations Can Be Full of Strife: The Life of Jonathan Edwards and Handling Conflict," *Reformation and Revival Journal* 21, no. 3 (2003): 25–42; Jonathan Edwards, *The Works of Jonathan Edwards*, vol. 12, *Ecclesiastical Writings*, ed. David D. Hall (New Haven: Yale University Press, 1994).

a respect for the elderly and, in the days before amplification systems, to a sensitivity for those who might not hear as well as they once did. But in Northampton, for this new meetinghouse, wealth trumped age. Pew boxes were assigned hierarchically by wealth.[10] Edwards had his hands full, plagued by a congregation with misplaced priorities. In this context, Edwards had a curious task as minister: to preach the gospel to "Christians."

"Divinity's Design": Edwards on the Purpose of a Sermon

Edwards understood the sermon to be God's gracious gift of calling sinners to the gospel. In his understanding of things, the inner call (the work of the Holy Spirit) softened hearts and "readied the ground" for the external call (God's gracious invitation proclaimed by his servants).[11] Helen Westra explains how this gets worked out in Edwards's view of preaching: "Ever attentive to preaching as a means of redemption and as his professional imperative, Edwards underscored the importance of his pulpit efforts by noting that 'the word commonly used in the New Testament that we translate "preach," properly signifies to proclaim aloud like a crier.'"[12] Westra then runs through the many multiform sermons Edwards preached throughout his ministry, including sermons for children, sermons for the elderly, sermons for deacons, sermons for fellow ministers, sermons to mark special occasions in the life of the colonies, sermons on the sacraments, sermons on theological topics—and the list goes on. Westra argues that the key theme that runs throughout these various types of sermons is Edwards's oft-repeated phrase "Divinity's design." By this Edwards meant God's chief end for the world and for humanity, namely, God's glory and the salvation and happiness of his creatures. Westra then draws an interesting conclusion: Edwards preached of Divinity's design by boldly proclaiming, like a loud crier, "God's dreadful justice *and* saving grace."[13]

Edwards recognized the gospel was a two-sided coin, with the wages of sin on one side and the treasures of grace on the other. The question for Edwards was which one to preach. Able to recognize a false dilemma, Edwards preached both sides of the coin. For example, preach-

---

[10]See Marsden, *Jonathan Edwards: A Life*, 186.

[11]Jonathan Edwards, "The Duty of Hearkening to God's Voice," sermon on Psalm 95:7–8, in *The Works of Jonathan Edwards*, vol. 10, *Sermons and Discourses, 1720–1723*, ed. Wilson H. Kimnach (New Haven: Yale University Press, 1992), 438–50.

[12]Helen P. Westra, "Divinity's Design: Edwards and the History of the Work of Revival," in *Edwards in Our Time: Jonathan Edwards and the Shaping of American Religion*, ed. Sang Hyun Lee and Allen C. Guelzo (Grand Rapids: Eerdmans, 1999), 134. The Edwards citation is from *Some Thoughts concerning the Revival*.

[13]Ibid., 155, her emphasis.

ing at funerals, Edwards would use the occasion to preach direct sermons designed to awaken the unregenerate and the spiritually lax. And there's always exhibit A, "Sinners in the Hands of an Angry God." But Edwards also spoke of the other side of the coin, the commending of the "sweetness"—one of his favorite words—of Christ and the gospel. In his early days of preaching to his first congregation in New York City—a few years before he went to Northampton and perhaps owing somewhat to his youthful outlook—Edwards told his congregation that "'tis worth the while to be religious if it were only for the delight and pleasantness of it."[14] Of course, that likely doesn't surprise anyone familiar with Edwards. What needs to be pointed out is that Edwards was not just speaking of some future joy, some future pleasure for Christians in heaven. In this sermon, Edwards was speaking of pleasure now, of delights in this life.

Edwards the Christian Hedonist

Christian thinkers from Augustine to C. S. Lewis, as well as points in between, have commended the faith by giving prominent place to the notions of joy, delight, and pleasure. So did Edwards. I once referred to Edwards's use of this as the "pleasure argument."[15] Apologists use all types of arguments for the existence of God and the veracity of the Christian faith. These arguments tend to be heavy on philosophy and long on rational argument. One that speaks significantly to the human condition often gets overlooked among this pile of philosophical syllogisms that apologists like to heap up. God, in the words of Augustine, made us for himself, and apart from him we are restless and anxious; we are unfulfilled and empty. God, Augustine also observed, made us to desire; he made us to love. When those desires are oriented away from God and toward our own selves, they result ultimately in pain and destruction. When those desires are aimed at God, however, they bring about joy and pleasure. They bring about peace in the place of that nagging anxiety, in the place of that eerie feeling that something's awry. They bring about fulfillment in the place of the sense that, try as one might, nothing brings genuine satisfaction.[16]

---

[14]Jonathan Edwards, "The Pleasantness of Religion," in *The Sermons of Jonathan Edwards: A Reader*, ed. Wilson H. Kimnach, Kenneth P. Minkema, and Douglas A. Sweeney (New Haven: Yale University Press, 1999), 13.

[15]See Stephen J. Nichols, *Heaven on Earth: Capturing Jonathan Edwards's Vision of Living in Between* (Wheaton, IL: Crossway, 2006), 48–60.

[16]See Augustine *Confessions* bk. 1.

In the hands of John Piper, this emphasis on pleasure and joy and delight became "Christian hedonism."[17] This phrase has already been deftly treated by Sam Storms in an earlier chapter in the book, so I will direct readers there.[18] In the hands of Jonathan Edwards, this emphasis on pleasure and joy and delight may be summed up rather nicely in the word "happified." Though archaic, it nevertheless speaks well to Edwards's understanding of the goal of preaching. In a sermon on the Beatitudes, Edwards extols, "It is a thing truly happifying to the soul of men to see God." He later adds, "To see God is this: it is to have an immediate and certain understanding of God's glorious excellency and love." He expounds even a bit further, explaining, "He that sees God, he has an immediate view of God's great and awful majesty, of his pure and beauteous holiness, of his wonderful and enduring grace and mercy."[19]

Consider as well these doctrines from sermons that Edwards preached on 1 Peter. In a sermon on 1 Peter 1:8, Edwards declares, "They live the happiest life in this world, that live a life of love to Jesus Christ, beholding him with an eye of faith." In a sermon on 1 Peter 2:2–3 he reasons, "If persons have ever tasted the sweetness of the word and grace of Christ, they will be longing for more and more of it."[20]

In a sermon in 1754 Edwards declares that Christ died on the cross "for the salvation and the happiness of the souls of men."[21] In the preaching of the gospel the salvation piece usually gets the attention, as it should. But the "happiness" piece that Edwards refers to here more often than not gets overlooked or left out altogether. The gospel truly shouts good news, but in our presenting and preaching it, we sometimes mute the good news by failing to extol the happiness and joy that are found in God. This is the gospel, the message of salvation *and* happiness, that both non-Christians and Christians need to hear.

This gospel, however, sometimes goes unpreached. Or the happiness piece is twisted into personal fulfillment or prosperity or something akin to psychological babbling. Edwards clearly distances his sense of being happified from what passes in most of American culture as the "pursuit of happiness." It is not about worldly goods or worldly honor or pomp; it is about the end of our salvation, our union with Christ and fellowship

---

[17]See John Piper, *Desiring God: Meditations of a Christian Hedonist*, 3d ed. (Sisters, OR: Multnomah, 2003). For many of those introduced to Jonathan Edwards by John Piper, this was the book that made the introduction.

[18]Sam Storms, "Christian Hedonism: Piper and Edwards on the Pursuit of Joy in God."

[19]Jonathan Edwards, "The Pure in Heart Blessed," in *The Works of Jonathan Edwards*, vol. 17, *Sermons and Discourses, 1730–1733*, ed. Mark Valeri (New Haven: Yale University Press, 1999), 61, 64.

[20]These unpublished sermons may be seen at the Jonathan Edwards Center at Yale University, www.yale.edu/wje.

[21]Bailey and Wills, eds., *The Salvation of Souls*, ed. Bailey and Wills, 159.

with the Trinity.[22] Listening to Edwards will quickly and acutely impress upon us the need to proclaim the gospel message of salvation *and* happiness and to proclaim it in a way that gets it right.

Edwards on Commending Christians to the Gospel

There is one more piece to preaching the gospel to Christians in the sermons of Jonathan Edwards. Namely, not only should preaching be aimed at proclaiming the gospel to Christians, but preaching should also be aimed at commending Christians to the gospel. In one of his many recent books, *Finally Alive*, John Piper, perhaps with a hint of frustration in his voice, offers the following observation concerning a survey by the Barna Group:

> I want to say loud and clear that when the Barna Group uses the term *born again* to describe churchgoers whose lives are indistinguishable from the world, and who sin as much as the world, and sacrifice for others as little as the world, and covet things as greedily as the world, and enjoy God-ignoring entertainment as enthusiastically as the world—when the term *born again* is used to describe these professing Christians, the Barna group is making a profound mistake. It is using the biblical term *born again* in a way that would make it unrecognizable to Jesus and the biblical writers.[23]

In thinking about Edwards's congregation at Northampton we might be well within the mark to say that not much has changed since the eighteenth century. The solution is, at least in part, to be found in the pulpit. The solution may be found in the type of preaching that Paul commends in 2 Timothy 3 and 4, in clear contradistinction to the type of preaching he condemns in that same text. Such preaching consists of, at times, the stick as opposed to the carrot. In the face of real danger, mollifying words only appear to offer peace. In fact, they offer only a false assurance and far more harm than good. Sinners are best helped by being told they are sinners; Christians are best helped when they are convicted of their sin and their lukewarm love and their lackluster worship. "Let us offer to God acceptable worship, with reverence and awe," the author of Hebrews warns, "for our God is a consuming fire" (Heb. 12:28b–29).

Such preaching as commended by Paul also consists of, at other times, the carrot. The gospel is the only solution to the human dilemma of sin.

---

[22]See Edwards's sermon "The Value of Salvation," in *Sermons and Discourses 1720–1723*, 308–36. See also John Piper, *God Is the Gospel: Meditations on God's Love as the Gift of Himself* (Wheaton, IL: Crossway, 2005).

[23]John Piper, *Finally Alive: What Happens When We Are Born Again* (Fearn, Ross-shire: Christian Focus, 2009), 13.

The work of Christ, in the words of Paul in Romans 5, accomplishes much more than merely undoing what Adam did. It is in Christ that we are complete; in Christ we "have been filled" (Col. 2:10). Christ himself tells us that as we abide in him and abide in his love, evidenced by keeping his commandments, our joy will be full (John 15:11). Pastoral wisdom knows when to condemn and when to commend, when to ply the law and when to proclaim grace. This may surprise those who know only of Edwards by way of the Puritan caricature, but he likely erred on the side of grace (though I suspect he would quibble with the word "erred"). The minister is "a loud crier" of the joy, delight, and pleasure that flow to us from the love and grace of the triune God. That kind of preaching can make a significant difference in the life of a congregation. Sometimes, though, it doesn't.

When Preaching the Gospel to Believers Doesn't Work Out
Edwards faced such disappointment, perhaps the deepest disappointment a pastor can face: to labor in love for the gospel to a congregation of yawns and sighs. We shouldn't be much surprised by the statistics of ministers who drop out. The story may work itself out differently, but the main strokes look something like this. A young minister, fueled by the ideals of changing the world, ascends to the pulpit week in and week out, extolling God's Word and calling for commitment. A few years later, after listening to petty bickering and endless complaining and seeing no excitement about the things of God, the pastor resigns. Even to these pastors, Edwards has some advice, more in the testimony of his perseverance than in his words. The minister's duty is to proclaim the gospel, faithfully and persuasively and as if all eternity depended on it. God's role is to change hearts. In the face of disappointment, Edwards didn't drop out, but instead turned to God. His happiness was not in the success of his congregation or, to be quite anachronistic, in the numbers who logged on to his Web site to hear his sermons. His happiness was found in God, and so he was able to persevere even in challenging and utterly disappointing times in his ministry.

There's an application for those who listen to sermons. Life change can sometimes be more glacial when we would prefer it to be meteoric. This is true of others and it is true of ourselves. The good news is that God's grace is not only sufficient to save us; it is also sufficient to keep us and to sanctify us.

Edwards reminds pastors that preaching is primarily the proclamation of the gospel, the town crier shouting good news for all the people to hear.

Perhaps ironically, this preaching of the gospel is as much for Christians as it is for non-Christians. All of us in our collective humanity run headlong into the exact wrong things for our fulfillment, joy, pleasure, and happiness. God has made us for himself and we are only happy in him, to put an Edwardsean twist on an Augustinian phrase. This may not be the only piece of Edwards's legacy for preaching, but it is a significant one. Another is to see how Christ factors into preaching. The minister, in Edwards's view, is to be an imitator—an imitator of the one who not only proclaimed joy but is our joy.

Edwards on Christ and Preaching

Over the years, Jonathan Edwards drew a number of young ministerial candidates to his home and his church at Northampton. They were there to learn, like apprentices, the craft of preaching and being a pastor. They also earned their keep, chopping his wood and doing all sorts of odd jobs around his home. This was true on-the-job training. A number of them went on to ministries of their own. Many times they called on their mentor to preach their ordination or installation services. One example is Job Strong. Strong had been in Edwards's Northampton congregation before heading off to Yale for his education and before returning to the Rev. Edwards's parsonage for his apprenticeship. On June 28, 1749, Edwards traveled to Portsmouth, New Hampshire, to preach his ordination sermon.

Perhaps aware of the influence he wielded over his protégé, Edwards pointed Strong past himself to a far better example to imitate as Strong began his pastoral ministry. Edwards titled the sermon "Christ the Great Example of Gospel Ministers." It was published in Boston in 1750, the year Edwards was dismissed from his church at Northampton, which was also Strong's home church.

"It is the duty of ministers of the gospel," Edwards declares in the doctrine section of the sermon, "to follow the example of their great Lord and Master."[24] Edwards then develops this, in typical Puritan sermon fashion, with points and subpoints all logically flowing from this single proposition. Edwards starts by explaining that ministers, like all Christians, are to follow Christ in terms of cultivating personal holiness. But then he gets to a matter for ministers in particular. He exhorts, "More particularly should ministers of the gospel follow the example of their great Master, in the manner in which they seek the salvation and the

---

[24]Jonathan Edwards, "Christ the Great Example of Gospel Ministers," in *Sermons and Discourses, 1743–1758*, 335.

happiness of the souls of men. They should follow his example of love to souls." He concedes that such love will not be to the degree of Christ's love, yet ministers "should have the same spirit of love to them, and concern for their salvation." The reason is that "the love to men's souls in Christ was far above any regard he had to his temporal interest, his ease, his honor, his meat and drink." Then Edwards puts it plainly and directly: "So it should be with his ministers."[25] Edwards was preaching from John 13:14–16, which contains the phrase "a servant is not greater than his master."

Edwards also offers examples of some particulars of how Christ's love provides the standard for ministers. He mentions prayer, diligent labors, suffering ("to spend and to be spent"), and zealousness—tempered with gentleness.[26] Jesus even condescended by "preaching the gospel to the poor, and taking a gracious notice from time to time of little children."[27] Edwards also sees the minister's imitation of Christ in broad strokes. Ministers imitate Christ in his prophetic office.

The Reformed tradition had long since used the threefold office of Christ as a means to summarize the grand sweep of biblical teaching concerning his work. Christ is Prophet, Priest, and King. These different mediatorial roles were all instituted by God in the Old Testament. Christ is not only all three; he is all three perfectly and ultimately. Edwards makes a direct and significant application of Christ's function as Prophet to ministers. Prophets not only foretold, prophesying in the sense of prediction, but they also forthtold, proclaiming the Word of God. Christ, the Logos, spoke and indeed was and is that Word perfectly (John 1:1–18 and Heb. 1:1–4). Ministers are to imitate Christ in his prophetic role. Edwards puts it this way: the work of ministers is "the same with the work Christ does in his prophetical office." Then he adds, "Only with this difference, that ministers are to speak and act wholly under Christ, as taught of him, as holding forth his word, and by light and strength communicated from him."[28] He keeps pressing the connection as the sermon unfolds. Reading it, you can hear him building the momentum before he concludes this section of the sermon: "The work that ministers are called and devoted to, is none other than the work of Christ, or the work that Christ does."[29]

This is Edwards's vision of preaching. For some this may open whole new vistas never before considered. For others this may confirm an already

---

[25]Ibid., 337.
[26]Ibid., 338–40.
[27]Ibid., 340.
[28]Ibid., 341.
[29]Ibid., 342.

established view of preaching. For all those who step into the pulpit, it serves as a powerful summons not only to preach Christ, but to preach like Christ: to be consumed by the salvation and happiness of souls, motivated solely by love.

But Edwards isn't finished quite yet. He still has the application of the sermon, which he splits down the middle for ministers on the one side and for congregations on the other. First, he speaks to or, better, continues speaking to ministers. He points out that imitating Christ is the source of the minister's joy. He explains:

> Our following the example of Christ in the work of the ministry is the way to enjoy the sensible, joyful presence of Christ with us. The disciples had the comfort of Christ's presence and conversation by following him, and going where he went. When we cease to follow him, he will go from us, and we shall soon lose sight of him.

Conversely, following Christ is "the way for us to have his joy fulfilled in us." He adds, "Our imitating Christ in our ministry will be the way for us to be partakers with him in his glory."[30]

This means a devoted life; it also means doctrinal preaching. Edwards explains that for ministers who desire to imitate Christ, they must "take heed that the religion we promote be the same religion that Christ taught and promoted, and not any of its counterfeits and delusive appearances, or anything substituted by the subtle devices of Satan, or vain imaginations in lieu of it." Ministers must be zealous in distinguishing "true from false religion," or they risk "doing much more hurt than good with all [their] zeal and activity."[31]

Ministers imitate Christ in their preaching by proclaiming both love and truth. Knowing that the conflict with Northampton was at full boil in 1749 puts Edwards's exhortations in a revealing light. He found himself in the throes of controversy, trying to preach faithfully, trying to proclaim both love and truth. Perhaps Edwards persevered at Northampton so long, through many years of conflict and trial, because he was buoyed up by precisely what he commended to Job Strong. The minister, motivated by love, seeks the salvation and happiness of souls, regardless of what faces him in the pews.

Maybe Edwards has his own congregation in mind as he ends the sermon, for his last words are devoted to those who listen to ministers.

---

[30]Ibid., 345.
[31]Ibid., 346.

Up to this point in the sermon, he has been speaking directly to ministers and even more directly to Job Strong. To those who would be listening to Strong week in and week out, Edwards challenges, "Encourage and help him, and strengthen his hands, by attending diligently to his ministry, receiving the truth in love, treating him with the honor due to a messenger of Christ." Then, drawing upon his own personal experiences, Edwards adds, "carefully avoiding all controversy with him, and one with another."[32] Edwards then ends on a brighter note. His very last words are that, as Job Strong imitates Christ in his preaching, minister and congregation will be a mutual encouragement and comfort "each other's crown of rejoicing in the day of the Lord Jesus Christ."[33]

Edwards on the Atonement and Preaching

Edwards preached many more ordination and installation sermons. Two of them were for Edward Billing. The first one was in 1740, when Billing began his ministry at Cold Springs, Massachusetts. Twelve years later, Billing was voted out of his church for holding the same view on the Lord's Supper as Edwards. After a few years, Billing received a call to Greenfield, Massachusetts. Edwards preached the installation sermon on March 28, 1754. He again returns to the theme of Christ and the ministry, but he adds something unique. Edwards based the sermon on Acts 20:28, which teaches that Christ has purchased the church with his own blood. Edwards expresses the doctrine this way: "My design from these words is to consider Christ's expending his own blood for the salvation and happiness of the souls of men, in the view both of an inducement and a direction of ministers to exert themselves for the same end."[34] Here Edwards not only looks to Christ; he looks to Christ's work on the cross. Ministers are not only to preach Christ, but according to Paul, to preach him crucified (cf. 1 Cor. 1:23). Edwards takes that seriously and looks to the atonement to see what he can learn about preaching.

One of the first things the atonement means for preaching is that ministers take sin seriously and present sin in all its profound depth. "The very nature of sin," Edwards reminds us, "is enmity against God." Sin is hell-bent in opposition to God and to "the design of God in the creation of the world, which was his own glory and the spiritual and eternal excellency and happiness of his creatures."[35] If sin is opposition to Divinity's design,

---

[32] Ibid., 348.
[33] Ibid.
[34] Jonathan Edwards, "The Work of the Ministry Is Saving Sinners," in *The Salvation of Souls*, ed. Bailey and Wills, 159.
[35] Ibid., 165.

then the atonement is absolutely central and essential to overcoming that opposition and to accomplishing Divinity's design.

Edwards makes two interesting applications to preaching based on what the atonement conquered and achieved. First, Christ died for us when we were at our worst, when we were odious and vile. And while we were in that precise state and condition, he gave his life for us. Second, Christ died to purchase us as his own possession, as "his peculiar treasure."[36] The first point offers a strong inducement to the minister to love his congregation. Edwards makes a direct corollary to Christ's demonstration of love and the minister's willingness to love his congregation: "Now Christ loved the souls of men, and had so great a regard to their salvation, that he thought it worthy for him so to lay out himself. Shall not his ministers and servants be willing to do the same?"[37] We need to remember that these words were spoken *by* a minister who was ousted from his congregation *to* a minister who was also ousted by his congregation.

The second point offers a strong inducement to the minister to preach Christ and him crucified to his congregation and to be ever mindful of Divinity's design. Edwards inextricably links the gospel (the salvation and happiness of souls) with God's glory (the display of his beauty and excellence). Preaching, in his understanding of things, should always exude this design, like the fragrant aroma of life to life (2 Cor. 2:14–17). Consequently, sermons can never be too cross-centered or never be too focused on the glory of God. Edwards makes the point this way: "Seeing Christ manifested so great a regard to the honor of God in the salvation of souls, surely his ministers ought earnestly to seek that they may be the instruments of promoting the glory of God in the same thing."[38]

Edwards drives the imitation of Christ a bit further when he observes that Christ offered himself up in love and humility. These become cardinal virtues for ministers, who "in the whole course of their labors should have a constant regard to the example of Jesus Christ."[39] It is an example to be followed in word and in deed, in the minister's life and in the minister's preaching.

Preachers as Subordinate Agents

Edwards brings this to a close by encouraging Edward Billing, and by extension, encouraging pastors today in their task of being "subordinate agents" to Christ, who serve him by proclaiming "that great offer of the

---

[36]Ibid., 167.
[37]Ibid., 170.
[38]Ibid., 169.
[39]Ibid., 175.

salvation and happiness of men's souls."[40] This idea of course is in complete agreement with Edwards's other main idea, Divinity's design. Right after George Whitefield visited Northampton in 1740, Edwards preached a sermon on 2 Corinthians 2:15–16, in which he declares directly, "The preaching of the gospel is the principal means of glorifying Christ."[41] These two symbiotic and intertwined ideas of glorifying Christ and the salvation and happiness of souls are at front and center of Edwards's charge to pastors in their preaching. This is ultimately his example for those who, week in and week out, step into the pulpit and proclaim God's Word.

It is also, by even further extension, the goal for those who, week in and week out, listen to sermons. Marsden, it may be recalled, spoke of Edwards's intention to jolt his congregation. We need to be jolted, for our vision tends to be far too inward and far too short-sighted. The type of preaching that Edwards practiced and commended jolts us past our self and past our narrow horizons. It jolts us to look to Christ. In one of his sermons, Edwards urges his listeners to come to Christ, who "has flung the door of mercy wide open." Coming to Christ, he continues, results in being in "a happy state," with our "hearts filled with love to him that has loved [us] and washed [us] from [our] sins in his own blood." The chief end of which, he continues in the sermon, leaves us "rejoicing in hope of the glory of God" (Rom. 5:2). And this wasn't just any sermon of Jonathan Edwards. These words in fact are to be found in "Sinners in the Hands of an Angry God."[42]

The goal of preaching is ultimately an eternal goal. In the ordination sermon of Edward Billing, at its very conclusion, Edwards turns to God's Word. He allows Paul to have the final say in the matter: "For what is our hope or joy or crown of boasting before our Lord Jesus at his coming? Is it not you? For you are our glory and joy" (1 Thess. 2:19–20).

---

[40]Ibid., 176.
[41]Jonathan Edwards, "Ministers a Savor of Life or Death," in *The Works of Jonathan Edwards*, vol. 22, *Sermons and Discourses, 1739–1742*, ed. Harry S. Stout and Nathan O. Hatch with Kyle P. Farley (New Haven: Yale University Press, 2003), 206.
[42]In *Sermons of Jonathan Edwards: A Reader*, ed. Kimnach, Minkema, and Sweeney, 103.

20

THE PASTOR AND THE TRINITY

C. J. Mahaney

I t happened in my hometown, in a Washington DC Metro station. And I'm sure, had I been there, I would have walked past it without a single glance.

In 2007, the *Washington Post* organized an experiment. During the morning rush hour, world-famous violinist Joshua Bell stood incognito in the entrance to the L'Enfant Plaza Metro station and played a brilliant classical repertoire for forty-five minutes. It was, as *Post* reporter Gene Weingarten explained, "an experiment in context, perception and priorities—as well as an unblinking assessment of public taste."[1]

Joshua Bell routinely fills up concert halls worldwide. Days before, an audience in Boston had paid around $100 apiece to see him perform. In L'Enfant Plaza, he was playing a Stradivarius made in 1713, reportedly worth $3.5 million. On that Washington morning, the virtuoso collected exactly $32.17 from the few passersby who stopped. Most of the 1000-plus commuters who hurried through the station that morning didn't even slow down.

---

[1]Gene Weingarten, "Pearls before Breakfast," *Washington Post*, Sunday, April 8, 2007, p. W10, http://www.washingtonpost.com/wp-dyn/content/article/2007/04/04/AR2007040401721.html (accessed February 24, 2009).

I don't think I would have slowed my pace either. If I had been rushing through L'Enfant Plaza that morning, I might not have even noticed him. He was hidden in plain sight.

It's quite possible for us to rush past certain verses of Scripture in a similar fashion. Sadly, I often do. We are busy, we've read this before, and we assume we understand the important stuff anyway. We do not perceive the wealth of God-glorifying, grace-magnifying, life-transforming truth before us.

This is one of many reasons I am grateful for the personal example of my friend John Piper. John doesn't rush past the words of Scripture. He doesn't assume he understands what he reads the first time around. He reads slowly, contemplates a single paragraph or sentence or phrase, examines a single word. As Mark Dever eloquently puts it:

> While too many of us are saying a lot of things quickly and running on to the next, John stops and stands and stays and stares at God's Word. Sometimes he stares at something that seems so obvious, but he keeps staring until it begins to expand and fill the horizon of his sight. . . . John prays and thinks until a part of God's Word which seemed simple and obvious becomes fresh and powerful.[2]

John has taught me to slow down, to read my Bible carefully, to ponder the meaning and implications of every line, every word. So following his example, let's stop and stare at a single verse that's easily overlooked. It's only one sentence. In these few words, however, we'll discover in Paul's example a model for pastoral ministry.

Hidden in Plain Sight

In the closing words of Paul's second letter to the Corinthian church, we read, "The grace of the Lord Jesus Christ and the love of God and the fellowship of the Holy Spirit be with you all" (2 Cor. 13:14).

Have you ever paused to contemplate this verse? Until recently, I hadn't. For me, these words were hidden in plain sight.

I've often been guilty of racing past the closing verses of New Testament letters. Sometimes we approach these passages like the last few seconds of a phone conversation: "OK. Yep. Thanks. See ya later." We assume these verses are a mere formality, an expression of ancient etiquette and nothing more.

---

[2]Mark Dever, "Introduction," in Mark Dever, J. Ligon Duncan III, R. Albert Mohler Jr., and C. J. Mahaney, *Preaching the Cross* (Wheaton, IL: Crossway, 2007), 15.

But in Scripture there are no throwaway lines. This final sentence was divinely inspired, carries divine purpose, and has particular relevance for pastoral ministry. In this simple verse, just twenty Greek words, we find a biblical model for pastoral ministry. It is right before our eyes, if we do not race past it.

Gordon Fee cautions us not to neglect or overlook the importance of this benediction. He writes:

> In many ways this benediction is the most profound theological moment in the Pauline corpus. . . . It is not difficult to see why such a profound moment of theology—in the form of *prayer* for the Corinthians—should be the single most appropriate way to conclude this letter. What Paul wishes for them is all of this, and nothing less.[3]

"In many ways . . . the most profound theological moment in the Pauline corpus." And we so easily rush past it.

Paul's benediction would deserve our attention no matter where in Holy Scripture it appeared, but it is particularly striking when we consider the original audience. Paul was writing to the Corinthian church, and if there ever was a church of self-absorbed sinners, these folks were it. They had been seduced by human wisdom. They had drifted from the centrality of the cross. They were splitting into four factions. The church was allowing sexual immorality of a kind, Paul wrote, "not tolerated even among pagans" (1 Cor. 5:1). Lawsuits among church members were common. They were desecrating the Lord's Supper—some were even getting drunk there. They misunderstood and misused the gifts of the Spirit. In fact, Paul told them, their meetings did more harm than good (1 Cor. 11:17). So in two letters Paul exhorts this church, rebukes them, appeals to them, and admonishes them. The second letter is his most passionate—reading it in one sitting will leave you emotionally exhausted.

And yet, as he draws the letter to a close, what does he wish for them? "The grace of the Lord Jesus Christ and the love of God and the fellowship of the Holy Spirit."

All of this, and nothing less.

I don't think that would have been my closing wish for the Corinthian church. I'd have had a different wish altogether.

---

[3]Gordon Fee, *God's Empowering Presence: The Holy Spirit in the Letters of Paul* (Peabody, MA: Hendrickson, 1994), 363–64.

Is Paul's prayer what you wish for your church? If not, perhaps you need to reexamine the model of pastoral ministry provided in his closing benediction.

A Model for Pastoral Ministry

In this chapter I want to draw your attention to this Trinitarian benediction of 2 Corinthians in order to remind you of what has always been true: the character and work of the triune God define and inform the heart of pastoral ministry. In 2 Corinthians 13:14, hidden in plain sight, is a wonderfully succinct model for pastoral ministry.

Paul's pastoral ministry was theologically informed. Moreover, it was thoroughly Trinitarian—he references each member of the Godhead in his benediction. And it was shaped by a clear understanding of the Trinity's disposition toward the church: in the gospel, the triune God extends to us his amazing grace, his immeasurable love, and his gracious fellowship.

Are you looking for a model upon which to build your ministry? If you have been a pastor for more than a few weeks, no doubt you have heard the calls for a new kind of ministry to meet the challenges of a modern world. Hardly a week goes by without a new article, another survey, a large conference, or a new book on church growth, all proclaiming that time-tested ways of doing ministry no longer work. Something entirely new is needed, they tell us. Stephen Wellum captures the current mood: "Around us on every side are calls to 'revision' Christian theology, to 're-imagine' evangelism, to 're-think' how we do church, and even to 're-articulate' the very nature of the gospel for our postmodern times."[4]

But as John Piper has proclaimed for decades, a biblically faithful ministry model needs no revising. What we are after is not novelty but faithfulness, not new paths but old ones, not the power of cool but the power of the gospel. Scripture is not silent on what leadership in the church should look like. And in a volume dedicated to Dr. Piper—who for thirty years has provided for all of us a compelling model of faithful pastoring—it is fitting for us to reexamine a biblical definition of ministry.

Pastor, if you are looking for a model for ministry, you'll find it here: 2 Corinthians 13:14. Through our prayers, our preaching, our counseling, and all facets of our leadership, we must position those we serve to experience the grace of the Son, the love of the Father, and the fellowship of the Holy Spirit.

---

[4]Stephen J. Wellum, "Learning from John Today," *Southern Baptist Journal of Theology* 10, no. 3 (Fall 2006): 2.

The Grace of the Lord Jesus Christ

Paul's benediction for the Corinthian church is consistent with all his letters, and indeed with his entire ministry: he points his readers to the grace of Jesus Christ. Paul did not rely on leadership styles popular in his day, the strength of his own personality, or the quickest way to increase membership numbers. His definition of ministry was rooted in theology, and at its center was the grace of Jesus Christ. For Paul there was no other foundation. And for us it should be no different.

The order of the Trinity as Paul presents it here is striking. He begins with the Lord Jesus Christ, then references God the Father, and concludes with a reference to God the Holy Spirit. Why does he not begin with the Father, the first person of the Trinity?

This verse is not intended to describe the relationships within the Trinity, but rather appears to describe for us the chronological order of our experience of the triune God. It is on the basis of the person and work of Christ that we are reconciled to God. And this priority remains consistent throughout the Christian life. All of the mercy, all of the grace, all of the blessings a Christian receives in this life and throughout eternity derive from the saving work of Jesus Christ.

So it is no surprise that Paul begins by referencing the grace of God, which is revealed through the gospel. The grand centerpiece of "the grace of the Lord Jesus Christ" is the salvation of sinners through the death and resurrection of Christ. This is where Paul always begins. He is gospel-centered, he is cross-centered, and he consistently reminds the Corinthians of the content and the centrality of the gospel.

Paul begins 1 Corinthians with the gospel:

> I give thanks to my God always for you because of the grace of God that was given you in Christ Jesus. (1:4)

> For Christ did not send me to baptize but to preach the gospel, and not with words of eloquent wisdom, lest the cross of Christ be emptied of its power. For the word of the cross is folly to those who are perishing, but to us who are being saved it is the power of God. . . . But we preach Christ crucified, a stumbling block to Jews and folly to Gentiles. (1:17–18, 23)

> For I decided to know nothing among you except Jesus Christ and him crucified. (2:2)

Near the end of the letter, Paul once again reminds the Corinthians of the gospel: "For I delivered to you as of first importance what I also received:

that Christ died for our sins in accordance with the Scriptures, that he was buried, that he was raised on the third day in accordance with the Scriptures" (15:3–4).

And in 2 Corinthians, Paul continues with the gospel: "For you know the grace of our Lord Jesus Christ, that though he was rich, yet for your sake he became poor, so that you by his poverty might become rich" (8:9).

And although Paul addresses the Corinthians on diverse topics, he remains steadily cross-centered. At every turn Paul's instruction is derived from the gospel, revealing a man who never assumed the gospel, and who refused to allow the Corinthian church to drift from Christ and him crucified. Down to the final words of the concluding benediction, Paul reinforces the primacy of the gospel.

All pastors have the privilege and joy of emulating Paul's example in every area of pastoral responsibility. Paul's example reminds me that:

- I must never assume the gospel.
- I must never assume the church I serve sufficiently understands the gospel.
- I must inform every aspect of pastoral ministry with the proclamation and celebration of the grace of our Lord Jesus Christ revealed in the gospel.
- I must never teach on any topic without explaining how it relates to the gospel.
- I must preach to reveal the grace of our Lord Jesus Christ.
- I must counsel to impart the grace of our Lord Jesus Christ.
- I must help those vulnerable to legalism and condemnation to experience the justifying grace of our Lord Jesus Christ.
- I must help those fighting a besetting sin to experience the sanctifying grace of our Lord Jesus Christ.
- I must help the suffering to experience the comforting grace of our Lord Jesus Christ.
- I must help the weary to experience the sustaining grace of our Lord Jesus Christ.
- I must help those who persist in disobedience to experience the convicting and cleansing grace of our Lord Jesus Christ.

In short, I must labor so the grace of our Lord Jesus Christ will be with them all. This is the pastor's privileged task. This is our joy and our call.

Yet if we understand our message and are committed to proclaiming it, why does the grace of Jesus Christ often seem to be an elusive experience for those we serve? If we're preaching this week after week, why don't some folks seem to grasp it? Why isn't the message of grace taking root in every member's life?

Let me offer one possible reason.

The Doctrine of Sin: Handle with Care

Grace is what God extends to sinners. So preaching grace can be a complex task: in order to proclaim grace, we must address sin.

We face two possible errors when addressing the doctrine of sin. One is to preach grace while neglecting sin. This we must not do. The doctrine of sin is of immeasurable value to our churches. We must never minimize its importance, nor should we apologize for preaching it. Our hearers must understand that sin is pervasive, subtle, deceptive, and deadly. Only then will grace have any meaning.

The other error, one to which many of us are prone, is to teach and apply the doctrine of sin while neglecting grace. It is possible to teach this doctrine and not reveal the grace of our Lord Jesus Christ. This is also a sobering possibility, one we must avoid at all costs.

It takes great skill to teach the doctrine of sin in a way that reveals, rather than obscures, the grace of Christ. Sinclair Ferguson captures this challenge:

> Only by seeing our sin do we come to see the need for and wonder of grace. But exposing sin is not the same thing as unveiling and applying grace. We must be familiar with and exponents of its multifaceted power, and know how to apply it to a variety of spiritual conditions.
>
> Truth to tell, exposing sin is easier than applying grace; for, alas, we are more intimate with the former than we sometimes are with the latter. Therein lies our weakness.[5]

Have you seen this weakness in your own life and ministry? In your church? When was the last time you thought deeply about it? We are all more familiar with sin than we are with grace—therein lies our weakness.

So we must handle the doctrine of sin with great care. We must teach it with humility and apply it with wisdom. Remember: this doctrine is a means, not an end. Preaching about sin is not the same as preaching grace. If we do not unveil and apply grace, our emphasis on the doctrine

---

[5]Sinclair Ferguson, "A Preacher's Decalogue Part II," *Reformation21*, http://web.archive.org/web/20070812061418/www.reformation21.org/Past_Issues/2006_Issues_1_16_/2006_Issues_1_16_Articles/Decalogue_II/149/ (accessed March 27, 2009).

of sin will leave the members of our churches devoid of hope, without joy, and aware only of their sin, not of the grace of Christ.

Pastors, our goal is not simply to convict our hearers of sin, but to convince them of the grace of our Lord Jesus Christ. So which are you more aware of: the pervasiveness of sin, or the power of grace? Which is your church more aware of? If someone were to study your sermon notes, would he find more space devoted to exposing sin than to unveiling and applying grace?

It requires little skill merely to expose sin. But it takes great skill to unveil grace and apply it to the wide variety of spiritual conditions represented in our churches. Merely addressing sin or exposing sin is not sufficient; we must labor to show the stunning magnitude and power of the grace of Christ toward those he has redeemed. The message we deliver is the message of the grace of our Lord Jesus Christ, which saves us from all our sin.

Make Calvary Your Landmark

Since as pastors we must handle the doctrine of sin, how do we avoid misusing this doctrine? How do we proclaim and unveil and apply the grace of our Lord Jesus Christ? Here is how: never lose sight of Calvary. What happened in Christ's death gives the greatest possible hope for sinners. There we find forgiveness for sin, freedom from condemnation, salvation from God's wrath, power to put sin to death and to grow in godliness, strength in weakness, perseverance in suffering, certainty amid mystery, and hope for eternity.

Some facet of gospel truth is the ultimate answer for every pastoral situation you confront—every one. But it requires discernment and skill to unveil the gospel and apply it to the apparent complexity of people's lives, the circumstances in our congregations, and the situations we face in counseling. This is what we have been called to do, and this is what we can do, if we never lose sight of Calvary.

In his study of the Puritans, J. I. Packer writes, "The preachers' commission is to declare the whole counsel of God; but the cross is the centre of that counsel, and the Puritans knew that the traveller through the Bible landscape misses his way as soon as he loses sight of the hill called Calvary."[6] This is how to avoid misusing the doctrine of sin: never lose sight of Calvary. Keep this landmark firmly in your view.

---

[6] J. I. Packer, *A Quest for Godliness: The Puritan Vision of the Christian Life* (Wheaton, IL: Crossway, 1990), 286.

It is frighteningly easy to lose sight of Calvary. We drift away from the cross, not toward it. And when this happens, we become aware only of our sin, the sins of our wives and children, the sins of our church members. So we must establish practices that enable us to maintain a clear view of the gospel.

Make this a priority in your spiritual disciplines. Dwell on some aspect of Christ and him crucified as revealed in your daily Scripture reading. Use your supplemental reading to refocus your gaze on the cross. Like Paul, resolve to know nothing except Christ and him crucified (1 Cor. 2:2).

Let the cross be central in your public ministry as well. As you prepare your sermons, ensure that at some point you give your church a clear sighting of Calvary. No matter how obscure the passage seems to be, however unrelated to the cross it appears, we must work at it until we can show how the text fits into the redemptive storyline of Scripture. Your sightings of Calvary should be so consistent that your church expects them in every sermon. When they arrive on Sunday to hear you preach God's Word, they should be filled with anticipation. They should be able to say to someone who has never attended your church, "Regardless of what text our pastor begins with, regardless of whether he preaches from the Old Testament or the New, regardless of how obscure the text appears to be, I guarantee you that at some point in this sermon you will be led to the cross."

And when you are counseling, although you must discuss heart issues, address sin, and carefully diagnose sinful cravings, at some point there must be a sighting of Calvary. Apart from the gospel, we have no basis on which to offer people hope for change. And we could continue on to every area of pastoral responsibility. No arena is exempt.

Paul never lost sight of Calvary. The man celebrated grace even more intensely than he grieved over sin. Even when writing to the Corinthian church—a church with more deficiencies than you will likely ever encounter in ministry—Paul reminded them that the grace of God was present and active among them as a result of the gospel. Paul wasn't unaware of their sins. He was just more aware of the grace of the Lord Jesus Christ.

Which are you more aware of? As you think about your church, pray for them, preach to them, and counsel them—even in your casual conversations with them—which carries more weight in your soul: their sins, or the grace of Christ toward them?

Let us, like Paul, center our ministries on the cross of Christ. Let us labor that our churches may become more aware of the grace of God.

The Love of God

After praying that the Corinthian church will experience the grace of Christ, Paul prays that they will experience "the love of God." It is a simple phrase, easy to rush past. But I appeal to you to slow down, to ponder this prayer, to ask what Paul means when he says, "The love of God . . . be with you all." How should the model Paul provides here shape our pastoral ministry?

In the Trinitarian structure of this benediction, "God" specifically refers to the Father, the first person of the Trinity. And it is clear that Paul has in mind God's love for us, not our love for God.

Paul's closing benediction demonstrates what our prayer should be for those we love and serve: that through our ministry they might encounter the love of God the Father. True pastoral ministry seeks to convince Christians of the love of God the Father for them, a love that is specific, personal, and passionate.

And many Christians need convincing. Over the years I have spoken with many genuine Christians who are not certain of God's love for them. They tend to think of God as merely tolerating them, often frustrated with them, eager to punish them. Countless genuine Christians are suspicious of God.

How are we to convince these believers of God's love for them? I believe J. I. Packer gives us wise guidance. In his outstanding book *Knowing God*, Packer writes, "The New Testament gives us two yardsticks for measuring God's love. The first is the cross (see Rom 5:8; 1 Jn 4:8–10); the second is the gift of sonship [1 John 3:1]."[7] We convince God's people of his love for them by leading them to the cross and by reminding them of their adoption as sons of God.

Let us acknowledge right here that to fully measure God's love is an unending and impossible (and joyous) task. Who can mark off the height and breadth and length and depth of God's love for us? Elsewhere Paul prays for the Ephesians that they will "know the love of Christ *that surpasses knowledge*" (Eph. 3:19). When we survey the love of God for us, we are plumbing the unfathomable, measuring the immeasurable. But let us use these two yardsticks, the cross and the gift of sonship, to attempt to do just that.

The Father's Love in the Cross

How do we lead those we love and care for to experience the love of God the Father? First, we proclaim God the Father's plan to send his

---

[7]J. I. Packer, *Knowing God* (Downers Grove, IL: InterVarsity, 1973), 214.

only Son to us, and to sacrifice him on the cross for sinners like you and me. Scripture is clear: the love of God the Father for sinners is supremely demonstrated on the cross.

In fact, the Father's love cannot be understood apart from the cross. John writes, "For God so loved the world, that he gave his only Son" (John 3:16). Later he writes, "In this the love of God was made manifest among us, that God sent his only Son into the world" (1 John 4:9). Paul adds to the chorus: "God shows his love for us in that while we were still sinners, Christ died for us" (Rom. 5:8).

The Father's love for sinners like you and me was the divine motivation for the cross. As John Stott writes:

> It cannot be emphasized too strongly that God's love is the source, not the consequence, of the atonement. . . . God does not love us because Christ died for us; Christ died for us because God loved us. If it is God's wrath which needed to be propitiated, it is God's love which did the propitiating.[8]

Dr. Stott offers serious wisdom here to those committed to preaching faithfully on the topic of God's wrath. Our sermons and our songs must not neglect the holiness and the wrath of God. We must not soften these topics or apologize for preaching them. But we must never teach about God's holiness and wrath in isolation from his love.

One reason we cannot separate God's wrath from his love is simple: they are joined at the cross. We must never leave the impression that it was the loving Son who placated the angry Father. Rather it was the Father's love—his love for sinners who richly deserved his righteous wrath—that moved him to sacrifice his only Son as our substitute. At the cross, the Father both satisfies his wrath and displays his love for sinners. Pastors, we must remind those we care for that before the cross and behind the cross and through the cross, the love of the Father is revealed. If we do this well, their contemplation of the cross will bring a fresh experience of the personal and passionate love of the Father toward them.

Sinclair Ferguson says this well:

> When we think of Christ dying on the cross we are shown the lengths to which God's love goes in order to win us back to himself. We would almost think that God loved us more than he loves his Son! We cannot measure such love by any other standard. He is saying to us: I love you this much. . . . The cross is the heart of the gospel. It makes the gospel good news:

---

[8]John R. W. Stott, *The Cross of Christ* (Downers Grove, IL: InterVarsity, 1986), 174.

Christ has died for us. He has stood in our place before God's judgment seat. He has borne our sins. God has done something on the cross which we could never do for ourselves. But God does something *to us* as well as *for us* through the cross. He persuades us that he loves us.[9]

Is that what your church thinks? Have you ever preached so clearly about the Father's love as revealed in the cross that your church wondered if God loved them more than he loves his Son?

The cross convinces us of the Father's love because it is here that the voice of the Father says to us:

I will crush my Son under the full fury of my righteous wrath for you. In the Garden of Gethsemane, my Son will cry out for this bitter cup to pass from him. And I will remain silent. Why? Because I love you that much.

And when my Son utters that shriek on the cross, unlike any other protest in all of history, "My God, my God, why have you forsaken me?" I will again remain silent. Why? To convince you that I love you.

Behold the supreme demonstration of my love—the cross—the death of my Son. What more can I say? What else do you require to be convinced of my love for you?

Behind the death of the Son for us stands the love of a Father toward us. And there is no more effective way to persuade your church of God the Father's love than to remind them of the cross, the supreme demonstration of the Father's personal love for them.

The Father's Love in Adoption

The second yardstick for measuring the immeasurable—as if we required more convincing—is our spiritual adoption. God the Father not only sacrifices his only begotten Son for us; he also adopts us as his children. "See what kind of love the Father has given to us," John writes, "that we should be called children of God; and so we are" (1 John 3:1). In our adoption, the Father's love is on full display.

Does your heart resonate with those words? How would the members of your church respond to this verse? Are they convinced that God the Father, in his great love, has adopted them as his children? J. I. Packer asks us this question in his book *Knowing God*:

If you want to judge how well a person understands Christianity, find out how much he makes of the thought of being God's child, and having God as his Father. If this is not the thought that prompts and controls his wor-

---

[9]Sinclair B. Ferguson, *Grow in Grace* (Carlisle, PA: Banner of Truth, 1989), 56, 58.

ship and prayers and his whole outlook on life, it means that he does not understand Christianity very well at all. . . .

To those who are Christ's, the holy God is a loving Father; they belong to his family; they may approach him without fear and always be sure of his fatherly concern and care. This is the heart of the New Testament message. . . .

Adoption is a *family* idea, conceived in terms of *love*, and viewing God as *father*. In adoption, God takes us into his family and fellowship—he establishes us as his children and heirs. Closeness, affection and generosity are at the heart of the relationship. To be right with God the Judge is a great thing, but to be loved and cared for by God the Father is a greater.[10]

Do the words "closeness, affection and generosity" describe your church's perception of God? If not, perhaps your church is more aware of their sin than they are of adopting grace.

It is indeed a great thing to be right with God the Judge through the person and work of Jesus Christ. It is a great thing to be forgiven of sin, to be free from the fear of God's wrath. But it is possible to grasp these great realities and remain unaware of what is even greater: we are adopted and loved by God the Father. In Christ, God the Father justifies us, but he does not stop there: he adopts us as his sons.

Does your church understand the great, but not the greater? Do they know about justification, but not adoption? Do they celebrate being made right with God, while unaware that they have been adopted by God?

The doctrines of justification and adoption are related, but they are not the same. We must distinguish between them without ever separating them. In fact, the doctrine of justification must always be foundational to our teaching and ministry, because all the saving benefits we receive depend upon justification alone. But we must also help our churches understand and celebrate the doctrine of adoption. We are not only declared righteous; we are made God's children. We are not only right with God the Judge; we are loved by God the Father. And the more we teach on adoption, the more our churches will experience God's fatherly love, affection, care, closeness, and generosity.[11]

So are those you serve certain of the Father's love for them? Are you laboring to convince them of it? How do you leave your church at the end of a sermon? Where do you leave them at the end of a counseling

---

[10]Packer, *Knowing God*, 201, 203, 207.

[11]As you study the doctrine of adoption, let me recommend three books: Sinclair Ferguson's *Children of the Living God* (Carlisle, PA: Banner of Truth, 1989), particularly the chapter "Adopted Children"; J. I. Packer's classic *Knowing God*, particularly the chapter titled "Sons of God"; and Trevor Burke's *Adopted into God's Family: Exploring a Pauline Metaphor* (Downers Grove, IL: InterVarsity, 2006).

appointment? What is the effect of even a casual conversation with you? Does a member of your church leave your presence more aware of his sin, or more aware of the love of God the Father? Is your church more secure in the Father's personal and passionate love as a result of your ministry?

Let me ask a more personal question: Are you convinced of the Father's love for you? He crushed his Son for you so that he might adopt you, so that he might convince you of his holy love for you. Pastor, are you more aware of your sin, the weaknesses in your pastoral ministry, the deficiencies in your church, or of the Father's love? You cannot convince your church of the Father's love if you are not convinced yourself.

As Paul concludes his letter to the Corinthians, in spite of all their faults, he closes not with a parting correction but with a reminder of the Father's love for them. As pastors, we are called to lead our churches to experience the love of God the Father. And this begins with experiencing the love of the Father ourselves.

If your church is not persuaded of God's love for them, I recommend that you lead them in studying the doctrine of adoption until they are secure in the Father's love. You may even want to restrict the teaching diet of your church to this topic for a time. As you immerse yourself and your church in an extended study of this topic, you can expect to be freshly aware of, and overwhelmed by, the Father's immeasurable love for you and those you serve.

The Fellowship of the Holy Spirit

As Paul closes his letter to the Corinthians, his final prayer is that they will experience "the fellowship of the Holy Spirit" (2 Cor. 13:14). He wants nothing less than that they experience the Holy Spirit's presence, participate in his work, and partake of his fellowship—that they grow in relationship with the third person of the Trinity.[12] Pastors, as we follow Paul's model for ministry, this must be our burden as well.

We must remain dependent upon the Holy Spirit, pursue his presence and power for sanctification and service, and grow in eagerness to experience his gifts as described in Scripture. Scripture does not permit us merely to affirm the existence of the Holy Spirit. Scripture calls us to grow in our relationship with him and our experience of his presence and work.

---

[12]Although it is possible that the phrase "fellowship of the Spirit" refers to fellowship among the Corinthians created *by* the Spirit (a genitive of source), the evidence seems to favor the interpretation chosen here. See Murray J. Harris, *The Second Epistle to the Corinthians*, New International Greek Testament Commentary (Grand Rapids: Eerdmans, 2005), 939–41.

I know what some of you are thinking at this point: "Wait, this guy's charismatic! You mention the third person of the Trinity, and bingo! suddenly this chapter becomes an apologetic for the charismatic view." I can already feel the nervousness of my cessationist friends—just when you thought this was a safe volume, the charismatic guy shows up!

It's true, I represent an odd combination: I am Reformed and charismatic. Some would say that's an oxymoron, like being a Presbyterian televangelist or a humble Duke basketball fan. But although being Reformed and charismatic may sound historically odd, there is nothing theologically strange about it. Believing in God's sovereignty over all things and seeing God's glory as the end of all things provide motivation for the pursuit of the gifts, guidance for the exercise of the gifts, and evaluation for the practice of the gifts.

As a Reformed and charismatic pastor, I am aware of the many theological and practical deficiencies of the charismatic movement. When some Christians hear the word *charismatic*, they think of the nutty things they have seen on television, or stories of large healing meetings that resemble a WWF Ultimate Challenge on pay-per-view. I sympathize with all who are troubled by the theological deficiencies and goofy practices present in the charismatic movement. This stuff disturbs me as well. One reason it disturbs me is that it reflects a disregard for the authority and sufficiency of Scripture.

So let there be no misunderstanding: as we lead our churches in their experience of the Holy Spirit, we must always uphold the unique authority of Scripture.

Scripture Is Our Final Authority

Scripture alone is our final authority in all matters of life and doctrine. And Scripture is our only basis for helping our churches to grow in their appreciation and pursuit of the Holy Spirit's work. It is the Bible that calls us to grow in our relationship with the Spirit, to eagerly desire and practice the gifts, and to experience his power and presence. We must study Scripture carefully, and lead our churches to do the same.

A weakness to which charismatics can be prone is the tendency to put more confidence in subjective impressions and feelings than in the Bible. And you don't have to be a charismatic to have this weakness. All of us tend to assign more authority to subjective thoughts and feelings than we should.

I am grateful for Dr. Piper's wise teaching in this area. I still remember the first time I read his provocatively titled article, "The Morning I Heard the Voice of God." He begins:

Let me tell you about a most wonderful experience I had early Monday morning, March 19, 2007, a little after six o'clock. God actually spoke to me. There is no doubt that it was God. I heard the words in my head just as clearly as when a memory of a conversation passes across your consciousness. The words were in English, but they had about them an absolutely self-authenticating ring of truth. I know beyond the shadow of a doubt that God still speaks today.

As soon as I read that paragraph I wondered what had taken place in the life of my good friend. Apparently something unprecedented! John does not usually write this openly about his personal experiences (for which he has my respect).

So I kept reading until I came upon this explanation:

It was through the Bible that I heard these divine words, and through the Bible I have experiences like this almost every day. . . . If you would like to hear the very same words I heard on the couch in northern Minnesota, read Psalm 66:5–7. That is where I heard them. O how precious is the Bible. . . . This is the very voice of God.

John concludes, "Something is incredibly wrong when the words we hear outside Scripture are more powerful and more affecting to us than the inspired word of God."[13]

Pastors, we must not build churches in which the words we hear outside of Scripture are more powerful and more affecting to our members than the words of Scripture. The words of Scripture must always speak to us most powerfully and move us most deeply. Let us study the Bible, celebrate it, honor its unique authority, and teach our churches to understand and treasure and obey it as their final authority.

Only when we uphold the authority of Scripture can we grow in our experience and pursuit of the Holy Spirit. The Holy Spirit speaks to us primarily through Scripture, and never in contradiction of Scripture. And we lead our churches to grow in their relationship with the Spirit by leading them to understand, treasure, and obey the Scriptures.

Celebrate the Breadth of God's Work

As we examine what Scripture teaches us about the Holy Spirit, we see that his work in the church is multifaceted. As is evident in Paul's letters to the Corinthians, the Spirit's work is diverse and broad. I think Gordon Fee got it right in his summary of Paul's understanding of the person and

---

[13]John Piper, "The Morning I Heard the Voice of God," blog posted March 21, 2007, www.desiring-God.org.

work of the Spirit. He writes, "In Paul, power is not to be thought of merely in terms of the miraculous, the extraordinary. . . . Paul understood the Spirit's power in the broadest possible way."[14]

This is a perspective on the spiritual gifts that the Corinthians failed to grasp. It appears they exaggerated the importance of the gift of tongues and saw all the other gifts as secondary. For them, the gift of tongues was exciting, spectacular, the mark of true spirituality. The other gifts were good, but not truly spectacular.

So Paul sought to expand their understanding. To illustrate the diversity of the Spirit's work, Paul gave the Corinthians two lists of gifts, neither of them exhaustive (1 Cor. 12:4–11, 27–31). In each list, Paul intentionally placed tongues last, not because tongues were the least of the gifts, but because the Corinthians exaggerated the importance of this gift. In a few brilliant chapters Paul adjusted their perspective, broadened their understanding, and taught them to perceive the breadth of the Spirit's work.

Like the Corinthians, we are sometimes inclined to see the Holy Spirit's work only in gifts or events that appear spectacular. Like them, we sometimes emphasize only one gift of the Spirit, or only one kind of gift. Make no mistake: I am convinced that the Holy Spirit does give spectacular gifts, including prophecy, healing, and miracles. I thank God for the spectacular, wherever and whenever it genuinely occurs. But Scripture teaches us that God is at work in countless ways, whether it appears spectacular to us or not.

So let us understand the Spirit's work in the broadest possible way. Let us cultivate our appreciation for, and celebration of, the diverse work of the Spirit as defined in Scripture. If you understand the multifaceted work of the Holy Spirit, your eyes will be opened to discover his work. He is at work all around you. Do not confine his work to what appears to be spectacular. And do not dismiss his work because of your particular views on the spiritual gifts.

In fact, Scripture gives us two very easy ways to identify the Holy Spirit's work in our churches. Here's your "starter kit" for recognizing his work: study the fruit of the Spirit (Gal. 5:22–23) and the gifts of the Spirit (1 Cor. 12:4–11, 27–31; Eph. 4:11–16; 1 Pet. 4:10–11). Read these lists carefully. Then look up, and look at your church. You will see the Holy Spirit at work everywhere you look. I'd recommend you teach your church to do the same.

---

[14]Fee, *God's Empowering Presence*, 8.

The Spirit is at work in you, and in the lives of those you care for. It may be easy to recognize his work when you witness the spectacular (and let's be clear: it doesn't get any more spectacular than the miracle of regeneration[15]). But it requires a different kind of discernment to recognize his work in daily life. When the elderly lady serves consistently and faithfully in your church year after year; when parents endure the loss of a child and continue to trust in God; when a single man gives away his time and energy to serve in a small group; when the businessman's portfolio takes a hit but he keeps giving joyfully and generously—there is only one explanation for these. It is the presence and the work of the Holy Spirit that brings the fruit and the gifts of the Spirit in your church. And that is truly spectacular.

The Spirit Leads Us to the Cross

As we lead our churches to grow in the fellowship of the Spirit, we must remember that the Holy Spirit always glorifies the Son. The primary role of the Holy Spirit is to reveal the Savior and to testify to the gospel. Our pneumatology must never take precedence over—and in fact cannot be understood apart from—the gospel of Jesus Christ.

Let's avoid adopting the Corinthians' erroneous definition of spirituality. They equated maturity with giftedness, spirituality with the spectacular. They thought of themselves as "people of the Spirit," yet they lacked the primary evidence of the Spirit's work: love. This is why Paul labors to redefine spiritual maturity for them in both of his letters. D. A. Carson summarizes Paul's point:

> What it means to be "spiritual" is profoundly tied to the cross, and to nothing else. More precisely, to be spiritual, in this passage [1 Cor. 2:6–16], is to enjoy the gift of the Holy Spirit—and this means understanding and appropriating the message of the cross, "God's secret wisdom." . . . Indeed, those who are most mature are most grateful for the cross and keep coming back to it as the measure of God's love for them and the supreme standard of personal self-denial.[16]

What does it mean for your church to grow spiritually? They must become always more grateful for the cross, always returning to Calvary. Let the glorious truth of Christ and him crucified define maturity for your church.

---

[15]See John Piper, *Finally Alive: What Happens When We Are Born Again* (Fearn, Ross-shire: Christian Focus, 2009).
[16]D. A. Carson, *The Cross and Christian Ministry: An Exposition of Passages from 1 Corinthians* (Grand Rapids: Baker, 1993), 62.

Let us foster an appreciation for the broad work of the Spirit and pursue the Spirit, ever and always with Calvary in view.

The Holy Spirit unfailingly testifies to Christ. Let this be the work of the Spirit that we treasure the most.

Conclusion

The concluding sentence of 2 Corinthians provides a wonderful summation of the pastor's priorities. Here Paul shows us that it is the character and work of the triune God that define and shape the heart of pastoral ministry.

May this definition of pastoral ministry govern us and guide us. May this triune priority be the increasing experience of each of those entrusted to our care. May the Lord equip us to passionately proclaim the grace of Jesus Christ, faithfully teach the love of God the Father, and consistently cultivate the fellowship of the Spirit. What a privilege we share in caring for, serving, and leading those the Savior "obtained with his own blood" (Acts 20:28).

Pastor, take this Trinitarian benediction and pray it for your people, desire it for them, pronounce it over them, and labor to see it take root in their hearts. Do everything you can to position them to experience all of this, and nothing less.

21

THE PASTOR AS WORSHIPER

Ray Ortlund

"There was a man sent from God whose name was John" (John 1:6). We thank God for sending to us the man Dr. John Piper. We honor John for his steady, courageous, articulate faithfulness to his mission. But it isn't his mission alone. This collection of essays bears witness to our united commitment to "spreading a passion for the supremacy of God in all things for the joy of all peoples through Jesus Christ."[1] What else is there?

"The Pastor as Worshiper" is my responsibility here. The topic raises at least these questions. Can and should a pastor, as a pastor, worship the Lord Jesus Christ in a way distinct from the worship offered by his people? If so, how? And can that uniquely pastoral worship bring a man closer to his people rather than put him at a distance from them? If so, how?

These questions are answered in Philippians 2:17–18, where the apostle Paul writes: "Even if I am to be poured out as a drink offering upon the sacrificial offering of your faith, I am glad and rejoice with you all. Likewise you also should be glad and rejoice with me." Three themes converge here, themes central to Dr. Piper's ministry: joy, suffering, and

---

[1]The mission statement of Bethlehem Baptist Church and John Piper.

worship. My own thinking is deeply marked by the following assertions in John's books:

> *Joy*—"No act is truly virtuous—that is, truly loving—that does not come from and aim at joy in the glory of God."[2]

> *Suffering*—"The suffering that seems to threaten future grace is, in reality, grace upon grace."[3]

> *Worship*—"Missions exists because worship doesn't."[4]

Anyone remotely familiar with John's ministry will recognize these truths, and even their expression, as unmistakably Piperian. But far better, they are Pauline. Joy, suffering, and worship lay at the heart of the apostle's ministry, they lie at the heart of all pastoral ministry, because they lie at the heart of the biblical gospel. Philippians 2:17–18 will take us there more deeply.

The Context of Philippians 2

The context in Philippians 2 is Paul's presentation of the poured-out life. This Christlike way of life bears witness to a mentality so counterintuitive, so improbable, that Paul must show it to us from four different angles of vision. First and foremost, the eternal Son exemplifies the poured-out life. Though he was in the form of God, he emptied himself and took the form of a servant, humbling himself all the way down, down, down to a tortured death on a bloody cross of shame. Therefore, God highly exalted him above all others as the One to whom every created being is destined to give a final reckoning, with either indescribable joy or unspeakable dread (vv. 6–11). The Lord Jesus himself incarnates, as no one else can, the poured-out life in its painfully deep but temporary humiliation and its glorious and endless exaltation.

With this vision of King Jesus immediately before them, compelling their reverent attention, the Philippians have a reason not to quit in the face of persecution but to persevere, working out their salvation with confidence in God's overruling power (vv. 12–13). They must not become cynical toward their persecutors, nor should they turn in exasperation on one another, reduced to shameful grumbling and questioning (v. 14). Instead,

---

[2]John Piper, *God's Passion for His Glory: Living the Vision of Jonathan Edwards* (Wheaton, IL: Crossway, 1998), 35.
[3]John Piper, *Future Grace* (Sisters, OR: Multnomah, 1995), 350.
[4]John Piper, *Let the Nations Be Glad: The Supremacy of God in Missions*, 3d ed. (Grand Rapids: Baker, 2010), 15, 35.

looking to that coming day of Christ when every knee will bow to him and every tongue will confess his majesty, they must keep their witness radiant and bold. That way, Paul's ministry to the then-glorified Philippians will prove to be the eternal triumph he is hoping for (vv. 15–16).

Secondarily, after the Lord Jesus Christ, Paul himself (vv. 17–18), Timothy (vv. 19–24), and Epaphroditus (vv. 25–30) also illustrate, imperfectly but really, the beauty of the poured-out life. It is Paul's own personal reflections in verses 17–18 that reveal a pastor's worship and attract our interest here.

The apostle looks into the events of his life with the eyes of a seer. He perceives the true significance of his sufferings. He is in prison and may suffer martyrdom (1:19–25). But even if he is released, as seems to him likely, he still dies daily. His friends in Philippi could be thinking, "Paul doesn't deserve the wretched treatment he keeps suffering. And we need this man protected from stress and danger. He is too valuable to us, too valuable to the cause of Christ." They might see his sufferings as nothing but defeat. But Paul is thinking more profoundly. He is not frustrated by the political powers in apparent control of his life; he is not feeling confined by his imprisonment; he is not angrily looking for someone to blame; he is not frantically pleading for intervention. He discerns in the course his life is taking, whatever hardships he encounters, a joyous opportunity to contribute to what he values most. Suspended in that confident thought, he opens his heart and mind to his friends who are so concerned for him.

Paul Is Being Poured Out as a Drink Offering

"But even if I am being poured out as a drink offering . . ." (Phil. 2:17, my translation). The ESV translates, "Even if I am to be poured out . . . ," apparently following the RSV.[5] But the particle ἀλλὰ deserves to register its presence. The sudden shift in Paul's vision from the future day of glorious triumph (v. 16) to his present struggles in pastoral ministry (v. 17) prompts his insertion of the adversative particle. The contrast between the difficult present and the glorious future, far from warranting a spirit of complaint, provides the occasion for a surprising joy even in the present. Moreover, the nature of the concessive clause, as Paul states it, is actual rather than hypothetical.[6] Therefore, I adjust the wording of the ESV from "to be poured out" to "being poured out."

---

[5] The NRSV translates, "But even if I am being poured out . . . ."
[6] See Ernest De Witt Burton, *Syntax of the Moods and Tenses in New Testament Greek* (Edinburgh: T. & T. Clark, 1898), section 284.

Paul has just described his ministry to the Philippians as a kind of athletic running toward a goal and strenuous exertion in laboring (v. 16). Now he changes the metaphor to a drink offering being poured out. This is the language of worship. A drink offering appears in both pure Old Testament worship[7] and in pagan and corrupted worship.[8] Here is an example of the drink offering in legitimate worship: "You shall offer with the burnt offering, or for the sacrifice, a quarter of a hin of wine for the drink offering for each lamb. . . . a pleasing aroma to the LORD" (Num. 15:5, 7). The precise quantity of a hin appears to be uncertain,[9] but a quarter of a hin may have approximated a modern quart. This drink offering of wine was a secondary "enhancement,"[10] accompanying the larger, more costly animal offering. Together, the elements of this worship rose to the Lord as "a pleasing aroma," suggesting his pleasure in receiving the worship. The drink offering functioned in connection with various demonstrations of personal and corporate devotion: ". . . a food offering or a burnt offering or a sacrifice, to fulfill a vow or as a freewill offering or at your appointed feasts, to make a pleasing aroma to the LORD" (Num. 15:3). It was a frequent supplementary act of worship.[11]

How then is Paul being poured out as a drink offering? The analogous imagery in 2 Timothy 4:6 is clear: "For I am already being poured out as a drink offering, and the time of my departure has come." Here Paul's drink offering before his Lord is to be poured out in death. But in Philippians 2:17 the reality Paul intends by his figure of speech is not obvious. Peter O'Brien interprets the drink offering as Paul's martyrdom,[12] while Gordon Fee construes it as Paul's imprisonment.[13] Each case is argued well, but on balance I find Fee's reasoning more forceful, primarily because Paul seems to expect deliverance (1:19) with continued service to the Philippians (1:25) and even a return visit to Philippi in the near future (2:24).

---

[7]See especially Numbers 28–29, where the drink offering is scripted pervasively into both the daily and the special-occasion worship of Israel, summarized in 29:39.

[8]Deuteronomy 32:38; Psalm 16:4; Jeremiah 44:17–19, 25; Ezekiel 20:28; cf. Othmar Keel, *The Symbolism of the Biblical World: Ancient Near Eastern Iconography and the Book of Psalms* (New York: Seabury, 1978), 330.

[9]See Marvin A. Powell, "Weights and Measures," in *The Anchor Bible Dictionary* (New York: Doubleday, 1992), 6:904.

[10]R. K. Harrison, *Numbers* (Chicago: Moody, 1990), 222.

[11]Gordon J. Wenham, in his notes on Numbers 28:1–29:40 in *The ESV Study Bible*, calculates that, over the course of a year, the prescribed sacrifices required 113 bulls, 1086 lambs, over a ton of flour, and 1000 bottles of oil and wine.

[12]Peter T. O'Brien, *The Epistle to the Philippians: A Commentary on the Greek Text* (Grand Rapids: Eerdmans, 1991), 305–6.

[13]Gordon D. Fee, *Paul's Letter to the Philippians* (Grand Rapids: Eerdmans, 1995), 252–54.

Jean-François Collange broadens the referent to Paul's ministerial sufferings in general, which satisfies me still further.[14] Paul has already drawn the Philippians' attention there, proposing a clear parallel between his and their respective sufferings as Christians: "For it has been granted to you that for the sake of Christ you should not only believe in him but also suffer for his sake, engaged in the same conflict that you saw I had and now hear that I still have" (1:29–30). Moreover, the immediately preceding verse of our nearer context has Paul reminding them of the price he has paid in ministry for their sakes: "so that in the day of Christ I may be proud that I did not run in vain or labor in vain" (2:16). In the coherence of the passage, the metaphor of the drink offering here in verse 17 seems to refer broadly and inclusively to the lifestyle of exertion, risk, opposition, dishonor, controversy, and all the other afflictions his ministry required.

One is struck all the more, therefore, with the almost casual tone with which Paul mentions his life of hardship in ministry: "But even if I am being poured out as a drink offering . . . ." The selflessness implicit here goes a long way toward explaining the joy in the apodosis of this verse and elsewhere in this letter. This man was the pastor who said, "I do not account my life of any value nor as precious to myself" (Acts 20:24). This pastor also said, "I will most gladly spend and be spent for your souls" (2 Cor. 12:15). But the remarkable feature of our passage in Philippians is that his selfless care for others goes even deeper than compassion; it is worship.

The Sacrificial Offering of Your Faith

"Even if I am being poured out as a drink offering upon the *sacrificial offering* of your faith" (Phil. 2:17). The ESV correctly interprets the two nouns θυσίᾳ and λειτουργίᾳ coordinated with καὶ and marked by the single definite article τῇ as one compound increment of meaning.[15] Paul continues to use the language of worship. The "sacrifice" covers a range of gifts brought to the altar, while the "offering" may evoke the ministry of the Levites.[16] Together the two terms dignify the Philippians' faith as sacred, costly, and God-focused. Undoubtedly for them the practical realities of the poured-out life were not pretty. It meant many common

---

[14]Jean-François Collange, *The Epistle of Saint Paul to the Philippians*, trans. A. W. Heathcote (London: Epworth, 1979), 113–14.

[15]Maximilian Zerwick, *Biblical Greek Illustrated by Examples* (Rome: Pontifical Biblical Institute, 1963), section 184.

[16]Cf. Numbers 8:22; 16:9 LXX; Luke 1:23; Hebrews 8:6, where the ESV translates λειτουργίας as "ministry"; 9:21, where the ESV paraphrases τὰ σκεύη τῆς λειτουργίας as "the vessels used in worship."

yet demanding tasks of undramatic self-giving. But Paul wants them to know this encouraging truth: their Lord above is receiving their lifestyle of faith as a pleasing aroma.

I am reminded of William Bradford's account of how the Pilgrims cared for one another as they struggled through that first horrible winter of 1620–21:

> But that which was most sad and lamentable was that in two or three months' time half of their company died, especially in January and February, being the depth of winter, and wanting [i.e., lacking] houses and other comforts; being infected with the scurvy and other diseases which this long voyage and their inaccommodate condition had brought upon them. So as there died sometimes two or three persons of a day in the foresaid time, that of 100 and odd persons, scarce fifty remained. And of these, in the time of most distress, there was but six or seven sound persons who to their great commendations, be it spoken, spared no pains night nor day, but with abundance of toil and hazard of their own health, fetched them wood, made them fires, dressed them meat, made their beds, washed their loathsome clothes, clothed and unclothed them. In a word, did all the homely and necessary offices for them which dainty and queasy stomachs cannot endure to hear named; and all this willingly and cheerfully, without any grudging in the least, showing herein their true love unto their friends and brethren; a rare example and worthy to be remembered. Two of these seven were Mr. William Brewster, their reverend Elder, and Myles Standish, their Captain and military commander, unto whom myself and many others were much beholden in our low and sick condition. And yet the Lord so upheld these persons as in this general calamity they were not at all infected either with sickness or lameness. And what I have said of these I may say of many others who died in this general visitation, and others yet living; that whilst they had health, yea, or any strength continuing, they were not wanting [i.e., unavailable] to any that had need of them. And I doubt not but their recompense is with the Lord.[17]

This story of poured-out love began in heaven, came down into this self-centered, grasping, angry world through Christ and has reappeared by the power of the gospel in countless lives and churches, including the Philippians. They cared sacrificially for Paul himself.[18] Now he wants them to see that their demonstration of the poured-out life clothes them, as it were, with the priestly garments of the Levites active in worship.

---

[17]William Bradford, *Of Plymouth Plantation*, ed. Samuel Eliot Morison (New York: Alfred A. Knopf, 1953), 77–78.
[18]Philippians 1:5; 2:30; 4:10–18.

He names their service to him through their member Epaphroditus as λειτουργὸν (2:25). He calls the gifts they sent him "a fragrant offering, a sacrifice acceptable and pleasing to God" (4:18). Paul is painting a picture of the Philippian church as a new covenant priesthood under Christ, worshiping God with a lifestyle of sacrifice for others motivated by the gospel. Their faith is taking action, τῆς πίστεως [2:17] functioning as a subjective genitive.[19]

Faith as their motivation raises a question. What certainties does their faith have to lay hold of in order to inspire and sustain them in their shared lifestyle of a "sacrificial offering"? Taking into account only this letter from the apostle, they have reason to believe that:

- he who began this good work in them will bring it to completion at the day of Jesus Christ (1:6);
- they are all partakers of grace together (1:7);
- they are experiencing the affection of Christ Jesus himself through their relationship with Paul (1:8);
- they will be pure and blameless for the day of Christ (1:10);
- human opposition, far from defeating the gospel, is serving to advance the joyous spread of the gospel (1:12–18);
- should life be lost, Christ is gained (1:21);
- temporary survival is gospel opportunity (1:22);
- to depart and be with Christ is far better than this life (1:23);
- the further one goes with Christ, the more joy one experiences (1:25);
- the gospel of Christ is an uplifting power (1:27);
- opposition to gospel witness presages the doom of the opponents and the glorious destiny of the faithful (1:28);
- it is a God-given privilege to suffer for the sake of Christ (1:29);
- union with Christ brings encouragement, comfort from love, participation in the Spirit, affection, and sympathy (2:1);
- Christ Jesus himself is living proof that the arrogance of this world is doomed and that gospel humility is the path of great reward (2:6–9);
- Jesus is King, and he will have every rational creature in the universe know it and own it, to the greater glory of God the Father (2:10–11);

---

[19]According to Moisés Silva, *Philippians* (Grand Rapids: Baker, 1992), 151; cf. Galatians 3:2, 5; 1 Thessalonians 1:3; 2 Thessalonians 1:11.

- the Philippians do not need Paul always present to lead them by the hand; God himself is deeply at work in them (2:12–13);
- knowing Christ Jesus the Lord redefines all trophies of self-exaltation as "rubbish," for he gives true righteousness and participation in his death and resurrection; he is so superior to all things in this world that, whatever path one may take into the resurrection of the dead, the price to be paid is small in comparison (3:7–11);
- in conversion, Christ Jesus takes eternal possession of the believer (3:12);
- the call of God in Christ Jesus offers a prize far beyond this world, worthy of the believer's all (3:14);
- to whatever extent any believer struggles to grasp the upward call, God will reveal all that that believer needs revealed (3:15);
- to settle for the rewards of this world is to make oneself an enemy of the cross of Christ and to make a god of one's earthly appetites, which is the path of destruction and the reversal of a truly human life (3:18–19);
- those who worship by the Spirit of God and glory in Christ Jesus and put no confidence in the flesh also find their citizenship in heaven, from which they await a Savior, the Lord Jesus Christ, who will raise even their lowly bodies into his immortal glory by his power over all things (3:3, 20–21);
- their names are written in the book of life (4:3);
- the Lord is at hand (4:5);
- God receives the prayers of his people and sends his overruling peace to guard their hearts when the circumstances of life would have them frantic (4:6–7);
- if believers will follow the apostolic example of lovely heavenly-mindedness, they will experience the presence of the God of peace (4:8–9);
- Christ strengthens his people to accept with contentment whatever life may bring (4:11–13);
- when the Philippians support Paul's ministry, the fruit increases to their own credit (4:17);
- God receives their partnership with Paul as a sacrifice pleasing to himself (4:18);
- God is committed to the Philippians' own needs with all his riches in glory in Christ Jesus (4:19);
- in it all, God will get glory for himself forever and ever (4:20);

- in the meantime, the grace of the Lord Jesus Christ will steadfastly be with their spirit (4:23).

Setting aside, for the sake of our present considerations, the grandeur of Romans, of Ephesians, of Hebrews, and so forth, the faith of the Philippian church, armed with this letter alone, was well supplied with ample resources for continuing boldly in the lifestyle of a "sacrificial offering."

Glad Rejoicing Together

"I am glad and rejoice with[20] you all. Likewise you also should be glad and rejoice with me" (Phil. 2:17–18). Paul's verbally repetitious and emotionally extravagant exuberance is obvious in the text. Something remarkable is happening in Paul's psychology. I am reminded of George Marsden's assessment of Jonathan Edwards's outlook on life: "In the Edwardses' world, the meaning of life was found in intense loves, including earthly loves."[21] And so it was with Paul. The meaning of his life—the sacred center which, if served and satisfied and fulfilled, rendered all else happy—was intensely joyous love for Christ: "the surpassing worth of knowing Christ Jesus my Lord" (3:8). Nothing less makes sense of this man's astonishing heart. He is pouring his life out for others. It is costing him dearly—though less, in his own eyes, than the Philippians' "sacrificial offering." The idol of self within is being deeply denied. Rather than wallowing in despair, Paul is not only willing but is overflowingly happy. This man is no self-pitying "wounded hero," manipulating people emotionally for strokes. He is glad to give himself away, so that he can add, in some small degree at least, to the Philippians' worship of Christ.

H. A. A. Kennedy paraphrases Paul's mentality this way: "I rejoice on my own account because I have been the instrument of your salvation. I also share in the joy which you experience in the new life you have received."[22] His reverence for Christ flows over into deep emotional identification with the Philippian church, freeing him from the narrow prison of self-centered brooding. His heart is empowered to make the first move emotionally. He does not fish for their sympathy, so that they will cheer

---

[20]Lightfoot interprets συγχαίρω as "congratulate," not "rejoice with." The former is valid, according to the classical lexicon of Liddell-Scott-Jones, and allowable, according to the New Testament lexicon of Bauer-Arndt-Gingrich. New Testament usage, however, does not seem to strengthen Lightfoot's case. Indeed, in 1 Corinthians 13:6 the compound carries the same force, mutatis mutandis, as the simple form: "It does not rejoice at wrongdoing, but *rejoices with* the truth."

[21]George M. Marsden, *Jonathan Edwards: A Life* (New Haven: Yale University Press, 2003), 497.

[22]In *The Expositor's Greek Testament*, ed. W. Robertson Nicoll (repr., Grand Rapids: Eerdmans, 1970), III:443.

him up. On the contrary, he is firmly happy in the Lord, entirely on his own terms. That sets the tone. Then he insists that the Philippians join him in the sacred environment of gospel gladness. He has no intention of waiting to see how everything is going to turn out, in case unpleasant eventualities might veto his joy. No, the matter is already settled, because his sufferings can only add to the sacrificial offering of their faith in Christ. This is how Paul not only mortifies the natural temptation to self-pity but also reinforces the triumph of holy joy by demanding that his friends join him in his enthusiasm.

I see here not a particle of a martyr complex, isolating Paul from others; far otherwise, I see clearly, both in the main clause of verse 17 and in the rapid follow-up thought of verse 18, marked explicitly as the corollary with τὸ αὐτὸ, the poured-out life creating a community of shared joy, suffering, and worship to the greater glory of Christ. Paul is showing us how the pastoral ministry extends into the world today the continuing redemptive impact of the incarnation, suffering, death, and resurrection of the Son of God, increasing and intensifying the volume of worship rising to his honor until he returns. "For me to live is Christ" (1:21) is the key to doing all things without grumbling or questioning (2:14).

> If God is most glorified in us when we are most satisfied in him, . . . then living for the glory of God must mean that we live to gladly make others glad in God. . . . By gladly pursuing the gladness of others in God—even at the cost of our lives—we love *them* and honor *God*. This is the opposite of a wasted life.[23]

This is also the definition of a poured-out life, which is a pastor's worship. Philippians 2:17–18 proves it.

The Day the Philippians First Heard These Words
Moving now from the principial to the historical, we can reconstruct in our imaginations the key moment in Philippi when this Christ-exalting outlook came home to those who first heard these words. It is the Lord's Day in that great Macedonian city sometime in A.D. 62. During the previous week Epaphroditus has returned from Paul in Rome, with this letter from the apostle in hand. The buzz has gone around the Christian network in town, and everyone is excited to hear the letter read aloud when the church gathers for worship. They meet in Lydia's home this

---

[23]John Piper, *Don't Waste Your Life* (Wheaton, IL: Crossway, 2003), 102–3. Italics his.

Sunday, seated together throughout the inner courtyard.[24] Euodia is there, as is Syntyche, but not yet sitting together (cf. 4:2). This is a lovely but imperfect church.

As the believers gather, exchanges of greetings and small talk draw each one into the circle of fellowship. Eventually, an elder stands and welcomes them all, prays, and leads them in a hymn of praise. Then he asks Epaphroditus to step forward and join him at the front. Everyone claps and cheers, receiving him in the Lord with all joy (2:29). Epaphroditus, after giving a brief account of his journey and of Paul and his situation, relays Paul's greetings and formally presents the letter to the elders of the church. He resumes his seat. The presiding elder then reads aloud Paul's letter, which requires only about fifteen minutes—less than a typical sermon in our churches today.

As the letter is read to everyone, in rapt attention, the Holy Spirit is speaking to their hearts. They start changing, at least a little, under the ministry of this letter. They become more willing than ever before, some of them dramatically more willing, to offer themselves to God by faith as a Christlike sacrificial offering. A hush settles over that courtyard, a solemn happiness, as the Spirit imparts a wonderful sense of the glory of Christ. They are worshiping.

Paul knew this would happen. He meant it to happen. He wanted to share in it. Back in Rome, Paul is sitting in his prison cell on that same Lord's Day. He and Epaphroditus have discussed how long the return journey to Philippi may take. Paul figures that Epaphroditus is likely there by now. He goes there himself in memory and joins the meeting of his dear Philippian friends in heart and mind. Their faces—elders, deacons, members, children—pass before his mind's eye. He longs for them. He prays for them. And his deepest emotion, having years before settled the matter in his own heart that he is himself a living sacrifice—his deepest thought and feeling at this moment constitute a drink offering upon the sacrificial offering of their faith. The humility of the poured-out life has taken its rightful place of happy authority at the center of Paul's soul. The great apostle does not feel that he is the important figure around which the Philippians ought to rally. They are the important ones. Their sacrifices seem to him greater than his own. He views their daily faith with awe, as they stand firm in one spirit, striving for the gospel, not running from conflict but engaged in it, shining as lights in their world, holding fast to the word of life.

---

[24]A virtual tour of such a house is available online at http://www.youtube.com/watch?v=WCo5nA4rZag.

Paul remembers how he first met them—pagans living as pagans must. He has watched the gospel transform them into "the saints of Christ Jesus who are at Philippi" (Phil. 1:1). Though Paul has witnessed these gospel miracles over and over again around the Mediterranean world (Col. 1:6), he is always moved by the saving power of God. At this moment of quiet thought in his cell, his heart is swallowed up with a sense of privilege that he is being drawn into the only sacred and saving thing on the face of the earth. That he, a former blasphemer, persecutor, and insolent opponent (1 Tim. 1:13), is directly and personally participating in the outspreading grace of God in the world, raising up a bright new church out of the former human devastations of pagan Philippi—his sense of amazement exceeds his powers of utterance. Oh, that he would indeed be a drink offering on such a holy sacrifice! Sitting there in his prison cell that day, Paul too is worshiping, as only a pastor can. Far from this removing him from his people, he feels bound to them profoundly.

The Two Men Who Taught Me the Most about Worship
Now, if I may, I would like to say something personal to Dr. Piper. John, I have known two men who, more than others, have taught me about such worship. My dad was one; you are the other. You will remember my dad, of course, as your pastor at Lake Avenue Congregational Church during your seminary years. Dad left to me a compelling example of pastoral selflessness, humble admiration of others, cheerfully putting them first, paying a personal price for their progress and joy in the faith. But it was more than friendship on a horizontal level. It was his worship of his Savior. And my dad was the most ruggedly happy, even radiant, man I have ever seen. I know for a fact that worship was his deepest motive and intention. In the final hours of his dying day, July 22, 2007, as he lay in that hospital bed in California, God gave him the privilege of speaking patriarchal blessings and exhortations to his family gathered around. Sadly, Jani and I were ministering in Northern Ireland that day. But his final message to me, minutes before he fell asleep, was, "Tell Bud that ministry isn't everything. Jesus is." Obviously, there are tragic reasons for taking that into account. A church can and will break a pastor's heart. But there are also deeper, richer reasons why that is so. Pastoral ministry is more than caring for people. It is worship. It must be pursued as worship, because Jesus really is everything. He certainly was to my dad.

He is to you too, John. You show it. We see it. With perhaps unequaled influence, as far as I can discern, you have changed the conversation among the gospel-loving pastors of our generation and of the rising generation. You have borne a compelling witness that Christ has called us to a life of worship—above all else, worship. This sacred lifestyle of pastoral ministry calls us to embrace suffering. We are not stuck with suffering. We choose it, following Christ, because he himself is living proof that the poured-out life is the only pathway to true and everlasting joy. The Lord Jesus Christ has gone before us in this way, and we see the gloriously happy outcome in his eternal triumph. So, looking to Jesus, now we pastors know what to do. Along with others, John, you have helped me understand this with growing clarity. You have even gotten up in my face a time or two, though you may not have known it at the time. But your ministry has, by God's grace, increased the flow of the pastoral drink offerings being poured out upon the sacrificial offerings of the church's faith in our generation and the next. I know you are glad and rejoice with us, even as we are glad and rejoice with you.

A Challenge for Pastors of the Next Generation

Finally, I want to challenge you pastors of the next generation, you stallions for Christ in your twenties and thirties who are reading this essay. You have read Dr. Piper's books. You have heard him preach. You have watched him on YouTube. But realize this. He and his entire generation will soon be gone and forgotten. The stalwarts of my dad's generation are already fading quickly from view. So will Dr. Piper and I and all of us in our generation. And before you feel entirely prepared for it, the cause of the gospel will fall upon you. The baton will be placed in your hand, to run the race through the next generation. You must settle the matter of your worship right now.

So here are the questions that demand a clear answer in every generation of pastors. I ask you in the name of Jesus Christ and for his sake: Have you surrendered your life completely to your Lord and Savior, with no preconditions? Are you a living sacrifice? Or is your ministry really about you? Have you humbled yourself to the point that, for the sake of Christ, you count others more significant than yourself? Are you happy to be poured out as a drink offering upon the sacrificial offering of the church's faith? Or do you proudly scorn the church as beneath you? Do you consider her unworthy of your best? There is only one entry point into the ageless community of worship and joy: following Jesus in his humility and suffering. That community will be built up in your generation. Here is the only question. *Will you answer his call to enter in? And will you decide right now?*

Where are the young men . . . who will hold their lives cheap and be faithful even unto death? Where are those who will lose their lives for Christ's sake—flinging them away for love of him? Where are those who will live dangerously and be reckless in his service? Where are his *lovers*—those who love him and the souls of men more than their own reputations or comfort or very life? Where are the men who will say "no" to self, who take up Christ's cross to bear it after him, . . . willing, if need be, to bleed, to suffer and to die on it? . . . Where are the adventurers, the explorers, the buccaneers for God who count one human soul of far greater value than the rise or fall of an empire? . . . Where are God's men in this day of God's power?[25]

---

[25]Howard Guinness, *Sacrifice* (Chicago: InterVarsity, 1947), 59–60.

22

THE PASTOR AS COUNSELOR

David Powlison

P astor, you *are* a counselor. Perhaps you don't think of yourself that way. Perhaps you don't want to be a counselor. But you are one.

Perhaps preaching, leadership, and administration keep you preoccupied, and you do not do much hands-on pastoral work. You don't take time for serious talking with people. In effect, you are counseling your people to think that most of us don't need the give-and-take of candid, constructive conversation. Apparently, the care and cure of wayward, distractible, battered, immature souls—people like us—can be handled by public ministry and private devotion. The explicit wisdom of both Scripture and church history argues to the contrary.

Perhaps you are a poor counselor. Are you shy, tentative, passive? Are you aggressive, controlling, opinionated? Do you sympathize with strugglers so much that you have trouble shifting the conversation into forward gear? Do people feel you don't listen well and don't really care, so they don't find reasons to trust you?

Unlike the proverbs, do you moralize, unhinging advice from deeper insight and deeper reasons? "Read your Bible. . . . Just get accountable. . . . Have your quiet time. . . . Get involved in a ministry."

Unlike the psalms, are you pietistic? "Just pray and give it all to Jesus. Claim back your inheritance from Satan. Learn mindfulness and listen for the voice of God in your inner silence."

Unlike Jesus, do you speak in theological abstractions and generalities? "The Sovereignty of God. . . . Justification by faith. . . . The synergy of God's initiative and man's response in the sanctification process."

Unlike Paul—no two letters and no two sermons ever the same!—do you offer the predictable boilerplate of pat answers and pet truths?

Do you talk too much about yourself—or too little? Does your counsel sound like a self-help book? There are innumerable ways to run off the rails. But even if your counseling is ineffectual, off-putting, or harmful, you are still a counselor.

If you are a good counselor, then you're learning how to sustain with a word the one who is weary (Isa. 50:4). This is wonderful, nothing less than your Redeemer's skillful love expressed in and through you. You've learned to speak truth in love, conversing in honest, nutritious, constructive, timely, grace-giving ways (Eph. 4:15, 25, 29). You deal gently with the ignorant and wayward because you know you are more like them than different (Heb. 5:2–3). You don't only do what comes naturally, but have gained the flexibility to be patient with all, to help the weak, to comfort the fainthearted, to admonish the unruly (1 Thess. 5:14). You bring back those who wander (James 5:19–20), just as God brings you back time and again. You're engaged in meeting the most fundamental human need, both giving and receiving encouragement every day (Heb. 3:13). In becoming a better counselor, you are growing into the likeness of Jesus Christ.

Pastor, you are a counselor—and much more than a counselor. A pastor also teaches, equips, supervises, and counsels other counselors. Is your preaching worth the time you put into it and the time others spend listening? The proof lies in whether they are growing up into wise mutual counselors. That is the call and challenge of Ephesians 3:14–5:2. Hands-on pastoral counseling never means that you become the only counselor in the body of Christ. You are training Christ's people how to walk in the image of the Wonderful Counselor. This is a refreshing vision for the care and cure of souls! It is a distinctively Christian vision.

This chapter focuses on the counseling aspect of a pastor's calling. But other readers are most welcome to listen in. All human beings are counselors, whether wise, foolish, or mixed. *All* Christians are meant to become wiser counselors. God intends that *every* word you ever say to anyone is actively constructive in content, intention, tone, and appropriateness

(Eph. 4:29). Those who face *any* affliction should find you a source of tangible comfort (2 Cor. 1:4). Wisdom sets the bar high. We are to become a community in which substantial conversations predominate. You who are not pastors will grow in wisdom by considering how pastoral work particularizes the wisdom of Christ in the cure of souls wherever the body of Christ is working well.

This chapter has two parts. First, we will discuss how to understand the word *counseling* within a pastoral frame of reference. Second, we will unpack a few of the distinctives that make a pastor's counseling so unique.

What Is "Counseling"?

The psychotherapeutic conception of counseling operates in a different universe from the pastoral conception. The human problems are the same, of course: broken, confused, distressed, distressing people who need help. How should we define the "talking cure" for the ills that beset us?

A therapist's treatment typically means a private relationship confined to an appointed hour once a week. Like medicine or law, the mental health professions treat patients/clients on a fee-for-service basis. State-licensure recognizes education and experience that presumably grant esoteric explanatory insight and exceptional interventive skills. Like medical professionals, mental health professionals present themselves as possessing objective scientific knowledge and offering value-neutral technical expertise. The ostensibly healthy treat the definedly sick. A client's difficulties and distress are susceptible to diagnosis in morally neutral categories: a DSM-IV syndrome, dysfunction, or disorder.

Therapeutic professionalism serves a distinct ethos. Clinical detachment intentionally avoids the mutuality of normal social existence: willing self-disclosure, dual relationships that live outside the office as well as inside, the candid give-and-take of story, opinion, persuasion, and mutual influence. Professional reserve dictates that "the therapist will not impose or otherwise induce his personal values on the patient. . . . The exploration and acquisition of more constructive and less neurotically determined values [are] conducted without ethical or moral pressure or suasions of any kind."[1] Psychotherapeutic faith roots in "the assumption that in every human being there is a core selfhood that if allowed free and unconflicted expression would provide the basis for creative, adaptive, and productive living."[2] Religion is recognized as a factor that might be

---

[1]W. W. Meissner, "The Psychotherapies: Individual, Family, and Group," in *The Harvard Guide to Psychiatry*, ed. Armand Nicholi (Cambridge, MA: Belknap Press of Harvard University Press, 1999), 418–19.
[2]Ibid., 418.

individually compelling for some clients, either a comforting resource or an aspect of pathology. But "God" has no objective significance or necessary relevance either in explanation or treatment of dysfunctional emotions, behaviors, and thoughts.

This constellation of assumptions and expectations expresses the professional self-image of the talking-cure professions. It shapes our culture's implicit belief that psychotherapy/counseling is essentially analogous to medical doctoring. But this complex of meanings profoundly misshapes assumptions of what counseling really is and ideally ought to be. Counseling per se is not like medical doctoring. It is pastoring. It is discipling. If we want to use the physician analogy, counseling is the "bedside manner" part of doctoring, not the medical part. It expresses the influence human beings have on one another's thoughts, values, moods, expectancies, and choices. Counseling is not essentially a technical enterprise calling for technical expertise. It is a relational and pastoral enterprise engaging in care and cure of the soul. Both psycho-therapy and psych-iatry attempt pastoral work, engaging in "care and cure of the soul" as their etymologies accurately signify. Sigmund Freud rightly defined therapists as "secular pastoral workers."[3]

Personal factors—who you are, how you treat people, what you believe—are decisive in pastoral work. The key ingredients in pastoring another human being are love, wisdom, humility, integrity, mercy, authority, clarity, truth speaking, courage, candor, curiosity, hope, sane humanity, wide experience, much patience, careful listening, responsive immediacy, and willingness to live with uncertainty about process and outcome. Therapists also know this, deep down, and say as much when they doff the professional persona.[4] These are terrific personal qualities. They express nothing less than how the image of God lives in human flesh while going about the work of redeeming broken, confused, distressed, distressing people who need help. The mental health professions intuit well when they say that personal factors are the essential factors. But they serve in pastorates with no God and no church. They aim to restore straying, suffering, willful, dying human beings. But they consider Christ unnecessary to their pastoral work. As a matter of principle, they will not lead strugglers to the Savior of strays. You know better. But the secularized-medicalized definition of "counseling" powerfully intimidates

---

[3]Sigmund Freud, *The Question of Lay Analysis* (1926; repr., New York: W. W. Norton, 1969), 108.
[4]Readers interested in doing some digging will appreciate Armand Nicholi, "The Therapist-Patient Relationship," in *The Harvard Guide to Psychiatry*, 7–22. See also Peter Kramer, *Moments of Engagement* (New York: W. W. Norton, 1989), esp. 182–218; and Perry London's classic *The Modes and Morals of Psychotherapy* (New York: Holt, Rinehart & Winston, 1964).

pastors and laypersons alike. If the habits, instincts, outlook, and goals of therapeutic pastorates define "counseling," then you had better not pretend or aspire to be a counselor.

Consider four ways that you as a pastor must redefine "counseling."

For starters, if the psychotherapeutic definition controls our vision, *what pastor could ever provide the necessary care and cure of even thirty souls, let alone one hundred, five hundred, or five thousand souls? What pastor has time to get the presumably necessary secularized education?* Having labored long toward your ordination by the church, who has time or inclination to labor for a second ordination by the mental health system? What pastor could ever invest so much time in one-on-one counseling? A pastor needs a very different vision for what counseling is and can be.

Second, *what true pastor believes that the love of Christ and the will of God are value-free?* You will never say to anyone (except ironically), "You are free to discover your own values, whatever works for you, whatever way of living with yourself and others brings you a sense of personal satisfaction." God has chosen to impose his values on the entire universe. First Timothy 1:5 bluntly asserts nonnegotiable goals: "love . . . from a pure heart and a good conscience and a sincere faith." God insists on the supreme worth and glory of who he is and what he has done. God insists that self-centered people learn love—not coping skills, not self-actualization, not meeting felt needs, not techniques of managing emotions or thought life, not fulfilling personal goals. God's morally charged categories heighten human responsibility. His willing mercy and sheer grace give the only real basis for true compassion and patience. He insists that we learn love by being loved, by learning Jesus: "In this is love . . . that he loved us and sent his Son to be the propitiation for our sins" (1 John 4:10). On the last day, every knee bows to God's values.

The whole nature of ministry is to "impose" light into darkness, to induce sanity, to form Christ's life-nourishing values within us. Pastoral counseling openly brings ethical or moral suasions as expressions of genuine love that considers the actual welfare of others. The conscious intentions of Christless counselors are kindly, but they do not consider the true welfare and needs of actual human beings. A pastor has a systematically brighter vision for what counseling is all about.

Third, *what honest pastor would ever buy into the arm's-length professional reserve of the therapist?*[5] Ministry is self-disclosing by necessity

---

[5]Not all therapists buy into the reserve valued by psychodynamic psychotherapists. For example, a Virginia Satir or Albert Ellis or Fritz Perls or Steven Hayes brings a dynamic and charismatic presence into the

and as a matter of principle. After all, we follow David, Jeremiah, Jesus, and Paul. Shouts of delight along with loud cries and groaning are part of the whole package. No real pastor can be clinically detached. The Paul who wrote 1 Thessalonians 2:7–12 is far too emotionally involved. Like Jesus, he cares too much to ever stand at arm's length from people and their troubles. If Jesus had entered into purely consultative, professional relationships, he'd have had to stop being a pastor. Pastoral self-disclosure is one part of wise love. It is not self-indulgent. It is neither impulsive venting nor exhibitionistic transparency nor a pontificating of private opinions. It includes proper reserve. But Christian openness is a different ballgame from the ideal of dispassionate professionalism. Ministry expresses the honest emotional immediacy of team sports and contact sports. It is full-court basketball, not chess or poker.

How about you? Don't people know you in all sorts of other roles besides counselor?—proclaimer of words of life, friend at the dinner table, bedside visitor in the hospital, second baseman on the softball team, mere man and leader who can't help but show how he faces financial pressure or handles interpersonal conflict, object of uproarious roasting at the church retreat, public speaker who tells a good story on himself, host and landlord to the struggler staying in your spare bedroom, husband of a woman who is well known in her own right, father of kids in Sunday school, fellow sufferer who needs what he asks of God, fellow worshiper who candidly gives thanks for what he receives, fellow servant who yearns to love better than he does. You not only have a dual relationship with the people you counsel; you have multiple relationships. And that's as it should be. Christianity is a different counseling ethos.

Finally, *what good pastor could ever in good conscience adopt the ethos by which the ostensibly well presume to treat the evidently sick?* Aren't we all in this together, facing the same temptations, sorrows, and threats? Aren't we all prone to the same sinfulness? "Behavioral medicine" (as the HMOs label it) claims to cure a patient's character disorder, identity confusion, mood disorder, thought disorder, maladaptive behavior, relational dysfunction, and post-traumatic-stress syndrome. Ministry addresses the same problems, but humanizes the struggle. A dark disease deranges our character, identity, emotions, thoughts, behaviors, and relationships. A

---

counseling moment, freely expressing opinions, emotions, reactions, assertions, personal testimony. In their case, what gives them the right to so freely push their values and perspectives onto others? The more detached psychotherapists rightly see the danger of charlatanism endemic to the more intrusive psychotherapies. But the more intrusive counselors rightly see that values are induced in every form of counseling, and that a pretense of neutrality only makes that process covert. Only Christian faith embodies a principle by which values can be openly and continuously induced without either bullying or manipulation.

bright Savior sets about curing such souls. Endemic sinfulness deranges our reactions to both traumatic and everyday sufferings. Psalm 23 infuses a different way of suffering. Our derangement is fundamental, rooting in dedicated attentiveness to our own inner voice, the liar we find most persuasive—Proverbs 16:2 and 21:2. But our Pastor's voice heals us: "My sheep hear my voice" (John 10:27). Don't you have the same kinds of problems as those you minister to, and aren't our differences matters of degree not kind? Aren't you part of the same ongoing healing? Real ministry addresses deeper problems than the psychotherapies address. It goes after problems that they don't even know exist, hidden cancers that we all share, whether our symptoms are florid or mild. And any healing is *our* healing, one and all.

Where does this pastoral ethos come from? Jesus himself was touched with the weaknesses, struggles, and temptations of those with whom he spoke and for whom he died. Jesus eschews clinical detachment. He chooses frank self-disclosure and the multirelationships intrinsic to pastoral love. He was never value-neutral. He used every form of loving suasion, right down to publicly dying for those he sought to persuade.

The Uniqueness of Pastoral Counseling

We have sketched a vision for counseling as pastoral work. What does it look like? We will consider five unique aspects of the pastor as counselor. Your responsibility, opportunity, method, message, and context are each unique.

You Have a Unique Responsibility to Counsel

You must counsel. It's not optional. You can't say no as if it were simply a career choice, a matter of personal preference, or an absence of gifting. This does not mean that every pastor will have the same balance between public and private aspects of ministry. How much you'll formally counsel (i.e., meet with particular persons at agreed-on times) depends on many factors. Some pastors will do a great deal of hands-on cure of souls, some relatively little. But every pastor ought to dedicate some percentage of his ministry to the delicate art of intentional conversation, as well as being continually on the lookout for the informal opportunities latent in every human interaction.[6]

A pastor's calling to counsel is significantly different from any of the other counseling professions. We'll consider several aspects of this uniqueness.

---

[6]For discussion of how much time a pastor should give to counseling and the sorts of people to whom he should give himself, see "Pastoral Counseling," in David Powlison, *Speaking Truth in Love* (Greensboro, NC: New Growth, 2005), 127–32.

Your Call to Personal Ministry Is Woven into All the Scriptures
Many passages express the significance of hands-on cure of souls. The classic texts include Acts 20:20; Galatians 6:1–2; Ephesians 3:14–5:2; 1 Thessalonians 5:17; Hebrews 3:12–14; 10:24–25; and scores of other "one-anothering" passages. In fact, every place that addresses the specific concerns of a named individual can be considered a counseling passage. A pastor's counseling responsibility is unique. What other counselor is called by God himself both to counsel and to train others to counsel! Briefly consider three passages.

The Second Great Commandment says, "Love your neighbor as yourself." Love engages your neighbor's specific personal needs and struggles. Love encompasses many things: attitudes of patience and kindness; actions that meet material needs and offer a helping hand. And love includes honest conversation about what matters. Interestingly, the original context for the command (Lev. 19:17–18) makes a personal counseling illustration and application: "You shall not hate your brother in your heart, but you shall reason frankly with your neighbor, lest you incur sin because of him. You shall not take vengeance or bear a grudge against the sons of your own people, but you shall love your neighbor as yourself: I am the Lord."

God chooses to go after one of the most difficult of all matters: how will you love kith and kin in their shortcomings? Love of neighbor is illustrated by an example of candid, verbal problem solving, in contrast with the judgmentalism, avoidance, bitterness, and aggression that come so easily. You yourself act on this command by doing personal pastoring with your neighbors. Whenever their problems involve interpersonal conflict, you will also help those you counsel to learn constructive, verbal love. What a promise you have! "I am the Lord" (gracious, compassionate, slow to anger, abounding in steadfast love and faithfulness, forgiving . . . while honestly reckoning intransigence). Personal pastoring depends on this God, and then lives out the very image of this God amid the exigencies of helping broken people. You live out what is inside that last parenthesis. Exodus 34:6–7 displays the goodness and glory of God . . . and goodness and glory are communicable attributes, the image of Jesus forming in us.

Conversational love takes many other forms as well. You will ask: How are you really doing? Would you like to talk? How can I pray for you? Where are the pressure points? What are your joys and your sorrows? Any secret gardens? Conscious struggles? Delightful victories? How are you doing with God and with your nearest and dearest? What burdens are weighing on you? When you did/said_____, what were you after? How are you processing anxiety, anger, or escapism? How are you handling this wonderful achievement or blessing? In asking and answering such questions, we enter each other's lives. These are doors for grace, because these are the places Jesus meets people. As a pastor, your most obvious neighbors (beyond family) are the flock for which you have personal responsibility. "Love your neighbor as yourself" calls you to counsel.

Second, consider the Proverbs as a whole. It's not wrong to preach from Proverbs. Wisdom herself calls out in the streets, inviting all comers to listen (Proverbs 8–9). But you must *counsel* from Proverbs. Verbal wisdom is highly esteemed, and most of what Proverbs commends reads as warmly personalized individual counsel: like a father, like a wife and mother, like a true friend, like a good king, like any wise person. Wisdom is a counseling gift. When it comes to distributing this most valuable, life-renewing gift, God's generosity is blind to differences of gender, ethnicity, age, wealth, status, or education. Surely he will not lavish the desirable gift of counseling skill only to everyone else in the body of Christ, while leaving out pastors! You are called to become one of the wise men.

Finally, consider the Pastoral Epistles. Paul's letters to Timothy, Titus, and Philemon are examples of personal counseling captured on paper for all time. Each is addressed to a named individual, discusses particular circumstances, considers specific strengths and weaknesses, builds on the actual relationship between counselor and counseled. As counselor, Paul is tender, knowledgeable, self-disclosing, pointed, relevant, encouraging, challenging. Can you legitimately preach on what amounts to a personal counseling text? Of course. But would you only preach on a personal pastoring text and not also do personal pastoring? Pastor, the Pastoral Epistles call you to pastor.

You Are Called to Do the Impossible
It is curiously comforting to know that your calling is beyond your capability. This is another way that a pastor's call to counsel is unique. You can place no confidence in your gifts, experience, education, techniques, professional persona, credentials, maturity, wisdom. You are called to do what God must do.

In 1 Timothy 4:6–16, Paul exhorts Timothy, "Immerse yourself in revealed truth, in a life of faith, in active love, in the work of ministry, in serving Jesus Christ. Exercise, devote, practice, persist. Watch closely over yourself and what you teach." Why does Paul so carefully drive this home? The reason is astonishing: "By so doing you will save both yourself and your hearers" (v. 16) Come again? You will *save* yourself and your hearers? It's so. Who is sufficient for such things? God alone saves from death, from sin, from tears, from weakness, from ourselves. Christ alone saves by grace, mercy, and patience at immediate personal cost (1 Tim. 1:14–16). The Spirit alone cures the soul of suicidal selfishness, making a person and a people alive to faith and love. Yet this great and good Physician willingly uses Timothy, a mere pastor, as a physician's assistant in the curing process. He also uses you.

It is hard to shepherd souls, to combat intricate moral evil, to help people walk through pain and anguish. Gregory the Great called it the art of arts in his great treatise on pastoral care.[7] He thought the task of guiding souls far more difficult than the tasks performed by a mere medical doctor. Think about that. The body is relatively accessible. It is often explicable by cause-and-effect reasoning and treatable by medication or surgery. But the "more delicate art deals with what is unseen,"[8] the irrational madness in our hearts (Jer. 17:9; Eccles. 9:3). When you consider the challenge, how is it that most churchly counseling seems slapdash, pat answer, and quick fix? A good MD spends a lifetime in acquiring case-wise acumen. A mature psychotherapist pursues continuing education. Can a pastor be content with one-size-fits-all boilerplate? *Kyrie eleison*. People are not served when the Christian life is portrayed as if some easy answer will do—a pet doctrine, religious strategy, involvement in a program, spiritual experience—and presto!, case solved. Again, hear Gregory's words: "One and the same exhortation is not suited to all, because they are not compassed by the same quality of character. . . . In exhorting individuals great exertion is required to be of service to each individual's particular needs."[9] A pastor's work is the art of arts.

You Are Called to Do Something So Simple Only a Christian Can Do It

Hearts may be unsearchable and insane, but the Word of God reveals the thoughts and intentions of the heart (Heb. 4:12–13). My self-righteous reaction to criticism may be an unsearchable morass of iniquity, but I can learn to name it for what it is, to turn for needed mercies, to seek and find the God who humbles me. We can come to know ourselves truly (though never wholly). Similarly, though the purposes and intentions of another's heart are deep water, a man of understanding draws it out (Prov.

---

[7]St. Gregory the Great, *Pastoral Care*, trans. Henry Davis (591; repr., New York: Newman, 1950), 21 (1.1).
[8]Ibid., 229.
[9]Ibid., 89, 226.

20:5). You can learn what you need to know. Though you have no privileged access into any soul, though every strategy or truth can be resisted, though you have no power to open blind eyes or to make deaf ears listen, God uses your ministry to cure souls. Human beings are idiosyncratic in every detail, yet there is no temptation that is not common to all; you can comfort others in any affliction with the comfort that you receive in your particular affliction (1 Cor. 10:13; 2 Cor. 1:4). Fundamental unities make us comprehensible enough to significantly help each other. These are things a mere Christian can do.

Dietrich Bonhoeffer was raised in a sophisticated, modern psychological culture, and his father was a psychiatrist. Like all educated Germans, Bonhoeffer thoroughly absorbed the psychological models and psychotherapeutic practices of the great twentieth-century psychiatrists. But he had this to say about the knowledge and wisdom that make the decisive difference:

> The most experienced psychologist or observer of human nature knows infinitely less of the human heart than the simplest Christian who lives beneath the Cross of Jesus. The greatest psychological insight, ability and experience cannot grasp this one thing: what sin is. Worldly wisdom knows what distress and weakness and failure are, but it does not know the godlessness of man. And so it does not know that man is destroyed only by his sin and can be healed only by forgiveness. Only the Christian knows this. In the presence of a psychiatrist I can only be a sick man; in the presence of a Christian brother I can dare to be a sinner. The psychiatrist must first search my heart and yet he never plumbs its ultimate depth. The Christian brother knows when I come to him: here is a sinner like myself, a godless man who wants to confess and yearns for God's forgiveness. The psychiatrist views me as if there were no God. The brother views me as I am before the judging and merciful God in the Cross of Jesus Christ.[10]

You might want to read that again, slowly—I speak as someone prone to skim block quotes. As a Christian brother to those you counsel, you know depths that other counselors cannot and will not see. You can go where they never go. You can bring the Savior of the world.

Where Ministry Is Strong, Pastors Practice in Private What They Preach in Public

Your calling uniquely combines public and private ministry. The Christian message preaches well to crowds. The Christian message converses

---

[10]Dietrich Bonhoeffer, *Life Together and Prayerbook of the Bible*, Dietrich Bonhoeffer Works, vol. 5 (Minneapolis: Fortress, 1996), 115.

well with individuals. Preaching and counseling stand in a complementary relationship, and no other kind of counselor does both. A pastor's working vocabulary and intentional activity must counsel the Word as well as preach the Word.

Of course, up-front proclamation and in-private conversation bring the message home in very different ways. A talk is relatively planned, scripted, and structured. It usually involves one-way communication—though Jesus did have a way of flexing his message after an outburst from the crowd, or launching a message based on a question someone was asking! In a sermon, you usually have a rough idea what you'll say next and where you'll end up. But giving a talk is different from the give-and-take of just talking. Conversations are extemporaneous, improvised, unpredictable, back and forth, messy—even when you come with a game plan. You never know what a person will say next. Since what you say is usually a response, you almost never know what you'll say next. It's a bad sign when either party reverts to boilerplate, delivering a set piece or shtick. Counseling usually starts with immediate, troubling experience, and moves toward the God whose person, words, and actions bring light. In contrast, preaching usually moves from Bible exposition toward life application. The two aspects of ministry demand different, but complementary, skill sets. The Lord and his prophets and apostles move freely in both directions. Pastors need the complete skill set.

The church has a long tradition of well-reasoned practical theology and skillful pastoral care. Like any legacy of art and wisdom, without continual use and updating, ideas become cobwebbed, applications get out of date, and skills are forgotten. Several factors internal to the church blind our eyes to the pointed counseling implications of Christian faith. Among those who take Scripture seriously, ecclesiastical habits focus almost exclusively on the pastor as public proclaimer, team leader, and administrator. Skill in cure of individual souls is optional—and sometimes is even discouraged as a waste of time. These assumptions structure seminary education, ordination requirements, job descriptions, role models, and the priorities of actual church practice. They shape the illustrations used in books about ministry, the relative dearth of books on how to counsel biblically, and the common associations that treat the phrase "ministry of the Word" as synonymous with "the pulpit."

In your preparation and testing to become a pastor, perhaps no one ever said that firsthand understanding of people and firsthand skill in counseling are essential aspects of your pastoral calling. But it must be said and taken to heart.

You Already Are a Counselor—All the Time

A pastor is unavoidably a public person. Other people are always reading you, taking cues from you, sizing you up. Unlike other counselors, in an essential way your work life is not spent out of sight in an office behind a closed door. Whether in casual interaction, a called meeting, or public worship, your attitudes, core values, and functional beliefs are continually on display. Other people listen, learn, watch, and decide whether to tune you in or tune you out. The fact that you are not hidden is a unique aspect of your pastoral calling.

People know how you treat people. They know (or have an inkling) if you are honest (or dishonest). They know if you are kind (or indifferent, even unkind). They know if you are wise (or foolish). They know how you handle (or mishandle) the pressures of life. They know if you are humble (or proud). They know if you care (or couldn't care less). They know if you want their welfare in God's kingdom (or if you are building a kingdom for your ego). They know (or have a fairly good idea) if you are a good counselor (or a busybody, a pontificator, a slacker, a pat-answer man). They know if you are the real deal (or a religious role player). Since you fall short, they intuit your flaws already. They have some inkling of how you handle your failings and how you'll handle theirs. Are you honest with yourself before God, a person who finds the grace and mercy of Jesus? They know (or have an inkling) because you are not a professional counselor isolated in an office and self-protected by clinical detachment. You live, move, and have your being in public space. If you fail the test, they won't seek you out, and they'll be guarded when you seek them out. If you pass, your counseling will gain a power for good that is unimaginable to other counselors.

It is daunting to know that your sins miscounsel others. Richard Baxter famously observed, "I publish to my own flock the distempers of my own soul."[11] He warned of the danger that "you unsay with your lives what you say with your tongues."[12] But it is a corresponding delight to know that God uses your honest faith and love to publicly counsel others, so that both publicly and privately you might bring others under the sweet rule of his voice.

If You and the Church Don't Do Counseling, Who Will?

It is unique to your calling that it matters whether or not people find help in the church. Psychotherapists want to make a living, but in principle,

---

[11]Richard Baxter, *The Reformed Pastor* (1656; repr., Edinburgh: Banner of Truth, 1974), 61 (1.1.2).
[12]Ibid., 63 (1.1.3).

as a professional courtesy, they are just as happy to have a struggler go to anyone else for help, even if another practitioner operates with a very different counseling philosophy. But the church must not give over the care and cure of troubled souls to other voices. Those voices may be well intended, but when they try to fix "with God" problems using a "without God" message, you have a problem. The fear of the Lord is the beginning of wisdom. Consciousness of God is the starting point, the system-aligning principle, the architectonic prerequisite for making good sense of life. When friends, family, coworkers, the mass media, self-help books, or psychotherapeutic professionals ignore reality, they inevitably miscounsel. In Jeremiah's metaphor, they heal wounds lightly, "saying, 'Peace, peace,' when there is no peace" (Jer. 8:11). I will say it again. Pastors must not hand over care and cure of souls to other voices. Any number of people, paid and unpaid, are more than willing to do your work for you.

You Have Unique Opportunities to Counsel
Pastoral counseling is unlike any other form of counseling because of the many unusual opportunities a pastor has to engage lives. Here are seven unique facets of the pastoral life that open doors.

You Have Opportunity to Pursue People
Jesus Christ goes looking for people. He takes the initiative in loving. Even when people sought him out with their sufferings and sins, they were responding to what they'd heard about who he was, what he said, how he cared, and what he could do. In a fundamental way, our Redeemer always makes the first move, and his entire modus operandi is active. The Good Shepherd goes after "the one that is lost, until he finds it" (Luke 15:4). Good shepherds do likewise, creating counseling opportunities. You can ask, "How are you really doing?" or "How may I pray for you?" in any context. The person's answer, whether candid or evasive, can become an opportunity for a significant conversation. When you hear that someone is facing trouble or going through a hard patch, you can stop by to care.

In contrast, all other counseling models are passive, responding rather than initiating. Psychotherapists must wait until a troubled person seeks aid or a troublesome person is referred by a concerned third party. But a pastor pursues, and people respond in a unique way to being actively loved.

You Have Opportunity in Crucial Life Situations
You have natural access into people's lives at decisive moments of transition, hardship, and joy. They invite you in. You have license to simply show up. The door is open to you whenever important events unfold:

- engagement and marriage
- injury, illness, and hospitalization
- dying, death, bereavement, and funeral
- birth of a baby
- moving into a new neighborhood
- loss of a job or retirement
- betrayal, adultery, and divorce
- a child on drugs or in trouble with the law
- catastrophic victimization by house fire, crime, or storm

No other counselor has natural access at the most significant moments.

It so happens that these events are the major stressors on every stress scale. It also happens that the inner reality of a person becomes more obvious and more accessible in exactly such circumstances. Is he living for true hopes or false? Are her fears realistic or distorted? Are their joys and sorrows appropriate, inordinate, or oddly absent? What do these insecurities or angers reveal? Where is this confusion coming from? The heart lies open. Furthermore, it so happens that people become unusually open to seeking and receiving counsel at exactly such times.

Consider one example. God says, "set your hope fully on the grace that will be brought to you at the revelation of Jesus Christ" (1 Pet. 1:13). Those are nice-sounding words, pleasant to repeat. But when the heat is on, previously covert false hopes show up in high-definition video and audio. You have a counseling moment, and life-changing reorientation can occur. The combination of high significance, strong feeling, and unusual openness means that you have privileged access into the God-sent circumstances when people can grow up in faith and love.

You Have Opportunity with Both the Struggling and the Strong
Biblical ministry is not only for troubled or troublesome people. Pastoral care serves both weak and strong, able and disabled, talented and limited, successful and failing. The gospel speaks life-rearranging truth into every person's life, "comforting the disturbed and disturbing the comfortable." Those whose lives overflow need to learn gratitude, humility, generosity— and alertness to temptations of presumption, superiority, and pride. Those whose lives run on empty need to learn hope, courage, patience—and alertness to temptations of despair, grumbling, and covetousness. All of us need to learn what lasts and what counts, whatever our conditions of life. All of us need to learn to comfort others with the comfort we receive from God. The Vinedresser's pruning shears are in every life. As a pastor you understand that every person you meet today needs to awaken, to

turn, to trust, to grow, to love God and others. Everyone needs counseling every day (Heb. 3:12–14). Even God's thriving children need counsel (and counseling training) in order to better help their struggling brethren who are straying, discouraged, or helpless (1 Thess. 5:14).

No other counseling role has a vision for everybody. Other counseling models define some class of human beings as needing help, and others as essentially okay. Christian faith defines every human being as needing the cure of soul that is a pastor's unique calling.

You Have Opportunity with Both Rich and Poor

A pastor has a huge advantage over other counselors in that the counseling relationship is founded on loving concern, not fee for service. Pastoral counseling is a gift to the needy. It is funded by free-will offerings of the people of God, whether or not they are counsel seekers. Broken and distressed people rightly wonder about professional counselors, "Do you really care? Are you really my friend?" The gift of ministry takes off the table questions about divided or suspect motives. The exchange of money for time, care, attention, and friendship always brings a high potential for warping a relationship.

In contrast, a pastor has great freedom to work. With people who have money, you are in the unusual position of not allowing them to buy the services they want. With people who lack money, you are in the unusual position of not excluding them from receiving the help they need. A pastor is uniquely able to incarnate God's freely given mercies and wisdom. Counseling is caring candor (Eph. 4:15). When no fee is involved, your care is less ambiguous and your candor less constrained.

It makes a great difference that you come free. When the tithes and offerings of many people underwrite how the church meets counseling needs, it creates the best of all possible delivery systems for care and cure.

You Have Opportunity with People Who Already Trust You

What is the first issue in every counseling conversation? Though it is rarely verbalized, every person who sits down to talk with someone is always asking: "Why should I trust you? . . . Are you giving me good reason to trust you? . . . Do I trust you?" If the bottom-line answer is yes, the conversation might head somewhere constructive. Basic trust leads to two further questions that also determine the success or failure of the conversation: "Can I be completely honest with you?" and, then, "Will I listen to what you say to me?"

Of course, questions of trust, willing honesty, and willingness to listen are often worked out gradually. But it is a unique aspect of pastoral work that you will counsel people who have already decided to trust you. They come committed to be honest and willing to listen. This trust arises because you are a known quantity. Preanswering these questions in the affirmative gives an incalculable boost to the efficacy and efficiency of your counseling. You don't need to spend months building trust. You can cut to the chase, because counsel seekers cut to the chase.

The fact that you are known and trusted also means you'll be the first person that others seek out to talk over their problems. They will be honest about the most delicate things: grave sins, deep fears, heartbreak, disappointment, fragile aspirations, underlying confusion. Otherwise unspeakable matters find words where there is trust. After you have listened well to these most vulnerable utterances—quick to hear, careful to ponder, slow to speak—you also find that people listen to you if your words are kind, illuminating, and true. What comes to the light can become light.

Other counselors rarely enjoy this privilege, but you may find it is a regular occurrence.

You Have Opportunity with People You Already Know

Not only do others know and trust you, but you know them. For you as a pastor, this creates another unique opportunity. If you've made any kind of effort, you already know your people. You are continually getting to know them better. Such firsthand knowledge gives you an incalculable advantage over the office-bound professional counselor. You know people by name, personality, and life context. You've seen them in action. You already have a sense for strengths and weaknesses, besetting sins and flourishing graces, good habits and bad. How does a man treat his family? Does this woman pitch in to help? Is this a man who keeps his word or have you learned to wait and see what he does? What is her reaction when she faces frustration, hardship, and conflict? How does he talk about the blessings he receives? How does she worship? You may know significant history and circumstances. You may know someone's family. You have natural access to many involved parties.

Wide-ranging knowledge helps protect you from some of the pitfalls that beset counselors. For example, counselors often hear only one side of any story. They are always vulnerable to spin and disinformation—facts and reactions may be true and plausible as far as they go, but may steadily mislead and prevent accurate, balanced assessment. Given various instincts of our fallen hearts, counselors are easily tempted to side with whomever they happen to be counseling (Prov. 18:17). When an aggrieved twenty-five-year-old paints her mother as a monster, is it so? Perhaps. But if you happen to know both mother and daughter, you may have more nuanced insight into what's going on. The fact that you may already know people and know them in context is a unique strength of the pastoral setting for counseling ministry.

No other counselor has a regular opportunity to get both a head start and a reality check on what you hear in private conversation.

You Have Opportunity with People Who Already Have a Wise Change Agenda

Not only do people know you and you know them, but as a pastor you will counsel people who already have a pretty good idea of what's wrong and of where they need to grow. Such upfront acuity is never guaranteed, but when it happens, it gives your counseling another huge head start.

We mentioned earlier the basic questions of trust, willingness to be honest, and willingness to listen. The next watershed question in all counseling concerns agenda: "Why are we here? What are we aiming to accomplish?" In general, most counsel seekers come with defective goals:

- "Change how I feel."
- "Change my circumstances."
- "Vindicate me."
- "Give me a formula."

Counseling with any modicum of wisdom works patiently to change that agenda into "Help me to change." Christian faith and ministry flesh out the change agenda in a particularly rich way. "Help me to change, both inwardly and outwardly. Let me see where I run astray. Let me grasp how Christ's grace and truth actually connect to my struggles. Help me learn how to turn to God, how to trust, how to love. Help me take refuge in the Lord. I need to set my hopes on what is indestructible, rather than pursuing obsessive schemes for earthly joy. Help me see more clearly how I contribute to conflict and alienation. I need forgiveness. Help me to forgive and constructively love my enemies." It's a counselor's dream whenever a person comes with such an agenda already more or less operative. If your church has any clear-thinking vitality, you'll sometimes—often?—counsel people who already have a feel for what's really at stake. Even having a roughly accurate agenda makes a big difference.

Good public ministry, robust small groups, meaningful friendships, and relevant private devotion form people who already know the framework of reality. They know the contours of the soul's struggles. They know something of how God connects. But all of us need help connecting the dots. We always need help overcoming the contradictions between what we know and how we live. Those you counsel need the wonderful surprises that always come when an honest seeker sits down for a patient, probing conversation with a wise pastor.

No other counselor gets regular opportunities to work with people who already have an inkling of what they most need.

Like your responsibility to cure souls, your opportunities are unique. I hope this vision thrills you. I hope it nerves you for the long fight to bring pastoral achievement closer to pastoral aspiration.

The Way You Do Counseling Is Unique

From a distance, it looks as if most counselors do the same things. They talk with people experiencing some sort of trouble. The conversation focuses on the concerns of the troubled party. Would-be helpers demonstrate kind and constructive intentions. They ask questions, elicit personal honesty, listen attentively. They give feedback intended to illuminate, challenge, give hope, reorient, affect, or redirect. Troubled people who take the conversation to heart and act on it experience some alteration of mood, thought, or action. But apparent similarities are like similarities between different religions. When you get up close, you realize profound systematic differences.

Your counseling methods are unique. Your line of questioning moves in atypical directions. Your interpretation of the etiology/causality of problems takes the conversation to places no one else goes. Your self-disclosure and proper reserve obey a different set of principles, reveal a different set of purposes. You bear witness to the testimony of God himself, who made, sustains, judges, and saves. You act as physician's assistant, not the Great Physician. That affects a conversation in countless details of tone and content. The image you have of your calling as a counselor—pastor-shepherd, minister-servant, responsible brother, peer in the body of Christ, fellow sinner and sufferer needing a Savior—subtly and openly affects everything that happens.[13] This section could be book-length, but I will highlight only one unique aspect of how you approach the art of arts: *You pray with and for those you counsel.*

Do you realize how unusual this is? Have you ever considered how significant it is that you pray as a matter of course, while other counselors don't pray? The designated psychotherapists in our culture—psychiatrists,

---

[13]For a discussion of how the counselor's role is conceived both in Christian ministry and in secular psychotherapies, see my "Familial Counseling: The Paradigm for Counselor-Counselee Relationships in 1 Thessalonians 5," *Journal of Biblical Counseling* 25, no. 1 (Winter 2007): 2–16.

clinical psychologists, social workers, licensed professional counselors, marriage and family therapists, etc.—in principle do not pray with and for people.[14] This lacuna in their practice signifies that they believe no outside help is needed, wanted, or available. They and those they counsel presumably possess everything they might need for making sense of problems and choosing to live fruitfully. The answers lie within the individual, combined with a supportive, insightful, and practical therapist, perhaps with a boost from psychoactive medication.

You as a pastor do not believe that an explanation and cure of human difficulties can leave out the active intentional heart that is always loving either the true God or something else. Only an outside agent can turn a wandering heart into an attentive heart. A true cure of the soul can't ignore the active malice of the deceiver, enemy, and slave master of souls. In the fog of war, who will help you see clearly? Wisdom does not suppress knowledge of the living God. Who will deliver us from evil? When you and those you counsel lack wisdom, who will give what is needed? You need and want available help. Therefore, you pray with and for others. Teaching others to voice honest believing prayers is one prime counseling goal. You pray because people need forgiveness for their sins—you cannot grant that. They need a Shepherd who will never leave them—you are not that person. They need the power that raised Jesus from the dead—so do you. They need the hope of the resurrection, that one day all tears will be wiped away and all sins washed away—you share the same necessity. They need faith-working-through-love to become truer in their lives, to run deeper, to take hold of everything.

- You pray for people before you sit down to talk.
- You pray inwardly while you are talking.
- You pray with people as an appropriate aspect of the conversation.
- You pray for people after you say goodbye.

Your way of counseling is unique.

You Counsel a Unique Message
The uniqueness of your message is easy to see. But you already know this. I won't rehearse the unsearchable riches of Christ, or the ten thousand pertinent implications.

---

[14]The odd counselor, out of personal religious convictions, might walk out of step with the professional ethos, and step out of role. But as a rule, there is no prayer.

But I do want to note the uniqueness of your message by contrast. Every counselor brings a message: an interpretation of problems, a theory that weighs causalities and context, a proposal for cure, a goal that defines thriving humanness. How does your message compare with their messages? Simply consider what our culture's other counselors do *not* say.

- They never mention the God who has a name: YHWH, Father, Jesus, Spirit, Almighty, Savior, Comforter.
- They never mention that God searches every heart, that every human being will bow to give final account for each thought, word, deed, choice, emotion, belief, and attitude.
- They never mention sinfulness and sin, that humankind obsessively and compulsively transgress against God.
- They never mention that suffering is meaningful within God's purposes of mercy and judgment.
- They never mention Jesus Christ. He is a standing insult to self-esteem and self-confidence, to self-reliance, to self-salvation schemes, to self-righteousness, to believing in myself.
- They never mention that God really does forgive sins.
- They never mention that the Lord is our refuge, that it is possible to walk through the valley of the shadow of death and fear no evil.
- They never mention that biological factors and personal histories exist within the providence and purposes of the living God, that nature and nurture locate moral responsibility but do not trump responsible intentionality.
- They never mention our propensity to return evil for evil, how hardships tempt us to grumbling, anxiety, despair, bitterness, inferiority, and escapism.
- They never mention our propensity to return evil for good, how felicities tempt us to self-trust, ingratitude, self-confidence, entitlement, presumption, superiority, and greed.
- They never mention that human beings are meant to become conscious worshipers, bowing down in deep sense of personal need, lifting up hands to receive the gifts of the body and blood of Christ, lifting voices in heartfelt song.
- They never mention that human beings are meant to live missionally, using God-given gifts to further God's kingdom and glory.
- They never mention that the power to change does not lie within us.

In other words, they always counsel true to their core convictions.

As a pastor, you mention all these things, or you are no pastor. Even more, you are never content merely to mention or list such realities, as if a troubled person simply needed the bare bones of didactic instruction. Like a skilled musician, you develop a trained ear. In every detail of every person's story, you learn to hear the music of these unmentioned realities. You help others hear what is actually playing. A relevant, honest pastoral conversation teaches another person how to listen, and then how to join the song. Need I say more? No one else is listening to what you hear. No one else is saying what you have to say. No one else is singing what you believe. No one else is giving to others what you have been given that you might freely give. Every person who needs counseling actually needs your unique message.

You Counsel in a Unique Community Context

As a pastor, you counsel within the church. That doesn't just mean that your office is located in a different building from other counseling offices. Your setting contains unique potentials. God intends that churches serve as schools of counseling wisdom. You serve a congregation of potential members of the pastoral care team. Furthermore, every person whom you successfully counsel becomes in some way a better counselor of others. I've witnessed this development hundreds of times.

Other kinds of counselors operate as private professionals in an office or as members of a treatment team in a quasi-medical institution. But therapists sometimes dream that counseling services might become truly community-based. For example, Sigmund Freud dreamt that psychoanalytically trained community workers would fan out into every community to offer their services.[15] Over the past century many thoughtful psychiatrists and psychotherapists have candidly recognized the limitations of office-based professional practice and have longed for community-based "mental health services." It makes all the sense in the world, given that people's problems play out in the home, in the workplace, on the street, amid the relationships, exigencies, and contingencies of daily life. But secular counselors have been almost powerless to realize their dream of what is needed to get the job done.

You are living their dream.

You work within the ideal community context. The church's DNA includes wise counseling in daily life by people who already know and love each other. Troubled people find meaning and relationship in a natural

---

[15]Freud, *The Question of Lay Analysis*, 98–99.

social context, and people who find meaning and relationship are no longer troubled. The body of Christ is the ideal home for counseling practice.

I'm not denying that our churches fall short of this sweet dream—far short. When it comes to handling problems well and wisely, church can seem more like a coma, a sleepless night, or a nightmare. But our failures as the church always stand next to Ephesians 4. The dream will come true. Community-based counseling practice is in our eschatology as well as our DNA. Your task right now is simply to take the next step in the right direction.

I will close with a final perspective on your unique community setting. You stand in a tradition of pastoral care reaching back through centuries. Wise Christians have come before you. Set out to learn from your brethren.

Every pastor will profit by reading Gregory the Great's *Pastoral Care*, written almost fifteen hundred years ago. We may have better hermeneutics, wider doctrinal understanding, and more awareness of the richness of the gospel of Jesus. But Gregory has more awareness of "the Truth in person," more case-wisdom, more flexibility in adapting to human differences, more sense of pastoral responsibility, more humility about his achievements, more alertness to the subtlety of sin. Stand on his shoulders.

Every pastor will profit from reading Richard Baxter's *The Reformed Pastor*. Baxter is dense, and, like all old books, dated. You won't do ministry in the same way he did. But if you sit with Baxter, you will become a wiser pastor. Similarly, every pastor will profit from reading Thomas Oden's *Pastoral Counsel*[16] and Dietrich Bonhoeffer's *Life Together*. Oden's digest of ancient wisdom will introduce you to wise pastors you never knew existed. Your church history class likely explored the development of doctrine and events in church politics. Oden explores how pastors pastored. Bonhoeffer's twentieth-century wisdom and example will inform and nerve you as you take up your unique counseling calling. Every pastor would also profit from carefully pondering Alan Paton's *Cry, the Beloved Country* and Marilynne Robinson's *Gilead*. Why fiction? In both books, the protagonist is a pastor, and you will learn how Christian life and ministry work on the inside amid the untidy details of life lived.

Of course, I think that every pastor profits by reading and hearing teachers in the contemporary resurgence of biblical counseling. Ministry never simply recovers wise nuggets from the past. Pastoral theology undertakes fresh work. Current writers address questions and problems the church has

---

[16]Thomas C. Oden, *Classical Pastoral Care*, vol. 3, *Pastoral Counsel* (Grand Rapids: Baker, 1987).

never before addressed, or has never addressed in quite such a fine-grained way. Not all of it will stand the tests of time, ministry, and Scripture. You will become part of the winnowing of wheat from chaff.

Finally, in a book honoring the ministry of John Piper, it is fitting to close by commending to you an article from Piper himself: "God's Glory Is the Goal of Biblical Counseling." He writes eloquently of how your life and your counseling must express the faith that you preach. He shows how you must involve the body of Christ in this calling to counsel, because perseverance in faith is, always has been, and always will be a community project. "According to Hebrews, perseverance of the saints is a community project, therefore we need biblical counseling as the lifeblood of church life. . . . Perseverance is a community project. I say it again, because this is the reason counseling *must* be in the church."[17] O pastor, your responsibility, your opportunities, your methods, your message, and your context are unique because perseverance of faith in Christ is, always has been, and always will be a community project.

---

[17]John Piper, "God's Glory Is the Goal of Biblical Counseling," *Journal of Biblical Counseling* 20, no. 2 (Winter 2002): 13, 17, available online at ccef.org/goal-of-biblical-counseling.

23

THE PASTOR AS SHEPHERD

Mark Dever

omeone has well described "superpastor":

Superpastor is always available to everyone and accomplishes great
things but always has time to stop and talk and never misses anyone's
birthday and if you are sick he's at the hospital and you can call him at home
whenever you need advice and he loves meetings and spends hours studying
and praying and yet you can interrupt him if you need something—did I
mention he always puts his family first?[1]

A more realistic picture comes from the novel *Gilead*. The protagonist
is an elderly pastor in Iowa who writes out his life so that his young son
will know him when he grows up. This pastor reflects:

I get much more respect than I deserve. This seems harmless enough in most
cases. People want to respect the pastor and I'm not going to interfere with
that. But I've developed a great reputation for wisdom by ordering more
books than I ever had time to read, and reading more books, by far, than
I learned anything useful from, except, of course, that some very tedious

---

[1] Rob Bell, *Velvet Elvis* (Grand Rapids: Zondervan, 2005), 115.

gentlemen have written books. This is not a new insight, but the truth of it is something you have to experience to fully grasp. . . . Often enough when someone saw the light burning in my study long into the night, it only meant I had fallen asleep in my chair. My reputation is largely the creature of the kindly imagining of my flock, whom I chose not to disillusion.[2]

Ah, the life of the pastor! What really is a pastor? When I introduce myself as a pastor, people most often hear that as simply preacher. And preaching is certainly my most important single function as a pastor. But it's inaccurate as a summary of the whole role of the pastor.

Some ignorance about pastors today is because the role has increasingly been so modified in churches that it bears little resemblance to the kindly white-haired pastor many of us grew up watching. George Barna wrote a few years ago that this traditional idea of a pastor is "rapidly losing ground."[3] However accurate Barna may be in his reading of trends, I don't think we're going to see pastors vanishing. In Scripture they are a regular part of the church, and therefore we should expect to see them in churches that are self-consciously subservient to the Bible.

So what is this pastor? David Wells has observed that changing patterns in church life often obscure the biblical role of pastor from our view:

Across much of evangelicalism, but especially in the market-driven churches, one . . . sees a new kind of leadership among pastors now. Gone is the older model of the scholar-saint, one who was as comfortable with books and learning as with the aches of the soul. This was the shepherd who knew the flock, knew how to tend it, and Sunday by Sunday took that flock into the treasures of God's Word. This has changed. In its place is the new "celebrity" style. What we typically see now, Nancy Pearcey suggests, is the leader who works by manipulating the feelings of the audience, enhancing his own image with personal anecdotes, modeling himself after the CEO, and adopting a domineering management style. He (usually) is completely results-oriented, pragmatic, happy to employ any technique from the secular world that will produce the desired results. And this leader has to be magnetic, entertaining, and light on the screen up front.[4]

Is this what a pastor is to be? It's important for Christians to be clear on this. It is worth your while to work to better understand your pastor or your elders. I hope that this chapter helps you to pray for those of us

[2]Marilynne Robinson, *Gilead* (New York: Farrar, Straus and Giroux, 2004), 45.
[3]George Barna, *Revolution* (Carol Stream, IL: Tyndale, 2005), 62.
[4]David Wells, *The Courage to Be Protestant* (Grand Rapids: Eerdmans, 2008), 40.

who serve in such roles, to hold us accountable, to recognize new elders, and perhaps even decide if you, too, should aspire to serve in this role.

Several Shepherds and a Head Shepherd?

Most fundamentally, all true bishops, elders, ministers of the Word, overseers, pastors, and shepherds have the same office. But whatever you call him, the Bible teaches that the pastor has many roles. That's expressed in Scripture by some of the different names he's given. We see in the New Testament that the same set of people are referred to as pastors, elders, and overseers or bishops (e.g., Acts 20; Titus 1:5–7). They are also called leaders and servants or ministers (e.g., Hebrews 13; Acts 6). Any of these names can be applied to all elders in a congregation, regardless of how often they preach in the main gathering. But if they are true of all the elders, they are especially true of the senior pastor, that elder who provides the largest portion of the public teaching, the one who is most singularly the leader of the congregation. In the New Testament there is not the distinction that grew up later in the church's history between one elder (called the bishop) and the other elders. Whether an elder is employed by the church for pay is not the point. The shepherding office is distinguished by fulfilling the role of leading by teaching God's Word.

The senior pastor is to provide leadership for the congregation as a whole. In many churches, he will have no fellow elders to help him. Even where he does, he will normally form a unique relationship with the congregation over time, as he teaches, counsels, cares for, leads, guides, and protects them—supremely as preacher, but also as a counselor of his people. He is the congregation's theological guide, and, you could even say, its lead worshiper. He normally provides the largest section of their teaching.

But does the Bible really teach that there is to be a senior pastor figure alongside, or inside, the eldership? I think the answer to that question is "No, not directly." Having said that, I think that we can discern a distinct role among the elders for the one who is the primary public teacher of the church.

Behind the English word "pastor" is the Greek word *poimēn*, which is related to "shepherd." You have the related word for shepherd appearing a few times (e.g., in 1 Pet. 5:2; Acts 20:28). But in none of these examples does a separate position from elder seem to be indicated. Indeed in Acts 20:17, 28 it is clear that "elder," "overseer [bishop]," and "shepherd [pastor]" are all used interchangeably of the same group of people.

Having said that, I think the New Testament does seem to indicate a kind of distinct role for one of the elders, for the following reasons.

1. Even in the New Testament, we find that there were some elders who moved from place to place (like Timothy or Titus), and some who didn't (presumably like those appointed by Titus in every town [Titus 1:5]). Timothy wasn't from Ephesus. He had come with Paul. And yet he clearly became an elder there. On the other hand, the elders that Titus was to appoint in the towns of Crete were, we presume, from there.

2. There were some elders who were supported full-time by the flock (e.g., 1 Tim. 5:17–18; Phil. 4:15–18), and others who worked at another job (as Paul often did when he was first establishing the gospel in an area). One would think that new church plants like those Titus established in the towns of Crete could probably not fully financially support multiple elders, at least initially.

3. It is interesting to note that Paul wrote to Timothy alone with instructions for the church there, when we know from Acts 20 that there were other elders in the Ephesian church. But Timothy seems to have had a unique function among them.

And this fits with a fourth glimpse we see:

4. The letters of Jesus to the seven churches in Revelation 2 and 3 seem to be addressed to the messenger (singular) of each of these churches.

None of these are air-tight commands; but they are descriptions that are consistent with the practice of setting aside some among the elders who are not necessarily from the church's own community, supporting them, and, even among them, giving one elder the primary teaching responsibility in the church. And these are often the elements that make up the unique role of what we call a senior pastor.

Even if you don't find these observations from New Testament examples persuasive, I think that we certainly have freedom to set aside men full-time for the teaching of the Word, to provide for their support, and, if necessary, to bring in someone from elsewhere to serve.[5] And such a one is essentially a full-time pastor, whether senior or associate.

However, we must remember that the preacher, or pastor, is also fundamentally one of the elders of his congregation. Their service together has the immense benefits of rounding out the pastor's gifts, making up

---

[5]Such freedom has historically been defended by Protestants. So the Westminster Confession, 1.6 reads: "The whole counsel of God, concerning all things necessary for his own glory, man's salvation, faith, and life, is either expressly set down in Scripture, or by good and necessary consequence may be deduced from Scripture . . . . and there are some circumstances concerning the worship of God, and government of the Church, common to human actions and societies, which are to be ordered by the light of nature and Christian prudence, according to the general rules of the Word, which are always to be observed."

for some of his defects, supplementing his judgment, and creating support in the congregation for decisions, leaving leaders less exposed to unjust criticism. It also makes leadership more rooted and permanent, and allows for more mature continuity. It encourages the church to take more responsibility for the spiritual growth of its own members and helps make the church less dependent on its employees.

The Nature of a Shepherd

Robert Murray M'Cheyne once observed that "a holy minister is an awful weapon in the hands of God."[6] But how can we tell what faithfulness is? One image that the Scriptures use to comprehend and communicate the role of the pastor is that of a shepherd. That's what the word *pastor* means. This is an important image in both Scripture and the history of Christianity. So to help us think about the role of the pastor, we want to turn now to considering the nature of a shepherd.

God's Old Testament people were an agrarian people. In Genesis 47:3, when Pharaoh asks Joseph's brothers what they do for a living, they respond that they are shepherds.[7] And that's how God reveals himself to them. When Jacob is praying for Joseph's children in the next chapter, he describes God as "the God who has been my shepherd all my life to this day" (Gen. 48:15). And in the next chapter, when Jacob is blessing Joseph himself, he again describes God as the Shepherd, and ascribes Joseph's faithfulness to God's care for him (Gen. 49:24). This image of God as shepherd goes deep in the history of God's people.

It's therefore no surprise that leaders over God's people come to be represented by this same image. So when Moses is told by the Lord that it will soon be time for him to die, Moses prays that God would raise up a man "over this community to go out and come in before them, one who will lead them out and bring them in, so the LORD's people will not be like sheep without a shepherd" (Num. 27:16–17). This is when the Lord instructs Moses to take Joshua and commission him in front of the people. So Joshua will be Moses' successor in order that the people will not be "like sheep without a shepherd." Joshua will become their shepherd—their undershepherd—when the Lord takes Moses. In 1 Chronicles 11:2, King David is likewise referred to by the Lord as one who will "shepherd my people Israel."

---

[6] Andrew Bonar, *Memoir and Remains of Robert Murray M'Cheyne* (repr., Grand Rapids: Baker, 1978), 258.
[7] All Scripture quotations in this chapter are from the NIV.

The image of God's people without a leader, being like sheep without a shepherd, is meant to be a pathetic image, one that would bring to mind the confusion, fear, and slow, meandering self-destruction of the flock. And God repeatedly presents his people like this. Centuries later when Ahab of Israel and Jehoshaphat of Judah are allying themselves for war, God's prophet Micaiah prophesies that if they do, Ahab will be killed and "all Israel scattered on the hills like sheep without a shepherd" (1 Kings 22:17; 2 Chron. 18:16). The prophets would use the same image about the judgment that was to come on Babylon—the Babylonians would be "like sheep without a shepherd" when God judged them (Isa. 13:14). In Jeremiah 10:21 the house of Israel is condemned with these words:

> The shepherds are senseless
>   and do not inquire of the LORD;
> so they do not prosper
>   and all their flock is scattered.

You can begin to see how important good leadership is. No wonder a few chapters later, in Jeremiah 23, the Lord says, "'Woe to the shepherds who are destroying and scattering the sheep of my pasture!' . . . Therefore this is what the LORD, the God of Israel, says to the shepherds who tend my people: 'Because you have scattered my flock and driven them away and have not bestowed care on them, I will bestow punishment on you for the evil you have done,' declares the LORD" (Jer. 23:1–2; cf. 25:35–36; 50:6; Ezekiel 34). Indeed, being without good leaders is presented as part of God's judgment in this fallen world. And how appropriate that is, that God would withdraw such a sign of himself—his fruitful authority—when his favor is withdrawn from a people.

We can understand how meaningful this image would have been. For most of their history, the Israelites were simple herders. They weren't the cosmopolitan coastal Phoenicians—merchants with trading ships plying the sea, bringing goods and sophistication from all over! No, God's Old Testament people were the folks who settled up in the mountains of Canaan. Jerusalem, their capital from the time of David, was a city in the hills high above the plains of the Phoenicians, where the armies of Egypt, Assyria, and Babylon would march. Theirs was not even the merchant culture of river cities like those of Egypt and Babylon. The Israelites were hillbillies; they were shepherds.

This image is also used by God when he shows compassion on a people who are defeated and destitute. So when the Lord describes the people of Judah who are in thrall to idols, he prophesies through Zechariah:

> The idols speak deceit,
>   diviners see visions that lie;
> they tell dreams that are false,
>   they give comfort in vain.
> Therefore the people wander like sheep
>   oppressed for lack of a shepherd. (Zech. 10:2)

And then, in Zechariah 13, in the midst of a wonderful prophecy of restoration, there is this abrupt and violent prophecy in verse 7:

> "Awake, O sword, against my shepherd,
>   against the man who is close to me!"
>   declares the LORD Almighty.
> "Strike the shepherd,
>   and the sheep will be scattered."

The Lord Jesus uses this image on multiple occasions, first about the Jewish nation: "When Jesus landed and saw a large crowd, he had compassion on them, because they were like sheep without a shepherd. So he began teaching them many things" (Mark 6:34). And then Jesus cites, as a prophecy about his own disciples, Zechariah 13:7, "Strike the shepherd" (quoted in Mark 14:27 and Matt. 26:31). This is how Jesus shows them that even their own fearful desertion of him was prophesied. The Lord had promised in the Old Testament that, after he had judged his people, he would himself come and shepherd them (Jer. 25:35–36; 31:10; Ezek. 34:5; 37:24; cf. Jer. 3:15).

Of course, Jesus was the fulfillment of God's promises to come and shepherd his people himself. So Matthew 2:6 presents Jesus as fulfilling the Lord's promise in Micah 5:2 to raise up from Bethlehem a ruler, a Shepherd of his people. And in his own ministry, Jesus presents himself, the Son of Man, sitting in judgment separating "the people one from another as a shepherd separates the sheep from the goats" (Matt. 25:32). And, supremely, Jesus speaks of himself openly to his disciples as the Good Shepherd.

> I am the good shepherd. The good shepherd lays down his life for the sheep.
> The hired hand is not the shepherd who owns the sheep. So when he sees

the wolf coming, he abandons the sheep and runs away. Then the wolf attacks the flock and scatters it. The man runs away because he is a hired hand and cares nothing for the sheep. I am the good shepherd; I know my sheep and my sheep know me—just as the Father knows me and I know the Father—and I lay down my life for the sheep. (John 10:11–15)

So Peter can write to young Christians: "For you were like sheep going astray, but now you have returned to the Shepherd and Overseer [Bishop] of your souls" (1 Pet. 2:25). And, when speaking to the elders of the churches (the shepherds in 1 Peter 5), he says, "And when the Chief Shepherd appears, you will receive the crown of glory that will never fade away" (1 Pet. 5:4). And in the vision that God gives John of the last day, we read of a heavenly elder describing to John the final glory of the saved in Christ: "For the Lamb at the center of the throne will be their shepherd; he will lead them to springs of living water. And God will wipe away every tear from their eyes" (Rev. 7:17).

With all of that as background, we note that one of the gifts of Christ to his church is the shepherd or pastor. Paul explains, "It was he who gave some to be apostles, some to be prophets, some to be evangelists, and some to be pastors [shepherds] and teachers" (Eph. 4:11). What does it mean to serve as a pastor, an elder? Peter himself gives the following charge to fellow elders and pastors:

To the elders among you, I appeal as a fellow elder, a witness of Christ's sufferings and one who also will share in the glory to be revealed: Be shepherds of God's flock that is under your care, serving as overseers—not because you must, but because you are willing, as God wants you to be; not greedy for money, but eager to serve; not lording it over those entrusted to you, but being examples to the flock. And when the Chief Shepherd appears, you will receive the crown of glory that will never fade away. (1 Pet. 5:1–4)

And Paul, probably after this, on his way to Jerusalem—on the trip that will finally land him in a Roman jail—meets with the elders of the church in Ephesus (Acts 20:17). And what are such elders to do? Paul charges these elders, these bishops (as they're also called), to be shepherds. Here is his charge to them—a kind of prototypical charge to the elders, the pastors:

"Keep watch over yourselves and all the flock of which the Holy Spirit has made you overseers. Be shepherds of the church of God, which he bought with his own blood. I know that after I leave, savage wolves will come in among you and will not spare the flock. Even from your own number men will arise and distort the truth in order to draw away disciples after them. So be on your guard! Remember that for three years I never stopped warning each of you night and day with tears.

"Now I commit you to God and to the word of his grace, which can build you up and give you an inheritance among all those who are sancti-fied. I have not coveted anyone's silver or gold or clothing. You yourselves know that these hands of mine have supplied my own needs and the needs of my companions. In everything I did, I showed you that by this kind of hard work we must help the weak, remembering the words the Lord Jesus himself said: 'It is more blessed to give than to receive.'"

When he had said this, he knelt down with all of them and prayed. They all wept as they embraced him and kissed him. What grieved them most was his statement that they would never see his face again. Then they accompanied him to the ship. (Acts 20:28–38)

My church has used a series of vows to induct both me, as senior pastor, and others into service as pastors, elders, shepherds of our congregation:

1. Do you reaffirm your faith in Jesus Christ as your own personal Lord and Savior? I do.
2. Do you believe the Scriptures of the Old and New Testaments to be the Word of God, totally trustworthy, fully inspired by the Holy Spirit, the supreme, final, and the only infallible rule of faith and practice? I do.
3. Do you sincerely believe the Statement of Faith and Covenant of this church contain the truth taught in the Holy Scripture? I do.
4. Do you promise that if at any time you find yourself out of accord with any of the statements in the Statement of Faith and Cov-enant you will on your own initiative make known to the pastor and other elders the change which has taken place in your views since your assumption of this vow? I do.

After these four doctrinal vows, we then turn to what we might call more practical vows.

5. Do you subscribe to the government and discipline of the Capitol Hill Baptist Church? I do.
6. Do you promise to submit to your fellow elders in the Lord? I do, with God's help.

7. Have you been induced, as far as you know your own heart, to accept the office of elder from love of God and sincere desire to promote His glory in the Gospel of His Son? I have.

8. Do you promise to be zealous and faithful in promoting the truths of the Gospel and the purity and peace of the Church, whatever persecution or opposition may arise to you on that account? I do, with God's help.

9. Will you be faithful and diligent in the exercise of all your duties as elder, whether personal or relative, private or public, and will you endeavor by the grace of God to adorn the profession of the Gospel in your manner of life, and to walk with exemplary piety before this congregation? I will, by the grace of God.

10. Are you now willing to take personal responsibility in the life of this congregation as an elder to oversee the ministry and resources of the church, and to devote yourself to prayer, the ministry of the Word and the shepherding of God's flock, relying upon the grace of God, in such a way that the Capitol Hill Baptist Church, and the entire Church of Jesus Christ will be blessed? I am, with the help of God.

And then we ask the following questions of the congregation:

1. Do you, the members of Capitol Hill Baptist Church, acknowledge and publicly receive this man as an elder, as a gift of Christ to this church? We do.

2. Will you love him and pray for him in his ministry, and work together with him humbly and cheerfully, that by the grace of God you may accomplish the mission of the church, giving him all due honor and support in his leadership to which the Lord has called him, to the glory and honor of God? We will.

In the ninth question, the prospective shepherd is asked if he will be "faithful and diligent in the exercise of all your duties as elder." In the rest of this chapter, I want to turn to consider what the duties of the shepherd are.

The Duties of the Shepherd
The Shepherd Should Feed the Sheep
Do you remember Jesus' postresurrection appearance to the disciples where he first talks with Peter after Peter had denied him? Peter becomes the prototype shepherd, charged with shepherding the sheep.

When they had finished eating, Jesus said to Simon Peter, "Simon son of John, do you truly love me more than these?"

"Yes, Lord," he said, "you know that I love you."

Jesus said, "Feed my lambs."

Again Jesus said, "Simon son of John, do you truly love me?"

He answered, "Yes, Lord, you know that I love you."

Jesus said, "Take care of my sheep."

The third time he said to him, "Simon son of John, do you love me?"

Peter was hurt because Jesus asked him the third time, "Do you love me?" He said, "Lord, you know all things; you know that I love you."

Jesus said, "Feed my sheep." (John 21:15–17)

This is our main work as elders. This is why in 1 Timothy 3:2 there is only one qualification that is uniquely for elders. Every other qualification listed for elders is something that all Christians—not just elders—are commanded to pursue. But elders alone are said also to need to be able to teach.

We feed our people by their ears! This is why Paul can exhort Timothy so firmly in 2 Timothy 4:2: "Preach the Word; be prepared in season and out of season; correct, rebuke and encourage—with great patience and careful instruction."

Bad shepherds don't do this. In his little letter, Jude warns of such deadly shepherds. "These men are blemishes at your love feasts, eating with you without the slightest qualm—*shepherds who feed only themselves*. They are clouds without rain, blown along by the wind; autumn trees, without fruit and uprooted—twice dead" (v. 12). This is so terrible, of course, because shepherds are called to feed the sheep. What most churches simply call the pastor is chiefly a shepherd, and the primary way the pastor is called to shepherd is by proclaiming God's Word. This, in varying ways, is the duty of all pastors and elders. Unfaithfulness as a shepherd is defined by God in the Old Testament as speaking something other than God's Word to his people. That's why pastors should usually preach expositionally rather than topically.

This is how Christians have always understood the call of the shepherd. So for Ambrose of Milan, who baptized Augustine in the fourth century,

> the most essential task of a bishop was at all times Biblical instruction and preaching. However many duties his office imposed upon him in the course of the years, duties of administration and pastoral care, the education of his clergy, and ecclesiastical and civil politics, Ambrose never neglected or

failed in his obligations as a preacher. In this, above all, he saw the meaning of his spiritual calling.[8]

Such feeding is the duty of every elder, and especially of the pastor or the senior pastor. I understand that my main task as a senior pastor is to give myself to the expositional preaching of God's Word. All the oversight and teaching that an eldership provides should be driven by God's Word, and by the elders' prayerful consideration of the implications of it.

Do you understand that? Christian, do you feed on the teaching of God's Word? This is how you are to mature in Christ. What a great legacy of teaching God has entrusted to us in our churches. In this cursed and fallen world, we, as God's people, are to learn as God's ancient people did in the wilderness, to "not live on bread alone but on every word that comes from the mouth of the LORD" (Deut. 8:3). And it is the joy and privilege of pastors to so serve, to so feed other Christians by teaching God's Word.

But this isn't all that we're to do.

The Shepherd Should Know the Sheep

When God promises in Ezekiel 34 to come himself to shepherd his people, he clearly presents himself as knowing and caring for the sheep individually. And this is clearly in the background of what Jesus did and taught. This is how Jesus lived out his messiahship. He didn't mutely conquer. He didn't just impersonally address faceless masses. He called his disciples by name. He cultivated relationships with them where he knew them personally, and they knew him. This is how Jesus said it would be with the Good Shepherd. That's why he cares even if only one wanders off. Jesus taught that "his sheep follow him because they know his voice" (John 10:4). He says, "I am the good shepherd; I know my sheep and my sheep know me" (John 10:14). And Jesus tells his foes, "My sheep listen to my voice; I know them, and they follow me" (John 10:27).

Sometimes congregations become too large for a single shepherd to know all the sheep. That's why we follow the biblical model of having multiple shepherds (elders) in a single congregation. So, too, we should work to create a culture of discipleship in our churches where members care for each other and where helping others follow Jesus is taken as a basic part of our own discipleship. Within the congregation, we should

---

[8]Hans von Campenhausen, *Men Who Shaped the Western Church*, trans. Manfred Hoffman (New York: Harper and Row, 1965), 93.

recognize some men as shepherds to help in the task of knowing and caring for the sheep.

The Puritans were remarkable at this. William Gouge, pastor of St. Ann's, Blackfriars, in London in the mid-seventeenth century, gave himself to preaching, but he also regularly examined the members to make sure they were ready to be admitted to the Lord's Table. And Richard Baxter famously

> mapped out the parish so that he could interview and catechize every member of every household. Two days each week Baxter and his assistant took between them fourteen families, his assistant going through the parish, and the town coming to Baxter. He would carefully examine them in the catechism which he had prepared for the purpose: then he would take each one apart for a personal interview and would urge them "tenderly and earnestly to immediate decision." There were few who left him before they had been moved to tears.[9]

Such personal care and interest is the duty of every elder, and I think I would say not just even the senior pastor, but especially the senior pastor. So we must labor to do this. Should we not follow the example of the Good Shepherd here? If you are the single pastor in your congregation (as is the case with most congregations), pray and teach to raise up other elders. Brother pastor, don't, by your neglect of the biblical office of elder, force yourself into choosing between making this, or teaching, your top priority. They should both be done. Both are parts of shepherding. Teach your congregation to pray for and recognize other elders.

The Shepherd Should Guide the Sheep Personally and by Example

This is how Joshua's role of leading the people in and out is described in Numbers 27:16–17. We shepherds are to give our time to leading and counseling with wisdom. One part of this leadership means being an example. This is why Paul in Acts 20:28 first tells the elders to keep watch over themselves; and he tells Timothy in 1 Timothy 4:16: "Watch your life and doctrine closely. Persevere in them, because if you do, you will save both yourself and your hearers." So Peter in 1 Peter 5:3 instructs elders to serve "not lording it over those entrusted to you, but being examples to the flock." This is why Hebrews 13:7 instructs Christians to "remember your leaders, who spoke the word of God to you. Consider the outcome of their way of life and imitate their faith." The qualifications Paul gives

---

[9]Marcus L. Loane, *Makers of Puritan History* (Grand Rapids: Baker, 1961), 187.

for bishops and elders in 1 Timothy 3:2–7 and in Titus 1:5–8 are exemplary for all Christians.

One important question about the role of an elder is Can you be an example and be humble at the same time? We should probably ask, Can you be an example without being humble? A good pastor shares his life. The flock needs to be able to see into the life of a faithful man (and his family) and see the truths of Scripture lived out. This is always a challenge, especially as congregations grow. But as congregations grow, so we should pray that Christ give more elders. Elders are, by the nature of their ministry, local. They, like good shepherds, must be within reach of the flock. Internet podcasts of even the best preachers will never replace the teaching and learning that God means to go on from live pastors.

So this kind of exemplary living is the duty of every elder, especially the pastor or the senior pastor. As an elder I am to live, not a life without trials, but a life in which I regularly turn to Christ for my strength, for wisdom, for hope—and I must be seen to do this. Pray for the life of and wisdom for your elders. Pray that elders model well what it means to be a Christian. Pray that elders apply Scripture well in teaching. And pray that God would help you both to seek and to submit yourself to advice and counsel of those godly friends and especially elders that God has put in your life.

The Shepherd Should Guard the Sheep

Sheep are not a stationary commodity. They have legs and must be guarded and watched over. Remember the little parable that Jesus told: "If a man owns a hundred sheep, and one of them wanders away, will he not leave the ninety-nine on the hills and go to look for the one that wandered off?" (Matt. 18:12). Shepherds are to protect sheep from their own dangerous wandering off by themselves. This means saying no to, contradicting, warning, and correcting someone who wants to wander off, so to speak. And this takes courage. It takes courage, not least, because the very small percentage of sheep who do wander off are precisely the ones with the least disposition to listen to their elders. But this is the duty of every elder, and especially the pastor or the senior pastor.

And along with steely backbones, in order to do this guarding well, elders need soft hearts. So pray for your elders. Pray that they not get discouraged. Shepherds spend far less time dealing with the 90 percent of the flock that is prospering. No, the time of the elder is—and is supposed to be—taken up with the sick, the weak, the wounded, those wanting in and those wanting out, and those who Paul in Galatians 6:1 says are "caught in sin."

If you are reading this and you are an elder, then consider carefully the nature of the work you are called to. And if this kind of work discourages you, then you should think about getting off the eldership. Doctors can't be squeamish about blood, or scared of being around sick people.

And if you are not an elder, pray for your own humility. Realize, too, that you may not always know when you are in spiritual danger. So be honest and open, and keep spiritually mature friends and especially your elders informed about how you're doing.

The Shepherd Should Protect the Sheep from Attackers

Our problem isn't only that the sheep might wander off. You recall what Jesus said in John 10:27–29: "My sheep listen to my voice; I know them, and they follow me. I give them eternal life, and they shall never perish; no one can snatch them out of my hand. My Father, who has given them to me, is greater than all; no one can snatch them out of my Father's hand." So, then, the sheep must be protected, even from attackers within our own number, including the eldership. Did you notice Paul's warning to the Ephesian elders in Acts 20:29–31? Paul later told Timothy that false teachers would be coming to the Ephesian church (2 Tim. 4:3–4). So here in Acts 20 he says:

> I know that after I leave, savage wolves will come in among you and will not spare the flock. Even from your own number men will arise and distort the truth in order to draw away disciples after them. So be on your guard! Remember that for three years I never stopped warning each of you night and day with tears.

And that's why Paul specifically instructs Titus that an elder "must hold firmly to the trustworthy message as it has been taught, so that he can encourage others by sound doctrine and refute those who oppose it" (Titus 1:9).

If you are an elder, ask yourself if this is an aspect of your own ministry you've considered much. I regularly think of this as part of my pastoral ministry. John Sampey, an Old Testament professor and president of Southern Seminary back in the 1930s and 1940s, said:

> I came to have a peculiar feeling for my flock. There is no animal more helpless than a sheep, and my large flock could not organize resistance against one vicious dog. The shepherd is everything to a flock of sheep. I know of

no figure used by Jesus to picture what he means to us that so appeals to me as does his affirmation, "I am the good shepherd."[10]

Brother pastors, will we take the time to prepare to defend the flock as it's needed? It's part of our calling.

The Shepherd Should Love the Sheep to the Point of Laying Down His Life for Them

Again, remember the example of Christ as the Good Shepherd in John 10. This is why we are willing, even "eager" as Peter says in 1 Peter 5:2, to serve as a shepherd, that is, because we love the sheep. Paul speaks of one's setting his heart on being a bishop, an overseer (1 Tim. 3:1). Brother elder, is your heart set on the honor of the office, or the greater service of the sheep? The elder must not be selfish. That's why Paul gives us qualifications like "not given to drunkenness, not violent but gentle, not quarrelsome, not a lover of money" (1 Tim. 3:3). Drunkenness, violence, quarrelsomeness, and money loving are all expressions of a dominating self-concern. Instead we are to have a more selfless love. As Calvin said, "No man will ever be a good pastor, unless he shows himself to be a father to the church entrusted to him."[11] Brother pastors and elders, do you see the way we are to combine authority and love in our office? And this love is not to be the selfish love of the Pharisees for money (e.g., Luke 16:14). We're not to love the honor we receive in public, but rather we're to love the very ones we're called to exercise authority over. We're to realize that our authority is to be used for them and their benefit, never for our own gain.

Edward Griffin, a faithful pastor in New Jersey in the early nineteenth century, had these words to say to his congregation in his farewell sermon to them as he tried to help prepare them for the new minister they had chosen:

> For your own sake, and your children's sake, cherish and revere him whom you have chosen to be your pastor. Already he loves you; and he will soon love you as "bone of his bone, and flesh of his flesh." It will be equally your duty and your interest to make his labors as pleasant to him as possible. Do not demand too much. Do not require visits *too* frequent. Should he spend, in this way, half of the time which some demand, he must wholly neglect his studies, if not sink early under the burden. Do not report to him all the unkind things which may be said against him; nor frequently, in his

---

[10]John R. Sampey, *Memoirs of John Sampey* (Nashville: Broadman, 1947), 11.
[11]John Calvin, *Calvin's New Testament Commentaries*, vol. 8, *The Epistles of Paul to the Romans and Thessalonians* (Grand Rapids: Eerdmans, 1995), 345.

presence, *allude* to opposition, if opposition should arise. Though he is a minister of Christ, consider that he has the feelings of a man.[12]

Pray that elders would have hearts full of affection for their congregation members, their flock. And church members, pray that God would help you recognize elders as the gifts of Christ to you that they are. Submit to your elders. Even defend them when that is needed. Share your troubles and temptations with your elders. Share your wealth, resources, time, and talents with them to enable them to glorify God by serving you. Stand by them in difficult times and agree with them as you are able with a good conscience. So return to them the love the Lord has given your elders for you.

This kind of mutual love begins to show you what Christianity is all about. We read in Paul's letter to the Romans:

> You see, at just the right time, when we were still powerless, Christ died for the ungodly. Very rarely will anyone die for a righteous man, though for a good man someone might possibly dare to die. But God demonstrates his own love for us in this: While we were still sinners, Christ died for us. (Rom. 5:6–8)

The Good Shepherd lays down his life for the sheep.

Conclusion

Why should shepherds do all this? The shepherd should do all this because he loves the Savior. Our love shows itself in a number of ways.

We *obey* him. We, like Peter, want to feed Christ's sheep because he's told us to in his Word. Can you imagine a more solemn basis for action? "Be shepherds of the church of God, which he bought with his own blood" (Acts 20:28)!

We are *grateful* to him. We realize that the Good Shepherd has laid down his life for us (John 10:11–15).

We *delight* in him! We enjoy and delight in the One we most love, like Paul in Philippians 1:23, when he says that to be with Christ is best; or Jesus himself in Hebrews 12:2 ,where we read that he endured this laying down of his life for the joy set before him—the joy of unbroken eternal fellowship with God, and perhaps with those whom he purchased by his blood.

---

[12]Edward D. Griffin, *A Tearful Farewell from a Faithful Pastor* (1809; repr., Amityville, NY: Calvary, 1993), 6–7.

And finally, we are *humbled* before him.

1. We are humbled by thinking of the *sheep*. We remember that we must give an account of our shepherding (Heb. 13:17). And he will reward us if we care well for the sheep (1 Pet. 5:4). The congregation may have recognized our ministry, but it was God the Holy Spirit who gave it to us (Acts 20:28). The sheep belong to the Lord, not to us (remember Jesus' repeated references to "my sheep," "my flock" in his words to Peter in John 21:15–17). The pastor doesn't own the sheep. Your poor undershepherds feed you. But it is God who has purchased you with his blood (Acts 20:28). We undershepherds belong to him!

2. And we are humbled by thinking of *ourselves*. We shepherds remember that we are more fundamentally sheep than we are shepherds. The Lord is our Shepherd.[13] In that sense, any good pastor exercises authority, shares authority, and is certainly under authority.

As we make our own lives partial pictures of Christ's love for his church, we are doing no more than what he has called and equipped us to do.

What can lead us to trust Christ so much that we will obey him, to regard Christ as one to whom we owe thanks, to desire him so much that we rejoice in him, and to understand him and his holiness and his love so much that we are humbled before him? Remembering how God has loved us in Christ. Focusing on his cross, the greatest act of the Good Shepherd for us. Here at the cross we find our motivation, our foundation, our own earthly goal, and our own pride's end. This is true for pastors, for all elders, for all Christians.

What a privilege it is to be a pastor! I can't finish this consideration without sharing with you the way Charles Spurgeon conceived of his own pastoral ministry. I love his description. It is how I feel too.

> I am occupied in my small way, as Mr. Great-heart was employed in Bunyan's day. I do not compare myself with that champion, but I am in the same line of business. I am engaged in personally-conducted tours to Heaven; and I have with me, at the present time, dear Old Father Honest: I am glad he is still alive and active. And there is Christiana, and there are her children. It is my business, as best I can, to kill dragons, and cut off giants' heads, and lead on the timid and trembling. I am often afraid of losing some of the weaklings. I have the heart-ache for them; but, by God's grace, and your kind and generous help in looking after one another, I hope we shall all travel safely to the river's edge. Oh, how many have I had to part with there! I have stood on the brink, and I have heard them singing in the midst

---

[13]See Psalms 23:1; 100:3; cf. Isaiah 40:11.

of the stream, and I have almost seen the shining ones lead them up the hill, and through the gates, into the Celestial City.[14]

What a privilege to be engaged in the pastoral work of the shepherd, shepherding the sheep safely home!

A Personal Postscript

One man who in our own day has exemplified pastoral ministry is John Piper. Many may first think of John as a passionate preacher, or as a careful student of the Scriptures, or as a disciple of Jonathan Edwards, or as a prolific and influential author. But John is also a pastor, whose ministry personifies much that this chapter has presented.

We can tell this from his public ministry. For decades now, John has been the moving force behind the Bethlehem Pastor's Conference, where hundreds of pastors gather each year (in the sunshine of a Minneapolis February!) to enjoy preaching, fellowship, prayers, and books. John has always had a special concern for pastors. His 2002 book *Brothers, We Are Not Professionals* sounded themes that can be found in John's sermons and writings but are especially appropriate for pastors. There he applies them carefully and searchingly to the work of the minister—application he can do only because he knows that work so well himself.

How would I know that John is such a good pastor when I've never been a member of his congregation? Well, I've benefited many times from his public teaching. But I've also been on the receiving end of his care. Two examples come to mind.

A few years ago, John heard that my father had died. He sent me this note:

Dear Mark,
You are a dear friend. Your loss of your father is huge. I feel a fraction of it as I ponder the loss of my own—which could happen in the not too distant future. What a gaping hole a father's death leaves in our lives. There is nothing like it. He was there as the head, no matter what he was like. His very existence is a great reality in a son's life. You are doing well to build life with your son. I pray that your loss will make you an even better dad and that most of all your heavenly father will become more precious and powerful than he ever has.

Affectionately,
John

---

[14]C. H. Spurgeon, *The Autobiography of Charles Spurgeon*, vol. 2, *1854–1860* (London: Curts and Jennings, 1899), 131.

That e-mail was a great encouragement, but I can't say that it was a surprise. A few years earlier when my family had been through another crisis, John and Noël both separately (and the night before John was to preach in the morning) wrote to us. My wife and I got e-mails from them—Connie from Noël, and I from John. Among other things, this is what John advised me about the family member I was so concerned about:

> Continue to glory in your own salvation by grace. Let her see that you are mainly enjoying the Lord's goodness to you in sustaining you in this pain. We do Christ wrong when our pursuit of others feels like we are mainly angry at how they let us down or broke the rules. They need to see in us a resting in the gospel so that it looks better than what they have. It is an irony. To win those who are breaking our heart, we must strive to enjoy the great heart-sustainer more than ever. Savor these truths especially: Psalm 103:8–10, "The LORD is merciful and gracious, slow to anger and abounding in steadfast love. He will not always chide, nor will he keep his anger forever. He does not deal with us according to our sins, nor repay us according to our iniquities."

If you've ever wondered if John is only an author, or a convention speaker, I hope this brief postscript throws a new light on John's ministry, to God's praise and glory. I know from personal experience that, by God's grace, John is an example of a shepherd, a pastor.

24

THE PASTOR AS LEADER

John MacArthur

The secular first-century archetype of leadership was, of course, the Roman emperor. Every culture under Rome's influence was dominated by autocratic leaders and despotic leadership structures. Political rulers, military commanders, slave masters, heads of households, and even the priests and teachers of religion were all variations on the same theme. Authority was generally administered with an iron fist. That style ran through the chain of command from the emperor's office right down into the family unit. The typical Roman paterfamilias was a minor dictator in his own home, and family members were viewed as his chattel. If he chose to do so, he had the right to sell his own children into slavery.

Israel in particular was oppressed by multiple layers of harsh and heavy-handed leadership. Some sixty-five years before the birth of Christ, Rome had conquered Judea. By the time of Christ's birth, the Roman senate had named Herod the Great "King of the Jews," and for several generations after Christ the Herodian dynasty wielded power in Israel with efficient ruthlessness. The occupying Roman armies and Roman procurators (including Pontius Pilate) were likewise renowned for their brutal tyranny. Even the Sanhedrin, the ruling council of the Jewish religion, commonly employed force and intimidation as the main tools of their leadership. The council was ruled by the high priest and heavily weighted with members of a priestly aristocracy who lorded it over people with threats of excommunication (John 9:22) or stoning (John 8:59; 10:31–33; Acts 23:12–14).

So it was highly significant (and profoundly countercultural) for the early church to revere the figure of a shepherd as the chief model of spiritual leadership. The word *pastor* means "shepherd," of course, and it is laden with implications about how leadership in the church is supposed to function—contrary to all worldly patterns. In Jesus' own words:

> You know that the rulers of the Gentiles lord it over them, and their great ones exercise authority over them. *It shall not be so among you.* But whoever would be great among you must be your servant, and whoever would be first among you must be your slave, even as the Son of Man came not to be served but to serve, and to give his life as a ransom for many. (Matt. 20:25–28)

Of course, Christ himself is "the chief Shepherd" (1 Pet. 5:4), and elders in the church are undershepherds, tending sheep that belong to their Lord. He is their singular example, and the shepherding paradigm perfectly epitomizes what they are called to do. It is not an authoritarian role but a service-oriented one. In fact, the apostle Peter's admonition to his fellow undershepherds stresses that very point:

> I exhort the elders among you, as a fellow elder and a witness of the sufferings of Christ, as well as a partaker in the glory that is going to be revealed: shepherd the flock of God that is among you, exercising oversight, not under compulsion, but willingly, as God would have you; not for shameful gain, but eagerly; *not domineering over those in your charge, but being examples to the flock.* (1 Pet. 5:1–3)

Indeed, the shepherd's task was the extreme antithesis of the harsh, tyrannical top-down style of a political dictatorship. In that part of the world especially, shepherding involved constant hands-on care from shepherd to sheep. Middle Eastern flocks (even today) aren't generally herded by dogs as in most Western sheep ranching; they are *led* by the shepherd. "He goes before them, and the sheep follow him, for they know his voice" (John 10:4). Sometimes they are *carried* by him (Isa. 40:11; Luke 15:4–5).

Mark Dever wonderfully unpacks the implications of shepherding in chapter 23, and this is a key point: leadership in the church is not about raw authority administered by force. The fruits of true, Christlike leadership are humility, tenderness, self-sacrifice, and affection for the sheep. A good shepherd embodies what every leader in the church should strive to be: personal, patient, gentle, hands-on, and self-giving—leading and feeding the flock and watching out for the welfare of the sheep, even to the point of giving his life for them if necessary (John 10:11).

In other words, he leads by serving them, not by driving them.

That principle has far-reaching implications. It means the badge of a true Christian leader is not an office, clerical garb, or a title, but the influence he has through his example and his service to the flock. True leaders stand out from the crowd for precisely this reason: people follow them.

By that measure, John Piper has distinguished himself as a leader of leaders and a pastor's pastor. His passion for the truth is matched by his affection for the flock of God, and it shows in the sacrificial way he lives and ministers. It's a privilege to honor Dr. Piper with this brief survey of leadership from a biblical perspective.

In the Beginning . . .
The idea of humble servant leadership did not originate with the metaphor of shepherding. Much less was it a novel invention when Jesus washed the disciples' feet in John 13. This is how human leadership was supposed to work from the very beginning of creation, even before Adam fell. Human society was ordered by God's own design, and the family was the first unit of human government—the building block for all other social structures. Adam was the head and Eve his helper (Gen. 2:18).

Moreover, by the mystery of divine foreknowledge, Adam's relationship with Eve was designed specifically to illustrate Christ's sacrificial love for the church (Eph. 5:23). Christ's care for his people is therefore the model for every husband (1 Cor. 11:3). And since the husband was the original, prototypical leader in the human realm, Christlike loving-kindness is a defining element of true leadership as God designed it.

That's why in God's own plan for the family, the husband, not the wife, is the designated head. While the husband-wife relationship is a true, loving, mutual partnership, the roles are not reversible. Scripture expressly and repeatedly says the husband is to take the leadership role in the family (1 Cor. 11:3–10; Eph. 5:22–23; Col. 3:18; 1 Pet. 3:1–6). For similar reasons, men, not women, are to be leaders in the church (1 Tim. 2:11–14; 1 Cor. 11:5; 14:34–36).

The principle of male headship has been badly abused at times, and of course it is at odds with the feminist agenda embraced by today's secularized Western cultures. The wife's role properly understood does not diminish her; it exalts her. Again, headship as God designed it is nothing like dictatorship. The godly husband loves his wife as Christ loves the church: with the heart of a servant, not a slave master. His chief duties to her include tenderness, service, honor, and self-sacrifice. He sets her welfare above his, and her protection, purity, and satisfaction mean more to him than his personal comforts.

The faithful wife is her husband's devoted helper, committed to him alone, just as the church is faithful to Christ.

Together, husband and wife oversee and care for the children. When marriage and family are functioning according to God's design, the parents' authority over the children is the perfect expression of gentle, loving, well-balanced leadership. The caring nurture and affection of a devoted mother exemplify the tender side of leadership. The faithful provision and protective supervision of a loving father exemplify the strong yet self-sacrificial aspect of leadership. Every true leader and shepherd of God's flock must possess both maternal and paternal qualities. In other words, a balanced picture of how leadership should function was woven into the very fabric of the family from the start of creation.

Apostolic Maternal and Paternal Leadership Qualities
The apostle Paul clearly saw it that way, and his own leadership style reflected both maternal and paternal qualities in full measure. Writing to the Galatians, he pictured himself as an expectant mother in labor: "My little children, for whom I am again in the anguish of childbirth until Christ is formed in you!" (Gal. 4:19). That was the perfect imagery through which to convey the intensity of his desire for them to become what they were destined to be—conformed to the image of Christ.

On the other hand, in 1 Corinthians 4:15, he described himself as the Corinthians' spiritual father: "Though you have countless guides in Christ, you do not have many fathers. For I became your father in Christ Jesus through the gospel." He was the human instrument through which they were brought into the kingdom—their father in the faith. He was their teacher and protector. He deeply cared about them, earnestly desiring to see them prosper spiritually—and with good reason, because he was their spiritual father.

Paul, of course, had full apostolic authority (1 Cor. 9:1–19). He wrote Galatians and 1 Corinthians mainly to correct significant problems in those churches. He could have dealt with the false doctrines, the troublemakers, and the rivalries between believers simply by invoking his office and issuing bare apostolic decrees. But that is not the approach Paul took. He used familial metaphors to stress his care and loving-kindness. He pleaded tenderly and patiently with his people, modeling the very best and most important aspects of authentic leadership.

In his first epistle to the Thessalonians, Paul employs both parental figures side by side to describe his style of leadership. This brief passage in 1 Thessalonians 2:7–12 is one of the most important statements in all of Scripture about faithful church leadership. This is how spiritual leaders ought to see their role:

> We were gentle among you, like a nursing mother taking care of her own children. So, being affectionately desirous of you, we were ready to share with you not only the gospel of God but also our own selves, because you had become very dear to us.
>
> For you remember, brothers, our labor and toil: we worked night and day, that we might not be a burden to any of you, while we proclaimed to you the gospel of God. You are witnesses, and God also, how holy and righteous and blameless was our conduct toward you believers. For you know how, like a father with his children, we exhorted each one of you and encouraged you and charged you to walk in a manner worthy of God, who calls you into his own kingdom and glory.

There we see two sides of spiritual leadership in perfect balance: the tenderness of compassionate, motherly care alongside the fortitude and strength of fatherly supervision. Each of those warrants our careful understanding.

The Maternal Aspect

There is perhaps no more gentle, sensitive, tenderhearted relationship than that of "a nursing mother taking care of her own children" (v. 7). The Greek noun is *trophos*, which literally means "nurse" (and that's how the expression is translated in the King James Version). Still, this is no wet nurse or day-care worker. Paul stresses the intimacy of the relationship with the expression "her *own* children."

Unlike a nanny or babysitter tasked with the duty of caring for someone else's children, a mother has the most intimate personal connection with her own children. She is therefore more gentle, more affectionate, and more sensitive to the needs of her infant than any babysitter.

Paul's use of such imagery suggests a crucial lesson about spiritual leadership. Those whom God places in positions of responsibility in the church are to approach the task not with the indifference of a surrogate caretaker, but with the single-minded, wholehearted empathy of a mother.

No matter how many children a mother has, she loves them and cares for them as individuals. She has a special affection and concern for each child. Thus it should be in the church. Pastors and church leaders must see beyond the flock as a congregation and minister to the sheep as individuals.

Paul is reminding the Thessalonians of how honorably he dealt with them. He contrasts his gracious conduct toward them with the behavior of the typical religious quack or false teacher. Invariably, the charlatan's aim is to exploit people. Such men are motivated by greed, lust, a thirst for power, or similar evil motives. They abuse people. They manipulate them and take advantage of them. They are users, not givers; they seek to be overlords, not servants.

Paul was the polar opposite: "For we never came with words of flattery, as you know, nor with a pretext for greed—God is witness. Nor did we seek glory from people, whether from you or from others, though we could have made demands as apostles of Christ" (vv. 5–6). Again, even though he had full apostolic authority, he never invoked it for personal gain, or as a tool with which to manipulate people.

What's intriguing is that "gentle" is the key word Paul chooses to sum up his own leadership style and to contrast himself with spiritual impostors who only exploit people. It is a beautiful word, translated from the Greek expression *ēpios*. That word is used only here and in 2 Timothy 2:24, where the word is translated "kind." In that text, *ēpios* stands at the head of several characteristics that define what the Lord's servant is supposed to be like in contrast to those who are quarrelsome. So the word has overtones of kindness, gentleness, heartfelt concern about someone else's well-being, and sensitivity to others' needs. It denotes acceptance, respect, compassion, patience, tenderheartedness, loyalty, understanding, and tolerance of another's imperfections. It is the extreme antithesis of every kind of domineering abuse. It is the perfect word to describe a loving mother's sympathetic fondness for her own children.

In all the human realm, there is no human relationship more self-giving and affectionate than that of a nursing mother toward her own infant. It is an illustration of personal care and loving self-devotion from someone in authority toward someone under authority. At the same time it is an image utterly devoid of any idea of force or dominion. The mother cradles the little one with great tenderness and affection, not with the grip of authority. She is not seeking honor from the child. On the contrary, she is willing to spend herself completely for the child's sake. Hers is a love that spares nothing.

The English text of 1 Thessalonians 2:7 understates the potency of the words Paul uses to paint the verbal portrait of a mother "taking care" of her children. The Greek verb *thalpō* (often translated "cherish") conveys the idea of warming the infant with body heat. As the mother takes the little one in her arms, her warmth helps to sustain that little life. The exquisite intimacy and tenderness of the metaphor have no equal.

This, Paul says, is a fitting emblem for spiritual leadership. The true leader must have qualities analogous to the tender, caring heart of a nursing mother. Overbearing autocrats who seem incapable of empathy or kindness are not fit leaders at all. The key to effective leadership has very little to do with wielding authority and much to do with giving oneself.

From that opening picture in verse 7, Paul proceeds to unfold the maternal aspect of leadership in verses 8 and 9. He applies the nursing-mother analogy to himself, connecting the thought with an adverb meaning "in this way." He writes, "So [in the manner of a nursing mother,] being affectionately desirous of you, we were ready to share with you not only the gospel of God but also our own selves." He underscores two ideas inherent in the nursing-mother analogy: affectionate desire and the sharing of oneself.

The affectionate desire of a mother for her child is the quintessential emotion of motherhood. Though it may seem inexplicable under a purely rational analysis, it is a natural, God-given aspect of the mother's relationship with her child. The mother with an infant in her arms has such a fond affection for her little one that she will go to amazing extremes of self-sacrifice and inconvenience to nurture and care for that child. As every mother knows, there are no kudos for this, no laurels, no public recognition, and no riches to be gained from mothering. The payback includes lots of crying, dirty diapers, sleepless nights, runny noses, frequent illnesses, and loads and loads of laundry. It's hard work and nonstop duty. Yet faithful mothers are motivated by affectionate desire for that little life in their arms.

In a similar way, the faithful spiritual leader is driven by affectionate desire for those in his care. It is a yearning for their welfare, a zeal for their spiritual well-being that motivates the leader to impart not only the gospel but also his very life (v. 8).

Paul is not describing a mere sense of duty. It wasn't just a commitment to his God-given responsibility that motivated him as a leader; it was a passion for the people themselves. He had such a fond affection for them that he was "ready to share" his whole self with them. The expression Paul used speaks of zeal, eagerness, and enthusiasm about serving them. Ministering to them was a joy for him, not a drudgery, even though many aspects of Paul's ministry were anything but pleasant duties. But to Paul, it wasn't a burden; it was a joy, because of his affectionate desire for the people.

How far was Paul willing to go in self-sacrifice? "We were well-pleased to impart to you . . . our own lives" (v. 8 NASB). The Greek word for "life" is *psychē*, "soul." Paul was willing to sacrifice the totality of his earthly existence on their behalf. Again, that is precisely what the faithful mother does. She sets aside her life for the life of her beloved baby. She is sacrificial. She is utterly unselfish. She is generous. She is willing to give anything and everything for that little life. And the baby consumes her thoughts, her time, her energy—her very life.

Why does a mother do this? The end of verse 8 gives the answer, and it is the very same reason a faithful spiritual leader devotes his life to his people: "because you had become very dear to us." Paul uses the Greek word *agapētos* to describe his affection for the Thessalonians. That word is used sixty times in the New Testament and is translated "beloved" in all but two instances. In Romans 1:7, the word is used to address "those in Rome who are *loved* by God." And in our text, of course, it is rendered "very dear." It is precisely the same word used by the heavenly Father at Christ's baptism and at his transfiguration: "This is my *beloved* Son, with whom I am well pleased" (Matt. 3:17; 17:5). It is perhaps the strongest possible expression of affection and personal love, with the focus on a strong, compelling sense of the preciousness of love's object. That is the nature of the Father's love for the Son; it is the essence of a mother's love for her child; and it is the same kind of love a true spiritual leader has for his people.

Paul carries the metaphor into verse 9, with the conjunction "for" making the connection between thoughts, thus logically attaching what he says in verse 9 to that phrase at the end of verse 8: "You had become very dear to us. For . . ." A casual reader might at this point expect Paul to explain why the Thessalonians were so precious in his estimation with something like this: "You became very dear to us, for you served us day and night." Instead, the conjunction introduces not the *reason* for Paul's deep affection for them, but rather the *proof* of it: "For you remember, brothers, our labor and toil: we worked night and day, that we might not be a burden to any of you, while we proclaimed to you the gospel of God" (v. 9).

He is further developing the analogy of motherhood. Like a devoted mother, he worked night and day for their benefit. He was no burden to them; indeed, he gladly bore the full burden of the ministry in Thessalonica—even to the extent of supporting himself financially on the side, so that no one could possibly think he had made himself a spiritual leader to them with the motive of getting something out of the relationship for himself.

Such sacrifice always characterized the apostle Paul's ministry. In 2 Corinthians 6:10 he described himself "as poor, yet making many [spiritually] rich; as having nothing, yet possessing everything." His life was marked by poverty, hardship, disrespect, disrepute, hard labor, frequent dangers, hunger, thirst, exposure, trouble, and persecution (2 Cor. 11:23–30). Paul was not a taker; he was a giver.

The first part of Acts 17 describes Paul's early difficulties in Thessalonica. There was a synagogue there, and "as was his custom" (v. 2), that is where Paul began his ministry to the Thessalonians. Luke writes:

> On three Sabbath days he reasoned with them from the Scriptures, explaining and proving that it was necessary for the Christ to suffer and to rise from the dead, and saying, "This Jesus, whom I proclaim to you, is the Christ." And some of them were persuaded and joined Paul and Silas, as did a great many of the devout Greeks and not a few of the leading women. (vv. 2–4)

That was the start of the church in Thessalonica.

This was during a very turbulent time in Paul's life and ministry. Acts 16:19–40 describes how Paul had been beaten and imprisoned in Philippi. When the officials of that town learned that Paul was a Roman citizen and therefore their treatment of him was illegal and unjust, they released him and urged him to leave their district. That is what brought Paul and his missionary team to Thessalonica.

Paul was evidently in Thessalonica only for a very short time, and he was more or less run out of town by the enemies of the gospel. The leaders in the synagogue there began to accuse him and tried to foment violence against Paul and his traveling companions. So the Christians in that fledgling church had to send Paul away by night to Berea (Acts 17:10).

Nevertheless, during his brief time there, Paul founded that church and formed lasting, affectionate relationships with the people whom he had brought to Christ. In fact, the intimacy of the nursing-mother analogy is all the more remarkable in light of how quickly Paul's ministry among those people ended. If we take Luke's account at face value, Paul's first visit to Thessalonica lasted only a few weeks at most. But the believers in that city knew very well that Paul had literally sacrificed everything for the sake of bringing them the gospel.

Moreover, during the time he was with them, Paul supported himself financially. Acts 18:3 says he was a tentmaker by trade, so evidently during those weeks in Thessalonica, he was able to earn money by hiring his services out to a tentmaking business in Thessalonica. He literally worked day and night so that he could bring the gospel to the Thessalonians free of charge.

That is the maternal spirit. That's what a godly mother does, working day and night for the sake of her infant and never taking anything from the infant in return.

That is also the temperament of a godly spiritual leader—willing to labor long hours for the sake of his people in order to keep them receiving the life-giving truth of the gospel and the nourishment of God's Word. It is a life of sacrifice and self-giving, carrying the load for others, ministering to their needs with tenderness, gentleness, and long-suffering.

The Paternal Aspect

Obviously, the delicate traits of motherhood don't exhaust what it means to be a leader. True leadership is anything but effeminate. There's an indispensable balance to the equation, and it is embodied in manly attributes such as strength, valor, and boldness. Accordingly, as the apostle Paul describes his own approach to leadership, he compares himself not only to a gentle nursing mother, but also to a watchful, concerned father.

He writes:

> You are witnesses, and God also, how holy and righteous and blameless was our conduct toward you believers. For you know how, like a father with his children, we exhorted each one of you and encouraged you and charged you to walk in a manner worthy of God, who calls you into his own kingdom and glory. (1 Thess. 2:10–12)

Paul sets the mother and father analogies side by side deliberately. He is stressing the importance of a balanced approach to leadership. He is also vividly affirming the most vital principle of Jesus' teaching about leadership: that the tyrant who wants to exalt himself and be served rather than care for his people is no true leader at all (Matt. 20:25–28; 23:8–12; Mark 9:35; Luke 9:48; 22:25–27).

What do tenderhearted mothers and loving fathers have in common? The motive that drives them is a desire for their children's maturity and well-being. A good father is no less self-giving than a nursing mother. But his role is different. The mother tenderly nurtures the infant; the father is the principal guardian and guide.

Of course, modern secular society sneers at the notion that men and women are designed with different qualities and appointed by God to fill different roles in the family. Secular culture desperately tries to make gender neutrality the norm, even in the family. But it is a stubborn biological fact that the sexes are different and that the most vital aspects of their distinctive, God-given roles are not interchangeable. Mothers are naturally better suited to nurture infants; and men in general are physically stronger and therefore better equipped to shoulder the task of protecting and providing for the family.

Furthermore, it ought to be obvious to all but the most determined feminist that the differences between men and women go beyond merely physical distinctions. Characteristics like compassion, gracefulness, and gentleness are commonly found in greater abundance among women; while qualities like courage, stamina, and strength of conviction are the hallmarks of masculinity.

Scripture recognizes and affirms these gender differences. In 1 Corinthians 16:13 Paul writes, "Act like men." There he uses a Greek verb in the middle voice, *andrizō*. The word appears only once in all of Scripture, but it was fairly common in the Greek literature of that time, and it made a dual contrast—between masculinity and femininity, as well as between manhood and childhood. The sense of Paul's command, therefore, is this: "Be manly, not childish or effeminate. Be like grown men."

Scripture is full of similar commands: "Be strong and courageous" (Josh. 1:6, 7, 9, 18). "Take up the whole armor of God, that you may be able to withstand in the evil day, and having done all, to stand firm. Stand therefore" (Eph. 6:13–14). "Share in suffering as a good soldier of Christ Jesus" (2 Tim. 2:3). "O man of God . . . pursue righteousness, godliness, faith, love, steadfastness, gentleness. Fight the good fight of the faith" (1 Tim. 6:11–12). "Brothers, do not be children in your thinking. Be infants in evil, but in your thinking be mature" (1 Cor. 14:20).

Notice the recurring themes of fortitude, conviction, steadfastness, preparedness, and militancy. Of course, when the apostle speaks of "the good fight of the faith," he is not advocating flesh-and-blood combat (2 Cor. 10:3–5). He is talking about a spiritual battle for righteousness' sake (Eph. 6:13–18). Scripture condemns men who are self-willed, quick-tempered, or pugnacious (Titus 1:7). The biblical command to be a good soldier is not a call to be contentious. In fact, elders in the church are to be "not violent but gentle, not quarrelsome" (1 Tim. 3:3).

Nevertheless, there is a true sense in which men (and leaders in particular) need to be strong, bold, courageous, steadfast, devoted to defending the safety and purity of those in their care, and above all willing to stand, fight, or perhaps even die for the truth. Such qualities, rightly applied, are the true hallmarks of mature masculinity.

As a matter of fact, when Paul commanded believers in 1 Corinthians 16:13 to "act like men," those were precisely the characteristics he had in mind. The full verse makes his meaning clear: "Be watchful, stand firm in the faith, act like men, be strong." Watchfulness, strong convictions, and strength are the kinds of characteristics Paul has in mind. The context indicates the strength Paul has in mind is not merely physical strength but toughness of character, courage and stamina, fortitude. Those are of course the very features human societies have traditionally associated with masculinity.

And those are likewise vital characteristics of every truly godly father. When Paul speaks of the paternal aspect of leadership in 1 Thessalonians 2:11, such qualities are precisely what he has in mind.

The text itself makes that clear. Paul introduces the father analogy by reminding the Thessalonians how he and his associates in ministry behaved in their midst: "You are witnesses, and God also, how holy and righteous and blameless was our conduct toward you believers" (v. 10). Paul's motives were clearly not self-serving. All could see that his goal was the advancement of the gospel among the Thessalonians, not personal gain for himself at their expense. His conduct reflected the highest level of holiness and integrity.

That is every father's duty: to set the standard of integrity in the family. That is also every spiritual leader's responsibility.

Paul uses three significant adjectives in that statement: "holy and righteous and blameless." Holiness has to do with the purity of one's life before God. Righteousness has a dual focus, encompassing one's duty to God as well as one's duty to fellow humans. (The Mosaic law, of course, reflects both aspects of righteousness. The first four of the Ten Commandments spell out our duty to God; the rest outline how we should treat others.) Blamelessness refers to one's reputation—how others perceive his character. Paul's behavior among the Thessalonians was the very model of what every leader's character should be: before God, holy; before God and men, righteous; and before men, blameless.

But being a true leader (and a good father) is not just modeling; it's also teaching. Therefore, Paul says, "like a father with his children, we exhorted each one of you and encouraged you and charged you to walk in a manner worthy of God, who calls you into his own kingdom and glory" (vv. 11–12).

Here's another triad of fatherly characteristics: "we exhorted . . . and encouraged . . . and charged you." Exhortation tells children the proper way to walk. Encouragement helps them along when the way gets difficult. The Greek verb Paul uses to speak of charging the people under his care is *martyromenoi*, a word that speaks of giving testimony, or summoning a witness. (It's the source of our English word *martyr*, used because the martyrs sacrificed their lives giving testimony to the truth of the gospel.) It's a powerful expression, evoking the image of a father who admonishes his children with affection and compassion, using his own life as a witness to the lesson he wants to convey, illustrating the point from his own experience and testimony. Paul reminds the Thessalonians that he gave such exhortations to them individually, instructing "each one of you" in the same way a father leads his children.

Like a wise father, the godly spiritual leader lives the virtuous pattern his children are supposed to follow. But he doesn't stop with that. He carefully instructs and exhorts them—individually when necessary. He also encourages them and helps them along.

There is obviously a large element of authority in the father's role, but a godly father doesn't wield that power in an authoritarian way. He is patient, encouraging, and personally involved with his children, showing them love in the process—even when it is necessary to rebuke or discipline them.

This balance is absolutely crucial to all spiritual leadership. Christ embodied it. Paul modeled it for us. Every spiritual leader ought to aspire to maintain the balance, and not lean too far to one side or the other. The true spiritual leader has a tender, compassionate side; and he has a strong, courageous side in which he himself is righteous and uncompromising, and exhorts his people to be holy and steadfast as well. He is at once tender and loving like a nursing mother, as well as firm and courageous like a confident father. He maintains on the one hand a concern for the person, on the other hand a concern for the process; on the one hand a concern for kindness, on the other hand a concern for control; on the one hand a concern for affection, on the other hand a concern for authority. He is on the one hand embracing, on the other hand exhorting; on the one hand cherishing, on the other hand challenging.

It is a beautiful, robust balance that God has designed right into the fabric of our families. It is the perfect epitome of what all leaders in the church should aspire to be. And where there is that balance in our leaders' lives, the church is greatly blessed.

We are indeed blessed by the ministry and leadership of John Piper, and I am grateful to the Lord for such an example.

25

The Pastor and His Study

William D. Mounce

At the 1998 national meeting of the Evangelical Theological Society in Orlando, Florida, John Piper was invited to speak on the topic "Preparing the Next Generation of Preachers and Missionaries."[1] Dr. Don Carson led off by speaking on preparing the next generation of teachers and scholars. It was an excellent discussion of the challenges that lay ahead. And when John got up to speak, we expected much the same. We were mistaken.

At this point in time, many in the audience—about fourteen hundred college and seminary professors, graduate school students, and some pastors—did not know who John was. Wayne Grudem, the vice president of ETS that year, introduced him first with his academic credentials (German DTheol, thesis published in a distinguished series, then professor at Bethel College) and then with his ministerial credentials (preaching pastor at Bethlehem Baptist Church in Minneapolis, Minnesota). I can still hear Wayne say, "He is one of us." And certainly John had the academic credentials to speak to this particular audience. But thankfully John did

---

[1]The manuscript and audio for this talk are available at www.desiringGod.org, under the title "Training the Next Generation of Evangelical Pastors and Missionaries." In what follows I will be quoting from both the prepared remarks and the oral presentation of them.

not care to impress us with his academic acumen; he had quite a different message to deliver.

I remember the two professors sitting next to me. One of them had seen John preparing to speak, and evidently John was facing a wall and swaying back and forth, much like what is done before the Wailing Wall in Jerusalem today. They thought it was rather strange that a man would face a wall and sway. I turned to them and said, "He was praying." That stopped the gossip. And yet it is the contrast between those two teachers and what John said that drove his address home to my heart and forever changed the way I study.

John's basic message was this: "The greatest need of every pastor and every missionary is . . ." Let's stop right there. How would you finish his sentence? Based on your training, gifting, experience, and culture, what do you think would be most important? Certainly they should have a working knowledge of Greek and Hebrew! A solid grasp of systematics grounded in biblical exegesis. An appreciation for solid expositional preaching. An awareness of culture and its points of intersection with the church. I would guess that most would complete John's sentence that way. How did you?

That is not how John finished the sentence. "The greatest need of every pastor and every missionary is . . . to know God better than they know anything and enjoy God more than they enjoy anything." He explained:

> The supreme challenge of every scholar and teacher who would prepare these pastors and missionaries is: How shall I study, how shall I teach, and how shall I write, and how shall I live . . . so as to help pastors and missionaries know God better than they know anything, and delight in God more than they delight in anything? That is the supreme challenge of your life. . . . There are hundreds of other things to talk about in the ministry if we are to do our job well, but nothing comes close to the magnitude of the importance of this.

There were other statements John made during the hour that have stuck in my mind and have had a significant impact on my ministry. The one that cut closest to my heart was this:

> It would not have occurred to *anybody* to create a course in spiritual formation if students were walking out of biblical classes aflame with a passion for the glory of God standing forth from the exegesis of the Greek text. [I was currently running the Greek Language Program at Gordon-Conwell Theological Seminary.] It wouldn't have entered anybody's *mind*! It would

not have occurred to anyone to add courses in spiritual formation if students were coming out of systematic theology and church history with their minds amazed at the majesty of God and their hearts burning like the men on the road to Emmaus (Luke 24:32).

John's opposition was not aimed toward the whole area of spiritual formation, but it was aimed at professors who taught their respective disciplines apart from any idea or goal of the student's spiritual transformation into Christlikeness.

At the end of his address, I am not sure there was a dry eye in the conference room. The Spirit had worked mightily through John, answering his swaying prayers, and had cut through the academic mask that we often wear at these meetings and gone to the joint and marrow of our bones. Wayne had trouble regaining his composure when he had to go through the perfunctory "thank you" after John's talk. I suspect my two neighbors felt a bit like Eli after his similar comments toward Hannah.

When I returned to Gordon-Conwell, I brought a tape of John's address. For every year after that I played John's talk to all my Greek teaching assistants as part of their preparation for the new year. The impact on each of them was the same as I had experienced in Orlando. But how would we do it? How would we teach Greek in such a way that the spiritual formation classes would be just a review? Don't get me wrong; I enjoy books on spiritual formation. The works by Dallas Willard, J. P. Moreland, and John Coe have been instrumental in my thinking, my study, and especially my preaching. But I realized that if students in Greek classes, of all classes, could be exposed to their teacher going all the way from Greek paradigms and vocabulary drills through exegesis and homiletics and eventually to the goal of all things—loving God and being changed into Christlikeness—then they would have a better chance of doing it themselves.

Seminary education is quite committed to specialization: Old Testament versus New Testament, hermeneutics versus homiletics, Gospels versus Paul, 1 Thessalonians versus 2 Thessalonians. One professor said that the academy is committed to "infinite differentiation"; we can never define something too specifically. But if the TA's and I could go the other direction, if we could show how to move smoothly from the beginning to the end, if the students could see the entire cycle happen in the ministry of one person (their teacher or TA), then they would more likely catch the vision and the passion. How powerful it is to see your Greek teacher use his or her craft in the languages to proclaim with power the counsel of God in chapel. How powerful it is to see your systematics professor struggle with the Greek text and then work to integrate the text with his overall theology. Students must see this full cycle at work in one person.

After all, isn't this the point? Shouldn't all knowledge move us to wonder at the majesty of God? Shouldn't all endeavors be done to God's glory? Isn't it wrong to stop short, as if biblical study is done for its own sake and not God's? Shouldn't all theology move to doxology?

This was my first real exposure to John Piper, and in this article I would like to lay out how I worked through the questions he raised as I taught in seminary and then preached in church.

Teaching Greek Students to Love God

My first step was to incorporate devotional studies into class. I would come to class fifteen minutes early, and the students could do the same if they wished. Every day I would take a passage in Greek, translate it, and then try to move through the vocabulary and grammar to meaning, application, and ultimately to issues of transformation (i.e., spiritual formation). I found it to be one of the most difficult tasks I accepted. It had not been part of my training. I didn't think in these terms when I wrote my grammar and taught class. But John's voice haunted me.

In retrospect, this was one of the most important things I ever did, and I would encourage you to do the same. It forced me to face my educational weaknesses and to shift my paradigm for what I was trying to accomplish. I had taken for granted that the students would use their Greek to more accurately and powerfully proclaim the glories of Christ. But as John also said at the ETS address, "God does not like being taken for granted." When we take God for granted, it often means we are ignoring him altogether. If my students were going to move from exegesis to proclamation, they needed to see me do it. If your students are going to love God, they need to see you love God more than academic degrees, books published, or the praise of men.

I remember a conversation with John years later. I had mentioned the book *Light on the Path*,[2] and John suggested I write a similar book that would move from Greek exegesis to spiritual formation. He said, "It will be easy. You do all your devotions in Greek, so just write your thoughts down every day." His assumption about my devotional life was unfortunately incorrect. I still struggle today with keeping devotional time from

---

[2]Heinrich Bitzer, *Light on the Path: Daily Scripture Readings in Hebrew and Greek* (1969; repr., Grand Rapids: Baker, 1982). See John's stirring meditation about being in the text, "Brothers, Bitzer Was a Banker!" in *Brothers, We Are Not Professionals* (Nashville: Broadman and Holman, 2002), 81–88.

turning into browsing through a Greek lexicon, looking for just the right meaning of a Greek word. But this is one of the challenges we all face, of using our disciplines well and at the same time remembering that the ultimate goal is not increased knowledge but increased love for God.

The TA's and I also started to focus on community. Greek is hard enough to learn as it is, and it is even harder for most if we try to learn it by ourselves. How much better to learn together. After all, seminaries should be about training future leaders of communities. I also recognized that the better the students learned Greek, the more likely they would actually use it in ministry; so we looked for any and all means possible to encourage students to work together. We had mixed results, but it was worth the effort.

If I could skip ahead a decade, I am still trying to find ways to meet John's goal of Greek classes' being a place of spiritual formation. I was recently asked to blog once a week on issues raised in first- and second-year-Greek class as well as in translations. As I was the chair of the New Testament committee for the English Standard Version, I thought this would be a good exercise for me, and I would have many stories to recount about Dr. J. I. Packer and other members of the translation team.

But even in writing this blog, John's words continue to haunt. What can I do to help prepare the next generation of preachers and teachers? How can I use Greek to encourage them to love God more? It is amazing how many times I am done with a blog, and John (in my head) says, "Will this help them love God?" Many times the answer is no, and that means I am not done with the blog. I always try to make the full hermeneutical cycle, starting with a tidbit of grammar or vocabulary and moving to how it can be used to proclaim the majesty of God. I have mixed results, but that is my goal. And I trust that I am helping others use their Greek to more accurately and powerfully proclaim the message of our King.

Is the Bible True?

Anyone who has heard John preach will come away with the same impression. He preaches with absolute authority—not his own authority but the authority of the author of Scripture. When you leave Bethlehem or one of his conferences, you have heard, "Thus saith the Lord." How does he do it? How could I do it? I am not talking about issues of style. My style of preaching is somewhat different from his, as is probably yours. But John brings a refreshing and unashamed sense of truth to the pulpit, reminding us that we are hearing the very words of God as he understands them.

There are several answers to this question of preaching with authority, and the least important is knowing Greek. But let me start at the beginning.

John believes the Bible is true. There is no question about his confidence in the revealed Word of God. When he speaks the words of Scripture, he speaks the words of God. And when he speaks the words of God, they are true even if every person is a liar (my adaptation of Rom. 3:4).

All of the Greek homework in the world will not enable you to trust the Bible; and if you do not trust the Bible, you will not preach it with conviction; and if you do not hold to the total trustworthiness of Scripture, you will mix God's ideas with yours, and eventually you will get tired of coming up with your own good ideas every Sunday morning. I wonder how nonexpository preachers do it. Week after week, month after month, year after year, trying to think of some good way to convey some good human truth (at least they think it is true). Is this not what happens? Is not part of the plight of the American pulpit due to an egregious lack of conviction that Scripture is true? And if you are not convinced that the Bible is true, then why spend time learning it in its original languages? There is no reason, and hence the appalling lack of solid biblical study behind many sermons preached every Sunday.

I am convinced that the foundation of a preacher is a bedrock conviction of the truth of Scripture. Every person who is going to step into the pulpit needs to wrestle with the questions of the text. Are there errors? Where? How do I deal with the problem passages? Can meaning be conveyed with words? These are important questions, and no amount of Greek study will convince you that the Bible is true. And if you are not convinced of its truth, you will probably lack the fierce determination necessary to learn Greek and use it in your ministry, and the books on your shelves will age with dust.

Is God True?

Is there a difference between loving the Bible and loving its author? Absolutely. When I hear someone say, "I love the Word," I always ask, "Do you also love its author?" The Pharisees loved the Hebrew Testament; but unless our righteousness exceeds theirs, we are doomed to hell, Jesus says. (I rarely add the second clause, but I think it.)

John's message has always been that we are to love God, the person of God, and not just good things from God (like forgiveness, joy, and heaven). In fact, if we stop short of loving God, then these good things become idols. Bible study can be one of the greatest idols of all times if we stop at study and do not move on to loving the author. In fact, Satan is quite content if we love to study our Bible and don't move on. He can work with that. He can push us toward Pharisaism. He knows that knowledge puffs up.

But Paul does not say that he wants to know God's Word. He says that he wants to "know *him* and the power of his resurrection, and . . . share his sufferings, becoming like him in his death, that by any means possible I may attain the resurrection from the dead" (Phil. 3:10–11). Jesus defines eternal life as "knowing God" (John 17:3). We cannot know God apart from the perfect revelation of the invisible God in the visible Jesus. Yes, this involves knowledge. But knowledge is a means to an end—the ultimate end of knowing God, living in union and in relationship with him.

So how does this impact the pastor and his study, and specifically knowing Greek? The languages are a means to an end. There may be people who want to learn languages for languages' sake, and that is fine. But that is not true of most of us. Greek and Hebrew are a means of knowing God better, of understanding his revelation more clearly, and of moving through the text to the author.

As the pastor engages with the text, as he puts it to the test, as he pushes through hermeneutics to homiletics, he comes face to face with God. Not just his Word, but God himself. And the text challenges us to trust him, believe in him, endure all things for him. Stopping short at parsing and sentence diagramming will never move a pastor to powerful proclamation. But using study, and especially a study of the Greek text, with the goal being an experiential knowledge of the person of God, results in a level of preaching that many pastors never experience.

The Value of Translations
If a person is convinced that the words of the text are the very words of God, and that God himself is true and just and good and faithful, then the next step in powerful preaching is to know what the text *says* and what it *means*. These are two different things.

What does the text say? Before moving to Greek, let me say something about translations. Translations are good. They are done—as far as I know—by godly men (and in some cases women) who love the Lord and are committed to his church. The general adage is to pick one translation as your primary text, and read others for insight and clarity. John has become a strong advocate of the ESV, as am I, but I enjoy reading how other scholars understand the text in other translations. Do you have to know Greek to know what God says? Of course not. A careful and

critical use of different translations goes a long way in understanding the
ambiguities of the Greek text.

The Value of Greek

No translation is infallible. We all make mistakes, but a working knowledge of Greek and Hebrew is essential for an accurate and powerful
proclamation of the character and activity of God. Does knowing Greek
mean that you will never make mistakes? Of course not. Does not knowing Greek ensure that you will make mistakes? Absolutely.

I do not trust my abilities with Hebrew. When I preach out of the
Hebrew Testament, there is always a level of insecurity. The computer
tools assure me of the parsing of a form (assuming they are inerrant,
which they are not); but I do not have an intuitive feel for the language,
and it is hard for me to follow a detailed discussion of the grammar of a
passage. So how do I stand before my people and preach the whole word
of God, including the first four-fifths?

I am in a fortunate situation. I have friends who are Hebrew experts,
whether they were colleagues at Gordon-Conwell, translators I have
worked with on the ESV and the New International Version, or other
scholars I have met. It is a tad humiliating to have to call them and ask
them to help me understand the text or a commentator's argument. At
least I can call them, but most pastors do not have access to this type of
expertise.

It struck me a while back that this is how many pastors feel even when
preaching from the Greek Testament. I know a scholar who has repeatedly
said, "If you have only read the _____ [and he names a translation], you
have never read the Bible." While that is not true,[3] there is a point at which
if all you have is the English, you will most certainly step into the pulpit
with some degree of apprehension and uncertainty, not only because you
could not read the actual words of God, but because you probably were
not able to read the best commentaries in your sermon preparation since
they rely heavily on a working knowledge of Greek. It is hard for me to
consider preaching a sermon on Romans without reading the Greek text,
doing my sentence flows, and then reading the commentaries by C. E. B.
Cranfield and Douglas Moo, and if I am still not clear, the commentary
by Thomas Schreiner. These three commentaries are indispensable tools

---

[3]As John has said, "I would rather have people read any translation of the Bible—no matter how weak—
than to read no translation of the Bible. If there could be only one translation in English, I would rather
it be my least favorite than that there be none. God uses every version to bless people and save people."
See "Good English with Minimal Translation: Why Bethlehem Uses the ESV," a sermon at Bethlehem
Baptist Church, January 1, 2004, available at www.desiringgod.org.

for the pastor; but without a working knowledge of Greek, some of the discussion will be beyond your reach.

In my own experience, when I have done my homework in both the Greek text and the critical commentaries, and when I have been able to come to a clear understanding of the text, and when I can see how that text fits into my overall theology, only then am I able to preach with absolute conviction and power. I don't have to be imprecise so as to hide my lack of understanding; I don't have to raise my voice so as to bully people into believing what in fact I neither fully understand nor can defend. And I don't have to tell stories so as to fill up the time.

Have I made mistakes? Absolutely. Several times over the years I have had to start a sermon by correcting my previous sermon. But my prayer before every sermon is the same: "Father, would your Spirit do today what my words cannot do. Would my words be correct, clear, persuasive, and filled with grace. May I say nothing in any way that would hinder the work of your Spirit in changing lives this morning. For your glory. Amen." But the only way I can say that prayer with a clear conscience is if I have spent the time in study. At times I want to add the same type of qualification in my prayer that most authors do when thanking their editors. "I especially want to thank my editor_____ who helped make this book better than I could have done on my own, and yet all mistakes are my responsibility." I want to tell my people, "I have done the best job I can do in preparing this talk, and it is my prayer that the Spirit of God will flow through your minds, convicting and challenging as he sees fit. But any and all errors or ungracious words are my fault."

My point is this: the pastor must make a resolute commitment to study if he is going to stand before his church and declare, "Thus saith the Lord." He is going to have to spend the time to let the sermon trickle down into his own life and convict him of his own sin, so he can preach from a clear conscience. It is difficult for me to see how this can be done without reading the actual words of God, and God did not speak his words in English.

Once again John Piper has been an encouragement to me in this area. The other day he wrote me an e-mail, frustrated with the new Bible search program he was learning. Knowing that I have worked with the main programer of the software, he thought that I would have some insight into the dilemma. He was searching for a rare inflected Hebrew term. John has evidently been able to keep up his Hebrew much better than I.

Greek and Translations

One of the ways in which a pastor can use his knowledge of the biblical languages is to help his people understand the nature of translations, why they are different, and the value in studying from several.

All translations have a translation philosophy. They all have made basic decisions on issues such as where on the continuum they sit between formal and functional equivalence, minimum age group of their readership, what to do with ambiguities, gender language, how transparent to be to the Hebrew and Greek grammar and vocabulary, etc. The ESV translators wanted to be in the translation stream from the King James Version through the American Standard Version and the Revised Standard Version. We wanted people to see that they are reading an ancient book that reflects ancient culture. We were content with people having to work a bit to come to an understanding of a passage, assuming that the original readers would have had to work to understand as well. We were comfortable requiring readers to learn a technical vocabulary, such as "righteousness," "saints," and even "propitiation."

Other translations choose a different philosophy. They want the Bible to be read in the current vernacular. They want the meaning of the passage to be immediately apparent. They don't want to force a new vocabulary on people, so "saints" becomes "God's people." They may be concerned that their readership will not engage with the text if "man" and "he" are used generically, and so their translation is significantly different from the ESV.

My position is that we need different types of translations. A more formally equivalent version such as the New American Standard Bible or ESV is a better base Bible from which to study, and the other more dynamic versions are good to show what other translators think the passage means. But in all these discussions, the people in our churches need to understand why their Bibles are different and, most importantly, that they can be trusted.

This raises a tremendously significant issue. In my preaching prior to the ESV, I used another version that most of the people in the church used. It was nice knowing that when I read the passage or talked about a specific word, the wording was the same in their Bibles. But I went through a few weeks of sermons where I thought the version had really missed the translation, and so I corrected it. After the third week of corrections, a young Christian came to me and asked if she could no longer trust her Bible. Her words sent a shiver through my body. No matter how much I disagreed with a particular translation's handling of a passage, I never wanted to call into question the overall value of a Bible or a person's trust in God's Word.

I resolved never to do the same again. Fortunately, the ESV is sufficiently transparent to the Greek and Hebrew that I don't find myself correcting it; and often if there is a real question in the text, it says so in the footnote. A working knowledge of Greek allows you to say something like, "This is a difficult passage to translate, and my preference is to agree with the footnote." No one's faith in the Bible is disturbed.

But in all this, a working knowledge of Greek is essential. Without it, your people may not understand why their Bibles are so different in places, and consequently they may not trust them.

One of my favorite stories is of the snake people of the Appalachian Mountains. My family is from Gravelswitch, Kentucky. I guess that makes us hillbillies. Grandpa left when he was young, and so I didn't see my distant relatives until I was in high school. It was strange to drive into a town and see most of the businesses named "Mounce's____." But it is the people from this area that you may have studied in high school sociology class. They drink poison and handle snakes, and they don't die from it. To the question why they do this, you might expect a rather bizarre answer, but it's not. The answer is, "This is what Christians do. Have you not read the Bible, Mark 16:17–18? 'And these signs shall follow them that believe; In my name shall they cast out devils; they shall speak with new tongues; They shall take up serpents; and if they drink any deadly thing, it shall not hurt them; they shall lay hands on the sick, and they shall recover' [KJV]." It is a religious expression of faith for them.

The preceding verse is likewise troubling. "Whoever believes and is baptized will be saved, but whoever does not believe will be condemned." And so all unbaptized believers will stop short of the heavenly gates on judgment day. After all, that is what the text seems to say!

The question is one of textual criticism, discerning whether these verses were in the original Greek manuscript of the Gospel according to Mark or were added later by a scribe (as many evangelical scholars now believe). But if a pastor does not know Greek and is unable to think through issues of textual criticism, how can he respond to the questions and doubts that people in the pew might raise? This whole issue of text criticism can become a contentious one (e.g., see the "King James only" debate), and it requires clarity, grace, and strength of conviction.

My point is not so much that a working knowledge of the biblical languages can solve church disagreements. The real issue is whether your people can trust their Bible. Will they go to it to determine their theology?

Will they go to it for encouragement in difficult times? Will they go to it for hope in the midst of great pain? These decisions are all made before the times of stress come, and part of the pastor's job is to build into people the commitment and trust that the Bible is true and helpful, a source of joy and contentment such that when the pains of life come, they have a place to turn. And then, of course, they are to go through the text to him who is encouragement and hope and truth itself.

How Not to Use Greek from the Pulpit

My one blog post that has generated perhaps the most discussion had to do with using Greek from the pulpit. Is there ever a place to say, "In the Greek it says . . ."? I am going to cite some of that blog in the following paragraphs, but my point is one of humility. I know it is tempting, especially for younger preachers, to show that they have done their homework and know what they are talking about, but putting yourself up on a pedestal by flaunting Greek is never a good idea. People put you up there easily enough as it is. (Just remember, they may be doing it to get a better shot at you, but that is a different topic.)

Some time ago I was listening to a sermon by a fairly good preacher. He was talking about the ending to the Sermon on the Mount and how the builders of both houses were working with the same materials, but one was wise and one was foolish; one built his house on a solid foundation and the other on sand. The storms could not destroy the first, but they washed away the latter. The person who builds on the good foundation is the person who not only hears Jesus' words but also does them. The foolish person (Greek, *mōros*) hears them but does not do them, does not apply them to his or her life.

The speaker stressed that in a church everyone hears the same words, fills in the same sermon notes, but that does not make them wise. All the people have the same building blocks, both houses in the story may have looked alike on the outside, but the wise pew-sitter (my word) is the person who takes the words and applies them. Good point.

But in the process of making the point, he committed a basic blunder, one that unfortunately has been repeated in pulpits across this land innumerable times, but should never be repeated. It is very easy to prevent: never define a Greek word by its English cognate. Never! He said the Greek word is *mōros*, from which we get our English _____, and he let the people fill in the blank. "Moron," they replied, engaging in the sermon and working to turn a monologue into a dialogue. Again, a good practice. And then he added, "That is a good word picture."

Actually, it is a terrible word picture. It is totally wrong, and the pew-sitters may forever have an incorrect understanding of an incredibly important biblical concept.

What is a "moron"? Wikipedia says it is a "disused term for a person with a mental age between 7 and 12," with a slang meaning of a "stupid person." Is that what a "fool" is in biblical theology? When the psalmist says, "The fool says in his heart, 'There is no God'" (Ps. 53:1), is he thinking of a mentally deficient person? When Proverbs says,

> The one who conceals hatred has lying lips,
>   and whoever utters slander is a fool (Prov. 10:18),

is the author thinking of people with IQs below 70? I know of several people who are quite bright (at least in IQ tests) but are unable to guard their mouths against slanderous gossip. Are they fools? When Proverbs says,

> The way of a fool is right in his own eyes,
>   but a wise man listens to advice (12:15),

does it mean that true biblical wisdom is an issue of intelligence? Of course not. And yet, when you tell pew-sitters that the English "moron" is a good word picture of the Greek *mōros*, that is exactly what you have done.

The fact of the matter is that a fool is not a mentally deficient person but a morally deficient person. A fool is someone who does not recognize the majesty and grandeur of God, a person who does not stand in fear of God. Fools are so blinded by their own sin that they cannot see God for who he is and therefore who they truly are. My dictionary defines it as "ignorance of, and willful rebellion against, God and his will."[4]

It is such an easy rule to remember. English was not a language until the second millennium A.D. You cannot define a Greek word by what a cognate meant a thousand years later. How many times have we heard that *dynamis* means "dynamite," and people leave thinking that the "power of God" is explosive? I wonder, does God have a fuse?

I know it is tempting to show a little Greek knowledge and try to create a helpful word picture, but unless you are completely confident that

---

[4]William D. Mounce, *Mounce's Complete Expository Dictionary of Old and New Testament Words* (Grand Rapids: Zondervan, 2006), 262.

your Greek is absolutely right, I strongly urge you not to display your Greek knowledge.

This brings me to the general point. I discourage my students from ever saying, "In the Greek . . . ." Why would you want to say that? To impress your listeners with your academic acumen? To convince them that you are right when you can't prove your point with biblical logic? Perhaps I am being a little harsh, but I am sensitive to pastors claiming to be authorities and putting themselves on a pedestal. That's not where servants belong.

I have always found a way to describe what the Greek text says without running the risk of placing myself above the people. Often you can reference the footnote or another translation that will help you make the point. Even saying something like "the word translated 'foolish' has the basic meaning . . . ." Again, maybe I am a little harsh on this point. I remember after one sermon my older son Tyler saying to me, "Dad, I would like it better if you would actually teach us some of the Greek words and what they mean." And in a recent sermon series I did teach two Hebrew words, *Yahweh* and *hesed*.

People want to place their pastors on a pedestal. Please do not help them do this. Do your homework. Be sure of the meaning of the Greek words. And then proclaim the power of God's word with humility and care. And please do not give your people an inaccurate word picture that significantly confuses important biblical themes.

Very smart people can still be biblical fools, and many of the wisest people around could never pass a Greek exam. Fools are people who have no fear of God, and wisdom begins with fearing the Lord. Let's not cloud the picture with issues of intellectual deficiencies.

A related topic is ecclesiology. How do you think of the church? Is it a top-down hierarchy with the pastor at the top, the head of the church, the Lord's anointed? I use Gordon Fee's illustration of a circle. Inside the circle are lots of little circles representing all the various gifts God has given to the church to meet the diverse needs of the body. Preaching or teaching is one of those gifts. But just as important are the gifts of mercy, and giving, and administration. I don't believe in congregational rule and I do believe that Paul gives us a hierarchical structure for the church, but my gifts do not put me outside the circle of the church. Only Christ is outside the circle. Only Christ is the Head of the church, the Lord's Anointed.

The church has become so layered with different hierarchies of authority and responsibility that it gives the false impression to most lay people that all they have to do is sit and soak (and then sour if they don't exercise). This is wrong. We are all gifted and all called to serve one another. This is one of my driving principles, and it is what lies behind my strong preference that you not say, "Now in the Greek . . . ." Holding yourself up as an authority that must be obeyed works against biblical ecclesiology.

If you are wondering about whether to use technical language, ask yourself why. Is it to make much of yourself, or to make much of God? Can you find a humbler way of saying it, and if so why wouldn't you do it that way? Motives are a hard thing to assess, especially in yourself, but the effort is worth it.

God's call for humility and gentleness does not stop at the classroom door. They are not qualities only for the uninitiated pew-sitters. Humility, gentleness, and kindness must first and foremost be demonstrated from the pulpit. If your church is struggling with arrogance, perhaps all of us who stand before people should watch a video of how we preach and what we say. Maybe that is where the problem starts.

How to Use Greek from the Pulpit

Having said how not to use Greek, let me move to the more positive and ask how it should be used. It starts with your homework. The most important place to use biblical languages is behind the scenes in doing your research, whether in sermon preparation or in planning a Bible study. The languages give you access to tools that are far beyond the reach of English.

The International Critical Commentary series is inaccessible without Greek and Hebrew, but it is hard for me to imagine preparing a talk on Romans without checking Cranfield carefully. Even a series like Eerdman's New International Commentary on the New Testament requires a working knowledge of Greek. Though the Greek is relegated to the footnotes, I can't imagine being able to follow the commentator's line of reasoning without having a working knowledge of Greek. When a writer argues that argument A is stronger than argument B, behind those decisions almost always lies not just knowledge of Greek but a feel for the language and how it functions.

Or how about a discussion of the flow of a biblical author's thought? All translations (to varying degrees) simplify sentence structure. Passages like Ephesians 1 and Colossians 1 demand it. But when the commentator starts talking about dependent and independent constructions, and what words a phrase or clause modifies, English-only readers will struggle to keep up with the discussion.

How many commands are in the Great Commission? Even if a subordinate construction ("go") picks up the force of the governing finite verb ("make disciples"), there is still only one primary command. And then how do we accomplish the commission? The answer is conveyed partly by two dependent constructions ("baptizing," i.e., evangelism, and "teaching," i.e., spiritual formation). If you aren't doing your homework in Greek, or if you don't have some facility in Greek, this type of discussion is almost meaningless.

And then there are word studies. The tools such as Accordance and BibleWorks, or one of my interlinears, give you the Strong's or GK number behind the English so that you can at least do your word studies in Greek and Hebrew, never in English. At one level it does not take an extended knowledge of the languages to use *Mounce's Expository Dictionary* or Verbrugge's *Dictionary of New Testament Theology*, and yet when the dictionary gives a word's range of meaning, how do you make a determination as to which nuance is present in a particular context? This is an ability, perhaps even an art, that you develop over time in using the languages.

So learn your languages, do your homework, read the best commentaries, struggle with the Greek and Hebrew text, check various translations, and then express yourself with simplicity and humility, and let the power of the sermon be the power of the Spirit working through your words. But please do not hold yourself up as an authority who must be believed because you know what the Greek says.

How Do You Best Love Your People?

I would like to challenge some basic misconceptions of the pastor because they have a significant impact on the area of study.

We often characterize a person as being a "pastor" (warm, friendly, relational, available), a "rancher" (a successful pastor who now has too many people to spend time with), or a "preacher" (speaker, powerful, teacher, removed). How many times have you asked somebody about their pastor; their response is something like, "He's a great guy, we love him, but he's not much of a speaker." Or, "He's a dynamic speaker, challenging, but removed from most people." As the stereotypes often go, the "pastor" is viewed as a friendly person and the "preacher" as not friendly.

After seven years in pulpit ministry I understand how this happens. There is so much to do, staff to manage and encourage, elders to train, people to visit, parking lots to plow, and lawns to mow. The pastor spends his energies loving people one-on-one, and come Saturday night he takes long hot baths trying to think of something to speak on the next day (true story I heard).

The preacher on the other hand is committed to his craft, spends time in his study, rehearsing Greek paradigms, reading generally, staying up on culture, pushing his way through exegesis, crafting the sermon, and trying to determine how he is going to be misunderstood so he can massage the message and avoid foreseen pitfalls. But then the assault on his time comes. He's not available as much for counseling. He is focused on his sermon between services, and so he is criticized for not being friendly. He wouldn't sit by the bedside of a person nursing the latest hangnail. And he doesn't have time to argue about the color selection for the bathroom. And when he suggests that a person go to his or her small-group leader for support and encouragement, the preacher is labeled uncaring and the gossip starts.

But I would like to suggest that the preacher is as loving as the pastor, and my hope is that this will encourage you to study. What is the most important thing you can do? What are the most significant obstacles that need to be overcome in people's lives? I submit that regardless of the size of a church, the mission of the pastor-preacher is to "proclaim the excellencies of him who called you out of darkness into his marvelous light" (1 Pet. 2:9). Nothing is as important as that. Not the territorial thinking in the missions committee, not the latest disagreements among parishioners, and not the latest board controversy.

Some of these may be (or may not be) important, but when the music has led people to take their eyes off themselves and train on God, when the responsive reading has drawn people into dialogue, when the announcements have reminded people that they are family, and when you stand before your people to preach, there is nothing more important than what you did in the quiet of your study. All of the preparation, from the first day in Greek class to your rehearsing the sermon to an empty room Saturday morning, all your hard work comes to the forefront, and with confidence and humility you stand before the expectant people and proclaim the glory of God. At that moment, you aren't the church's plumber. You aren't the person who has to go to the store to buy more paper for the copier. You are the herald of the King, proclaiming clearly and truthfully the wonders of God. If you have done your work, and if God's Spirit is so inclined to move, your words will encourage the downtrodden and chasten the sinners. If you are faithful to your King's decree, you will love your people the most important way, because there is nothing more important than the clear, powerful, rooted-in-truth, Spirit-inspired proclamation of a vision of the glory of God. Nothing. Preachers love their people every bit as much as do pastors. Their love is just shown differently, but it is just as real and just as powerful.

Fervency in the Pulpit

I would like to end this chapter with one more story about John Piper. As you will see, he has had a phenomenal influence on my life; everything I have been advocating I have seen modeled in his life.

Gordon-Conwell Theological Seminary is one of the top academic evangelical institutions in the United States. It is where you want to end up at the end of your academic career (if you are a teacher). So when I started thinking about leaving the school to find a pulpit, it was a hard decision. I had spent much of my life learning to teach Greek, and this was as good as it would get. But there was something lacking in my heart, a hole if you will. I found myself enjoying teaching my Sunday school class more than my academic classes. I knew that John had made a similar move from podium to pulpit, so I arranged some time to talk with him. He flew to Gordon-Conwell for a chapel address, and I was able to drive him from the airport.

"Why did you leave Bethel College and move to a pulpit ministry?" I will never forget his answer. He said he was coming to the end of his sabbatical and had just finished his book *The Justification of God*. It is a treatise on Romans 9 and the freedom of God to act as he chooses. Romans 9 is a biblical chapter that lifts your heart and mind to the glory of God, and John had been immersed in it for six months. But on a sleepless night, October 14, 1979, something happened. I'll let John describe it in his own words:

> I was 34 years old. I had two children and a third on the way. As I studied Romans 9 day after day, I began to see a God so majestic and so free and so absolutely sovereign that my analysis merged into worship and the Lord said, in effect, *"I will not simply be analyzed, I will be adored. I will not simply be pondered, I will be proclaimed. My sovereignty is not simply to be scrutinized, it is to be heralded. It is not grist for the mill of controversy, it is gospel for sinners who know that their only hope is the sovereign triumph of God's grace over their rebellious will."* This is when Bethlehem contacted me near the end of 1979. And I do not hesitate to say that because of Romans 9 I left teaching and became a pastor.[5]

---

[5] John Piper, "The Absolute Sovereignty of God: What Is Romans 9 All About?" Sermon preached at Bethlehem Baptist Church, November 3, 2002; my emphasis.

No single statement I have ever heard has had more impact on me than John's. "I am not a God to be pondered, I am a God to be proclaimed." God is most glorified in us when we are most satisfied in him. We will never be content merely describing God, listing his attributes, cataloging his activities; and this type of approach to learning will never satisfy the human soul or the jealousy that God has for his own name. Ever. If in your studies you never move beyond the Greek, you have not preached. But if your studies become one of the weapons in your arsenal to "proclaim the excellencies of him who called you out of darkness into his marvelous light" (1 Pet. 2:9), then you will have moved beyond description to proclamation.

This is John's legacy for me—and I am forever thankful to my Lord for the gracious gift of John Piper in my life—preaching with informed passion about what matters most: God.

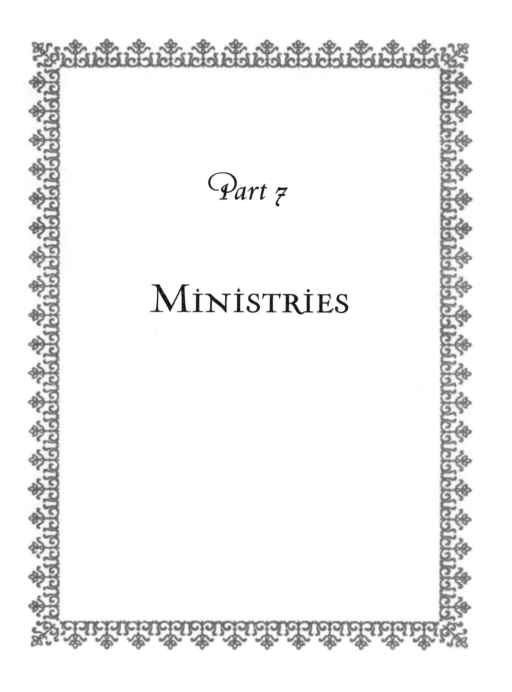

Part 7

Ministries

26

THE VISION AND MINISTRY
OF DESIRING GOD

Jon Bloom

The unplanned birth of Desiring God Ministries happened in March of 1994.

I had been John Piper's ministry assistant for about nine months when he stepped into my office and informed me that the elderly couple who had operated the cassette tape ministry at Bethlehem Baptist Church for sixteen years had suddenly announced their retirement. They would be finished in three weeks. Someone needed to take it over. "I want you to make it happen," John said. "Okay," I replied, more confidently than I felt.

The seed of DGM was actually planted in early 1987. That February, John's book *Desiring God: Meditations of a Christian Hedonist* had recently been released by Multnomah Publishers. In it he devoted a whole chapter to money as "the currency of Christian Hedonism." He argued that Christians should be content with the simple necessities of life because we could invest the extra we make for what really counts. . . . 26.5 percent of the world's population live in people groups that do not have indigenous evangelizing churches. This does not count the third of the world that does live in evangelized peoples but makes no profession of faith. If the unevangelized are to hear—and Christ commands that they hear—then cross-cultural missionaries will have to be sent and paid for. All the wealth needed to send this new army of good news ambassadors is already in the church.[1]

But beyond that, John emphasized how dangerous wealth can be for the soul. He pointed to Paul's warning in 1 Timothy 6:9–10:

> But those who desire to be rich fall into temptation, into a snare, into many senseless and harmful desires that plunge people into ruin and destruction. For the love of money is a root of all kinds of evils. It is through this craving that some have wandered away from the faith and pierced themselves with many pangs.

So to avoid the peril of wealth and to alleviate the spiritual and physical suffering in the world, John exhorted Christians to adopt a "wartime lifestyle," living modestly in order to free up financial resources to invest in kingdom work. He closed the chapter with this challenge to his readers:

> You want life which is life indeed, don't you ([1 Timothy 6] verse 19)? You don't want ruin, destruction and pangs of heart, do you (verses 9–10)? You do want all the gain that godliness can bring, don't you (verse 6)? Then use the currency of Christian Hedonism wisely: do not desire to be rich, be content with the wartime necessities of life, set your hope fully on God, guard yourself from pride and let your joy in God overflow in a wealth of liberality to a lost and needy world.[2]

But in the release of this book about delighting in God above everything else, with such strong words about money, John recognized a test of his own resolve. If *Desiring God* had broad readership, it could potentially make him a lot of money on top of his salary as a pastor.

John felt the enticing power of that additional income. A host of previously unavailable options awakened cravings he recognized as dangerous. And there were legitimate reasons to keep significant portions for himself.

---

[1]John Piper, *Desiring God: Meditations of a Christian Hedonist*, 3d ed. (Sisters, OR: Multnomah, 2003), 190.
[2]Ibid., 203.

He had four young sons and future college costs to think about. He had a mortgaged house. He drove an older car. And at forty-one, he wasn't as far from retirement as he used to be.

But this was the very temptation he had written about. It was not to be played with. God was calling him to practice what he preached. So he and Noël decided that they would live off John's salary from the church and not receive any book royalties as personal income.

With the counsel and support of Bethlehem's leaders, John set up a charitable fund in the spring of 1987 that would receive the book royalty payments. These would then be invested in strategic efforts to help as many people as possible understand and embrace the truth that God is most glorified in us when we are most satisfied in him. John named it the Christian Hedonism Expansion Fund (CHEF).

The genesis of my partnership with John in Desiring God occurred on Sunday, June 5, 1988. That was the first time I heard John preach. I remember right where I was sitting in Bethlehem's old sanctuary with Pam, my bride of barely two weeks, and my brother Jim and his wife, Raquel. John preached a sermon titled "Unless You Repent You Will Likewise Perish," from Luke 13.

I was twenty-two years old and had been an earnest Christian since I was about ten. I had been raised in a loving, supportive, evangelical church and had attended a solid Christian college. But spiritually I was restless. I was grateful for the practical teaching on Christian living I had received. But the God I read about in the Bible and had begun to experience was breathtaking. I really wanted to know this person and to be near others who were enthralled by him.

That June Sunday, in both the preaching and the congregational singing, I experienced God-entranced worship like never before. God was weighty, holy, majestic, and beautiful. And it changed the course of my life. When Pam and I walked out of Bethlehem that day, I said to her, "That's it! That's what we've been talking about!" We knew we had just found a new church home.

In 1991, about a thousand people were attending Bethlehem. Pam and I didn't know the Pipers personally. So a phone call in January caught me completely off-guard. It was Noël Piper. "Johnny and I would like to know if you and Pam would be interested in renting our basement apartment." I think my jaw dropped to the floor.

For years the Pipers have rented their basement to young couples. The current renters were moving out. My brother Jim, who by this time was leading Bethlehem's college ministry, had suggested us to John and Noël. Bless him.

I tried not to sound too eager. "Yes, Noël, Pam and I would be very interested in looking at the apartment."

My hand was shaking when I hung up the phone. I think I knew immediately that our answer was supposed to be yes. Something about that invitation seemed significant and life-directional. But Pam and I were living with her parents, both trying to finish college, and had barely any income to pay rent. So we fasted and prayed and sought counsel—then said yes!

For two precious years we lived with the Pipers. We shared Sunday lunches, cereal suppers, family birthdays, apple cider by the fire, and family devotions. And the Pipers became good friends.

In the spring of 1993, as we were preparing to move out of the Pipers' house into our first little home, I heard from Jim that John was contemplating hiring his first full-time administrative assistant. He wanted a male, someone who could travel with him and uniquely care for the growing number of inquiries and ministry demands.

This news landed on me with the same weighty sense I had about the apartment. I couldn't get it out of my mind. At age twenty-seven, an administrative assistant position may have appeared an unwise career choice. But I knew I was supposed to do it. This was the next step. A few days later I walked upstairs to John's home office and simply asked him to consider me for the job. He did. I began in July.

By March of 1994, the Christian Hedonism Expansion Fund had been receiving and dispersing royalties from the sales of John's growing list of books for seven years.[3] As John's assistant, my job was to administer

---

[3]The entity that now receives John's book royalties is the Desiring God Foundation.

this fund and dream of creative strategies to spread the vision of Christian hedonism.

Now suddenly the tape ministry had just been handed to me. Again I felt that sense of significance. God was up to something. What was it?

As I spent a few days praying and pondering over this, I observed that increasing numbers of people were contacting the church requesting John's books, sermon recordings, articles, and other resources, and these requests were all being handled by different staff members. It hit me that if we created a coordinated, proactive strategy for using resources to spread the vision of God we loved, we could reach far more people.

So I went to John and suggested that we combine my CHEF responsibilities with the tape ministry and literature inquiries and create a single vision-spreading resource ministry. He responded, "That's a great idea! We could call it Desiring God Ministries."

And DGM was born.

What Desiring God Is

In John's own words, Desiring God

> exist[s] to spread a passion for the supremacy of God in all things for the joy of all peoples through Jesus Christ. We do this mainly by proclaiming and explaining the joyful truth that God is most glorified in us when we are most satisfied in him, especially as unfolded in *Desiring God: Meditations of a Christian Hedonist*.[4]

We are a people who have found the surpassing triune Treasure and seek to point as many people as possible to him so that they too will find eternal delight in him. And because the Lord has used John Piper's preaching and writing ministry so powerfully in our lives, we want others to benefit from them as well. So we seek to put them into the most accessible, portable, transferable, and economical formats we can produce.

And when I say we are a people, I mean Bethlehem Baptist Church. Desiring God is not a parachurch ministry. We are an extension of a local church that seeks to serve as much of the global church as the Lord grants. We have our own 501(c)3 status with the I.R.S. But Desiring God

---

[4]John Piper with Jon Bloom, *Money, Markets and Ministry* (Minneapolis: Desiring God, 2007), 2.

is owned by Bethlehem. Bethlehem's council of elders oversees our work and installs our board of directors.

Here is what we are seeking to accomplish:

> We want to see millions of people around the world more accurately understand the Bible and increase in their love for Jesus Christ by reading, listening to, and watching our resources at the times and locations that are most helpful to them, and eagerly sharing these resources with others.[5]

Every word in this statement has been prayerfully and carefully chosen to help us determine what we should and shouldn't do. We can't do everything. So we are focusing on a few things that we believe will most effectively accomplish this vision:

> **Internet:** We are not only trying to make our Web site (www.desiringGod. org) a large, easy-to-use, enjoyable storehouse of theological delights available for free, but we are also trying to harness the best communications tools proliferating in the Internet world to maximize gospel spreading.

> **Resources:** Besides distributing hundreds of thousands of books, CDs, and DVDs, as well as millions of electronic audio and video files every year, we are increasingly using creative media, such as film, to help people outside of our current networks see and savor Jesus Christ.

> **Conferences:** Since probably the most effective way of spreading Christian hedonism is helping people hear John preach, we coordinate John's speaking schedule and sponsor numerous events during the year.

> **International Outreach:** The fastest growing part of DG's outreach is outside of the English-speaking West. With the rapid growth of the church in the global south and east, and the great need for resources that exists in these regions, we desire to serve the church there by making our resources as accessible as possible, especially to leaders, in the languages and formats most appropriate to each region.

> **Children Desiring God:** A very precious part of our work is passing the vision of God we love so much to the next generation. So we publish the curricula that have been developed for Bethlehem Baptist's children's ministry so that other churches and families are also able to point their children to the greatest Treasure that exists.

---

[5]This statement comes from an internal document titled "The Mission and Vision Statements of Desiring God."

Over time our strategies have changed to adapt to new technologies, opportunities, and demands. In our early days, cassette duplication was a major focus of our time. Today we don't even own tape duplicators. CDs replaced cassettes, and now most people prefer electronic files directly downloaded from our Web site or podcasts.

From 2000 to 2005, we experimented with a small office based in Northern Ireland to make our resources more affordably available in Europe. Our partnership with our UK friends was precious. But as the Internet evolved, it became clear that international offices would not be the most cost-effective long-term way to distribute resources around the world.

We also experimented with radio broadcasting. But in the years we were on the air (2004–2006), we watched radio quickly lose ground to the Internet as the medium of choice for the vast majority of the people listening to John. Radio was not the most accessible, portable, transferable, and economical strategy. So we decided to broadcast only on the Internet.

If the Lord gives us another fifteen years of ministry, Desiring God may look very different than it does now. But, Lord willing, our passion for God's glory and commitment to serve the global church will be even greater.

Freely Give

John's early commitment to a war-time approach to life and ministry has not diminished. It has become part of Desiring God's DNA. It shapes everything we do and frees us for radical generosity. John describes it beautifully in this word to the DG staff:

> The radical nature of what we are called to spread profoundly shapes the way we spread it. We are called to spread gospel-based passion for the supremacy of God which satisfies the trusting heart and inclines it to renounce all sinful and many innocent comforts in this world for the sake of giving more freely, loving more deeply, and displaying the infinite worth of Christ more truly.
>
> Along with the content of what we teach, *how* we spread a passion for God is crucial for our integrity and authenticity. A radical message calls for radical strategies in ministry. God will, I believe, honor a risk-taking, counter-cultural, God-centered mission-orientation in DESIRING GOD. I tremble at the prospect of being, or appearing like, just another middle-class, comfortable, domesticated ministry which reflects the values of American consumerism more than the values of the One who had no

place to lay his head and said, "Freely you have received; freely give" [cf. Matt. 10:8 NIV].[6]

This is why from day one we've had a "whatever you can afford" policy for DG's resources. We adopted it from the late musician/evangelist Keith Green, who had this policy for his records. It is a constant reminder that we serve God, not money.

It's also why we decided to encourage (rather than forbid) people to copy our audio or video sermon recordings to freely give away. If they're giving it away, they have our blessing. We want to release, not restrict, gospel spreading.

And when it became possible to make all of our audio and video resources available for free online, it was this approach to ministry that pushed us over the edge to do it. We weren't exactly sure how the economics would work. But we were sure that far more people around the world would listen to or watch our resources and share them with others if they were free. And we believed that God would honor this risk-taking venture by bringing us the support we needed.

And he has, so very faithfully. We have always sensed that when it came to fund-raising, God wanted us to cultivate a prayerful dependence on him; we were not to draw much attention to money but humbly make needs known when necessary. And as we've done that, God has provided a small army of supporters who have helped DG grow from what began with just me and a few volunteers to over forty paid staff and over fifty regular volunteers at the time of writing. And we've been able to devote tens of thousands of dollars every year to supply thousands of leaders, churches, schools, language translators, prison inmates, armed forces personnel, and others with needed resources. And we've never gone into debt. Second Corinthians 9:8, 10 has been a precious reality for us:

> And God is able to make all grace abound to you, so that having all sufficiency in all things at all times, you may abound in every good work. . . . He who supplies seed to the sower and bread for food will supply and multiply your seed for sowing and increase the harvest of your righteousness.

John Piper's influence on my life is incalculable. Because of John I am more deeply in love with Jesus and his church. My marriage, my children, my

---

prayers, my love of Scripture, my vocation, my possessions, where I live, how I lead, what I read—all have been profoundly influenced by him.

And I'm just one person. As I reflect on what God has done in the lives of thousands, I am overwhelmed.

Desiring God is not the result of brilliant planning, managerial excellence, or savvy marketing. It is God's grace. It's his grace in providing remarkable men and women who have served at DG over the years. They are "the excellent ones, in whom is all my delight" (Ps. 16:3). And, I believe, it is one of God's gracious blessings on the life and ministry of a rare man who really treasures him supremely. It has been my unspeakable joy to benefit from that blessing.

27

The Vision and History of the Bethlehem Institute

Tom Steller

The Bethlehem Institute (TBI) is a church-based training center. We seek to provide God-centered, Christ-exalting, Spirit-empowered, Bible-saturated training to equip men, women, and young adults for effective leadership in the twenty-first century. Our aim is to win and preserve worshipers of Jesus Christ from every tribe, tongue, people, and nation. In other words, TBI exists to spread a passion for the supremacy of God in all things for the joy of all peoples through Jesus Christ by equipping men, women, and young adults in the context of the local church to serve as family, business, and community leaders, full-time Christian workers, missionaries, pastors, and teachers.[1]

The Bethlehem Institute (now evolving into Bethlehem College and Seminary[2]) has its roots in a relationship between one particular mentor and one particular student. John Piper is the mentor. I am the student. I came to Bethel College in 1973 as a newly converted product of the 1960s. I had been involved for the first two years of my Christian life in

[1]For more information, see http://www.thebethleheminstitute.org/.
[2]See http://www.bethlehemcollegeandseminary.org/.

a dynamic charismatic church where I fell in love with an all-satisfying Christ. I was passionate to worship him and live for his glory but had very little understanding of what that meant. My hunger for the Bible was awakened, and I read it with increasing delight and intrigue. So many answers and so many more questions emerged out of my study. By God's grace I was led to Bethel College because my parents wanted me to go to a liberal arts school. I was not particularly interested in a college education. The only thing I could imagine studying was the Bible. Bethel was the solution because it was a liberal arts college with a Bible department.

During my freshman year we heard that a new professor was coming to Bethel who just finished his doctorate of theology in Germany. I signed up for Dr. Piper's first class in the fall of 1974. But when it turned out that this new twenty-eight-year-old professor looked younger than some of the students, I decided to transfer to the Greek class taught by the seasoned chair of the Bible department. My next opportunity to study under Dr. Piper came during interim when I could have taken his intensive course on Ephesians. But I chose to take a course on "Contemporary Spirituality" in hopes that it would deepen my prayer life. While I was learning how to use Jesus beads and other innovative spiritual aids gleaned from the world's religions, my lifelong friend, Scott Hafemann, was taking the Ephesians course. Our classes were across the hall from each other and let out at the same time. I would come out of my class confused about integrating Buddhist techniques into my prayer life, while Scott's feet were barely touching the ground. Day after day we would walk down the hall, and he would tell me what he was seeing in the apostle Paul's magisterial epistle. One day, he looked at me and said, "I think I was converted this morning in class." The spiritual impact of Dr. Piper's teaching on my friend made it impossible for me not to sign up for a Piper course the next semester.

I ended up taking seven courses from Dr. Piper. My charismatic heart was drawn class after class to his humble, earnest passion for the glory of Christ. He would begin class with a brief devotional from his Greek New Testament, something he just saw that morning in his devotions. Then he would pray a deep and rich prayer and then lead seamlessly into the most rigorous exegesis and reflection on the text of Scripture. He taught us to look methodically at the text and to diagram the Greek sentences, and then he taught us to lay out each clause or proposition of the text on its own line and pay special attention to the connecting words and to the flow of the author's thought. He taught us a way to display the flow of thought through a method he learned from his mentor, Daniel Fuller, called arcing.[3] Dr. Piper's great passion was that his students would see the beauty of Scripture with their own eyes. And what beauty we saw together! He was as interested in what his students were seeing as in what he was seeing, celebrating our insights and oftentimes modifying his own arcs. We saw beauty together in a community of hungry students and mentor. One climactic moment came after we drew the big arc over Romans 9–11 and the class spontaneously started singing the doxology—Scott Hafemann striking the first note.

Through Dr. Piper's influence, I went to Fuller Seminary to study with Daniel Fuller, who had so deeply impacted John. I wasn't disappointed, but only further captivated by the beauty and intricacy of apostolic revelatory thought. Diagraming and arcing were solidified as the methods I would use and teach wherever God might lead me.

One day in the winter of 1980 my wife, Julie, and I received a letter from Dr. Piper telling us that he felt "irretrievably called to leave teaching and go into pastoral ministry." He then asked in the letter, "Am I crazy?" to which I responded with a loud voice in my San Marino apartment, "YES!" It wasn't that I didn't think Dr. Piper would make a great preacher and pastor, but I didn't want the evangelical community to lose him as a scholar. I remember him saying, "God's Word is not only to be analyzed, but it must be proclaimed!" As much as Dr. Piper loved investing in college students, his growing desire to preach to all ages in all situations of life the glories of Christ that he was seeing in his study and in the classroom became overwhelming. A short while later, we received another letter from Dr. Piper, saying that Bethlehem Baptist Church in downtown Minneapolis called him to serve as their pastor. The next sentence changed my life forever. "Would you like to come and serve with me?"

Julie's and my first Sunday at Bethlehem was two weeks before Pastor John preached his first sermon. When we walked in the door of the old sanctuary, we saw a sea of gray hair on mostly Swedish heads. Bethlehem was founded in 1871 as the First Swedish Baptist Church of Minneapolis. After a fire destroyed its first sanctuary, the young church bought the building on 13th Avenue and 8th Street. All services were in Swedish until 1893 when bimonthly services in English were added. Swedish services were discontinued in the mid-1930s. But the Swedish heritage at Bethlehem remained strong when the German Piper and Steller families moved in.

What a joy to be a ministry colleague with my professor and mentor— a bit intimidating as well! The process of "Dr. Piper" becoming "John"

---

[3]For more information on this method, visit http://www.biblearc.com.

to me is still ongoing—three decades later! In one sense I was the first TBI apprentice. I was still finishing my Fuller seminary degree at Bethel Seminary—one course a quarter—and was teaching Greek at Bethel College. This still left Julie and me many hours a week to pour into our "part-time" job of pastoring the college and young adults who now started streaming into Bethlehem. The sea of gray hair was now being speckled with almost an equal number of students in their late teens and twenties. Pastor John would regularly meet with me and with the youth interns. I remember our times arcing our way through the Pastoral Epistles trying to learn together what it means to shepherd the flock of God. Integrating theological discourse and original language exegesis along with hands-on ministry experience was priceless as we earnestly sought to care for the flock entrusted to us.

Out of the richness of my own experience of learning Greek, sentence diagraming, arcing, and a growing understanding of the big picture of God and his purpose, mingled with pastoral mentorship amidst substantial ministry involvement, the idea for an Apprenticeship Program for Ministerial Candidates was birthed in the mid-1980s. In addition to providing pastoral supervision to a growing number of seminary students, we were also seeking to impart to them the biblical truths that had most gripped us. As a means to that end, we were teaching them God's Word in the original languages using the method of inductive Bible study that helped us to see these truths emerging from our own rigorous exegesis of the text. Each year we would welcome in a new group of seminary students, plug them into ministry, and spend time teaching them arcing and the unity of the Bible.

In 1983 a missions renewal began at Bethlehem which twenty-five years later has not yet subsided. John and I were more the victims of it than its cause. However, we did come to see that our theology of God's sovereign purpose that

> the earth will be filled
> with the knowledge of the glory of the LORD,
> as the waters cover the sea (Hab. 2:14 NASB)

is indeed a missions theology. Our passion to help people worship God with white-hot affection through the proclamation and teaching of his Christ-exalting Word was enlarged to embrace the unreached peoples of the world. The prayer of the psalmist increasingly became our prayer:

Let the peoples praise You, O God;
let all the peoples praise You. (Ps. 67:3 NASB)

In April of 1984 the church changed my job description to pastor for students and missions. That summer over twenty people joined Julie and me in driving our old cars out to Pasadena to take the Perspectives on the World Christian Movement Course[4] offered at the U.S. Center for World Missions. We brought this course back to Bethlehem that fall, and over 120 people took the course. The Perspectives Course has been foundational in our leadership development efforts ever since and is a crucial course in The Bethlehem Institute today. More and more people from Bethlehem were sensing God's call to missions, so a Nurture Program for Missionary Candidates[5] was established, designed to nurture men, women, and young people from the first inkling of a missionary call until their commissioning to the mission field.

Meanwhile, as these efforts to equip pastors and missionaries were being implemented, there was always a heartfelt longing to impart these precious truths to emerging leaders within the church and to anyone (not just pastors and missionaries!) who was hungry to grow in understanding the whole counsel of God. Early on in my ministry I saw the value of leading church members (about a dozen or so) in cohort-based journeys into the Word of God by teaching a mini–systematic theology class called Leadership Training Through Theological Reflection (affectionately called LTTTR). In addition I would regularly teach Bible study method classes and a unity of the Bible class. Toward the end of the 1980s this grew into The Bethlehem Institute and Training Center (BITC), which recruited additional instructors, enrolled more and more people from Bethlehem and beyond, and multiplied the number of classes offered.

In 1997 we sensed God's leading to try to bring these streams of leadership development together and proposed to Bethlehem's elders a vision for what I initially proposed as the Desiring God Institute. The elders affirmed the vision and sent me on a study leave to the Billy Graham Center on the Wheaton College campus in Wheaton, Illinois. I spent several months praying and dreaming and writing, and returned with the first class of six men recruited for the seminary-level training. I also returned with a catalog highlighting the three tracks of what has been known for ten years as The Bethlehem Institute. Track One consisted of our leadership development courses and seminars designed for motivated

---

[4]See http://www.perspectives.org.
[5]Http://www.hopeingod.org/NurtureProgram.aspx.

lay leaders, missionary candidates, and other Christian workers who yearned for solid biblical teaching and ministry preparation. Track Two was our apprenticeship program for vocational eldership. In this track our aim was to prepare men for pastoral ministry and other elder-level vocational ministries where teaching Scripture would be central to their calling. Track Three made use of the World Christian Foundations curriculum inspired by Ralph Winter, a course of study leading students from creation to consummation, providing insights through the disciplines of Bible, exegesis, theology, history, anthropology, linguistics, world religions, and more.

As the vision was developing, John and I deliberated further over the name and decided on The Bethlehem Institute to emphasize that this effort in leadership development was church-based. We wanted it to be serious theological education in the context of the local church—designed to be a crucial means of helping Bethlehem accomplish her mission of spreading a passion for the supremacy of God in all things for the joy of all peoples through Jesus Christ.

In the fall of 1998 The Bethlehem Institute was officially launched. In ten years, our lay leadership development courses and seminars have influenced thousands. TBI has graduated eight classes from its seminary-level program since the year 2000 (seventy-five graduates). While some of these men are pursuing further education elsewhere, many of our graduates are serving as pastors, church planters, missionaries, college or seminary professors, and parachurch workers on university campuses and in the inner city. Several of our graduates have gone on to PhD programs at Wheaton Graduate School, Southern Baptist Theological Seminary, Cambridge, Durham, Oxford, St. Andrews, Harvard, Boston University, and the University of Minnesota. TBI has also graduated two classes from the INSIGHT program (twenty-seven graduates). Most of these students are going on for further education as they prepare to impact the world for Christ.

When we say TBI is a church-based theological education and ministry training program, we mean that TBI is a ministry of Bethlehem Baptist Church. We are not just housing theological education coming from somewhere else (though we welcome many adjunct professors and lectures from the greater Christian community); but we as a church are wholeheartedly investing in this intentional leadership development through preaching, teaching, mentoring, and many other ministries of the church. The TBI students (we call them "apprentices"), both undergraduate and graduate, are folded into the life of the church, using their gifts to benefit the body and benefiting from the gifts of others in the body.

In October of 2008 the TBI board voted to become Bethlehem College and Seminary. We also affirmed Pastor John as the chancellor. We hesitate to say that TBI is becoming a college and seminary because that implies to many that we will offer multiple majors and multiple degrees and a varsity sports program and endless growth of the student body. TBI is what it is! TBI has been an innovative, refreshing alternative to the traditional college and seminary programs. In no way do we indict the traditional college and seminary programs. God has transformed both John's life and my life through such programs. Bethlehem College and Seminary is intending to be a serious center of church-based theological education and ministry training. We plan to offer only one undergraduate degree with two majors and only one very focused graduate degree. There will be minimal variations in what will be a very established curriculum.

Why another theological educational institution when there are so many others? We are envisioning an accredited institution of Christian higher learning that

- offers a consistent theological perspective throughout its entire curriculum,
- utilizes only faculty who gladly embrace the affirmation of faith undergirding Bethlehem College and Seminary and who teach with contagious conviction aimed at persuasion while teaching students to be Bereans—to see truth for themselves and not to be "second-handers,"
- has as one of its key aspects the mentoring and holistic discipling of each student—head, heart, and hands,
- does not foster the prolonging of adolescence, but strongly encourages students to seriously pursue Christlike leadership development,
- uses time, space, and resources so effectively and efficiently that undergraduate and graduate students are able to earn their degrees with an efficient use of time and resources,
- is so affordable that it allows students to graduate without incurring the crippling debt that plagues many graduates of Christian institutions,
- is anchored in a vibrant, local church congregation that provides a dynamic context for all learning and a place to apply what they

are learning for the benefit of the church and the advancement of her mission,

- has credits that are transferable virtually anywhere,
- targets the needs of current pastors by offering them a continuing education experience that restores the soul, enlightens the heart, and renews the mind,
- prepares future pastors and elders to lead their churches toward powerful, gospel-advancing, life-transforming ministry,
- equips the global church for more effective service by training national pastors and by fostering a "world Christian" mind-set in all of our students.

But we are not calling it John Piper College and Seminary, even though his fingerprints are more far-reaching than I have space to articulate. What consumes the administration, faculty, and students of TBI is not a man, but a vision of our triune God as revealed in Scripture, which alone will satisfy the deepest longings of the human soul, no matter what race or culture or place in society. Pastor John/Dr. Piper has trumpeted this vision for close to four decades of faithful teaching and preaching. He is living out this vision in his home, his urban neighborhood, his church, and through his wider ministry of speaking and writing. But it's not about him. What he embodies is a sinner saved by grace and transparent about his own ongoing battle with indwelling sin, who has tasted the sweetness of the blood and righteousness of Jesus Christ and the endless riches of the Word of God. My appreciation for the gift of partnering with this man only deepens with time.

Subject Index

abortion, 293, 294n1, 307, 328–50
absurdity, 124–25, 169
acedia, 335
acknowledgment of truth as source of motivation, 96–98
Acts 29, 42
adolescence, 19, 514
adoption, 34, 338, 395, 397–99
adultery, 224, 258–62, 315, 433
affirmation of faith, 514
aim of our existence, 51
aim of the authors of this book, 13
all people desire happiness, 52–54
anger, 35, 97n55, 221, 224, 304, 370, 426–27, 433, 462
antinomy, 114n
anxiety, 32n24, 85, 94n50, 376, 427, 439,
apostolic maternal and paternal leadership qualities, 466–76
arcing, 510–11
Arminian, 29, 116, 118, 129
Arminianism, incipient, 29
art of arts, 428, 437
assurance, 62, 81, 97n54, 124, 133, 210, 363, 378
atonement, 73n5, 172, 175, 184n27, 185, 363, 383–84, 396
  "dramatic view," 175–76, 185
  Edwards on, 383–84
  Fathers on, 173–74

penal substitutionary, 161, 165, 175, 183, 185, 205, 211, 362
"ransom to Satan" view, 174, 178
Reformed tradition on, 171–73

Baby Boom(ers), 24, 42
baptistic Reformed theology, 39
below-average memory, 41
Bereans, 514
"best is yet to come," 33
Bethel College, 17, 19, 31–32, 235, 272, 477, 494, 508–9, 511
Bethel Seminary, 511
Bethlehem Baptist Church, 11–12, 17–19, 26n6, 29n18, 33–34, 36–38, 40, 42, 44n7, 45, 123, 205, 293, 299n9, 306, 329, 330n2, 330n3, 405n, 461, 477, 481, 484n, 494, 499, 501–4, 510–13
Bethlehem College and Seminary, 38n, 508–15
Bethlehem Institute, The (TBI), 38, 508–15
  vision and history of, 508–15
Bethlehem Institute and Training Center (BITC), 512
Bible. *See* Scripture
Bible Belt, 38
biblical theology, 176n17, 190n, 215–34, 236, 237n, 238n5, 244n, 249n15,

516

PERSON INDEX

Scripture Index